MEGARRY'S MANUAL
OF
THE LAW OF REAL PROPERTY

ALSO BY R. E. MEGARRY
THE RENT ACTS
SNELL'S EQUITY, 23rd edition
   (with P. V. Baker) 24th–27th editions
LECTURES ON THE TOWN AND COUNTRY PLANNING ACT 1947
MISCELLANY-AT-LAW
A SECOND MISCELLANY-AT-LAW
LAWYER AND LITIGANT IN ENGLAND
   (The Hamlyn Lectures, 1962)
ARABINESQUE-AT-LAW
INNS ANCIENT AND MODERN
   (The Selden Society Lecture, 1971)

WITH H. W. R. WADE
THE LAW OF REAL PROPERTY

ALSO BY M. P. THOMPSON
CO-OWNERSHIP
INVESTIGATION AND PROOF OF TITLE

AUSTRALIA
The Law Book Company
Brisbane • Sydney • Melbourne • Perth

CANADA
Carswell
Ottawa • Toronto • Calgary • Montreal • Vancouver

Agents:
Steimatzky's Agency Ltd., Tel Aviv;
N.M. Tripathi (Private) Ltd., Bombay;
Eastern Law House (Private) Ltd., Calcutta;
M.P.P. House, Bangalore;
Universal Book Traders, Delhi;
Aditya Books, Delhi;
MacMillan Shuppan KK, Tokyo;
Pakistan Law House, Karachi, Lahore

A MANUAL OF
THE LAW OF
REAL PROPERTY

BY

THE RT. HON. SIR ROBERT MEGARRY,
M.A., LL.D. (Cantab.), Hon. LL.D. (Hull, Nottingham,
The Law Society of Upper Canada and London),
Hon. D.U. (Essex), F.B.A.
an Honorary Fellow of Trinity Hall, Cambridge;
a Bencher of Lincoln's Inn; sometime the
Vice-Chancellor of the Supreme Court

SEVENTH EDITION

BY

SIR ROBERT MEGARRY

and

M. P. THOMPSON
LL.B. (Leicester), LL.M. (Keele)
Professor of Law in the Newcastle Law School
at the University of Newcastle upon Tyne

LONDON
SWEET & MAXWELL LIMITED
1993

First Edition	1946	By R. E. MEGARRY
Second Impression, revised	1947	" "
Third Impression, revised	1949	" "
Fourth Impression	1951	" "
Second Edition	1955	" "
Second Impression	1960	" "
Third Edition	1962	" "
Second Impression	1967	" "
Fourth Edition	1969	By P. V. BAKER
Second Impression	1972	" "
Third Impression	1973	" "
Fifth Edition	1975	" "
Sixth Edition	1982	By D. J. HAYTON
Second Impression	1989	" "
Seventh Edition	1993	By R. E. MEGARRY and M. P. THOMPSON

Published in 1993 by Sweet & Maxwell Limited
of South Quay Plaza, 183 Marsh Wall, London E14 9FT
Computerset by MFK Typesetting Limited, Hitchin
Printed in Great Britain by The Bath Press, Bath, Avon.

A CIP catalogue record for this book
is available from The British Library

ISBN 0 420 479600 (PB)

PREFACE

It is now over ten years since the last edition of this book appeared, and in that time both Parliament and the courts have been active. Usually they have added to the material to be included, but there has been one notable reduction: with the repeal of section 40 of the Law of Property Act 1925 over three centuries of a luxuriant but not very elevating jurisprudence have vanished. This, together with the rewriting of some of the more expansive passages, has made it possible to avoid any increase in length; indeed, there has been a reduction of nearly 40 pages. The number of authorities cited has substantially increased, but this is less formidable than it seems. Many of the authorities mainly provide examples or qualifications of the principles stated, and so they are but different aspects of a single point; yet this function is valuable. "Define, and your reader gets a silhouette; illustrate, and he has it 'in the round'."[1] We have sought to avoid citing multiple authorities for a single proposition, and instead to carry out the precept of Dodderidge J., uttered over three centuries ago, that "every string ought to give his sound."[2] Invasions of the footnotes by textual material have been repelled, and the reader may confidently give undivided attention to the text.

We have left the framework of the book unchanged, though the number of chapters has been reduced by one. The isolated chapter on rectification and indemnity for registered land, now rewritten and shortened, has rejoined the rest of the material on registered land in Chapter 4, and the 12-page chapter on covenants affecting leasehold land, as revised, now forms part of the chapter on landlord and tenant. On the other hand, licences and proprietary estoppel have been given a chapter of their own. In the end, over half the text for this edition has been rewritten or newly-written, and a greater uniformity of style has been attained. Throughout, the object has been to use language that is as clear and direct as the subject permits. The system of headings and sub-headings, so important as a focus both for initial comprehension and for ultimate revision, has been reconsidered and, we hope, improved. The generous supply of cross-references in the footnotes, essential for so complex and interlocking a subject, has been augmented. Each of us is editorially responsible for the whole book, with juniority producing the first draft, seniority the revised draft, and, geography notwithstanding, combined operations the final draft.

[1] H.W. Fowler, Preface to the *Concise Oxford Dictionary* (2nd ed. 1929).
[2] (1615) 3 Bulstr. 103.

For one of us, acute memories of the initial difficulty of the subject have been revived by the close and prolonged re-reading and reconsideration of much that was written over fifty years ago. The attempt, made while the difficulties were still fresh, was to provide explanations and reasons that would ease those difficulties. The book remains a work of moderate compass which, as the preface to the first edition asserted, is "primarily intended for the examination candidate whose main anxiety is not whether he will head the list but whether he will appear in it at all." In its present form, with an increased citation of authority and periodicals, our hope is that it will also satisfy the needs of some of those with less modest examination prospects; for them, the references will at least give access to further and better particulars.

We are indebted to the publishers for preparing the index and the tables, and for seeing the book through the press. We are especially grateful to the typesetters, in conjunction with the publishers and printers, whose skill and despatch has enabled us to state the law as at the date of this preface.

Lincoln's Inn, and
University of Newcastle
*   upon Tyne*   R.E.M.
October 1, 1992   M.P.T.

CONTENTS

CHAPTER 1

INTRODUCTION

CHAPTER 2

ESTATES

CHAPTER 6

FUTURE INTERESTS

CHAPTER 7

SETTLED LAND AND TRUSTS FOR SALE

CHAPTER 10

INCORPOREAL HEREDITAMENTS

CHAPTER 11

RESTRICTIVE COVENANTS

CHAPTER 14

LIMITATION

CHAPTER 15

OWNERSHIP AND ITS LIMITS

TABLE OF CASES

TABLE OF STATUTES

TABLE OF STATUTORY INSTRUMENTS

ABBREVIATIONS

STATUTES

A.E.A.: Administration of Estates Act.
A.H.A.: Agricultural Holdings Act.
C.A.: Conveyancing Act.
H.A.: Housing Act.
I.E.A.: Intestates' Estates Act.
J.A.: Supreme Court of Judicature (Consolidation) Act.
L.C.A.: Land Charges Act.
L.P.A.: Law of Property Act.
L.P.(Am.)A.: Law of Property Amendment Act.
L.P.(M.P.)A.: Law of Property (Miscellaneous Provisions) Act.
L.R.A.: Land Registration Act.
L.R.R.: Land Registration Rules.
L. & T.A.: Landlord and Tenant Act.
R.P.A.: Real Property Act.
S.L.A.: Settled Land Act.
T.A.: Trustee Act.

CASES

B.S.: Building Society.
D.C.: District Council.
I.R.C.: Commissioners of Inland Revenue.
In b.: (In bonis) In the Goods of, In the Estate of.
L.B.C.: London Borough Council.
R.D.C.: Rural District Council.
S.E.: Settled Estate(s).
S.T.: Settlement Trust(s).
W.T.: Will Trust(s).

BOOKS AND PERIODICALS

Bl.Comm.: Blackstone's Commentaries on the Laws of England, 15th ed., 1809.
Camb.L.J. (or C.L.J.): Cambridge Law Journal.
Challis R.P.: Challis's Law of Real Property (3rd ed. 1911).
Co.Litt.: Coke's Commentary upon Littleton (19th ed., 1832).
Conv.(N.S.) (or Conv.): The Conveyancer, New Series, 1936–
Conv.(O.S.): The Conveyancer, Old Series, 1916–36.
Conv.Y.B.: Conveyancers' Year Book.
Cru.Dig.: Cruise's Digest of the Laws of England respecting Real Property (4th ed., 1835).
Gray, *Perpetuities*: Gray's Rule against Perpetuities (4th ed., 1942).
Halsbury: Halsbury's Laws of England (4th ed.).
Harv.L.R.: Harvard Law Review.
Hayton: Hayton's Registered Land (3rd ed., 1981).
H.E.L.: Holdsworth's History of English Law, 1922–66 (see (1945) 61 L.Q.R. 346).
Law Com.: Law Commission.
Litt.: Littleton's Tenures: see Co.Litt.
L.J.News.: Law Journal Newspaper.
L.Q.R.: Law Quarterly Review.
L.R.Ann.Rep.: Land Registry Annual Report.
L.S.G.: The Law Society's Gazette.

Maitland, *Equity*: Maitland's Equity (2nd ed., 1936).
　　　　Forms of Action: Maitland's Forms of Action at Common Law, 1936.
Mod.L.R. (or M.L.R.): Modern Law Review.
M. & W.: Megarry and Wade's Law of Real Property (5th ed., 1984).
N.L.J.: New Law Journal.
P. & M.: Pollock & Maitland's History of English Law (2nd ed., 1898) (reprinted with new introduction 1968).
Preston, *Estates.*: Preston's Elementary Treatise on Estates (1820–27).
Ruoff & Roper: Ruoff & Roper's Law and Practice of Registered Conveyancing (6th ed., loose-leaf, 1991).
Sanders, *Uses*: Sanders' Essay on Uses and Trusts (5th ed., 1844).
Shep.: Sheppard's Touchstone of Common Assurances (7th ed., 1820).
S.J.: Solicitors' Journal.
Snell: Snell's Principles of Equity (29th ed., 1990).
Theobald, *Land*: Theobald's Law of Land (2nd ed., 1929).
Tudor L.C.R.P.: Tudor's Selection of Leading Cases on Real Property, Conveyancing and the Construction of Wills and Deeds (4th ed., 1898).
Williams R.P.: Williams' Principles of the Law of Real Property (23rd ed. 1920).
　　　　V. & P.: Williams' Treatise on the Law of Vendor & Purchaser (4th ed., 1936).
W.P.: Working Paper.

GLOSSARY

The object of this glossary is to provide a ready source of reference to the meanings of some of the more troublesome technical expressions used in the text. For the most part, brief but not necessarily exhaustive definitions have been given, with references by means of numerals in brackets to the pages of the text where further information can be obtained and the terms may be seen in their context; references which are essential to a proper understanding of the terms are in heavy type. Where the text contains a convenient collection and explanation of a number of contrasting terms, a simple reference to the appropriate pages is given instead of setting out the definitions.

Abstract of title: an epitome of documents and facts showing ownership (**126**).

Ademption: the failure of a gift by will, *e.g.* because the property ceases to exist or to belong to the testator (154).

Ad hoc settlement or trust for sale: one with special overreaching powers (**262**).

Administrators: persons authorised to administer the estate of an intestate (164); compare Executors.

Advowson: a right of presenting a clergyman to a vacant benefice (72).

Alienation: the act of disposing of or transferring.

Allodial land: land not held of a lord (19).

Ante-nuptial: before marriage.

Appendant: attached to land by operation of law (376); compare Appurtenant.

Approvement: the appropriation of a portion of the manorial waste free from rights of common (398).

Appurtenant: attached to land by act of parties (376); compare Appendant.

Assent: an assurance by personal representatives vesting property in the person entitled (165).

Assignment: a disposition or transfer, usually of a lease.

Assurance: the documentary or other evidence of a disposition or transfer.

Beneficial owner: a person entitled for his own benefit and not, *e.g.* as trustee.

Beneficiaries: those entitled to benefit under a trust or will.

Betterment levy: see Development charge.

Bona vacantia: goods without an owner.

Borough English: a special form of descent whereby on an intestacy before 1926 land descended by ultimogeniture and not primogeniture, *i.e.* to the youngest son instead of the eldest (23).

Cestui que trust: a beneficiary under a trust.

,,   ,,   *use*: a person to whose use property was conveyed (63).

,,   ,,   *vie*: a person for whose life an estate *pur autre vie* lasted (46).

Charge: an incumbrance securing the payment of money.

Collaterals: blood relations who are neither ancestors nor descendants.

Consolidation: a requirement that a mortgagor shall not redeem one mortgage without another (460).

Contingent: operative only upon an uncertain event (**175**); compare Vested.

Contractual tenancy: a tenancy under a lease or agreement which is still in force; contrast Statutory tenant.

Conversion: a change in the nature of property either actually or notionally (**218**).

Conveyance: an instrument (other than a will) transferring property.

Co-parceners: persons together constituting the heir (**281**).

Corporeal: accompanied by physical possession (66).

Covenant: a promise contained in a deed.

Coverture: the continuance of a marriage.

Curtesy: a widower's life estate in his wife's realty (156).

Customary heir: the heir according to a local custom.

Deed: a document which shows that it is intended to be a deed and has been signed and delivered (127).

Deed poll: a deed with only one party (129); compare Indenture.

Defeasance: the determination of an interest on a specified event.

Demise: a transfer, usually by the grant of a lease.

Desmesne: land occupied by the feudal lord (20).

Determine: terminate, come to an end.
Development charge; development gains tax; development land tax; betterment levy (511, 512).
Devise: a gift of real property by will.
Distrain, distress: the lawful extra-judicial seizure of chattels to enforce a right, *e.g.* to the payment of rent (343).
Dominant tenement: land to which the benefit of a right is attached (367); compare Servient tenement.
Dower: a widow's life estate in one-third of her husband's realty (156).
Durante viduitate: during widowhood.

Emblements: crops still growing which an outgoing tenant may take (51).
Enceinte: pregnant.
Engross: prepare a fair copy (127).
En ventre sa mère: conceived but not born.
Equities: equitable rights (60).
Equity of redemption: the sum of a mortgagor's rights in the mortgaged property (**430**).
Escheat: a lord's right to ownerless realty (162).
Escrow: a document which upon delivery will become a deed (129).
Estate: 1. the *quantum* of an interest in land (20).
        2. an area of land (20).
        3. the whole of the property owned by a deceased person (20, 164).
Estovers: wood which a tenant may take for domestic and other purposes (48).
Execute: 1. to perform or complete, *e.g.* a deed.
         2. to convert, *e.g.* to transform the equitable interest under a use into a legal estate (64).
Executors: persons appointed by a testator to administer his estate (164); compare Administrators.
Executory: not yet completed (contrasted with "executed") (180, 287).
Executory interest: a valid future interest not complying with the legal remainder rules (**180**).
Executory trust: a trust the details of which remain to be set out in some further document (287).

Fee: base (44), conditional (35), determinable (35), simple (24), tail (39).
Feoffee to uses: a person holding property to the use of another (63).
Feoffment: a conveyance by livery [delivery] of seisin (66).
Fine: 1. a collusive action partially barring an entail (40); compare Recovery.
      2. a premium or a lump sum payment, *e.g.* for the grant of a lease.
Foreclosure: proceedings by a mortgagee which free mortgaged property from the equity of redemption (449).
Freehold: 1. socage tenure (22).
          2. an estate of fixed but uncertain duration (**24, 25**).

Gavelkind: a special custom of descent whereby land descended on intestacy to all sons and not to the eldest son alone (23).
General equitable charge: an equitable charge on a legal estate not protected by a deposit of title deeds (78).
Good consideration: natural love and affection for near relatives (59).

Hereditaments: inheritable rights in property (66).
Heritable issue: descendants capable of inheriting.
Hold over: remain in possession after the termination of a tenancy (316).
Hotchpot: the bringing into account of benefits already received before sharing in property (160).

Improved value: the value of land together with improvements to it.
In capite: in chief, immediately holding of the Crown (19).
Inclosure: the appropriation of the whole of a manorial waste free from rights of common (399).
Incorporeal: not accompanied by physical possession (66).
Incumbrance: a liability burdening property.

Indenture: a deed between two or more parties (129); compare Deed poll.
Infant: a person under 18 years of age.
In gross: existing independently of a dominant tenement (368, 377).
Instrument: a legal document.
Interesse termini: the rights of a lessee before entry (**315**).
Intestacy: the failure to dispose of property by will.
Issue: descendants of any generation (33).

Jointure: provision by a husband for his widow, usually under a settlement (215).
Jus accrescendi: right of survivorship (282).

Lapse: the failure of a gift, especially by the beneficiary predeceasing the testator (145).
Letters of administration: the authorisation to persons to administer the estate of a deceased person (164).
Licence: a permission, *e.g.* to enter on land (427).
Limitation, words of: words delimiting the estate granted to some person previously mentioned (**29, 34**); compare Purchase, words of.

Marriage articles: the preliminary agreement for a marriage settlement (288).
Merger: the fusion of two or more estates or interests (333).
Mesne: intermediate, middle (20).
Minor: see Infant.
Minority: the state of being an infant.

Next-of-kin: the nearest blood relations (156).
Nuncupative: oral (of wills) (145).

Overreach: to transfer rights from land to the purchase money therefor (5, 6).
Override: to render rights void, *e.g.* against a purchaser (92).

Parol: by word of mouth.
Particular estate: an estate less than a fee simple (178).
Per capita: by heads; one share for each person (160); compare *Per stirpes*.
Personal representatives: executors or administrators (164).
Per stirpes: by stocks of descent; one share for each line of descendants (160); compare *Per capita*.
Portions: provisions for children, especially lump sums for the younger children under a settlement (215).
Possibility of reverter: the grantor's right to the land if a determinable fee determines (35).
Post-nuptial: after marriage.
Prescription: the acquisition of easements or profits by long user (386).
Privity of contract: the relation between parties to a contract (348).
Privity of estate: the relation of landlord and tenant (349).
Probate: the formal confirmation of a will, granted by the court to an executor (164).
Procreation, words of: words confining the persons mentioned to issue of a particular person (32).
Puisne mortgage: a legal mortgage not protected by a deposit of title deeds (78).
Pur autre vie: for the life of another person (25).
Purchase, words of: words conferring an interest on the person they mention (30); compare Limitation, words of.
Purchaser: a person who takes land by act of parties and not by operation of law.

Que estate: dominant tenement (388).

Recovery: a collusive action completely barring an entail (40); compare Fine, 1.
Remainder: the interest of a grantee subject to a prior particular estate (178).
Rent: chief rent (367), fee farm rent (367), ground rent (123), quit rent (367), rack rent (123), rent of assize (367), rentcharge (366), rent seck (366), rent service (366).
Restraint on anticipation: an obsolete restriction preventing a married woman from disposing of capital or future income.

Restrictive covenant: a covenant restricting the use of land (65).
Reversion: the interest remaining in a grantor after granting a particular estate (178).
Riparian owner: the owner of land adjoining a watercourse (507).
Root of title: a document from which ownership is traced (62).

Satisfied term: a term of years created for a purpose which has since been fulfilled (333).
Seisin: the feudal possession of land by a freeholder (**27**).
Servient tenement: land burdened by a right such as an easement (367); compare Dominant tenement.
Settlement: provisions for persons in succession (or the instruments making such provisions) (215, 233).
Severance: the conversion of a joint tenancy into a tenancy in common (299).
Severance, words of: words showing that property is to be held in distinct shares (286).
Spes successionis: a possibilty of succeeding to property (30).
Squatter: a person occupying land without any title to it (502).
Statutory owner: persons with the powers of a tenant for life (224).
Statutory tenant: a person holding over under the Rent Acts (535); compare Contractual tenancy.
Statutory trusts: certain trusts imposed by statute, especially—
    1. the trust for sale under co-ownership (**289**).
    2. the trusts for issue on intestacy (**160**).
Sub-mortgage: a mortgage of a mortgage (475).
Sui juris: "of his own right," *i.e.* subject to no disability.

Tenement: anything which may be held by a tenant.
Tenure: the set of conditions upon which a tenant holds land (20); compare Estate, 1.
Term of years: a period with a defined minimum for which a tenant holds land (74).
Terre tenant: a freehold tenant in possession (364).
Title: the evidence of a person's right to property.
Trust: bare (267), completely constituted (269), constructive (269), executed (288), executory (287), express (268), implied (269), incompletely constituted (269), precatory (268), resulting (270).
Trust corporation: one of certain companies with a large paid-up capital, or one of certain officials (260).

Undivided share: the interest of a tenant in common or co-parcener (281, 284).
Use: benefit (64), resulting (270), shifting (180), springing (180).
User: use, enjoyment (Note: *not* the person who uses).

Vested: unconditionally owned (**175**); compare Contingent.
Vesting assent (226), declaration (276), deed (225), instrument (225).
Voluntary conveyance: a conveyance not made for valuable consideration.
Volunteer: a person taking under a disposition without having given valuable consideration.

Waste: ameliorating (47), equitable (48), permissive (47), voluntary (47).

CHAPTER 1

INTRODUCTION

Sect. 1. Prefatory

THE English law of real property, traditionally described by Oliver Cromwell as "an ungodly jumble," is justly recognised as being a difficult subject for the beginner, partly because of the intricate interlocking of its component parts and partly because of the complexity of the language, which involves the use of many technical terms. For these reasons, those coming new to the subject must not expect to understand everything at a first reading. In this subject more than any other it is economical of time and effort to read fast and often. Much that is almost incomprehensible at first will become clear on a second reading and perhaps obvious on a third. In order to understand complex ideas expressed in unfamiliar language it is necessary to master the language as soon as possible, and for this purpose a generous use should be made of the glossary which immediately precedes this page.

1. Objects of learning the subject. The objects of learning the law of real property are—

(a) to acquire a knowledge of the rights and liabilities attached to interests in land; and
(b) to lay a foundation for the study of conveyancing.

It is not easy to distinguish accurately between real property and conveyancing. In general, it can be said that the former is static, the latter dynamic; real property deals with the rights and liabilities of landowners, conveyancing with the art of creating and transferring rights in land. Yet inevitably the two overlap, and often the exact place at which to draw the line is ultimately a matter of taste. But although this is a book on the law of real property, it is built upon a conveyancing foundation. In deciding what to include and what to exclude, conveyancing has played a large part. The reader's knowledge of land law has to be carried to the point when it will be possible for him to embark with profit on a study of conveyancing; the joints must be true and the overlapping restrained within due limits. It is, indeed, best to regard real property and conveyancing not as two separate though closely related subjects, but as two parts of the one subject of land law; it is convenience of teaching rather than any essential difference of nature that dictates the division.

Conveyancing necessarily influences any book on real property in another way, namely, by making it essential to include some historical element. A conveyancer must deal both with ownership and incumbrances; in other

1

words he must see not only that his client gets what he has agreed to buy but also that he gets it free from any burdens such as mortgages or rights of way which would make it less valuable. (In parenthesis, it must be noted that this division between ownership and incumbrances is not rigid; what in one transaction appears as an incumbrance may appear in another as the subject-matter of ownership. If A owns a mortgage on X's land, the mortgage is regarded as an incumbrance if X sells his land, but as the subject-matter of ownership if A sells his mortgage. Nevertheless, in any particular transaction the distinction is clear). A conveyancer acting for a client who is purchasing property must investigate the title to the land, both as to ownership and as to incumbrances, for a period which is usually at least the last 15 years. Those who are engaged in this work must consequently know the law not only as it is but also as it was.

Modern conveyancing is based upon the 1925 property legislation, enacted some 70 years ago. The title to land may either be registered at the Land Registry, or else be unregistered. In unregistered conveyancing, a purchaser need only investigate the vendor's title as far back as a good "root of title" (*e.g.* a conveyance on sale) at least 15 years old.[1] It is therefore relatively uncommon for knowledge of the pre-1925 law to be required. For registered land (and there are now over 12 million registered titles) the register sets out, subject to "overriding interests,"[2] the current state of the title. Accordingly, comparatively little attention will be paid to the pre-1926 law on subjects that fall within the system of registration of title.[3] Instead, the emphasis will be on registration of title.

2. The common law basis of the subject. The law of real property is part of the common law of England. The phrase "common law" or "at law," which will frequently be encountered, is used in three senses:

   (i) in contrast with local custom;
   (ii) in contrast with statute law; and
   (iii) in contrast with equity.

The third is the most usual sense, the second less usual, the first comparatively rare; the context will normally make it plain which is meant. A word must be said on the third meaning. As will be seen later,[4] certain rights could be enforced in the common law courts (*i.e.* the King's ordinary courts), and these were known as legal rights. Other rights were not protected by the common law courts, but in time came to be protected by the Chancellor if he deemed this equitable. It was the Chancellor who first compelled trustees to carry out their trusts, and remedied wrongs which, because of non-compliance with some formality, the common law courts would not redress. Rights enforced by the Chancellor were known as equitable rights, for the

---

[1] *Post*, p. 9.
[2] *Post*, pp. 10, 102 *et seq.*
[3] Where such knowledge is required, see Megarry and Wade, *The Law of Real Property* (5th 1984, cited as "M. & W.") or the fifth or earlier editions of this book.
[4] *Post*, pp. 52 *et seq.*

Chancellor's Court, the Court of Chancery, was known as the Court of Equity. Equitable rights were (and still are) inferior to legal rights, in that a legal right would be enforced against everyone, whereas an equitable right would be enforced only against a person whom the Chancellor considered was unable in good conscience to deny liability. Thus not only would a trustee be compelled to carry out his trust, but also if he gave or sold the trust property to a third person who knew that the trustee was committing a breach of trust, the equitable rights of the beneficiaries under the trust would be enforced against that third person, who would thus be compelled to carry out the trust. Ultimately, equitable rights became enforceable against the whole world except a bona fide purchaser for value of a legal estate without notice of the equitable right, or someone claiming title under such a person[5]; in the language of more spacious days, he was "equity's darling." Legal rights, on the other hand, were enforceable against everyone, without this exception.

The common law affecting real property has in the course of time been profoundly affected by equity, and today most questions on real property law fall for decision in the Chancery Division of the High Court; yet this is merely a procedural arrangement which must not be allowed to obscure the common law basis of the law of real property, though much affected by statute law.

Sect. 2. The Scope of the Subject

1. The complex functions of land. A principal reason for the complexity of the law of real property lies in the physical nature of land itself. Land is both virtually indestructible and uniquely immovable, with the result that various people can have different interests in it and rights over it. This is not generally true in the case of chattels. Thus if a person buys a car, he does not find that it is subject to obligations such as a prohibition on driving it to Exeter, or a limit to what can be carried in it or what alterations he may make to it. He may, of course, by contract impose such obligations on himself, but they will not flow from his ownership of the car. Nor will such a person find that by reason of owning the car he has acquired rights over other people's property, such as a right to drive over their land. Again, he will not find that the boundaries of his car are uncertain or that it is liable to be compulsorily purchased. He will not find that another person has a life interest in the car or a 99-year tenancy or a 21-year sub-tenancy of it.

In contrast, because of the nature of land, it is quite feasible that an owner of land may be concerned with matters of this nature. Land may be settled upon A for life, then to A's eldest son for life and, finally to A's eldest grandson absolutely. Alternatively, it may be leased to X for 99 years, who sub-leases it for 21 years to Y, who further sub-leases it for a year to Z. Laws have to regulate not only the relationships between A and the remaindermen, and between X, Y and Z, but also the position of a purchaser of the

---

[5] See *post,* pp. 58 *et seq.*, where this is more fully discussed.

property in which they are interested. Land is also especially apt for satisfying concurrent needs, whether of spouses or businessmen. Land may be
owned by H and W as joint tenants or by P and Q as tenants in common. In
the former case, by the *jus accrescendi* (right of survivorship), the survivor
will become the sole owner, whereas in the latter instance the share of the
deceased will pass under his will or under the rules for intestacy.

Land may also be subject to adverse rights. For example, a neighbour may
have a right of light over the land. The land may also be subject to restrictive
covenants, as by limiting the number of buildings that may be erected upon it
or prohibiting their use except as private dwellings. Land also provides ideal
security for a loan of money where such money is lent by way of mortgage or
charge.

Land and buildings thereon, which are treated as part of the land under
the maxim *"quicquid plantatur solo, solo cedit"* (whatever is attached to the
soil becomes part of it), are divisible vertically (*e.g.* semi-detached or
terraced houses) or horizontally (*e.g.* maisonettes and flats), thus creating
many problems as to mutual rights and obligations. Further difficulties arise
from the unique inelasticity of the supply of land, and this has provoked
much legislation.

2. Legal estates and equitable interests. Before 1926, there were many
different legal estates and legal interests that could exist in land; and a
corresponding range of estates and interests could exist in equity. After
1925, only two legal estates in land can exist, and the number of legal
interests has been limited. The two legal estates are the "fee simple absolute
in possession" and the "term of years absolute." In lay terms, A will be
called the "owner" of Greenacre; in legal terminology, A holds the fee
simple absolute in possession in Greenacre. If A has granted a lease to B
(*e.g.* for 21 years), A's fee simple is still "in possession," for "possession"
includes the right to receive the rent from the land. Although B has a "term
of years absolute" in the land, he will commonly be called the leaseholder or
tenant of it.

Legal interests are rights over someone else's land, such as easements
(*e.g.* rights of way or rights of light), rentcharges (*i.e.* rights to a rent where
there is no lease or tenancy) and legal charges (*i.e.* certain types of mortgage). All other interests are equitable. These include the right to enforce
restrictive covenants (*e.g.* that the land will not be built upon) and interests
under trusts. Further, any of the estates and interests that can exist at law
may instead exist in equity, as where they have been created without the due
formalities.

By reducing the number of legal estates and legal interests, the legislature
has reduced the number of estates and interests which will bind a purchaser
without notice of them.

3. The estate owner and overreaching. Before 1926, the legal estate in land
could be divided between two or more persons in succession, so that X might

have a legal life estate and Y the fee simple subject to that life estate. After 1925, this is no longer possible. The entire legal estate in fee simple will be vested in one person, and the life interest can exist only in equity. By following the correct procedure, the owner of the fee simple can sell the land, free from the rights that others have in it; yet their rights will not be destroyed, for they will be transferred to the purchase money, which will be held by trustees. The process whereby rights in the land are detached from it and attached instead to the proceeds of sale is known as "overreaching."[6] This is quite distinct from the process whereby equitable rights are held to be void as against a purchaser without notice of them; rights that are over-reached are merely transferred, and not invalidated.

4. Settlements. Some of the complications of land law arise from cases where land has been settled upon a succession of persons. A somewhat complex (and not very realistic) example may be taken so as to give a bird's eye view of the matter, though many readers will probably not fully comprehend the example until most of this book has been read.

(a) *Beneficial interests.* By his will a testator gives Greenacre to his son H for life, with remainder to W for life, and remainder in tail for such child of H and W as H shall appoint by deed or will, but in default of appointment to the first of the sons of H and W to attain 21 years of age, in tail. This provision gives H a life interest in possession, W a life interest in remainder, and H a special power of appointment that enables him to appoint an entailed interest to any child of H and W. Such an interest is one that can continue as long as the child or any of his descendants is living. Each child of H and W is an "object" of the power of appointment, taking no estate or interest in the land but having a mere hope (*spes*) that the power will be exercised in his or her favour. Each of the sons of H and W has a contingent entailed interest in remainder, the contingency being the attainment of 21 years of age; and the interest of each son is subject to the exercise of the power of appointment and to the interests of any older sons. When a son is 21, he has a vested entailed interest, subject to the interests of H and W and any exercise of the power of appointment, and also, while H is still alive, subject to being divested by any future exercise of the power of appointment. As the testator has not disposed of the whole of the fee simple (for H and W may die without issue, or the entails may not take effect), the testator retains the fee simple in reversion, and this will pass under his will or intestacy.

(b) *The Settled Land Acts.* Greenacre would be virtually unsaleable if a purchaser had to deal with everyone who had any interest in it. Accordingly, the Settled Land Acts made it possible for a purchaser to acquire Greenacre in fee simple, free from the interests of H, W, their children, and the testator's estate, without having to deal with anyone except the tenant for life for the time being. Under the Settled Land Act 1882, this was achieved by giving the tenant for life (H) a statutory power which in effect enabled

[6] *Post*, p. 6.

him to gather together all the fragments of the fee simple under the settlement and transfer it to the purchaser. Under the Settled Land Act 1925 the result is similar but the process different. The whole fee simple is vested in the tenant for life on trust for himself and all the other beneficiaries under the settlement, so that he will convey to a purchaser an estate that is vested in him, rather than exercising a statutory power to convey a fee simple in which he has only a limited interest. Each Act laid down a procedure that must be followed, and under each Act the rights of all the beneficiaries under the settlement were overreached, becoming corresponding interests in the purchase money held by the trustees of the settlement. Rights outside the settlement are not affected. Easements, mortgages and other rights existing when the settlement was made will bind the purchaser, and will not be overreached.[7]

(c) *Trusts for sale.* The trust for sale is an alternative to settled land under the Settled Land Act 1925. Under a trust for sale, the same beneficial interests may be created as under the Act; but the legal estate will be vested in the trustees, and not the tenant for life. A trust for sale is created by conveying the land to two, three or four trustees (or a trust corporation) to hold it on trust for sale but with power to postpone sale. Normally the trustees will be expected to retain the land under the power of postponement, rather than selling it; and while they retain it they have all the powers of management and control that a tenant for life has under the Act. When they sell the land, they will convey to the purchaser the fee simple that is vested in them, and will receive and hold the purchase money on trust for all the beneficiaries under the trust for sale. When settling land, an important factor in deciding whether to make the land settled land under the Act or whether to settle it by way of trust for sale is who it is that will make the decisions and exercise the powers: for settled land, it is the tenant for life, whereas for trusts for sale it is the trustees.[8]

(d) *Rights not overreached.* Both for settled land and land held on trust for sale, a purchaser is naturally concerned with any rights in the land that are not overreached. Thus tenancies, mortgages, easements and other rights existing when the settlement was made continue to bind the land even when it has been sold by the tenant for life or trustees for sale. Further, any such rights created by the tenant for life or trustees for sale under their statutory powers remain in force despite any sale.

5. Co-ownership

(a) *Fragmentation of title.* Land, as well as being held for persons in succession, may be held for persons concurrently: ownership may be divided not only vertically but also laterally. Even though Greenacre may be free from any successive interests in it, it may be held by two or more co-owners.

---

[7] See generally *post*, pp. 263, 264.
[8] See generally *post*, p. 265.

There might be dozens of co-owners of the fee simple in Greenacre, either as joint tenants or tenants in common. Joint tenants tended to be reduced in numbers, for when one died, the *jus accrescendi* would in effect carry his interest to his fellow joint tenants. On the other hand, tenants in common tended to increase in number, since when one died his interest would pass under his will or intestacy, perhaps to his ten children. Land might be owned by dozens of tenants in common living in different parts of the world; and even if all of them could be traced, some might be minors or mental patients. Until 1926, a would-be purchaser of such land might face such formidable and expensive difficulties that he would abandon his venture.

(b) *Integration of title.* In 1925 the problem was resolved.[9] There can now never be more than four co-owners of the *legal* estate. They must hold the legal estate as *joint tenants*, so that on death the legal estate remains in the survivors, by the *jus accrescendi*. They can appoint others to be joint tenants of the legal estate with themselves so long as their number does not exceed four. The legal estate is held by the joint tenants on *trust for sale* with power to postpone sale, and so the property may remain unsold for a long time. They may hold on trust for any number of co-owners, who may be minors or mental patients or live in remote countries, and who have *equitable* interests which may be joint tenancies or tenancies in common. So long as a purchaser pays his purchase moneys to the joint tenants holding the legal estate as trustees and takes a conveyance of the legal estate from them, he obtains a good legal title free from all the equitable interests of the beneficial co-owners. They exist instead in the proceeds of sale.[10]

(c) *Undisclosed title.* Difficulties arise when it is found that there is an undisclosed co-owner. If H purchases a house and his wife contributes one-third of the purchase price, normally the proper course to adopt is to have the house conveyed to H and W as joint tenants to hold on trust for sale for themselves as tenants in common in equity, as to two-thirds and one-third respectively. If instead the house is conveyed to H alone, with nothing to reveal W's contribution, W is still entitled to a one-third share in equity but there is nothing to disclose this to a purchaser. If a purchaser (P) pays the purchase money to H, thinking him to be solely entitled, W's equitable rights will not be overreached, for the purchase money has not been paid to trustees for sale, being at least two in number, or a trust corporation. W's rights will therefore bind P unless he can show that he is a bona fide purchaser for value of the legal estate without notice of W's rights, and so will take free from them under the general equitable principles.[11] P had no actual knowledge of W's rights, but he will be treated as having notice of them if they would have come to his knowledge had he made such inquiries and inspections as he ought reasonably to have made.[12]

[9] *Post*, pp. 288–292.
[10] *City of London B.S.* v. *Flegg* [1988] A.C. 54.
[11] L.P.A. 1925, s.199(1)(ii).
[12] *Post*, pp. 60 *et seq.*

There are difficulties in this concept. At one time the tendency was to construe it somewhat narrowly. Thus if H was in possession of the property, it was not thought reasonable to require P to make inquiries of H's wife or other occupiers if their presence was consistent with H being the sole owner.[13] Today, this view is discredited, and failure to inquire of other occupiers will at least in some cases constitute notice.[14] This difficult question is more fully considered later.[15]

6. Registration of land charges. There are two separate systems for the registration of certain charges over land.

(a) *Land charges.* Many of the difficulties of the equitable doctrine of notice can be avoided by making certain equitable rights registrable in a register of land charges. This system, begun in a very restricted form in 1839, was much extended in 1888, and further important extensions were made in 1925. The present statute is the Land Charges Act 1972, replacing the Land Charges Act 1925. If such a right is duly registered, all persons are deemed to have actual notice of it for all purposes.[16] If it is not registered, it will normally be void against a purchaser for value, even if he knows of it.[17] What is decisive is thus the indisputable state of the register and not the arguable state of the purchaser's mind. Equitable interests registrable in this way include equitable easements and restrictive covenants. In addition, the system has been extended to certain legal interests, such as mortgages not protected by a deposit of the title deeds. Such interests do not, of course, depend on notice for their protection, but nevertheless they are made void against a purchaser for value if they are not registered. Land charges are registered against the names of the persons who created them, in a national computerised system at Plymouth.

(b) *Local land charges.* In addition to the land charges register, there are separate registers of local land charges under the Local Land Charges Act 1975 (replacing provisions in the Land Charges Act 1925). These charges are of a local public nature, such as prohibitions or restrictions on the use of land under planning law, and charges for the cost of making up a private road. Individual registers are maintained by each district council in England and Wales, each London borough, and the Common Council of the City of London. Registration is against the address of the land and not the name of the landowner.

7. Investigation of title

(a) *Title.* A purchaser of land must investigate the title of the vendor in

---

[13] See *Caunce* v. *Caunce* [1969] 1 W.L.R. 286.
[14] See *Williams & Glyn's Bank Ltd.* v. *Boland* [1981] A.C. 487; *Kingsnorth Finance Co. Ltd.* v. *Tizard* [1986] 1 W.L.R. 783.
[15] *Post*, pp. 60–62.
[16] See Judgments Act 1839; Land Charges Registration and Searches Act 1888.
[17] L.P.A. 1925, s.198.

order to confirm that the vendor is able to convey it. He does this by examining the documents under which the vendor holds the land, going back to a "good root of title" at least 15 years old. A good root of title is a document which deals with the whole legal and equitable interest in the land, describes the land adequately, and contains nothing to throw any doubt on the title. If the title consists of a series of conveyances on sale made 4, 14 and 30 years ago, the purchaser must go back to the 30-year old conveyance. If he fails to do this (*e.g.* by accepting the 14-year old conveyance as the root of title), he will be fixed with constructive notice of all that he would have discovered had he investigated the title for the full period.

(b) *Incumbrances.* In addition to confirming that the vendor has power to convey the land, the purchaser must see that there are no burdens on the land that will affect him. For this purpose, he must consider anything that is disclosed by his investigation of title, and inspect the land; and he must make due inquiries of any tenant or other person in occupation of the land.[18] He must also search the local land charges register and the land charges register. Local land charges, being registered against the land, present no special problem. But the land charges register, being a names register, sometimes creates difficulties. The purchaser will know the names of all the estate owners back to the good root of title at least 15 years old, and so he can search against their names. But usually he will not know and cannot discover who were the estate owners prior to that root of title, and so he cannot search against their names. Registration remains valid indefinitely, even against the names of persons hidden behind the root of title. Since 1969, however, a person who is adversely affected by such a charge may obtain compensation out of public funds.[19]

8. Registration of title

(a) *The system.* Although modern legislation has mitigated the defects of the ancient system of investigating title to some extent, in other respects it has aggravated them. There was also much duplication of work: a purchaser had to investigate the title anew even though many previous purchasers had fully investigated it and found it satisfactory. Under the system of registration of title, there is an official investigation of title, and thereafter the land could be transferred without any further investigation of title. The register also notes certain rights held for the benefit of the land, and contains entries that protect certain rights adverse to the land. At first Parliament merely provided a system for the voluntary registration of titles, but in 1897 the registration of title on dealings with land in London became compulsory.[20] Not until the Land Registration Act 1925 came into force did the compulsory registration of title on dealings with land become general, with the system

---

[18] *Hunt* v. *Luck* [1902] 1 Ch. 428.
[19] L.P.A. 1969, s.25. See *post*, p. 86.
[20] See Land Registry Act 1862; Land Transfer Act 1875; Land Transfer Act 1897.

being gradually extended throughout England and Wales, reaching over 12 million registered titles today. In time the system will entirely replace unregistered conveyancing. This extension made it possible to end the limited and unsatisfactory system for the registration of deeds for land in Yorkshire and Middlesex that had been established early in the 18th century as a safeguard against the loss, destruction or suppression of deeds; and by 1976 these registers had been closed.[21]

(b) *Registrable estates.* Two estates in land are capable of being registered: the fee simple absolute in possession, and a leasehold which has at least 21 years to run. On registration, a land certificate is issued to the owner of the estate, who thereupon becomes the "registered proprietor." He then become the legal estate owner, holding subject to entries on the register and any "overriding interests," but free from all other interests. The land certificate shows the title that is recorded in the register of title maintained at the appropriate District Land Registry. The certificate and the register are divided into three parts.

(i) The property register: this describes the property by reference to a filed plan, and notes certain rights held for the benefit of the property.
(ii) The proprietorship register: this sets out the name of the registered proprietor. It also records any "restrictions" on his powers of disposition (*e.g.* that no disposition will be effective unless the purchase money is paid to at least two trustees or a trust corporation), together with any "caution" protecting an adverse claim which cannot be protected by a "restriction" or "notice."
(iii) The charges register: this sets out "notices" of certain incumbrances on the title, such as a lease exceeding 21 years, or a mortgage, restrictive covenant or easement.

"Overriding interests" are interests that will bind a purchaser even though they are not protected by any entry on the register. In general, they are rights which usually can easily be discovered by inspecting the land, making inquiries of occupiers and searching the local land charges register: the land charges register plays no part in registered land. Overriding interests include rights being acquired by adverse possession of the land for at least 12 years under the Limitation Act 1980; the rights of any person "in actual occupation" of the land (or in receipt of the rents and profits thereof) save where his rights are not disclosed after enquiry of him; leases for 21 years or less granted at a rent without taking a premium; and local land charges.

(c) *Overriding interests.* In most respects the system of registered land is plainly an improvement on the old system for unregistered land; but it is not free from difficulties. One difficulty lies in the rights of a person "in actual occupation" of the land as constituting an overriding interest. If H is registered as the sole proprietor of Greenacre but W is entitled to a one-third share in it as an equitable tenant in common, the question when H sells the

[21] See M. & W. 170.

land to P is whether P will be bound by W's rights. For unregistered land, it has been seen that this depends on whether P had notice of W's rights.[22] For registered land it depends on whether W was "in actual occupation" of the land and so has an overriding interest. One view is that this is merely a question of fact; another view is that only occupation that is reasonably discoverable is "actual occupation." Each view has some judicial support; the question is considered later.[23]

(d) *Conclusiveness of registration.* One important difference between the two systems lies in the greater security of title given to registered land. If V has no title to Greenacre but forges deeds that show him to be the owner, a conveyance by V to P vests nothing in P: a person cannot transfer what is not his (*nemo dat quod non habet*). In the case of registered land, if V becomes the registered proprietor of Greenacre and later sells it to P, on registration P will become the estate owner and can validly dispose of the land. Subject to the powers of rectification of the register, the registration of P as the registered proprietor is conclusive.

(e) *Rectification and indemnity.* The court and the registrar have wide powers to rectify the register where there is an error or omission, though these powers are restricted if the registered proprietor is in possession.[24] There are corresponding provisions for compensation out of public funds if any person suffers loss by reason of any rectification, or by reason of an error or omission in the register which is not rectified.[25] Unregistered land lacks any similar provisions.

(f) *The concurrent systems.* Ultimately, all land will become registered land. After successive extensions over nearly a century, the whole of England and Wales is now subject to the compulsory registration of title. But that does not mean that all the land is registered land. Registration is not required until the fee simple is sold or a lease for not less than 21 years is granted or assigned. Much land remains unregistered because it has not been sold or leased since registration became compulsory in the area. Land vested in companies or other corporations or bodies may remain unsold for centuries. Further, when unregistered land is sold, the sale is usually carried out under the system for unregistered land, and the purchaser then registers the title after completion. A knowledge of both systems of law will thus be needed for a long while.

9. A balance of interests. The complexity of land law is in large measure due to the complexity of the rights in land which have grown up to meet many different human needs. A single plot of land may be subject to a wide

---

[22] See *ante*, p. 7.
[23] *Post*, pp. 104, 105.
[24] See the *Haigh* case: Ruoff & Roper, *The Law and Practice of Registered Conveyancing*, 6th ed. 1991 (cited as "Ruoff & Roper"), p. 2–08 (murderer dissolves victims in acid bath and obtains registered title to a victim's land by forgery).
[25] See *post*, pp. 114, 115.

variety of rights, and the extent and validity of these rights may be tested from time to time, and especially when the land is sold. The interests of a purchaser would be served if all such rights were made void against him if not registered. Yet such a provision would be oppressive, not only in the scale of registration that would be required but also in respect of rights that could not reasonably be expected to be registered. The question is one of balance.

Sect. 3. Historical Outline

The history of the law of property in land can be divided into six periods.

1. Formulation of principles. This was the early period during which the common law courts formulated many of the fundamental rules of land law. A number of important statutes were passed during this period, which extended from the Norman Conquest to the end of the fourteenth century.

2. Growth of Equity. This was the period from about 1400 to 1535, when the jurisdiction of the Chancellor to give relief in cases not covered by the common law rules was firmly established and developed.

3. The Statute of Uses. This was the period from 1535 to the middle of the seventeenth century, when the great changes made by the Statute of Uses 1535 were being worked out.

4. Development of trusts and the rules against remoteness. This encompassed the end of the seventeenth century and the eighteenth century, when trusts, which had been considerably restricted by the Statute of Uses 1535, were once more enforced. The modern form of a strict settlement of land, by which land was "kept in the family" from one generation to another, was fully developed during this period, as were rules preventing interests vesting in persons at remote future dates.

5. Statutory reforms. This period consists of the nineteenth and twentieth centuries, when far-reaching reforms were made by Parliament. Many reforms were made during the nineteenth century, particularly between 1832 and 1845 and again between 1881 and 1890; but important though these were, they could not rival the 1925 property legislation in complexity and comprehensiveness. The Law of Property Act 1922 laid the foundation for the Acts of 1925, but most of it, together with extensive amendments of the law made by the Law of Property (Amendment) Act 1924, was repealed and replaced before it came into force. The provisions of these two Acts and of much of the earlier reforms were consolidated and divided up into six Acts; and these Acts and the unrepealed portions of the Act of 1922 all came into force on January 1, 1926. The "1925 property legislation" thus consists of:

The few unrepealed portions of the Law of Property Act 1922.

The Settled Land Act 1925.
The Trustee Act 1925.
The Law of Property Act 1925.
The Land Registration Act 1925.
The Land Charges Act 1925.
The Administration of Estates Act 1925.

In addition, some amending statutes were subsequently passed, altering details in the principal Acts.

The genesis of the 1925 property legislation is important when construing it. The Acts of 1925 are all consolidating Acts, and a consolidating Act is presumed to change the law no more than the language necessarily requires. However, the Acts of 1922 and 1924 are professedly amending Acts, so that the presumption is not that the Acts of 1925 have not changed the old law, but that they have not changed the changes in that law made by the Acts of 1922 and 1924. Accordingly, where the Acts of 1922 and 1924 have left the old law unchanged, the Acts of 1925 are presumed not to have changed the law.[26] But where the Acts of 1922 and 1924 have changed the old law, it is those provisions which, though repealed, must first be construed.[27]

Since 1925 a number of statutes directed to specific reforms have appeared. These include the Perpetuities and Accumulations Act 1964, the Law of Property (Joint Tenants) Act 1964, the Matrimonial Homes Act 1967, the Law of Property Act 1969, the Charging Orders Act 1979, the Limitation Act 1980 and the Law of Property (Miscellaneous Provisions) Act 1989. Furthermore, in 1972 the Land Charges Act 1925 was replaced by a new consolidating Act, the Land Charges Act 1972.

6. Social control and registration of title. This period overlaps the last. It consists of the last 75 years. During this period Parliament enacted drastic provisions, sometimes varying with the political party in power, which curtailed and restricted the rights of landowners in the interests of tenants and the public. During this period there was also a great extension of the compulsory registration of title, especially since 1965.

Sect. 4. Meaning of "Real Property"

1. Land. The natural division of physical property is into land (sometimes called "immovables") and other objects known as chattels or "movables." This simple distinction is inadequate. In the first place chattels may become attached to land so as to lose their character of chattels and become part of the land itself.[28] Second, a sophisticated legal system of property has to provide not simply for the ownership of physical property,

---

[26] See, *e.g. Beswick* v. *Beswick* [1968] A.C 58.
[27] *Re Turner's W.T.* [1937] Ch. 15; *Grey* v. *Inland Revenue Commissioners* [1960] A.C. 1; *Lloyds Bank Ltd.* v. *Marcan* [1973] 1 W.L.R. 339 at 344 (affirmed [1973] 1 W.L.R. 1387).
[28] For "fixtures," see *post*, p. 15.

but also for the ownership of a wide variety of *interests* in such physical property, and also for the ownership of interests in non-physical or intangible property such as shares in companies or copyright.[29] Third, for historical reasons English law has developed a distinction between "real property" and "personal property" which only approximately corresponds to that between "land" and other types of property.

2. History. In early law, property was deemed "real" if the courts would restore to a dispossessed owner the thing itself, the "*res*," and not merely give compensation for the loss.[30] Thus if X forcibly evicted Y from his freehold land, Y could bring a "real" action whereby he could obtain an order from the court that X should return the land to him. But if X took Y's sword or glove from him, Y could bring only a personal action which gave X the choice of either returning the article or paying the value of it. Consequently, a distinction was made between real property (or "realty"), which could be specifically recovered, and personal property (or "personalty"), which was not thus recoverable. In general, all interests in land are real property, with the exception of leaseholds (or "terms of years"), which are classified as personalty.

At first, a dispossessed leaseholder had no right to recover his land from anyone except the lessor who had granted him the lease. Against third parties, he remained without remedy until late in the thirteenth century, when he was enabled to recover damages but not possession. Not until 1468 was this rule seriously questioned, and when in 1499 it was finally decided that he might recover the land itself,[31] leaseholds had become too firmly established as personalty for this change to make any difference to their status. Thus, if a testator dies today, leaving a will giving all his realty to R and all his personalty to P, the reason for the leaseholds being included in the property passing to P lies in a rule which ceased to exist some 500 years ago.

3. Reasons for distinction. In early times there were no opportunities for investing in stocks and shares such as there are today. Money was therefore often employed in buying land and letting it out on lease on order to obtain an income from the capital. Further, the relationship between landlord and tenant was regarded as being mainly contractual, the tenant on his part agreeing to pay rent, and the landlord on his side agreeing to allow the tenant to occupy the land.[32] These conceptions were so far removed from the feudal system of landholding that leaseholds remained outside that system[33] and for a long time were hardly regarded as being rights in the land at all.

4. Classification. Although leaseholds are still classified as personalty, they differ from most of the other kinds of personalty in that they fall under

---

[29] For interests in land, see *post*, p. 21.
[30] 3 H.E.L. 3, 4; and see T.C. Williams (1888) 4 L.Q.R. 394.
[31] See 3 H.E.L. 213–216.
[32] 2 P. & M. 106.
[33] Challis R.P. 63.

the heading of "land" or "immovables" as opposed to "pure personalty," or "movables," such as furniture or stocks and shares. They are accordingly classified as "chattels real," the first word indicating their personal nature (cattle were the most important chattels in early days, hence the name), the second showing their connection with land.[34] The three types of interests may therefore be classified thus:

$$\left. \begin{array}{l} \textit{Land} \\ \textit{Personalty} \end{array} \right\} \left\{ \begin{array}{l} \text{(i) Realty.} \\ \text{(ii) Chattels real.}^{35} \\ \text{(iii) Pure personalty.} \end{array} \right.$$

Although strictly a book on real property should exclude leaseholds, it has long been customary and convenient to include them, and that course is adopted here.

5. Modern distinction. The legislation of 1925 has abolished many of the remaining differences between the law governing realty and that governing personalty.[36] For example, before 1926, if a person died intestate (*i.e.* without a will), all his realty passed to his heir, while his personalty was divided between certain of his relatives; again, realty could be entailed and personalty could not. After 1925, however, realty and personalty both pass on intestacy to certain relatives, and both kinds of property can be entailed. Thus the modern emphasis is on the distinction between land and other property, though the term "real property" still has some significance and is still widely used.

Sect. 5. Fixtures

In law, the word "land" extends to a great deal more than "land" in everyday speech. The general rule is "*quicquid plantatur solo, solo cedit*" (whatever is attached to the soil becomes part of it). Thus if a building is erected on land and objects are attached to the building, the word "land" prima facie includes the soil, the building and the objects affixed to it; and the owner of the land becomes owner of the building, even if it is built with bricks stolen by the builder.[37] The word "fixtures" is the name applied to anything which has become so attached to land as to form in law part of the land. A mortgage or devise of Greenacre or a contract to sell it thus passes rights to the fixtures to the mortgagee or devisee or purchaser.

A. Definition of Fixtures

In deciding whether or not an object has become a fixture, there are two main elements to be considered, namely—

---

[34] See *Ridout* v. *Pain* (1747) 3 Atk. 486 at 492.
[35] For other chattels real, of no importance today, see Co. Litt. 118b and M. & W. 16.
[36] See A.E.A. 1925, ss.45–47; L.P.A. 1925, ss.60, 130.
[37] *Gough* v. *Wood & Co.* (1894) 10 T.L.R. 318.

(1) the degree of annexation, and
(2) the purpose of annexation.

1. Degree of annexation. In general, for an article to be considered a fixture, some substantial connection with the land or a building on it must be shown. An article which merely rests on the ground by its own weight, such as a cistern or a "Dutch barn" which rests upon timber laid on the ground, is prima facie not a fixture.[38] On the other hand, a chattel attached to the land or a building on it will prima facie be a fixture even if it would not be very difficult to remove it.[39]

2. Purpose of annexation. The degree of annexation is useful as showing upon whom the onus of proof lies[40]; thus if the article is securely fixed, the burden of proof lies on the party contending that it is not a fixture. The purpose of the annexation, however, is the main factor; the modern tendency is to regard the degree of annexation as being chiefly of importance as evidence of the purpose of annexation.[41] The more securely an object is affixed and the more damage that would be caused by its removal, the more likely it is that the object was intended to form a permanent part of the land.[42] An object which is not affixed at all is unlikely to be held a fixture.[43]

In determining the purpose of annexation, the question to be asked is: "Was the intention to effect a permanent improvement of the land or building as such; or was it merely to effect a temporary improvement or to enjoy the chattel as a chattel?"[44] In the first case, the chattel is a fixture, in the second it is not. Thus, a wall composed of blocks of stone, or statues forming part of a general architectural design,[45] or movable dog-grates substituted for fixed grates,[46] or tapestries and portraits in a room designed as an Elizabethan room, have all been held to be fixtures.[47] In each case, the evident intention was to effect a permanent improvement to the land. But tapestry attached by tacks to wooden strips fastened to the wall by two-inch nails,[48] panelling screwed into wooden plugs let into the wall, a collection of stuffed birds attached to movable wooden trays in glass cases attached to the walls of a bird gallery,[49] and pictures recessed into panelling[50] have all been held not to form part of the premises. Although in these cases there was a

---

[38] See *Wiltshear* v. *Cottrell* (1853) 1 E. & B. 674.
[39] See *Buckland* v. *Butterfield* (1820) 2 Brod. & B. 54; *Jordan* v. *May* [1947] K.B. 427.
[40] *Holland* v. *Hodgson* (1872) L.R. 7 C.P. 328 at 335.
[41] *Leigh* v. *Taylor* [1902] A.C. 157 at 162. See also *Hynes* v. *Vaughan* (1985) 50 P. & C.R. 444.
[42] *Spyer* v. *Phillipson* [1931] 2 Ch. 183 at 209, 210.
[43] *H.E. Dibble Ltd.* v. *Moore* [1970] 2 Q.B. 181; *Berkley* v. *Poulett* [1977] E.G.D. 754; *Deen* v. *Andrews* (1985) 52 P. & C.R. 17. Contrast *Hamp* v. *Bygrave* [1983] E.G.D. 1000, not citing *Berkley* v. *Poulett*.
[44] See *Hellawell* v. *Eastwood* (1851) 6 Exch. 295 at 312.
[45] *D'Eyncourt* v. *Gregory* (1866) L.R. 3 Eq. 382. See now *Berkley* v. *Poulett, supra.*
[46] *Monti* v. *Barnes* [1901] 1 Q.B. 205.
[47] *Re Whaley* [1908] 1 Ch. 615.
[48] *Leigh* v. *Taylor* [1902] A.C. 157.
[49] *Viscount Hill* v. *Bullock* [1897] 2 Ch. 482.
[50] *Berkley* v. *Poulett, supra.*

substantial degree of annexation, the only way in which the chattels could be properly enjoyed was to attach them to the house in some way, and thus it was easy to infer an intent to affix them for the better enjoyment of them as chattels and not for the permanent improvement of the building.[51] So, too, a drainpipe serving a house and laid in adjoining land has been held not to be a fixture; it was put there for the commodious occupation of the house and not for the benefit of the land in which it lay.[52] Similar articles may in individual cases remain chattels or become fixtures, depending on the circumstances, *e.g.* tip-up seats fastened to the floor of a cinema or theatre,[53] statues, and tapestries.[54]

B. Right to Remove Fixtures

If according to the above rules an article is not a fixture, it can be removed by the person bringing it on to the land or by his successors in title; but if it is a fixture, prima facie it cannot be removed from the land and must be left for the fee simple owner, although there are some important exceptions to this. Questions of the right to remove fixtures arise between the following parties.

I. LIMITED RIGHT OF REMOVAL

1. Landlord and tenant. Prima facie, all fixtures attached by the tenant are "landlord's fixtures," *i.e.* must be left for the landlord. But the exceptions which have arisen nearly swallow up the rule; and fixtures which can be removed under these exceptions are known as "tenant's fixtures." These fixtures can be removed while the tenancy continues, and even after it has ended if the tenant remains in possession as a tenant under some statutory or other right.[55] If the tenancy is brought to an end by a notice which does not allow enough time to remove the fixtures, the tenant is allowed a reasonable time in which to remove them.[56] When removing fixtures, the tenant must make good any damage caused to the property either on their removal or on their initial installation.[57]

The following have been held to be tenant's fixtures, though in some cases it is not clear whether the article is removable because it has not become a fixture or because, though a fixture, it is a tenant's fixture.

(a) *Trade fixtures.* Fixtures attached by the tenant for the purpose of his

---

[51] See *Young* v. *Dalgety Plc.* [1987] 1 E.G.L.R. 116 (carpeting and light fittings).
[52] *Simmons* v. *Midford* [1969] 2 Ch. 415; contrast *Montague* v. *Long* (1972) 24 P. & C.R. 240 (bridge over river).
[53] Contrast *Lyon & Co.* v. *London City & Midland Bank* [1903] 2 K.B. 135 with *Vaudeville Electric Cinema Ltd.* v. *Muriset* [1923] 2 Ch. 74.
[54] Compare *Re Whaley* [1908] 1 Ch. 615 with *Leigh* v. *Taylor* [1902] A.C. 157, and *D'Eyncourt* v. *Gregory, supra*, with *Berkely* v. *Poulett, supra*.
[55] *New Zealand Government Property Corporation* v. *H.M. & S. Ltd.* [1982] Q.B. 1145.
[56] *Smith* v. *City Petroleum Co. Ltd.* [1940] 1 All E.R. 260. See G. Kodilinye [1987] Conv. 253.
[57] *Mancetter Developments Ltd.* v. *Garmanson Ltd.* [1986] Q.B. 1212.

trade or business have long been removable by the tenant.[58] Vats, fixed steam engines and boilers, a shed for making varnish, shrubs planted by a market gardener and the fittings of a public house have all been held to come within the category of trade fixtures.[59] A tenant does not surrender his right of removal by surrendering his existing tenancy in return for the grant of a new tenancy.[60] Nor is the value of tenant's fixtures taken into account for the purposes of a rent review.[61]

(b) *Ornamental and domestic fixtures.* This exception appears to be rather more limited than the previous one, and seems to extend only to chattels perfect in themselves which can be removed without substantial injury to the building.[62] An article which can be moved entire is more likely to fall within this exception than one which cannot.[63] Thus while a conservatory on brick foundations has been held not to be removable, looking glasses, ornamental chimney pieces, window blinds, stoves, grates and kitchen ranges have all been held to be removable during the tenancy.

(c) *Agricultural fixtures.* At common law, agricultural fixtures were not regarded as falling within the exception of trade fixtures,[64] for agriculture was regarded as a normal use of land and not as a trade. But by statute[65] a tenant of an agricultural holding who has attached fixtures to the land may remove them before, or within two months after, the determination of the tenancy, provided the following conditions are observed:

(i)   one month's written notice is given to the landlord;
(ii) all rent due is paid and all the tenant's obligations under the tenancy are satisfied by him;
(iii) no avoidable damage is done in the removal, and any damage done is made good; and
(iv) the landlord is allowed to retain the fixtures if he pays a fair price for them.

2. Tenant for life and remainderman. If land is settled on A for life with remainder to B, on the death of A the question arises whether fixtures which A has attached to the land can be removed and treated as part of A's estate or whether they must be left for B. The position here is similar to that between landlord and tenant. Prima facie, all the fixtures must be left for B, with the common law exceptions of trade, ornamental and domestic fixtures[66]; but the statutory exception of agricultural fixtures does not apply.

---

[58] *Poole's Case* (1703) 1 Salk. 368.
[59] See M. & W. 735.
[60] *New Zealand Government Property Corporation* v. *H.M. & S. Ltd.* [1982] Q.B. 1145.
[61] See *Young* v. *Dalgety Plc.* [1987] 1 E.G.L.R. 116.
[62] See *Martin* v. *Roe* (1857) 7 E. & B. 237 at 244.
[63] *Grymes* v. *Boweren* (1830) 6 Bing. 437.
[64] *Elwes* v. *Maw* (1802) 3 East 38.
[65] A.H.A. 1986, s.10, replacing provisions in statutes from L. & T.A. 1851, s.3, onwards.
[66] See *Re Hulse* [1905] 1 Ch. 406 at 410.

II. NO RIGHT OF REMOVAL

3. Devisee and personal representative. If the land is given by will, the rule is that all fixtures pass under the devise; the testator's personal representatives are not entitled to remove them for the benefit of the testator's estate, whether they are ornamental, trade or any other kind of fixture.[67]

4. Vendor and purchaser. Without exception, all fixtures attached to the land at the time of a contract of sale must be left for the purchaser[68] unless otherwise agreed. The conveyance will be effective to pass the fixtures to the purchaser without express mention[69] though not structures or erections which are not fixtures.

5. Mortgagor and mortgagee. If land is mortgaged, all fixtures on it are included in the mortgage without special mention; the exceptions as between landlord and tenant do not apply.[70] The mortgagor is not even entitled to remove fixtures which he has attached after the date of the mortgage.[71]

Sect. 6. Tenures and Estates

The basis of English land law is that all land in England is owned by the Crown. A small part is in the Crown's actual occupation; the rest is occupied by tenants holding either directly or indirectly from the Crown.[72] "*Nulle terre sans seigneur*" (no land without a lord): there is no allodial land in England,[73] *i.e.* no land owned by a subject and not held of some lord.

1. Lord and tenant. This position can be traced from the Norman Conquest. William I regarded the whole of England as his by conquest. To reward his followers and those of the English who submitted to him, he granted and confirmed certain lands to be held of him as overlord.[74] These lands were granted not by way of an out-and-out transfer, but to be held from the Crown upon certain conditions. Thus, Greenacre might have been granted to X on the terms that he did homage and swore fealty, that he provided five armed horsemen to fight for the Crown for 40 days in each year, and the like. Whiteacre might have been granted to Y on condition that he supported the King's train in his coronation. X and Y might each in turn grant land to others to hold of them in return for services. Those who held directly of the King (such as X and Y in the examples above) were known as "tenants *in capite*" or "tenants in chief." Those who in fact

---

[67] See *Re Lord Chesterfield's S.E.* [1911] 1 Ch. 237.
[68] *Colegrave* v. *Dias Santos* (1823) 2 B. & C. 76; *Phillips* v. *Lamdin* [1949] 2 K.B. 33.
[69] L.P.A. 1925, s.62(1); *H.E. Dibble Ltd.* v. *Moore* [1970] 2 Q.B. 181.
[70] *Monti* v. *Barnes* [1901] 1 Q.B. 205; L.P.A. 1925, s.62(1).
[71] *Reynolds* v. *Ashby & Son* [1904] A.C. 466.
[72] 1 P. & M. 232, 233.
[73] Co. Litt. 1b.
[74] Williams R.P. 12.

occupied the land were called tenants in desmesne, and the tenant or tenants (if any) who stood between the King and the tenant in desmesne were called mesne lords, or mesnes.[74a] In days when land and its rents and profits constituted nearly the whole tangible wealth of a country,[75] it was more usual to secure the performance of services by the grant of land in return for those services than it was to secure them by payment; the whole social organisation was based on landholding in return for services.[76]

2. Services. These services became to a certain extent standardised. Thus there was one set of services (which included the provision of armed horsemen for battle) which became known as knight service; there was another set (which included the performance of some honourable service for the King in person) which was known as grand sergeanty; and there was a set (which included performing agricultural services) known as socage. Each of these sets of services was known as a *tenure*, for it showed how the land was held (*tenere*, to hold).

3. Time. A further essential is the length of time for which the land was held. Land might be granted for life (for as long as the tenant lived), in tail (for as long as the tenant or any of his descendants lived), or in fee simple (for as long as the tenant or any of his heirs, whether descendants or not, were alive). Each of these lengths of tenancy was known as an *estate*, a word derived from *status*.[77] Thus the Crown might grant land to A for an estate in fee simple, and A in turn might grant it to B for life. But the ownership of the land remained in the Crown. A man might own one or more estates in land, yet he never owned any of the land itself. Ownership of the largest estate in land, the fee simple, has come more and more to resemble ownership of the land itself, but even today it is technically true to say that the whole of the land in England is owned by the Crown; a subject can own only an estate. Both in popular speech and in legal parlance, however, the word "estate" is often used in other senses. Thus it may describe an area of land ("the Blank Estate is for sale") or assets generally ("the testator left a net estate of £50,000"). The context will usually leave little doubt about which sense is intended.

4. Basic doctrines. There are thus two basic doctrines in the law of real property. These are known as—

   (i) the doctrine of tenures: all land is held of the Crown, either directly or indirectly, on one or other of the various tenures; and
   (ii) the doctrine of estates: a subject cannot own land, but can merely own an estate in it, authorising him to hold it for some period of time.

In short, the tenure answers the question "How is it held?", the estate the question "For how long?"

[74a] Pronounced "demain" (domain) and "mean".
[75] Challis R.P. 1.
[76] Williams R.P. 10.
[77] 2 H.E.L. 351, 352.

5. Effects of doctrines. This doctrine of estates, coupled with the permanence of land as opposed to mere destructible chattels, is one reason why the law relating to land is so much more complex than the law governing chattels. At common law, it can in general be said that only two distinct legal rights can exist at the same time in chattels, namely, possession and ownership. If A lends his watch to B, the ownership of the watch remains vested in A, while B has possession of it. But in the case of land, a large number of legal rights could and still can exist at the same time. Thus the position of Greenacre in 1920 might have been that A was entitled to the land for life, B to a life estate in remainder (*i.e.* after A's death), and C to the fee simple in remainder. At the same time, D might own a lease for 99 years, subject to a sub-lease in favour of E for 21 years, and the land might be subject to a mortgage in favour of F, a rentcharge in favour of G, easements such as rights of way in favour of H, J and K, and so on, almost *ad infinitum*. Before 1926, all these estates and interests could exist as legal rights, and most, but not all, can exist as legal rights today.

It may thus be said that in the case of pure personalty, the unit of ownership is the chattel or other thing itself; it is either owned by one person (or several persons jointly or in common with each other), or it is not owned at all. In the case of land, however, the unit of ownership is not the land itself (which is necessarily owned by the Crown), but the estates and interests which have been artificially created in the land. In popular speech, one may refer to X's ownership of Greenacre; but technically, one should speak of X owning a lease of Greenacre, or holding Greenacre in fee simple. This conception of the subject-matter of ownership being an abstract estate rather than the corporeal land was a remarkable and distinctive achievement of early English legal thought; it contributed greatly both to the triumphant flexibility of the English system and to its undoubted complexity.

The doctrine of tenures, now greatly attenuated, is briefly described in the following section, while the doctrine of estates, still of great significance, is considered in greater detail in the next chapter.

Sect. 7. Tenures

The disappearance of the social organisation based on landholding in return for services has led over the centuries to extensive changes in the rules of tenure, so that many tenures, formerly important, have now vanished.

1. Extinct tenures. The tenancies which existed at common law were divided into two main classes, free and unfree.

(a) *Free tenures*. There were three classes of free tenures:

    (1) Tenures in chivalry (or military tenures).
    (2) Tenures in socage (generally involving agricultural services).
    (3) Spiritual tenures (involving religious services).

Each of these categories was subdivided, but it is unnecessary to consider

in detail the different incidents and services to which each gave rise.[78] The
statute *Quia Emptores* 1290, which prohibited the creation of new tenures
by anyone except the Crown, the Tenures Abolition Act 1660, which converted tenures in chivalry into common socage, and the Law of Property Act
1922, which abolished almost all[79] the remaining incidents of the free
tenures, have reduced all free tenures to one class, namely socage,[79a] now
usually called "freehold." The process of attrition of tenures has also
brought about the disappearance of all intermediate tenures, so that the
courts will now readily act on the presumption that all freehold land is held
directly of the Crown.[80]

(b) *Unfree tenures.*[81] The two unfree tenures were villein tenure and,
somewhat confusingly, "customary freehold." Their main distinguishing
features were the uncertain varying nature of the services to be rendered to
the lord, and the absence of protection by the King's Courts. The tenant had
to look for his protection to the court of his lord. Both these features
disappeared in later centuries, but not before it had been established that
land held on an unfree tenure could be transferred only by a surrender and
admittance made in the lord's court. The transaction was recorded on the
court rolls and the transferee was given a copy of the entry to prove his title;
he thus held "by copy of the court roll," and the tenure became known as
"copyhold."

(c) *Enfranchisement of copyholds.* Before 1926, provision had been made
by statute for the enfranchisement of copyholds, *i.e.* the conversion of land
of copyhold tenure into socage. The Copyhold Acts of 1841, 1843 and 1844
provided for voluntary enfranchisement, *i.e.* enfranchisement where both
lord and tenant agreed. The Copyhold Acts of 1852, 1858 and 1887 (consolidated in the Copyhold Act 1894) enabled either lord or tenant to secure
compulsory enfranchisement. But apart from any proceedings taken under
these Acts, the various tenures remained substantially unaltered until the
legislation of 1925 came into force. Finally, by the Law of Property Act
1922,[82] all remaining copyhold land was converted into land of freehold
tenure. However, the incidents of copyhold land, unlike those of freehold
land, remained important and effective in 1925, and therefore could not be
simply abolished without causing injustice to the lord. Some were abolished
forthwith subject to the payment of compensation.[83] Others, including quit
rents and chief rents, were preserved temporarily, a class which disappeared
on or before December 31, 1935.[84] Lastly, there are a few which continue

---

[78] See M. & W., Chap. 2.

[79] A survival is escheat where the trustee in bankruptcy of a landowner disclaims, or a
   corporation holding land is dissolved: see M. & W. 34.

[79a] From "soc," meaning either "plough-share," or, more probably, "seek," for the tenant must
   seek his lord's "soke," or court.

[80] See, *e.g. Re Lowe's W.T.* [1973] 1 W.L.R. 882.

[81] See M. & W. 22–27.

[82] s.128, Sched. 12, para. (1).

[83] L.P.A. 1922, Sched. 12, para. i; Sched. 13, Pt. II, as amended.

[84] *Ibid.* ss.128, 138, 140, Sched. 13, Pt. II. See M. & W. 35.

indefinitely unless abolished by written agreement between lord and tenant. These are:

  (i) Any rights of the lord or tenant to mines and minerals;
 (ii) Any rights of the lord in respect of fairs, markets and sporting;
(iii) Any tenant's rights of common (*e.g.* to pasture beasts on the waste land of the manor); and
 (iv) Any liability of lord or tenant for the upkeep of dykes, ditches, sea walls, bridges and the like.

2. Modern tenures. As a consequence of the developments outlined above, there is only one feudal tenure left today, namely, socage, now called freehold. By contrast, leasehold land has increased in importance,[85] and although leaseholds stood outside the feudal system of tenures, they have long been the most important modern form of tenure. Thus at the present time there are only two forms of tenure, namely, freehold and leasehold.

Today little trace remains of the former varieties of tenure and the customs that went with them. Yet some reference must be made to gavelkind and borough English.[86] These were not separate tenures, but customs which applied to certain land of socage tenure and copyhold tenure. The most striking feature of gavelkind, which was mainly found in Kent, was partibility, *i.e.* that on intestacy the land descended to all sons equally and not to the eldest son alone. The main feature of borough English, which was found in Nottingham and places in Sussex and Surrey, was ultimogeniture, *i.e.* that on intestacy the land descended to the youngest son instead of the eldest. These customs no longer apply, for the rare cases where the old rules of intestacy still operate after 1925 are governed by the general law, without these customs.[87]

[85] See *post*, pp. 26, 28 and Chap. 9 (pp. 306–360).
[86] See M. & W. 19–21.
[87] See *post*, p. 163.

CHAPTER 2

ESTATES

Part 1

CLASSIFICATION

THE nature of an estate has already been discussed[1]; it is essentially an interest in land of defined duration. It is now necessary to consider the different kinds of estate. In doing this, much of the discussion will be in the past tense, for as will be seen[2] some of the estates can no longer exist as such, although corresponding rights can exist as interests (instead of estates) in land.

Estates were divided into two classes:

1. Estates of freehold; and
2. Estates less than freehold.[3]

It should be noted that "freehold" here has nothing to do with freehold (or socage) tenure; it is merely that the same word is used to express sometimes the quality of the tenure, and sometimes the quantity of the estate. "Freehold", as normally used by the man in the street, unconsciously combines these senses; thus when a house agent advertises "a desirable freehold residence," he refers to a fee simple estate in land of freehold tenure.

Sect. 1. Estates of Freehold

There were three estates of freehold:

   (a) fee simple;
   (b) fee tail; and
   (c) life estate.[4]

The fee simple and the life estate have always existed in English law; the fee tail was introduced by statute in 1285. Before considering the estates in any detail a brief account of each must be given.

1. Fee simple. Originally a fee simple was an estate which endured for as long as the original tenant or any of his heirs survived. "Heirs" comprised any blood relations, although originally ancestors were excluded; not until

---

[1] *Ante*, p. 20.
[2] *Post*, p. 71.
[3] 1 Preston, *Estates*, 22.
[4] Co. Litt. 43b.

24

the Inheritance Act 1833 could a person be the heir of one of his descendants. Thus at first a fee simple would terminate if the original tenant died without leaving any descendants or collateral blood relations (*e.g.* brothers or cousins), even if before his death the land had been conveyed to another tenant who was still alive. But by 1306 it was settled that where a tenant in fee simple alienated the land, the fee simple would continue as long as there were heirs of the new tenant and so on, irrespective of any failure of the original tenant's heirs.[5] Thenceforward a fee simple was virtually eternal.[6]

2. Fee tail. A fee tail was an estate which continued for as long as the original tenant or any of his descendants survived. Thus if the original tenant died leaving no relatives except a brother, a fee simple would continue, but a fee tail would come to an end. The terms "fee tail," "estate tail," "entail" and "entailed interest" are often used interchangeably, although "fee tail" is the correct expression for a legal entail[7] and "entailed interest" is usually reserved for an equitable entail.[8]

3. Life estate. As its name indicates, a life estate lasted for life only. The name "life estate" usually denoted that the measuring life was that of the tenant himself, *e.g.* when the grant was to A for life. The form of life estate where the measuring life was that of some other person was known as an estate "*pur autre vie*" (pronounced "per *oh*ter vee," and meaning "for the life of another"), *e.g.* to A for so long as B lives.

A common feature of all estates of freehold was that the duration of the estate was fixed but uncertain.[9] Nobody could say when the death would occur of a man and his heirs, or a man and all his descendants, or a man alone. But the duration was not wholly indefinite; the estate was bound to determine if some pre-ordained event occurred. In the case of the fee simple and the fee tail, the word "fee" denoted (a) that the estate was an estate of inheritance, *i.e.* an estate which, on the death of the tenant, was capable of descending to his heir[10]; and (b) that the estate was one which might continue for ever.[11] A life estate, on the other hand, was not a fee. It was not an estate of inheritance and it could not continue for ever. On the death of the tenant, an ordinary life estate determined, and an estate *pur autre vie* did not descend to the tenant's heir, but until 1926 passed under the special rules of "occupancy."[12] Life estates were sometimes called "mere freeholds" or "freeholds," as opposed to "freeholds of inheritance."

[5] Y.B. 33–35 Edw. I (R.S.) 362.
[6] 1 Preston, *Estates*, 429; but see T. Cyprian Williams (1930) 69 L.J. News. 369, 385; 70 *ibid.* 4, 20; (1931) 75 S.J. 843 at 847.
[7] Litt. 13; 1 Preston, *Estates*, 420; Challis R.P. 60.
[8] See *post*, p. 42.
[9] Williams R.P. 65.
[10] 1 Preston, *Estates*, 262, 419; Challis R.P. 218.
[11] 1 Preston, *Estates*, 419, 480.
[12] See M. & W. 94.

Each estate of freehold could exist in a number of varied forms which will be considered in due course.

Sect. 2. Estates Less than Freehold

At first, the three estates of freehold were the sole estates recognised by law; the only other lawful right to the possession of land was known as a tenancy at will,[13] under which the tenant could be ejected at any time, and which therefore hardly ranked as an estate at all. Terms of years grew up outside this system of estates; the lack of protection given to them by the courts, and early doubts whether terms for longer than 40 years were valid,[14] placed leaseholders in a position of inferiority from which they never recovered. Although by the sixteenth century terms of years had become recognised as legal estates[15] and were fully protected, yet they ranked below the three estates of freehold.[16] Leaseholders were regarded as holding their land in the name of their lords, the possession of the leasehold tenant being regarded as the possession of the lord.[17]

Today, the various forms of leasehold estate are of the first importance. Nevertheless, it is still not easy to find any satisfactory common element in them; perhaps it is not possible to evolve a more precise definition than "an estate not a freehold." The principal categories are as follows: they are dealt with more fully later.[18]

1. Fixed term of certain duration. The tenant may hold the land for a fixed term of certain duration,[19] as under a lease for 99 years. The possibility of the term being extended or curtailed under some provision in the lease to this effect does not affect the basic conception, which is one of certainty of duration in the absence of steps being taken for extension or curtailment. A lease for "99 years if X so long lives" also fell under this head; it was not an estate of freehold,[20] for although X might well die before the 99 years had run, the maximum duration of the lease was fixed. For all practical purposes, there was no chance of X outliving the 99 years, so that the duration of the lease would be the same as an estate granted "to X for life"; yet in law the former was less than freehold and the latter freehold. Partly as a result of the intervention of statute, such leases are comparatively rare today.[21]

2. Fixed term with duration capable of being rendered certain. A lease of land "to A from year to year," with no other provision as to its duration, will

---

[13] Challis R.P. 63.
[14] See Co. Litt. 45b, 46a.
[15] Challis R.P. 64.
[16] Co. Litt. 43b; and see *Re Russell Road Purchase Moneys* (1871) L.R. 12 Eq. 78 at 84.
[17] 1 Preston, *Estates*, 205, 206.
[18] *Post*, pp. 314–318.
[19] 1 Preston, *Estates* 203.
[20] 1 Cru.Dig. 47.
[21] See *post*, p. 319.

continue indefinitely unless either landlord or tenant takes some step to determine it. But either party can give half a year's notice to determine it at the end of a year of the tenancy, and thus ensure its determination on a fixed date. This, coupled with the fact that originally the lease was for an uncertain term of uncertain duration, classifies the estate as less than freehold. The same applies to quarterly, monthly, weekly and other periodical tenancies.[22]

3. Uncertain period of uncertain duration. A tenancy at will is a tenancy which may continue indefinitely or may be determined by either party at any time; it is thus less than freehold. In the same way, a tenancy at sufferance, which is similar in nature, is less than freehold.[23] Indeed, such tenancies are perhaps not estates at all.[24]

Sect. 3. Seisin

1. Meaning. One distinction between freeholders and owners of estates less than freehold was that only a freehold could carry seisin with it. It is difficult to define seisin satisfactorily.[25] It has nothing to do with the word "seizing," with its implication of violence. To medieval lawyers it suggested the very opposite: peace and quiet. A man who was put in seisin of land was "set" there and continued to "sit" there.[26] Seisin thus denotes quiet possession of land, but quiet possession of a particular kind.

2. Freeholder. Although at first the term was applied to the possession of a leaseholder as well as that of a freeholder, during the fifteenth century it became confined to those who held an estate of freehold.[27] A leaseholder merely had possession: only a freeholder could be seised.[28] And since the possession of a leaseholder was regarded as the possession of the freeholder from whom he held, a freeholder remained seised even after he had granted a term of years and had given up physical possession of the land: receipt of the rent was evidence of seisin. Further, only land of freehold tenure carried seisin with it. A copyholder could not be seised, even if he held a fee simple.

From this it will be seen that a person was seised only if—

(i) he held an estate of freehold,
(ii) the land was land of freehold tenure, and
(iii) either he had taken physical possession of the land, or a leaseholder or copyholder held the land from him.

3. Definition. Although it seems impossible to frame a satisfactory definition of seisin, to call it "that feudal possession of land which only the owner

[22] For these tenancies see *post*, pp. 315–318.
[23] For these tenancies see *post*, p. 318.
[24] Consider *Wheeler* v. *Mercer* [1957] A.C. 416 at 427, 428; M. & W. 129.
[25] See, generally, Maitland's *Collected Papers*, Vol. 1, pp. 329, 358, 407.
[26] 2 P. & M. 30.
[27] Challis R.P. 99.
[28] Litt. 324; Co. Litt. 17a, 200b.

of a freehold estate in freehold land could have" is to express the most important elements. A man might be seised of many plots of land at the same time, whether or not he had granted any leases of them, for the requirement of physical possession did not mean that the person seised had to be in continuous occupation: seisin was not lost merely because he went away on a visit. Once seisin was acquired, it continued until another person acquired it.

4. Importance. The importance of seisin, which has greatly diminished in modern times, is shown in many ways. For example—

> (i) Feudal services could be claimed only from the tenant seised of the land.[29]
> (ii) A real action (one in which the land itself could be recovered and not merely damages) could be brought only against the tenant seised.[30]
> (iii) Curtesy and dower (the rights of a surviving spouse under the rules for intestacy before 1926) could be claimed only out of property of which the deceased had been seised.[31]
> (iv) Conveyances of freehold land could originally be made only by a "feoffment[32] with livery of seisin." This was a solemn ceremony carried out by the parties entering on the land, and the feoffor, in the presence of witnesses, delivering the seisin to the feoffee either by some symbolic act, such as handing him a twig or sod of earth, or by uttering some words such as "Enter into this land and God give you joy," and leaving him in possession of the land.

For these and other reasons, the common law abhorred an abeyance of seisin. Any transactions whereby one person lost seisin without transferring it to another was void.

Sect. 4. Position of Leaseholds Today

As has been seen, leaseholds were at first regarded as mere contractual rights to occupy land.[33] Despite their subsequent recognition as legal estates, they always remained outside the feudal system of landholding. Today, it is possible to regard leasehold as a tenure. Only in the case of leaseholds does there now arise a relationship of lord and tenant which has any practical importance. The one remaining feudal tenure, socage, has been shorn of all the incidents of any consequence, whereas in the case of leaseholds a valuable rent is nearly always payable, and the lord usually has power to forfeit the lease if the tenant does not fulfil his obligations. Further, the position as regards creating successive interests in leaseholds is substantially the same as for land held in socage. Thus just as socage land may be given "to A for life, remainder to B in tail, remainder to C in fee simple," so leasehold

---

[29] Challis R.P. 100.
[30] *Freeman d. Vernon* v. *West* (1763) 2 Wils. K.B. 165 at 166.
[31] See M. & W. 543–546.
[32] Pronounced "feffment"; and similarly for "feoffor" and "feoffee."
[33] *Ante*, p. 14.

land may be given "to A for life, remainder to B in tail, remainder to C absolutely." Nevertheless, leaseholds also retain the principal characteristic of an estate, for they mark out the length of time for which the land is held. Consequently, although it may be true that for all practical purposes lease-holds have completed the transition from contract via estate to tenure, it is better to regard them as being in a class by themselves, having features of both estates and tenures.

The details of leaseholds will be considered later.[34]

Part 2

ESTATES OF FREEHOLD

The two main points to be considered concerning estates of freehold are—

  (1) the words required to create each of the estates, and
  (2) the characteristics of each estate.

Sect. 1. Words of Limitation

"Words of limitation" is the phrase used to describe the words which limit (*i.e.* delimit, or mark out) the estate to be taken. Thus in a conveyance today "to A in fee simple," the words "in fee simple" are words of limitation, for they show what estate A is to have.

1. Inter vivos. The rule at common law was that a freehold estate of inheritance could be created in a conveyance *inter vivos* (*i.e.* a transfer of land between living persons) only by a phrase which included the word "heirs." A life estate could be created without using this word, but a fee simple or fee tail could not[35]: no other word would do. "Heirs" was the sanctified word of limitation, and had a magic which no other word possessed.

2. Wills. In the case of gifts by will, the attitude of the courts was different. A conveyance was a solemn transaction that was enforced by the courts of law, whereas wills were less formal and were at first enforced by the Court of Chancery; and that court looked to the intent rather than the form. When the Statute of Wills 1540 compelled the common law courts to give effect to wills, both the words of the statute (authorising the testator to dispose of land "at his free will and pleasure"[36]) and the practice of Chancery encour-aged the courts to interpret wills liberally. Thus strict words of limitation were not required in wills. Provided the intention of the testator was clear, it would be effectuated.[37]

---

[34] *Post*, Chap. 9, pp. 306 *et seq.*
[35] Co. Litt. 20a, 20b.
[36] Statute of Wills 1540, ss.1, 2.
[37] *Throckmerton* v. *Tracy* (1555) 1 Plowd. 145 at 162, 163.

The rules will now be considered, taking the fee simple, fee tail and life estate in turn and dealing separately under each head with conveyances *inter vivos* and wills.

A. Words of Limitation for a Fee Simple

I. CONVEYANCES INTER VIVOS

1. At common law

(a) *Natural persons.* At common law, the proper expression to employ was "and his heirs" following the grantee's name, *e.g.* "to A and his heirs."[38] "Heir" in the singular would not do, and the word "and" could not be replaced by "or"[39]: "to A or his heirs" gave A a mere life estate, and so did expressions not containing the word "heirs," *e.g.* "to A for ever," or "to A in fee simple."[40]

It is important to note that the words "and his heirs" gave no estate in the land to the heirs. The words were mere words of limitation, delimiting or marking out the estate which A was to take; they were not words of purchase, that is to say, they were not words which conferred any estates on the heirs themselves. ("Purchase" is here used in the technical sense as referring to any transaction, whether for value or not, whereby property is acquired by act of parties, as by gift, and not merely by operation of law, as on intestacy[41]). Thus if A had a son at the time of the conveyance, the son acquired no estate by it, but had merely a *spes successionis*, *i.e.* a hope of succeeding to the fee simple if A died without having disposed of it.[42] Although A's eldest son is his "heir" in the popular sense, the legal maxim is "*nemo est heres viventis*" (a living person has no heir).[43] A living person may have an heir apparent, *i.e.* a person who, if he survives A, will be A's heir, such as his eldest son; or he may have an heir presumptive, *i.e.* a person who, if he outlives A, and no person with a better claim comes into existence, will be A's heir, such as his daughter: but not until A's death can his heir be ascertained.[44]

(b) *Corporations.* In the case of conveyances to corporations, different rules applied. A corporation aggregate consists of two or more persons united together under some name to form a new legal person having perpetual existence, *e.g.* a Dean and Chapter, or a limited company. No words of limitation were needed in such a case; a conveyance to the corporation *simpliciter*, *e.g.* "to the Alpha Co. Ltd.," sufficed to pass the fee simple, for there was no reason to give it any other estate.[45] A corporation sole, on the

---

[38] 2 Preston, *Estates*, 1.
[39] Co. Litt. 8b; Challis R.P. 221, 222.
[40] Litt. 1.
[41] See M. & W. 540.
[42] *Re Parsons* (1890) 45 Ch.D. 51 at 55.
[43] 2 Preston, *Estates* 35.
[44] See 3 Cru.Dig. 328.
[45] 2 Preston, *Estates*, 43–47.

other hand, comprises only one natural person. Thus the King, a bishop or a parson are all corporations sole in their official capacities. In such cases, a life estate to the individual holder of the office was a conceivable alternative to a fee simple, and so to create a fee simple a formula had to be used which indicated that the corporation rather than the individual should benefit.[46] This formula was "and his successors," *e.g.* "to the Vicar of Bray and his successors."[47] Failure to use this phrase resulted in a mere life estate passing to the individual, though the use of "heirs" perhaps gave a fee simple to the individual.[48]

2. By statute

(a) *After 1881.* It has been seen that at common law a conveyance "to A in fee simple" would create not a fee simple, but only a life estate.[49] This was remedied by the Conveyancing Act 1881[50] enacting that in deeds executed after 1881 the words "in fee simple" would suffice to pass the fee simple. The expressions available at common law still remained effective: the Act merely supplied an alternative, and this alternative had to be employed as strictly as the older expression.[51]

(b) *After 1925.* By the Law of Property Act 1925, the necessity for words of limitation in creating a fee simple was abolished in the case of all deeds executed after 1925, for the grantee takes "the fee simple or other the whole interest which the grantor had power to convey in such land, unless a contrary intention appears in the conveyance."[52] This effect will be produced even if the conveyance is to a corporation sole.[53] In practice, the words "in fee simple" are always inserted to make it clear that there is no contrary intention.

II. GIFTS BY WILL

1. Before 1838. Before 1838, no formal words of limitation were required in a will, but it was necessary for the will to show an intent to pass the fee simple.[54] Thus "to A for ever," "to A and his heir," or "to A to dispose at will and pleasure" all sufficed to pass the fee simple.[55] But it was for the devisee to show that a fee simple was intended to pass; a devise "to A" prima facie carried merely a life estate.[56]

---

[46] See *Ex p. Vicar of Castle Bytham* [1895] 1 Ch. 348 at 354.
[47] Co. Litt. 8b, 94b; and see *Bankes* v. *Salisbury Diocesan Council of Education Incorporated* [1960] Ch. 631.
[48] 2 Preston, *Estates*, 48; Co. Litt. 94b, n. (5).
[49] Shep. 106.
[50] s.51.
[51] See *Re Ethel and Mitchells and Butlers' Contract* [1901] 1 Ch. 945 ("in fee" not enough).
[52] s.60(1).
[53] s.60(2).
[54] 2 Preston, *Estates*, 68.
[55] See, generally, 6 Cru.Dig., Chap. XI.
[56] 2 Preston, *Estates*, 78.

2. After 1837. By the Wills Act 1837[57] the fee simple or other the whole interest of which the testator has power to dispose passes in a gift by any will made or confirmed after 1837[58] unless a contrary intention is shown. This reverses the onus of proof; a devise "to A" now passes the fee simple unless a contrary intention is shown. But the old rule still applies if the will is creating some new interest, *e.g.*, a rentcharge.[59]

B. Words of Limitation for a Fee Tail

I. CONVEYANCES INTER VIVOS

1. At common law. The expression required to create a fee tail at common law was the word "heirs" followed by some words of procreation,[60] *i.e.* words which confined "heirs" to descendants of the original grantee; an example is "to X and the heirs of his body." The word "heirs" was essential, but any words of procreation sufficed. Thus "to A and the heirs of his flesh" or "to A and the heirs from him proceeding" sufficed to create entails. But expressions such as "to A and his issue" or "to A and his seed" would not create a fee tail in a deed, for the vital word "heirs" was missing.

By the addition of suitable words, an entail could be further restricted so that it descended only to a particular class of descendants. There were thus the following types of entail[61]:

(i) a tail general, *e.g.* "to A and the heirs of his body," where any descendants of A, male or female, could inherit;

(ii) a tail male, *e.g.* "to A and the heirs male of his body," in which case only male descendants of A who could trace an unbroken descent from him through males could inherit, and not, *e.g.* a son of A's daughter; and

(iii) a tail female, *e.g.* "to A and the heirs female of his body," where corresponding rules applied.

In addition a "special tail" could be created, confining the heirs entitled to those descended from a specified spouse, such as "to A and the heirs of his body begotten upon Mary," when only issue of A and Mary could inherit; Mary, of course, took nothing. A special tail could exist in any of the three above forms.

As in the case of a fee simple, the words following A's name were mere words of limitation. "To A and the heirs of his body" gave A a fee tail; it gave his heir apparent or heir presumptive no estate but only a *spes successionis*.

2. By statute. In the case of deeds executed after 1881 the Conveyancing Act 1881[62] made provisions for entails similar to those made for a fee simple.

[57] s.28.
[58] s.34.
[59] See *post*, p. 363.
[60] 2 Preston, *Estates*, 477, 478.
[61] See Litt. 21–29.
[62] s.51.

In addition to the expressions which sufficed to create an entail at common law, the words "in tail" (not "in fee tail," it will be noted) following the name of the grantee would create a fee tail: *e.g.* "to X in tail." If it was desired to restrict the entail to a particular class of descendants, apt words could be added, *e.g.* "to A in tail male."

These rules still apply after 1925, the provisions of the Conveyancing Act 1881 being now replaced by the Law of Property Act 1925.[63] The effect of using informal words such as "to A and his issue" is to pass the fee simple either to A, or to A jointly with such of his issue as are alive at the time of the gift; the former seems the better view.[64]

II GIFTS BY WILL

1. Before 1926. The rule before 1926 was that in a will any words showing an intent to create an entail sufficed, even if no technical expressions were used. Thus "to A and his seed," "to A and his heirs male,"[65] "to A and his descendants," and "to A and his issue,"[66] all usually sufficed to create entails. A devise "to A and his children" sometimes gave A an entail and sometimes gave the property to A and his children jointly, depending on the circumstances.[67] "Children" prima facie meant descendants of the first generation only, and so was less apt to create an entail than words such as "issue," which prima facie included descendants of any generation and were thus the informal equivalent of "heirs of his body."[68]

2. After 1925. The above rule remained unaffected until the Law of Property Act 1925[69] laid down that informal expressions would no longer suffice to create an entail in a will, but that expressions which would have been effective to create an entail in a deed before 1926 must be employed. Thus in deeds and wills alike either "heirs" followed by words of procreation, or "in tail," must now be used. As in the case of conveyances *inter vivos*, it seems that the effect of using informal expressions such as "to A and his issue" is to pass the fee simple either to A or to A jointly with such of his issue as are alive when the testator dies.[70]

C. The Rule in Shelley's Case

A rule, known as the Rule in *Shelley's Case*,[71] applied to deeds and wills taking effect before 1926. Under the rule, a conveyance "to A for life, remainder to his heirs" operated to vest the fee simple in A, while his heirs

---

[63] ss.60, 130.
[64] See (1936) 6 Camb. L.J. 67; (1945) 9 Camb. L.J. 46; *ibid.* (1946) p. 185.
[65] In a deed this created a fee simple: *Idle* v. *Cook* (1705) 1 P.Wms. 70 at 77.
[66] *Slater* v. *Dangerfield* (1846) 15 M. & W. 263 at 272.
[67] *Wild's Case* (1599) 6 Co. Rep. 16b at 17a, b. See M. & W. 537, 538.
[68] *Re Lord Lawrence* [1915] 1 Ch. 129 at 146.
[69] s.130.
[70] *Supra*, n. 64.
[71] (1581) 1 Co. Rep. 88b; and see Challis R.P. 152–167.

took nothing. The words "remainder to his heirs" were treated as being words of limitation to A, so that the effect was the same as for a limitation "to A and his heirs"; instead of the land being tied up, it was immediately alienable. The rule was abolished for all instruments coming into operation after 1925,[72] and is now solely of historical interest.[73]

D. Words of Limitation for a Life Estate

I. CONVEYANCES INTER VIVOS

In a conveyance before 1926, a life estate was created either by words showing an intention to create a life estate, such as "to A for life," or by the use of expressions insufficient to create a fee simple or fee tail, as "to A" or "to A for ever."[74]

After 1925, a fee simple (or the whole of the interest that the grantor has power to convey, if it is less than a fee simple) passes unless a contrary intention is shown.[75] Thus to create a life interest, words showing an intention to do so must normally be used, *e.g.* "to A for life."

II. IN WILLS

Before the Wills Act 1837, a devise passed only a life estate unless an intention to create a fee simple or fee tail was shown. That Act provided that the fee simple passes unless a contrary intention is shown,[76] so that in this case also, words showing an intent to pass only a life interest are now essential.

Sect. 2. Nature of the Estates of Freehold

A. The Fee Simple

The fee simple is the most ample estate which can exist in land. Although in theory it still falls short of absolute ownership, in practice it amounts to this, for nearly all traces of the old feudal burdens have disappeared. A fee simple normally exists in a defined area of land, and all that is above or below it; but it can exist in the upper storey of a building, without the soil beneath it, and it may even be movable, shifting from plot to plot within a defined area (*e.g.* as settled by lot annually), or varying with boundary changes, as where the sea gradually invades or retreats.[77] Subject to provisions against racial discrimination,[78] a tenant in fee simple has long been free to dispose of his

[72] L.P.A. 1925, s.131.
[73] See M. & W. 1161–1163.
[74] *Re Irwin* [1904] 2 Ch. 752.
[75] *Ante*, p. 31.
[76] s.28; see *ante*, p. 32.
[77] See Co. Litt. 48b; *post*, p. 507.
[78] See Race Relations Act 1976, ss.21–24.

estate in whatever way he thinks fit, either by will[79] or *inter vivos*, though this has not always been so.

A fee (or fee simple) may be absolute or modified; a modified fee is any fee except a fee simple absolute. There are four types of fee.

1. Fee simple absolute. This is the type normally encountered in practice. It is an estate which continues for ever. "Fee" denotes inheritability,[80] "simple" excludes entails, and "absolute" distinguishes modified fees.

2. Determinable fee. A determinable fee is a fee simple which will automatically determine on the occurrence of some specified event which may never occur. If the event is bound to happen at some time, the estate created is not a determinable fee. Thus before 1926 a grant "to A and his heirs until B dies" gave A an estate *pur autre vie*, and a grant "to C and his heirs" for a fixed term of years gave C a mere tenancy for a term of years. A grant to X and his heirs until a specified lease was made, or to Y and his heirs "as long as such a tree stands," however, created determinable fees.[81] The estates of X and Y might continue for ever, but if the specified state of affairs came about, the fee determined and the land reverted to the original grantor. The grantor thus had a "possibility of reverter," *i.e.* a possibility of having an estate at a future time. If the occurrence of the determining event became impossible, the possibility of reverter was destroyed and the fee simple became absolute,[82] as where land was given "to A and his heirs until B marries" and B died a bachelor.

Determinable fees are rarely encountered in practice except under marriage settlements,[83] where the settlor grants land to himself until the solemnisation of the marriage. A fee simple limited to a corporation does not determine merely because the corporation is dissolved.[84]

3. A fee simple upon condition. In making a grant of a fee simple, a clause may be added providing that the fee simple is not to commence until some event occurs, or that it is to determine on the occurrence of some event. Conditions of the first type are conditions precedent[85]: a gift "to X in fee simple if he attains 21" is a gift of a fee simple with a condition precedent that X must attain 21 before he can take the land. These limitations are dealt with under future interests.[86] A condition subsequent is one which operates to defeat an existing interest, *e.g.* a devise of land to X "on the condition that he never sells it out of the family."[87] Here the land passes to X, but it is liable to

---

[79] Subject to possible claims under the Inheritance (Provision for Family and Dependants) Act 1975: see *post*, pp. 135 *et seq*.
[80] See *ante*, p. 25.
[81] *Idle* v. *Cook* (1705) 1 P.Wms. 70 at 78.
[82] Challis R.P. 83, 254.
[83] *Post*, p. 215.
[84] *Re Strathblaine Estates Ltd.* [1948] Ch. 228.
[85] Pronounced "preeseedent," with the accent on the second syllable.
[86] *Post*, pp. 174, *et seq*.
[87] *Re Macleay* (1875) L.R. 20 Eq. 186.

be forfeited if the condition is broken: X has a vested interest, liable to be divested.

The difference between a determinable fee and a fee simple defeasible by condition subsequent is not always easy to discern. The essential distinction is that the determining event in a determinable fee is included in the words marking out the limits of the estate, whereas a condition subsequent is a clause added to a limitation of a complete fee simple absolute which seeks to defeat it. Thus a devise to a school in fee simple "until it ceases to publish its accounts" would create a determinable fee, whereas a devise to the school in fee simple "on condition that the accounts are published annually" creates a fee simple defeasible by condition subsequent.[88] Words such as "while," "during," "as long as," "until" and so on are apt for the creation of a determinable fee, whereas words which form a separate clause of defeasance, such as "provided that," "on condition that," "but if," or "if it happen that," operate as a condition subsequent.[89]

It will be seen that the difference is primarily one of wording; the determining event may be worked into the limitation in such a way as to create either a determinable fee or a fee simple defeasible by condition subsequent, whichever the grantor wishes. The question is whether the words limit the utmost time of continuance of the estate, or whether they mark an event which, if it takes place in the course of that time, will defeat the estate: in the first case the words form a limitation, in the second a condition. In short, a limitation marks the bounds or compass of the estate, a condition defeats the estate before it attains its boundary.

There are some practical differences between the two forms of fee.

(a) *Determination*: a determinable fee automatically determines when the specified event occurs, for the natural limits of its existence have been reached.[90] A fee simple upon condition merely gives the grantor (or whoever is entitled to his realty, if the grantor is dead) a right to enter and determine the estate when the event occurs; until entry is made, the fee simple continues.[91]

Since a right of forfeiture arises from a condition subsequent the condition is void (and so the grantee takes a fee simple absolute) unless it can be seen from the outset distinctly and precisely what events will cause a forfeiture.[92] The concepts of continuing to reside in Canada[93] and of marrying a person "not of Jewish parentage and of the Jewish faith"[94] have been held to be uncertain, whilst the concepts of continuing in permanent residence in England[95] and of being or becoming a Roman Catholic have been held to be

---

[88] See *Re Da Costa* [1912] 1 Ch. 337.
[89] See 1 Sanders, *Uses* 156; Shep. 121.
[90] *Newis* v. *Lark* (1571) 2 Plowd. 403.
[91] *Matthew Manning's Case* (1609) 8 Co.Rep. 94b at 95b.
[92] *Sifton* v. *Sifton* [1938] A.C. 656.
[93] *Ibid.*
[94] *Clayton* v. *Ramsden* [1943] A.C. 320.
[95] *Re Gape* [1952] Ch. 743: "permanent residence" is a concept used in the doctrine of domicile in the conflict of laws.

sufficiently certain.[96] This strict rule for conditions subsequent may be contrasted with the more relaxed rule for conditions precedent, where the question is one not of forfeiture but of entitlement. Thus under a gift to the eldest son of X who is "a member of the Church of England,"[97] or an option to purchase given to "any friends of mine,"[98] the impossibility of defining who is or is not a "member" or "friend" will not invalidate the gift for any person who on any possible meaning of the words is indisputably a "member" or "friend." The court is reluctant to hold a provision void for uncertainty.[99]

(b) *Remoteness*: if a condition subsequent may possibly become operative at too distant a date, it is void, and the fee simple is absolute, whereas at common law a determinable limitation was probably valid no matter how far in the future the estate might determine.[1] But determinable limitations made since July 16, 1964 are now subject to the same rules as conditional interests.[2]

(c) *Existence at law*: a determinable fee cannot, it seems, exist as a legal estate after 1925; but a fee simple subject to a condition subsequent apparently can.[3]

(d) *Flexibility*: a determinable fee is more flexible than a fee simple upon condition. There are certain restrictions upon the conditions on which a fee simple may be made liable to be defeated. A condition subsequent is void, and the fee simple is absolute, if the condition infringes any of the following rules.

(i) It must not take away the power of alienation. One of the incidents of ownership is the right to sell or otherwise dispose of the property. A condition against alienation is said to be repugnant to this right, and contrary to public policy, if it substantially takes away the tenant's power of alienation; such conditions are thus void.[4] For example, conditions prohibiting all alienation, or all alienation during the life of some person, or alienation to anyone except X, have all been held void.[5] But certain partial restraints have been held valid; thus where land was devised to A "on the condition that he never sells it out of the family," the condition was held valid on the grounds that it did not prohibit any form of alienation except sale, it did not prohibit sales to members of the family, and it bound only A and not subsequent owners of the land.[6] Moreover, a mere covenant not to alienate is not

---

[96] *Blathwayt* v. *Lord Cawley* [1976] A.C. 397.
[97] *Re Allen* [1953] Ch. 810.
[98] *Re Barlow's W.T.* [1979] 1 W.L.R. 278.
[99] See *Brown* v. *Gould* [1972] Ch. 53 at 56.
[1] *Post*, p. 198.
[2] *Ibid*.
[3] *Post*, p. 73.
[4] *Bradley* v. *Peixoto* (1797) 3 Ves. 324.
[5] See *Re Cockerill* [1929] 2 Ch. 131.
[6] *Re Macleay* (1875) L.R. 20 Eq. 186; *cf. Re Brown* [1954] Ch. 39; and see (1954) 70 L.Q.R. 15.

repugnant to the power of alienation; the covenantee may recover damages (which might be nominal) for breach of the covenant, but the alienation is valid and gives rise to no right of forfeiture.[7]

(ii) It must not be directed against a course of devolution prescribed by law. A condition rendering a fee simple liable to be defeated if the tenant dies intestate, becomes bankrupt, or has the estate seized in execution, is void, for on each of these events the law prescribes that a fee simple shall devolve in a particular way, and this course of devolution cannot be altered by condition.[8]

(iii) It must not be illegal, immoral or otherwise contrary to public policy. The condition under this head most frequently encountered is a condition in restraint of marriage. Partial restraints, prohibiting marriage with a Papist, or a Scotsman, or a person who had been a domestic servant, have been held good.[9] But total restraints (or restraints which are virtually total, *e.g.* against marrying a person who has not freehold property worth £500 per annum in 1795) are void unless the intent is not merely to restrain marriage but simply to provide for the tenant until marriage,[10] or unless the tenant has already been married once.[11]

A determinable fee, on the other hand, is not so strictly confined. A devise of freeholds on trust for X "until he shall assign charge or otherwise dispose of the same or some part thereof or become bankrupt... or do something whereby the said annual income or some part thereof would become payable to or vested in some other person" has been held to give X a determinable fee.[12] On any of the events occurring X's estate would determine; if he died before any of them occurred, the fee simple would become absolute, for it would then cease to be possible for any of them to occur. But although a fee may thus be made determinable on alienation or on bankruptcy or on similar events, a limitation would probably be void if it were contrary to public policy for the fee to be determinable on the stated event, *e.g.* if the event is the return to X of his wife who is separated from him.

(e) *Effect of condition or limitation becoming void or impossible.* If a condition subsequent is void or becomes impossible, the donee takes a fee simple absolute, free from any condition[13]; but if a fee is made determinable upon an event contrary to law, the whole gift fails.[14]

4. A base fee. A base fee is a particular kind of determinable fee. The two essentials of a base fee are (a) it continues only so long as the original grantor

[7] *Caldy Manor Estates Ltd.* v. *Farrell* [1974] 1 W.L.R. 1303.
[8] *Re Machu* (1882) 21 Ch.D. 838 (bankruptcy).
[9] *Jenner* v. *Turner* (1880) 16 Ch.D. 188 (domestic servant).
[10] See *Jones* v. *Jones* (1876) 1 Q.B.D. 279.
[11] *Newton* v. *Marsden* (1862) 2 J. & H. 356.
[12] *Re Leach* [1912] 2 Ch. 422.
[13] *Re Greenwood* [1903] 1 Ch. 749.
[14] Consider *Re Moore* (1888) 39 Ch.D. 116 (personalty).

or any heirs of his body are alive; and (b) there is a remainder or reversion after it.[15] Such estates are more fully dealt with below.[16]

5. Nature of modified fees. In general, the owner of a modified fee has the same rights over the land as the owner of a fee simple absolute: thus the common law refused to restrain him from committing acts of waste,[17] such as opening and working mines. Equity, on the other hand, intervened to prevent the commission of equitable waste, *i.e.* acts of wanton destruction,[18] whereas the owner of a fee simple absolute is under no such restraint.

At common law the owner of a modified fee could not convey a fee simple absolute but merely a fee liable to determination, for a man cannot convey more than he has. Statute has qualified this position.[19] Further, such a fee may become enlarged into a fee simple absolute, *e.g.* by the determining event becoming impossible[20]; and there are special rules for the enlargement of base fees.[21]

B. The Fee Tail

I. HISTORY

1. Origin. The fee tail is a creature of statute. Before the Statute *De Donis Conditionalibus* 1285 no such estate existed; the common law recognised only two estates of freehold, the fee simple and the life estate, each existing in varying forms. Before the statute, the courts had treated a gift of land to X and the heirs of his body as empowering X to alienate the land in fee simple as soon as any issue was born to him. The exercise of this power would not only defeat the expectations of the issue but also destroy any possibility of the land reverting to the donor when X's line died out.[22] It was to remedy this that the statute created a new estate.

The name "fee tail" was given to the estate since the word "tail" showed that the fee was *talliatum* or *taillé*, *i.e.* cut down; unlike the fee simple, which would descend to any class of heirs, a fee tail could descend to only one class, namely, issue of the donee. Notwithstanding any act of the original tenant or his issue the land was bound to descend to the issue in tail in the proper way. The statute did not prevent a tenant in tail from alienating the land, but the estate so created could be defeated by his issue after his death. Nor could the rights of the issue be prejudiced by the tenant levying a fine (a fine being a collusive action which was compromised[23]) or by any act of escheat or forfeiture.

[15] See *post*, pp. 40, 179.
[16] *Post*, pp. 40, 44.
[17] For waste, see *post*, p. 47.
[18] *Re Hanbury's S.E.* [1913] 2 Ch. 357 at 365.
[19] *Post*, p. 242.
[20] *Ante*, p. 38.
[21] *Post*, p. 44.
[22] See M. & W. 76.
[23] See *infra*.

2. The barring of entails. For nearly two centuries landowners were able to secure the unbroken descent of their land. However, freedom of alienation was ultimately secured by the ingenuity of practitioners and the courts. Two methods of "barring the entail" were evolved: the common recovery and the fine.

(a) *The common recovery. Taltarum's Case,*[24] decided in 1472, shows that there was then in full working order a process whereby a tenant in tail could bar the entail by means of a recently invented collusive action known as a "common recovery." The process employed was that an action claiming the land was brought against the tenant in tail with his consent; the court was prepared to allow this claim, provided judgment was entered against some third party for land of equal value to compensate the disappointed heirs. Consequently some "man of straw" was found against whom the second judgment could be given, and the matter could then proceed. The result of the action was that the tenant in tail was able to dispose of the whole fee simple, thus defeating the claims not only of the heirs of his body, but also those of any person entitled to any subsequent remainder, reversion or other estate. However, the action could be brought only by, or with the concurrence of, the person seised of the land: if land was given "to A for life, remainder to B and the heirs of his body," B could not suffer a recovery without the co-operation of A.

(b) *The fine.* A fine was a solemn form of conveyance whereby an agreement to convey the land was entered in the court records in the form of a final compromise of an action (*finalis concordia*). It was of earlier origin than the common recovery, but it did not become available for barring entails until some time later. The judges' dislike of unbarrable entails gave rise to judicial decisions which made it possible for entails to be barred by common recoveries, but as the Statute *De Donis* 1285 expressly prohibited the barring of entails by fines, legislation was necessary to make fines effective. The Statutes of Fines 1489 was thought to have made a fine effective to bar the issue in tail unless they asserted their rights within five years of the fine, and the Statutes of Fines 1540 confirmed this construction and made the fine immediately effective to bar the issue.

A fine could be levied without the concurrence of the person seised; but it was not so effective as a common recovery, for although it barred the rights of the issue in tail, it did not bar the owner of any subsequent remainder, reversion or other estate.[25] The estate produced by a fine was known as a "base fee." In effect a base fee was a fee simple which endured for as long as the entail would have continued if it had not been barred, and determined when the entail would have ended.[26] Thus, if land was limited to A for life, remainder to B in tail, remainder to C in fee simple, and B barred his entail by a fine in favour of X, X took a base fee. X remained entitled to the land

[24] Y.B. 12 Edw. 4, Mich., pl. 25, f. 19a.
[25] *Margaret Podger's Case* (1613) 9 Co.Rep. 104a.
[26] *Ante*, p. 38.

for as long as B or any of his issue lived, but when they were all dead, C became entitled to the land.

A fine could be levied by one who had no entail but merely a *spes successionis*, or only a contingent or executory interest in tail, *i.e.* an entail to which he would be entitled only if some specified event occurred.[27] Such a person could not suffer a recovery.

(c) *Differences between fines and recoveries*. The main differences between fines and recoveries may be summarised as follows:

FINE	RECOVERY
(i) Action compromised.	(i) Action proceeded to judgment.
(ii) Consent of freehold tenant in possession not required.	(ii) Consent of freehold tenant in possession essential.
(iii) Not confined to owners of vested entails.	(iii) Available only to owners of vested entails.
(iv) Produced a base fee.	(iv) Produced a fee simple absolute.

Both these methods of barring entails became purely formal; all that a tenant had to do was to instruct his lawyers to take the necessary steps. However, although there was no legal obstacle to the barring of an entail, fines and recoveries were dilatory, complicated and expensive. By the Fines and Recoveries Act 1833 fines and recoveries were abolished and replaced by a simple method of barring entails.

3. The Fines and Recoveries Act 1833. This Act substantially preserved the distinction between fines and recoveries, although the actions themselves were abolished. The Act provided that an entail could be barred by any assurance (*i.e.* any conveyance or other transfer) by which a fee simple could be disposed of, except a will. It was essential, however, that the assurance should be either made or evidenced by a deed; and a mere declaration by deed that the entail was barred was not enough, for an assurance was what the Act required.[28] If the tenant barring the entail wished to retain the land himself, he conveyed it to some trustee for him; if he wished to dispose of it, he made the disentailing assurance in favour of the grantee. It was necessary for every disentailing assurance to be enrolled within six calendar months of execution, formerly in the Court of Chancery, and later in the Central Office of the Supreme Court.[29] A conveyance which did not comply with the Act did not bar the issue or the reversioner or remainderman.

---

[27] *The Case of Fines* (1602) 3 Co.Rep. 84a at 90a, b.
[28] Fines and Recoveries Act 1833, ss.15, 40; see *Carter* v. *Carter* [1896] 1 Ch. 62 (declaration of trust sufficient).
[29] Fines and Recoveries Act 1833, s.41.

A disentailing assurance transferred a fee simple absolute if it was executed either by a tenant in tail in possession or else by a tenant in tail in remainder with the consent of the "protector of the settlement." Unless a special protector had been appointed, the protector was the beneficial owner of the first subsisting estate under the settlement which was not a mere lease for years. Usually the protector was the tenant for life in possession. A disentailing assurance that was executed without the consent of the protector would pass only a base fee. The distinction between fines and recoveries was thus in effect preserved. A contingent or executory interest in tail may still be barred, but not a mere hope of becoming entitled.[30]

II. RIGHTS OF A TENANT IN TAIL

In general, a tenant in tail in possession has the same rights of enjoyment of the land as a tenant in fee simple. He may thus commit all kinds of waste, including equitable waste, even if he is restrained from barring the entail by statute.[31] His position is considered further in the chapter dealing with the Settled Land Act 1925.

III. TYPES OF ENTAIL

The various types of entail, such as special tail and tail male, have already been considered.[32]

IV. PRESENT LAW

The Law of Property Act 1925 has made important amendments to the law of entails, but the general principles remain unchanged. The following are the chief points to note.

1. Existence only in equity. It is no longer possible for a legal fee tail to exit.[33] After 1925, all entails must exist behind a trust; this means that the legal estate in fee simple must be vested in some trustees or trustee (who may be the tenant in tail himself) on trust for the person entitled in tail and everyone else interested in the land. This does not impair the benefits accruing from the land; only the bare legal ownership is affected. Since an entail is no longer an estate in the land itself, but only an interest under a trust, the proper title for an entail is no longer "estate tail" or "fee tail," but "entailed interest." Similarly a "base fee" can no longer be a legal estate but exists only as an equitable interest in the nature of a base fee. The Fines and Recoveries Act 1833 applies to these equitable interests in the same way as it applied to the legal estate before 1926.[34]

---

[30] *Ibid.*, ss.15, 20; contrast *Re St. Albans' W.T.* [1963] Ch. 365 with *Re Midleton's W.T.* [1969] 1 Ch. 600.
[31] *Lord Glenorchy* v. *Bosville* (1733) Ca.t.Talb. 3 at 16; *Att-Gen* v. *Duke of Marlborough* (1818) 3 Madd. 498.
[32] *Ante*, p. 32.
[33] L.P.A. 1925, s.1; *post*, pp. 71, 72.
[34] L.P.(Am.)A. 1924, Sched. 9.

2. Personalty entailable. Any property, real or personal, may be entailed after 1925.[35] This was not so before 1926, for the Statute *De Donis* 1285 applied only to "tenements."[36] Thus the land itself, and inheritable rights in realty such as perpetual rentcharges (*e.g.* £100 per annum charged on Blackacre), could be entailed, but life estates (which were not inheritable) and leaseholds and other personalty could not be entailed.[37] Before 1926, a gift of personalty "to A and the heirs of his body" or "to A in tail" gave A the absolute ownership of the personalty, whether the gift was by deed or by will.[38] Informal words such as "to A and his issue" or "to A and his descendants" usually gave the property to A and such of his issue or descendants as were alive at the relevant date.[39]

Since 1925, entails can be created in personalty, and all the rules applying to entails of realty (*e.g.* as to the words of limitation required, barring the entails, interests equivalent to a base fee, and the like) apply to entails of personalty. However, it is expressly provided that if after 1925 personalty is directed "to be enjoyed or held with, or upon trusts corresponding to trusts affecting," land which is already held in tail, this will be sufficient to entail the personalty.[40]

3. No enrolment. A disentailing assurance made after 1925 need not be enrolled.[41]

4. Barring by will. Under the Law of Property Act 1925, s.176, a tenant in tail can now bar his entail by will, and thus dispose of the fee simple. However, this power is subject to a number of limitations:

(a) It applies only to entails in possession: there is no power to bar an entail in remainder by will, even if the protector consents.
(b) The tenant in tail must be of full age.
(c) The will must be either executed after 1925 or confirmed by a codicil executed after 1925.
(d) The will must refer specifically either to—
    (i) the property (*e.g.* "Greenacre"),[42]
    (ii) the instrument under which it was acquired (*e.g.* "all the property to which I succeeded under X's will"), or
    (iii) entails generally (*e.g.* "all property to which I am entitled in tail").

This power extends to all entailed property, whether real or personal, whenever the entail was created. Further, it allows the owner of a base fee in

---

[35] L.P.A. 1925, s.130.
[36] Challis R.P. 43, 47, 61.
[37] But see M. & W. 95 on quasi-entails of life estates.
[38] *Dawson* v. *Small* (1874) 9 Ch.App. 651; and see *Portman* v. *Viscount Portman* [1922] A.C. 473. See also *post*, p. 257.
[39] *Re Hammond* [1924] 2 Ch. 276.
[40] L.P.A. 1925, s.130(3).
[41] *Ibid.* s.133.
[42] See *Acheson* v. *Russell* [1951] Ch. 67.

possession to enlarge it by a disposition by will, provided he complies with the above conditions, and provided he is capable of enlarging it into a fee simple absolute without the consent of anyone else. But the section does not apply to a tenant in tail after possibility or to a tenant in tail restrained by statute from barring his entail.[43] Except so far as is necessary to give effect to the will, the entail or base fee is unaffected; thus if instead of disposing of the fee simple in the entailed land the testator merely devises a life interest, the entail will resume its natural devolution when the life interest ceases.

V. BASE FEES

The nature and mode of creation of base fees have already been considered.[44] The uncertainty of the duration of a base fee makes it an unsatisfactory interest in land, but it can be enlarged into a fee simple absolute in a number of ways. If land is given to A for life, remainder to B in tail, reminder to C in fee simple, a base fee created by B can be enlarged in four ways.

(1) *New disentailment*: by the former tenant in tail (*i.e.* B) executing a fresh disentailing assurance with the consent of the protector or after the protectorship has ceased (*e.g.* after A's death). This can be done even after the base fee has been conveyed to a purchaser.[45]

(2) *Acquisition of reversion*: by the owner of the base fee acquiring the whole of the remainder or reversion in fee simple (*i.e.* by B, or any person to whom he has conveyed the base fee, acquiring C's fee simple). This does not merge the base fee in the remainder or reversion and so subject the owner of the base fee to any burdens attached to the remainder or reversion, such as a mortgage, but enlarges the base fee into a fee simple absolute, free from any incumbrances on the remainder or reversion.[46]

(3) *Long possession*: by the owner of the base fee (*i.e.* B or anyone to whom he has conveyed it) remaining in possession of the land for 12 years after the protectorship has ceased.[47]

(4) *Devise*: by a gift by will complying with section 176 of the Law of Property Act 1925.[48] This power is exercisable only by a person who is entitled to a base fee in possession and who could enlarge it without the concurrence of any person. Thus B can enlarge the base fee by will if the protectorship has ceased before he dies; but if B has conveyed the base fee to some third person, neither that person nor B can enlarge it by will in any circumstances.

[43] For these, see *post*, p. 45.
[44] *Ante*, pp. 38, 40, 42.
[45] Fines and Recoveries Act 1833, ss.19, 35; *Bankes* v. *Small* (1887) 36 Ch.D. 716.
[46] Fines and Recoveries Act 1833, s.39.
[47] Limitation Act 1980, s.27.
[48] *Ante*, p. 43.

VI. INTERESTS IN TAIL AFTER POSSIBILITY

On the death of the specified spouse of a tenant in special tail without leaving any issue capable of inheriting the entail, the tenant becomes "a tenant in tail after possibility of issue extinct," the last three words usually being omitted for brevity. For example, if land is given "to A and the heirs of his body begotten on Mary," on the death of Mary without leaving issue A is a tenant in tail after possibility. Such a tenant is in a peculiar position. For—

(i) He cannot bar the entail.[49]
(ii) Yet although he is virtually in the position of a tenant for life, he is still technically a tenant in tail. Thus like all tenants in tail he is not liable for voluntary waste (damage to the land), although a tenant for life is. However, he will be restrained from committing equitable waste (wanton destruction).[50]

An interest in tail after possibility can arise only on the death of the spouse specified in the limitation; it cannot arise out of a tail general, for even if the tenant in tail is unmarried and of a great age, it is always deemed possible that he or she will marry and have issue.[51]

VII. UNBARRABLE ENTAILS

1. No unbarrable entails. The common law rule which developed at the end of the sixteenth century was that it was impossible to create an unbarrable entail. By means of fines and recoveries, all entails could be barred, and any attempt to restrain the tenant from doing this was ineffective. Thus a condition that the tenant should not suffer a common recovery was repugnant to the entail and so void.[52] This rule was not affected by the Fines and Recoveries Act 1833.

2. Exceptions. Despite this general rule, there are certain entails which cannot be barred. These are:

(i) An interest in tail after possibility.
(ii) Entails created by the Crown for services rendered to the Crown, the reversion being in the Crown.[53]
(iii) Entails made unbarrable by special Acts of Parliament, such as the entails given to reward the first Duke of Marlborough and the first Duke of Wellington.[54]

3. Persons. Certain persons are unable to bar an entail, even if the entail is one which can be barred.

---

[49] Fines and Recoveries Act 1833, s.18.
[50] *Williams* v. *Williams* (1810) 12 East 209; *Cooke* v. *Whaley* (1701) 1 Eq.Ca.Abr. 400. For waste, see *post*, p. 47.
[51] Co. Litt. 28a.
[52] *Sir Anthony Mildmay's Case* (1605) 6 Co.Rep. 40a.
[53] Fines and Recoveries Act 1833, s.18.
[54] 6 Anne, cc. 6, 7, 1706; 54 Geo. 3, c. 161, 1814.

(i) A minor is generally regarded as being unable effectively to bar an entail. This disability has been exploited to keep settled property tied up for as long as possible.[55]

(ii) A person of unsound mind (under the Mental Health Act 1983 called a "patient") cannot bar his entails; but his receiver[56] can do so, under an order of the Court of Protection.[57]

(iii) A bankrupt cannot bar his entails; this can be done only by his trustee in bankruptcy.[58]

C. The Life Estate

After 1925 an interest in land for life can no longer exist as a legal estate but only as an equitable interest.[59] In general, the law of life estates set out below applies equally to the corresponding life interests after 1925.

I. TYPES OF LIFE ESTATE

The two types of life estate were the ordinary life estate and the estate *pur autre vie*.

1. Estate for the life of the tenant. The normal type of life estate was one for the life of the tenant. This arose either—

(i) by express limitation, as by a grant "to A for life"[60]; or
(ii) by operation of law, as in the case of a surviving spouse's rights on an intestacy before 1926 to curtesy and dower.[61]

2. Estate pur autre vie. An estate *pur autre vie* was an estate for the life of someone other than the tenant,[62] the person whose life measured the duration of the estate being called the "*cestui que vie*" (pronounced "setty ker vee"). An estate *pur autre vie* could arise either—

(i) by the owner of a life estate assigning it to another: *nemo dat quod non habet* (nobody can give what he has not got), so that the assignor could create no interest which would last for longer than his own life; or
(ii) by express grant, *e.g.* "to A for the life of X."

Both types of life estate were estates of freehold, but neither was a freehold of inheritance, for they were not capable of descending to the tenant's heir on his death. A life estate ceased automatically when the tenant died, and

[55] See *post*, p. 215.
[56] See *post*, 170.
[57] Mental Health Act 1983, s.96(1).
[58] Insolvency Act 1986, s.314, Sched. 5. The former disability of married women is obsolete.
[59] *Post*, p. 71.
[60] *Ante*, p. 34.
[61] See M. & W. 543–546; *post*, p. 156.
[62] See, generally, *Doe* d. *Jeff* v. *Robinson* (1828) 2 Man. & Ry. 249.

although an estate *pur autre vie* continued during the life of the *cestui que vie* despite the tenant's death, before 1926 it did not descend to the tenant's heir as such but passed on intestacy according to special rules of occupancy.[63] Since 1926 it passes like other property under a will or intestacy.

Both types of life estate could be made determinable or subject to conditions subsequent[64] and were in general subject to similar rights and burdens.

II. POSITION OF A TENANT FOR LIFE AT COMMON LAW

In considering the position of a tenant for life at common law, an important part is played by the law of waste (particularly as to timber and minerals), and the rules governing emblements and fixtures.

(a) Waste

Although the law of waste is of importance in other connections, notably in the law of landlord and tenant, it is most suitably considered in relation to life interests, where it is applicable both to ordinary life interests and to interests *pur autre vie*. Technically, waste consists of any act which alters the nature of the land, whether for the better or for the worse, *e.g.* the conversion of arable land into a wood or *vice versa*. Four types of waste must be considered, namely, ameliorating, permissive, voluntary and equitable.

1. Ameliorating waste. Alterations which improve the land, such as converting dilapidated store buildings into dwellings, or a farm into a market garden, constitute ameliorating waste. Since the decision of the House of Lords in *Doherty* v. *Allman*[65] in 1878 the court is unlikely to grant an injunction to restrain such waste or to award any damages.

2. Permissive waste. This consists of the failure to do that which ought to be done, as by the non-repair of buildings or the failure to clean out a ditch or moat so as to prevent the foundations becoming rotten.[66] But mere non-cultivation of land is not permissive waste.[67] A tenant for life is not liable for permissive waste unless an obligation to repair is imposed upon him by the terms of the limitation under which he holds.[68]

3. Voluntary waste. Voluntary waste is positive in nature: "the committing of any spoil or destruction in houses, lands, etc., by tenants, to the damage of the heir, or of him in reversion or remainder."[69] Literally, this would

---

[63] On this, see M. & W. 93, 94.
[64] *Brandon* v. *Robinson* (1811) 18 Ves. 429; and see *Re Evans's Contract* [1920] 2 Ch. 469; see also *ante*, pp. 36–38.
[65] 3 App.Cas. 709 (conversion of dilapidated barracks into dwelling-houses by tenant for years).
[66] See, *e.g. Powys* v. *Blagrave* (1854) 4 De G.M. & G. 448.
[67] *Hutton* v. *Warren* (1836) 1 M. & W. 466 at 472.
[68] *Re Cartwright* (1889) 41 Ch.D. 532.
[69] Bacon's *Abridgement* (7th ed.), Vol. 8, p. 379, definition of waste.

include equitable waste, but the term voluntary waste is usually reserved for such voluntary waste as does not amount to equitable waste. Such acts as opening and working a mine in the land (but not merely working a mine already open),[70] or cutting timber,[71] are examples of voluntary waste. Timber consists of oak, ash and elm trees which are at least 20 years old and not too old to have a reasonable quantity of usable wood in them. Other trees may rank as timber by local custom, such as beech in Buckinghamshire and willow in Hampshire; and custom may also prescribe some qualification other than an age of 20 years for the trees to be considered timber.[72]

A tenant for life is liable for voluntary waste unless his interest was granted to him by an instrument exempting him from liability for voluntary waste, as under a grant "without impeachment of waste."[73] Where there is such an exception the tenant is said to be "unimpeachable of waste": otherwise he is said to be "impeachable of waste." Thus if nothing is said about waste, the tenant is impeachable; in practice, however, he is usually made unimpeachable.

4. Equitable waste. "Equitable waste is that which a prudent man would not do in the management of his own property."[74] Acts of wanton destruction, such as stripping a house of all its lead, iron, glass, doors, boards, etc., to the value of £3,000,[75] or pulling down houses, or cutting timber planted for ornament or shelter (unless this is necessary for the preservation of part of the timber), fall under the head of equitable waste. A tenant for life is liable for equitable waste unless the document conferring his interest upon him shows an intention to allow him to commit equitable waste. It is not enough that his interest has been given to him without impeachment of waste: he must show that it is intended that he should be allowed to commit equitable as well as voluntary waste.[76]

(b) Timber and minerals

Although largely governed by the general law of waste, the rights of a tenant for life with regard to timber and minerals are important enough to merit separate treatment.

1. Timber. There are many relevant factors.

(a) *Estovers.* Whether impeachable of waste or not, a tenant for life can take reasonable estovers (or botes) from the land. These consist of wood and timber taken as—

(i) house-bote, for repairing the house or burning in it;

---

[70] See *Dashwood* v. *Magniac* [1891] 3 Ch. 306 at 360.
[71] *Honywood* v. *Honywood* (1874) L.R. 18 Eq. 306.
[72] *Ibid.* at p. 309; *Countess of Cumberland's Case* (1610) Moo.K.B. 812.
[73] *Re Ridge* (1885) 31 Ch.D. 504 at 507.
[74] *Turner* v. *Wright* (1860) 2 De G.F. & J. 234 at 243.
[75] *Vane* v. *Lord Barnard* (1716) 2 Vern. 738.
[76] L.P.A. 1925, s.135.

(ii) plough-bote, for making and repairing agricultural implements; and
(iii) hay-bote, for repairing fences.

The tenant's right to house-bote does not entitle him to cut down timber in excess of his present needs in order to use it for any repairs which may become necessary in the future, nor does it authorise him to sell the timber, even if he employs the proceeds in repairing, or the timber proves unfit for repairs.[77]

(b) *Timber estate.* On a timber estate (an estate cultivated mainly for the produce of saleable timber which is cut periodically), the tenant can cut and sell timber according to the rules of proper estate management even if he is impeachable of waste. The reason for this rule is that the timber properly cut on such an estate is part of the annual fruits of the land rather than part of the inheritance.[78]

(c) *Timber planted for ornament or shelter.* As has been seen,[79] it is equitable waste to cut timber planted for ornament or shelter, and only a tenant unimpeachable of equitable waste is permitted to do this.

(d) *Trees.* In general, a tenant for life, even if he is impeachable of waste, may cut dotards (dead trees not fit for use as timber) and all trees which are not timber, *e.g.* in most cases willows or larches.[80] But there are a number of exceptions to this. It is voluntary waste to cut trees which would be timber but for their immaturity (unless the cutting is necessary to thin them out and so allow proper development) or to cut fruit trees in a garden or orchard.[81] Further, it is voluntary waste to cut wood which a prudent man would not cut, such as willows which help to hold a river bank together; and it is equitable waste to cut trees planted for ornament or shelter, or to grub up an entire wood. Where by reason of abnormal circumstances, such as extraordinary gales or wartime conditions, trees are severed before they are ripe for cutting, the court will direct that the tenant for life is to receive only part of the proceeds, the balance being held in trust for those entitled after his death.[82]

(e) *Normal rules.* Subject to the above special rules, the position is that a tenant for life who is unimpeachable of waste may cut and sell timber and keep all the proceeds.[83] But if the tenant is impeachable of waste, his only right to cut timber is that given to him by statute.[84] This authorises him to cut and sell timber ripe and fit for cutting, provided—

[77] Co. Litt. 41b, 53b.
[78] *Honywood* v. *Honywood* (1874) L.R. 18 Eq. 306 at 309, 310; *Dashwood* v. *Magniac* [1891] 3 Ch. 306.
[79] *Ante.* p. 48.
[80] *Re Harker's W. T.* [1938] Ch. 323.
[81] *Kaye* v. *Banks* (1770) Dick. 431.
[82] *Re Terry* (1918) 87 L.J. Ch. 577.
[83] *Lewis Bowles's Case* (1615) 11 Co.Rep. 79b.
[84] S.L.A. 1925, s.66, replacing S.L.A. 1882, s.35.

> (i) the consent of the trustees of the settlement under which he holds his life interest, or an order of the court, is obtained; and
>
> (ii) three-quarters of the proceeds are set aside as capital money: this means that the trustees hold this portion of the price on trust for all persons having any interest in the land, paying only the interest to the tenant for life. The remaining quarter of the proceeds is paid to the tenant for life.

(f) *Ownership of severed timber*. Until timber is severed, a tenant for life has no claim to it, so that if land is sold with the uncut timber on it, the life tenant cannot claim any share of the price even though he could lawfully have cut the timber.[85] Once the timber is severed it belongs to the life tenant if he was entitled to cut it, whether the severance was effected by the tenant, a stranger or an act of God, such as a storm; but if he was not entitled to sever it, it belongs not to him but to the owner of the next vested estate or interest of inheritance.[86]

2. Minerals. The mineral rights of a tenant for life depend on two factors, namely, whether the mine was already open when his tenancy began, and whether he is impeachable of waste.

(a) *Right to work mines*. A tenant for life may work a mine and take all the proceeds unless—

> (i) he is impeachable of waste, and
> (ii) the mine was not open when his tenancy began.

Where both these conditions are satisfied, he cannot work the mine at all, for to open and work an unopened mine is voluntary waste. But it is not waste to continue working a mine already open[87]; even if new pits are made on different parts of the same plot of land to pursue the same or a new vein; for the grantor, by opening or allowing the opening of the mines, has shown an intent that the minerals should be treated as part of the profits of the land.

(b) *Right to lease mines*. The Settled Land Act 1925[88] authorises a tenant for life to grant mining leases for one hundred years or less, whether the mine is open or not, and whether or not the tenant is impeachable of waste. In each case, subject to any contrary intention in the settlement, the tenant for life is entitled to three-quarters of the rent, except that if he is impeachable of waste and the mine is unopened, he is entitled to only one-quarter. The balance of rent is capital money, and is held for the benefit of all those interested under the settlement.[89]

---

[85] *Re Llewellin* (1887) 37 Ch.D. 317.
[86] *Bewick* v. *Whitfield* (1734) 3 P.Wms. 267.
[87] See *Re Hall* [1916] 2 Ch. 488 at 493.
[88] ss.41, 42, 45–47, replacing earlier Acts; see *post*, pp. 243 *et seq.*
[89] S.L.A. 1925, s.47.

(c) Emblements and fixtures

A tenant cannot foresee the date on which an estate *pur autre vie* or for his own life will determine, and so to encourage him to cultivate his land by assuring him of the fruits of his labour, the law gives him a right to emblements (pronounced *em*-blem-ents). This means that the tenant's personal representatives, or in the case of an estate *pur autre vie* the tenant himself, may enter the land after the life estate has determined and reap the crops which the tenant himself has sown.[90] This applies only to annual crops artificially produced, such as corn, hemp and flax, and not to things such as fruit trees and timber; further, it extends only to the crops actually growing at the determination of the tenancy.[91] Where the end of the tenancy is brought about by the tenant's own act (*e.g.* where a life estate is granted to a widow until remarriage and she remarries) there is no right to emblements.[92]

Prima facie any fixtures attached to the land by a tenant for life must be left after his death for the person next entitled to the land; but trade fixtures and ornamental and domestic fixtures are excepted.[93]

---

[90] Co. Litt. 55b; *Grantham* v. *Hawley* (1615) Hob. 132.
[91] *Graves* v. *Weld* (1833) 5 B. & Ad. 105 at 119.
[92] *Oland's Case* (1602) 5 Co.Rep. 116a.
[93] See *ante*, p. 18.

CHAPTER 3

LAW AND EQUITY

Part 1

GENERAL PRINCIPLES

THE difference between Law and Equity, which has already been mentioned in brief outline,[1] must now be considered in greater detail.

Sect. 1. The Historical Basis of Equity

1. The common law courts. The existence of Equity can best be explained historically. At the end of the thirteenth century the principal courts were (a) many local courts, held by feudal lords and others; and (b) the Royal courts known as the Courts of Common Law, consisting of the courts of King's Bench, of Common Pleas, and of Exchequer. Each of the Royal courts at first had its own proper sphere, but by the end of the Middle Ages their jurisdiction overlapped so much that a plaintiff often had a choice between the three courts. By this time, too, they had attracted much of the litigation of the country, and although many of the local courts survived into the eighteenth century, most of them were in decline, or moribund.

2. The writ system. In general, no action could be commenced in any of the common law courts until a writ had been issued by the Chancellor. The Chancellor, who was usually an ecclesiastic, was the head of the King's Secretarial Department. As keeper of the Great Seal with which writs were sealed, he was at the head of the English legal system.

The writs issued by the Chancellor differed for each different kind of action. Today, anyone claiming to be entitled to some remedy, such as the recovery of possession of land of which he had been dispossessed, or the payment of money owed to him, can issue a writ claiming the appropriate relief. The writ is in a form which leaves it to the plaintiff to state his claim in his own words. The same form can equally well be filled up with a claim for the possession of land as for payment of a debt, or damages for trespass: there is no special writ of ejectment, or debt, or trespass or any other matter. But in medieval days this was not so. Each different kind of action had its own writ, often with its own special procedure.[2] Often causes of action which seemed very similar in principle had separate writs. Thus if a tenant of land died and before his heir could enter the land a stranger took it, the heir could

---

[1] *Ante*, p. 2.
[2] Maitland, *Forms of Action*, 5.

bring an action against the stranger for possession of the land. If the heir were a son of the tenant the action had to be started by a writ of *mort d'ancestor*; if he was a grandson a writ of *aiel* had to be used, while if he was the great-grandson a writ of *besaiel* was required. No action could succeed unless the correct writ was chosen.

The selection of the correct writ was thus of great importance. Not until the Common Law Procedure Act 1852 were the old writs replaced by a single form of writ for all actions, and even then, until the Judicature Acts 1873–75 came into force, it was necessary to observe the form of action based on the old writs which was appropriate to the case. Sometimes there were two or more writs appropriate to the plaintiff's claim. Where this was so one writ usually had procedural advantages over the other or others. A writ which had already been settled was known as a writ *de cursu*, a writ "of course," obtainable simply on paying the prescribed fee. But sometimes there was no known writ to fit the case, and the plaintiff would have to ask for the invention of a new writ.

At first new writs were invented with comparative freedom. But it did not follow that the courts would accept each new writ as being valid. Even if a suitor had surmounted the first obstacle by obtaining a writ, he might still fall at the second fence by failing to obtain the court's recognition of its validity. Nevertheless the Register of Writs rapidly increased during the latter half of the twelfth century and the first half of the thirteenth: many new writs became writs *de cursu*, duly recognised by the courts.

This power to invent new writs was assailed by the barons. Recognising that the power to invent new remedies was a power to create new rights and duties, they procured the making of the Provisions of Oxford 1258, in which the Chancellor swore that he would seal no writ, except a writ *de cursu*, without the command of the King and his Council. Had this remained fully effective, it would have stifled the growth of the common law. But the Statute of Westminster II 1285 provided in the famous Chapter 24, *In Consimili Casu*, that the clerks in Chancery should have a limited power to invent new writs.[3] If there already existed one writ and in a like case (*in consimili casu*), falling under like law and requiring like remedy, there was none, the clerks in Chancery were authorised to agree in making a writ, or else they were to refer the matter to the next Parliament. Consequently a suitor whose grievance was not covered by a writ *de cursu*, or one *in consimili casu*, was still left without a remedy unless he could persuade Parliament to intervene.

3. Petitions to the King referred to the Chancellor. The result of this was that there were a number of cases where suitors could obtain no remedy from the courts. In addition to the problems associated with writs, there was the possibility that a rich and powerful adversary would bribe or intimidate

---

[3] It is controversial how far the statute was responsible for this development: see S.F.C. Milsom, *Historical Foundations of the Common Law* (2nd ed.) pp. 284, 344, collecting the literature.

jurors. The only way to obtain relief was then to petition the King and his Council; for the King, as the Fountain of Justice, was regarded as having a residue of judicial power left in his hands. Such petitions were heard by the King's Council, of which the Chancellor was an important member. The Chancellor, as keeper of the King's Conscience, was particularly well fitted to deal with such petitions, and during the reigns of Edward II and III many were referred to him. After the reign of Edward III petitions were often addressed to the Chancellor alone. But although the Chancery became recognised as a court during the fourteenth and fifteenth centuries, the decisions upon the petitions were made either in the name of the King's Council or else with the advice of the serjeants and judges. Not until 1474, it seems, did the Chancellor make a decree on his own authority; but after that date such decrees became frequent.[4]

4. The Court of Chancery. In this way there gradually came into existence a Court of Chancery in which the Chancellor, acting independently of the King's Council, sat as a judge administering a system of justice called Equity. After the end of the seventeenth century only lawyers were appointed to the office of Chancellor. Equity, which had varied with each Chancellor, began with Lord Ellesmere (1596–1617) to develop into a code of principles, and the work of Lord Nottingham (1673–82) in systematising the rules earned him the title of the Father of Equity. When Lord Eldon retired in 1827 the rules of equity had become as fixed as those of the common law.

In the course of time various subsidiary officials were appointed to assist the Chancellor (including the Master of the Rolls and, later, Vice-Chancellors), a system of appeals grew up, and finally in 1875 the Chancery system was merged with the common law courts to form the present Supreme Court of Judicature. In short, what was once a method of petitioning the King for justice in exceptional cases gradually became a way of starting an action before a regular court of justice. But there were important differences between Chancery and the common law courts. The latter decided cases according to strict common law rules, and technicalities often played an important part. Chancery, on the other hand, mitigated the rigour of the common law, deciding cases in the light of what had seemed just and equitable to generations of Chancellors, and technical pleas were usually unsuccessful. Further, the common law courts were mainly concerned with enforcing the strict rights of the plaintiff regardless of his conduct, whereas Chancery was a court of conscience. In Chancery, the court might cleanse the conscience of the parties, compelling a defendant to disgorge any ill-gotten gains by acting *in personam* (on his person), *e.g.* by imprisoning him; and a remedy might be withheld from a plaintiff who was guilty of unconscionable conduct. There were also important differences in the remedies available. In the courts of common law a plaintiff might recover his land or

---

[4] 1 H.E.L. 400–404.

be awarded damages, but he could not obtain injunctions or orders for the specific performance of contracts, or the other remedies that were available in Chancery. The Court of Chancery might even grant an injunction to restrain a plaintiff who had succeeded in a court of common law from inequitably enforcing his judgment.[5] There was thus a marked difference between legal rights, the name for rights enforced by the courts of law, and equitable rights, enforced only by equity. This will be examined later.[6]

5. Fusion of the Courts of Law and Equity. By the Judicature Act 1873,[7] the superior courts of law and equity were fused into one Supreme Court, divided into a High Court and Court of Appeal. For convenience, the High Court was divided into five Divisions, each of which had certain matters assigned to it. In 1880 the Common Pleas Division and Exchequer Division were merged into the Queen's Bench Division, and in 1972 the Probate, Divorce and Admiralty Division was re-named the Family Division, with some adjustments of jurisdiction. There are now three Divisions:

the Chancery Division,
the Queen's Bench Division, and
the Family Division.

The Queen's Bench Division hears common law cases, the Chancery Division hears equity cases, and the Family Division deals with matrimonial matters and minors. But it is important to notice that these are only divisions of one court, the High Court, and not separate courts; each division of the High Court has jurisdiction to enforce both legal and equitable rights and give both legal and discretionary equitable remedies. This means that it is no longer necessary to go to two separate courts to enforce legal and equitable rights or to obtain legal and equitable remedies. If a point of equity arises in an action in the Queen's Bench Division, for example, the court can deal with it; and it will not be fatal to an action if it is started in the wrong division, for the case will be transferred to the proper division.

Law and equity nevertheless remain distinct: the systems have not been fused, although they are now both administered by the same court.[8] A legal right is still enforceable against a purchaser without notice, while an equitable right is not. Equitable rights are still enforceable only by equitable remedies, though there is now power to award damages in place of or in addition to an injunction or specific performance.[9] Indeed, the distinction between the two systems is emphasised by the provision that where there is any conflict between the rules of law and those of equity, the rules of equity shall prevail. Conflicts rarely occur: but there have been cases where this

---

[5] *Earl of Oxford's Case* (1615) 1 Rep.Ch. 1.
[6] *Post*, pp. 57 *et seq.*
[7] Which, by the Supreme Court of Judicature (Commencement) Act 1874, s.2, came into force on November 1, 1875. See now Supreme Court Act 1981.
[8] *Salt* v. *Cooper* (1880) 16 Ch.D. 544 at 549.
[9] Supreme Court Act 1981, s.50, replacing Chancery Amendment Act 1858, (Lord Cairns' Act), s.2.

provision has been operative, and the most important will be considered later.[10] The Court of Chancery is a ghost, but like many other English legal ghosts, its influence can be seen on every side.

Sect. 2. Equity Follows the Law

In equity, there could exist a whole range of equitable estates or interests corresponding to the legal estates and interests in land. A fee simple, fee tail, life estate, mortgage, easement and nearly every other interest might be either legal or equitable. Thus if A granted a lease to B to hold on trust for C, B had a legal term of years and C an equitable term. If the fee simple owner of Greenacre granted Y a lease for 99 years, Y's lease would be legal if it was granted by deed, equitable if merely in writing. If a person held an equitable interest it would usually be found either that his interest arose under a trust or else that it was created without employing the formalities necessary at law.

Certain interests could exist only in equity: if Greenacre was bound by a restrictive covenant, this could never cast a legal burden on anyone who subsequently acquired the land, although it might well bind him in equity. But apart from these cases, there was a strict parallel in law and in equity. In most cases the maxim "Equity follows the law" applied: "the Chancery moulded equitable estates and interests after the fashion of the common law estates and interests."[11] The courts tended to treat an interest in the land in the same way whether it was legal or equitable.[12] Thus equitable entails had to be barred in the same way as legal entails[13]; equitable interests passed on intestacy to the same persons as legal estates; an equitable tenant for life was in the same position as regards equitable waste as a legal tenant for life, and so on. But in certain matters, equity considered that there was good reason for refusing to follow the law, often to avoid hardship. Thus equitable remainders were not liable to destruction in the same way as legal remainders; and equity allowed a mortgagor to recover the property mortgaged if he paid all that was due, even though he no longer had any legal right to redeem the property.

With regard to words of limitation, equity followed the law in part only. If the grantor used informal words showing a clear intention to create a fee simple or fee tail, *e.g.* a limitation on trust for A "absolutely,"[14] these were as effective as formal words. But if strict conveyancing language was employed, the limitation was construed in the same way as a legal limitation and in the absence of proper words of limitation only a life estate passed. This was so even if a general intention to pass some other interest could be gathered from the instrument,[15] although in this case if the court was asked

[10] *Post*, pp. 311 *et seq.*
[11] Maitland, *Equity*, p. 108.
[12] See *Re Somerville and Turner's Contract* [1903] 2 Ch. 583 at 588.
[13] *Kirkham* v. *Smith* (1749) Amb. 518.
[14] *Re Arden* [1935] Ch. 326.
[15] *Re Bostock's Settlement* [1921] 2 Ch. 469.

to rectify the instrument and not merely construe it, words of limitation necessary to carry out the grantor's intention would be inserted.[16]

It will thus be seen that in some important points equity refused to follow the law. Nevertheless it has been said with some justice that "the cases, where the analogy fails, are not numerous; and there is scarcely a rule of law or equity, of a more ancient origin, or which admits of fewer exceptions, than the rule, that equity followeth the law."[17]

Sect. 3. The Nature of Equitable Rights

A. Distinction Between Legal and Equitable Rights

At first sight it might seem that as long as a person had a right which would be enforced by some court, it mattered little which court it was. But there is a great difference between legal and equitable rights. This is sometimes expressed by saying that "legal rights are rights *in rem*, equitable rights are rights *in personam*." A legal interest in land is a right in the land itself, so that whoever acquires the land is bound by that right, whether or not he knew of it. Equity, on the other hand, would enforce equitable rights only against certain persons. For example, if land was conveyed to T in fee simple on trust for A in fee simple, there was at first no court which would compel T to carry out his trust. Equity, however, began to intervene on behalf of A if T was guilty of a breach of trust, and so A's interest, being enforceable in equity but not at law, was merely equitable. It was a right *in personam* enforceable against T alone, so that if he died or conveyed the land to another, the trust would not be enforced against the new tenant.

Then successive extensions were made. In 1465 it was laid down that a trust would be enforced against anyone who took a conveyance of the land with notice of the trust.[18] In 1483 the Chancellor said that he would enforce a trust against the trustee's heir,[19] and in 1522 it was said that a trust would be enforced against anyone to whom the land had been given.[20] After it had been decided that others such as the executors and creditors of the trustees would be bound by the trust, it finally became established as one of the most important rules of equity that trusts and other equitable rights would be enforced against everyone except a bona fide purchaser of a legal estate for value without notice of these rights, or somebody claiming through such a person. Equitable rights thus gradually came to look less and less like mere rights *in personam* and more and more like rights *in rem*. Although it is possible still to regard them as rights *in personam*, it is perhaps best to treat them as hybrids, being neither entirely one nor entirely the other. They have never reached the status of rights *in rem*, yet the class of persons against whom they will be enforced is too large for mere rights *in personam*.

[16] *Banks* v. *Ripley* [1940] Ch. 719.
[17] Co. Litt. 290b, n. 1, xvi.
[18] Y.B. 5 Edw. 4, Mich., pl. 16.
[19] Y.B. 22 Edw. 4, Pasch., pl. 18.
[20] Y.B. 14 Hen. 8, Mich., pl. 5, fo. 7.

The difference between legal and equitable rights as regards a purchaser without notice may be illustrated as follows. In 1920 X bought the fee simple in Greenacre. In 1921 he granted a legal easement of way across one corner to L, and an equitable easement of way across the other corner to E.[21] As long as X still owned Greenacre, no substantial difference appeared between the rights of L and E: both were enforceable against X. But as soon as the land was conveyed to a third party, Y, the distinction between the rights of L and E became apparent. Even if Y purchased the land without notice of L's easement, it bound him, for it was a right *in rem*.[22] But if Y could prove that he was a bona fide purchaser for value of a legal estate without notice of E's easement, he took free from it.

This doctrine of purchaser without notice, so fundamental to property law (the "polar star of equity"[23]), must now be considered more fully.

B. The Purchaser Without Notice

The plea of purchaser of a legal estate for value without notice is "an absolute, unqualified, unanswerable defence."[24] The onus of proof lies on the person setting it up: it is a single plea, and cannot be regarded as a plea of a purchase for value, to be met by a reply of notice.[25] The principal points are as follows.

1. Bona fide. The purchaser must act in good faith. Although this is a separate requirement from the absence of notice,[26] there is no clear example of it doing more than emphasising the requisite innocence of notice.

2. Purchaser for value. The words "for value" are included to show that value must have been given, because "purchaser" in its technical sense does not necessarily imply this. A "purchaser" is a person who acquires property by act of parties, as under a gift *inter vivos* or by will, and not by mere operation of law, as by descent on intestacy. "Value" includes money, money's worth (*e.g.* other land, or stocks and shares) and marriage.[27] The value need not be full value,[28] but it must all have been actually paid or given before the purchaser receives notice of the equity.[29] "Money or money's worth" usually consists of some present consideration in the sense used in the law of contract, but it also includes the satisfaction of an existing debt.[30] "Marriage," however, extends only to a future marriage: an ante-nuptial

---

[21] For the registration of equitable easements created after 1925, see *post*, p. 80.

[22] See, *e.g. Wyld* v. *Silver* [1963] Ch. 243 (purchaser bound by undiscovered legal rights of others to hold an annual fair or wake on the land even though none had been held for over 80 years).

[23] *Stanhope* v. *Earl Verney* (1761) 2 Eden 81 at 85, *per* Lord Henley L.C.

[24] *Pilcher* v. *Rawlins* (1872) 7 Ch.App. 259 at 269.

[25] *Wilkes* v. *Spooner* [1911] 2 K.B. 473 at 486.

[26] *Midland Bank Trust Co. Ltd.* v. *Green* [1981] A.C. 513 at 528.

[27] *Wormald* v. *Maitland* (1866) 35 L.J.Ch. 69 at 73.

[28] *Bassett* v. *Nosworthy* (1673) Rep.t. Finch 102; *Midland Bank Trust Co. Ltd.* v. *Green*, *supra*.

[29] *Tourville* v. *Naish* (1734) 3 P.Wms. 307.

[30] See *Thorndike* v. *Hunt* (1859) 3 De G. & J. 563.

agreement (*i.e.* a promise made in consideration of future marriage) is deemed to have been made for value, but a promise made in respect of a past marriage (a post-nuptial agreement) is not. When an ante-nuptial marriage settlement is made, valuable consideration is deemed to have been given both by the spouse and by the unborn issue of the marriage.[31] "Good consideration" (the natural love and affection which a person has for his near relatives) is of small importance and does not amount to value. "Purchaser" is not confined to a person who acquires a fee simple; it includes, for example, mortgagees and lessees, who are purchasers *pro tanto* (to the extent of their interests).[32]

3. Of a legal estate. The purchaser normally must show that he has acquired some legal estate in the land and not a mere equitable interest.[33] If the purchaser acquires merely an equitable interest, his equity is later in time than the prior equitable interest, and as between competing equities the first in time normally prevails; where part of the equitable interest is already vested in the owner of the prior equity, the subsequent purchaser can take only what remains.[34]

There are three qualifications to this rule.

(a) *Better right to legal estate.* A purchaser without notice who acquires only an equitable interest will nevertheless take free from equities if his purchase gives him the better right to a legal estate. Thus if a legal estate is conveyed not to the purchaser but to a trustee for him and the trustee is also without notice, the purchaser takes free from equities.[35]

(b) *Subsequent acquisition of legal estate.* A purchaser without notice who at the time of his purchase fails to obtain either a legal estate or the better right to one will nevertheless prevail over a prior equity if he subsequently gets in a legal estate, even if he then has notice of the equity. As between himself and the owner of the prior equity, there is equal equity, and the legal estate will prevail.[36] But if the purchaser knowingly acquires the legal estate in breach of trust, he will not take free from the interests of the beneficiaries under that trust.[37]

(c) *Mere equities.* Although a purchaser of an equitable interest without notice of prior equitable interests does not take free from them, he takes free from any "mere equities" of which he has no notice.[38] Mere equities fall

---

[31] *Macdonald* v. *Scott* [1893] A.C. 642 at 650.
[32] See *Goodright* d. *Humphreys* v. *Moses* (1774) 2 Wm.Bl. 1019.
[33] See *Pilcher* v. *Rawlins* (1872) 7 Ch.App. 259 at 268, 269.
[34] *Phillips* v. *Phillips* (1862) 4 De G.F. & J. 208 at 216; *Cave* v. *Cave* (1880) 15 Ch.D. 639; *post*, p. 487.
[35] See *Assaf* v. *Fuwa* [1955] A.C. 215.
[36] *Bailey* v. *Barnes* [1894] 1 Ch. 25; and see *post*, p. 487.
[37] *Harpham* v. *Shacklock* (1881) 19 Ch.D. 207; *McCarthy & Stone Ltd.* v. *Julian S. Hodge & Co. Ltd.* [1971] 1 W.L.R. 1547.
[38] *Phillips* v. *Phillips* (1862) 4 De G.F. & J. 208; *Cave* v. *Cave* (1880) 15 Ch.D. 639 at 647; *Allied Irish Banks Ltd.* v. *Glynn* [1973] I.R. 188.

short of being actual interests in the land, and in the main are rights to equitable relief in respect of property. They include the right to have a transaction set aside for fraud,[39] or to have an instrument rectified for mistake.[40] Mere equities are not purely personal rights. They are ancillary to the land, and the benefit of them will pass with the land to a purchaser.[41] The burden of them will also pass with the land, but they will not bind a purchaser of an equitable interest without notice of them as he is acquiring the entire equitable interest, and the mere equities are only burdens on that interest.[42] For brevity, equitable interests in land are often included in the term "equities," but they are not "mere" equities.

4. Without notice. There are three kinds of notice.

(a) *Actual notice.* A person has actual notice of all facts of which he has[43] actual knowledge, however that knowledge was acquired; but he is not regarded as having actual notice of facts which have come to his ears only in the form of vague rumours.[44] As seen above, statute has made a number of rights registrable as land charges, and registration of them constitutes actual notice.[45]

(b) *Constructive notice.* A person has constructive notice of all facts of which he would have acquired actual notice had he made those inquiries and inspections which he ought reasonably to have made, the standard of prudence being that of men of business under similar circumstances.[46] A purchaser has constructive notice of a fact if he—

(i) had actual notice that there was some incumbrance and a proper inquiry would have revealed what it was, or

(ii) has, whether deliberately or carelessly, abstained from making those inquiries that a prudent purchaser would have made.[47]

A purchaser's duties of prudence fall under two main heads, namely, inspecting the land and investigating the title.

(1) INSPECTION OF LAND. It has long been accepted that a purchaser should inspect the land with the object of discovering whether it is affected by any adverse interest (*e.g.* a right of way that is suggested by a footpath over the land) and whether any of the land is occupied by any other person.[48]

---

[39] *Ernest* v. *Vivian* (1863) 33 L.J.Ch. 513.

[40] *Smith* v. *Jones* [1954] 2 All E.R. 823; *Re Colebrook's Conveyance* [1972] 1 W.L.R. 1397.

[41] L.P.A. 1925, s.63 (*post*, p. 130); *Boots the Chemist Ltd.* v. *Street* [1983] E.G.D. 251.

[42] See *National Provincial Bank Ltd.* v. *Ainsworth* [1965] A.C. 1175 at 1238, 1253; and see *Westminster Bank Ltd.* v. *Lee* [1956] Ch. 7. See also *Latec Investments Ltd.* v. *Hotel Terrigal Pty. Ltd.* (1965) 113 C.L.R. 265; and see generally M. & W. 145–147.

[43] For facts forgotten, see *Re Montagu's Settlement* [1987] Ch. 264 at 284.

[44] *Lloyd* v. *Banks* (1868) 3 Ch.App. 488; *Barnhart* v. *Greenshields* (1853) 9 Moo.P.C. 18 at 36.

[45] *Ante*, p. 8; more fully, *post*, p. 85.

[46] L.P.A. 1925, s.199; *Bailey* v. *Barnes* [1894] 1 Ch. 25 at 35.

[47] *Jones* v. *Smith* (1841) 1 Hare 43 at 55; *Oliver* v. *Hinton* [1899] 2 Ch. 264.

[48] *Taylor* v. *Stibbert* (1794) 2 Ves.Jun. 437 at 440; *Barnhart* v. *Greenshields* (1853) 9 Moo.P.C. 18 at 32, 33.

A purchaser has constructive notice of all the equitable rights[49] of a tenant in occupation of any of the land, though not of the rights of the tenant's landlord.[50]

Where the vendor is not in sole occupation of the land himself but there are others who occupy it as well, there are sometimes questions whether a purchaser is to be treated as having constructive notice of the rights of those other occupants. At one time the view was that a purchaser was not required to make inquiries of any occupants whose presence was consistent with the vendor being in occupation: the presence of the vendor's spouse would normally be explicable in terms of the vendor being in occupation, and as being a mere shadow of that occupation.[51] This view facilitated conveyancing by reducing the burden of inquiries that a purchaser had to make, but it also failed to give proper protection to any rights that those occupants might have.[52] In particular, in recent years it has become increasingly common for a wife to own some equitable interest in the matrimonial home (*e.g.* through having contributed to the purchase price), even though the house has been put in the husband's sole name; and the husband may sell or mortgage the house without disclosing his wife's interest.[53] There has thus been some criticism of the "easy-going practice of dispensing with enquiries as to occupation beyond that of the vendor."[54]

Today, the approach is different. A purchaser who omits to inquire of any occupier of the land or any part of it will probably be held to have constructive notice of all the rights of that occupier, at all events so far as his occupation is in conflict with the vendor's title.[55] This approach has many difficulties for purchasers, especially mortgagees. Some houseowners have large families of varying ages, and some houses have "floating populations," making full inquiries burdensome. Again, a mortgagee may be held to have constructive notice of the rights of an estranged wife who only intermittently occupies the matrimonial home and is absent when the mortgagee inspects the house under an appointment arranged by the husband, the mortgagor.[56] The limits of this new approach have yet to be worked out.

Sometimes the position is affected by the doctrine of estoppel. Where an occupier has represented to the purchaser (whether by words, conduct or silence) that the property will pass free from any claim by the occupier, the

---

[49] Including at least some mere equities: see *Green* v. *Rheinberg* (1911) 104 L.T. 149 and *Blacklocks* v. *J.B. Developments (Godalming) Ltd.* [1982] Ch. 183 at 196, and contrast *Smith* v. *Jones* [1954] 1 W.L.R. 1089.

[50] *Hunt* v. *Luck* [1902] 1 Ch. 428.

[51] *Caunce* v. *Caunce* [1969] 1 W.L.R. 286; *Bird* v. *Syme-Thomson* [1979] 1 W.L.R. 440 (see at p. 444).

[52] See *Northern Bank Ltd.* v. *Henry* [1981] I.R. 1.

[53] See, *e.g. Hodgson* v. *Marks* [1971] Ch. 892.

[54] See *Williams & Glyn's Bank Ltd.* v. *Boland* [1981] A.C. 487 at 508, *per* Lord Wilberforce; and see *Hodgson* v. *Marks*, *supra*.

[55] *Midland Bank Ltd.* v. *Farmpride Hatcheries Ltd.* [1981] E.G.D. 985 (directors residing in their company's property).

[56] *Kingsnorth Finance Co. Ltd.* v. *Tizard* [1986] 1 W.L.R. 783, a case in which there was notice of the wife's rights from other sources. See the criticism at [1986] Conv. 283 (M.P. Thompson).

occupier will be precluded from claiming any interest adverse to a purchaser who has relied on the representation.[57] Similarly, the owner of an equity who permits the legal owner to mortgage the land without disclosing the equity will be precluded from claiming priority for the equity over the mortgage.[58]

(2) INVESTIGATION OF TITLE. A purchaser has constructive notice of all rights which he would have discovered had he investigated the title to the land for the period allowed by law in the case of an open contract, *i.e.* one which (*inter alia*) prescribes no special length of title. This period was originally at least 60 years, but it has been successively reduced by statute: in 1874 to at least 40 years, in 1925 to at least 30 years, and in 1969 to at least 15 years.[59] The period is "at least" 15 years, so that the purchaser must call for a good root of title which is at least 15 years old, and see all documents subsequent thereto which trace the dealings with the property. A good root of title is a document which deals with the whole legal and equitable interest in the land, describes the property adequately, and contains nothing to throw any doubt on the title. Thus if the title consists of a series of conveyances respectively 3, 14, 41 and 45 years old, as well as older deeds, a purchaser under an open contract can require the production of the conveyance 41 years old and all subsequent conveyances. If in fact he fails to investigate the title at all, or else investigates it for only part of this period (*e.g.* because he has agreed to accept a shorter title), he is fixed with constructive notice of everything that he would have discovered had he investigated the title for the full statutory period.[60]

(c) *Imputed notice.* If a purchaser employs an agent, such as a solicitor, any actual or constructive notice which the agent receives may be imputed to the purchaser.[61] Before the Conveyancing Act 1882, notice received by an agent in a previous transaction was occasionally imputed to a purchaser; but this discouraged the employment of local solicitors with knowledge of local affairs[62] and was modified by the Act. Only actual or constructive notice which the agent acquires as such in the particular transaction in question is now imputed to a purchaser.[63] Where the same solicitor acts for both parties, any notice he acquires may be imputed to both parties, except where he enters into a conspiracy with one to conceal something from the other.[64]

---

[57] *Abigail* v. *Lapin* [1934] A.C. 491; *Spiro* v. *Lintern* [1973] 1 W.L.R. 1002; *Midland Bank Ltd.* v. *Farmpride Hatcheries Ltd.*, *supra*. See also *Wroth* v. *Tyler* [1974] Ch. 30 at 47.
[58] *Bristol and West B.S.* v. *Henning* [1985] 1 W.L.R. 778; *Paddington B.S.* v. *Mendelsohn* (1985) 50 P. & C.R. 244 (registered land); *Abbey National B.S.* v. *Cann* [1991] 1 A.C. 56 at 94. For criticism, see (1986) 49 M.L.R. 245 and [1986] Conv. 57 (M. P. Thompson); (1986) 16 Fam.Law 315 (J. Martin).
[59] Vendor and Purchaser Act 1874, s.1; L.P.A. 1925, s.44; L.P.A. 1969, s.23.
[60] See *Re Cox and Neve's Contract* [1891] 2 Ch. 109 at 117, 118.
[61] *Re The Alms Corn Charity* [1901] 2 Ch. 750.
[62] See *Re Cousins* (1886) 31 Ch.D. 671.
[63] L.P.A. 1925, s.199, replacing C.A. 1882, s.3. See *Kingsnorth Finance Co. Ltd.* v. *Tizard* [1986] 1 W.L.R. 783.
[64] *Sharpe* v. *Foy* (1868) 4 Ch.App. 35; *Meyer* v. *Chartres* (1918) 34 T.L.R. 589.

5. Successors in title. The protection given to a purchaser without notice extends also to his successors in title, even if they take with notice[65]; for otherwise the owner of the equitable interest could, by widely advertising his right, make it difficult for the purchaser without notice to dispose of the land for as much as he had paid for it. To this rule there is one exception, which prevents it being abused. If a person bound by the interest sells to a purchaser without notice and later acquires the property again, he cannot shelter behind the immunity of that purchaser.[66]

Part 2

SPECIES OF EQUITABLE RIGHTS

Sect. 1. Trusts

1. Origin. Everyone today is familiar with the nature of trusts, whereby the ownership of property is vested in one or more persons (the trustees) who hold it for the benefit of others (the beneficiaries). The ancestor of the trust is the use, which had substantially the same nature. The word "use" was not derived from the Latin "*usus*" but from the Latin "*opus*" in the phrase "*ad opus*" (on his behalf) *via* the Old French "*al oes*" or "*al ues*" and hence "to the use of": thus land was conveyed "to A and his heirs to the use of B and his heirs."[67]

Although there are records of uses having been created even before the Norman Conquest, the only uses found for some time after the Conquest appear to have been merely temporary uses, so that a landowner could secure the protection of his land and his family while he went on a crusade. In about 1225 the Franciscan friars came to England. The rules of their Order prevented their owning property, and so land was conveyed, for example, to some town to the use of the friars.[68] After this, uses of a permanent nature became more common, and by the middle of the fourteenth century they were frequent.

2. Enforced by equity. After early hesitations, the common law courts refused to recognise uses. If land was conveyed by A "to B and his heirs to the use of C and his heirs" the common law courts refused to compel the feoffee to uses, B, to hold the land for the benefit of C, the *cestui que use* (pronounced "setty ker use"). B was the person seised, and the common law would take notice of his rights alone; C had no interest which the law would recognise, for "uses were but imaginations."[69] Nevertheless, many uses were created in reliance on the honour and good faith of the feoffees to uses, and

---

[65] *Harrison* v. *Forth* (1695) Prec. Ch. 51; *Wilkes* v. *Spooner* [1911] 2 K.B. 473.
[66] *Gordon* v. *Holland* (1913) 82 L.J.P.C. 81.
[67] Maitland, *Equity*, p. 24.
[68] 2 P. & M. 231–238.
[69] *Chudleigh's Case* (1595) 1 Co.Rep. 113b at 140a; and see Maitland, *Equity*, p. 28.

consequent breaches of trust occurred. Towards the end of the fourteenth century the Chancellor's aid was sought, and although there is no record of a decree in favour of a *cestui que use* until 1446, probably relief was given in the first quarter of the fifteenth century.[70]

3. Duties. The duties of the feoffees to uses towards their *cestui que use* were threefold: they were bound—

   (i) to permit him to take the profits of the land ("pernancy of profits");
  (ii) to dispose of the land in accordance with his instructions; and
 (iii) to take all necessary proceedings to protect or recover the land.[71]

Although at first the *cestui que use* was regarded as merely having a right to compel the feoffees to uses to carry out their duties, the rights of the *cestui que use* were so extensive that it was soon recognised that he had an estate in the land.[72] The legal estate was in the feoffees to uses, the equitable estate in the *cestui que use*: the former had the husk, the latter the kernel. With some qualifications, it could be said in Chancery that "the equity is the land."

4. Legal and equitable interests. Frequently the legal and equitable interests in property go together; a person who has had the legal fee simple in Blackacre conveyed to him normally receives the equitable fee simple as well. But although there is often no need to consider separately the legal and equitable estate in land, in some cases this is the only way to arrive at a proper understanding of the subject.[73] The ability of the beneficial owner of a legal estate (*i.e.* one who has the equitable interest as well as the legal estate for his own benefit) to separate the legal from the equitable interest is one of the fundamentals of English law.

5. The Statute of Uses 1535. It was possible by conveying lands to uses to evade most feudal liabilities, as they fell only upon the person or persons who were seised of land. All that was needed was the selection of suitable and sufficient feoffees so that the land was never vested in a single feoffee whose death would give rise to the feudal incidents which became due upon the death of the tenant. The evasion seriously affected the King, who was always lord and never tenant. After various manoeuvres, in 1535 "the Statute of Uses was forced upon an extremely unwilling parliament by an extremely strong-willed king."[74] The effect of this was to "execute" all uses to which it applied, taking the legal estate out of the feoffees to uses and converting the equitable interests of the *cestuis que use* into corresponding legal estates. Thus, if land were conveyed to A, B, C and D and their heirs to the use of X and his heirs, the effect was to vest the legal fee simple in X, so

---

[70] Ames, *Lectures on Legal History*, p. 237.
[71] 4 H.E.L. 431.
[72] *Brent's Case* (1583) 2 Leon. 14 at 18.
[73] Consider, *e.g.* joint tenancies and tenancies in common; *post*, pp. 285 *et seq*.
[74] Maitland, *Equity*, 34; the King was Henry VIII.

that if X attained majority or married or died the feudal incidents would fall due.

6. The use upon a use. Soon after the statute was passed it was held that a use upon a use was void,[75] so that a conveyance "to A and his heirs to the use of B and his heirs to the use of C and his heirs" gave the whole legal and equitable interest to B and nothing to A or C. After the Restoration the feudal incidents were mainly abolished,[76] and by 1676 the Chancellor was enforcing the use in C's favour as a trust,[77] so that B held the legal estate on trust for C. In time, the shorter formula "unto and to the use of B and his heirs in trust for C and his heirs" was normally used. The statute survived until its repeal by the Law of Property Act 1925.[78]

7. After 1925. A trust of land is now created by conveying land "to A and B in fee simple in trust. . . . " The legal estate is thus in A and B, while those named as beneficiaries will have equitable interests.[78a] Since 1925 life interests and entailed interests can only exist as equitable interests under a trust of the legal estate.

Sect. 2. Other Equitable Rights

The Chancellor did not confine his intervention to the enforcement of uses or trusts, though that always remained the most important part of his jurisdiction. There were other important areas of real property in which he intervened.

1. Mortgages. If A conveyed his land to B as security for a loan, equity would allow A at any time after repayment of the loan fell due, despite any contrary provisions in the mortgage, to recover his land by paying B what was due to him under the loan. The development of this equitable right of redemption, exercisable after expiry of the legal date for redemption, is described later.[79]

2. Restrictive covenants. Normally a contract is binding upon and enforceable by the parties alone. But during the nineteenth century it was held that if a landowner covenants not to use his land in a certain way for the benefit of neighbouring land, the covenant could be enforced in equity against successors in title of the covenantor, thus imposing an equitable burden on his land.[80] This is confined to covenants that are negative in nature, prohibiting certain acts; it does not apply to positive covenants.

[75] *Tyrrel's Case* (1555) 2 Dy. 155a.
[76] *Ante*, p. 22.
[77] *Grubb* v. *Gwillim* (1676) 73 S.S. 347; *Symson* v. *Turner* (1700) 1 Eq. Ca. Abr. 383. For a full treatment of the Statute of Uses and developments therefrom, see M. & W. 1164–1175.
[78] Sched. 7.
[78a] For the categories of trusts today, see *post*, pp. 267 *et seq.*
[79] *Post*, p. 440.
[80] *Post*, p. 409 *et seq.*

3. Estate contracts. Where a person contracts to purchase a legal estate in land, he is at once considered to have an equitable interest in that land, even before he has paid the price and has had the legal estate of the vendor conveyed to him.[81] This also applies to an option to purchase an interest in land, but not to a mere right of pre-emption.[82] If P has an option to purchase land, he has the right, on exercising the option, to compel the landowner to sell the land to him in accordance with the terms of the option, and the landowner cannot deal with the land inconsistently with the option. If instead P has a right of pre-emption (often called a right of first refusal), he has no more than the right to be offered the land if the landowner decides to sell it; and although the right will become an interest in the land as soon as the landowner decides to sell it, until then it is no more than a mere *spes* (hope).[83]

Sect. 3. Creation of Equitable Rights

Equitable rights in land arose under three heads:

(i) Informality: where the proper formalities for the creation or con-veyance of a legal estate were not observed.

(ii) Inability: where the grantor had power only to create or convey an equitable interest.

(iii) Intention: where the grantor provided that only an equitable interest should arise.

1. Informality. At law, in order to create or transfer a legal estate, certain formalities had to be observed. The rule was that "Corporeal hereditaments lie in livery, incorporeal hereditaments lie in grant." A corporeal heredita-ment was an inheritable right in realty which was accompanied by physical possession of the land, *e.g.* a fee simple in possession; for such estates, a feoffment with livery of seisin was essential.[84] An incorporeal hereditament was an inheritable right in land not accompanied by physical possession, such as a fee simple in remainder or an easement; for such interests, a feoffment was inappropriate but a deed of grant was essential. Leases for a term of years were not hereditaments and at first could be created orally, but the Statute of Frauds 1677[85] made writing necessary in nearly all cases. The Real Property Act 1845[86] made a deed essential for most leases; it also made a deed an alternative to a feoffment of corporeal hereditaments, and pro-vided that if a feoffment was employed it would be void unless evidenced by a deed. Thus after the Act it became substantially true to say that without a

---

[81] *Lysaght* v. *Edwards* (1876) 2 Ch.D. 499; *post*, p. 122.
[82] *Pritchard* v. *Briggs* [1980] Ch. 338; *post*, p. 79.
[83] See *Pritchard* v. *Briggs*, *supra*, criticised at (1980) 96 L.Q.R. 488 (H.W.R.W.). Yet it is registrable: *post*, p. 79.
[84] *Ante*, p. 28.
[85] s.1.
[86] ss.2, 3, now L.P.A. 1925, s.54.

deed no legal estate could be created or transferred, even if it was merely an oral tenancy.[87]

Equity, on the other hand, was not so strict. In two important respects, what was ineffective at law might be effective in equity.

(a) *Contract*. In accordance with the maxim "Equity treats that as done which ought to be done," equity regarded a specifically enforceable contract to create or convey an interest in land as being as effective as if the transaction had been properly carried out. But it would not take effect at law, since with few exceptions (including certain leases for not more than three years), any conveyance of land or any interest therein is void for the purpose of conveying or creating a legal estate unless it is made by deed.[88] Equity, however, treated an attempt to convey or create a legal estate which failed at law through lack of a deed as being a contract to carry out the transaction, and thus, if it was specifically enforceable, as being effective in equity. Formerly, the transaction would be specifically enforceable if it was supported either by sufficient evidence of it in writing (such as a letter referring to it) or by a sufficient act of part performance.[89] In this way, many informal transactions, including leases and mortgages by deposit of the title deeds,[90] took effect in equity. Now, however, under the Law of Property (Miscellaneous Provisions) Act 1989, contracts for the sale or disposition of land or any interest in land must actually be in writing, incorporating all the terms of the contract.[91] This seems to invalidate the contractual basis on which equity acted.[91a] Yet if it was intended to abolish an important range of long-established equitable interests, it may be questioned whether Parliament would have adopted the oblique method of merely removing their theoretical foundation. It is possible that the doctrine of proprietary estoppel[92] may be adapted so as to prevent informal transactions from losing their status in equity[93]; but there are obvious difficulties.

(b) *Proprietary estoppel*. Proprietary estoppel is an important equitable doctrine of considerable antiquity.[94] The essence of the doctrine is that if A has acted to his detriment in reliance on the belief or expectation that he owns or will acquire an interest in O's land, and O has either encouraged that belief or expectation or has acquiesced in A's action, it is unconscionable for O to deny a proper fulfilment of A's belief or expectation.[95] An equity arises in A's favour and it is then in the court's discretion as to how that equity

---

[87] *Crago* v. *Julian* [1992] 1 W.L.R. 372; see *post*, pp. 310, 322.
[88] L.P.A. 1925, ss.52(1), 54; for the leases, see *post*, p. 310.
[89] L.P.A. 1925, s.40; *post*, p. 116.
[90] *Post*, p. 446.
[91] s.2.; see *post*, p. 117.
[91a] See [1990] Conv. 441 (J. Howell).
[92] *Infra*; and see *post*, p. 122.
[93] See (1987) Law Com. No. 164, para. 5.4.
[94] See *Hunt* v. *Carew* (1649) Nels. 47; *Hobbs* v. *Norton* (1682) 1 Vern. 137.
[95] *Taylors Fashions Ltd.* v. *Liverpool Victoria Trustees Co. Ltd.* [1982] Q.B. 133n.

should be satisfied.[96] Thus if O knows that A is spending money on improving O's land in the belief that the land is A's, O's silence may result in the land being held to be A's,[97] or A may be held to have some lesser right.[98] Equity is at its most flexible here.[99]

2. Inability. If X owned only an equitable interest, *e.g.* a right under a trust, he had no power to create a legal interest out of it. So far as the common law was concerned, he had no interest in land at all, and thus could create nothing that the common law would recognise. But he could create or transfer interests in equity.

3. Intention. Even if a deed was employed, and the grantor had power to create or convey a legal interest, if the grantor provided that only an equitable interest should be created or transferred, no legal estate would pass.

Sect. 4. The Borderline between Personal and Proprietary Rights

The boundary between rights that are merely personal and rights in the land itself is not always distinct. A fundamental rule of the common law is that a contract binds only the parties to it, creating merely personal rights and liabilities. But as has been seen,[1] when equity intervened to grant specific performance of a contract to sell land, the purchaser's rights came to be treated as equitable rights in the land itself: the purchaser's personal rights became proprietary.[2]

This well-settled impact of remedies upon rights has now been carried further. Under the law of tort, merely personal rights may sometimes become enforceable against third parties, and so produce something of the same effect as if they were rights in land. If G Ltd., the owner of a garage, covenants with P Ltd. that for five years G Ltd. will sell only P Ltd.'s petrol at the garage (a "solus" agreement), and that if G Ltd. sells the garage a similar covenant will be extracted from the purchaser, the obligations of G Ltd. to P Ltd. are merely personal: as the restrictions are not for the benefit of any land owned by P Ltd., they cannot be enforced against others under the equitable doctrine of restrictive covenants.[3] If T Ltd. then buys all the shares in G Ltd. and makes G Ltd. sell the garage to a subsidiary of T Ltd., the subsidiary, being no party to the covenants, is not bound by them. Yet if T Ltd. and its subsidiary have committed the tort of wrongful interference in

---

[96] *Crabb* v. *Arun D.C.* [1976] Ch. 179.
[97] *Pascoe* v. *Turner* [1979] 1 W.L.R. 431.
[98] *Inwards* v. *Baker* [1965] 2 Q.B. 29.
[99] See *Crabb* v. *Arun D.C.*, *supra*, at p. 189; and see Snell 562, 563. On the doctrine generally, see *post*, pp. 429, 434 *et seq.*
[1] *Ante*, p. 67.
[2] *See Swiss Bank Corporation* v. *Lloyds Bank Ltd.* [1979] Ch. 548 at 565 (reversed on a different point: [1982] A.C. 584).
[3] *Post*, p. 411.

the execution of the contract between G Ltd. and P Ltd., the court may grant a mandatory injunction compelling the subsidiary to transfer the garage back to G Ltd., to be held subject to the covenants.[4] In this way the merely personal rights of P Ltd. against G Ltd. have in effect been enforced against third parties in respect of the garage. But mere uncertainties or suspicions about the contract are not enough[5]; actual knowledge must be shown.[6] Nor is there any tort if the interference is justifiable.[7] Thus if V contracts to sell land to X and then contracts to sell the same land to Y, X will be justified in requiring V to convey the land to him, despite the interference with Y's contract; for X has the prior right.[8] Again, a person who interferes with a contract appears to be justified if the contract is void against him for want of registration.[9]

Such cases are not yet recognised as forming part of property law, but they illustrate the effect of remedies on rights, and the need to look outside the sometimes narrow bounds of property law, *e.g.* in protecting the rights of contractual licensees.[10] In general, a right can be admitted to the category of property rights only if it is definable, identifiable by third parties, capable in its nature of assumption by third parties, and has some degree of permanence or stability.[11] What is relevant is the nature of the right and not the remedy which exists for its enforcement.[12]

---

[4] *Esso Petroleum Co. Ltd.* v. *Kingswood Motors* (*Addlestone*) *Ltd.* [1974] Q.B. 142.
[5] *Smith* v. *Morrison* [1974] 1 W.L.R. 659.
[6] *Grieg* v. *Insole* [1978] 1 W.L.R. 302; *Swiss Bank Corporation* v. *Lloyds Bank Ltd.* [1979] Ch. 548 at 575 (reversed on other grounds [1982] A.C. 584).
[7] *Grieg* v. *Insole, supra*, at pp. 340–342; and see (1977) 41 Conv.(N.S.) 318 (R. J. Smith).
[8] See *Pritchard* v. *Briggs* [1980] Ch. 338 at 415.
[9] Consider *Miles* v. *Bull* (*No. 2*) [1969] 3 All E.R. 1585 at 1590; *Midland Bank Trust Co. Ltd.* v. *Green* [1981] A.C. 513.
[10] See *post*, p. 434.
[11] *National Provincial Bank Ltd.* v. *Ainsworth* [1965] A.C. 1175 at 1248.
[12] *Ibid.*

CHAPTER 4

THE STRUCTURE OF LAND LAW AFTER 1925

Part 1

THE POLICY OF THE 1925 LEGISLATION

THE dominant policy of the 1925 legislation was to facilitate the transfer of land by easing the burden on purchasers without defeating the interests of others unfairly. The different methods by which this was achieved have already been considered in outline, but it is convenient to consider them together here. There are five main points.

1. Reduction in number of legal estates. A purchaser of a legal estate in land without notice of adverse claims takes subject to those which are legal but free from those which are equitable. The position of a purchaser has been substantially improved by reducing the number of legal estates and interests which can exist in land.[1]

2. Extension of registration of land charges. The width of constructive and imputed notice sometimes made it difficult for an innocent purchaser to establish that he had no notice, and offered scope for argument. Where a right was registrable as a land charge the question was one not of notice but of the state of the register; and this was discoverable by a search. The extension of the system of registration of land charges often substituted certainty for contention. But not all interests were made registrable, and the exceptions continue to bind a purchaser without notice only if they are legal.[2]

3. Extension of registration of title. The system of registration of title simplifies the task of a purchaser by enabling him to obtain the title to land that is shown in the Land Register rather than the title which appears to him to be disclosed by his examination of often bulky title deeds. The extension of this system under the 1925 legislation has brought many within its benefits.[3]

4. Extension of overreaching. A purchaser takes free from rights which are overreached and so transferred to the purchase money; and there has been a substantial expansion of the system of overreaching. This is of particular importance in what may be called "family" matters, where land is held for

---

[1] *Ante*, p. 58.
[2] *Ante*, pp. 8, 58 *et seq.*
[3] See *ante*, p. 9.

members of a family or others under a settlement, as distinct from "commercial" dealings with land.[4]

5. Simplification of title for co-ownership. The ownership of land by co-owners, and particularly tenants in common, often led to difficulties in making title. These difficulties were met by a combination of prohibiting the ownership of a legal estate by tenants in common and providing for the legal estate to be vested in trustees as joint tenants on trust for sale. The trustees could then make a good title to the land and the rights of the co-owners would be overreached.[5]

Part 2

THE STRUCTURE OF UNREGISTERED LAND LAW

Sect. 1. Reduction in the Number of Legal Estates

Section 1 of the Law of Property Act 1925 reduced the number of legal estates that can exist in land to two, and the number of classes of legal interests to five. The distinction, broadly, is that a legal estate confers full rights to use and enjoy land as one's own, while a legal interest is a right over the land of another. The terms of the first three subsections of section 1 are as follows:

"1.—(1) The only estates in land which are capable of subsisting or of being conveyed or created at law are—

(*a*) An estate in fee simple absolute in possession;

(*b*) A term of years absolute.

(2) The only interests or charges in or over land which are capable of subsisting or of being conveyed or created at law are—

(*a*) An easement, right, or privilege in or over land for an interest equivalent to an estate in fee simple absolute in possession or a term of years absolute;

(*b*) A rentcharge in possession issuing out of or charged on land being either perpetual or for a term of years absolute;

(*c*) A charge by way of legal mortgage;

(*d*) Land tax, tithe rentcharge,[6] and any other similar charge on land which is not created by an instrument;

(*e*) Rights of entry exercisable over or in respect of a legal term of years absolute, or annexed, for any purpose, to a legal rentcharge.

(3) All other estates, interests, and charges in or over land take effect as equitable interests."

---

[4] See *ante*, pp. 5 *et seq.*
[5] See *ante*, p. 7.
[6] These four words have been repealed: *post*, p. 76.

It should be noted that the section does not provide that the estates and interests mentioned in subsections (1) and (2) are *necessarily* legal, but merely that they alone *can* be legal. If they are to be legal the proper formalities must be employed, *i.e.* a deed must be used except in the creation of leases taking effect in possession for a term not exceeding three years.[7]

Probably the incidents of equitable interests are similar to those attaching to corresponding legal estates before 1926. Thus the position of a tenant for life as regards waste seems to have remained unchanged despite the conversion of his legal life estate into an equitable life interest at the beginning of 1926. There is no express provision on this point but "equity follows the law."[8]

The general scheme of the section is to deal with the legal rights of ownership in the land itself in subsection (1) and with legal rights over the land of another in subsection (2). However, this is complicated by the definition of "land" given by the Act. "Land" is defined as including, unless the context otherwise requires, any corporeal or incorporeal hereditament, and among the latter is mentioned an advowson.[9] An advowson is the right of presenting a clergyman to a living[10] and, oddly enough, is a species of real property. By reading subsection (1) in the light of the definition of "land," it seems clear that a fee simple in possession in an advowson is a legal estate and so is a term of years absolute in an advowson.

It will be noted that the rights mentioned in subsection (1) are called legal estates and those mentioned in subsection (2) are called legal interests or charges. This is a convenient distinction between rights over a person's own land and rights over the land of another, but both types of right are referred to in the Act as "legal estates," and have the same incidents attached to them as attached to legal estates before 1926.[11] The title "estate owner" is given to the owner of a legal estate.[12] Before 1926, equitable rights in land were frequently and properly called equitable estates, but they should now be called equitable interests, and the name "estate" reserved for legal rights.

The various legal estates and interests must now be examined more closely.

1(a). "Fee simple absolute in possession." The meaning of "*fee simple*" has already been considered.[13]

"*Absolute*" is used to distinguish a fee simple which will continue for ever from a modified fee,[14] such as a determinable fee or a base fee. A fee simple

---

[7] L.P.A. 1925, ss.52, 54; *post*, p. 310.

[8] *Ante*, p. 56.

[9] L.P.A. 1925, s.205(1)(ix).

[10] It is subject to important restrictions, *e.g.* no advowson may be sold after two vacancies of the benefice have occurred after July 14, 1924: see Benefices Act 1898; Benefices Act 1898 (Amendment) Measure 1923.

[11] L.P.A. 1925, s.1(4).

[12] *Ibid.*

[13] *Ante*, p. 24.

[14] See *ante*, p. 35.

defeasible by condition subsequent[15] would also not be "absolute" but for the Law of Property (Amendment) Act 1926. A fee simple defeasible by condition subsequent used to arise most frequently in connection with rentcharges until the Rentcharges Act 1977 prohibited the creation of rent-charges in most cases. In some parts of the country, particularly Manchester and the north, it was a common practice to sell a fee simple for a compara-tively small sum in cash and a perpetual rentcharge (an annual sum charged on the land). The remedies for non-payment of a rentcharge include a right to enter on the land temporarily to collect the rents and profits; further, in a number of cases an express right of re-entry is reserved by the conveyance, entitling the grantor to enter and determine the fee simple and thus regain his old estate if the rent is a specified number of days in arrear. The reservation of a right of re-entry clearly made the fee simple less than absolute, and it was thought by some that even a temporary right of entry might have this effect. This meant that those who had purchased land in this way before 1926 and had obtained legal estates suddenly found that their estates might no longer be legal and that it was doubtful who had the legal estate. Further, the complicated provisions of the Settled Land Act 1925 probably applied.[16]

To remedy this state of affairs the Law of Property (Amendment) Act 1926[17] provided that "a fee simple subject to a legal or equitable right of entry or re-entry is for the purposes of [the Act of 1925] a fee simple absolute." While this undoubtedly meets the difficulty it was meant to deal with, the wide terms in which it was drawn appear to have done more than was intended. The effect of a condition subsequent annexed to a fee simple is to give rise to a right of re-entry exercisable on breach of the condition, and until the right of re-entry is exercised the fee simple continues.[18] Conse-quently, by virtue of the Amendment Act, every fee simple defeasible by condition subsequent appears to rank as a legal estate (unless created under a trust), even though it is far from being "absolute" in the ordinary sense of the word. Further, by statute, certain land held for special purposes, such as schools or highways, would be divested and revert to (usually) the grantor when the special purpose was at an end. Such a fee simple was nevertheless declared to be absolute.[19] But now, at the end of the special purpose, the legal estate remains vested in the existing owners, though they hold it on trust for sale for those entitled under the reverter.[20]

"*In possession*" means that the estate is a present estate and not in remainder or in reversion.[21] It includes not only physical possession of the

---

[15] *Ante*, p. 35.

[16] *Post*, pp. 236 *et seq.*

[17] Sched., adding words to L.P.A. 1925, s.7(1).

[18] *Ante*, p. 36.

[19] L.P.A. 1925, s.7(1).

[20] Reverter of Sites Act 1987, s.1, resolving the difficulty shown by *Re Clayton's Deed Poll* [1980] Ch. 99 and *Re Rowhook Mission Hall, Horsham* [1985] Ch. 62. See [1987] Conv. 408 (D. Evans).

[21] See *District Bank Ltd.* v. *Webb* [1958] 1 W.L.R. 148.

land but also the receipt of rents and profits or the right to receive them, if any. Thus a fee simple is still "in possession" even though the owner has granted a lease, for he is entitled to the rent reserved by the lease. But if land has been granted "to A for life, remainder to B in fee simple," the interests of both A and B are necessarily equitable, for a life interest cannot now be legal and B's fee simple is not in possession.[22] Yet a mortgagor's legal estate is not converted into an equitable interest merely by the mortgagee exercising his power to take possession of the mortgaged property.[22a]

1(b). "Term of years absolute." "*Term of years*" is defined as including a term of less than a year, or for a year or years and a fraction of a year, or from year to year.[23] In effect, "terms of years" seems to mean a term for any period having a fixed and certain duration as a minimum. Thus, in addition to a tenancy for a specified number of years (*e.g.* "to X for ninety-nine years"), such tenancies as a yearly tenancy or a weekly tenancy are "terms of years" within the definition, for there is a minimum duration of a year or a week respectively. But a lease "for the life of X" cannot exist as a legal estate, and the same, perhaps, applies to tenancies at will or at sufferance (if they are estates at all[24]), for their duration is wholly uncertain.

"*Absolute*." This has very little effect since a term of years is not prevented from being absolute merely by being liable to determination by notice, re-entry, operation of law or by a provision for cesser on redemption or in any other event (other than the dropping of a life, or the determination of a determinable life interest).[25] This means that a term of years may be absolute even if it contains a clause enabling the parties to determine it at certain specified periods, such as at the end of the first five or 10 years, or if it provides (as is almost always the case) that the landlord may determine it if the rent is not paid or a covenant is broken. "Operation of law" is illustrated by the doctrine of satisfied terms,[26] and a proviso for cesser on redemption by the law of mortgages.[27]

It will be seen from this that by the express provisions of statute, a term of years absolute may consist of a tenancy which is neither a "term of years" nor "absolute" according to the natural meaning of the words, *e.g.* a monthly tenancy liable to be forfeited for non-payment of rent. "Absolute" really has very little meaning here.

Unlike a fee simple absolute, a term of years absolute may be a legal estate even though not "in possession." A lease to commence in five years' time may thus be legal, although there is now a 21 year limit to the length of time which may elapse between the grant of a lease and the commencement of the

---

[22] See, however, the Welsh Church (Burial Grounds) Act 1945, s.1, for a curious qualification of L.P.A. 1925, s.1.
[22a] L.P.A. 1925, s.95(4). See *post*, p. 454.
[23] *Ibid.* s.205(1)(xxvii).
[24] See *ante*, p. 27.
[25] L.P.A. 1925, s.205(1)(xxvii).
[26] *Post*, pp. 333, 441.
[27] *Post*, p. 441.

term.[28] There is no limit to the length of a term of years absolute; thus terms of 3,000 years are common in the case of mortgages.[29] But there is no such thing as a lease in perpetuity.[30]

2(a). "An easement, right, or privilege in or over land for an interest equivalent to an estate in fee simple absolute in possession or a term of years absolute." This head includes both easements and, it seems, profits *à prendre*.[31] An easement confers the right to use the land of another in some way, or to prevent it from being used for certain purposes. Thus rights of way, rights of water and rights of light may exist as easements. A *profit à prendre* gives the right to take something from the land of another, *e.g.* peat, fish or wood. These rights can be legal only if they are held for interests equivalent to one of the two legal estates. Thus a right of way for 21 years may be legal but a right of way for life must be equitable.

2(b). "A rentcharge in possession issuing out of or charged on land being either perpetual or for a term of years absolute." A rentcharge is a right which, independently of any lease or mortgage, gives the owner the right to a periodical sum of money, with the payment of which some land is burdened,[32] as where the fee simple owner of Blackacre charges the land with a payment of £50 per annum to X. With some exceptions, no new rentcharges could be created after August 21, 1977, and any existing rentcharge will be extinguished 60 years after it first became payable, and in any case by July 22, 2037.[33]

"In possession." Under the subsection a rentcharge to start at a date subsequent to that on which it was granted could not be legal, whether it was perpetual or for a term of years absolute. But the Law of Property (Entailed Interests) Act 1932[34] declared that a rentcharge was "in possession" notwithstanding that the payments were limited to commence or accrue at a date subsequent to its creation, unless the rentcharge was limited to take effect in remainder after or expectant on the failure or determination of some other interest.[35] Thus if X conveyed land to Y in consideration of a perpetual rentcharge becoming payable one year after the conveyance, the rentcharge could nevertheless have been legal; but if a perpetual rentcharge was granted "to A for life, remainder to B absolutely," B's interest could not be legal until A's death.

"Issuing out of or charged on land." "Land" includes another rentcharge.[36] Thus if P charged his fee simple estate in Blackacre with the

---

[28] *Post*, p. 315.
[29] See L.P.A. 1925, ss.85(2), 87(1).
[30] See *Sevenoaks, Maidstone and Tunbridge Ry.* v. *London, Chatham and Dover Ry.* (1879) 11 Ch.D. 625 at 635.
[31] For easements and profits, see *post*, pp. 367 *et seq.*
[32] For rentcharges, see *post*, p. 361 *et seq.*
[33] Rentcharges Act 1977, ss.2, 3. See *post*, pp. 363, 366.
[34] s.2.
[35] See (1932) 73 L.J. News. 321.
[36] L.P.A. 1925, ss.122, 205(1)(ix); see *post*, p. 362.

payment to Q of £100 per annum in perpetuity, Q could formerly create a legal rentcharge of £50 per annum in favour of R, charged on his rentcharge of £100.

"*Being either perpetual or for a term of years absolute.*" "Perpetual" is used here in place of "fee simple absolute" used in 2(a) above. This verbal difference seems to be of no practical importance.

2(c). "A charge by way of legal mortgage." This needs no comment here save to point out that this is one of the ways of creating a legal mortgage today, the other being by the grant of a term of years absolute on certain conditions. Both forms are dealt with later.[37]

2(d). "Land tax, tithe rentcharge, and any other similar charge on land which is not created by an instrument." This group comprises periodical payments with which land is burdened by operation of law (*e.g.* by statute) and not by some conveyance or other voluntary act of parties. The words "land tax, tithe rentcharge" have now been repealed,[38] but they are printed here in order to explain the word "similar."

Land tax was a small annual tax on land first imposed in 1692. It was abolished in 1963.[39]

Tithe rentcharge was abolished by the Tithe Act 1936. It was a type of rentcharge imposed by statute in lieu of the former right of parsons and others to one-tenth of the produce of land. Under the Act of 1936, tithe owners were compensated with government stock, and there was imposed on the land formerly burdened with tithe rentcharge a "tithe redemption annuity" payable to the Crown, originally for 60 years[40]; but this was extinguished on October 2, 1977.[41] Although a tithe redemption annuity was not expressly stated to be a legal interest, it clearly fell within that category as being a "similar charge on land which is not created by an instrument."

2(e). "Rights of entry exercisable over or in respect of a legal term of years absolute, or annexed, for any purpose, to a legal rentcharge." As already mentioned,[42] a legal term of years absolute is usually subject to the right of the landlord to re-enter if the tenant fails to pay rent or comply with the covenants. Such a right may be a legal right, and the same applies to any right of re-entry attached to a legal rentcharge, *e.g.* if the rent is not paid. By contrast, a right reserved on an assignment of a lease for the assignor (who retains no other interest in the land) to re-enter and retake the land for

[37] *Post,* pp. 441, 442.
[38] Tithe Act 1936, Sched. 9; Finance Act 1963, Sched. 14, Pt. VI.
[39] Finance Act 1963, s.68, Sched. 14, Pt. V, VI.
[40] Tithe Act 1936, s.3.
[41] Finance Act 1977, s.56. See M. & W. 830–833 for further details about tithe, tithe rentcharge and tithe redemption annuity.
[42] *Ante,* p. 74.

breach of covenant by the assignee is merely an equitable interest,[43] even, perhaps, if it is for a defined or indefinite term.[44]

Concurrent legal estates. Any number of legal estates may exist concurrently in the same piece of land.[45] Thus A may have the legal fee simple in Greenacre, subject to a legal mortgage in favour of B, a legal rentcharge in favour of C, a legal lease in favour of D, and so on.

Sect. 2. Registration of Land Charges

The system of registration of land charges, already considered in outline,[46] must now be examined in some detail. There are two categories of registers, each governed by its own Act. They are:

(1) The registers maintained by the Land Charges Department of the Land Registry under the Land Charges Act 1972, replacing the Land Charges Act 1925; and
(2) The registers of Local Land Charges maintained by various local authorities under the Local Land Charges Act 1975, replacing provisions in the Land Charges Act 1925.

This section of the book will be confined to the registers maintained by the Land Charges Department of the Land Registry, which are held in a computerised form at Plymouth. For brevity, this is usually called the land charges register. Local land charges will be considered later.[47] For the land charges register, the two basic principles are that for any registrable interest—

(1) due registration of the interest constitutes actual notice of the interest registered[48]; and
(2) non-registration makes the interest void against certain purchasers.[49]

A. Registrable Interests

Five separate registers and an index are kept in the Land Charges Department of the Land Registry.[50] The first of these is much more important than the others.

1. Land charges. Land charges,[51] strictly so called, are divided into six classes, A, B, C, D, E and F. The most important classes are C and D (which

[43] *Shiloh Spinners Ltd.* v. *Harding* [1973] A.C. 691. For assignments of leases, see *post*, p. 322.
[44] *Ibid.* at p. 726.
[45] L.P.A. 1925, s.1(5).
[46] *Ante*, p. 8.
[47] *Post*, p. 91.
[48] L.P.A. 1925, ss.198, 199.
[49] See *post*, pp. 87 *et seq.* for the details.
[50] L.C.A. 1972, s.1.
[51] *Ibid.* ss.2–4.

are subdivided) and F.[52] Most of the interests are equitable interests affecting another's land.

Class A consists of charges imposed on land by some statute, but which come into existence only when some person makes an application. Thus where a landlord who is not entitled to land for his own benefit has to pay compensation to an agricultural tenant, the landlord may apply to the Minister of Agriculture, Fisheries and Food for a charge on the land for the amount of compensation.[53] Class A charges are registrable whenever created.

Class B consists of charges which are similar to those in Class A except that they are not created on the application of any person, but are automatically imposed by statute. Most charges thus imposed are registrable as local land charges, and so few are registrable in Class B. An example is a charge on property recovered or preserved for a legally aided litigant in respect of unpaid contributions to the legal aid fund.[54]

Class C land charges are divided into four categories.

C(i): A PUISNE MORTGAGE. A puisne (pronounced "puny") mortgage is a legal mortgage not protected by a deposit of documents relating to the legal estate affected. This has been made registrable because by taking the title deeds a mortgagee puts a subsequent mortgagee or purchaser on inquiry, whereas a mortgagee who does not obtain the deeds does not.

C(ii): A LIMITED OWNER'S CHARGE. This is an equitable charge which a tenant for life or statutory owner acquires under any statute by discharging inheritance tax or other liabilities to which the statute gives special priority. Thus inheritance tax is payable on the death of a tenant for life of settled land, and if his successor finds the money out of his own pocket instead of leaving the burden on the settled property itself, he is entitled to a charge on the land in the same way as if he had lent money to the estate on mortgage.[55] Such a charge is registrable under this head.

C(iii): A GENERAL EQUITABLE CHARGE. This is any equitable charge which—

(a) is not included in any other class of land charge;
(b) is not protected by a deposit of documents relating to the legal estate affected; and
(c) does not arise, or affect any interest arising, under a trust for sale or settlement (and so be overreachable).

This is a residuary class which catches equitable charges not registrable elsewhere, *e.g.* an unpaid vendor's lien on the land.[56] It includes equitable

---

[52] *Ibid.* s.2.
[53] A.H.A. 1986, s.86. For a full list of such charges, see L.C.A. 1972, Sched. 2.
[54] Legal Aid Act 1988, s.16(6).
[55] Inheritance Tax Act 1984, s.212(2); L.C.A. 1972, s.2(4), as amended by Inheritance Tax Act 1984, Sched. 8, para. 3. See Finance Act 1986, s.100.
[56] *Uziell-Hamilton* v. *Keen* (1971) 22 P. & C.R. 655. For the lien, see *post*, p. 438.

mortgages of a legal estate but not equitable mortgages of an equitable interest under a settlement or trust for sale or other charges on the proceeds of sale of land.[57] It also includes certain annuities created after 1925.[58]

C(iv): AN ESTATE CONTRACT. This is a contract to convey or create a legal estate, made by a person who either owns a legal estate or is entitled at the date of the contract to have a legal estate conveyed to him. Oral contracts formerly sufficed if sufficiently supported by evidence in writing or part performance,[59] but contracts made after July 27, 1989, must be in writing.[60] It suffices if the person who makes the contract owns any legal estate in the land, even if it is less substantial than the estate he has agreed to convey or create, as where a yearly tenant agrees that if he acquires the reversion he will grant his sub-tenant a lease for 10 years.[61]

In addition to ordinary contracts, options to purchase, rights of pre-emption[62] and other like rights are expressly included by the statute. Thus an option given to a tenant to purchase the freehold reversion is registrable,[63] and so is an option to renew a lease, even though such an option runs with the land at law[64] and so there seems little point in making it registrable.[65] An obligation to offer to surrender a lease to the landlord before seeking to assign it is also included,[66] and so is a tenant's notice exercising his statutory right to purchase the freehold or take an extended lease.[67] At least some conditional contracts seem to be registrable,[68] and it has been held that a contract with an agent to convey the land to whoever the agent directs is also included.[69] But a contract with an agent to make an estate contract is not registrable,[70] nor is a notice to treat under the process for the compulsory acquisition of land.[71] A boundary agreement is registrable only if it clearly transfers land.[72]

Class D land charges fall into three categories.

D(i): INLAND REVENUE CHARGES. Originally this class comprised charges for estate duty on death (often called "death duty"). But in 1975 it was replaced by the different system of capital transfer tax,[73] and after 1984

---

[57] *Georgiades* v. *Edward Wolfe & Co. Ltd.* [1965] Ch. 487 (estate agent's commission charged on proceeds of sale not a C(iii) land charge); and see *Thomas* v. *Rose* [1968] 1 W.L.R. 1797.
[58] *Post*, p. 81.
[59] L.P.A. 1925, s.40; *Universal Permanent B.S.* v. *Cooke* [1952] Ch. 95 at 104.
[60] L.P.(M.P.)A. 1989, s.2; *ante*, p. 67.
[61] *Sharp* v. *Coates* [1949] 1 K.B. 285.
[62] See *ante*, p. 66.
[63] *Midland Bank Trust Co. Ltd.* v. *Green* [1981] A.C. 513.
[64] *Phillips* v. *Mobil Oil Co. Ltd.* [1989] 1 W.L.R. 888.
[65] See (1981) 125 S.J. 816 (M. P. Thompson).
[66] *Greene* v. *Church Commissioners for England* [1974] Ch. 467.
[67] Leasehold Reform Act 1967, s.5; *post*, p. 549.
[68] See *Haslemere Estates Ltd.* v. *Baker* [1982] 1 W.L.R. 1109 at 1118; and see *Williams* v. *Burlington Investments Ltd.* (1977) 121 S.J. 424.
[69] *Turley* v. *Mackay* [1944] Ch. 37, doubted in *Thomas* v. *Rose* [1968] 1 W.L.R. 1797.
[70] *Thomas* v. *Rose, supra.*
[71] *Capital Investments Ltd.* v. *Wednesfield U.D.C.* [1965] Ch. 774.
[72] *Neilson* v. *Poole* (1969) 20 P. & C.R. 909.
[73] Under Finance Act 1975, Pt. III, Sched. 4.

this tax, in a revised form, was renamed "inheritance tax."[74] The tax creates a charge on land in favour of the Board of Inland Revenue, though it does not apply to leaseholds or undivided shares in land under a trust for sale which were owned by the deceased beneficially.[75] It is chargeable on freeholds, and must be registered in order to bind purchasers; but in practice it is rarely registered.

D(ii): RESTRICTIVE COVENANTS. Under this head, any covenant or agreement restrictive of the user of land may be registered, provided it—

(a) was entered into after 1925, and
(b) is not between a lessor and a lessee.

Restrictive covenants in leases are never registrable even where they relate not to the demised land but to adjoining land owned by the lessor.[76] For leases, the normal rules as to privity of contract and privity of estate apply, and when there is neither, the question, as usual, is one of notice. Similarly, restrictive covenants made before 1926 still depend upon notice, being enforceable against everyone except a purchaser for value of a legal estate without notice.

D(iii): EQUITABLE EASEMENTS. Any "easement, right or privilege over or affecting land" is registrable under this head, provided—

(a) it is merely equitable, and
(b) it was created or arose after 1925.

Thus a perpetual easement created without using a deed and an easement for life, being equitable, are both registrable.[77] Similarly, a specifically enforceable contract to create an easement is also registrable as an equitable easement,[78] or perhaps as an estate contract.[79] Equitable *profits à prendre* also seem to be included under this head.[80]

The apparent width of the term "right or privilege" is restricted by the context. The modern approach is to construe this head narrowly, and it has been held that it does not include a requisition of land under Defence Regulations,[81] an interest by proprietary estoppel,[82] a right to remove fixtures at the end of a lease[83] or a right of entry to secure compliance with the covenants contained in an assignment of a lease.[84] The result is that a number of informal rights fall within the scope of the old doctrine of notice.

---

[74] Under Capital Transfer Act 1984, now named Inheritance Tax Act 1984: see Finance Act 1986, s.100.
[75] Inheritance Tax Act 1984, s.237; and see Sched. 8, para. 3.
[76] *Dartstone Ltd.* v. *Cleveland Petroleum Co. Ltd.* [1969] 1 W.L.R. 1807.
[77] See *ante*, pp. 66, 71.
[78] *E. R. Ives Investment Ltd.* v. *High* [1967] 2 Q.B. 379 at 403 (contrast pp. 395, 396); [1986] Conv. 31 at 34–37 (M. P. Thompson).
[79] *Huckvale* v. *Aegean Hotels Ltd.* (1989) 58 P. & C.R. 163 at 165; (1947) 11 Conv.(N.S.) 165 at 176 (E. O. Walford); and see *E. R. Ives Investment Ltd.* v. *High, supra.*, at p. 397.
[80] *E. R. Ives Investment Ltd.* v. *High, supra*, at p. 395.
[81] *Lewisham Borough Council* v. *Maloney* [1948] 1 K.B. 50.
[82] *E. R. Ives Investment Ltd.* v. *High, supra*; but see *post*, p. 93.
[83] *Poster* v. *Slough Estates Ltd.* [1969] 1 Ch. 495 at 506, 507.
[84] *Shiloh Spinners Ltd.* v. *Harding* [1973] A.C. 691; *ante*, p. 77.

Class E: Annuities created but not registered before 1926.[85] An annuity is a rentcharge or an annuity for life or lives, or for an estate determinable on a life or lives (*e.g.* to X for 99 years if he so long lives) not created by a marriage settlement or a will.[86] This class is thus small and diminishing. Annuities as thus defined created after 1925 are registrable in Class C(iii) as general equitable charges.

Class F: A spouse's statutory right to occupy a house owned by the other spouse.

In a series of cases in the 1950's,[87] a controversial[88] doctrine was evolved under which a wife who had been deserted by her husband was held to have an equitable right to remain in occupation of the matrimonial home vested in her husband. This right, which was held to be a mere equity[89] rather than an equitable interest, was enforceable against her husband and everyone else except a bona fide purchaser for value of a legal or equitable interest in the house.[90] In 1965, the House of Lords held that this "deserted wife's equity" did not exist, and that the wife had a mere personal right that would not bind a purchaser.[91] This led to the enactment of the Matrimonial Homes Act 1967 (now the Matrimonial Homes Act 1983) which gave statutory rights of occupation to both husbands and wives.

The statutory "rights of occupation" conferred by the Act arise automatically, and are not dependent on desertion or anything else. The rights are given only to a spouse who has neither the legal fee simple nor a term of years in the matrimonial home, and either has no right to occupy it (whether by virtue of any estate, interest, contract or statute) or else has only an equitable interest in it, or in the proceeds of sale.[92] The statutory rights are the right not to be excluded from the home, and the right, with the leave of the court, to enter into occupation of it.[93] The rights are a charge on the other spouse's estate or interest in the home as from the date when that spouse acquired the home, or the date of the marriage, or January 1, 1968, whichever is the latest.[94] These rights are registrable as a Class F land charge even before the court has granted any leave to enter into occupation of the home[95]; and once registered, the rights will bind purchasers, and also the trustee in bankruptcy of the owning spouse.[96] But a registration effected not for the protection of rights of occupation but for some ulterior purpose (*e.g.*

---

[85] For annuities registered before 1926, see *post*, p. 84.
[86] L.C.A. 1972, s.17(1).
[87] *Bendall* v. *McWhirter* [1952] 2 Q.B. 466; *Street* v. *Denham* [1954] 1 W.L.R. 624.
[88] See (1952) 68 L.Q.R. 379 (R.E.M.).
[89] See *ante*, p. 59.
[90] *Westminster Bank Ltd.* v. *Lee* [1956] Ch. 7.
[91] *National Provincial Bank Ltd.* v. *Ainsworth* [1965] A.C. 1175. See also *post*, p. 433.
[92] Matrimonial Homes Act 1983, s.1.
[93] *Ibid.*
[94] *Ibid.* s.2.
[95] *Watts* v. *Waller* [1973] Q.B. 153; [1976] Current Legal Problems 26 at 31–33, 43–50 (D. J. Hayton).
[96] Insolvency Act 1986, s.336(2).

to put financial pressure on the other spouse) is improper and will be set aside.[97]

The statutory rights of occupation are not absolute. They end when the marriage ends, and the court has wide powers at any time to restrict or terminate them, or to prohibit, suspend or restrict the exercise of the right of occupation by either spouse, including the owning spouse.[98] In making orders under the Act the court has a wide discretion, and must consider all the circumstances of the case, including the position of a purchaser from the owning spouse.[99]

While married couples are living together, it is unusual for any rights of occupation to be registered. Registration, when discovered, is likely to be seen as a hostile act, and it is not the practice of the Land Registry to inform the owning spouse of any registration.[1] This is liable to create difficulties for an owning spouse who sells the home without knowing of the registration of a Class F charge either prior to the contract or between contract and completion.[2] A prudent purchaser will therefore obtain the written concurrence of the non-owning spouse to any sale, both for this reason and in case that spouse claims some beneficial interest in the home.[3]

Companies. Most charges on land created by a company for securing money (including a charge created by deposit of title deeds[4]) require registration within 21 days in the Companies Charges Register maintained under the Companies Act 1985 and earlier legislation.[5] For floating charges and charges created before 1970, this suffices, and takes effect as registration under the Land Charges Act 1972[6]; other charges require registration in both registers.[7]

2. Pending actions. This head comprises pending land actions and petitions in bankruptcy. A pending land action (often called a *lis pendens*) is any action or proceeding pending in court relating to land or any interest in land or charge on it.[8] This definition is not so wide as it may seem. It is confined to claims for some proprietary right in specific land.[9] This includes a claim to an easement over the land,[10] an application for an access order,[11] and an

[97] *Barnett* v. *Hassett* [1981] 1 W.L.R. 1385.
[98] Matrimonial Homes Act 1983, s.1.
[99] *Ibid.* ss.1, 2; *Kashmir Kaur* v. *Gill* [1988] Fam. 110.
[1] See Ruoff and Roper, 39–11.
[2] See *Wroth* v. *Tyler* [1974] Ch. 30.
[3] See *Williams & Glyn's Bank Ltd.* v. *Boland* [1981] A.C. 487; (1974) 38 Conv. 110 (D. J. Hayton).
[4] *Re Wallis & Simmonds (Builders) Ltd.* [1974] 1 W.L.R. 391.
[5] Companies Act 1985, s.396, as inserted by Companies Act 1989, s.93 (when brought into force); see *Re Molton Finance Ltd.* [1968] Ch. 325.
[6] L.C.A. 1972, s.3(7); see *Property Discount Corporation Ltd.* v. *Lyon Group Ltd.* [1981] 1 W.L.R. 300.
[7] See [1982] Conv. 43 (D. M. Hare and T. Flanagan).
[8] L.C.A. 1972, ss.5, 17.
[9] *Calgary and Edmonton Land Co. Ltd.* v. *Dobinson* [1974] Ch. 102; and see *Whittingham* v. *Whittingham* [1979] Fam. 9.
[10] *Greenhi Builders Ltd.* v. *Allen* [1979] 1 W.L.R. 156.
[11] See *post*, p. 408.

application for leave to bring proceedings for forfeiture of a lease which would terminate the lease.[12] But it does not include an action for damages for breach of a repairing covenant in a lease (even if coupled with a claim for a mandatory order to effect the repairs),[13] an action to restrain a nuisance emanating from land,[14] or a claim to restrain the sale of land[15] or to receive the proceeds of sale if it is sold.[16] Nor does it include a claim based on proprietary estoppel with the mere hope that, if it succeeds, the court will satisfy the estoppel by creating a charge on the land.[17]

A claim in divorce proceedings for a property adjustment order is registrable if it specifies the particular land claimed,[18] or, if it does not, when the land is specified on the application for registration.[19] But there is no *lis pendens*, and so nothing is registrable, before the proceedings have been commenced[20]; and a registration will be vacated when the proceedings have terminated on the making of the order, even if other proceedings to set aside the order have been commenced.[21] Registration lasts for five years, and it may be renewed for successive periods of five years if the *lis* is still pending.[22]

3. Writs and orders affecting land. This register[23] does not include writs commencing an action relating to land, but is confined to writs and orders *enforcing* judgments and orders of the court. There are three heads.

(i) Writs and orders affecting land issued or made by a court for the purpose of enforcing a judgment or recognisance. This head includes access orders,[23a] and also charging orders, whereby the land of a judgment debtor is charged with the payment of the money due (in place of the old writ of elegit).[24] But even though a charging order may now be made against a beneficial interest under a trust for sale,[25] such an interest is not "land,"[26] and so a charging order against it still appears not to be registrable.[27] Nor is a *Mareva* injunction[28] registrable, for it merely prevents a litigant from disposing of his assets pending the trial.[29]

---

[12] *Selim Ltd.* v. *Bickenhall Engineering Ltd.* [1981] 1 W.L.R. 1318 (under Leasehold Property (Repairs) Act 1938; *post*, p. 347).
[13] *Regan & Blackburn Ltd.* v. *Rogers* [1985] 1 W.L.R. 870.
[14] See *Calgary and Edmonton Land Co. Ltd.* v. *Dobinson*, *supra*, át p. 105.
[15] *Calgary and Edmonton Land Co. Ltd.* v. *Dobinson*, *supra*.
[16] *Taylor* v. *Taylor* [1968] 1 W.L.R. 378.
[17] *Haslemere Estates Ltd.* v. *Baker* [1982] 1 W.L.R. 1109. For proprietary estoppel, see *ante*, p. 67; *post*, p. 434.
[18] *Whittingham* v. *Whittingham*, *supra*.
[19] *Perez-Adamson* v. *Perez-Rivas* [1987] Fam. 89.
[20] *Kemmis* v. *Kemmis* [1988] 2 F.L.R. 223 at 239.
[21] *Sowerby* v. *Sowerby* (1982) 44 P. & C.R. 192.
[22] L.C.A. 1972, s.8.
[23] *Ibid*. s.6.
[23a] See *post*, p. 408.
[24] Charging Orders Act 1979, s.3.
[25] *Ibid*. ss.1, 2. See *National Westminster Bank Ltd.* v. *Stockman* [1981] 1 W.L.R. 67.
[26] See *post*, p. 416; and see *Irani Finance Ltd.* v. *Singh* [1971] Ch. 59.
[27] Contrast *National Westminster Bank Ltd.* v. *Allen* [1971] 2 Q.B. 718 (joint judgment against both joint tenants).
[28] *Mareva Compania Naviera S.A.* v. *International Bulk Carriers S.A.* [1975] 2 Ll.Rep. 509.
[29] *Stockler* v. *Fourways Estates Ltd.* [1984] 1 W.L.R. 25.

(ii) An order appointing a receiver or sequestrator of land. Sometimes a receiver is appointed in cases where no charging order can be made[30]; and in a dispute between the landlord and tenants of a block of flats, a receiver may be appointed to manage the flats pending trial.[31]

(iii) A bankruptcy order, whether or not the bankrupt's estate is known to include land.[32]

Registration remains effective for five years, but may be renewed for successive periods of five years.[33]

4. Deeds of arrangement.[34] The Deeds of Arrangement Act 1914[35] elaborately defines deeds of arrangement. For the present purpose, a deed of arrangement may be taken as any document whereby control over a debtor's property is given for the benefit of his creditors generally, or, if he is insolvent, for the benefit of three or more creditors. A common example is an assignment by a debtor of all his property to a trustee for all his creditors, made in the hope of his trading out of his actual or expected insolvency.

Registration is effective for five years and may be renewed for successive periods of five years.[36] The registration may be effected by the trustee of the deed or by any creditor assenting to or taking the benefit of the deed.[37]

5. Annuities.[38] This register, opened in 1855, was closed in 1925.[39] There can be few registered annuities left now.

B. Mode of Registration

1. Land charges. All land charges must be registered in the name of the estate owner whose estate is to be affected.[40] The estate owner is the owner of a legal estate.[41] Normally this does not give rise to any difficulty as the estate owner usually creates the charge. Charges created by beneficiaries of their beneficial interests under trusts are not registrable.[42] However in one common case there is a trap. If V contracts to sell land to P who then contracts to sell it to S, it is against V, the estate owner, and not P, that S must register his estate contract; registration against P will not be effective even if P later acquires the legal estate.[43] Yet S will often be ignorant of the

---

[30] See *Levermore* v. *Levermore* [1979] 1 W.L.R. 1277; Supreme Court Act 1981, s.37(4).
[31] *Clayhope Properties Ltd.* v. *Evans* [1986] 1 W.L.R. 1223.
[32] L.C.A. 1972, s.6(1), as amended by Insolvency Act 1985, Sched. 8, para. 21.
[33] L.C.A. 1972, s.8.
[34] *Ibid.* s.7.
[35] *Ibid.* s.1.
[36] *Ibid.* s.8.
[37] *Ibid.* s.7.
[38] *Ibid.* s.1, Sched. 1.
[39] See M. & W. 172, 173. For the registration of annuities created after 1925, see *ante*, p. 79.
[40] L.C.A. 1972, s.3(1).
[41] *Ibid.* s.17(1), applying the definition in L.P.A. 1925, s.205(1)(v).
[42] See *ante*, p. 79.
[43] *Barrett* v. *Hilton Developments Ltd.* [1975] Ch. 237.

identity and even the existence of V. To be safe S should stipulate for the name of the estate owner to be disclosed as soon as contracts are exchanged.[44]

2. Other registers. Pending actions and writs and orders affecting land are registrable in the name of the estate owner or other person whose estate or interest is intended to be or is affected.[45] It will be noted that this is not limited to estate owners. Deeds of arrangement are registrable in the name of the debtor.[46]

3. The name. Registration should be against the estate owner's full correct name as it appears in the conveyance to him, even if he is generally known by another name, or another name appears in his birth certificate.[47] This ensures that the name will appear in its correct place in the index and will be revealed on a search made in the correct name. A registration in a name which may fairly be described as a version of the correct name (*e.g.* "Frank" for "Francis") is not a nullity but will bind all except those who make an official search in the correct name and obtain a certificate which does not disclose the entry.[48] But registration is ineffective if it omits one of the names of the estate owner.[49] If the estate owner is dead, registration should be effected not against his name but against the names of his personal representatives or, if there are none and he died intestate, against the President of the Family Division.[50]

C. Effects of Registration and Non-Registration

1. Effect of registration

(a) *Notice.* By the Law of Property Act 1925,[51] registration under the Land Charges Acts constitutes actual notice of the interest registered to all persons and for all purposes connected with the land affected. There are statutory exceptions to this rule,[52] and it does not apply to a purchaser entering into a contract for the sale of land, where only actual or imputed knowledge suffices.[53] But in general it prevents any person claiming to be a purchaser without notice of a registered interest.

---

[44] See *Patman* v. *Harland* (1881) 17 Ch.D. 353 at 359.
[45] L.C.A. 1972, ss.5(4), 6(2).
[46] *Ibid.* s.7(1).
[47] *Standard Property Investment Plc.* v. *Plastics Federation* (1985) 53 P. & C.R. 25.
[48] See *Oak Co-operative B.S.* v. *Blackburn* [1968] Ch.730, where the system of indexing is described. See *post*, p. 89, for searches.
[49] *Diligent Finance Co. Ltd.* v. *Alleyne* (1972) 23 P. & C.R. 346.
[50] See [1979] Conv. 249 (A. M. Pritchard); [1986] Conv. 237 (J. E. Adams); (1986) 83 L.S.Gaz. 2127 (E. J. Pryer). A proposed reform is to validate registration against the name of the deceased: (1989) Law Com. 184, para. 2.7.
[51] s.198.
[52] See *post*, pp. 86 (compensation scheme), 460 (mortgage deeds).
[53] L.P.A. 1969, s.24, removing for land charges (but not local land charges) the difficulty arising from *Re Forsey and Hollebone's Contract* [1927] 2 Ch. 379: see *Rignall Developments Ltd.* v. *Halil* [1987] 1 E.G.L.R. 193.

(b) *Names register*. The most serious defect of the system from the point of view of a purchaser is that the registers are registers of the names of persons; an incumbrance is registered against the name of the estate owner at the time and not against the land. Thus on a purchase of 14 Newcastle Street it is not possible to search against 14 Newcastle Street, and a search must be made against the names of all previous owners of the land. The rights most likely to concern a purchaser, namely, Classes C and D, only became registrable after 1925, but in course of time the cost of searches has become considerable. It assists if each purchaser in turn preserves the certificate of the search he made when purchasing the land, and hands the certificates on with the title deeds so that the subsequent owners can rely upon them.

(c) *Compensation scheme*. In 1955, when 30 years had elapsed since 1925, the possibility arose that the names of persons against whom charges were registered might lie behind the root of title. The situation was aggravated in 1969 when the length of title was reduced to 15 years.[54] A purchaser may be unable to discover the relevant names, but yet will be deemed to have actual notice of the charges registered against them. As it is now impossible to reorganise the registers on a territorial basis, the only long-term solution is to press on with registration of title, and this is taking place.[55] As an interim measure financial compensation at public expense was introduced for purchasers saddled with registered but undisclosed land charges. The two main requirements are that the purchaser should not have any actual or imputed knowledge of the charge (the deemed actual notice from registration is disregarded), and that the estate owner against whom the charge is registered should not be a party to any transaction in the relevant title or be concerned with any event in it.[56]

(d) *Lessees*. The doctrine that registration constitutes notice *per se* may work especial hardship in the case of lessees. Where a lease is granted by a tenant in fee simple at a low rent in consideration of a fine, the lessee usually stipulates that he shall be entitled to investigate the lessor's title, whereas if the lease is granted at a rack rent, the lessee usually takes it for granted that the lessor is able to grant it and so does not investigate his title. Further, by statute,[57] under an open contract[58] to grant a lease the lessee is not entitled to investigate the freeholder's title; and similarly for assignments. In *Patman* v. *Harland*[59] it was held that since a lessee under an open contract might have made a special contract entitling him to investigate the lessor's title, he was fixed with notice of all that he would have discovered had he made a proper investigation.

The rule in *Patman* v. *Harland*, which caused some hardship and was

---

[54] L.P.A. 1969, s.23; *ante*, p. 62.
[55] See Report of Committee on Land Charges 1956 (Cmd. 9825).
[56] L.P.A. 1969, s.25. For the first claim, see Chief Land Registrar's Report (1988–89) para. 56.
[57] L.P.A. 1925, s.44, replacing Vendor and Purchaser Act 1874, s.2.
[58] *Post*, p. 123.
[59] (1881) 17 Ch.D. 353.

much criticised, has been abolished for all leases made after 1925.[60] However, the provisions for the registration of land charges such as restrictive covenants made after 1925 have created a new difficulty due to registration being effected against the name of the person making the covenant and not against the land. A prospective lessee will be able to search against the name of the lessor, but if he is not entitled to investigate the lessor's title he will not know the names of the previous owners of the land and so will not be able to discover restrictive covenants registered against their names. Nevertheless, registration is notice to all persons and for all purposes connected with the land,[61] and so the lessee is deemed to have notice of the covenants. He is, moreover, excluded from the compensation scheme.[62] The position may be summarised thus:

(i) Lease and restrictive covenant both made before 1926: the lessee is caught by *Patman* v. *Harland*.

(ii) Lease and restrictive covenant both made after 1925: the lessee is caught by the provisions for registration.

(iii) Restrictive covenant made before 1926, lease made after 1925: here alone is the lessee's position improved. The lessee is safe unless he has notice in some other way, for *Patman* v. *Harland* does not apply and the restrictive covenant, being made before 1926, is not registrable.[63]

2. Effect of non-registration

(a) *Categories*. The effect of non-registration varies according to the interest. There are two main categories:

(a) The incumbrance may be void against a purchaser for value of any interest in the land; or

(b) The incumbrance may be void against a purchaser for money or money's worth of a legal estate in the land.

One difference between (a) and (b) is that a purchaser of an equitable interest is protected by (a) but not by (b). Another is that marriage is "value" but is not "money or money's worth," and consequently in the case of land settled on an ante-nuptial marriage settlement the spouses and issue will be protected by (a) but not by (b). In each case "purchaser" has an extended meaning and includes a lessee, mortgagee or other person taking an interest in land for value.

(b) *Effect*. The effect of non-registration may be expressed as follows.[64]

(i) In general, whichever register is concerned, non-registration of any

[60] L.P.A. 1925, s.44(5).
[61] *Ibid.* s.198. This prevails over s.44(5): see *White* v. *Bijou Mansions Ltd.* [1937] Ch. 610 at 619.
[62] L.P.A. 1969, s.25(9), (10). For the scheme see *ante*, p. 86.
[63] See, *e.g. Shears* v. *Wells* [1936] 1 All E.R. 832.
[64] L.C.A. 1972, ss.4, 5(7), (8), 6(4), (5), (6), 7(2), Sched. 1, para. 4, as amended by Insolvency Act 1985, Sched. 8, para. 21, Sched. 10, Pt. III.

registrable matter in the appropriate register makes it void against a purchaser for value of any interest in the land.

(ii) If, however, a land charge falls within Class C (iv) (estate contracts) or Class D, and was created after 1925, non-registration makes it void only against a purchaser of a legal estate for money or money's worth.

(iii) Bankruptcy petitions (registrable as pending actions) and the title of trustees in bankruptcy under bankruptcy orders (registrable as writs and orders) are void only against a bona fide purchaser of a legal estate for money or money's worth.

(iv) Any other pending action is void against a purchaser for value of any interest in the land, provided he had no express notice of it.

(c) "*Void*." The courts have given full and literal effect to the word "void"; "void" really does mean void. An unregistered interest will be void against a purchaser even if he had full knowledge of it, even if he was not acting in good faith, and even though the owner of the interest was in possession of the land concerned.[65] In the leading case,[66] a son was the tenant of a farm owned by his father. The father then granted the son an option for 10 years to purchase the farm at a fixed price. Some six years later, after the farm had nearly doubled in value and family disputes had arisen, the father conveyed the farm to his wife for £500, with the common intention of defeating the son's option, which had not been registered. It was held that the option was void against the wife. The son had a claim for breach of contract against the father,[67] a claim for conspiracy against the father and the wife[68] (provided a sufficient intent to injure was shown[69]), and a claim against his solicitor for negligence in failing to register the option[70]: but he had no claim to the farm. For registered land, actual occupation of the land confers adequate protection[71]; but there is no corresponding provision for unregistered land. A section of the Law of Property Act 1925[72] provides that the interest of any person in possession or in actual occupation of land is not to be prejudiced by Part I of the Act; but Part I does not contain the provisions relating to land charges.[73] In any case, the section is confined to interests to which the person is entitled "in right of such possession or occupation," and that would not include the option above. By construing "void" simply and strictly all concerned are relieved of the burden of litigious enquiries into the motives and state of mind of the purchaser; a clear and definite system for the

---

[65] L.P.A. 1925, s.199; *Midland Bank Trust Co. Ltd.* v. *Green* [1981] A.C. 513.
[66] *Ibid.*
[67] *Ibid.*, at p. 526.
[68] *Midland Bank Trust Co. Ltd.* v. *Green* (*No. 3*) [1982] Ch. 529; but see [1985] C.L.J. 280 at 293–295 (M. P. Thompson).
[69] See *Lonrho Ltd.* v. *Shell Petroleum Co. Ltd.* [1982] A.C. 173 at 189.
[70] *Midland Bank Trust Co. Ltd.* v. *Hett, Stubbs & Kemp* [1979] Ch. 384: see *Midland Bank Trust Co. Ltd.* v. *Green* [1981] A.C. 513 at 526; but contrast *Bell* v. *Peter Browne & Co.* [1990] 2 Q.B. 495.
[71] *Post*, p. 104.
[72] s.14.
[73] Originally it did: see L.P.A. 1922, ss. 14, 32, Sched. 7. The change seems to have been an oversight.

protection of title to land is not to be destroyed by reading into the Act provisions to protect a person who has failed to protect himself by registering his land charge.[74]

D. Searches and Priority Notices

1. Searches. The means by which an intending purchaser of land can discover registrable incumbrances is by a search. This may be made in person,[75] but it is advisable to obtain an official certificate of search, for—

(i) it is conclusive in favour of a purchaser or intending purchaser whose application correctly specifies the persons[76] and the land,[77] and so frees him from registered rights which it fails to disclose[78];

(ii) it protects a solicitor or trustee who makes it from liability for any error in the certificate[79]; and

(iii) it provides protection against incumbrances registered in the interval between search and completion. If a purchaser completes his transaction before the expiration of the fifteenth working day after the date of the certificate he is not affected by any entry made after the date of the certificate and before completion, unless it is made pursuant to a priority notice[80] entered on the register before the certificate was issued.[81]

If the official certificate of search mistakenly fails to disclose a charge properly registered before the search, the owner of the charge will be wrongly deprived of his rights and may suffer loss. Damages for negligence against those responsible may be obtained,[82] though in the absence of fraud, individual employees of the Registry are not liable for any discrepancy between what is shown by the official search certificate as the particulars in the request for search and those actually stated in the request for a search.[83]

A single search is effective for all divisions of all registers.

2. Priority notices. Special provision has been made to provide for a rapid sequence of transactions, such as the creation of a restrictive covenant followed immediately by the creation of a mortgage before there has been time to register the covenant. Thus if V is selling land to P, who is raising the purchase-money by means of a loan on mortgage from M, and is to enter into a restrictive covenant with V, the sequence of events will be—

---

[74] See *Midland Bank Trust Co. Ltd.* v. *Green* [1981] A.C. 513 at 528, 530.
[75] L.C.A. 1972, s.9.
[76] See *Oak Co-operative B.S.* v. *Blackburn* [1968] Ch. 730; *ante*, p. 85.
[77] See *Du Sautoy* v. *Symes* [1967] Ch. 1146.
[78] L.C.A. 1972, s.10(4): see *Stock* v. *Wanstead and Woodford B.C.* [1962] 2 Q.B. 479 (local land charge).
[79] L.C.A. 1972, s.12.
[80] See *infra.*
[81] L.C.A. 1972, s.11(5), (6). For corresponding provisions for registered land, see *post*, p. 108.
[82] See *Ministry of Housing and Local Government* v. *Sharp* [1970] 2 Q.B. 223 (local land charge), not invalidated by *Murphy* v. *Brentwood D.C.* [1991] 1 A.C. 398: see at p. 486.
[83] L.C.A. 1972, s.10(6).

    (i) conveyance from V to P, creating the restrictive covenant, followed a
         few minutes later by
    (ii) mortgage by P to M.

In such a case, the restrictive covenant could not be registered in the few
minutes between its creation and the making of the mortgage, and so it will
be void against M, a purchaser for money or money's worth of a legal estate,
unless V has availed himself of the machinery of the priority notice. To do
this, he must give a priority notice to the registrar at least 15 days before the
creation of the restrictive covenant, and then, if he registers his charge
within 30 days of the entry of the priority notice in the register, the registration dates back to the moment of the creation of the restrictive covenant, *i.e.*
to the execution of the conveyance from V to P; once again, days on which
the registry is not open to the public are excluded.[84] It will be noted that the
notice must be given 15 days before completion: this is to allow the expiry of
the 15 days' period of protection given to those who made official searches
before the priority notice was lodged.[85]

    Priority notices are not, of course, confined to restrictive covenants, but
apply to all land charges.

E. The Vacation of Entries

An entry on the various registers at the Land Registry may be effected
merely by making an application in the proper form[86]; registration is automatic, without the Land Registry investigating whether there is anything to
justify the entry. As registration may effectively paralyse dealing with the
land by the owner, provision is made for the court to order the vacation (*i.e.*
removal) of any entries on the registers. There is an inherent jurisdiction to
do this,[87] and also a wide statutory jurisdiction which now applies to all the
registers and not only the land charges register.[88] This jurisdiction may be
used to vacate entries not only of unjustified claims but also of interests that
have ceased to be effective, such as contracts which have expired or have
been rescinded; but in these cases the person registering the charge will
usually apply to have the entry cancelled.[89] There is also power to vacate the
entry of a pending land action if the proceedings are not being prosecuted in
good faith.[90] Applications under the jurisdiction can be made speedily, on
motion, and the jurisdiction is exercised with a certain robustness.[91] Sometimes the court will refuse to order the entry to be vacated only if the person

---

[84] *Ibid.* s.11.
[85] *Supra.*
[86] Land Charges Rules 1974, rr. 5, 6.
[87] *Calgary and Edmonton Land Co. Ltd.* v. *Dobinson* [1974] Ch. 102.
[88] L.C.A. 1972, s.1(6); *Northern Developments (Holdings) Ltd.* v. *U.D.T. Securities Ltd.*
[1976] 1 W.L.R. 1230; and see *Tucker* v. *Hutchinson* (1987) 54 P. & C.R. 106 at 112.
[89] See Land Charges Rules 1974, rr. 9–12.
[90] L.C.A. 1972, s.5(10).
[91] *The Rawlplug Co. Ltd.* v. *Kamvale Properties Ltd.* (1969) 20 P. & C.R. 32 at 40; *Woolf
Project Management Ltd.* v. *Woodtrek Ltd.* [1988] 1 E.G.L.R. 179.

making it will undertake to pay the landowner damages if at the trial it is established that the entry was wrongly made.[92]

Sect. 3. Registration of Local Land Charges

In addition to the registers kept by the Land Charges Department of the Land Registry, a register of local land charges is kept by each district council, each London Borough, and the Common Council of the City of London.[93] These registers, which are divided into 12 Parts,[94] differ from those kept by the Land Charges Department in that the charges are registered against the land itself[95] and not against the owner of an estate in it. Thus a series of searches against successive owners is unnecessary. Official searches may be made.[96]

There is a wide range of interests that are registrable.[97] In general, they are charges acquired by statute by a local authority or, in some cases, by a government department; and they have the general nature of being public rights, rather than the private rights registrable in the Land Charges Department of the Land Registry. They may for the most part be classified as being either financial or restrictive. Some examples may be given: charges for making up a road that are imposed on the frontagers; the cost of certain sewerage works; prohibitions or restrictions on the use of land imposed or enforceable by a local authority or government department; closing or demolition orders for houses; conditions in a planning permission; and tree preservation orders. But some private rights are registrable, such as light obstruction notices.[98]

Failure to register a local land charge no longer makes it void against a purchaser. Instead, the charge remains valid, but the purchaser is normally entitled to compensation for any loss that he suffers; and similarly for omissions from an official search certificate.[99]

Sect. 4. Effect of a Conveyance

Before summarising the effect of a conveyance on legal and equitable interests in the land, the greater complexity of equitable interests requires them to be considered first.

---

[92] See *Tucker* v. *Hutchinson* (1987) 54 P. & C.R. 106, citing the cases (all on registered land).
[93] Local Land Charges Act 1975, s.3.
[94] Local Land Charges Rules 1977 (No. 985), r. 3.
[95] *Ibid.* r. 6.
[96] Local Land Charges Act 1975, s.9.
[97] *Ibid.* ss.1, 2. See J. F. Garner, *Local Land Charges* (10th ed. 1987).
[98] *Ibid.* s.1, Sched. 1; Local Land Charges Rules 1977, r. 10, Sched. 1, Forms A, B. For these notices, see *post*, p. 396.
[99] Local Land Charges Act 1975, s.10.

A. Equitable Interests

In determining whether or not a purchaser of land takes subject to equitable interests in it, there are three major heads to consider;

(i) Overreaching;
(ii) Non-registration of land charges; and
(iii) The purchaser without notice.

The broad picture is that the expansion of (i) and (ii) has reduced but not destroyed the importance of (iii).

1. Overreaching. The system of overreaching, whereby rights in land become corresponding rights in the purchase money, has considered mainly in relation to settled land and trusts for sale.[1] But there are other overreaching conveyances which take effect if the purchase money is paid to trustees or others in accordance with the law.[2]

(i) If a mortgagee exercised his power of sale on some default by the mortgagor, this overreaches the rights of all subsequent mortgagees (even if legal) and of the mortgagor, and these become attached to the money in the hands of the mortgagee, under a trust, though subject to the mort-gagee's right to repayment.[3]

(ii) A conveyance by personal representatives overreaches the rights of the beneficiaries under the will or intestacy.[4]

(iii) A conveyance made under an order of the court, (*e.g.* to remove incumbrances) overreaches all equitable interests and powers which are bound by the order.[5]

2. Non-registration of land charges. If a land charge is not duly registered it is void against a purchaser; the charge is overridden, not overreached. The varying details of this have already been considered.[6]

3. The purchaser without notice. The doctrine of purchaser without not-ice, though greatly reduced in its ambit, can still apply in a somewhat motley collection of cases. These can perhaps be classified as follows.

(a) *Excluded interests.* Some interests have been expressly made not registrable, as apparently being otherwise protected.

(i) A mortgage protected by a deposit of documents relating to the legal estate affected is not registrable[7]; the absence of the deeds will normally

---

[1] *Ante*, pp. 5, 6.
[2] L.P.A. 1925, s.2(1).
[3] *Ibid.* ss.2(1), 104, 105; *post*, p. 453.
[4] *Post*, p. 166.
[5] L.P.A. 1925, ss.2(1), 50.
[6] *Ante*, pp. 87 *et seq.*
[7] *Ante*, p. 78.

put the purchaser on inquiry, and so, if the mortgage is equitable, he cannot claim to be a purchaser without notice.

(ii) Restrictive covenants and equitable easements are not registrable if they arose before 1926, or, in the case of restrictive covenants, if they are between a lessor and a lessee,[8] when the lease will normally disclose them to a purchaser. Yet where the covenant binds not the lessor's reversion in the land, but other land of his, a purchaser of that other land will usually not see the lease.[9]

(b) *Omitted interests.* Some interests, without being expressly excluded, have simply been omitted from the provisions for overreaching and registration.

(i) Equitable rights of entry have not been made registrable. Thus the grant of a right to enter land and remove fixtures from it is not registrable,[10] nor is a right reserved on an assignment of a lease for the assignor (who retains no interest in the land) to re-enter the land and retake it for breach of covenant.[11]

(ii) Where A holds land on trust for B absolutely (B being *sui juris*) there is nothing to make B's equitable interest under the bare trust either registrable or overreachable.[12]

(c) *The fringes of overreaching and non-registration.* Various equitable interests which appear to fall within the provisions for overreaching or non-registration will nevertheless fall outside their operation.

(i) An overreachable interest will not be overreached if the statutory requirements are not observed,[13] as where the purchase money is not properly paid to the trustees.[14]

(ii) A registrable interest will not be void against a purchaser who merely gives value (such as marriage) where the statute requires money or money's worth to be given,[15] as for estate contracts.[16]

(iii) An equitable easement for an uncertain period, such as so long as certain foundations stand on certain land, created by proprietary estoppel or acquiescence, has been held not to be registrable as an equitable easement on the ground that it could not have existed at law before 1926.[17]

---

[8] *Ante*, p. 80.
[9] *Dartstone Ltd.* v. *Cleveland Petroleum Co. Ltd.* [1969] 1 W.L.R. 1807.
[10] *Poster* v. *Slough Estates Ltd.* [1969] 1 Ch. 495.
[11] *Shiloh Spinners Ltd.* v. *Harding* [1973] A.C. 691.
[12] Consider *Hodgson* v. *Marks* [1971] Ch. 892. A must obey B's directions.
[13] Consider *Caunce* v. *Caunce* [1969] 1 W.L.R. 286; (1969) 33 Conv. 240 (J. F. Garner); also *Williams & Glyn's Bank Ltd.* v. *Boland* [1981] A.C. 487.
[14] Consider *Kingsnorth Finance Co. Ltd.* v. *Tizard* [1986] 1 W.L.R. 783.
[15] See *McCarthy & Stone Ltd.* v. *Julian S. Hodge & Co. Ltd.* [1971] 1 W.L.R. 1547 (no legal estate); [1976] Current Legal Problems 26 (D.J. Hayton).
[16] *Ante*, p. 77.
[17] *E. R. Ives Investment Ltd.* v. *High* [1967] 2 Q.B. 379. L.P.A. 1925, ss.1(2)(a), 1(3), 4(1) (as cited at p. 395), seem to provide little support.

B. Legal and Equitable Interests: A Summary

In the briefest possible form, the effect of a conveyance on sale on legal and equitable interests in the land may be shown as follows.

1. The purchaser takes subject to all legal rights.

Exceptions: He takes free from—

(a) the few legal rights which are void against him for want of registration; and
(b) the few legal rights which are overreached.

2. The purchaser takes subject to all equitable rights.

Exceptions: He takes free from—

(a) equitable rights which are void against him for want of registration: notice is irrelevant;
(b) the many equitable rights which are overreached, *e.g.* under a settlement or trust for sale: again, notice is irrelevant; and
(c) other equitable rights, relatively few in number, in respect of which he can show either that he is a bona fide purchaser of a legal estate for value without notice, or else that he claims through such a person.

Part 3

REGISTRATION OF TITLE

Sect. 1. Introductory

1. History. Today, registration of title is of great and increasing importance; but it is by no means new. Acts were passed in 1862 and 1875,[18] providing for voluntary registration of title, but not until the Land Transfer Act 1897 made registration of title compulsory on dealings with land in the County of London were any substantial numbers of titles registered. The present principal Act is the ill-drafted Land Registration Act 1925, which, with a series of amending Acts, may be cited as the Land Registration Acts 1925 to 1986.[19] These Acts are supplemented by the Land Registration Rules 1925, as amended, and a number of other statutory rules.[20] Most of the work

---

[18] Land Registry Act 1862; Land Transfer Act 1875.
[19] See Land Registration Act 1936; Land Registration Act 1966; Land Registration and Land Charges Act 1971; Land Registration Act 1986. See also Administration of Justice Act 1977; Land Registration Act 1988; and certain Acts on special subjects, such as Housing Acts 1980 and 1985.
[20] They are printed in the standard book, Ruoff & Roper, *The Law and Practice of Registered Conveyancing*, 6th ed. 1991 (cited as "Ruoff & Roper"), Appendix B.

of conveyancing today is estimated to concern registered land, so that this has become an important branch of the law.

2. Basis of the system. The basic idea is to replace the separate investigation of title that takes place on every purchase by a title guaranteed by the State. In the case of unregistered land, a purchaser must satisfy himself from the abstract or epitome of title, the deeds, his requisitions on title, his searches and his inspection of the land that the vendor has power to sell the land and that it is subject to no undisclosed incumbrances. In the case of registered land, on the other hand, the purchaser can discover from the mere inspection of the register whether the vendor has power to sell the land and what the more important incumbrances are; the other incumbrances must be investigated in much the same way as in the case of unregistered land. The complexity of rights in land is such as to render it impossible to make the transfer of registered land as simple as the transfer of shares registered in the books of a company, but the present system of registration of title may be said to go almost as far on that road as is practicable.

3. Classification of rights. The system of registration of title in no way amounts to a separate code of land law. In the main it is concerned with the conveyancing aspects of land law, *i.e.* actual or potential transfers of rights existing under the general law, and in the main it leaves the basis of this unaffected. In this connection, the differing classes of interests in land must be distinguished.

(a) *Unregistered land*. In very broad terms, on a purchase of unregistered land, rights in the land fall into three main categories.

(i) There is the estate that the purchaser is buying.

(ii) There are rights adverse to the land which, being legal, will bind the purchaser except in the few cases where they are overreached or void for want of registration.

(iii) There are other rights adverse to the land which are equitable, and so, if not overreached or void for want of registration, will bind the purchaser unless he takes without notice of them.

(b) *Registered land*. In registered land, there is a similar but not exactly corresponding division.

(i) Registered estates, *i.e.* rights in respect of which a title has been granted by the registrar.

(ii) Overriding interests, *i.e.* rights which will bind a purchaser whether or not disclosed by the register or otherwise.

(iii) Minor interests, *i.e.* rights which need to be protected by some entry on the register.

4. Other registrations. If the title to land is registered, there is no question of registration in the Land Charges Department, for entries on the Land

Register take the place of this. But entries must still be made in the local land charges registers. Further, most charges created by a company for securing money require registration in the Companies Charges Register in addition to protection by an entry on the Land Register.[21]

5. Open Register. On December 3, 1990, the land register was opened to public inspection, with the right to obtain copies of it.[22] Previously, nobody could inspect it or obtain copies of it without the authority of the registered proprietor of the land,[23] though on a sale or other disposition (except a lease or charge) the vendor was obliged to give the purchaser an authority to inspect the register.[24] Further, an Index Map, a Parcels Index and a list of pending applications were[25] (and still are) open to public inspection, making it possible to discover whether or not any particular property has been or is about to be registered.

6. Fundamental principles. Two linked principles are fundamental to registered land.

(a) *Registration confers title*. In unregistered conveyancing, the vendor's estate in the land passes to the purchaser as soon as the conveyance is executed. In registered conveyancing, the execution of the transfer by the vendor confers no estate on the purchaser. It is registration that vests the title in the purchaser in accordance with the register.[26] Registration is treated as having effect "as of" the day when the purchaser delivers the relevant documents to the appropriate District Registry of the Land Registry.[27]

(b) *Registration is conclusive*. Registration is conclusive of title. When a title is first registered, the registration confers a new statutory title on the registered proprietor, even if his previous title was defective or he had no title at all, as where he claims under forged title deeds. The act of registration confers the statutory title on the proprietor,[28] and gives him "a new root of title."[29] He holds this title subject to any subsisting entries on the register, and subject to any overriding interests; but he holds free from all other interests,[30] even if he has full notice of them. The doctrine of notice for unregistered land has no application to registered land, even by analogy.[31] Subject to overriding interests, the register is conclusive. The one qualif-

---

[21] Companies Act 1985, ss.396, 397, as inserted by Companies Act 1989, s.93 (when brought into force).
[22] L.R.A. 1988, s.1; S.I. 1990 No. 1359. By March 1991 about 1,000 copies a day were being issued to enquirers: L.R.Ann.Rep. 1990–1991.
[23] L.R.A. 1925, ss.112, 112A.
[24] *Ibid.* s.110(1).
[25] L.R.R. 1925, rr. 8, 10, 12.
[26] L.R.A. 1925, s.69(1).
[27] L.R.R. 1925, r. 83(2).
[28] L.R.A. 1925, ss.5–12.
[29] *Kitney* v. *MEPC Ltd.* [1977] 1 W.L.R. 981 at 993.
[30] L.R.A. 1925, ss.20, 23, 33, 69; and see *Morelle Ltd.* v. *Wakeling* [1955] 2 Q.B. 379 at 411.
[31] *Williams & Glyn's Bank Ltd.* v. *Boland* [1981] A.C. 487 at 504.

ication to this doctrine is that there are limited powers to rectify the register in order to correct errors; but normally these are subject to the payment of compensation to any person thereby suffering loss.[32] Subject to this, a registered title is indefeasible.

Sect. 2. Interests in Registered Land

The three types of interest in registered land (namely, registered estates, overriding interests and minor interests) will now be considered in turn.

A. Registered Estates

1. Estates which can be registered. After 1925, the only estates in respect of which a proprietor can be registered are estates capable of subsisting as legal estates.[33] Thus a fee simple absolute in possession and a term of years absolute for more than 21 years are registrable interests. Although a lease for 21 years or less is not registrable, it takes effect as if it were a registered disposition.[34]

2. The register. The register itself is divided into three parts:

(a) *The property register.* This describes the land and the estate for which it is held, refers to a map or plan showing the land, and contains notes of interests held for the benefit of the land, such as easements or restrictive covenants of which the registered land is the dominant tenement, and other like matters. The boundaries shown on the map are general and are not so exact as to show on which side of a hedge or fence they run unless stated by the register to be "fixed."[35]

(b) *The proprietorship register.* This states the nature of the title (*i.e.* whether it is absolute, good leasehold, qualified or possessory[36]), states the name, address and description of the registered proprietor, and sets out any cautions, inhibitions and restrictions[37] affecting his right to deal with the land.

(c) *The charges register.* This contains entries relating to rights adverse to the land, such as mortgages or restrictive covenants, and in general all notices[38] protecting rights over the land.

The Land Registry, which is now a self-financing Executive Agency,[39] has its headquarters in Lincoln's Inn Fields in London. The register is kept at the appropriate District Land Registry; there are some 20 of these, dispersed

---

[32] See *post*, pp. 111 *et seq.*
[33] L.R.A. 1925, s.2.
[34] *Ibid.* s.19(2).
[35] *Ibid.* s.76; L.R.R. 1925, r. 278; *Lee* v. *Barrey* [1957] Ch. 251.
[36] See *post*, pp. 99, 100.
[37] *Post*, pp. 106–108.
[38] See *post*, p. 106.
[39] As from July 1990: see L.R.Ann.Rep. 1990–1991.

throughout the country. The three parts of the register in respect of each property are kept together. A copy of these entries is included in the "Land Certificate," and is given to each registered proprietor as his document of title for retention until he sells or charges the land.[40] The title deeds, stamped with a notice of registration, are also usually returned when the title is first registered. But the registered proprietor's proof of title is the register itself and not the Land Certificate, which may well be out of date owing to entries having been made in the register since the certificate was last in the registry.

3. Compulsory and voluntary registration

(a) *The compulsory areas.* During the years 1897 to 1990, the areas in which registration of title is compulsory were gradually extended, with a marked acceleration from 1965 onwards.[41] As from December 1, 1990, the compulsory areas have extended to the whole of England and Wales.[42]

(b) *Ambit of compulsory registration.* By no means all the land in the country has a registered title, for registration is compulsory only on the conveyance on sale of a fee simple, or on the grant or assignment of certain leases, made after the area became a compulsory area.[43] For many years much land is likely to remain unsold, such as land vested in corporate bodies or held on a family settlement; and gifts are not registrable.

(c) *Leases.* The provisions governing leases were formerly complex,[44] but they have now been simplified. Registration is now compulsory on the grant or assignment of a lease which has more than 21 years to run[45]; this is so even if it contains a prohibition or restriction against assignment, though this will be protected by an entry in the register.[46] Once the lease is registered, any future dealings with it must be registered.

(d) *Non-registration.* Where registration is compulsory, the transaction will be void as to the legal estate unless application for registration of it is made within two months[47]; but the registrar has power to extend this period for "sufficient cause."[48] In default of due registration, the vendor or lessor will hold the legal estate on a bare trust for the purchaser or lessee. There is no default in registration if an application is made but it misdescribes the land or omits part of it[49]; and where a title is registered, the time limit does not appear to apply to leases of the land.[50]

---

[40] See *post*, p. 109.
[41] See the map in L.R.Ann.Rep. 1990–1991.
[42] S.I. 1989 No. 1347.
[43] L.R.A. 1925, s.123(1).
[44] See M. & W. 199, 200.
[45] L.R.A. 1925, s.123(1), as amended by L.R.A. 1986, s.2(1); and see L.R.A. 1925, s.8(1A), inserted by L.R.A. 1986, s.2(2).
[46] L.R.A. 1925, s.8(2), inserted by L.R.A. 1986, s.3(1).
[47] L.R.A. 1925, s.123(1).
[48] *Ibid.*, a power used generously.
[49] *Proctor* v. *Kidman* (1985) 51 P. & C.R. 67.
[50] See L.R.A. 1925, ss.19(1), (2), 22(1).

(e) *Voluntary registration.* A voluntary application for registration may be made for any registrable interest.[51] The former restrictions on such applications if the land was outside the compulsory area[52] disappeared when the whole country was included within the compulsory area.

4. Titles. There are four classes of title with which an applicant for registration may be registered.

(a) *Absolute.* In the case of freeholds, an absolute title vests in the first registered proprietor, by force of statute and without any conveyance, a fee simple in possession (in equity[53] as well as at law) together with all rights and privileges (*e.g.* easements) belonging thereto, subject only to—

(i) entries on the register;
(ii) overriding interests, except so far as the register states that the land is free from them; and
(iii) as between himself and those entitled to minor interests, to minor interests of which he has notice, if he is not entitled to the land for his own benefit; thus trustees for sale who are registered as proprietors will still hold subject to the claims of the beneficiaries.[54]

In the case of leaseholds, an absolute title similarly vests the leasehold in the first registered proprietor subject to the rights set out above, and in addition to—

(iv) all the covenants, obligations and liabilities incident to the lease.[55]

An absolute title in the case of leaseholds guarantees not only that the registered proprietor is the owner of the lease but also that the lease was validly granted. Easements, restrictive covenants and other incumbrances affecting the superior title (but not mortgages or charges) will also appear on the leasehold title,[56] so that, in contrast with unregistered land,[57] a purchaser of the lease will be free from the risk of being bound by incumbrances which he cannot discover.

(b) *Qualified.* In the case of freeholds, a qualified title has the same effect as an absolute title except that the property is held subject to some defect or right specified in the register. This title is granted when an absolute title has been applied for but the registrar has been unable to grant it owing to some defect in the title. A qualified title to leaseholds has the same effect as an absolute or good leasehold title, as the case may be, except for the specified defect.[58]

[51] *Ibid.* ss.4, 8.
[52] L.R.A. 1966, s.1(2).
[53] The inference to the contrary from *Epps* v. *Esso Petroleum Co. Ltd.* [1973] 1 W.L.R. 1071 at 1075, 1078, is very slender; and see (1974) 38 Conv.(N.S.) 236 (S.N.L.Palk).
[54] L.R.A. 1925, s.5.
[55] *Ibid.* s.9.
[56] See Ruoff & Roper 5–09; and see *White* v. *Bijou Mansions Ltd.* [1937] Ch. 610 (affd. [1938] Ch. 351).
[57] See *ante*, p. 86.
[58] L.R.A. 1925, ss.7, 12.

(c) *Possessory*. In the case of either freeholds or leaseholds, first registration with possessory title has the same effect as registration with an absolute
title, save that the title is subject to all rights existing or capable of arising at
the time of first registration.[59] In short, the title is guaranteed as far as all
dealings after the date of registration are concerned, but no guarantee is
given as to the title prior to first registration, which must accordingly be
investigated by a purchaser in the same way as if the land were not
registered.

(d) *Good leasehold*. A good leasehold title applies only to leaseholds. It is
the same as an absolute title, save that the lessor's right to grant the lease is
not guaranteed.[60] If it appears that the lessor was never entitled to grant the
lease, the lessee is protected if he has an absolute title, but unprotected if he
has a good leasehold title. Since a lessee cannot investigate the freehold title
unless he stipulates for this in the contract,[61] he usually cannot give the
registrar evidence of the freehold title where it is or appears to be unregistered, and so he can apply only for a good leasehold title. The registrar may
nevertheless be able to grant an absolute title if the title to the freehold is in
fact registered, and, though unknown to the lessee, his landlord is the
registered proprietor.

Application may be made in the first instance for any of the above titles
except a qualified title, which can be applied for only if an absolute title is
refused.[62]

5. Conversion of titles. Where there has been registration with any title
other than absolute, the title may be converted subsequently, either on
application by the proprietor or by the registrar *ex mero motu*. There are
three categories.[63]

(i) *Good leasehold*: a good leasehold title may be converted to absolute
if the registrar is satisfied as to the title to the freehold and to any
intermediate leasehold.

(ii) *Possessory*: a possessory title may be converted to absolute or (if
leasehold) to good leasehold if the registrar is satisfied as to the title, or if
the possessory title has been registered for at least 12 years and he is
satisfied that the proprietor is in possession.

(iii) *Qualified*: a qualified title may be converted to absolute or (if
leasehold) to good leasehold if the registrar is satisfied as to the title.

Any person (other than the proprietor) who suffers loss by any conversion
of title is entitled to indemnity as if a mistake had been made in the register.[64]

6. Application for first registration. With the exceptions set out above, an

---

[59] L.R.A. 1925, ss.6, 11.
[60] *Ibid.* s.10.
[61] *Ante*, p. 86.
[62] See L.R.A. 1925, s.7(1).
[63] *Ibid.* s.77, as inserted by L.R.A. 1986, s.1.
[64] *Ibid.*; *post*, p. 114.

application for registration may be made by any estate owner, including those holding the estate as a trustee. Further, anyone entitled to call for a legal estate to be vested in him (except a mere purchaser under a contract, or a mortgagee) can apply for registration.[65] Thus if A holds land on a bare trust for B, B can apply for registration without first requiring a conveyance to be executed in his favour, though normally A will have to join or concur in the application.

The registrar examines the title and inquires into any objections that may be made to the proposed registration. He has power to accept a defective title if in his opinion it is "a title the holding under which will not be disturbed."[66] There is no appeal to the court from a refusal to register a title as absolute,[67] though it may be possible to challenge the registrar's action or inaction on an application for judicial review.[68]

7. Cautions against first registration. Any person interested in unregistered land who thinks that he may be prejudiced by an application to register any title to it may lodge a caution against first registration with the registrar.[69] This entitles him to be informed by the registrar of any application to register the title. Thus a person who claims that the execution by him of a conveyance of his unregistered land was obtained by fraud might lodge a caution against first registration to prevent the grantee registering the title without his knowledge. Cautions may also be lodged to prevent a conversion of the title, or against dealings by the registered proprietor.[70] Failure by the registrar to disclose a caution on an official search does not deprive the cautioner of his protection against subsequent purchasers or chargees.[71] Conversely, the lodging of a caution does not give the cautioner any priority over earlier chargees.[72]

The notice given to the cautioner requires him to make his objections to the registration or conversion within a fixed time, usually 14 days. Abuse of this procedure is discouraged by a provision that any person who causes damage to another by unreasonably lodging a caution is liable to pay him compensation.[73]

8. Registered charges. The formal way to mortgage registered land is to effect a registered charge by deed. Once registered, this operates as a charge by way of legal mortgage.[73a] A registered charge is *sui generis*. It is not an overriding interest or a minor interest, and it is not a registrable interest for which a land certificate can be issued. Instead, a charge certificate is issued,

[65] L.R.A. 1925, ss.4, 8.
[66] *Ibid.* s.13.
[67] *Dennis* v. *Malcolm* [1934] Ch. 244, considered in *Quigly* v. *Chief Land Registrar* [1992] 1 W.L.R. 834; see at p. 837.
[68] *Ibid.* at p. 253; R.S.C., Ord. 53.
[69] L.R.A. 1925, s.53.
[70] See *post*, p. 106 for cautions against dealings.
[71] *Parkash* v. *Irani Finance Ltd.* [1970] Ch. 101.
[72] *Barclays Bank Ltd.* v. *Taylor* [1974] Ch. 137.
[73] L.R.A. 1925, s.56.
[73a] *Ibid.* ss.25–27.

and the land certificate is retained in the registry. Registered charges will be considered with other mortgages in due course.[74]

B. Overriding Interests

1. Nature. Overriding interests are "all the incumbrances, interests, rights, and powers not entered on the register but subject to which registered dispositions are," by the Act, "to take effect.... "[75] They are interests which bind the proprietor even though he has no knowledge of them and the register does not refer to them. In general, they are the kinds of rights which a purchaser of unregistered land would not expect to discover from a mere examination of the abstract and title deeds, but for which he would make inquiries and inspect the land. Many are legal rights but some are equitable. Yet it is to be emphasised that for incumbrances on registered land, the issue in deciding whether or not a purchaser is bound is not whether the rights are legal or equitable, but whether they are overriding interests or minor interests.

2. The interests. The Land Registration Act 1925[76] sets out in 12 paragraphs a list of "subsisting" interests that are overriding interests. Only the most important of them will be considered here.

(1) *Para. (a)*: rights of common, public rights, profits *à prendre*, rights of way, watercourses, rights of water and other easements "not being equitable easements required[77] to be protected by notice on the register."[78] Despite these latter words, an equitable easement of way openly exercised and enjoyed for the benefit of adjoining land has been held to be an overriding interest.[79] "Easements, rights and privileges adversely affecting registered land" can be acquired by prescription in the same way as if the land was not registered.[80]

(2) *Para. (f)*: rights acquired or being acquired under the Limitation Acts.[81] A title to registered land may be acquired under these Acts by adverse possession in the same way as for unregistered land, though the operation of the Acts is different. For unregistered land, the adverse possession extinguishes the title of the landowner,[82] whereas for registered land the adverse possessor acquires no legal title until he has been registered as proprietor; until then, the registered proprietor holds the land on a bare

[74] See *post*, p. 447.
[75] L.R.A. 1925, s.3(xvi). The words omitted relate only to land registered before 1926.
[76] *Ibid.*, s.70(1).
[77] In the sense of "needing," it seems: there is no express requirement.
[78] L.R.A. 1925, s.70(1).
[79] *Celsteel Ltd.* v. *Alton House Holdings Ltd.* [1985] 1 W.L.R. 204 (in C.A. [1986] 1 W.L.R. 512), relying on L.R.R. 1925, r. 258. See [1986] Conv. 31 (M. P. Thompson). (1987) Law Com. No. 185, paras. 2.25–35 recommends changing this.
[80] L.R.R. 1925, r. 250.
[81] See Limitation Act 1980; *post*, pp. 493 *et seq.*
[82] See *post*, p. 502.

trust for him.[83] The adverse possessor may be registered with any of the four possible titles.[84]

(3) *Para. (g)*: the rights of every person "in actual occupation" of the land, or in receipt of the rents and profits thereof, unless the rights are not disclosed when enquiry is made of him. This important and difficult provision will be given detailed consideration shortly.[85]

(4) *Para. (h)*: where the title is not absolute, all estates, rights, interests and powers excepted from the effect of registration, such as rights existing at the time of first registration where only a possessory title has been granted.

(5) *Para. (i)*: rights under local land charges unless and until registered or protected on the register.

(6) *Para. (k)*: legal[86] leases for not more than 21 years, granted at a rent without taking a fine. Nearly all leases, however, unless entered on the register, will take effect as overriding interests under paragraph (g) above, even if they are for more than 21 years.[87]

3. "Actual occupation." As mentioned above. paragraph (g) is both important and difficult. It reads: "The rights of every person in actual occupation of the land or in receipt of the rents and profits thereof, save where enquiry is made of such person and the rights are not disclosed." The two main elements of this definition must be examined in turn.

(a) *"Rights."* The word "rights" here includes all proprietary rights, whether legal or equitable. Thus it includes a contract for the purchase of land[88]; an option to purchase the freehold reversion on a lease[89]; an unpaid vendor's lien[90]; a purchaser's lien for his deposit[91]; and the rights of a beneficiary under a bare trust,[92] or under a trust for sale of a house held for occupation by the beneficiary[93] rather than for sale.[94] Even a right which is a minor interest and so requires to be protected by an entry on the register[95] may instead be an overriding interest if the requirement of actual occupation is satisfied[96]; and derivative interests, carved out of overriding interests (such as a lease granted by the occupying beneficiary under a bare trust), have the protection of the overriding interest.[97] On the other hand, rights

---

[83] L.R.A. 1925, s.75. See *Bridges* v. *Mees* [1957] Ch. 475.
[84] L.R.A. 1925, s.75.
[85] *Infra.*
[86] *City Permanent B.S.* v. *Miller* [1952] Ch. 840.
[87] See *Strand Securities Ltd.* v. *Caswell* [1965] Ch. 958.
[88] *Bridges* v. *Mees, supra.*
[89] *Webb* v. *Pollmount Ltd.* [1966] Ch. 584.
[90] *London and Cheshire Insurance Co. Ltd.* v. *Laplagrene Property Co. Ltd.* [1971] Ch. 499.
[91] *Lee-Parker* v. *Izzet* [1971] 1 W.L.R. 1688.
[92] *Hodgson* v. *Marks* [1971] Ch. 892; *Marks* v. *Attallah* (1966) 110 S.J. 709.
[93] *Williams & Glyn's Bank Ltd.* v. *Boland* [1981] A.C. 487.
[94] See *Barclay* v. *Barclay* [1970] 2 Q.B. 677.
[95] See *post*, pp. 105 *et seq.*
[96] *Williams & Glyn's Bank Ltd.* v. *Boland, supra.*
[97] *Marks* v. *Attallah, supra.*

which are merely personal and not proprietary cannot be overriding interests even if they relate to land,[98] nor can rights that have been overreached,[99] or "mere equities" unless they are ancillary to some interest in land, or dependent on it.[1] There are also certain rights, with little in common, which by statute cannot be overriding interests, and must be minor interests. These include the rights of beneficiaries under a settlement within the Settled Land Act 1925[2]; rights under a mortgage which is not a registered charge[3]; a notice by a tenant exercising his statutory right to acquire the freehold or an extended lease[4]; and a spouse's statutory rights to occupy the matrimonial home.[5]

(b) *Actual occupation or receipt of rents and profits.* Nothing can be an overriding interest within paragraph (g) unless not only is it within the category of rights considered above, but also the owner of the right is "in actual occupation of the land or in receipt of the rents and profits thereof." Whether a person is "in actual occupation" is a question of fact[6] and degree. There must be some degree of permanence and continuity, and not a mere fleeting presence,[7] though this will not be destroyed by temporary absences, *e.g.* in hospital or on holiday. Prolonged but intermittent car parking on an unidentified part of the land will not suffice,[8] nor will a purchaser of a house be in actual occupation of it merely because, by permission, he has taken preparatory steps before completion, such as carrying out building works[9] or laying carpets or moving furniture in.[10] Mere physical presence may not be enough. Where a sole proprietor's spouse lives in a house with him or her, the spouse will be in actual occupation if he or she is entitled to some proprietary interest in the house,[11] but otherwise will be there merely by virtue of the actual occupation of the sole proprietor.[12] A purchaser will thus be at risk if he fails to make inquiry of all who are normally present on the premises, apart from young children; and the presence of furniture or other articles that suggest that the vendor is not the sole occupier may be impor-

---

[98] See *National Provincial Bank Ltd.* v. *Ainsworth* [1965] A.C. 1175 at 1238, 1240.
[99] *City of London B.S.* v. *Flegg* [1988] A.C. 54.
[1] See *National Provincial Bank Ltd.* v. *Ainsworth, supra,* at pp. 1238, 1240; *Blacklocks* v. *J.B. Developments (Godalming) Ltd.* [1982] Ch. 183 (rectification); and see (1976) 40 Conv. N.S. 209 (A. R. Everton).
[2] L.R.A. 1925, s.86(2).
[3] *Ibid.* s.106(2); see *post*, p. 447.
[4] Leasehold Reform Act 1967, s.5(5); but there is no corresponding provision for such rights under the Housing Act 1985, Pt. V.
[5] Matrimonial Homes Act 1983, s.2(8)(b).
[6] *Williams & Glyn's Bank Ltd.* v. *Boland* [1981] A.C. 487 at 506, 508, 511 ("a plain factual situation").
[7] *Abbey National B.S.* v. *Cann* [1991] 1 A.C. 56 at 93.
[8] *Epps* v. *Esso Petroleum Co. Ltd.* [1973] 1 W.L.R. 1071.
[9] See *Lloyds Bank Plc.* v. *Rosset* [1991] 1 A.C. 107, where the point was left undecided: see at p. 134.
[10] *Abbey National B.S.* v. *Cann, supra,* at p. 94.
[11] *Hodgson* v. *Marks* [1971] Ch. 892; see at p. 932.
[12] *Bird* v. *Syme-Thompson* [1979] 1 W.L.R. 440 ("as a shadow of occupation by the owner": p. 444).

tant.[13] Yet despite careful inspections and enquiries, a purchaser may be bound by the rights of some undiscovered third party.[14] Discovering who is in receipt of the rents and profits has its own difficulties.

The date for determining whether a person is in actual occupation is the date when the purchase is completed and the relevant documents executed, even though the estate will not vest in the purchaser until the title is registered.[15] If the occupation later ceases before there has been any relevant dealing with the land, the validity of the overriding interest remains unimpaired.[16]

4. Entries on register. The registrar *may* make entries on the register stating that the land is free from or subject to certain overriding interests. His only *obligation* is to enter a notice of the existence of any easement, right, privilege or benefit created by an instrument (and not, for example, an easement created by prescription) which appears on the title at the time of first registration.[17]

C. Minor Interests

1. Definition. The Act elaborately defines minor interests,[18] but for present purposes it may suffice to say that minor interests are those interests in land[19] which require protection by some entry on the register. The category excludes overriding interests and registered interests. The former require no protection and the latter are necessarily on the register either as a registered title or as a registered charge. All other interests are comprised in the class of minor interests and so need to be protected by an entry on the register, otherwise they will not bind a purchaser for value under a registered disposition, *i.e.* of the legal estate.[20] There are two classes of minor interests:

  (i) those which will not bind a purchaser even when protected by an entry on the register, but which will be overreached, such as the equitable interests of beneficiaries under a settlement or trust for sale; and
 (ii) those which will bind a purchaser provided they are protected in the appropriate way, *e.g.* restrictive covenants.

2. Protection of minor interests. A minor interest may be protected by a

---

[13] See *Chhokar* v. *Chhokar* (1983) 5 F.L.R. 313 at 317; [1989] Conv. 342 (P. Sparkes).
[14] See *Kling* v. *Keston Properties Ltd.* (1985) 49 P. & C.R. 212 at 222; and see *Hodgson* v. *Marks*, *supra*, at p. 923.
[15] *Abbey National B.S.* v. *Cann* [1991] 1 A.C. 56; *Lloyds Bank Plc.* v. *Rosset* [1991] 1 A.C. 107. See *ante*, p. 96.
[16] *London and Cheshire Insurance Co. Ltd.* v. *Laplagrene Property Co. Ltd.* [1971] Ch. 499.
[17] L.R.A. 1925, s.70(2), (3). See *Re Dances Way, West Town, Hayling Island* [1962] Ch. 490.
[18] L.R.A. 1925, s.3(xv).
[19] *Elias* v. *Mitchell* [1972] Ch. 652.
[20] *Miles* v. *Bull* (*No.* 2) [1969] 3 All E.R. 1585; contrast *Barclays Bank Ltd.* v. *Taylor* [1974] Ch. 137, where the purchaser took an equitable interest only.

notice, caution against dealings, inhibition or restriction.[21] Notices and restrictions normally can be entered only when the land certificate is in the registry.[22]

(a) *Notices*

(1) EFFECT OF NOTICE. In general, the effect of the entry of a notice is to ensure that any subsequent dealing with the land will take effect subject to the right protected by the notice[23]; the mere entry of a notice will not, of course, give validity to an invalid claim. A notice also serves to fix the registered proprietor with notice of the claim as from the moment of entry.

(2) RIGHTS PROTECTED. A wide and varied range of rights can be protected by notice.[24] These include leases for more than 21 years, land charges within the Land Charges Act 1972 (including a spouse's right of occupation within Class F, the right of a tenant under a long leasehold to serve notice for the acquisition of the freehold or an extended lease,[25] and Inland Revenue charges for inheritance tax[26]), legal rentcharges, legal easements, creditors' rights under a bankruptcy petition (when the notice is called a "creditors' notice"[27]), charging orders,[28] access orders,[28a] and the right of a beneficiary under a settlement or trust for sale to ensure that there are at least two trustees (though the beneficial interests themselves are not included).

(3) MODE OF ENTRY. Normally before the notice can be entered, the land certificate must be produced to the registrar. Thus unless the land is already charged so that the certificate has been deposited at the Land Registry,[29] a notice cannot be entered without the co-operation of the registered proprietor. But this does not apply to Class F land charges (spouse's right of occupation), creditor's notices, Inland Revenue charges for inheritance tax, or leases at a rent without a fine.[30]

(b) *Cautions against dealings*

(1) EFFECT OF CAUTION. Like cautions against first registration, considered above,[31] the main function of a caution against dealings is to ensure that the cautioner receives notice of a proposed transaction. Such cautions are sometimes used when the proprietor will not co-operate in the entry of a notice. Once a caution against dealings has been lodged, no dealing will be

---

[21] L.R.A. 1925, ss.48–62.
[22] *Ibid.* s.64(1).
[23] *Ibid.* s.52. See *Re White Rose Cottage* [1964] Ch. 483.
[24] L.R.A. 1925, ss.48–51, as amended.
[25] Leasehold Reform Act 1967, s.5(5); see *post*, p. 549.
[26] See *ante*, p. 79.
[27] L.R.A. 1925, s.61.
[28] Charging Orders Act 1979, s.3(3); see *ante*, p. 83.
[28a] See *post*, p. 408.
[29] L.R.A. 1925, s.65.
[30] *Ibid.* s.64, as amended. See *Strand Securities Ltd.* v. *Caswell* [1965] Ch. 958; *ante*, pp. 79, 81, 83.
[31] *Ante*, p. 101.

registered until notice has been served on the cautioner, warning him that registration will be effected unless he objects within (usually) 14 days.[32] A caution may be lodged by any person who claims any interest in registered land, including a beneficiary under a trust for sale[33] (though not a person with a mere contractual right to a share in the proceeds of sale[34]), and a tenant in a block of flats for which a receiver has been appointed.[35] The application must be supported by a statutory declaration.[36]

(2) DISPUTES. If the cautioner does duly object, the registrar has a wide discretion, after hearing the parties (and subject to a reference or appeal to the court), to do what he considers to be just.[37] Thus he may order the caution to be vacated, or refuse to do so; or he may allow the dealing to be registered subject to a notice protecting the cautioner's interest, or subject to the cautioner commencing legal proceedings within a fixed time. A person who lodges a caution without reasonable cause is liable to pay such compensation as is just to anyone who thereby suffers damage.[38] There is also both a general and a statutory jurisdiction[39] for the court on motion to rectify the register by vacating the caution. This jurisdiction will be exercised fairly robustly,[40] even if difficult questions of construction or law are involved,[41] but in case of doubt the court may order the entry to be vacated unless the cautioner undertakes to pay damages to the proprietor if the entry is later found to be unjustified.[42]

(c) *Inhibitions*. An inhibition is an order of the court, or an entry made by the registrar, which inhibits the registration of any dealing with the land, either for a fixed time or until some event occurs, or generally until further order or entry.[43] Any person interested may apply for an inhibition,[44] including the proprietor, as where his land certificate has been stolen. The entry is made after making such enquiries, giving such notices and holding such hearings as are thought expedient; and a notice or restriction may be placed on the register instead of an inhibition.[45] Inhibitions are rare. They are intended for use when there is no other way of protecting a claim; but

---

[32] L.R.A. 1925, s.55(1).
[33] *Ibid.* s.54(1); *Elias* v. *Mitchell* [1972] Ch. 652.
[34] *Lynton International Ltd.* v. *Noble* (1991) 63 P. & C.R. 452.
[35] *Clayhope Properties Ltd.* v. *Evans* [1986] 1 W.L.R. 1223; see *ante*, p. 84.
[36] L.R.R. 1925, r. 215, Form 14.
[37] *Ibid.* r. 220.
[38] L.R.A. 1925, s.56(3).
[39] *Lester* v. *Burgess* (1973) 26 P. & C.R. 536 (where an order operates *in personam*, rather than on the register); L.R.A. 1925, s.82; *post*, p. 111.
[40] *Rawlplug Co. Ltd.* v. *Kamvale Properties Ltd.* (1968) 20 P. & C.R. 32; and see *Price Bros. (Somerford) Ltd.* v. *J. Kelly Homes (Stoke-on-Trent) Ltd.* [1975] 1 W.L.R. 1512.
[41] *Alpenstow Ltd.* v. *Regalian Properties Plc.* [1985] 1 W.L.R. 721.
[42] *Tiverton Estates Ltd.* v. *Wearwell* [1975] 1 W.L.R. 146; *Tucker* v. *Hutchinson* (1987) 54 P. & C.R. 106.
[43] L.R.A. 1925, s.57(1).
[44] *Ibid.*
[45] *Ibid.* s.57(2), (4).

when a bankruptcy order is made, a "bankruptcy inhibition" is automatically registered, preventing any disposition of the land until a trustee in bankruptcy has been registered.[46]

(d) *Restrictions*

(1) EFFECT OF RESTRICTIONS. A restriction is similar to an inhibition in that it prevents any dealing with the land unless some condition has been complied with.[47] It differs from an inhibition in that the entry is normally made on the application of the registered proprietor himself (or with his consent),[48] either voluntarily or under the duty of trustees to protect their beneficiaries. If the registered proprietor fails to apply for the entry of restrictions, any other person may apply with his consent[49]; but the land certificate must be produced unless it is already in the registry.[50] In practice, the registrar sees that suitable restrictions are framed and entered. A restriction is a friendly entry, whereas inhibitions and cautions are hostile.

(2) RIGHTS PROTECTED. Restrictions are appropriate for the protection of the rights of beneficiaries under a settlement or trust for sale. Thus for settled land, there will be a restriction which prevents the registration of any disposition by the tenant for life which is not authorised by the Settled Land Act 1925, or one in which capital money arises unless it is paid to the trustees, being at least two in number or a trust corporation, or into court.[51] Restrictions are used in many other cases, such as restricting any disposition of a charity's land without the consent of the Charity Commissioners.[52] In this case, and where there are two or more registered proprietors but the survivor, not being solely beneficially entitled, will be unable to give a valid receipt for the purchase money on a sale, the registrar is required to enter a suitable restriction.[53]

3. Official searches. A purchaser may discover any entries which protect minor interests by making an official search of the register; and he may obtain an official search certificate.[54] This certificate will protect the purchaser during the "priority period," *i.e.*, the period of 30 working days after the application for the search.[55] This protection operates by providing that if the purchaser's application for registration is delivered to the registry during the priority period, any entries made during that period will be postponed to him,[56] thereby protecting him against last minute entries. A second search

[46] *Ibid.* s.61(3), as amended by Insolvency Act 1985, Sched. 8, para. 5.
[47] L.R.A. 1925, s.58(1).
[48] *Ibid.*
[49] L.R.R. 1925, r. 236.
[50] L.R.A. 1925, s.64(1).
[51] *Ibid.* s.86(3); L.R.R. 1925, rr. 56–58. See *post*, p. 260.
[52] L.R.R. 1925, r. 60.
[53] L.R.A. 1925, s.58(3); L.R.R. 1925, rr. 60, 213. See *post*, p. 290.
[54] Land Registration (Official Searches) Rules 1988 (No. 629), r. 3.
[55] *Ibid.* rr. 2, 3. For corresponding provisions for unregistered land, see *ante*, p. 90.
[56] Land Registration (Official Searches) Rules 1988, *supra*, r. 5.

made during the priority period will not extend that period, but merely create its own priority period.[57]

4. Competing minor interests. Minor interests take effect only as equitable interests,[58] and so where there is conflict between two or more minor interests they will normally take effect in the order of creation according to the general law[59]; the order in which they were protected by entries on the register does not affect this. Thus if A contracts to purchase land, and before he has entered a caution B contracts to purchase the same land and enters a caution, A will have priority over B[60]; the priority of cautions confers no priority of interests.

Sect. 3. Dealings with Registered Land

In general, the registered proprietor can deal with or dispose of his land to the same extent as an owner with an unregistered title. The Act expressly authorises a wide range of dealings, of which the most important are outlined below.[61]

A. Transfer Inter Vivos

1. Transfer. The transfer of registered land *inter vivos* is effected by a simple form of transfer[61a] which must be lodged at the appropriate District Land Registry together with the land certificate. The registrar makes the necessary entries on the register and the land certificate, and returns the latter to the new proprietor if the whole of the land has been sold. If part only has been sold, the original certificate is amended and returned to the vendor, and a new certificate for the part sold is issued to the purchaser.

2. Title. No legal estate passes until the title is registered,[62] though registration is treated as occurring when the purchaser delivers the relevant documents to the appropriate District Land Registry.[63] It is registration that confers on the transferee the legal estate,[64] despite any defect in the transferor's title or any irregularity in the transfer.[65] With the land, the transferee takes all easements and other rights for the benefit of the land.[66] Correspondingly the transferee takes subject to all entries on the register and to

---

[57] Land Registry Notice (1981) 131 N.L.J. 881.
[58] L.R.A. 1925, s.2(1).
[59] See *post*, p. 480.
[60] *Barclays Bank Ltd.* v. *Taylor* [1974] Ch. 137 (equitable mortgagee and contract for sale); and see *Abigail* v. *Lapin* [1934] A.C. 491 at 502; *Strand Securities Ltd.* v. *Caswell* [1965] Ch. 958 at 991.
[61] See L.R.A. 1925, ss.18, 21, 25, 40, 66.
[61a] See *post*, p. 134.
[62] *Ibid.* ss.19–23; and see *Grace Rymer Investments Ltd.* v. *Waite* [1958] Ch. 831 (charge).
[63] L.R.R. 1925, r. 83(2).
[64] L.R.A. 1925, ss.20, 69; *Morelle Ltd.* v. *Wakeling* [1955] 2 Q.B. 379 at 411.
[65] *Morelle Ltd.* v. *Wakeling* [1955] 2 Q.B. 379.
[66] L.R.A. 1925, s.20.

overriding interests, but free from all other estates and interests,[67] even if he has express notice of them.[68] It is otherwise if the transferee contracts to take the land "subject to" some other interest, for the court will not permit the Act to be used as an instrument of fraud.[69] A transfer made without valuable consideration has the same effect as a transfer for value, except that the transferee takes subject to any minor interests that bind the transferor.[70]

B. Mortgages

Mortgages of registered land may be created by a registered charge, by an unregistered mortgage, or by deposit of the land certificate. These transactions are considered later.[71]

C. Transfer on Death

On the death of a sole registered proprietor, his personal representatives may either[72]—

(i) apply for registration themselves, on producing to the registrar the grant of probate or letters of administration; or
(ii) without being themselves registered, transfer the land direct either to a purchaser or to the person entitled under the will or intestacy; in this case, both the transfer or assent and the probate or letters of administration must be lodged with the application for registration.

The name of a joint proprietor will be removed from the register on proof of death.[73]

D. Bankruptcy

The steps taken on bankruptcy, so far as they affect registered land, are briefly as follows.

(1) A bankruptcy petition is presented; this is protected by the entry of a creditors' notice, which prevents the debtor from selling the land free from the claims of the creditors.

(2) A bankruptcy order is made; this is protected by a bankruptcy inhibition, which prevents the registered proprietor from dealing with the land at all.

(3) The registered proprietor is adjudicated bankrupt. His trustee in bankruptcy (or, until a trustee is appointed, the official receiver) may be

---

[67] *Ibid.* s.20(1); *Freer* v. *Unwins Ltd.* [1976] Ch. 288.
[68] *Hodges* v. *Jones* [1935] Ch. 657 at 671; *De Lusignan* v. *Johnson* [1974] E.G.D. 76. Contrast *Peffer* v. *Rigg* [1977] 1 W.L.R. 285, which is unlikely to be followed.
[69] *Lyus* v. *Prowsa Developments Ltd.* [1982] 1 W.L.R. 1044.
[70] L.R.A. 1925, s.20(4).
[71] See *post*, pp. 447 *et seq.*
[72] L.R.A. 1925, ss.37, 41; L.R.R. 1925, rr. 168, 170.
[73] L.R.R. 1925, r. 172.

registered as proprietor in place of the bankrupt on production of an office copy of the adjudication, a certificate of his appointment as trustee and a declaration that the land is part of the bankrupt's estate.[74]

E. Limitation and Prescription

A title to registered land may be acquired under the Limitation Act 1980 by adverse possession in the same way as in the case of unregistered land. However, in the case of registered land, no legal title is acquired by the adverse possessor until he has been registered as proprietor; until then, the registered proprietor holds the land on trust for him.[75] Registration of the squatter's title may be made with absolute, qualified, good leasehold or possessory title as the case may be, but interests not extinguished by the adverse possession are not affected.

"Easements, rights and privileges adversely affecting registered land" are capable of being acquired by prescription in the same way as if the land were not registered.[76]

Sect. 4. Rectification and Indemnity

Although in general it may be said that a registered proprietor has a title guaranteed by the State, the guarantee is not absolute but relative. There is power to rectify the register so as to correct mistakes, and a registered proprietor may lose some or all of his land by rectification. If he does, he will instead have a right to compensation by way of indemnity. His title is, in effect, insured by the State: he will have either the land or compensation. The statutory provisions, which are somewhat complex, will be considered under the two heads of rectification and indemnity.

A. Rectification

1. Jurisdiction. The statutory power to rectify the register is confined[77] to eight statutory grounds. Rectification may be ordered by the court, or, except on the first two grounds, by the registrar.[78]

2. Grounds. The eight grounds for rectification may be summarised as follows.[79] In some cases, two or more of the grounds are applicable.[80]

---

[74] L.R.A. 1925, ss. 42, 61, as amended by Insolvency Act 1985, Sched. 8, para. 5; L.R.R. 1925, rr. 174–177.
[75] L.R.A. 1925, s.75. For limitation, see *post*, pp. 493 *et seq.* Contrast unregistered land, where the adverse possessor acquires an entirely new estate: *post*, p. 502.
[76] L.R.R. 1925, r. 250. For prescription, see *post*, pp. 386 *et seq.*
[77] *Norwich & Peterborough B.S.* v. *Steed* [1992] *The Times*, Mar. 18; cp. the general power: *ante*, p. 107.
[78] L.R.A. 1925, s.82(1), setting out the grounds in the eight lettered paragraphs considered below.
[79] *Ibid.*
[80] See, *e.g. Chowood Ltd.* v. *Lyall* (*No.* 2) [1930] 2 Ch. 156 (grounds (a), (g) and (h), and perhaps (b)).

(a) *Entitlement*: where the court has decided that a person is entitled to an estate, right or interest in the land, and as a consequence of the decision considers that rectification is required, and so orders. Thus an order may be made to rectify the register by entering notices, cautions or restrictions to protect some right.[81]

(b) *Person aggrieved*: where any person is aggrieved by the making or omission of an entry, or any default or unnecessary delay in making an entry. Rectification to expunge a caution may be ordered summarily on motion where there is no serious question to be tried.[82]

(c) *Consent*: where all persons interested consent.

(d) *Fraud*: where the court or the registrar is satisfied that any entry has been obtained by fraud. The requisite fraud is some actual dishonesty of the person obtaining the entry, and not (unless he knew of it at the time) the fraud of a predecessor in title of his.[83] But it is no fraud for the proprietor merely to take advantage of some legal right, as where statute invalidates some adverse interest.[84]

(e) *Duplication*: where two or more persons are mistakenly registered as proprietors of the same registered estate or charge.

(f) *Mortgage*: where a mortgagee has been registered as proprietor of the land instead of as proprietor of a charge, and a right of redemption still exists.

(g) *Non-owner*: where a legal estate has been registered in the name of a person who, if the land had not been registered, would not have been the estate owner. This will apply to the registration of a proprietor whose title has been extinguished under the Limitation Act 1980.[85]

(h) *"Just"*: in any other case where it is deemed just to rectify the register by reason of any error or omission in it, or by reason of any entry made under a mistake. "Mistake" is given a very wide meaning, and it covers the case where a title is registered for more land than the applicant owns[86]; but where a charge is correctly entered, there can be no rectification merely because the charge was obtained by fraud.[87] On an application made on this ground, the registrar has jurisdiction to determine the extent of a right of way.[88]

In addition, there are minor powers to correct or amend the register, such as for clerical errors or fixing boundaries.[89]

---

[81] *Orakpo* v. *Manson Investments Ltd.* [1977] 1 W.L.R. 347 (in H.L. [1978] A.C. 95).

[82] *Price Bros. (Somerford) Ltd.* v. *J. Kelly Homes (Stoke-on-Trent) Ltd.* [1975] 1 W.L.R. 1512.

[83] See *Assets Co. Ltd.* v. *Mere Roihi* [1905] A.C. 176 at 210; and see *Re Leighton's Conveyance* [1936] 1 All E.R. 667 (in C.A. [1937] Ch. 149).

[84] *Re Monolithic Building Co.* [1915] 1 Ch. 643 at 669; *Midland Bank Trust Co. Ltd.* v. *Green* [1981] A.C. 513 at 531.

[85] *Spectrum Investment Co.* v. *Holmes* [1981] 1 W.L.R. 221.

[86] *Chowood Ltd.* v. *Lyall (No. 2)* [1930] 2 Ch. 156.

[87] *Norwich & Peterborough B.S.* v. *Steed* [1992] *The Times*, Mar. 18.

[88] *Re Dances Way, West Town, Hayling Island* [1962] Ch. 490.

[89] See, *e.g.* L.R.R. 1925, rr. 13, 14, 131, 276, 277.

3. Proprietor in possession. The width of the overlapping grounds for rectification considered above is subject to an important qualification. The register cannot be rectified on any of the grounds "so as to affect the title of the proprietor who is in possession."[90] This is the nearest approach to indefeasibility in the Act. "Possession" seems to mean "physical occupation." The term is defined in the Act as including (unless the context otherwise requires) the right to receive the rents and profits[91]; but if that were to be applied here, every registered proprietor would be in possession, and there would be no special category.[92] Monetary compensation will usually be adequate in place of rents and profits; but for a proprietor in physical occupation it is no substitute for the land itself.

This protection for the proprietor in possession is subject to four exceptions.[93]

(a) *Overriding interests*: giving effect to an overriding interest. Every registered title is subject to overriding interests, and so rectification to give effect to them will not affect the rights of the proprietor. An overriding interest existing at the time of first registration is not affected if the proprietor later goes out of possession.[94]

(b) *Order of court*: giving effect to an order of the court.

(c) *Proprietor's fraud or lack of care*: the proprietor "has caused or substantially contributed to the error or omission by fraud or lack of proper care." This amended wording now excludes innocent mistakes such as misdescribing the land when applying for first registration[95]; but it includes intentionally misleading the registrar.[96]

(d) *Unjust not to rectify*: where "for any other reason, in any particular case, it is considered that it would be unjust not to rectify the register" against the proprietor. The question is not whether to order rectification would be "just," but whether refusing to order it would be "unjust": a positive case of injustice must be shown. This wide and general ground requires a broad survey of all the relevant facts. Thus rectification may be refused if the true owner of the land has no real use for it, so that an indemnity would be adequate to satisfy him, and the registered proprietor had spent money on the land.[97]

4. Discretion. Where jurisdiction to rectify the register is established, it is

---

[90] L.R.A. 1925, s.82(3), as amended by Administration of Justice Act 1977, s.24.
[91] L.R.A. 1925, s.3(xviii); and see *Freer* v. *Unwins Ltd.* [1976] Ch. 288 at 294, a dictum that is notably *obiter*.
[92] See (1968) 84 L.Q.R. 528 at 539, 540 (S. Cretney and G. Dworkin); Ruoff & Roper 40–10.
[93] L.R.A. 1925, s.82(3), as amended by Administration of Justice Act 1977, s.24.
[94] *London and Cheshire Insurance Co. Ltd.* v. *Laplagrene Property Co. Ltd.* [1971] Ch. 499.
[95] See, *e.g. Claridge* v. *Tingey* [1967] 1 W.L.R. 134.
[96] See *Re Leighton's Conveyance* [1936] 1 All E.R. 667 (in C.A. [1937] Ch. 149).
[97] *Re 139 High Street, Deptford* [1951] Ch. 884; see at p. 892; *Epps* v. *Esso Petroleum Co. Ltd.* [1973] 1 W.L.R. 1071; see at pp. 1082, 1083.

always a matter of discretion whether or not to exercise it.[98] Thus rectification may be refused where the applicant stood silently by while the proprietor was improving the land,[99] or where the consequences of rectification (including the level of any indemnity) would be substantially more serious to the proprietor than those of the refusal of rectification would be to the applicant.[1] On rectification, a new edition of the register is issued, and the rectification takes effect then, without relating back to any earlier date.[2]

B. Indemnity

The right to indemnity falls under three heads: the grounds, exceptions, and determination.

1. Grounds. The grounds on which a person may claim indemnity may be put under four heads.

(a) *Rectification*: loss by reason of any rectification of the register.[3] There is no indemnity for rectification which does not cause any loss but merely gives effect to a loss previously suffered, as where it gives effect to an overriding interest[4] such as a title acquired by a squatter under the Limitation Act 1980,[5] or the rights of a person in actual occupation of the land when the proprietor acquired his registered title.[6] However, where the title of a proprietor claiming in good faith under a forged disposition is rectified, he is deemed to have suffered loss by reason of the rectification and to be entitled to indemnity.[7]

(b) *Non-rectification*: loss by reason of an error or omission in the register which is not rectified. Thus if F by forgery obtains registration as proprietor of A's land, and then sells it to B, A will be entitled to indemnity if he cannot obtain rectification against B because B is a registered proprietor in possession.[8]

(c) *Conversion of title*: loss suffered by anyone except the registered proprietor by reason of any entry made on the conversion of titles.[9]

(d) *Errors*: loss by reason of various errors or omissions. These include errors in official searches or inaccuracies in various documents, and also the loss or destruction of documents lodged at the registry.[10]

[98] *Argyle B.S.* v. *Hammond* (1984) 49 P. & C.R. 148.
[99] *Claridge* v. *Tingey, supra.*
[1] *Epps* v. *Esso Petroleum Co. Ltd., supra.*
[2] *Freer* v. *Unwins Ltd.* [1976] Ch. 288.
[3] L.R.A. 1925, s.83(1).
[4] For these, see *ante*, pp. 102 *et seq.*
[5] *Re Chowood's Registered Land* [1933] Ch. 574.
[6] *Re Boyle's Claim* [1961] 1 W.L.R. 339 (boundary dispute).
[7] L.R.A. 1925, s.83(4).
[8] See *ante*, p. 113.
[9] L.R.A. 1925, s.77(6).
[10] *Ibid.* ss.83(3), 110(4), 113; and see *post*, p. 491 (tacking).

2. Exceptions. The main provision is that no indemnity is payable where the applicant or a predecessor in title of his (except under a disposition for value protected on the register) has "caused or substantially contributed to the loss by fraud or lack of proper care."[11] There are also exceptions for certain minerals and costs.[12]

3. Determination. Liability and amount are both determined by proceedings in court against the registrar; and payment is made out of moneys provided by Parliament.[13] The indemnity is for the amount of the loss, together with a reasonable amount for costs and expenses properly incurred by the claimant, though not the costs of any proceedings brought by the claimant against third parties (*e.g.* those who caused the loss) without the registrar's consent.[14] But where an estate or interest in land, or a charge on it, has been lost, the amount of the indemnity is restricted to its value. For rectification, it is the value immediately before rectification, but for non-rectification it is the value when the error or omission causing the loss was made[15]; and this may be much less than its present value.[16] Claims for indemnity are barred after six years, though time begins to run only when the claimant knew of the existence of the claim, or but for his own default might have known of it.[17] But when the claim arises from registration with an absolute or good leasehold title, the six years run from the date of registration, though there are some exceptions for infants, remaindermen, restrictive covenants and mortgages.[18]

Where an indemnity is paid, the registrar may recover the amount of it from any person who caused or substantially contributed to the loss by his fraud.[19]

---

[11] *Ibid.* s.83(5)(a), as substituted by Land Registration and Land Charges Act 1971 ("Act of 1971"), s.3.

[12] L.R.A. 1925, s.83(5)(b), (c); Act of 1971, s.2; for costs, see below.

[13] Act of 1971, ss.1, 2. In 1990–91, there were 293 payments amounting in all to £830,061, with a further £145,347 in costs: see Ruoff & Roper 40–32.

[14] L.R.A. 1925, s.85(3)(c), (8); Act of 1971, s.2(2), (4).

[15] L.R.A. 1925, s.83(6).

[16] See *Epps* v. *Esso Petroleum Co. Ltd.* [1973] 1 W.L.R. 1071 at 1081 (1959 values for non-rectification in 1973).

[17] L.R.A. 1925, s.83(11); Limitation Act 1980, Sched. 3, para. 1.

[18] *Ibid.*; see *Epps* v. *Esso Petroleum Co. Ltd.*, *supra*.

[19] L.R.A. 1925, s.83(9).

CHAPTER 5

DISPOSITIONS OF LAND

LAND may be disposed of in a variety of ways. The most common dispositions *inter vivos* are by sale, though gifts and settlements are sometimes made. On a sale, the formal conveyance or transfer of the land is almost always preceded by a contract for sale. Then on death, land may pass under the owner's will or, if none, under the rules for intestacy; and in each case, the executors or administrators of the estate of the deceased (his "personal representatives") have an important part to play. Finally, there are various disabilities which restrict certain persons or bodies in owning or disposing of land. In this chapter, these subjects will be considered under six headings.

1. Contracts.
2. Conveyancing.
3. Wills.
4. Intestacy.
5. Personal representatives.
6. Disabilities.

Part 1

CONTRACTS

The law governing contracts for the sale or disposition of any interest in land has recently been much changed. Under the Law of Property (Miscellaneous Provisions) Act 1989[1] contracts made before September 27, 1989, continue to be governed by the old law, but all other contracts are subject to the new law.[2] Although the former law is now of rapidly diminishing importance, it must be briefly summarised before turning to the new law.

Sect. 1. Contracts Made Before September 27, 1989

Before September 27, 1989, a contract for the sale or disposition of land or any interest in land could be validly made in any way. Although such contracts were usually made in writing, an oral contract was perfectly valid. But unless an oral contract was sufficiently evidenced in writing, or supported by a sufficient act of part performance, it could not be enforced by action.[3] Although deprived of its most important remedy, such a contract

---

[1] Cited as L.P.(M.P.)A. 1989. It is discussed at [1989] Conv. 431 (P. H. Pettit).
[2] L.P.(M.P.)A. 1989, ss.2(7), 5(3), (4).
[3] L.P.A. 1925, s.40.

remained valid, and it could be enforced by any means except an action, as where a vendor forfeited, (*i.e.* kept) the deposit made by a purchaser who later defaulted.[4] The law as to writing and part performance must be briefly summarised; it gave rise to much litigation.[5]

1. Evidenced in writing. The law required the agreement, "or some memorandum or note thereof," to be in writing, and to be signed by or on behalf of "the party to be charged,"[6] namely, the person against whom the action was to be brought. Any form of evidence of the contract sufficed if it was in writing; and it might come into existence long after the contract was made, and be made up of two or more connected documents. But the writing was required to state all the terms of the contract that the parties had agreed. Where the evidence in writing was signed by one party (V) but not by the other (P), V could not sue P, but P could sue V; for V was the party to be charged.

2. Part performance. If a party to an oral contract for the sale or disposition of land or any interest in land has done a sufficient act of part performance of it, equity would enforce it for him against the other party. The principle behind the doctrine[7] was that if the plaintiff had partly performed the contract, it would be fraudulent for the defendant to plead the lack of evidence as a defence. The acts done by the plaintiff raised an equity in his favour, and in satisfying that equity the court had to choose "between undoing what has been done (which is not always possible, or, if possible, just) and completing what has been left undone."[8] Part performance contrasted with evidence in writing in that the act of part performance had to have been done by the plaintiff, whereas the evidence in writing had to be signed by the defendant. What was required for part performance was some act which sufficiently indicated that there was some contract of the kind alleged. Thus if V agreed to sell land to P, and then allowed P to take possession of the land, the change of possession was a sufficient act of part performance both by V and by P.

Sect. 2. Contracts Made After September 26, 1989

For any contract made after September 26, 1989, the Act of 1989 repealed the law both as to evidence in writing and part performance.[9] Instead, it provided that "a contract for the sale or other disposition of an interest in land can only be made in writing and only by incorporating all the terms which the parties have expressly agreed in one document or, where contracts

---

[4] *Monnickendam* v. *Leanse* (1923) 39 T.L.R. 445.
[5] For details, see M. & W. 571–598.
[6] L.P.A. 1925, s.40(1), replacing part of Statute of Frauds 1677, s.4; and see *post*, p. 271.
[7] It had been recognised by L.P.A. 1925, s.40(2).
[8] *Maddison* v. *Alderson* (1883) 8 App.Cas. 467 at 476, *per* Earl of Selborne L.C.
[9] L.P.(M.P.)A. 1989, ss.2(1), (7), (8), 5(3), (4), Sched. 2.

are exchanged, in each."[10] A contract which does not comply with this provision is wholly void, and not merely unenforceable by action. The terms of this provision will be considered in turn, together with the requirement as to signature.

1. Sale or other disposition

(a) *Transactions included.* "The sale or other disposition" of an interest in land includes every type of disposition, whether sale, lease, mortgage or anything else[11]; and it applies both to disposing of existing interests and to the creation of new interests. It includes the sale of fixtures separately from the land to a stranger,[12] but not to the sale of fixtures to the landlord by a tenant who is entitled to remove them,[13] for in substance this is merely a waiver by the tenant of his right of removal, and so is no sale of either land or goods.[14]

(b) *Exceptions.* There are three classes of contract to which these statutory provisions do not apply.[15]

(i) SHORT LEASES: a lease for not more than three years at the best rent reasonably obtainable without taking a fine.[16]

(ii) PUBLIC AUCTIONS: a contract made in the course of a public auction.

(iii) FINANCIAL SERVICES: a contract regulated under the Financial Services Act 1986; this Act controls the conduct of investment business.

2. Interest in land. "Interest in land" is widely defined. It means "any estate, interest or charge in or over land or in or over the proceeds of sale of land."[16a] Interests under a trust for sale of land are thus plainly included, but the Act does not apply to annual crops, such as corn or potatoes, which require the periodical application of labour for their production; these are known as *fructus industriales*.[17] *Fructus naturales*, on the other hand, are sometimes included. This term applies to the natural products of the soil, such as grass and timber, and also the products of those plants and trees which, although needing attention at first, do not require it each year to produce a crop,[18] such as fruit from fruit trees.[19] *Fructus naturales* are treated as land within the statute unless either they are to be severed by the vendor

---

[10] L.P.(M.P.)A. 1989, s.2(1).
[11] *Ibid.* s.2(6); L.P.A. 1925, s.205(1)(ii).
[12] See *Underwood Ltd.* v. *Burgh Castle Brick and Cement Syndicate* [1922] 1 K.B. 123.
[13] See *ante*, p. 17.
[14] *Lee* v. *Gaskell* (1876) 1 Q.B.D. 700.
[15] L.P.(M.P.)A. 1989, s.2(6).
[16] See *post*, p. 310.
[16a] L.P.(M.P.)A. 1989, s.2(6).
[17] See *Duppa* v. *Mayo* (1669) 1 Wms. Saund. 275.
[18] *Marshall* v. *Green* (1875) 1 C.P.D. 35 at 40.
[19] *Rodwell* v. *Phillips* (1842) 9 M. & W. 501.

and not the purchaser,[20] or else the contract binds the purchaser to sever them as soon as possible.[21]

3. Made in writing. The Act requires the contract to be "made" in writing and not merely "evidenced" in writing.[22] An oral agreement is thus void, and no contract. Under an option to buy land, it could be said that there is no contract of purchase until the purchaser has exercised his option; but for the purposes of the Act the option is treated as being a conditional contract to sell the land, so that if the option satisfies the Act it is immaterial that the notice exercising it does not.[23] One consequence of this is that an option granted in 1988 and exercised in 1992 will be subject to the old law and not the new, even though not until 1992 did any obligation to buy and sell arise.

4. All the terms

(a) *The terms.* The writing must incorporate "all the terms which the parties have expressly agreed."[24] This does not extend to terms implied by law, such as the term that on a sale with vacant possession, vacant possession must be given at completion[25]; and perhaps the omission of an express term to this effect would be no breach of the statute.[26] Terms may be incorporated in a document either by being set out in it or by reference to some other document.[27] Formerly, although a memorandum in writing which did not accord with the true contract was bad if a term solely for the benefit of one party, or to his detriment, was omitted, he could cure the defect by offering to waive the term, or to perform it.[28] But no such cure seems possible now that the contract must include all the express terms.

(b) *Certainty.* The terms of the contract are sufficiently stated if they fall within the principle *id certum est quod certum reddi potest* (that is certain which can be made certain). Thus while it is essential that the document should disclose each party to the contract, or his agent,[29] it suffices if, without being named, each party is so described that his identity cannot be fairly disputed,[30] *e.g.* if the document refers to the "proprietor"[31] of the property, or states that "the vendor will convey as legal personal representative."[32] But references to the "vendor"[33] or "landlord"[34] or "my clients"[35] are

---

[20] *Smith* v. *Surman* (1829) 9 B. & C. 561.
[21] *Marshall* v. *Green* (1875) 1 C.P.D. 35 (and see the summary of decisions at p. 42).
[22] L.P.(M.P.)A. 1989, s.2(1).
[23] *Spiro* v. *Glencrown Properties Ltd.* [1991] Ch. 537.
[24] L.P.(M.P.)A. 1989, s.2(1).
[25] See *Topfell Ltd.* v. *Galley Properties Ltd.* [1979] 1 W.L.R. 446.
[26] See *Farrell* v. *Green* (1974) 232 E.G. 587.
[27] L.P.(M.P.)A. 1989, s.2(2).
[28] See M. & W. 581, 582.
[29] *Davies* v. *Sweet* [1962] 2 Q.B. 300.
[30] *Carr* v. *Lynch* [1900] 1 Ch. 613 at 615.
[31] *Rossiter* v. *Miller* (1878) 3 App.Cas. 1124.
[32] *Fay* v. *Miller, Wilkins & Co.* [1941] Ch. 360; but see (1941) 57 L.Q.R. 452.
[33] *Potter* v. *Duffield* (1874) L.R. 18 Eq. 4.
[34] *Coombes* v. *Wilkes* [1891] 3 Ch. 77.
[35] *Lovesy* v. *Palmer* [1916] 2 Ch. 233.

not sufficient by themselves, for these descriptions may fit many persons; the proprietor of land is not the only person who can be the vendor, for many other persons such as mortgagees or even complete strangers may enter into a contract to sell the land.[36] Similarly, when the land to be sold is sufficiently described, parol evidence is admissible to identify it and its boundaries.[37]

(c) *Rectification.* Where a document does not satisfy the requirements of the Act of 1989, it can sometimes be rectified by the court so as to cure the defect. Thus a term omitted by mistake can be inserted or mistaken language altered; but strong and convincing proof of the mistake must be adduced.[38] Rectification normally operates retrospectively, so that the document takes effect as if it had originally been in its correct form; but where a contract satisfies the Act of 1989 only by reason of the rectification of one or more documents, the contract comes into being at the time specified in the order of the court.[39]

5. "One document." Apart from an exchange of contracts, the terms expressly agreed must be incorporated in one document. But terms may be incorporated in a document either by being set out in it or by reference to some other document,[40] so that the terms may be found in two or more documents provided one of them sufficiently refers to the others. For exchanges of contracts, the usual practice is to prepare identical documents, and then, when the contract is ready to be made, to exchange the document signed by the vendor for the document signed by the purchaser.[41] But the statute does not invalidate an independent collateral warranty (*e.g.* as to title) given to induce the signing of the contract,[42] nor to an agreement which is supplemental to a contract (*e.g.*, to grant a lease) which has been duly carried out, and so is no longer executory.[43]

6. Signed. "The document incorporating the terms or, where contracts are exchanged, one of the documents incorporating them (but not necessarily the same one) must be signed by or on behalf of each party to the contract."[44]

(a) *Signature.* The words in brackets in this provision permit the continuance of the practice of exchanging contracts, with each part signed by only one party. Under the new law, there will normally be an ordinary signature at the end of the document; but previously, when only a note or memorandum was required, the courts gave an extended meaning to the

[36] *Donnison* v. *People's Cafe Co.* (1881) 45 L.T. 187.
[37] *Plant* v. *Bourne* [1897] 2 Ch. 281; *Harewood* v. *Retese* [1990] 1 W.L.R. 333.
[38] See generally Snell 626–636.
[39] L.P.(M.P.)A. 1989, s.2(4).
[40] *Ibid.* s.2(2).
[41] See *Eccles* v. *Bryant* [1948] Ch. 93.
[42] *Record* v. *Bell* [1991] 1 W.L.R. 853.
[43] *Tootal Clothing Ltd.* v. *Guinea Properties Management Ltd.* [1992] *The Times*, June 8.
[44] L.P.(M.P.)A. 1989, s.2(3).

word "signed," and this may still be of some relevance. Provided the name of the signatory appeared in some part of the document in some form, whether in writing, typewriting, print or otherwise, there was a sufficient signature if that person had shown in some way that he recognised the document as an expression of the contract.[45] Thus memoranda in the handwriting of A which began "I, A, agree"[46] or "A agrees"[47] or "sold A"[48] have, without any further signature, been held to have been sufficiently signed by A on the ground that he had shown by his writing that he recognised the existence of the contract mentioned in the document. But the mere occurrence of a person's name in a document written by him did not necessarily amount to a signature; thus if A wrote out a document beginning "Article of agreement made between A and B" and ending "As witness our hands," without any signatures, the statute was not satisfied[49]; for the names must be inserted in such a way as to "have the effect of authenticating the instrument,"[50] or "to govern what follows."[51]

(b) *Agents.* Where a party does not himself sign the contract, signature "on behalf of" him suffices. No provision is made about the mode in which an agent must receive his authority, and so it need not be given in writing.[52] But the mere existence of an agency is not enough; it must be shown that the agent had authority to sign the same kind of contract as that which in fact he signed.[53] The same person may be given authority to sign on behalf of both parties, as where a solicitor acts for both of them.[54] An auctioneer was treated as having authority to sign a note or memorandum on behalf of each party at an auction,[55] but now that there is no longer any requirement of writing for such contracts,[56] this has little importance today.

7. Abolition of part performance. Although there has been no express abolition of the doctrine of part performance, which had developed uncertainties,[57] it is plain that it no longer exists. As an oral agreement for the sale or other disposition of an interest in land cannot be a contract, there is no contract that could be partly performed. This may well cause hardship.[58] If V orally agrees to grant or sell some interest in land to P, V can can refuse to perform the agreement, however many and costly the acts that P has done in part performance of the agreement. This may be mitigated in some degree

---

[45] See *Halley* v. *O'Brien* [1920] 1 I.R. 330 at 339; and see *Leeman* v. *Stocks* [1951] Ch. 941.
[46] *Knight* v. *Crockford* (1794) 1 Esp. 190.
[47] *Bleakley* v. *Smith* (1840) 11 Sim. 150.
[48] *Johnson* v. *Dodgson* (1837) 2 M. & W. 653.
[49] *Hubert* v. *Treherne* (1842) 3 Man. & G. 743.
[50] *Ogilvie* v. *Foljambe* (1817) 3 Mer. 53 at 62, *per* Grant M.R.
[51] *Lobb* v. *Stanley* (1844) 5 Q.B. 574 at 582, *per* Coleridge J.
[52] *Heard* v. *Pilley* (1869) 4 Ch.App. 584; contrast L.P.A. 1925, s.53(1)(c) (*post*, p. 272).
[53] See *Thirkell* v. *Cambi* [1919] 2 K.B. 590 at 598.
[54] *Gavaghan* v. *Edwards* [1961] 2 Q.B. 220.
[55] See M. & W. 587.
[56] *Ante*, p. 118.
[57] See *Steadman* v. *Steadman* [1976] A.C. 536; Law Com. No. 164, para. 1.9.
[58] See also *post*, p. 446.

by the doctrine of proprietary estoppel,[59] to which the doctrine of part performance was related[60]; but this depends on the court's discretion as to the type of interest to be given to P, and that is more uncertain in its operation than the simple enforcement of the agreement between the parties.[61] Yet perhaps the court will regard the oral agreement, though void as a contract, as providing evidence of the appropriate way of satisfying P's equity.

Sect. 3. Effect of Contract

Once a contract for the sale of land has been made, the parties have many rights and become subject to many obligations. The detailed law on the subject is generally regarded as falling within the province of conveyancing rather than real property, but an outline of one particular aspect must be given here.[62]

1. The purchaser as owner in equity. As soon as a specifically enforceable contract for the sale of land has been made, the purchaser becomes "the real and beneficial owner of it."[63] Nearly all contracts for the sale of land are specifically enforceable, and Equity treats that as done which ought to be done. The purchaser is under many obligations, not least that of paying the purchase money at completion, and he normally has no right to possession until then; but in equity (though not in law) the land is his.

2. The vendor as trustee. On the same grounds, the vendor becomes a trustee of the land for the purchaser, and so is under a duty to take reasonable care of it.[64] Thus he is liable to the purchaser if he damages the land himself,[65] or if he fails to take reasonable care to prevent it being damaged by third parties[66] or by natural events.[67] His trusteeship is qualified by the various rights that he has, such as the right to retain possession until completion; but his powers to act as the owner in matters such as changing tenancies is suspended.[68]

3. Passing of risk. For similar reasons, the risks of the property pass to the purchaser as soon as the contract is made, unless it otherwise provides. Thus

---

[59] See *ante*, p. 67; *post*, p. 434; Law Com. No. 164, paras. 5.4, 5.
[60] See (1985) 36 N.I.L.Q. 358 at 359–364 (M. P. Thompson).
[61] See *ante*, p. 117.
[62] See the much fuller outline in M. & W. 601–627.
[63] *Shaw* v. *Foster* (1872) L.R. 5 H.L. 321 at 338, *per* Lord Cairns.
[64] *Wilson* v. *Clapham* (1819) 1 Jac. & W. 36 at 38.
[65] *Cumberland Consolidated Holdings Ltd.* v. *Ireland* [1946] K.B. 264 (abandonment of much rubbish on land).
[66] *Clarke* v. *Ramuz* [1891] 2 Q.B. 456 (trespasser removes soil); *Davron Estates Ltd.* v. *Turnshire Ltd.* (1982) 133 N.L.J. 937 (squatters).
[67] *Lucie-Smith* v. *Gorman* [1981] C.L.Y. 2866 (burst pipe from failure to turn off water in winter).
[68] *Raffety* v. *Scholfield* [1897] 1 Ch. 937 at 945.

if a house is destroyed by fire between contract and completion, the purchaser must still pay the vendor the full price, for the risk was his.[69] The purchaser should therefore either insure the house himself or arrange to take over the benefit of the vendor's policy. He can do this if the insurers consent and he pays the vendor a proportionate part of the premium, whereupon the vendor becomes liable to pay the insurance moneys to the purchaser on completion.[70] Otherwise the loss will fall on the purchaser, for he must pay the purchase money on completion, and as the vendor has suffered no loss, his insurers need not pay him.[71] However, these unsatisfactory provisions, which often led to a duplication of insurance,[72] usually do not apply today, for the Standard Conditions of Sale[73] that are generally used provide otherwise. Under these, the vendor retains the risk until completion; he is under no obligation to the purchaser to insure; the provision for taking over the benefit of the vendor's policy is excluded; and the purchaser has a right to rescind the contract if the physical state of the property has made it unusable for its purpose at the date of the contract as a result of damage against which the vendor could not reasonably have insured or which he cannot legally make good.[74]

Sect. 4. Contracts in Practice

A. *Cases where it is Usual to have a Contract*

Whenever a transaction involves a payment of a capital sum, it is usual for it to be governed by a contract. Thus where land is being sold in fee simple, or a lease at a ground rent (a rent representing the value of the land without the buildings on it) is being assigned in consideration of a capital payment, a formal contract is normally made. If, on the other hand, no capital payment is involved, there is usually no contract, *e.g.* on the grant or assignment of a lease at a rack rent (a rent representing the full value of the land and buildings). And a mortgage, although involving a capital payment, is rarely preceded by a contract.

B. *Types of Contract*

There are three main types of contract.

1. Open contracts. In these contracts, only the essential terms (the parties, the property to be sold and the price) have been expressly agreed. The remaining terms, such as the time for completion, are implied by the general law.

---

[69] *Lysaght* v. *Edwards* (1876) 2 Ch.D. 499 at 507; *Rayner* v. *Preston* (1881) 18 Ch.D. 1. See criticisms at [1984] Conv. 43 (M. P. Thompson).
[70] L.P.A. 1925, s.47.
[71] See *Castellain* v. *Preston* (1883) 11 Q.B.D. 380.
[72] See Law Com. W.P. No. 109, paras. 2.1–2.44.
[73] For these, see *post*, p. 124.
[74] See para. 5 of the Conditions.

2. Contracts by correspondence. In the case of contracts by correspondence for the sale of land, the Law of Property Act 1925[75] provides that the Statutory Form of Conditions of Sale 1925, made by the Lord Chancellor, are to govern the contract, subject to any modification or contrary intention expressed in the correspondence.[76] Such contracts were comparatively infrequent, and now that they must be in writing signed by both parties[77] they are likely to become even more rare; but they are not impossible, as where a copy of a letter signed by one party is signed by the other.

3. Formal contracts. It is always open to the parties to make a contract in such terms as they see fit, subject to the rule that certain provisions contrary to the policy of the law are void, such as any provision that the conveyance should be prepared by a solicitor appointed by the vendor.[78] In practice, various standard forms of conditions have been settled, the most recent being the new Standard Conditions of Sale,[79] introduced in 1990. Standard forms of conditions, with such emendations as are desirable to fit the particular case, are usually employed, since they avoid the labour of preparing a set of conditions for each case. It is common for standard forms of conditions to be supplemented by special conditions on a variety of matters, as by precluding the purchaser from objecting to some defect in the vendor's title.[80]

This division of the types of contract is not rigid; thus the parties may agree a few special conditions and leave the rest to the ordinary rules of law, thereby creating a contract which is in part formal and as to the remainder an open contract.

C. Terms of Contract

The following are examples of the matters usually dealt with in a formal contract for the sale of land.

1. Provision for the payment of a deposit (usually 10 per cent. of the purchase-money) and for the payment of interest on the purchase-money if completion is delayed.
2. Where the title is unregistered, the length and nature of the title to be deduced by the vendor, and any special conditions, *e.g.* as to making no objections to some specified defect in title or flaw in the evidence of title. Where the title is registered, the title number of the property, the

---

[75] s.46.
[76] See (1974) 90 L.Q.R. 55 (A. M. Prichard).
[77] *Ante*, p. 117.
[78] L.P.A. 1925, s.48(1).
[79] These conditions are an amended conflation of The Law Society's Conditions of Sale (20th ed.) and the National Conditions of Sale (20th ed.). They appear in the *Encyclopaedia of Forms and Precedents* (5th ed.), Service Volume C, (Vol. 35), as Form 21.1, in para. 442.2, and they are discussed in [1990] Conv. 179 (J. E. Adams). There is also a National Protocol which sets out the steps to be taken by each party: see *loc. cit.* Form 13.2 in para. 122.3.
[80] As should have been done in *Faruqi* v. *English Real Estates Ltd.* [1979] 1 W.L.R. 963.

class of title and copies of documents referred to on the register, *e.g.* as imposing restrictive covenants.[81]

3. The time within which the matters affecting the title must be dealt with.
4. The date and place for completion of the sale.
5. Power for the vendor to rescind the contract or re-sell the property in certain circumstances, such as the purchaser's insistence on objections to the title, or his failure to perform the contract.
6. Power for either party to serve a notice to complete, making time of the essence if the contract is not completed on the date specified in the contract.

D. Preliminaries to Contract

Whenever time permits, the proposed purchaser will usually send the proposed vendor "Inquiries before Contract," in order to obtain information on the state of the property. At the same time there will often be negotiations about the precise terms of the proposed contract. In addition, the purchaser will make the necessary searches before signing the contract.[82] The vendor may also be well advised to do the same in case some land charge has been registered against him without his knowledge[83]; for unless he contracts to sell expressly subject to the land charge, he will have to discharge it before completion.

Part 2

CONVEYANCING

Conveyancing may be regarded as the application of the law of real property in practice. It is an immense subject, and only a very brief outline of a few of the chief features can be given here.[84] Although conveyancing does not form part of the subject of real property, every student should have some idea of the relationship between the two subjects. The work of a conveyancer is twofold. First, he investigates titles by examining documents and making inquiries and searches. Secondly, he drafts conveyances and other legal documents. The drafting of legal documents demands great skill, though books of forms or "precedents" are widely used. The steps taken after a contract has been made will depend on whether the title is registered or unregistered.

[81] See *Faruqi* v. *English Real Estates Ltd.*, *supra.*
[82] See *ante*, pp. 89, 108.
[83] See *Newbery* v. *Turngiant Ltd.* (1991) 63 P. & C.R. 458.
[84] See generally M. & W. 153–169; M. P. Thompson, *Investigation and Proof of Title*, pp. 56–75.

Sect. 1. Unregistered Title

A. From Contract to Completion

The usual sequence of events on the sale of a freehold by V to P are as follows; most of the steps are normally taken by the solicitors for the parties rather than by the parties in person.

1. Delivery of abstract or epitome of title. Within the time mentioned in the contract, V must deliver to P the abstract of title. This document provides a consecutive story of the derivation of the title. It consists in part of a condensed version of the various documents, and in part of a recital of the relevant events, such as the births, deaths and marriages which affect the title. The abstract starts with a good root of title[85] and traces the devolution of the property down to V. Thus a very simple abstract might consist of—

   (i) a summary of a conveyance by A to B;
   (ii) a recital of B's death;
   (iii) a recital of probate of B's will being granted to X and Y;
   (vi) a summary of the assent by X and Y in favour of V.

In the age of the photocopier it is now customary, as an alternative, to provide an epitome of the title, setting forth the essential facts in the derivation of title, and supporting this by photocopies of the documents mentioned in the epitome.

2. Consideration of abstract. P then pursues the abstract or epitome of title, considers the validity of the title shown, and checks the abstract against V's title deeds.

3. Requisitions on title. P's examination of the abstract or epitome usually discloses a number of points upon which he requires further information. This further explanation is obtained by means of "requisitions on title," a series of written questions which P delivers to V. Requisitions usually consist of a mixture of genuine objections or requests for information (*e.g.* as to the date of some death, or as to the existence of some incumbrance which the abstract does not disclose), and statements of the obvious, *e.g.* that V, having agreed to sell free from incumbrances, must discharge a mortgage or obtain the concurrence of the mortgagee to the sale of the property free from the mortgage. Requisitions also usually seek confirmation of the answers to the inquiries on draft contract sent before conclusion of the contract.[86]

4. Replies to requisitions. V then answers the requisitions within the agreed time; if his answers are unsatisfactory on any point, P may make further requisitions.

[85] *Ante*, p. 19.
[86] *Ante*, p. 125.

5. Draft conveyance. P next prepares a draft conveyance in the form which he thinks it should take. He sends this draft to V for his approval; V makes in red ink any emendations he considers necessary, returns it to P, who makes any further amendments in green ink, and so on until the conveyance is agreed. P then engrosses the conveyance (*i.e.* prepares a fair copy of it) and sends it to V for execution.

6. Searches. A few days before the date fixed for completion, P searches the land charges register once more.

7. Completion. Completion[87] then takes place, usually at the office of V's solicitor, before expiry of the priority period afforded by the official search certificate.[87a] This involves V delivering to P the engrossment of the conveyance duly executed by V; only if P is entering into some obligation towards V, as by binding himself to observe restrictive covenants, will the conveyance be executed by P as well. In addition to receiving the conveyance, P is entitled to receive the title deeds. However, V may retain any deed which:

(i) relates to other land retained by him; or
(ii) creates a trust which is still subsisting; or
(iii) relates to the appointment or discharge of trustees of a subsisting trust.[88]

If V retains any deeds, he must give P an acknowledgment of P's rights to production of the deeds and, unless V is a mortgagee or trustee of the land, an undertaking for their safe custody.[89]

In return, P pays V the purchase money either in cash or by banker's draft. The exact amount due is settled by the "completion statement" which apportions the outgoings up to the exact day of completion.

B. The Conveyance

A conveyance of a legal estate must be by deed.[90] Formerly a deed required to be signed, sealed and delivered, but now the requirement of sealing, which had become an unimportant formality, has been abolished.[91] Instead, an instrument will be a deed only if[92]—

(i) it makes it clear on its face that it is intended to be a deed;
(ii) it is signed either by the person making it (or one of the parties to it) in the presence of a witness who attests the signature, or else at his direction

---

[87] For variations in the process of completion, for both unregistered and registered land, see [1991] Conv. 15, 81, 185 (D. G. Barnsley).
[87a] See *ante*, p. 89.
[88] L.P.A. 1925, s.45(9).
[89] For the effect, see L.P.A. 1925, s.64.
[90] L.P.A. 1925, s.52(1); and see *ante*, p. 67.
[91] Law of Property (Miscellaneous Provisions) Act 1989, s.1(1).
[92] *Ibid.* s.1(2)–(4).

and in his presence and the presence of two witnesses who each attest the signature; and

(iii) it is delivered[93] as a deed by him or by a person authorised to do so on his behalf.

I. PRECEDENT OF A CONVEYANCE

Commencement and date	THIS CONVEYANCE is made the 1st day of June 1992
Parties	BETWEEN John Bull of No. 1 Weelkes Street Farnaby in the County of Tye Composer (hereinafter called "the vendor") of the one part and Orlando Gibbons of No. 1 Morley Street Dowland in the County of Tallis Organist (hereinafter called "the purchaser") of the other part
Recitals	WHEREAS—
	(1) The vendor is the estate owner in respect of the fee simple of the property hereby assured for his own use and benefit absolutely free from incumbrances
	(2) The vendor has agreed with the purchaser to sell to him the said property free from incumbrances for the price of £29,750
Testatum Consideration Receipt clause Operative words	NOW THIS CONVEYANCE WITNESSETH that in consideration of the sum of £29,750 now paid by the purchaser to the vendor (the receipt whereof the vendor hereby acknowledges) the vendor As Beneficial Owner hereby conveys unto the purchaser
Parcels	ALL THAT messuage or dwellinghouse with the yard gardens offices and outbuildings thereto belonging known as No. 1 Byrd Street Purcell in the County of Norcome which premises are more particularly delineated and coloured pink on the plan annexed to these presents
Habendum	TO HOLD the same unto the purchaser in fee simple
Certificate of value	IT is hereby certified that the transaction hereby effected does not form part of a larger transaction or a series of transactions in respect of which the amount or value or the aggregate amount or value of the consideration exceeds £30,000
Testimonium	IN WITNESS WHEREOF the parties to these presents have hereunto set their hands the day and year first above written

[93] For delivery, see *post*, p. 129.

Attestation
clause

Signed and delivered by the ⎫
vendor in the presence of |
Edward Elgar Legal Executive |
with Messrs. Delius, Field and ⎬ JOHN BULL
Stanford solicitors |
|
⎭

EDWARD ELGAR

II. DETAILS OF THE CONVEYANCE

In considering the very simple form of conveyance set out above, the following points should be noticed.

1. Commencement. The old practice was for the initial words to be "This Indenture." An indenture was a deed with the top of the parchment indented, *i.e.* having an irregular edge. The deed was written out twice on a single sheet of parchment, which was then severed by cutting it with an irregular edge; the two halves of the parchment thus formed two separate deeds which could be fitted together to show their genuineness. This contrasted with a "deed poll," a deed to which there was only one party, which at the top had been polled, or shaved even. The modern practice is for the commencement to describe the general nature of the document, *e.g.* "This Conveyance," "This Mortgage" and the like.

2. Date. Whatever date is in fact inserted in the conveyance, the document takes effect from the date upon which it was signed and delivered by the parties to it.[94] A deed which has been signed but not delivered is ineffective; delivery is effected formally by uttering words such as "I deliver this as my act and deed," or informally by doing some act showing that the deed is intended to be operative. A deed may be delivered in escrow, *i.e.* delivered on the condition that it is not to become operative until some stated event occurs.[95] Usually a vendor of land will execute the conveyance some days before completion and deliver it to his solicitor in escrow, the condition being the completion of the purchase by the purchaser.[96] On satisfaction of the condition, the deed operates retrospectively to the date of delivery in escrow, though only as between the parties to it and not as to third parties.[97]

3. Parties. If any other person is an essential party to the transaction, such as a mortgagee who is releasing the property from his mortgage, he will be included as a party.

4. Recitals. These are of two types:

(a) *Narrative recitals*, which deal with matters such as how the vendor became entitled to the land; and

---

[94] Norton *Deeds* (2nd ed., 1928), p. 189.
[95] See *Beesly* v. *Hallwood Estates Ltd.* [1961] Ch. 105.
[96] *Glessing* v. *Green* [1975] 1 W.L.R. 863.
[97] *Alan Estates Ltd.* v. *W.G. Stores Ltd.* [1982] Ch. 511.

(b) *Introductory recitals*, which explain how and why the existing state of affairs is to be altered, *e.g.* that the parties have agreed for the sale of the property.

5. Testatum. This is the beginning of the operative part of the conveyance.

6. Consideration. The consideration is stated to show (*inter alia*) that the transaction is not a voluntary one.[98]

7. Receipt clause. This is inserted to save a receipt being given. Further, a solicitor who produces a conveyance containing such a clause which has been duly executed by the vendor thereby demonstrates that he has authority from the vendor to receive the purchase money.[99]

8. Operative words. These effect the actual conveyance of the property. They transfer all the rights which the vendor has in the land, or has power to convey.[1] A most important part of them is the phrase "As Beneficial Owner." It involves some consideration of the subject of covenants for title.

(a) *The covenants.* In order to shorten conveyances and other documents, the Law of Property Act 1925[2] provides that where for valuable consideration a person conveys *and*[3] is expressed to convey land "as beneficial owner" the following covenants for title are implied:

(i) Good right to convey: the vendor has power to convey the land.
(ii) Quiet enjoyment: the purchase shall have quiet enjoyment of the land.[4]
(iii) Freedom from incumbrances: the land is free from any incumbrances other than those subject to which the conveyance is expressly made.
(iv) Further assurance: the vendor will execute such assurances and do such things as are necessary to cure any defect in the conveyance.

In the case of a sale of leaseholds, the following additional covenants are implied:

(v) That the lease is valid.
(vi) That the rent has been paid and the covenants in the lease duly performed.[5]

Where a person conveys and is expressed to convey (whether or not for value) "as settlor" the only covenant implied is one for further assurance, binding that person and those claiming under him. Where a person conveys

---

[98] This excludes the possibility of a resulting trust.
[99] L.P.A. 1925, s.69.
[1] *Ibid.* s.63, obviating the former "All the estate" clause.
[2] s.76, Sched. 2, replacing C.A. 1881, s.7.
[3] See *Fay* v. *Miller, Wilkins & Co.* [1941] Ch. 360 (vendor must in fact be what he is expressed to be); but see M. & W. 160.
[4] See *post*, p. 335.
[5] L.P.A. 1925, s.76, Sched. 2.

"as trustee," "as mortgagee," "as personal representative," or "under an order of the court" the only covenant implied is that the grantor has not himself incumbered the land.[6]

(b) *Enforceability of the covenants.* The rules for enforcing covenants for title are as follows.

The benefit of the covenants runs with the land, so that each person in whom the land is for the time being vested is entitled to enforce the covenant.[7] Thus if V enters into the covenants with P, and later P sells the land to Q, Q is entitled to enforce the covenants for title against V even though Q was not a party to the conveyance from V to P which created the obligations.

As regards the burden of the covenant, the person liable is the person entering into the covenant. He does not, however, always make himself responsible for the acts of everyone. If land is conveyed "as beneficial owner" the general rule is that the vendor makes himself responsible for the acts and omissions of—

(i) himself, and
(ii) those claiming through, under, or in trust for him, and
(iii) those through whom he claims *otherwise than* by purchase for money or money's worth, and those claiming under them.[8]

Thus if V conveys land to P for value "as beneficial owner," and P subsequently discovers undisclosed incumbrances, he can sue V on the covenants for title if those incumbrances were created by V, or those claiming through, under or in trust for V, or those through whom V claims otherwise than by purchase for money or money's worth, and those claiming under them. This last phrase means that V will not be responsible for the acts of someone from whom he bought the land, but that he will be responsible for the acts of somebody who made a voluntary conveyance of the land to him, or gave it to him under a marriage settlement.

Where a person creates a mortgage "as beneficial owner," the covenants for title implied are absolute[9]; the mortgagor thus makes himself responsible for the acts of everyone. As stated under (a) above, the liability on the covenants implied by using phrases other than "as beneficial owner" is limited to the grantor's own acts.

9. Parcels. The parcels describe what is conveyed; often the conveyance employs a plan for this purpose, but this is not essential, *e.g.* if an accurate verbal description can be given, or the property can be described by reference to a plan on an earlier conveyance. The purchaser is entitled on completion to all fixtures attached to the land at the date of the contract,[10]

[6] *Ibid.* s.76, Sched. 2.
[7] *Ibid.* ss.76(6), 78.
[8] *Ibid.* Sched. 2; *David* v. *Sabin* [1893] 1 Ch. 523 at 532, 533. And see M. & W. 161–166.
[9] L.P.A. 1925, s.76, Sched. 2.
[10] For fixtures, see *ante*, pp. 15 *et seq.*

for they are part of it; and the conveyance will transfer them with the land, without special mention.

10. Habendum. This shows that the purchaser is to hold the land for his own benefit and not upon trust for a third party. It also contains the usual words of limitation.[11] It is followed by the acknowledgment and undertaking[12] where these are to be included.

11. Certificate of value. A certificate that the total consideration does not exceed certain specified amounts secures a reduction in stamp duty, or exemption from it.[13]

12. Testimonium, and

13. Attestation clause. These need no comment.

Sect. 2. Registered Title

A. From Contract to Completion

On the sale of a freehold in registered land by V to P, the sequence of steps (normally taken by their solicitors) is as follows.

1. Inspection. Now that the register is an open register,[14] P no longer requires V's authority to inspect it. But V must supply copies or abstracts of any documents noted on the register, *e.g.* as imposing restrictive covenants burdening the title.[15] If the registered title is only possessory or qualified then the pre-registration title or the qualification must be investigated as for unregistered land.[16] In every case, any possible overriding interests[17] must be carefully investigated.

2. Examination of title. The entries on the register must be examined to see that the purchaser will obtain what he is expecting. The register provides an instant title (subject to overriding interests) so there is obviously no need to examine past history.

3. Requisitions on title. If P's official search of the register reveals any untoward entries, *e.g.* a recent entry of a caution in favour of X, or if a copy of a document noted on the register is not supplied, then P will raise

---

[11] *Ante*, pp. 29 *et seq.*
[12] *Ante*, p. 127.
[13] Finance Act 1963, s.55, as amended by Finance Act 1984, s.109(1).
[14] See *ante*, p. 96.
[15] See *Faruqi* v. *English Real Estates Ltd.* [1979] 1 W.L.R. 963 (restrictive covenants not disclosed on first registration).
[16] L.R.A. 1925, s.110(2).
[17] See *ante*, pp. 102 *et seq.*

requisitions on these matters, as well as requiring confirmation of the answers given to his earlier inquiries on draft contract.

4. Replies to requisitions. V then answers the requisitions. If his answers are unsatisfactory on any point then P may make further requisitions until he is satisfied that he is obtaining what he contracted to purchase.

5. Draft transfer. P next fills in a standard form of draft transfer with such special clauses as he considers appropriate to give effect to the contract. He sends this to V for approval. When the draft transfer has been agreed (usually an easy matter), P sends a fair copy to V to be used as the engrossment for execution by V.

6. Searches. A few days before the date fixed for completion P makes an official search of the register to ensure that nothing has been entered against the title since the last search.

7. Completion. Before expiry of the priority period of 30 working days afforded by the official search certificate,[18] P will attend upon V to receive the duly executed transfer and the land certificate in return for P's banker's draft for the moneys due under V's completion statement. In contrast with unregistered land, the legal title does not pass until P is registered as proprietor, though registration will take effect from the day when he lodged his application to register the transfer with the appropriate District Land Registry[19]; and P must ensure that this is done before the priority period expires.

B. The Transfer

A registered proprietor can dispose of his registered estate, or deal with it, only as authorised by statute.[20] The forms set out in the Schedule to the Land Registration Rules 1925 must be used in all matters to which they are capable of being applied or adapted, with any alterations or additions which are necessary or desired and the registrar allows.[21] Some additions are expressly allowed, and others are customarily accepted. Thus expressions such as "as beneficial owner" and other words apt for creating covenants for title are authorised,[22] and additions such as a receipt for the purchase money are customary. The registrar has a wide discretion to refuse to register an instrument, as where it is not in the proper form, or is lacking in clarity, or is inconsistent with the principles of registered land; and he may require modifications.[23]

---

[18] See *ante*, p. 108.
[19] See *ante*, p. 96.
[20] L.R.A. 1925, s.69(4).
[21] L.R.R. 1925, r. 74. Many of the rules prescribe particular forms for particular transactions.
[22] *Ibid*. r. 76; and see *ante*, p. 130.
[23] *Ibid*. r. 78.

I. PRECEDENT OF A TRANSFER

The following is a simple form of transfer.[24]

H.M. LAND REGISTRY

LAND REGISTRATION ACTS 1925–1986

County and district *or* London Borough	Norcome, Purcell
Title Number	FT 034567
Property	1 Byrd Street Purcell in the County of Norcome
Date	1st June 1992

In consideration of twenty nine thousand seven hundred and fifty pounds (£29,750) receipt of which is acknowledged I JOHN BULL of No. 1 Weelkes Street Farnaby in the County of Tye Composer as beneficial owner transfer to ORLANDO GIBBONS of No. 1 Morley Street Dowland in the County of Tallis Organist the land comprised in the title above referred to.

It is hereby certified that the transaction hereby effected does not form part of a larger transaction or a series of transactions in respect of which the amount or value or aggregate amount or value of the consideration exceeds £30,000.

Signed and delivered by
the said John Bull in the   JOHN BULL
presence of Edward Elgar
Legal Executive with Messrs.
Delius, Field & Stanford
Solicitors

    EDWARD ELGAR

II. DETAILS OF THE TRANSFER

1. The date. The transfer must be dated, and, as between the parties to it, it takes effect from the date when it is signed and delivered.[25] But no legal estate passes until the transfer is registered, though when it is, it takes effect "as of" the date when the application for registration was lodged at the appropriate District Land Registry.[26]

2. Consideration and receipt. The statement of the consideration and the words of receipt are present for the same reasons as for unregistered land. So

---

[24] See Encyclopaedia of Forms and Precedents (5th ed.), vol. 36, p. 399, based on L.R.R. 1925, Sched., Form 19, required by r. 98.
[25] *Spectrum Investment Co.* v. *Holmes* [1981] 1 W.L.R. 221.
[26] *Ante*, pp. 96, 133.

far as the transferee is concerned, a disposition made without valuable consideration is subject not only to entries on the register and overriding interests but also to all minor interests.[27]

3. Operative words. The words "as beneficial owner" are intended to import the covenants for title,[28] and they probably would be held to do so, despite theoretical difficulties.[29]

4. The land comprised in the title. The purchaser obtains whatever title the vendor had in the land described in the Register.

5. Certificate of value. This is the same as for unregistered land.

Part 3

WILLS

Sect. 1. Freedom of Testation

From the fourteenth century until 1939 there was in general[30] no restriction upon a testator's power to dispose of property as he thought fit: for good reasons or bad he might give all his property to charities or other causes and leave his family penniless. This was changed by the Inheritance (Family Provision) Act 1938, which, after amendment, was replaced and extended by the Inheritance (Provision for Family and Dependants) Act 1975. The Act does not restrict a testator to disposing by will of only part of his estate, as some countries do, but instead makes dispositions subject to the court's discretionary power to vary their effect. Initially, the legislation applied only to wills, but now it applies to intestacy as well.

1. Ambit of the Act. The 1975 Act applies to the estate of any person who on or after April 1, 1976, has died domiciled in England and Wales. It enables certain persons to make an application to the court on the ground that reasonable provision has not been made for them out of the deceased's estate.[31]

(a) *Applicants.* The persons who can apply are the following[32]:

   (i) the wife or husband of the deceased, including a polygamous wife[33];

  (ii) a former wife or husband who has not remarried, including a remarriage that is void or voidable;

---

[27] L.R.A. 1925, ss.20(4), 23(5).
[28] See *ante*, p. 130.
[29] See the discussion in Farrand, pp. 276–280; and see Hayton, pp. 67–71; [1981] Conv. 32 (P. H. Kenny).
[30] For the limited restrictions that there were, see M. & W. 499, 500.
[31] Inheritance (Provision for Family and Dependants) Act 1975 ("Act of 1975"), s.1(1).
[32] *Ibid.* ss.1(1), 25(1), (4).
[33] *Re Sehota* [1978] 1 W.L.R. 1506.

    (iii) a child of the deceased, including a child who is *en ventre sa mère*, illegitimate or adopted, or was treated as a child of the deceased's family; and

    (iv) any other person who immediately before the death of the deceased was being maintained, either wholly or partly, by the deceased.

    (b) *"Maintained."* Under the last head above, a person is to be treated as being maintained by the deceased, whether wholly or partly, if the deceased (otherwise than for full valuable consideration) was making a substantial contribution towards the applicant's reasonable needs.[34] For persons living together, this requires the balancing of the respective contributions to the household expenses that they were making on a settled basis at the death of the deceased.[35] If one was the sole owner of the home, the provision of rent free accommodation for the other is a major factor which is subject to reduction to the extent that the applicant contributed to the acquisition and maintenance of the home.[36]

2. Applications

    (a) *Time.* Any application under the Act must be made not later than six months from the first grant of probate or letters of administration; but the court has a discretion to extend the period,[37] as may be done if a new will or codicil is found. The burden lies on the applicant to show sufficient grounds for extending the time.[38]

    (b) *No "reasonable financial provision."* The ground for making an application is that the disposition of the estate of the deceased by his will, or on his intestacy (or under both combined), does not make reasonable financial provision for the applicant.[39] The meaning of this falls under two heads.

    (i) For a spouse (unless separated under a decree of judicial separation), it means such financial provision as it would be reasonable in all the circumstances for a husband or wife to receive, whether or not it is required for his or her maintenance.[40] In such cases, the court must have regard to the provision which the spouse might reasonably have expected to receive if the marriage had been ended by divorce instead of death.[41]

    (ii) For others, it means such financial provision as it would be reasonable in all the circumstances for the applicant to receive for his or her maintenance,[42] thus restricting the amount.

---

[34] Act of 1975, s.1(3).
[35] *Jelley* v. *Iliffe* [1981] Fam. 128; *Bishop* v. *Plumley* [1991] 1 W.L.R. 582; and see *Malone* v. *Harrison* [1979] 1 W.L.R. 1353.
[36] *Ibid.*
[37] Act of 1975, s.4.
[38] See *Re Salmon* [1981] Ch. 167.
[39] Act of 1975, s.1(1).
[40] *Ibid.* s.1(2)(a).
[41] *Ibid.* s.3(2).
[42] *Ibid.* s.1(2)(b).

The test is objective: it is not whether the deceased acted unreasonably but whether any provision made was in fact not reasonable.[43] A will does not fail to make reasonable financial provision for a beneficiary merely because he can take nothing under it because he murdered the testator.[44]

(c) *"Net estate."* It is the "net estate" of the deceased that is available to satisfy any order under the Act. This consists of all the property of which the deceased had power to dispose by will, but after deducting his funeral, testamentary and administration expenses, and his debts and liabilities, including any inheritance tax.[45] Property over which the deceased had a power of appointment[46] is included if the power is general but not if it is special; and the court may order the deceased's interest under a joint tenancy which had passed from him by survivorship on his death to be treated as if he had had a share in it.[47] The court may also order the inclusion of property which has been subject to certain devices for evading the Act.[48]

3. Order. The court exercises a very wide discretion under the Act of 1975.

(a) *Circumstances.* If the court is satisfied that the disposition of the estate of the deceased does not make reasonable financial provision for the applicant, the court must consider all the relevant circumstances of the case when deciding whether to make an order, and what order to make. These circumstances include the present and future financial resources and financial needs of the applicant, of other possible applicants and of the beneficiaries of the deceased's estate, any obligation or responsibility of the deceased to any applicant or beneficiary, and any physical or mental disability that they have.[49] For spouses, children and persons maintained there are further special considerations.[50] Statements by the deceased, whether oral or written, are admissible as evidence of the facts stated.[51]

(b) *Terms of order.* The court has a wide discretion as to the provisions which are to be made out of the net estate.[52] The order may provide for paying a lump sum or some or all of the income, or for making periodical payments or transferring or settling property, or for varying marriage settlements. There are also powers to vary or discharge orders for periodical payments, and to make interim orders in case of immediate need.[53]

[43] See *Re Goodwin* [1969] 1 Ch. 283; *Re Coventry* [1980] Ch. 461.
[44] *Re Royse* [1985] Ch. 22.
[45] Act of 1975, s.25(1).
[46] See *post*, p. 199.
[47] Act of 1975, ss.9, 25(1).
[48] *Ibid.* ss.10–12, 25(1).
[49] *Ibid.* s.3(1).
[50] *Ibid.* s.3(2)–(4). See *Moody* v. *Stevenson* [1992] 2 W.L.R. 640.
[51] *Ibid.* s.21.
[52] *Ibid.* s.2.
[53] *Ibid.* ss.5, 6.

Sect. 2. Nature of a Will

1. A will is ambulatory. Until the death of the testator, a will has no effect at all, but operates as a mere declaration of his intention, which may be changed from time to time. For this reason, a will is said to be "ambulatory"; a beneficiary under it has merely a *"spes,"* and not any interest in property. This distinguishes a will from a conveyance, settlement or other dealing *inter vivos*, which operates at once or at some fixed time and confers an interest in property.

A will is also ambulatory in that it "speaks from death," *i.e.* it is capable of disposing of all property owned by the testator at his death, even if acquired after the date of the will.[54]

2. A will is revocable. Notwithstanding any declaration in the will itself or any other document, a will can be revoked at any time.[55] However, although a binding contract not to revoke a will does not prevent its revocation,[56] and will prima facie be construed as not extending to revocation by marriage,[57] such a contract binds the testator's assets, so that if the will is revoked, the beneficiaries thereunder can compel the person to whom the assets have passed to hold them on trust for them in accordance with the terms of the contract.[58]

3. Codicils. A codicil is similar to a will and is governed by the same rules. A testamentary document is usually called a codicil if it is supplementary to a will and adds to, varies or revokes provisions in the will: if it is an independent instrument, it is called a will. Although sometimes indorsed on a will, a codicil may be a separate document, and can stand by itself even after the revocation of the will to which it is supplementary.[59] Codicils are construed in such a way as to disturb the provisions of a will no more than is absolutely necessary to give effect to the codicil.[60]

Sect. 3. The Formalities of a Will

A. Formal Wills

I. EXECUTION

The present rules governing the execution of a formal will are as follows.[61]

1. Writing: the will must be in writing. Any form of writing, printing,

---

[54] Wills Act 1837, s.24; see further, *post*, p. 153.
[55] *Vynior's Case* (1610) 8 Co.Rep. 81b.
[56] *In b. Heys* [1914] P. 192.
[57] *Re Marsland* [1939] Ch. 820.
[58] *Re Cleaver* [1981] 1 W.L.R. 939.
[59] *In b. Savage* (1870) L.R. 2 P. & D. 78.
[60] *Doe* d. *Hearle* v. *Hicks* (1832) 1 Cl. & F. 20.
[61] Wills Act 1837, s.9, as substituted by Administration of Justice Act 1982, s.17.

typewriting and the like may be employed. No special form of words need be used: all that is required is an intelligible document.

2. Signature by testator: the will must be signed by the testator, or by someone else in his presence and by his direction. The testator's signature may be made in any way, provided there is an intention to execute the will. Thus initials,[62] a stamped name, a mark,[63] a signature in a former or assumed name,[64] or "your loving Mother,"[65] all suffice. But a seal is not enough, for the will must be signed and sealing is not signing.[66] Similar principles apply to signature by someone on behalf of the testator. Thus signature of his own name instead of that of the testator is sufficient.[67] But it is essential that the signature should be made in the testator's presence and authorised by him, either expressly or by implication.[68]

Effect will be given to dispositions contained in a document which has not been executed as a will if the document is incorporated in a will. For this to be the case—

   (i) the will must clearly identify the document to be incorporated;
  (ii) the will must refer to the document as being already in existence and not as one subsequently to be made; and
 (iii) the document must in fact be in existence when the will is executed.[69]

3. Position of signature. Before 1983, it was necessary for the signature to appear at the end of the will.[70] Any material which followed the signature in time or in space would be refused probate. This requirement caused various difficulties,[71] and the position has now been simplified. For those dying after 1982, the signature may be placed in any position in the will, provided that "it appears that the testator intended by his signature to give effect to the will,"[72] and that he was not, for example, merely identifying the document.[73] Thus T's will is duly signed if, as part of a single operation, he writes "My will by T" and then the dispositive words.[74]

4. Presence of witnesses: the testator must either make or acknowledge the signature in the presence of two witnesses present at the same time. Whether the signature to the will is made by the testator or by someone in his presence

---

[62] *In b. Savory* (1815) 15 Jur. 1042.
[63] *In b. Finn* (1936) 53 T.L.R. 153 (thumb-mark).
[64] *In b. Redding* (1850) 2 Rob. Ecc. 339.
[65] *In b. Cook* [1960] 1 W.L.R. 353.
[66] *Wright* v. *Wakeford* (1811) 17 Ves. 454.
[67] *In b. Clark* (1839) 2 Curt. 329.
[68] *In b. Marshall* (1866) 13 L.T. 643.
[69] See *University College of North Wales* v. *Taylor* [1908] P. 140.
[70] Wills Act 1837, s.9; Wills Act Amendment Act 1852.
[71] See M. & W. 507.
[72] Administration of Justice Act 1982, s.17, substituting a new s.9 of the Wills Act 1837.
[73] Contrast *In b. Mann* [1942] P. 146 with *In b. Bean* [1944] P. 83 and *Re Beadle* [1974] 1 W.L.R. 417 (the envelope cases).
[74] *Wood* v. *Smith* [1992] 3 All E.R. 556.

and by his direction, there is no need for witnesses to be present at the time of the signature if they are present when the testator subsequently makes a proper acknowledgement of the signature. But either the signature or the acknowledgement must be made in the *simultaneous* presence of two witnesses. An express acknowledgement is desirable but not essential,[75] and an acknowledgement by a third party is effective if it can be shown that it should be taken to be the acknowledgement of the testator.[76]

It is desirable but not essential that the witnesses should be of full age and sound intelligence; yet a blind person cannot be a witness, for the will cannot be signed in his "presence."[77]

5. Signature by witnesses: the witnesses must then sign in the presence of the testator. No form of attestation is necessary although a proper attestation clause showing that the will has been executed in accordance with the statutory requirements will facilitate the grant of probate. All that is necessary is that after the testator's signature has been made or acknowledged in the joint presence of two witnesses, they should sign their names or acknowledge their signatures in the testator's presence.[78] There is no need for the witnesses to sign in each other's presence,[79] although it is both desirable and usual.

II. ALTERATIONS

Every obliteration, interlineation or other alteration made after a will has been executed must itself be executed in the same way as a will; in default, it is ineffective unless it revokes any part of the will by rendering it illegible.[80] No alteration will therefore be effective unless it is signed or initialled by the testator and the witnesses.[81]

An obliteration or erasure of part of a will, even though unattested, is effective to revoke that part, since it amounts to a destruction of that part[82]; and the same applies to the pasting of paper over part of a will,[83] provided the words are not decipherable by any natural means, such as by the use of magnifying glasses or by holding the will up to the light.[84] The court will not permit physical interference with the will, as by using chemicals or removing paper pasted over the words[85]; and an obliteration is not ineffective merely because the original words can be deciphered by making another document, *e.g.* an infra-red photograph.[86]

---

[75] See *In b. Davies* (1850) 2 Rob. Ecc. 337.
[76] *Inglesant* v. *Inglesant* (1874) L.R. 3 P. & D. 172.
[77] *In b. Gibson* [1949] P. 434.
[78] Wills Act 1837, s.9, as substituted by Administration of Justice Act 1982, s.17, permitting acknowledgement by a witness and so reversing *Wyatt* v. *Berry* [1893] P. 5.
[79] *In b. Webb* (1855) Dea. & Sw. 1.
[80] Wills Act 1837, s.21.
[81] *Re White* [1991] Ch. 1.
[82] See *Townley* v. *Watson* (1844) 3 Curt. 761; and see below.
[83] *In b. Horsford* (1874) L.R. 3 P. & D. 211.
[84] *Ffinch* v. *Combe* [1894] P. 191.
[85] *In b. Horsford, supra*; contrast *In b. Gilbert* [1893] P. 183.
[86] *In b. Itter* [1950] P. 130.

III. REVOCATION

A will or codicil may be revoked by another will or codicil, by destruction, or by marriage.

1. By another will or codicil. A revocation clause expressly revoking all former wills is effective provided it is contained in a document executed with the proper formalities.[87] This is so even if the testator had been misled as to the effect of the clause,[88] but not if the testator did not know of the presence of the clause.[89] A will is not revoked merely because a later will is entitled (as is usual) "This is the last will and testament of me" or some similar phrase.[90]

A will is revoked by implication if a later will is executed which merely repeats the former will or is inconsistent with it, although if the repetition or inconsistency is merely partial, those parts of the former will which are neither repeated in the later will nor inconsistent with it remain effective.[91] Any number of testamentary documents may be read together, each being effective except so far as subsequently varied or revoked; the sum total constitutes the testator's will.[92]

2. By destruction animo revocandi. A will is revoked if it is destroyed by the testator, or by some person in his presence and by his direction, with intent to revoke it.[93] There are thus two elements, an act of destruction and an *animus revocandi* (intention to revoke).

(a) *Destruction.* It is not necessary that the will should be completely destroyed; there must, however, be some burning, tearing or other destruction of the whole will or some essential part of it, as by cutting off the signature of the testator or the witnesses.[94] It is not enough for the testator to draw a line through part of the will, indorse it "all these are revoked" and kick it into the corner.[95] Destruction of part of a will normally revokes that part alone,[96] unless the part destroyed is so important as to lead to the conclusion that the rest cannot be intended to stand alone.[97]

If a will has been destroyed without being revoked (*e.g.* because an *animus revocandi* was lacking), it is proved by means of a draft or copy, or even by oral evidence.[98] A will in the testator's possession which cannot be found at his death is presumed to have been destroyed by him *animo*

---

[87] Wills Act 1837, s.20.
[88] *Collins* v. *Elstone* [1893] P. 1.
[89] *In b. Moore* [1892] P. 378; and see *Re Phelan* [1972] Fam. 33.
[90] *Simpson* v. *Foxon* [1907] P. 54.
[91] *Lemage* v. *Goodban* (1865) L.R. 1 P. & D. 57.
[92] *In b. Fenwick* (1867) L.R. 1 P. & D. 319. For distributive revocation, see *Re Finnemore* [1991] 1 W.L.R. 793.
[93] Wills Act 1837, s.20.
[94] *Williams* v. *Tyley* (1858) Johns. 530.
[95] *Cheese* v. *Lovejoy* (1877) 2 P.D. 251.
[96] *Re Everest* [1975] Fam. 44.
[97] *Leonard* v. *Leonard* [1902] P. 243.
[98] *Sugden* v. *Lord St. Leonards* (1876) 1 P.D. 154.

revocandi and cannot be proved unless the presumption is rebutted by evidence of non-revocation.[99]

(b) *Intent to revoke.* The testator must have an *animus revocandi* at the time of destruction. If a will is intentionally torn up by a testator who is drunk[1] or believes the will to be ineffective, it is not revoked, for an intent to destroy the document is no substitute for the requisite intent to revoke the will. "All the destroying in the world without intention will not revoke a will, nor all the intention in the world without destroying: there must be the two."[2]

Revocation of a will may be conditional, in which case the will remains unrevoked until the condition has been fulfilled. One particular kind of conditional revocation is known as dependent relative revocation. If revocation is relative to another will and intended to be dependent upon the validity of that will, the revocation is ineffective unless that other will takes effect. Thus if a will is destroyed by a testator who is about to make a new will, and the evidence shows that he intended to revoke the old will only if he executed the new one, the old will remains valid if the new will is never executed.[3] Another example arises in the case of revival; if Will No. 1 is revoked by Will No. 2, the revocation of Will No. 2 is not sufficient to revive Will No. 1,[4] so that if the testator revokes Will No. 2 in the mistaken belief that he is thereby reviving Will No. 1, the doctrine of dependent relative revocation applies and the revocation of Will No. 2 is ineffective.[5] Again, if a testator obliterates a legacy and by unattested writing substitutes a new legacy, the old legacy remains effective if the court is satisfied that it was revoked only on the (erroneous) supposition that the new legacy would be effective.[6]

3. By marriage. Marriage automatically revokes all wills made by the parties to the marriage.[7] There are two exceptions to this.

(a) *Certain appointments.* An appointment by will under a power of appointment is not revoked by the marriage of the testator unless, in default of appointment, the property would pass to his personal representatives[8] and so become part of his estate. The general intention of this provision is that if the testator's new "family" will get the property even if the will is revoked, there is no harm in allowing the marriage to revoke it. But if the property would pass out of the "family" in default of appointment, the will is

---

[99] *Eckersley* v. *Platt* (1866) L.R. 1 P. & D. 281.
[1] *In b. Brassington* [1902] P. 1.
[2] *Cheese* v. *Lovejoy* (1877) 2 P.D. 251 at 253, *per* James L.J.
[3] *Dixon* v. *Treasury Solicitor* [1905] P. 42.
[4] *Post,* p. 143.
[5] *Powell* v. *Powell* (1866) L.R. 1 P. & D. 209; *In b. Bridgewater* [1965] 1 W.L.R. 416.
[6] *In b. Horsford* (1874) L.R. 3 P. & D. 211.
[7] Wills Act 1837, s.18, as substituted by Administration of Justice Act 1982, s.18.
[8] See *post,* p. 164.

allowed to stand so far as it exercises the power of appointment, and no farther.[9]

(b) *Contemplation of marriage.* A will made after 1925 that is expressed to be made in contemplation of a marriage is not revoked by the solemnisation of the particular marriage contemplated.[10] The contemplation may be inferential, such as a gift "to my fiancée" X,[11] but a mere general contemplation ("made in contemplation of marriage") is not enough,[12] nor is a contemplation expressed in relation to only some gifts in the will and not the will as a whole.[13] Wills made after 1982 are subject to similar provisions, with some variations.[14] It is now required that it should appear from the will that when it was made the testator was expecting to be married to a particular person, and that he intended that the will should not be revoked by the marriage. Further, if this intention applies only to some disposition in the will, the marriage will not revoke that disposition, nor, unless a contrary intention appears, will it revoke the rest of the will.

Where a testator dies after 1982, and his marriage is dissolved, annulled or declared void, any gift in his existing will to his former spouse will lapse,[15] and any appointment of his former spouse as an executor or trustee of the will is ineffective.[16] If a life interest lapses in this way, any remainder is accelerated.[17] A lapse under these provisions does not prejudice any right of the former spouse to apply for financial provision under the Inheritance (Provision for Family and Dependants) Act 1975.[18]

IV. REVIVAL

A will revoked by destruction *animo revocandi* can never be revived.[19] Any other will can be revived, but only by re-execution with the proper formalities or by a codicil showing an intention to revive it.[20] If a will has been revoked by a subsequent will, the first will is thus not revived merely by the revocation of the latter will.[21] If a will is first partially revoked, then wholly revoked, and then revived, the revival does not extend to the part partially revoked unless an intention to this effect is shown.[22]

---

[9] *In b. Russell* (1890) 15 P.D. 111; *In b. Gilligan* [1950] P. 32.
[10] L.P.A. 1925, s.177.
[11] *In b. Langston* [1953] P. 100; *Re Coleman* [1976] Ch. 1.
[12] *Sallis* v. *Jones* [1936] P. 43.
[13] *Re Coleman, supra.*
[14] Wills Act 1837, s.18, as substituted by Administration of Justice Act 1982, ss.18, 73(7).
[15] See *Re Sinclair* [1985] Ch. 446.
[16] Wills Act 1837, s.18A, inserted by Administration of Justice Act 1982, ss.18, 73(6).
[17] *Ibid.*
[18] *Ibid.* See *ante*, p. 135.
[19] *In b. Reade* [1902] P. 75.
[20] Wills Act 1837, s.22.
[21] *In b. Hodgkinson* [1893] P. 339.
[22] Wills Act 1837, s.22.

B. Informal Wills

Cetain persons are excepted from the rules that a testator must be of full age and must comply with the usual formalities.[23]

I. PRIVILEGED TESTATORS

1. A soldier in actual military service. The testator must not merely be in an army; when he makes the will he must be actually serving in connection with military operations which are or have been taking place or are believed to be imminent.[24] Thus service at a camp in England in August 1940 can suffice,[25] and so can service in Northern Ireland in 1978 during an armed and clandestinely organised insurrection.[26] A soldier is deemed to be in actual military service from the moment he receives mobilisation orders until the full conclusion of the operations. "Soldier" includes both officers and other ranks, a female army nurse,[27] and a member of the Air Force,[28] or Women's Auxiliary Air Force.[29]

2. A mariner or seaman at sea. This includes both members of the Royal Navy and merchant seamen, and extends to a female typist employed on a liner.[30] It includes an admiral directing naval operations on a river,[31] a master mariner in his ship lying in the Thames before starting on her voyage,[32] and a seaman whose ship is permanently stationed in harbour.[33] It also extends to a seaman on shore leave from his ship, or under orders to join a new ship.[34]

3. A member of Her Majesty's Naval or Marine Forces so circumstanced that, had he been a soldier, he would have been in actual military service.[35] This enables a member of the navy or marines who has been called up to make an informal will even though he has not joined his ship.[36]

II. EXTENT OF THE PRIVILEGE

A will made by a testator who at the time of making the will comes within one of the above categories has the following privileges.

[23] *Ibid.* s.11.
[24] *Re Wingham* [1949] P. 187.
[25] *In b. Spark* [1941] P. 115.
[26] *Re Jones* [1981] P. 7.
[27] *In b. Stanley* [1916] P. 192.
[28] Wills (Soldiers and Sailors) Act 1918, s.5.
[29] *In b. Rowson* [1944] 2 All E.R. 36.
[30] *In b. Hale* [1915] 2 I.R. 362.
[31] *In b. Austen* (1853) 2 Rob. Ecc. 611.
[32] *In b. Patterson* (1898) 79 L.T. 123.
[33] *In b. M'Murdo* (1867) L.R. 1 P. & D. 540.
[34] *In b. Newland* [1952] P. 71; *In b. Wilson* [1952] P. 92. Contrast *Re Rapley* [1983] 1 W.L.R. 1069.
[35] Wills (Soldiers and Sailors) Act 1918, s.2.
[36] *In b. Yates* [1919] P. 93.

1. It is immaterial that the testator is a minor. This has always applied to wills of personality, provided the minor is at least 14 years of age if a male and at least 12 if a female.[37] In the case of realty, this privilege seems to have been accidentally curtailed after 1925 in the case of minors who have never married.[38]

2. The will can be made or revoked informally. The will may be made in writing, with or without witnesses or signature, or it may be nuncupative; thus informal words of farewell spoken at a railway station may suffice.[39] The testator need not know that he is making a will, provided he gives deliberate expression to his wishes as to the destination of his property on his death,[40] *e.g.* "If I stop a bullet everything of mine will be yours."[41] Those entitled to make an informal will (including minors[42]) may also revoke a will, even if it has been made formally, in an informal manner, *e.g.* by an unattested letter to a relative asking that the will should be burned, "for I have already cancelled it."[43]

These privileges have always applied to wills of personalty, and extend to wills of realty if the testator dies after February 6, 1918.[44] A will properly made under the above conditions remains valid indefinitely unless revoked, even after the military or other service is over.[45]

Sect. 4. Operation of Wills

A. Lapse

I. GENERAL RULE

A legacy or bequest (*i.e.* a testamentary gift of personalty) or a devise (*i.e.* a testamentary gift of realty) is said to lapse if the beneficiary dies before the testator. In such a case, unless a contrary intention is shown, the gift fails and the property comprised in it falls into residue. This means that it passes under any general or residuary gift in the will,[46] such as "all the rest of my property I leave to X." If there is no residuary gift, or if the gift which lapses is itself a gift of all or part of the residue, there is a partial intestacy and the property passes to the persons entitled on intestacy.[47]

II. EXCLUSION OF THE GENERAL RULE

1. No lapse. The Wills Act 1837 excludes the general rule in two important

---

[37] *Hyde* v. *Hyde* (1711) Prec. Ch. 316.
[38] See A.E.A. 1925, s.51; *post* p. 170.
[39] *In b. Yates, supra.*
[40] *In b. Spicer* [1949] P. 441.
[41] *Re Stable* [1919] P. 7; contrast *In b. Knibbs* [1962] 1 W.L.R. 852.
[42] Family Law Reform Act 1969, s.3(3).
[43] *In b. Gossage* [1921] P. 194.
[44] Wills (Soldiers and Sailors) Act 1918, s.3.
[45] *Re Booth* [1926] P. 118.
[46] Wills Act 1837, s.25.
[47] *Ackroyd* v. *Smithson* (1780) 1 Bro.C.C. 503; *post*, pp. 156 *et seq.*

cases, though the operation of the Act has been altered for cases where the testator dies after 1982.

(a) *Entails.* By section 32, subject to any contrary intention in the will, there is no lapse if property is given to a person in tail and he predeceases the testator, leaving issue living at the testator's death capable of inheriting under the entail.

(b) *Gifts to issue.* By section 33, subject to any contrary intention in the will, there is no lapse if an interest in property not determinable at or before death is left to a child or other issue of the testator who left issue living (and not, it seems, merely *en ventre sa mère*[48]) at the testator's death. "Issue" includes legitimated issue[49] and, for testator's dying after 1969, illegitimate issue.[50]

2. Operation of the Act

(a) *Fictional survival.* Under neither section does the Act give anything to the issue whose survival prevented the lapse; it merely provides that the gift shall take effect as if the legatee or devisee had died immediately after the testator. Accordingly if T leaves £2,000 by his will to his daughter D, who dies some years before him, the legacy lapses unless she left issue who survived both herself and T, in which case the £2,000 forms part of D's estate. If D died a bankrupt, it passes to her trustee in bankruptcy[51]; if she was solvent but bequeathed all her property to charities or strangers, it passes to them under her will.[52] Only if D's issue is entitled under her will or intestacy will they benefit. But the fiction is applied only so far as is necessary to prevent a lapse. Thus where it saved from lapse a gift by a father who died in 1940 to a son who died intestate in 1920, the property carried to the son's estate passed under the rules of intestacy in force at the date of the son's real, and not his notional, death.[53]

(b) *Deaths after 1982.* When the testator dies after 1982, section 32 continues unchanged; but section 33 has been much revised, and there is a fictional survival no longer.[54] Subject to any contrary intention in the will, a gift to a child or remoter descendant of the testator who predeceased him, but left issue surviving him, takes effect as a gift to the issue living at the testator's death[55]; and they take in equal shares *per stirpes*.[56] For these purposes, illegitimacy is disregarded; and a person *en ventre sa mère* at the testator's death and born alive thereafter is treated as being alive at the testator's death.[57]

---

[48] See *Elliott* v. *Joicey* [1935] A.C. 209, disapproving *Re Griffiths' Settlement* [1911] 1 Ch. 246.
[49] *Re Brodie* [1967] Ch. 818; Family Law Reform Act 1969, s.16(2).
[50] Family Law Reform Act 1969, s.16.
[51] *Re Pearson* [1920] 1 Ch. 217.
[52] *Re Hayter* [1937] 2 All E.R. 110.
[53] *Re Basioli* [1953] Ch. 367.
[54] Wills Act 1837, s.33, as substituted by Administration of Justice Act 1982, ss.19, 73(6).
[55] *Ibid.* s.33(1).
[56] See M. & W. 520, 546; *post*, p. 160.
[57] Wills Act 1837, s.33(4), as substituted by Administration of Justice Act 1982, ss.19, 73(6).

3. Exceptions. In four cases section 33 does not apply to prevent a lapse.

(a) *Appointments under special powers.* Section 33 does not apply to an appointment by will under a special power,[58] for it is confined to cases where property is devised or bequeathed. It does, however, apply to appointments under general powers.[59]

(b) *Class gifts.* Where the testator died before 1983, section 33 does not apply to class gifts,[60] such as a gift to "all my children," even if in fact there is only one member of the class.[61] The reason is that membership of a class is normally ascertained at a testator's death, and those dying before the testator fail to become members of the class. Strictly, there is no question of lapse: it is merely that nothing has ever been given to those who predecease the testator. But a gift of property "to be equally divided between my five daughters" is not a class gift, for there is a gift to each individual alive at the date of the will; section 33 will accordingly apply if one of the children predeceases the testator.[62]

Where the testator dies after 1982, this rule no longer applies. Instead, subject to any contrary intention in the will, where there is a gift to a class of persons consisting of children or remoter descendants of the testator, and a member of the class predeceases him but leaves issue surviving him, the gift takes effect as if the class included the issue living at the testator's death.[63]

(c) *Interests terminable on donee's death.* Section 33 does not preserve gifts which would in any case terminate with the donee's death, *e.g.* gifts of a life interest or joint tenancy.[64]

(d) *Certain contingent gifts.* Section 33 does not preserve a contingent gift such as a bequest "to X as and when he is 25" if X dies aged 24, even if he would have attained the requisite age had he in fact outlived the testator.[65]

III. COMMORIENTES

Where a devisee or legatee dies at nearly the same time as the testator, it is necessary to determine which survived the other in order to know whether the gift lapsed. Similar questions between *commorientes* (those dying together) arise on intestacy and in respect of joint tenancies. Before 1926, there was no means of settling the question if there was no evidence of the order of deaths. Thus if two people perished in a shipwreck, in the absence of evidence of survivorship the estate of one could not benefit under the will or intestacy of the other, for it was impossible for the personal representatives to establish the survivorship essential to their case. In the case of deaths

---

[58] *Holyland* v. *Lewin* (1883) 26 Ch.D. 266; *post*, p. 201.
[59] *Eccles* v. *Cheyne* (1856) 2 K. & J. 676.
[60] See *post*, p. 154.
[61] *Re Harvey's Estate* [1893] 1 Ch. 567.
[62] *Re Smith's Trusts* (1878) 9 Ch.D. 117.
[63] Wills Act 1837, s.33(2), as substituted by Administration of Justice Act 1982, ss.19, 73(6).
[64] See *Re Butler* [1918] 1 I.R. 394.
[65] *Re Wolson* [1939] Ch. 780.

after 1925, however, where it is uncertain which survived the other, for all purposes affecting the title to property the younger is deemed to have survived the elder, subject to any order of the court.[66] This rule applies equally to cases of simple uncertainty, as where one of the parties is on a ship which founders with all hands on an uncertain date and the other dies at home during that period, and to common disasters, such as virtually simultaneous deaths in an air-raid.[67] But for the purpose of inheritance tax, the old rule remains, and each is deemed to have died simultaneously, so that there can be no second liability for tax on the death of a notional survivor.[68]

B. Gifts to Witnesses

1. Invalidation of gift. The Wills Act 1837[69] provides that the attestation of a beneficiary or his or her spouse is not to invalidate the will, but the beneficiary can claim no benefit under the will, either as to realty or personalty.

2. Limits of the rule. This rule does not apply in the following cases.

(a) *Informal wills*: where no witnesses at all are necessary for the validity of the will, as where the testator is a soldier in actual military service.[70]

(b) *Enough other witnesses*: where the testator dies after May 29, 1968, and the will would be validly executed without regard to the attestation by the beneficiary or his or her spouse.[71]

(c) *Signed not as a witness*: where the person has signed the will not as a witness but merely, for example, to show that he agrees with the testator's leaving him less than his brothers and sisters.[72]

(d) *Subsequent marriage*: where the marriage of the beneficiary to the witness occurred after the date of the will.[73]

(e) *Fiduciary gifts*: where the gift to the witness is to him as a trustee and not beneficially.[74]

(f) *Confirmation*: where the gift is made or confirmed by any will or codicil not attested by the beneficiary. Thus if there is a gift by will confirmed by codicil, a beneficiary who witnesses only one document is entitled to the gift since he can claim under the other document.[75]

(g) *Secret trusts*: where the beneficiary takes not under the will but under a

---

[66] L.P.A. 1925, s.184. For an exception, see *post*, p. 160 (intestate spouses).
[67] *Hickman* v. *Peacey* [1945] A.C. 304.
[68] Inheritance Tax Act 1984, s.4(2).
[69] s.15.
[70] *Re Limond* [1915] 2 Ch. 240.
[71] Wills Act 1968, s.1, reversing *Re Bravda* [1968] 1 W.L.R. 479.
[72] *Kitcat* v. *King* [1930] P. 266.
[73] *Thorpe* v. *Bestwick* (1881) 6 Q.B.D. 311.
[74] *Cresswell* v. *Cresswell* (1868) L.R. 6 Eq. 69.
[75] *Re Marcus* (1887) 56 L.J.Ch. 830; *Re Trotter* [1899] 1 Ch. 764.

secret trust in his favour binding property given by the will to another person.[76]

3. Effect. Where the rule applies, the effect is that the will is treated as if it had omitted the offending gift. Where the gift is of a limited interest, the effect is to accelerate the subsequent interests. Hence if property is given to A for life, with remainder to B, the effect of A attesting the will is that B is entitled to the property as soon as the testator dies.[77] Similarly if property is given to X, Y and Z as joint tenants, and X attests the will, Y and Z are entitled to the whole of the property.[78] The notional omission of the offending gift also means that a gift expressed to take effect if the offending gift fails is also void.[79]

C. Gifts to Persons Unlawfully Causing the Death

At common law, a person who unlawfully kills another can take no benefit under his victim's will[80]; and under the victim's intestacy the killer's prospective interest devolves as if he did not exist.[81] The rule applies to murder[82] even where there is a finding of diminished responsibility,[83] though not where the killer is found not guilty by reason of insanity.[84] In its application to manslaughter, a crime which varies almost infinitely in seriousness, there are two qualifications. First, the courts have confined the rule to cases of deliberate, intentional and unlawful violence or threats of violence.[85] Second, for manslaughter and any other unlawful killing except murder, such as infanticide or causing death by reckless driving, statute[86] has empowered the court to modify the rule if satisfied that in all the relevant circumstances "the justice of the case" requires this, provided application to the court is made within three months after the conviction.[87] Murder apart, the rule does not preclude certain applications for financial provision being made, for example, under the Inheritance (Provision for Family and Dependants) Act 1975.[88]

D. Rectification

Formerly the court had no power to rectify a will, however clear it was that

---

[76] *Re Young* [1951] Ch. 344.
[77] *Jull* v. *Jacobs* (1876) 3 Ch.D. 703.
[78] *Young* v. *Davies* (1863) 2 Dr. & Sm. 167.
[79] *Re Doland's W.T.* [1970] Ch. 267.
[80] *In b. Hall* [1914] P. 1; *Re Pollock* [1941] Ch. 219.
[81] *Re Sigsworth* [1935] Ch. 89; *Re Callaway* [1956] Ch. 559. For another application of the rule, see *post*, p. 301.
[82] *Re Pollock, supra.*
[83] *Re Giles* [1972] Ch. 544; *Re Royse* [1985] Ch. 22.
[84] *Re Pitts* [1931] 1 Ch. 546; compare *Re Pechar* [1969] N.Z.L.R. 574.
[85] *Re K.* [1986] Ch. 180 at 186; *Re H.* [1990] 1 F.L.R. 441.
[86] Forfeiture Act 1982.
[87] *Ibid.* ss.2, 5. See *Re K., supra.*
[88] *Ibid.* ss.3, 5; *ante*, pp. 135 *et seq.*

some clerical blunder had been made in it, as in writing or typing it from a draft. But where the testator died after 1982, the court now has a limited power to rectify a will, confined to cases where the court is satisfied that the will fails to carry out the testator's intention in consequence of a clerical error or a failure to understand his instructions.[89] This includes a solicitor's inadvertent omission of a clause when drafting a revised version of a will.[90] No application for rectification may be made more than six months after probate or letters of administration are first taken out unless the court extends the time[91]; and there is protection for personal representatives who distribute the estate after the six months have run without considering the possibility of time being extended.[92]

Sect. 5. Construction of Wills

The construction of wills is a vast subject; only a few of the more important rules can be mentioned here.

A. General Rule

The cardinal rule of construction is that effect must be given to the intention of the testator as expressed in the will, the words being given their natural meaning except so far as that leads to absurdities or inconsistencies.[93] The will alone must be looked at, and, in general, no evidence can be received to contradict the meaning of the words used in the will. "The will must be in writing, and the only question is, what is the meaning of the words used in that writing."[94] If the rule were otherwise, the requirement that a will should be in writing might largely be set at naught.

However, although words will usually be given their natural meaning, or the most appropriate of their several natural meanings, there is nothing to prevent words from being construed in some special sense if the will clearly shows that they are used in that sense; and in recent years the courts have been rather more ready to perceive that the testator has used words otherwise than according to their "strict" meaning.[95] Furthermore, statute may require a particular meaning to be given. For example, in wills made after 1969 a provision for the benefit of a child or relation of any kind is to be construed as including those illegitimately related, unless the contrary intention appears.[96] Again, if the will was made after 1949 or confirmed after April 1, 1959, children who were formally adopted before the testator died are included.[97]

---

[89] Administration of Justice Act 1982, s.20(1).
[90] *Wordingham* v. *Royal Exchange Trust Co. Ltd.* [1992] 2 W.L.R. 496.
[91] Administration of Justice Act 1982, s.20(2).
[92] *Ibid.* s.20(3), (4).
[93] See *Abbott* v. *Middleton* (1858) 7 H.L.C. 68 at 114.
[94] *Grey* v. *Pearson* (1857) 6 H.L.C. 61 at 106, *per* Lord Wensleydale.
[95] See *Perrin* v. *Morgan* [1943] A.C. 399 (meaning of "money").
[96] Family Law Reform Act 1969, s.15. This does not affect the meaning of "heir," or entailed interests.
[97] Adoption Act 1958, ss.16(2), 17(2), 59, Sched. 5, para. 4.

B. *Extrinsic Evidence*

Since only the words of the will may be considered, extrinsic evidence (*i.e.* evidence not gathered from the will itself) is normally inadmissible. However, this is subject to certain qualifications.

1. Surrounding circumstances. Evidence of facts and circumstances existing when the will was made is always admissible. "You may place yourself, so to speak, in [the testator's] arm-chair."[98] Thus extrinsic evidence is admissible to show that certain words had a peculiar meaning to the testator by the custom of the district or the usage of the class of persons to which he belonged. Again, nicknames, or symbols used by the testator in his trade, may be explained; thus it may be shown that a gift for "mother" was intended for the testator's wife, whom he always described thus,[99] or that a gift by a childless testator to "my children" was intended for his step-children.[1]

2. Equivocations

(a) *Ambiguity*. Evidence of the testator's intention is admissible to explain an equivocation. There is said to be an equivocation or ambiguity in a will when there is a description of a person or thing which can apply equally well to two or more persons or things. Thus if a testator devises his close (enclosed land) "in the occupation of W" and he has two such closes, there is an equivocation.[2]

(b) *Latent or patent*. An ambiguity is said to be latent when the will is apparently perfect on the face of it, but on attempting to apply it an ambiguity appears. Extrinsic evidence of the testator's intention is always admissible to explain such an ambiguity. Thus if a testator makes a devise "to my son John" and leaves two sons of that name, extrinsic evidence is admissible to show that the testator believed the elder son to be dead and intended the land for the younger son.[3] An ambiguity is said to be patent when the will itself discloses that the description fits more than one person or thing. Extrinsic evidence of the testator's intention is often said to be inadmissible in the case of patent ambiguities, but this is not universally true, and the position is far from clear. Thus evidence of the testator's intention was admitted in one case where there was a gift to "George Gord the son of Gord," and other parts of the will showed that there were two men called Gord with sons named George.[4]

(c) *Intention*. Once extrinsic evidence of the testator's intention is admitted, it will be given effect to even if it shows that someone apparently outside

---

[98] *Boyes* v. *Cook* (1880) 14 Ch.D. 53 at 56, *per* James L.J.
[99] Consider *Thorn* v. *Dickens* [1906] W.N. 54 (where the entire will consisted of the words "All for mother").
[1] *Re Jeans* (1895) 72 L.T. 834.
[2] *Richardson* v. *Watson* (1833) 4 B. & Ad. 787.
[3] *Lord Cheyney's Case* (1591) 5 Co.Rep. 68a at 68b.
[4] *Doe* d. *Gord* v. *Needs* (1836) 2 M. & W. 129. The sidenote misses the point.

the scope of the gift was intended. Thus in one case in 1932[5] a testatrix gave part of her property "to my nephew Arthur Murphy." She had two legitimate nephews of that name, and extrinsic evidence was admitted to explain this ambiguity. The evidence admitted showed that the testatrix intended to benefit an illegitimate nephew called Arthur Murphy, and it was held that he took to the exclusion of the two legitimate nephews. Had there been only one legitimate and one illegitimate nephew, there would have been no ambiguity, for "nephew" prima facie means "legitimate nephew"; consequently no extrinsic evidence would have been admitted and the legitimate nephew would have taken.[6]

(d) *Uncertainty.* If extrinsic evidence fails to resolve an ambiguity, the gift is void for uncertainty.[7] The same applies where the description is on the face of it indefinite, *e.g.* a gift by a testator "to one of the sons of X," X having at the time several sons.[8]

3. Deaths after 1982. The foregoing rules are relaxed if the testator dies after 1982. In such cases, extrinsic evidence (including evidence of the testator's intention) is admissible to assist in the interpretation of a will in so far as (i) any part of the will is meaningless, or (ii) the language in any part of the will is ambiguous on the face of it,[9] or (iii) evidence (not being evidence of the testator's intention) shows that any of the language is ambiguous in the light of surrounding circumstances.[10]

C. Contradictions

1. Inconsistency. Extrinsic evidence is not admissible to explain a contradiction in a will, *e.g.* a gift of "one hundred pounds (£500) to X." In such a case, the rule is that the second expression prevails over the first[11] since it is the latest in the testator's mind; this contrasts with a deed, where the former of two inconsistent expressions prevails, for what has once been done cannot be undone. Before resorting to such a rule of thumb, however, the court tries to reconcile the two provisions in some way.[12]

2. Engrafted gift. An important example of such a reconciliation is the rule in *Lassence* v. *Tierney*,[13] which applies to deeds as well as to wills.[14] This rule has been stated as follows: "If you find an absolute gift to a legatee in the first instance, and trusts are engrafted or imposed on that absolute interest which

---

[5] *Re Jackson* [1933] Ch. 237.
[6] *Re Fish* [1894] 2 Ch. 83.
[7] *Richardson* v. *Watson, supra.*
[8] *Strode* v. *Russel* (1708) 2 Vern 621 at 624, 625.
[9] See *Re Williams* [1985] 1 W.L.R. 905.
[10] Administration of Justice Act 1982, s.21.
[11] *Re Hammond* [1938] 3 All E.R. 308.
[12] See, *e.g. Re Gare* [1952] Ch. 80; and see *post*, p. 292.
[13] (1849) 1 Mac. & G. 551.
[14] See *Att.-Gen.* v. *Lloyds Bank Ltd.* [1935] A.C. 382.

fail, either from lapse or invalidity or any other reason, then the absolute gift takes effect so far as the trusts have failed to the exclusion of the residuary legatee or next of kin as the case may be."[15] Thus suppose a gift to X of a fee simple or an absolute interest in personalty, with a direction later in the will or in a codicil that the property given to X shall be held for X for life with remainder to his children. If the gift to the children wholly or partly fails (*e.g.* through there being no children or through the perpetuity rule being infringed), the gift of the fee simple or absolute interest to X takes effect, instead of the property passing under a residuary gift or as on intestacy.[16] For the rule to apply, there must be an initial absolute gift which is subsequently cut down; one continuous limitation containing both gift and restrictions will normally not bring the doctrine into play,[17] nor will a gift in which the names of the beneficiaries are immediately followed by the words "subject to the provisions hereinafter contained."[18]

3. Unintended life interest. Another form of contradiction has now been resolved by statute for deaths after 1982. If a testator gives property to his spouse in words that would carry the absolute interest in it but also gives an interest in it to his issue by the same will, (*e.g.* "I give my wife everything and then my children are to have it"), it is now presumed, subject to any contrary intention, that the gift to the spouse is absolute and the issue take nothing.[19] Previously, such words would usually have given the surviving spouse only a life interest, and many testators (especially those with small estates) probably did not realise the effect of giving the spouse merely the income, with no capital.

D. A Will Speaks from Death

There are two aspects of the rule that a will speaks from death: statute applies it to property, and the courts have applied it to persons.

I. AS TO PROPERTY

As already mentioned,[20] a will is ambulatory. Subject to any contrary intention, it is to be construed, with reference to the property in it, as if it had been executed immediately before the testator's death.[21] A will is therefore capable of disposing of all property owned by the testator at his death even if he acquired it only after making his will. Thus a gift of "my shares in the XYZ Co., Ltd." includes not only those owned when the will was made but also those acquired subsequently[22]; and a devise of land carries with it all

---

[15] *Hancock* v. *Watson* [1902] A.C. 14 at 22, *per* Lord Davey.
[16] See *Watkins* v. *Weston* (1863) 3 De G.J. & S. 434.
[17] *Re Payne* [1927] 2 Ch. 1.
[18] *Re Cohen's W.T.* [1936] 1 All E.R. 103.
[19] Administration of Justice Act 1982, s.22.
[20] *Ante*, p. 138.
[21] Wills Act 1837, s.24.
[22] *Trinder* v. *Trinder* (1866) L.R. 1 Eq. 695; contrast *Re Tetsall* [1961] 1 W.L.R. 938 ("my 750 shares").

fixtures attached to the land, even if they were affixed after the will was made.[23]

However, while the rule applies to all generic descriptions (*i.e.* descriptions of a class of objects which may increase or decrease) and is not confined to general or residual gifts, it has no application to a gift of a specific object existing at the date of the will. Thus if a testator makes a will giving "my piano" to X and subsequently sells his piano and buys another, X has no claim to it.[24] The bequest is said to have been adeemed, a term applied to the failure of a gift by the property concerned ceasing to exist, or ceasing to belong to the testator, between the date of his will and his death.

II. AS TO PERSONS

It is only in some respects that a will is construed as speaking from death as to persons.

1. Class gifts. A class gift is a gift of property to all who come within some description, the property being divisible according to the number of persons in the class, such as a gift of £10,000 "equally between X's children who attain full age."[25]

(a) *Class fixed at death.* The rule of construction adopted by the courts in determining the effect of class gifts is the same as in other cases, namely, to carry out the intention of the testator as expressed in the will. In the absence of any such intention being expressed, such as a gift to children "whenever born,"[26] the primary rule is that if any member of the class is in existence at the testator's death, membership of the class is fixed at that moment, so that persons dying before the testator[27] or born after his death are excluded.[28] Thus under a gift to "all of my sisters", the sisters alive at the testator's death take to the exclusion of any born afterwards. In short, the will speaks from death.

(b) *Rule excluded.* There are, however, a number of secondary rules which should be mentioned.[29]

(1) NO MEMBER LIVING. If no member of the class is alive at the testator's death, the gift prima facie includes all members born at any future date.[30] Thus if a testator gives property "equally among A's children," a child born after the testator's death can claim a share only if A had no children at the testator's death.

[23] For fixtures, see *ante*, pp. 15 *et seq.*
[24] *Re Sikes* [1927] 1 Ch. 364.
[25] See *post*, p. 195.
[26] *Re Edmondson's W.T.* [1972] 1 W.L.R. 183.
[27] *Fitzroy* v. *Duke of Richmond* (1858) 28 L.J.Ch. 750.
[28] *Viner* v. *Francis* (1789) 2 Cox Eq. 190.
[29] See the summary in *Re Chartres* [1927] 1 Ch. 466 at 471, 472.
[30] *Weld* v. *Bradbury* (1715) 2 Vern 705.

(2) LIFE INTEREST EXISTING. If a life interest precedes the class gift (*e.g.* "to X for life, remainder to Y's children"), all those alive when the life interest ceases are entitled to share in the gift.[31] Further, those who survive the testator but die before the life interest ceases are included and their shares will pass under their wills or intestacies.[32] Similarly, if a valid direction for accumulation is made, the class does not close until the accumulations cease.[33]

(3) REVERSIONARY INTEREST GIVEN. Again, if a reversionary interest[34] is given by will, the class remains open until the interest falls into possession. Thus if property is settled on S for life with remainder to T absolutely, and T dies in S's lifetime, leaving his interest to X's children, all of X's children born before S's death are entitled to share in the gift.[35]

(4) CONDITIONAL GIFT. If a gift is contingent upon the beneficiaries fulfilling some condition, such as attaining the age of 21 years, the Rule in *Andrews* v. *Partington*[36] applies, and the class remains open until one member has fulfilled the condition; it then closes.[37] If one member has fulfilled the condition at the testator's death, the class is ascertained then.[38]

(c) *The principle.* The principle behind these rules (which apply to realty and personalty alike) has been said to be one of convenience rather than of construing the testator's intention.[39] As soon as any member of a class is entitled to call for his share, the class must be closed, for otherwise the size of the share to be given to him cannot be ascertained. But subject to this requirement, the class is kept open for as long as possible. Thus if property is given to A for life, remainder to all the testator's grandchildren who attain the age of 21 years, the class remains open until A has died and a grandchild is 21 years old; neither event by itself suffices to close the class.[40] The rules apply to settlements *inter vivos* as well as wills; and although they yield to a contrary intention, the standard is high, so that nothing will oust them except an intention which is inescapably incompatible with their operation.[41]

2. Gifts to individuals. In the case of gifts to individuals, the date of the will, and not the date of the testator's death, is normally the relevant time. Thus a gift "to the eldest son of my sister" is a gift to the eldest at the date of the will; if he dies before the testator, the gift lapses and the eldest son at the testator's death has no claim. Similarly, a bequest "to Lord Sherborne" is a

[31] *Re Knapp's Settlement* [1895] 1 Ch. 91 at 96.
[32] *Greenwood* v. *Greenwood* [1939] 2 All E.R. 150.
[33] *Re Stephens* [1904] 1 Ch. 322.
[34] See *post*, p. 163.
[35] *Walker* v. *Shore* (1808) 15 Ves. 122.
[36] (1791) 3 Bro.C.C. 401.
[37] *Re Bleckly* [1951] Ch. 740.
[38] *Picken* v. *Matthews* (1878) 10 Ch.D. 264.
[39] *Re Emmet's Estate* (1880) 13 Ch.D. 484 at 490. See generally (1954) 70 L.Q.R. 61 (J. H. C. Morris).
[40] *Re Paul's S.T.* [1920] 1 Ch. 99; and see generally M. & W. 532–535.
[41] *Re Clifford's S.T.* [1981] Ch. 63; see *Re Tom's Settlement* [1987] 1 W.L.R. 1021.

gift to the holder of the title at the date of the will.[42] But like all rules of construction, this yields to a contrary intention, and a legacy "to the Lord Mayor of London for the time being" operates as a gift to the person holding that office at the testator's death,[43] while a gift "to the Mayor of Lowestoft for the benefit of poor and needy fisherman of Lowestoft" takes effect as a gift to the Mayor of Lowestoft for the time being, and not as a gift to a particular person who is Mayor at a particular time.[44]

E. Exercise of Powers of Appointment

A general devise or bequest (*e.g.* "I give all my property to X") operates to exercise a general power of appointment unless a contrary intention is shown by the will.[45] On the other hand, a special power (which for this purpose includes a power to appoint to "anyone except X"[46]) is not exercised by a general bequest or devise unless the will shows a contrary intention, as by referring to the power or to the property concerned.[47]

Part 4

INTESTACY

The rules relating to intestacy must now be considered. If the deceased died wholly intestate, leaving no effective will, these rules govern the devolution of all his property, while if he died partly testate and partly intestate, they apply to all the property which does not pass under his will.

Before 1926, realty and personalty descended differently. All the realty vested in the heir, whereas the personalty devolved on the next-of-kin. Thus if a widower died intestate leaving three sons and four daughters, the eldest son was the heir and took all the realty, but all seven children shared the personalty equally. For realty, the rights of the heir were subject to the rights of the surviving spouse. Subject to certain conditions, a widower was entitled to curtesy (more fully, "an estate by the Curtesy of England"), which was a life interest in the whole of his wife's realty, while a widow was entitled to dower, which was a life interest in one-third in her husband's realty.[48]

In the case of deaths occurring after 1925, both realty and personalty devolve in the same way under the new code for intestacy; and for those dying after 1952, the Intestates' Estates Act 1952 made some important modifications to the new code, though leaving it basically unchanged. Today, the former rules[49] have to be considered very rarely for realty, and

---

[42] *Re Whorwood* (1887) 34 Ch.D. 446.
[43] *Re Daniels* (1918) 87 L.J.Ch. 661.
[44] *Re Pipe* (1937) 106 L.J.Ch. 252.
[45] Wills Act 1837, s.27.
[46] Contrast *post*, p. 200.
[47] *Re Ackerley* [1913] 1 Ch. 510 at 515.
[48] For curtesy and dower, see M. & W. 543–546.
[49] For these, see M. & W. (4th ed.) 509–523; and for a full review of the existing rules, see Law Com. W.P. No. 108 (1988).

almost never for personalty. Accordingly, only the new rules will be considered here, with merely a brief indication of the few cases in which the old rules survive.

Sect. 1. Intestacy after 1925

Where a person dies intestate after 1925, no distinction is made between realty and personalty. By the Administration of Estates Act 1925,[50] all property, whether real or personal, which does not already consist of money is held on trust for sale. The personal representatives of the deceased have power to postpone sale for such periods as they think proper. However, unless required for the purpose of administration for want of other assets, "personal chattels" (see below) are not to be sold without special reason, and reversionary interests (such as an interest in a trust fund which will not fall into the intestate's estate until the life interest of some third person has ceased) are similarly not to be sold without special reason.

Out of the fund thus produced, the personal representatives must pay all funeral, testamentary and administration expenses, debts and other liabilities, and set aside a fund to meet any pecuniary legacies[51] in cases where the deceased was only partly intestate. The residue must then be distributed to the persons beneficially entitled. The rules for this distribution were in the main laid down by the Administration of Estates Act 1925, but they have been substantially modified by subsequent legislation, notably the Intestates' Estates Act 1952, which did much to improve the position of the surviving spouse.[52] References to sections of the Act of 1925 are to the sections as they stand amended, and the rules are stated as they apply to deaths after 1966.[53]

1. The surviving spouse. The rights of the surviving spouse,[54] whether widow or widower, depend on whether the intestate left issue or any "near relations," a convenient term to describe the parents and brothers and sisters of the whole blood or their issue; but any of them who die before attaining the age of 18 years or marrying thereunder are then disregarded.[55] As usual, "issue" means any descendant however remote; and for deaths since 1988, it is in general irrelevant whether any relationship is legitimate or illegitimate.[56] The surviving spouse's rights depend on whether the intestate left issue; or left no issue but "near relations"; or left neither.[57] The three heads will be taken in turn.

---

[50] s.33(1).
[51] A.E.A. 1925, ss.33(2), 34(3).
[52] See I.E.A. 1952, s.4; Family Provision Act 1966, s.1; Administration of Justice Act 1977, s.28.
[53] But certain of the amounts have since been varied, as will be seen below.
[54] See *Re Collins* [1990] Fam. 56 (divorce: still "spouse" until decree absolute).
[55] A.E.A. 1925, ss.46(1), 47(1), (4).
[56] Family Law Reform Act 1987, s.18.
[57] A.E.A. 1925, s.46(1).

(a) *Head 1: issue.* If the intestate left issue (whether or not there are also any "near relations") the surviving spouse takes the following interests.

(1) THE PERSONAL CHATTELS ABSOLUTELY. "Personal chattels" are elaborately defined. They include horses, cars, domestic animals, plate, linen, china, books, pictures, prints, furniture, jewellery, "articles of household or personal use or ornament," and wines and consumable stores, but not chattels used for business purposes, money, or securities for money.[58] Roughly speaking, the phrase includes everything that goes to make a home, and rather more besides, but not the house itself: the phrase has a meaning quite distinct from "personalty" or "personal property."

(2) £75,000 ABSOLUTELY: a fixed net sum of £75,000, free of death duties and costs, with 6 per cent. interest thereon from the date of death until it is paid or appropriated.[59] In 1925 the sum was fixed at £1,000 with interest at 5 per cent., but subsequently provision was made for these figures to be altered by statutory instrument,[60] and after successive revisions, they now stand at the above figures.[61] Both the £75,000 and the interest thereon are charged on the residuary estate, though the interest is payable primarily out of income and not capital.[62]

(3) A LIFE INTEREST in half the residuary estate, thereby providing income but not capital.

(b) *Head 2: near relations but no issue.* If the intestate left one or more "near relations" but no issue, the surviving spouse takes the following interests.

(1) THE PERSONAL CHATTELS ABSOLUTELY.
(2) £125,000 ABSOLUTELY: a fixed net sum of £125,000,[63] free of death duties and costs, with interest as above.
(3) HALF THE RESIDUE ABSOLUTELY: half the residuary estate absolutely, thereby providing capital.

(c) *Head 3: neither issue nor near relations.* If the intestate left no issue and no "near relations," the surviving spouse is entitled to the entire residuary estate absolutely.

These provisions are subject to a number of subsidiary rules.

(1) PURCHASE OF LIFE INTEREST. Within 12 months of probate or letters of administration being first taken out (or within such extended period as the court may grant), a surviving spouse who takes a life interest may (even if a

---

[58] *Ibid.* s.55(1)(x).
[59] *Ibid.* s.46(1), as substituted by Intestates' Estates Act 1952, s.1.
[60] *Ibid.*; Family Provision Act 1966, s.1; Administration of Justice Act 1977, s.28.
[61] S.I. 1983, No. 1374, 1987 No. 799. For deaths between March 1, 1981, and June 1, 1987, the fixed net sum is £40,000: S.I. 1981 No. 255.
[62] A.E.A. 1925, s.46(1), (4).
[63] S.I. 1987 No. 799. For deaths between March 1, 1981, and June 1, 1987, the fixed net sum is £85,000: S.I. 1981, No. 255.

minor) by notice in writing to the personal representatives elect that his or her life interest shall be purchased for a capital sum reckoned in accordance with special rules.[64] If the surviving spouse is the sole personal representative, written notice must be given to the Senior Registrar of the Family Division.[65]

(2) PURCHASE OF MATRIMONIAL HOME. The surviving spouse may by writing require the personal representatives (even if he or she is one of them) to appropriate to him or her any dwelling-house forming part of the residuary estate in which he or she was resident at the death of the intestate; usually this will be the matrimonial home.[66] This does not apply where the intestate's interest in the house is a mere tenancy which would determine (or could be determined by the landlord) within two years of his death, nor where the house is part of larger property held by the intestate unless the court is satisfied that the exercise of the surviving spouse's right is not likely to diminish the value of assets in the residuary estate or make them more difficult to dispose of. These provisions of the Act of 1952 in effect give the surviving spouse a power to compel the personal representatives to exercise in respect of the house the general discretionary power of appropriation conferred by the Act of 1925.[67] The property appropriated is taken, at a proper valuation when appropriated (not at the death),[68] to have satisfied to that extent the property to which the surviving spouse is absolutely entitled. However, if the house is worth more than the surviving spouse's interest such spouse can still require the house to be transferred to him or her partly in satisfaction of his or her interests in the estate and partly for money.[69] The personal representatives must not unnecessarily sell the house within 12 months after probate or letters of administration are first taken out, and the surviving spouse's right to require an appropriation is exercisable only during that period or any extension granted by the court.[70]

(3) PARTIAL INTESTACY. Under the Act of 1952, the sums of £75,000 or £125,000 mentioned above must be diminished by the value of any beneficial interest acquired by the surviving spouse under the will of the deceased.[71] If, for example, the surviving spouse is given a life interest under the will, and the rest of the property is undisposed of, the spouse may at once claim the £75,000 or £125,000 less the actuarial value of the life interest.[72] Alternatively, the surviving spouse may prefer to disclaim the testamentary life interest and take under the intestacy alone.[73]

---

[64] See Intestate Succession (Interest and Capitalisation) Order 1977, S.I. No. 1491.
[65] A.E.A. 1925, s.47A; Supreme Court Act 1981, Sched. 5.
[66] I.E.A. 1952, Sched. 2.
[67] By s.41.
[68] *Re Collins* [1975] 1 W.L.R. 309.
[69] *Re Phelps* [1980] Ch. 275.
[70] I.E.A. 1952, Sched. 2.
[71] A.E.A. 1925, s.49(1)(*aa*).
[72] *Re Bowen-Buscarlet's W.T.* [1972] Ch. 463.
[73] See *Re Sullivan* [1930] 1 Ch. 84; *Re Thornber* [1937] Ch. 29.

(4) SEPARATION. If husband and wife are separated by a decree of judicial separation and the separation is continuing, any property in respect of which either of them dies intestate will devolve as if the other were already dead.[74]

(5) COMMORIENTES. Although the general rule laid down for commorientes[75] applies in general to intestacy, the Act of 1952 has modified its application as between husband and wife. When the intestate and his or her spouse die in circumstances rendering it uncertain which survived the other, the rules of intestacy apply as if the spouse had not survived the intestate.[76] Thus if the wife, W, is younger than the husband, H, and both perish in a common disaster, then for the purposes of H's intestacy W will be treated as not having survived him. This avoids W taking benefits under H's intestacy which would almost instantly pass under her will or intestacy (probably to her side of the family if she had no issue). H's property accordingly passes as if no spouse had survived him, and so does W's. This exception to the general rule is confined to intestacy as between spouses; it does not affect wills, nor does it apply to other relations, *e.g.* issue.

2. The issue. Subject to the rights of the surviving spouse, if any, the property is held on the statutory trusts for the issue.[77] Under these trusts, the property is held upon trust for all the children of the deceased living at his death in equal shares, subject to three qualifications.

(a) *Subject to representation.* This means subject to the rule that issue of a deceased child stand in his shoes and take his share; descent is thus *per stirpes* (through the stocks of descent) and not *per capita* (one share for each head).

(b) *Subject to the rule that no issue attains a vested interest until he is 18 years old[78] or married.* This in effect means that if a minor dies without having married, the property must be dealt with from that moment as if the minor had never existed.[79] Thus if X dies leaving a widow and minor son, the widow takes a life interest in half of the residue. If the son dies before either marrying or attaining his majority, the widow forthwith takes absolutely either half the residue, or all, depending on whether any "near relations" survived X.

(c) *Subject to hotchpot.* There are two rules governing this.

(1) INTER VIVOS. If they wish to share in the distribution of the estate, children (but not remoter issue) must bring into account any money or property which the deceased has in his lifetime paid them or settled for their benefit by way of advancement or upon marriage.[80] For example, if the

---

[74] Matrimonial Causes Act 1973, s.18(2), replacing Matrimonial Proceedings and Property Act 1970, s.40, applying to deaths after July 31, 1970.
[75] See *ante*, p. 148.
[76] A.E.A. 1925, s.46(3), added by I.E.A. 1952, s.1(4).
[77] A.E.A. 1925, s.46(1).
[78] Family Law Reform Act 1969, s.3(2). For deaths before 1970 the age is 21.
[79] See A.E.A. 1925, s.47(2).
[80] *Ibid.* s.47(1).

estate is worth £160,000 and there are three children, one of whom has received an advancement of £20,000 in the intestate's lifetime, that child can claim only £40,000 out of the £160,000; the other two children each receive £60,000. Had the first child received an advancement of £100,000 he could not be compelled to refund any part of it for distribution between the others. The obligation to bring property into hotchpot is subject to any contrary intention appearing from the circumstances of the case. In determining what advances must be brought into hotchpot, a distinction must be made between payments made to start a child in life, and casual or periodical sums paid in the ordinary course of events, or so as to relieve the child from temporary difficulties; the former alone need be brought into hotchpot.[81]

(2) PARTIAL INTESTACY. In the case of partial intestacy, issue of the deceased, whether children or remoter descendants, must, subject to any contrary intention shown by the deceased, bring into hotchpot any benefit received by him or his issue under his will.[82] Thus if a grandchild of the deceased has received £10,000 from him, neither he nor his parent need bring it into hotchpot if it was an advancement made *inter vivos* (for he is not a child of the deceased), but it must be brought into account if it is given him by will.

If no issue attains a vested interest, then, subject to the claims of the surviving spouse (if any), the relatives of the deceased are entitled in the following order[83]; any member of one class who takes a vested interest excludes all members of subsequent classes.

3. The parents of the deceased are entitled in equal shares absolutely; if one is dead, the survivor is entitled absolutely.

4. The brothers and sisters of the whole blood, on the statutory trusts.

A division must be made here, for at this point the "near relations" end. Those included in the foregoing classes may take an interest even though the intestate left a surviving spouse; those in the subsequent classes cannot.

5. The brothers and sisters of the half blood, on the statutory trusts.

6. The grandparents, if more than one in equal shares.

7. The uncles and aunts of the whole blood, on the statutory trusts.

8. The uncles and aunts of the half blood, on the statutory trusts.

9. The Crown (or the Duchy of Lancaster or Duke of Cornwall) as *bona vacantia* in lieu of any right to escheat.

---

[81] See *Taylor* v. *Taylor* (1875) L.R. 20 Eq. 155 at 157; *Re Hayward* [1957] Ch. 528.
[82] A.E.A. 1925, s.49; see *Re Grover's W.T.* [1971] Ch. 168.
[83] A.E.A. 1925, s.46(1).

A number of points arise on the foregoing list.

(1) STATUTORY TRUSTS. The statutory trusts for the brothers, sisters, uncles and aunts are the same as those for the issue of the deceased, save that the provisions relating to hotchpot do not apply.[84] Thus deceased brothers, sisters, uncles and aunts are represented by their descendants, whose interests in every case are contingent upon their attaining full age or marrying. "Uncles" and "aunts" include only blood relations, and so the wife of a mother's brother, though called "aunt", has no claim: marriage is not blood.

(2) ILLEGITIMATE CHILDREN. Where the intestate dies after 1969 but before April 4, 1988, an illegitimate child (or his issue if he is dead) can take on the intestacy of either parent as if he had been born legitimate; and similarly on his intestacy each of his parents (if surviving) can take.[85] These provisions do not extend to other illegitimate relationships, or to any claim to an entailed interest. But for intestates dying after April 3, 1988, a far more general provision has been made. In such cases, it does not matter if the claimant, or anyone through whom his relationship is deduced, is illegitimate.[86] For these purposes, however, there is a rebuttable presumption that the father of an illegitimate person (and anyone related to him solely through his father) predeceased him.[87]

(3) ADOPTED CHILDREN. A formal adoption order (as distinct from a mere *de facto* adoption) puts both child and adoptive parents in the same position for all subsequent intestacies as if the child were their child, born in lawful wedlock, and not the child of any other person.[88] This does not apply to the descent of a peerage or of property limited to devolve with it.[89]

(4) CROWN DISCRETION. In practice, the Crown modifies its strict rights under head No. 9 by making provision for dependants of the deceased, whether related to him or not, and for others for whom he might reasonably have been expected to make provision. This purely discretionary power, which the Act of 1925 confirms,[90] is made all the more necessary by the Crown's increased prospects of succeeding to property of an intestate.[91] Before 1926, any relation, however remote, could claim as heir or next-of-kin, and mesne lords could claim land by escheat. After 1925, no relation more remote than a grandparent can claim, and there can be no escheat to a mesne lord on intestacy.

[84] A.E.A. 1925, s.47(3).
[85] Family Law Reform Act 1969, s.14.
[86] Family Law Reform Act 1987, ss.1, 18(1); S.I. 1988, No. 425.
[87] *Ibid.* s.18(2).
[88] Adoption Act 1976, ss.38–46; S.I. 1987, No. 1242.
[89] *Ibid.* s.44.
[90] A.E.A. 1925, s.46(1).
[91] See N. D. Ing, *Bona Vacantia* (1971) pp. 104–109.

Sect. 2. Survival of the Old Rules

I. REALTY

In the case of all persons dying after 1925, the foregoing rules supersede the old rules relating to intestacy, and no curtesy or dower can arise in favour of the surviving spouse.[92] However, the old general law of descent of realty still has to be applied in three cases.

1. Mental patient: any realty (including an interest under a trust for sale of realty[93]) which a mental patient of full age at the end of 1925 then owned, and as to which he subsequently dies intestate without having recovered testamentary capacity, descends according to the general law in force before 1926.[94] Curtesy and dower can still arise in such cases.

2. Entail: an entail not disposed of by the will of the deceased descends in accordance with the general law in force before 1926.[95] It is curious that while curtesy can still arise out of such an interest,[96] dower cannot.[97]

3. Limitation to heir: if property is limited after 1925, whether *inter vivos* or by will, to the heir of a deceased person, it passes to the heir according to the general law in force before 1926.[98] This is not a case of descent on intestacy, for the heir takes as purchaser.

II. PERSONALTY

In the case of personalty, the old rules[99] never apply to deaths after 1925. These rules still retain some of their importance, however, particularly in showing title to leaseholds, and in the practice of reversion conveyancing. Thus, if in 1920 personalty was settled upon A for life with remainder to B absolutely, and B died intestate in 1925, B's reversion (which is called by this name, although technically a remainder) passed to his next-of-kin. If the person at present entitled to B's reversion (A still being alive) wishes to sell or mortgage it, he will have to prove that he is duly entitled to it, thus invoking the old rules of intestacy.

[92] A.E.A. 1925, s.45(1).
[93] And including former copyholds: *Re Sirett* [1969] 1 W.L.R. 60.
[94] A.E.A. 1925, s.51(2); see *Re Bradshaw* [1950] Ch. 582.
[95] L.P.A. 1925, s.130(4); A.E.A. 1925, s.51(4).
[96] L.P.A. 1925, s.130(4).
[97] See A.E.A. 1925, s.45(1).
[98] L.P.A. 1925, s.132; A.E.A. 1925, s.51(1).
[99] See M. & W. 546–548, or 5th ed. of this book, pp. 274–277.

Part 5

PERSONAL REPRESENTATIVES

Sect. 1. Introductory

1. Vesting of property. The beneficial devolution of property on death has been considered above; it is now necessary to discuss the means by which the property becomes vested in those beneficially entitled. The general rule today is that all property first vests in the personal representatives of the deceased, who in due course (and normally within the "executor's year," *i.e.* one year from the death) are required to transfer to the beneficiaries any of the property not required in the due administration of the estate, *e.g.* for payment of debts. In this context "estate" is used not in the technical sense of an estate in land, but as a collective expression for the sum total of the assets and liabilities of the deceased.

2. Executors. "Personal representatives" is a phrase which includes both executors and administrators. If a person makes a will, he may (but need not) appoint one or more persons to be his executor or executors, with the duty of paying debts, inheritance tax and funeral expenses, and ultimately of distributing the estate to those entitled. The executor derives his powers from the will,[1] although he must obtain confirmation of his position by "proving the will," *i.e.* obtaining a grant of probate from the court. If a sole or only surviving executor who has obtained probate dies, having himself appointed an executor, the latter, on proving the original executor's will, becomes executor of the original testator also. This "chain of representation" may be continued indefinitely until broken by failure to appoint an executor, or failure of an executor to obtain a grant of probate.[2]

3. Administrators. If a person dies without having appointed an executor, or if none of the executors he has appointed is able and willing to act, application must be made to the court by some person or persons interested in the estate for "letters of administration" appointing an administrator or administrators. The duties of an administrator are substantially the same as those of an executor. If the deceased left no will, simple administration is granted; if he left a will, the grant is of administration *cum testamento annexo* ("with the will annexed").[3] A grant may be limited in any way the court thinks fit,[4] so that there may be a grant confined to settled land, or a grant "save and except" settled land,[5] or a grant *durante minore aetate* ("during the minority" of the sole executor).[6] There is no "chain of representation" for

[1] *Biles* v. *Caesar* [1957] 1 W.L.R. 156.
[2] See A.E.A. 1925, s.7.
[3] Supreme Court Act 1981, s.119.
[4] *Ibid.* s.113.
[5] See A.E.A. 1925, s.23.
[6] Supreme Court Act 1981, ss.116, 118.

administrators. If a sole or last surviving administrator dies without completing the administration of the estate, application must be made for a grant of administration *de bonis non administratis* (more shortly, *de bonis non*), which is a grant "in respect of the goods left unadministered."

Sect. 2. Devolution of Property on Personal Representatives

1. The background.[7] Before the Land Transfer Act 1897, all personalty (including leaseholds) vested in the personal representatives, whilst all realty passed immediately to the heir or devisee as the case might be. The Act made the "personal" representatives also "real" representatives, so that a testator's realty as well as his personalty vested in his executors.

2. Vesting. The Administration of Estates Act 1925 substantially repeats the provisions of the Land Transfer Act 1897. In the case of deaths after 1925, all land owned by the deceased, whether freehold or leasehold, vests in the personal representatives,[8] with the following exceptions:

  (i) Entails, unless disposed of by the deceased's will.[9]
 (ii) Property to which the deceased was entitled as a joint tenant.[10]
(iii) Property to which the deceased was entitled as a corporation sole.[11]
 (iv) Interests which ceased on the death of the deceased, such as an interest for his life.[12]

As before 1926, property subject to a general power of appointment exercised by the will of the deceased passes to his personal representatives.[13] On an intestacy, both realty and personalty vest in the Probate judge (*i.e.* the President of the Family Division) until administration is granted.[13a]

3. Assents. Before 1926 the personal representatives, subject to the due administration of the estate, held the property of the deceased on trust for those beneficially entitled, who could call for it to be transferred to them.[14] In the case of realty, any transfer to the heir had to be made by conveyance, but a transfer to a devisee could be by either a conveyance or an assent.[15] An assent did not even need to be in writing: any conduct by the executors which showed that they assented to the gift would suffice, as by letting the devisee take possession of the land.[16] This sometimes created difficulties, since an

---

[7] See further M. & W. 558–561.
[8] A.E.A. 1925, ss.1(1), 3(1). For legal estates in settled land, see *post*, pp. 231–233.
[9] *Ibid.* s.3(3).
[10] *Ibid.* s.3(4).
[11] *Ibid.* s.3(5).
[12] *Ibid.* s.1(1).
[13] *Ibid.* s.3(2).
[13a] *Ibid.* ss.9, 55(1) (xv), as amended by Administration of Justice Act 1970, s.1, Sched. 2, para. 5. See e.g. *Wirral B.C.* v. *Smith* (1982) 43 P. & C.R. 312.
[14] Land Transfer Act 1897, s.2(1); but see *post*, p. 166.
[15] *Ibid.* s.3(1).
[16] *Wise* v. *Whitburn* [1924] 1 Ch. 460.

essential link in a title might consist of disputable facts rather than a clear transaction on the face of the title deeds.

After 1925 an assent is no longer a mere recognition by the personal representatives that the land is not needed by them (*e.g.* for the payment of debts), but is a conveyance which vests the estate in the person named. Accordingly it was provided that no assent made after 1925 (even if the deceased died before 1926) will pass a legal estate in land unless it is in writing and signed by the personal representatives.[17] A written assent is also required when a legal estate is not transferred but is to be held in a different capacity, as where personal representatives, having completed their administration, begin to hold as trustees under any trusts in the will.[18] But an assent to the vesting of an equitable interest still need not be in writing, and may be inferred from conduct.[19] A bona fide purchaser for value is no longer concerned with the terms of the will; he can rely on the grant of probate or letters of administration, coupled with an assent or conveyance executed by the personal representatives, as constituting his title.[20]

4. Ownership of assets. While the administration is proceeding, the personal representatives are the legal and equitable owners of all assets not specifically devised and bequeathed. The beneficiaries entitled to residue have no interest, legal or equitable, in any specific assets. They merely have the right to compel the personal representatives to administer the estate properly.[21]

5. Powers. Personal representatives now have all the powers of trustees for sale,[22] and thus all the powers of a tenant for life and trustees under the Settled Land Act 1925.[23] On a sale they will thus overreach all the beneficial interests under the will or intestacy. Although they should sell the property only if this is necessary for the purposes of administration, a conveyance to a purchaser for value in good faith is not invalidated merely because he knows that all the debts and other liabilities have been met.[24] Nor is a conveyance to a purchaser for value in good faith invalidated merely because the probate or letters of administration under which the personal representatives acted are subsequently revoked.[25]

Personal representatives have joint and several powers over pure personalty but they have only joint authority over realty and leaseholds.[26]

---

[17] A.E.A. 1925, s.36(2), (4).
[18] *Re King's W.T.* [1964] Ch. 542, a controversial decision.
[19] *Re Edwards' W.T.* [1982] Ch. 30 at 40.
[20] A.E.A. 1925, ss.36(4), (7), 39(1).
[21] *Commissioner of Stamp Duties (Queensland)* v. *Livingston* [1965] A.C. 694; *Re Hayes' W.T.* [1971] 1 W.L.R. 758 at 764.
[22] A.E.A. 1925, s.39.
[23] *Post*, pp. 241 *et seq*. *Quaere* whether they have "*ad hoc*" powers (see *post*, pp. 262 *et seq*.) as being "approved or appointed by the court."
[24] A.E.A. 1925, ss.36(8), 55(1) (xviii).
[25] *Ibid*. ss.37, 55(1)(xviii), retrospectively confirming *Hewson* v. *Shelley* [1914] 2 Ch. 13.
[26] A.E.A. 1925, s.2(2); *Fountain Forestry Ltd.* v. *Edwards* [1975] Ch. 1.

Sect. 3. Number of Personal Representatives

1. Maximum. No grant of probate or letters of administration can be made to more than four personal representatives in respect of the same property.[26a] If a testator appoints more than four executors, they must decide among themselves who will apply for probate.

2. Minimum. Unlike trustees for sale, there is no provision preventing a sole personal representative from giving a valid receipt for purchase money; a sole personal representative, whether original or by survivorship, has full power to give valid receipts for capital money or any other payments.[27] However, if any person interested in the estate is a minor or has a life interest in it, the court must normally not appoint a sole administrator, other than a trust corporation.[28] A sole executor can act under such circumstances, but the court has power to appoint additional personal representatives.[29]

Part 6

DISABILITIES

Certain persons are subject to disabilities as to the interests in land which they can hold, create or alienate. Formerly, the list of such persons was more extensive than it is today, including married women, certain convicts and aliens.[30] These disabilities no longer exist, and this Part will be confined to those disabilities that remain.

Sect. 1. Minors

A minor (formerly called an infant[31]) is a person who has not attained full age. For centuries,[32] a person attained full age or "majority" at the first moment of the day preceding the twenty-first anniversary of his birth.[33] On January 1, 1970, the age of majority was reduced to 18 years,[34] and this is now reached at the first moment of the eighteenth anniversary of birth,[35] The following are the main points to note.

1. Ownership of land. Before 1926, a minor was capable of holding both

---

[26a] Supreme Court Act 1981, s.114.
[27] L.P.A. 1925, s.27(2).
[28] Supreme Court Act 1981, s.114(2).
[29] *Ibid.* s.114(4).
[30] See M. & W. 1020–1027.
[31] See Family Law Reform Act 1969, s.12.
[32] See 3 H.E.L. 510, 511 for the development of the rule in the Middle Ages.
[33] See, *e.g. Re Shurey* [1918] 1 Ch. 263.
[34] Family Law Reform Act 1969, s.1; S.I. 1969, No. 1140.
[35] Family Law Reform Act 1969, s.9.

legal estates and equitable interests in land. After 1925, a minor cannot hold a legal estate in land,[36] although he may still hold equitable interests.

2. Attempted conveyance to a minor. An attempt after 1925 to convey a legal estate to a minor alone or jointly with other minors operates as a contract for value to make a proper settlement by means of a vesting deed and trust instrument, and in the meantime to hold the land in trust for the minor or minors.[37] An attempted conveyance of a legal estate to a minor jointly with a person of full age vests the legal estate in the person of full age on the statutory trusts (*i.e.* the trust for sale implied in the case of a tenancy in common[38]) for himself and the minor.[39] These provisions do not apply to a conveyance to a minor as mortgagee or trustee, for which special provisions are made.[40]

3. Mortgages. A minor cannot be a legal mortgagee after 1925. An attempt to grant a legal mortgage to one or more persons who are all minors operates as an agreement for value to execute a proper mortgage when the minor or minors are of full age, and in the meantime to hold the beneficial interest in trust for those intended to benefit.[41] A mortgage to a minor and other persons of full age operates, so far as the legal estate is concerned, as if the minor were not named, although his beneficial interest is not affected.[42]

4. Personal representatives. A minor can be neither an executor[43] nor an administrator[44]; this was so before 1926.[45] If a minor would, but for his minority, be entitled to be an administrator, or is appointed sole executor, he cannot take a grant until he is of full age; in the meantime a grant may be taken by someone on his behalf, *e.g.* his guardian. In the case of administration, the grant must be made to at least two persons or a trust corporation on the minor's behalf, since a minor is interested in the estate.[46] If a minor is appointed one of several executors, the rest of whom are of full age, he must wait until he attains his majority, when he can join in the grant of probate previously made to the others.

5. Trustees. No minor can be appointed a trustee after 1925.[47] This applies

[36] L.P.A. 1925, s.1(6). Under elaborate transitional provisions, legal estates vested in minors at the end of 1925 became vested in persons of full age on January 1, 1926: L.P.A. 1925, Sched. 1, Pt. III; S.L.A. 1925, Sched. 2, para. 3.
[37] S.L.A. 1925, s.27(1) (a statutory exception to the equitable rule that an imperfect voluntary conveyance will not be treated as a declaration of trust: *post*, p. 269).
[38] *Post*, p. 289.
[39] L.P.A. 1925, s.19(2).
[40] See *infra.*
[41] L.P.A. 1925, s.19(6).
[42] *Ibid.*
[43] Supreme Court Act 1981, s.118.
[44] *In b. Manuel* (1849) 13 Jur. 664.
[45] J.A. 1925, s.165, replacing A.E.A. 1798, s.6, with amendments.
[46] See above.
[47] L.P.A. 1925, s.20.

to trusts of any property, real or personal. If there is a purported conveyance of a legal estate in land to a minor as trustee, the effect is as follows:

(i) If the minor is a sole trustee, the conveyance operates as a declaration of trust by the grantor; the effect is the same if the conveyance is to two or more trustees, all of whom are minors.[48]

(ii) If the minor is one of two or more trustees, at least one of whom is of full age, the conveyance operates as if the minor were not named, although this does not prejudice any beneficial interest thereby given to him.[49]

These provisions do not prevent a minor from becoming a trustee of property other than a legal estate in land in other ways, *e.g.* under a resulting or constructive trust.[50]

6. Settled land. As was the case before 1926, land to which a minor is entitled in possession is deemed to be settled land.[51] This is so even if the minor is absolutely entitled. In such a case, the statutory powers before 1926 were exercisable by the trustees of the settlement,[52] although the legal estate might still be vested in the minor. After 1925, both the legal estate and the statutory powers are vested in the statutory owner.[53]

7. Voidable dispositions. Any disposition by a minor of any interest in land is voidable at the option of the minor (but not of the grantee[54]) on the minor attaining his majority,[55] or within a reasonable time thereafter[56]; if the minor dies under age, his personal representatives may avoid the disposition within a reasonable time.[57] The same rule applied before 1926. As the disposition is voidable and not void, it is binding if the minor fails to repudiate it within a reasonable time after attaining his majority.[58]

8. Transfer on death. Although normally any equitable interest vested in a minor will pass on his death under his will (exceptionally) or intestacy, there is one exception. By the Administration of Estates Act 1925, s.51(3), if a minor who dies after 1925 without ever having married was entitled at his death under a settlement to a vested equitable interest in land in fee simple, or an absolute interest in property settled to devolve with such land or as freehold land, he is deemed to have had an entailed interest.

The objects of this somewhat strange subsection appear to be—

[48] *Ibid.* s.19(4).
[49] *Ibid.* s.19(5).
[50] *Re Vinogradoff* [1935] W.N. 68.
[51] *Post* p. 224.
[52] S.L.A. 1882, ss.59, 60.
[53] *Post*, p. 224.
[54] *Zouch* d. *Abbot* v. *Parsons* (1765) 3 Burr. 1794.
[55] *Ashfeild* v. *Ashfeild* (1628) W.Jo. 157.
[56] *Carnell* v. *Harrison* [1916] 1 Ch. 328.
[57] 4 Cru.Dig. 69.
[58] *Edwards* v. *Carter* [1893] A.C. 360.

    (i) to make it unnecessary always to take out a grant of administration to the minor's estate; and

    (ii) to make the land revert to the donor.

For example, if D settled land on A for life with remainder to B (a minor) in fee simple, and B died a minor without having married, he is deemed to have had an entail. Since he can have had no legitimate children, his notional entail comes to an end[59] and D is entitled to the fee simple, subject to A's life interest. This is probably closer to D's intentions than that the land should pass under B's intestacy to, perhaps, his father or uncle. Further, no grant of probate or administration to B's estate is needed in respect of the land. But if B had married, then whether or not he had issue, the subsection would not apply and the land would pass under his will or intestacy.

It is not clear to what extent this provision restricts the power of disposition over realty given by the Wills (Soldiers and Sailors) Act 1918 to minors who are soldiers or members of the Air Force in actual military service, or mariners at sea[60]; read literally, it deprives them of any testamentary power over realty until they marry, since a minor cannot bar an entail by will.[61]

9. Leases. Although a legal estate cannot be vested in a minor, a beneficial interest in a lease granted to a minor can only be enjoyed by him subject to the obligations attached to the lease. Further, unless he repudiates the lease within a reasonable time after attaining his majority, he is bound by it.[62] Even if he repudiates the lease, he cannot recover the rent he has paid.[63]

Sect. 2. Mental Patients

If a person is suffering from a mental disorder there are two points to consider: first, some control may have to be exercised over his person, and second, someone must be appointed to manage his property. Only the second of these points is relevant here.

1. Control over property

(a) *Jurisdiction.* Ever since the statute *De Prerogativa Regis* 1324 the Crown has exercised a jurisdiction over the property of mental patients (formerly called lunatics, and then persons of unsound mind). The current statute is the Mental Health Act 1983.[64] At present the jurisdiction is exercised by one or more nominated judges of the Chancery Division. In practice, the work is done by an office of the Supreme Court called "the Court of Protection" under a Master, subject to appeal to the judge.[65] The

---

[59] But consider Family Law Reform Act 1987, s.19.
[60] *Ante*, p. 144.
[61] *Ante*, p. 43.
[62] *Davies* v. *Beynon-Harris* (1931) 47 T.L.R. 424.
[63] *Valentini* v. *Canali* (1889) 24 Q.B.D. 166.
[64] Replacing Mental Health Act 1959, which in turn replaced Lunacy Act 1890.
[65] Mental Health Act 1983, ss.93, 94, 105.

jurisdiction is exercisable over any person who is "incapable, by reason of mental disorder, of managing and administering his property and affairs."[66] The normal course of events is for the Court of Protection to appoint a receiver for the patient (usually a near relation), and for the receiver to exercise wide powers under the supervision of the court, including the disposition of property, the management of a business and the conduct of litigation.[67]

(b) *Settlements.* As well as managing the property in the interests of the patient, the court is empowered to make dispositions and other transactions for the benefit of the patient's family or other persons for whom he might have been expected to provide whether in his lifetime or at his death.[68] Thus the court may authorise the making of a settlement[69] or a will[70] by the patient.

2. Capacity

(a) *After proceedings.* If a receiver has been appointed, the patient ceases to have any capacity to deal with his property.[71] He remains the owner but control has been taken from him. Thus even in a lucid interval, any disposition by him is void,[72] although a will made during a lucid interval is valid.[73]

(b) *Before proceedings.* If there are no proceedings on foot in the Court of Protection, a voluntary disposition of property by the patient is absolutely void unless made with a sufficient understanding of the effect of the gift.[74] A disposition for value is normally not void, but voidable, *i.e.* it remains valid until set aside; however, if the disposition is made during a lucid interval, or takes effect in favour of a person not aware of the mental disorder, it is valid.[75]

3. Enduring powers of attorney. The Enduring Powers of Attorney Act 1985 has now provided a means of avoiding some of the expense and complication of applying for the appointment of a receiver. Under this Act, a power of attorney may now be granted which, unlike an ordinary power of attorney, will not be revoked by any supervening mental incapacity of the donor.[76] Such a power must be granted in the prescribed form, and be executed by both donor and donee[77]; and such a power may be granted even

---

[66] *Ibid.* s.94(2).
[67] *Ibid.* s.99.
[68] *Ibid.* ss.95, 96.
[69] *Ibid.* s.96(1)(d).
[70] *Ibid.* s.96(1)(e). See *Re D.(J.)* [1982] Ch. 237 for the principles.
[71] *Re Walker* [1905] 1 Ch. 160; *Re Marshall* [1920] 1 Ch. 284.
[72] *Re Walker, supra.*
[73] *In b. Walker* (1912) 28 T.L.R. 466; *Re Beaney* [1978] 1 W.L.R. 770 at 772.
[74] *Re Beaney* [1978] 1 W.L.R. 770.
[75] *Imperial Loan Co. Ltd.* v. *Stone* [1892] 1 Q.B. 500; *Hart* v. *O'Connor* [1985] A.C. 1000.
[76] Enduring Powers of Attorney Act 1985, s.1.
[77] *Ibid.* s.2.

by a donor who is suffering from a mental disorder, provided he understands the nature and effect of the power.[78] It may confer an authority which either is general or is limited to specified matters.[79] If the attorney believes that the donor is, or is becoming, mentally incapable, he must promptly apply to the Court of Protection for registration of the power, giving notice of the application to the donor and specified relatives, and so enabling them to object on certain specified grounds.[80] Any supervening incapacity precludes the attorney from exercising any of his powers except under the authority of the court.[81] The Act thus enables a patient to arrange for his affairs to be managed by a person of his own choice, subject to safeguards.

Sect. 3. Corporations

1. Mortmain. By the Mortmain and Charitable Uses Act 1888, an assurance to a corporation which had no authority to hold land, either by statute or by licence from the Crown (called a licence in mortmain), made the land, whether freehold or leasehold, liable to forfeiture by the Crown[82]; but any mesne lords were entitled to enter within a reasonable time, and so secure the forfeiture instead.

2. Origin. This rule had its origin in Magna Carta 1215. Its purpose was to restrict conveyances to monasteries, for inasmuch as corporations never died or married and were never minors or convicted of felony, many valuable feudal incidents would have been lost by a conveyance into mortmain ("dead hand"). With changing conditions, many statutory exceptions were made, but although in modern times few corporations were caught by the rule, it could not be disregarded; in all cases it was essential to ascertain that the corporation concerned had authority to hold land.

3. Abolition. The law of mortmain was out of accord with modern ideas, and on July 29, 1960 it was abolished.[83] Today, no disposition to a corporation makes the land liable to forfeiture for mortmain.

4. Dispositions. In general, a corporation which has power to hold land has also the power to dispose of it. This rule is subject to certain exceptions: thus dispositions by the Universities and colleges of Oxford, Cambridge and Durham are restricted by provisions somewhat similar to those which regulate dispositions by tenants for life.[84]

---

[78] *Re K.* [1988] Ch. 310.
[79] Enduring Powers of Attorney Act 1985, s.3.
[80] *Ibid.* ss.4, 6(5), Sched. 1.
[81] *Ibid.* s.1.
[82] *Att.-Gen.* v. *Parsons* [1956] A.C. 421.
[83] Charities Act 1960, s.38.
[84] Universities and College Estates Acts 1925 and 1964.

Sect. 4. Charities

Formerly there were complex and far-reaching restrictions on dispositions to a charity and by a charity. These have been drastically curtailed by the Charities Act 1960. The present position is as follows.

1. Dispositions to a charity. Formerly assurances *inter vivos* to a charity were subject to one set of conditions and gifts by will to another. These have all been repealed, and there are now no special restrictions on such dispositions.[85]

2. Dispositions by a charity. Land held on charitable trusts is settled land, and the trustees have all the powers given by the Settled Land Act 1925 to a tenant for life and trustees of the settlement.[86] This provision does not make the land settled land for all purposes. Thus it does not require a conveyance to a charity to be made by a vesting deed and a trust instrument, nor does it disable a sole trustee from giving a good receipt for capital money if the scheme governing the charity authorises this.[87] But the powers that it gives are exercisable only subject to important restrictions. No land which forms part of the permanent endowment of the charity, or is or has been occupied by the charity, may be disposed of in any way without an order of the court or the Charity Commissioners. Other land (*e.g.* land held for investment purposes) is free from those restrictions; and even where they apply, leases granted for not more than 22 years without a fine, and any dispositions of an advowson, are excepted. Further, certain charities (*e.g.* the Universities of Oxford and Cambridge and their colleges) are exempt from the restrictions.[88]

---

[85] Charities Act 1960, s.38(2), (3), Sched. 7.
[86] S.L.A. 1925, s.29. See *post*, pp. 241 *et seq*.
[87] *Re Booth and Southend-on-Sea Estates Company's Contract* [1927] 1 Ch. 579.
[88] Charities Act 1960, s.29, Sched. 2.

CHAPTER 6

FUTURE INTERESTS

Part 1

NATURE OF FUTURE INTERESTS

Sect. 1. Introduction

1. Alienability of land. In feudal times land was the basis of wealth and status; and many men had dynastic ambitions. A landowner with full power to dispose of the fee simple in his lands would often seek to keep the land in his family by tying it up so that his heirs could not alienate it. From early days, however, the policy of the law was to make land freely alienable, so that it could be used to the fullest advantage; and this conflicted with the desire of landowners to keep land in the family. The creation of an estate tail was the most direct way of doing this; but by the fifteenth century the courts had evolved means whereby the entail could be barred and converted into a fee simple.[1] Again, if a fee simple was granted with a condition that the land was not to be alienated, the courts held the condition to be void.[2] Further, the feudal system required that there should always be some person who was seised of the land, and so be liable for the feudal services.[3] Thus a limitation which left a gap in the seisin after a tenant for life died (*e.g.* pending the birth or marriage of some person) was held to be void: the law abhorred any "abeyance of seisin."

2. Perpetuities. Out of these conflicting elements arose the law of future interests. Today, that law is far from simple; but formerly it was far more complicated. There is now rarely any need to consider in any detail the rules which failed to survive 1925, but something must be said of them, if only to make intelligible some of the case law that is still relevant to the present law. Today, future interests are mainly governed by three rules: the rule against perpetuities, the rule against inalienability, and the rule against accumulations. The first two rules prevent property from being tied up for longer than the perpetuity period: this consists of a life or lives in being, with a further 21 years. The rule against perpetuities is directed against remoteness of vesting: a future interest is void if it will take longer than the perpetuity period before it becomes a vested interest. The rule against inalienability prevents property from being made inalienable for longer than the perpetuity period. The rule against accumulations is similarly directed against the

[1] *Ante*, p. 40.
[2] *Ante*, p. 37.
[3] *Ante*, p. 28.

duration of restrictions, rather than remoteness of vesting. It prevents the compulsory accumulation of income for longer than one of the available accumulation periods: these are shorter than the perpetuity period. The three rules will be considered in due course.[4]

3. Tying up capital. Originally, the law did not prevent dispositions of the land itself being restrained, provided the relevant period was not exceeded. But the introduction of the system of overreaching,[5] first in the drafting of some settlements and then by statutes in the nineteenth century, meant that the land itself was always alienable, though if it was sold, the restraints attached to the purchase money instead. The rules governing future interests were then no longer required to secure the free alienability of land; but they continued to prevent a settlor or testator from tying up the land or the capital money representing it for an unreasonably long period.

Sect. 2. Vested and Contingent Interests

One of the fundamentals of the law of future interests is the distinction between vested and contingent interests.

1. Vested interests. A future interest in land is an interest which confers a right to the enjoyment of the land at a future time, such as a right to the land after the death of a living person. A future interest may be either vested or contingent. "Vested," when used by itself (as here), means "vested in interest," *i.e.* that there is a present fixed right of future enjoyment; this contrasts with a right "vested in possession," which carries with it a right of present enjoyment. Thus if land is devised on trust for X for life with remainder to his first and other sons successively for life, each son obtains a vested interest at birth, and it is immaterial that the interests of the younger sons may not vest in possession until long after X's death.[6]

2. Conditions for vesting. A future interest is vested if two conditions are satisfied:

  (i) that the person or persons entitled to the interest are ascertained; and
  (ii) that the interest is ready to take effect forthwith upon the determination of all the preceding estates and interests.[7]

(a) *Conditions satisfied.* Thus if land is given—

"to A for life, remainder to B for life, remainder to C in fee simple,"

the interests of B and C are both vested. Neither is vested in possession, for

---

[4] *Post*, pp. 181 *et seq.*
[5] *Ante*, p. 5.
[6] See *Evans* v. *Walker* (1876) 3 Ch.D. 211; and see *Pearson* v. *I.R.C.* [1981] A.C. 753.
[7] Fearne C.R. 9, 216; *Re Legh's S.T.* [1938] Ch. 39 at 52. For the purposes of the rule against perpetuities, there is an additional condition: see *post*, p. 177.

A has the only interest which is vested both in interest and in possession. But if A's life interest were to terminate forthwith, an ascertained person, B, is ready to take the land, and so B's interest is vested. Even if A is aged 23 and B 97, so that it is most improbable that B's interest will ever vest in possession, B nevertheless has a vested interest; an interest may be vested even if there is no certainty of its taking effect in possession at any time, for otherwise no future life interest or entail would be vested. If land is given to X in tail, remainder to Y in fee simple, Y's remainder is vested, not because X's entail is bound to determine at some time (for this is not the case), but because the whole fee simple has been split up between X and Y, and Y has been *invested* with a portion of it.

(b) *Person not ascertained.* If the person to take is not ascertained his interest is contingent, even though it is bound to take effect at some time. For example, if property is given—

"to A and B for their joint lives, with remainder to the survivor," the death of one before the other is bound to occur at some time, yet since it is uncertain who will be the survivor, the remainder is contingent.[8] Similarly, a gift to the heir of a living person is contingent, for until that person dies his heir cannot be ascertained.

(c) *Interest not ready.* Although the gift is in favour of a specified person, it will not be vested if it is made to depend upon some event occurring, *e.g.*—

"to A upon attaining 25 or marrying," or
"to B if he returns to take up permanent residence in England."

In such cases, the interests of A and B are contingent until the event occurs, when they become vested.

3. Size of interest.

(a) *General.* For most purposes[9] an interest will be vested even if the size of the beneficiary's interest has not been finally ascertained. For example, where land is devised in trust for—

"A for life, reminder to all his children who shall attain the age of 18 years,"

each child obtains a vested interest on attaining his majority; but these vested interests are liable to open to let in each child who subsequently attains full age.[10] Thus if X and Y are the only children who have attained their majority, they each have a vested interest in one-half of the property, subject to that interest being partially divested in favour of subsequent children. When Z becomes 18, the shares of X and Y each fall to one-third and Z has the other third; and so on for any other children. X and Y, having vested interests, can dispose of their shares either *inter vivos* or by will,

---

[8] See *Re Legh's S.T.* [1938] Ch. 39.
[9] For an exception, see below.
[10] See *Re Lechmere and Lloyd* (1881) 18 Ch.D. 524.

although even in the hands of the transferee the shares will be liable to be diminished by other children attaining full age. But any child of A who dies before he is 18 never has any interest in the property.[11]

(b) *Rule against perpetuities.* A long line of cases has established that the size of a beneficiary's interest must be ascertained before the interest is vested for the purposes of the rule.[12] Thus a gift before 1926 to trustees for such of the children of X as attained the age of 25 (X being alive at the date of the gift and having no child aged 25 or more) was totally void because, as will be seen, a child might attain the age of 25 outside the period allowed by the rule.[13] It mattered not that one or more children attained the age within the period, because until it was known how many children would ultimately reach the given age, the size of the share to be taken by each beneficiary was uncertain. This aspect of vesting is considered more fully later.[14]

4. Vesting subject to divesting. A remainder may be vested and yet subject to some provision which may operate to defeat the remainder completely. For example, if land is held on trust for A for life, remainder on trust for A's issue as A shall appoint, and in default of appointment on trust for all A's children equally, the remainder to the children is vested, subject to being divested to the extent of any appointment made by A.[15] In cases of doubt, the law favours early vesting, and every interest is construed as being vested forthwith if that is possible; if not, it is treated as becoming vested as soon as possible. A gift by will to X "if" or "when" he is 25 is *prima facie* contingent, but the addition of a gift over to Y if X dies before he is 25 indicates that X is intended to have all that is not given to Y, and so X's interest will *prima facie* be construed as being vested subject to being divested.[16]

5. Assignability. In the sense that all vested interests give a present right to future enjoyment, the name "future interests" is hardly appropriate. If land is given—

"to X for life, reminder to Y in fee simple,"

Y has a present interest in fee simple which is future only as to the possession of the land. Y can sell, give away, devise or otherwise dispose of his fee simple at any time he wishes. Nevertheless, for convenience, vested interests which are not coupled with a right of present enjoyment are usually dealt with under the head of future interests. Contingent interests are more clearly entitled to be described as future interests, for until the contingency occurs, the person entitled has no estate but merely a possibility of acquiring one. They can, however, be assigned, devised or otherwise disposed of.[17]

---

[11] See *Rhodes* v. *Whitehead* (1865) 2 Dr. & Sm. 532.
[12] See, *e.g.* *Pearks* v. *Moseley* (1880) 5 App.Cas. 714.
[13] *Boreham* v. *Bignall* (1850) 8 Hare 131.
[14] *Post*, pp. 195 *et seq.*
[15] *Re Master's Settlement* [1911] 1 Ch. 321; and see *Re Brooks' S.T.* [1939] Ch. 993.
[16] The rule in *Phipps* v. *Ackers* (1842) 9 Cl. & F. 583; *Brotherton* v. *I.R.C.* [1978] 1 W.L.R. 610.
[17] L.P.A. 1925, s.4(2).

Sect. 3. Classification of Future Interests

The two main categories into which future interests fall are reversions, and remainders. These will be considered in turn.

A. *Reversions*

1. Nature of reversions. A "particular estate" in land may be defined as some estate or interest less than a fee simple, *i.e.* either a fee tail, a life interest or a term of years: it is a mere part (*particula*) of the fee simple. If the owner of an estate in land creates one or more particular estates out of his own estate, the residue of his original estate which he retains is known as a reversion. Thus if a tenant in fee simple grants a life interest or a lease for a term of years, the fee simple which he retains is a reversion. If, on the other hand, the tenant creates a particular estate and by the same instrument disposes of some or all of the residue of his estate to one or more other persons, the interests of those other persons are not reversions but remainders. In the case of a reversion, the land reverts to the grantor when the particular estate determines; in the case of a remainder, it remains away from him for the benefit of some third party. It follows that while there may be many remainders created out of one estate, there can be but one reversion. Thus if X, a tenant in fee simple, grants land—

"to A for life, remainder to B for life, remainder to C in tail,"
he retains the reversion in fee simple, and yet has created two remainders, namely those of B and C. Further, a reversion arises by operation of law, a remainder by act of parties.

2. All reversions are vested. From its very nature, it follows that a reversion is always a vested interest[18]; the grantor, or, if he is dead, his representatives, stand ready to receive the land as soon as the particular estate determines. A freehold reversioner on a term of years has an estate which is vested both in interest and in possession, for the grant of a lease does not deprive the grantor of seisin, and he therefore has what is properly called a freehold in possession subject to the term. From this point of view, a reversion on a lease is not a reversion or, indeed, a future interest at all; but from a more practical point of view such interests are generally treated as reversions today. A possibility of reverter[19] cannot be a reversion as it is a mere possibility of having an estate and not an estate.

3. Reversions after 1925. Before 1926 a reversion might be legal or equitable, according to whether the estate out of which it was created was legal or equitable. After 1925, a reversion upon an entail or life estate is necessarily equitable; the land will be settled land and the legal estate will be vested in the tenant for life or statutory owner.[20] A reversion upon a term of years, however, can still exist as a legal estate, because—

[18] Challis R.P. 67.
[19] *Ante*, p. 35.
[20] *Post*, pp. 223 *et seq.*

(a) if the owner of a legal fee simple absolute in possession grants a lease, his estate remains a legal estate, for "possession" includes the right to receive the rents and profits, if any; and

(b) if the owner of a legal term of years absolute grants a sublease, there is nothing in this to render his estate any the less legal; any number of legal estate can exist concurrently in the same land.[21]

B. Remainders

In addition to reversions, before 1926 three principal types of future interest could exist, namely—

(1) Legal remainders;
(2) Future trusts; and
(3) Legal executory interests.

These will be considered briefly.

1. Legal remainders. As already mentioned,[22] if a landowner granted land "to A for life, with remainder to B and his heirs," B's interest was a remainder and not a reversion; for when the particular estate (*i.e.*, A's life interest) came to an end, the land remained away from the grantor and did not revert to him. If the grantor had a legal fee simple, before 1926 A's life interest and B's fee simple in remainder would both be legal.

A legal remainder was subject to strict rules, largely based on the sanctity of seisin. Thus no legal remainder could be granted which could cut short the particular estate, or spring up after the end of the particular estate; and there could be no remainder after a fee simple, even if it was a determinable or conditional fee.[23] The most strict rule was one that imposed a double requirement. This was the rule that a remainder must not only be *capable* of vesting by the time the particular estate ended, but must also in fact *do* this. Under a limitation to A for life with remainder to B when he was 25, B's remainder satisfied the first prong of the rule, but if A died before B was 25, the second prong destroyed B's remainder, and he got nothing. The same applied if before B was 25 A's life interest was artificially terminated, as by surrender or enlargement. The courts favoured such devices as counteracting the tendency to tie up estates for long periods. During the nineteenth century, however, statutory reforms were made which greatly curtailed the severity of these rules,[24] and left such cases to be dealt with by the more rational rule against perpetuities.

2. Future trusts. Future trusts were never subject to the rules for legal remainders, for the whole legal estate was vested in trustees, and the

---

[21] *Ante*, p. 77.
[22] *Ante*, p. 178.
[23] *Ante*, pp. 35–38. Base fees were an exception.
[24] For the rules and the statutory reforms, see M. & W. 1176–1185.

common law paid no regard to trusts. Equitable interests which would cut short a prior interest could thus be created, and so could interests which would spring up at some future date, leaving the beneficial interest in the grantor in the meantime. The price of this freedom was that the interests were merely equitable, and did not give the security of a legal estate. But such interests were subject to the rule against perpetuities.

3. Legal executory interests. The Statute of Uses 1535 made it possible to create future interests which had the best of both worlds. By conveying land to uses, interests could be created which at some future date would spring up ("springing uses") or shift from one person to another ("shifting uses"); and the Statute, by executing the uses,[25] would make the interests legal. Thus land could be conveyed "to X and his heirs to the use of A and his heirs in four years time," or "to X and his heirs to the use of A and his heirs until A evicts B from his house, and then to the use of B and his heirs." Such interests were called "executory" interests, "executory" being used in the sense of "yet to be executed or carried out"; but by virtue of the Statute they were legal estates, and not mere equitable interests. The Statute of Wills 1540[26] was construed so as to produce similar results for gifts by will, without employing any uses, thus producing a similar range of "executory devises." But the courts curtailed this apparent freedom by holding that every legal executory interest must be treated as being a legal remainder, and thus be subject to the rules for legal remainders, unless on the face of it the executory interest was from the outset incapable of complying with those rules.[27]

4. After 1925. For future interests, the two main statutory changes made by the 1925 legislation are—

    (1) the Statute of Uses 1535 has been repealed[28]; and
    (2) no future estates in real property can be legal, for the only legal estate in realty now possible is the fee simple absolute in possession.[29]

The result is therefore that—

    (i)   legal remainders can no longer exist, for the second reason above, and
    (ii) legal executory interests can no longer exist, for both reasons; but
    (iii) future trusts can still exist.

After 1925, therefore, all future interests in realty must necessarily be equitable. Legal remainders and legal executory interests existing before 1926 were automatically converted into equitable interests. Thus the comparatively simple law of future trusts, free from feudal rules and statutory modifications, now applies to all future interests. In all cases, the land will

---

[25] *Ante*, p. 64.
[26] *Ante*, p. 29.
[27] The rule in *Purefoy* v *Rogers* (1671) 2 Wms. Saund. 380.
[28] *Ante*, p. 65.
[29] *Ante*, p. 71.

either be settled land and subject to the code laid down by the Settled Land Act 1925, or else be subject to a trust for sale. This means that there is full freedom to dispose of the land itself, notwithstanding the rights of the beneficiaries, for their rights will be transferred from the land to the purchase-money which represents it.[30]

Sect. 4. Remoteness

The simplification of the common law rules governing future interests has left the group of rules governing remoteness as the principal body of law affecting them. These rules have already been mentioned in outline.[31] There are three sets of rules. First, there is the rule against perpetuities, sometimes called the rule against remoteness of vesting. This prevents future interests becoming vested after the perpetuity period has expired; the requirement is for vesting in interest within the period and not for vesting in possession or enjoyment within that time. The perpetuity period consists of a life or lives in being and a further 21 years. Second, the rule against inalienability prevents property from being made inalienable for longer than the perpetuity period. Third, the rule against accumulations prevents the compulsory accumulation of income for longer than one of the statutory accumulation periods: these are shorter than the perpetuity period. In very broad terms, the rule against perpetuities is concerned with commencement, while the other two rules restrict duration. From each of the rules there are various exceptions. The rules will be considered in turn.

Part 2

THE RULE AGAINST PERPETUITIES

Sect. 1. History

1. Need for a rule. The rules governing legal remainders usually made it difficult for a remainder to vest at a very remote date: a remainder after a life estate had to vest during the life, a remainder after an entail could be barred, and there could be no remainder after a fee simple.[32] But these rules did not apply to legal executory interests or future trusts, and they might spring up or shift at remote future dates, thus leaving the ultimate ownership and right of alienation uncertain for a long time. The courts sought to meet this danger by evolving several rules. The rule against remote possibilities struck down limitations that depended upon a remote or unlikely possibility; but remoteness proved hard to define. The rule against double possibilities held void a limitation that depended on more possibilities than one; but agreement on

[30] *Ante,* pp. 5, 6; *post,* pp. 258 *et seq.*
[31] *Ante,* p. 174.
[32] *Supra.*

the number of possibilities was often difficult, and an innocent remainder to
the first son of Z to be 21 might be attacked as containing the double
possibility that Z would have no son, and that even if he did, the son might
not live to be 21. Only the ancient rule which became known as the rule in
Whitby v. *Mitchell*,[33] from the modern case in which it was fully discussed,
ever became firmly established.

This rule was that if an interest in realty was given to an unborn person,
any remainder to his issue was void, together with all subsequent limitations.
This prevented the creation of the equivalent of an unbarrable entail by
means of an indefinite succession of life interests, as by giving land to X for
life, remainder to his son for life, remainder to the son's son for life, and so
on. When the rule against perpetuities began to emerge in the seventeenth
century, it adequately met the danger. The rule in *Whitby* v. *Mitchell*[34]
became a trap for unwary draftsmen, sometimes invalidating limitations
which plainly complied with the rule against perpetuities: *e.g.*, a gift by X, a
bachelor, to his eldest son for life, with remainder to the first of his sons to be
born in X's lifetime. The rule in *Whitby* v. *Mitchell*[35] was therefore abolished
for all instruments coming into operation after 1925.[36]

2. Development. The rule against perpetuities that finally emerged kept
future interests in land within reasonable and intelligible limits by allowing
settlors to leave the ultimate ownership uncertain for a maximum period of a
lifetime plus a further 21 years. This corresponded to the practice under a
strict settlement: if land was settled on H for life with remainder to his eldest
son in tail, the longest period that could elapse before the entail could be
barred was H's lifetime plus his son's minority, which, before 1970, was 21
years.[37]

Many years passed before the rule was finally settled. As early as 1662 the
limitation of a term of years to several living persons in succession had been
held good,[38] and in 1679 an executory devise which might not have vested
until the expiration of a lifetime plus 21 years was held valid.[39] But the rule
became firmly established only by stages. The *Duke of Norfolk's Case*[40] in
1685 settled beyond doubt that a shifting use bound to take effect, if at all,
during a life in being was valid. In 1797 it was settled that a child *en ventre sa
mère* (conceived but not born) might be treated as a life in being,[41] thus
extending the period by a possible further nine months or so; and by then it
had become accepted that the effect of a statute of 1698[42] was that the period
of 21 years after the life in being also might be extended to cover a further

---

[33] (1890) 44 Ch.D. 85.
[34] *Supra.*
[35] *Supra.*
[36] L.P.A. 1925, s.161.
[37] *Ante*, p. 167.
[38] *Goring* v. *Bickerstaffe*, Pollex. 31.
[39] *Taylor* d. *Smith* v. *Biddall*, 2 Mod. 287.
[40] 3 Ch.Ca. 1.
[41] *Long* v. *Blackall*, 7 T.R. 100.
[42] Statute of Posthumous Children 1698.

period of gestation, if it existed. In 1805 it was finally settled that the lives in being might be chosen at random and be unconnected with the property,[43] and by 1833 the rule was completed by the decision of the House of Lords in *Cadell* v. *Palmer*[44] that the period of 21 years was an absolute period without reference to any minority, but that the periods of gestation could be added only if in fact gestation existed.

3. Statutory reform. The rule was invented and developed by the judges without the intervention of Parliament. In the main it achieved a sound solution to the problem of perpetuity, but its undue rigidity produced anomalies requiring reform. Minor amendments were made by the Law of Property Act 1925, followed by revolutionary alterations under the Perpetuities and Accumulations Act 1964.[45] As is customary, these statutes did not sweep away the old law, but built upon it. Thus an understanding of the old law is still essential in order to appreciate the changes. Moreover, the former law still governs future interests taking effect under past dispositions, for the Act of 1964, which came into force on July 16, 1964, applies in general only to instruments taking effect after July 15, 1964.[46] Furthermore, there are many cases where pre-Act instruments have created special powers of appointment, and the exercise of such powers is governed by the old law.

Sect. 2. Operation of the Rule

The rule may be stated thus:

(1) A limitation of any interest in any property, real or personal, is void if by any possibility it might become vested after the perpetuity period has expired.

(2) The perpetuity period consists of a life or lives in being at the time of the gift, together with a further period of 21 years[47]; and where gestation actually exists, the period of gestation may be added.

The principal points must now be considered in some detail.[48]

1. Meaning of "vest." The meaning of "vest" has already been considered.[49] The rule does not require that an interest should be incapable of vesting *in possession* after the period has run, but only that it should be incapable of becoming vested *in interest* outside the period.[50] Thus if land is

---

[43] *Thellusson* v. *Woodford* (1805) 11 Ves. 112.
[44] 1 Cl. & F. 372.
[45] Based on the Fourth Report of the Law Reform Committee (Cmnd. 18, 1956).
[46] s.15(5). See *Re Holt's Settlement* [1969] 1 Ch. 100 (order of court).
[47] This is unaffected by the reduction of the age of majority to 18 under the Family Law Reform Act 1969.
[48] For a full consideration of the rule, see Maudsley, *Modern Law of Perpetuities* (1979) and Morris & Leach, *The Rule against Perpetuities* (2nd ed. 1962, with Supp. 1964). The classic text for the old law is *Gray on Perpetuities* (4th ed. 1942).
[49] *Ante*, p. 175.
[50] *Evans* v. *Walker* (1876) 3 Ch.D. 211.

devised on trust for X for life with remainder to his first and other sons successively for life, the limitations are valid even if X was a bachelor at the time of the gift. Each of X's sons obtains a vested interest at birth, and these interests are not invalidated by the fact that some of the sons may not be entitled to possession of the property until after the period has run[51]; it is thus immaterial that if X was a bachelor at the time of the gift and his eldest son outlives him by 50 years, the interest of the second son will not vest in possession until 29 years after the perpetuity period has expired.

2. No "wait and see" at common law. In general,[52] the unreformed rule deals with possibilities, not probabilities or actual events. Every limitation must be considered at the time when the instrument creating it takes effect. Thus a deed must be considered at the time when it is executed, while a will must be considered at the moment of the testator's death.[53] If at the relevant moment there is the slightest possibility that the perpetuity period may be exceeded, the limitation is void, even if it is most improbable that this in fact will happen and even if, as events turn out, it does not.[54] For example, if property is given—

"to A (a bachelor) for life, remainder to his widow for life, remainder to the eldest of his brothers living at the widow's death,"

the remainder to the brother is bad if A's parents are alive. It is just possible that A will marry someone who was not alive at the time of the gift, and if A's wife survived him for more than 21 years, the property might become vested outside the period in a brother born after the date of the gift. This possibility renders the gift to the brother void, even if A is very old and unlikely to marry or in fact marries someone alive at the time of the gift, and even if A's parents are so old that they are most unlikely to have any more children. For the purposes of the perpetuity rule, no person is ever deemed too old to have children,[55] though for other purposes the courts take a more realistic view of preternatural fertility[56]; but statute prevents the lawful marriage (and so lawful issue) of a person under the age of 16 years.[57] Again, a gift of property to certain persons "if the minerals under the said farm should be worked" offends the perpetuity rule and is void because of the possibility that the minerals will be worked after the perpetuity period has expired.[58]

It is immaterial that the gift may never vest at all; the question is whether if it does vest, it is capable of vesting *outside* the period. A gift to the first son of X, a bachelor, may never vest at all, for X may never have a son. But this possibility does not render the gift void for perpetuity; the gift is incapable of

[51] *Re Hargreaves* (1889) 43 Ch.D. 401.
[52] See *post*, pp. 186, 201, for qualifications of this rule.
[53] *Vanderplank* v. *King* (1843) 3 Hare 1 at 17.
[54] These words were approved in *Re Watson's S.T.* [1959] 1 W.L.R. 732 at 739.
[55] See *Ward* v. *Van der Loeff* [1924] A.C. 653 (persons aged 66).
[56] See, *e.g. Re White* [1901] 1 Ch. 570.
[57] *Re Gaite's W.T.* [1949] 1 All E.R. 459 (Age of Marriage Act 1929); but see (1949) 13 Conv. (N.S.) 289 (J.H.C. Morris).
[58] *Thomas* v. *Thomas* (1902) 87 L.T. 58.

vesting outside the perpetuity period, for if X does have a son, the son must be born or conceived during X's lifetime, and X is the life in being. In short, the gift is bound to vest, *if it vests at all*, within the perpetuity period. Again, a gift by will—

"to the first of my daughters to marry after my death,"

is valid, even though no daughter may marry; for if any daughter does marry, she must do so in her own lifetime, and since the testator is dead when the gift takes effect, no further daughters can be born and all those who are alive or *en ventre sa mère* rank as lives in being. Had the gift been made by deed, it would have been void, for the donor might have had further daughters after the date of the gift (who would not have been lives in being) and one of these might have been the first to qualify for the gift by marrying more than 21 years after the death of the donor and all his other daughters.

A gift which would otherwise be too remote may be validated by the insertion of an express clause confining its vesting to the proper period. Thus a gift by a testator to such of his issue as should be living when some gravel pits should become exhausted is void as it stands, even if it is highly probable that the pits will be worked out in five or six years.[59] The gift would have been valid, however, if worded "to such of my issue living 21 years after my death or when the gravel pits are exhausted, whichever first happens"; and a gift to bodies existing "when the residue of my estate is realised" has been construed as being confined to the "executor's year,"[60] *i.e.* one year from death.[61] But a clause seeking to confine the vesting within the period must do so clearly; a void gift is not validated merely by the addition of words providing that the vesting shall be postponed only "so far as the rules of law and equity will permit.[62]

3. Future parenthood. The Act of 1964 has replaced the rigid rule that no person is too old to have children with a statutory presumption—

  (a) that a male can have a child at the age of 14 or over, but not under that age, and
  (b) that a female can have a child at the age of 12 or over, but not under that age or over the age of 55.[63]

This presumption may be rebutted by showing that in a particular case a living person will or will not be able to have a child at the time in question.[64] "Having a child" extends to having a child "by adoption, legitimation or other means."[65]

[59] *Re Wood* [1894] 3 Ch. 381.
[60] See *ante*, p. 164.
[61] *Re Petrie* [1962] Ch. 355; and see *Re Atkins' W.T.* [1974] 1 W.L.R. 761.
[62] *Portman* v. *Viscount Portman* [1922] 2 A.C. 473; contrast *Re Vaux* [1939] Ch. 465; and see *I.R.C.* v. *Williams* [1969] 1 W.L.R. 1197 at 1202.
[63] s.2(1).
[64] *Ibid.* See *L.* v. *K.* [1985] Fam. 144.
[65] s.2(4).

If events falsify the presumptions, the High Court has a general discretion to make such order as it thinks fit for placing the persons interested in the property in the position in which they would have been if the presumptions had not been applied.[66]

4. "Wait and see" under the Act of 1964

(a) *The new rule.* The common law rule has one great advantage: one can see at the outset whether the gift is good or bad. But it frequently frustrates the intentions of settlors and testators by striking down limitations which almost certainly would vest within the period. To meet these cases the Act of 1964 has introduced the rule of "wait and see" for limitations in instruments taking effect after July 15, 1964,[67] which would be void at common law. For such a gift the Act provides that it is not to be treated as if it were subject to the rule against perpetuities until "it becomes established that the vesting must occur, if at all, after the end of the perpetuity period"[68]; until then, the gift is valid. It is now permissible to look at actual rather than possible events, so that the disposition does not become void until it is clear that it is going to vest, if it vests at all, outside the period.

(b) *Examples.* The previous example[69] of a gift "to the first of my daughters to marry" was bad at common law if the gift was made by deed and the donor had at the time no daughter who was married. Even if he had unmarried daughters at that time the gift would be bad, for he might have had further daughters, one of whom might have been the first daughter to marry, and that marriage might have occurred more than 21 years after the death of the donor and of all his daughters living at the date of the deed. But under the Act one can wait and see whether one of his daughters, whether living at the date of the deed or still unborn, marries within the period, that is the period which ends 21 years after the death of the donor and any daughters living at the date of the deed. If no daughter marries within that period the gift will fail, even though an after-born daughter marries thereafter.

Similarly, a gift by a testator to such of his issue as should be living when some gravel pits should become exhausted, which is void at common law, will be valid if the pits in fact become exhausted within 21 years of the death of the survivor of those of his issue who are living at his death.

(c) *Consequences.* The practical consequences of the new rule will not be so great as one might suppose from so radical an amendment of the rule. First, the great majority of limitations in fact comply with the old rule, and it is not to be expected that the Act will bring about a relaxation of the standards of drafting. Second, the new rule does not extend the period: it does not enable a donor to do anything which he cannot achieve within the framework of the common law rule by the use of an express clause confining

---

[66] s.2(2).
[67] See *ante*, p. 183.
[68] s.3(1).
[69] *Ante*, p. 185.

the vesting to the proper period, such as a period expiring 21 years after the death of all the descendants of King George VI living at the date of the instrument.

5. The perpetuity period. The perpetuity period must be considered as it stands at common law, as it has been varied by statute, and as it stands under the Act of 1964.

(a) *At common law*

(1) LIVES IN BEING. For a person to be a life in being for the purposes of the rule, it is unnecessary that he should receive any benefit from the gift or that he should be in any way connected with the beneficiaries.[70] Nor is there any restriction upon the number of lives selected, provided it is reasonably possible to ascertain who they are; "for let the lives be never so many, there must be a survivor, and so it is but the length of that life."[71] "If a term be limited to one for life, with twenty several remainders for lives to other persons successively, who are all alive and in being, so that all the candles are lighted together, this is good enough."[72] For example, gifts by a testator to such of his descendants as are living 21 years after the death of the last survivor of the members of a given school at the testator's death.[73] or 20 years after the death of the last survivor of all the lineal descendants of Queen Victoria living at the testator's death,[74] have been held valid. In the latter case, the testator died in 1926 when there were some 120 lives in being and it was reasonably possible to follow the duration of their lives; a similar limitation today might well be void for uncertainty,[75] though the living descendants of King George VI may safely be selected.[76]

From one point of view, everyone alive at the time of the gift is a life in being in the literal sense; but a gift depending on the dropping of all those lives would be void for uncertainty. Thus the only lives in being which have to be considered in relation to the perpetuity rule are those which are implicated in the gift, being mentioned in it either expressly or by implication in a way that is relevant to its vesting, governing the time when the gift is to vest. In the above examples, lives in being have been expressly mentioned; but this is not always the case. If a testator gives property to such of his grandchildren as attain the age of 21, his children can be taken as lives in being. They are all bound to have been born by the time of the testator's death, and a gift to grandchildren presupposes the existence of children. The gift is therefore good, for no grandchild can take longer than 21 years from its parent's death to reach the age of 21. But a gift to the grandchildren of a living person is bad, unless the class is restricted in some way, *e.g.* to those

---

[70] *Cadell* v. *Palmer* (1833) 1 Cl. & F. 372.
[71] *Scatterwood* v. *Edge* (1697) 1 Salk. 229.
[72] *Howard* v. *Duke of Norfolk* (1681) 2 Swans. 454 at 458, *per* Lord Nottingham L.C.
[73] *Pownall* v. *Graham* (1863) 33 Beav. 242 at 245, 247.
[74] *Re Villar* [1929] 1 Ch. 243.
[75] Consider *Re Moore* [1901] 1 Ch. 936.
[76] See *Re Leverhulme* [1943] 2 All E.R. 274.

living at the death of a life in being[77]; the living person might have another child after the date of the gift and then, long after all those alive at the date of the gift had died, that child might have a child.

Consequently, it can be said that everyone who—

(i) is alive at the time of the gift, and

(ii) is implicated in its vesting,

should be treated as a life in being. Others, the duration of whose lives have no bearing on the vesting of the gift, should be ignored. In the case of limitations made *inter vivos*, the date of the instrument, and, in the case of wills, the date of the testator's death, is the time when the period starts running and the facts must be ascertained; to be a life in being, a person must be alive at that moment.

The lives must be human lives, and not the lives of animals.[78]

(2) NO LIVES. If the limitation is made without reference to lives in being, the period is 21 years. A gift by a testator to all his issue living 50 years after his death, or to all the children of X (who is alive) living 28 years after the testator's death, is void.[79] It is true that in the first case the testator's children and in the second X could be taken as lives in being, but in neither case has the period selected any relation to their lives; it is a period in gross, and neither the immediate death nor the prolonged life of the testator's children or of X will alter the date of vesting. Consequently the gifts must be treated as if there were no lives in being, with the result that the period is 21 years.

(3) CHILD EN VENTRE. For the purposes of the perpetuity rule, a child *en ventre sa mère* is treated as if it had been born. Two cases can arise:

(i) A child may be *en ventre sa mère* at the beginning of the period, *i.e.* at the time of the gift. In this case, the child is treated as a life in being.[80] Thus if a testator gives property for life to the child with which his wife is enceinte, with a remainder contingent upon certain circumstances existing at that child's death, the remainder is good; for the contingency must be resolved at the child's death and the child is treated as the life in being.[81]

(ii) A child may be *en ventre sa mère* during the period. In this case, the period is extended as far as is necessary to include the period of gestation. Thus if property is given to the first of A's sons to be 21 years old, the gift is valid even if A's only son was unborn at A's death; the perpetuity period in such a case is A's lifetime plus the period of gestation and 21 years.

It will be seen from this that two periods of gestation may arise in the same case; both are allowed. If property is given to Jane's eldest child for life, with remainder to the first son of that child to be 21, and Jane is pregnant with her first child at the time of the gift, the remainder does not infringe the

[77] *Wetherell* v. *Wetherell* (1863) 1 De G.J. & S. 134 at 139, 140.
[78] See *Re Kelly* [1932] I.R. 255 at 260, 261.
[79] *Speakman* v. *Speakman* (1850) 8 Hare 180; *Palmer* v. *Holford* (1828) 4 Russ. 403.
[80] *Re Wilmer's Trusts* [1903] 2 Ch. 411 at 421.
[81] *Long* v. *Blackall* (1797) 7 T.R. 100.

perpetuity rule even though Jane's child may be a son who dies leaving his wife enceinte of an only son. Jane's child is treated as a life in being, and the perpetuity period will be extended to cover the period of gestation of the child's son.[82]

These rules do not allow the addition of any period or periods of nine months or so in all cases; they apply only where gestation actually exists.[83]

(b) *Statutory age reduction.* A frequent cause of gifts failing was that they were made contingent upon the beneficiary attaining an age greater than 21. Thus property might be given—

"to the first of A's children to attain the age of 25."

In certain circumstances, the gift would be good: if A was dead at the time of the gift, he could have no further children, and since every possible claimant was a life in being, the gift would be valid.[84] Further, even if A was alive, if one of his children had attained the age of 25 at the date of the gift, the limitation was valid as being an immediate gift to an ascertained person.[85] But if A was alive and no child had attained the age of 25, the gift was bad. This was so even if a child had attained the age of 24, for there was no certainty that he would not die before his twenty-fifth birthday, and a child born after the date of the gift might be the first child to reach the age of 25.[86]

To deal with cases such as this, section 163 of the Law of Property Act 1925 lays down that in certain circumstances the age of 21 may be substituted for the offending age. This may be done only if—

(i) the limitation is contained in an instrument executed after 1925, or in the will of a testator dying after 1925, but in either case before July 16, 1964[87]; and

(ii) the limitation would otherwise be void; and

(iii) the excess is in the age of the beneficiary or class of beneficiaries.

The first point needs no illustration; the second may be illustrated by considering the limitation mentioned above, namely, "to the first of A's children to attain the age of 25." Before 1926, if A was alive and no child had reached the age of 25, the gift failed; if made after 1925, section 163 substitutes "21" for "25" and the gift is good, the first child to attain the age of 21 taking the property at that age. But if A had been dead, the gift would have been valid without the aid of section 163 and so "25" remains undisturbed. In the result, if A's eldest child is aged 19 at the time of the gift, whether he must wait two years or six before becoming entitled depends upon whether A is alive or dead.

The third point may be illustrated by cases where vesting is postponed for

---

[82] See *Thellusson* v. *Woodford* (1805) 11 Ves. 112 at 143, 149, 150.
[83] *Cadell* v. *Palmer* (1833) 1 Cl. & F. 372 at 421, 422.
[84] *Southern* v. *Wollaston* (1852) 16 Beav. 276.
[85] *Picken* v. *Matthews* (1878) 10 Ch.D. 264.
[86] See, *e.g. Re Finch* (1881) 17 Ch.D. 211.
[87] Except in the case of an instrument made in the exercise of a special power of appointment created before July 16, 1964: Act of 1964, s.15(5).

a fixed period of years. A gift to the testator's issue living 50 years after his death was void before 1926[88] and was not validated by section 163, for the "50" is not the age of a beneficiary.

(c) *Act of 1964*

(1) LIVES IN BEING. It is controversial whether the introduction of the "wait and see" principle required any alteration in the rules for ascertaining the lives in being. Probably no alteration was needed, since the lives in being at common law are not confined to those which necessarily succeed in restricting the vesting of the gift to the perpetuity period, but include any lives sufficiently implicated in the vesting, whether or not they succeed in saving the gift.[89] Unfortunately, some took the view that at common law the only lives that rank as lives in being are those which save the gift by confining its vesting to the perpetuity period; only "salvation lives" count as lives in being. In consequence, where a gift is void at common law there are necessarily no salvation lives, and so there would be no lives in being which could save the gift on waiting and seeing.[90]

The draftsman of the Act of 1964 appears to have acted on this latter view. The Act provides four categories of lives, all of whom must be both in being and ascertainable at the date of the gift. Further, lives in the second and third categories which are defined by description are to be disregarded if they are so numerous as to render it impracticable to ascertain the death of the survivor.[91] If there are no lives in the four categories which satisfy the preceding conditions, the "wait and see" period is 21 years from the date of the gift.[92]

The four categories are as follows.[93]

(a) The donor: "the person by whom the disposition was made."
(b) A donee: "a person to whom or in whose favour the disposition was made, that is to say—
  (i) in the case of a disposition to a class of persons, any member or potential member of the class;
  (ii) in the case of an individual disposition to a person taking only on certain conditions being satisfied, any person as to whom some of the conditions are satisfied and the remainder may in time be satisfied;
  [(iii) and (iv) concern special powers of appointment, discussed below[94]];

---

[88] See *ante*, p. 188.
[89] (1964) 80 L.Q.R. 486 at 495–501 (J. H. C. Morris and H. W. R. Wade); (1981) 97 L.Q.R. 593 (R. L. Deech); (1986) 102 L.Q.R. 250 (J. Dukeminier). This was the assumption of the Law Reform Committee: *ante*, p. 183, n. 45.
[90] (1965) 81 L.Q.R. 106 (D. E. Allan); (1970) 86 L.Q.R. 357 (R. H. Maudsley); Maudsley, *Modern Law of Perpetuities*, pp. 87 *et seq.*
[91] s.3(4)(*a*).
[92] s.3(4)(*b*).
[93] s.3(5).
[94] *Post*, p. 200.

> (v) in the case of any power, option or other right, the person on whom the right is conferred."
>
> (c) A donee's parent or grandparent.
> (d) The owner of a prior interest.

In many cases these complicated provisions produce the same lives in being as the common law rule, but there are divergences. Often more lives are available under the Act. Thus a gift "to A's first grandson to attain 21" where A is alive and without such a grandson at the date of the gift is void at common law. Under the "wait and see" rule, the lives in being are the donor (under (a) above), A and any existing children of A and their spouses (under (c) above), and any existing grandchildren (under (b)(ii) above), so that one waits to see whether a grandchild reaches 21 within 21 years of the death of the survivor of those lives.

(2) STATUTORY AGE REDUCTION. For instruments taking effect after July 15, 1964,[95] the Act of 1964 has replaced the Law of Property Act 1925, s.163,[96] by a more flexible provision. It operates where a disposition satisfies the following conditions—

> (a) It is limited by reference to the attainment by any person or persons of a specified age exceeding 21 years.[97] The corresponding provision of section 163 applied only to the excessive age of a beneficiary; the new provision applies to the excessive ages of others as well, as in a gift to an unborn person "living when A's eldest son attains 25."
> (b) It is apparent when the disposition is made, or becomes apparent later—
>> (i) that it would otherwise be void for remoteness, but
>> (ii) that it would not be so void if the specified age had been 21 years.
> (c) It is not saved by the "wait and see" rule.

If these conditions are satisfied, the disposition is treated as if it had been limited by reference to the greatest age which would have prevented it from being void.[98] Here again the new provision diverges from section 163, for under that section the reduction was to a uniform 21 years in every case.

Thus if there is a gift by will to A's children at 25, and A is alive at the date of the testator's death, one first "waits and sees" whether the gift is valid without alteration. This will be so if A's children were all alive at the

---

[95] Except instruments made in the exercise of a special power of appointment created before July 16, 1964; s.15(5).
[96] *Ante*, p. 189.
[97] Act of 1964, s.4(1).
[98] *Ibid.* s.4(1), (7), added by Children Act 1975, Sched. 3, para. 43.

testator's death, or were all over four at A's death. If, however, A's youngest child was not alive at the testator's death but was a year old at A's death, the vesting age will be reduced to 22 years.[99]

Unlike section 163, the new provision also caters for gifts which specify two or more ages. If there is a gift by will to A's sons who attain 30 and his daughters who attain 25, and on A's death after the testator his youngest son is eight and his youngest daughter is three, the vesting ages will be reduced to 29 for sons and 24 for daughters.[1]

(3) SURVIVING SPOUSES. A gift to such of the children of A as are living at the death of the survivor of A and his widow frequently failed at common law because of the possibility that A might marry a person not born at the date of the gift but who might survive A by more than 21 years. The Act of 1964 eliminated this notorious trap of the "unborn widow." If a gift which refers to the death of the survivor of a person in being and his or her spouse is not saved by the "wait and see" rule, it is to be treated "as if it had instead been limited by reference to the time immediately before the end of" the perpetuity period.[2] Thus in the example above, if A is survived by his widow, the gift will vest 21 years after the death of A if the widow is then still living, so that the children then living will take even if one or more of them subsequently die before the widow.

(4) ALTERNATIVE FIXED PERIOD. The Act of 1964 contains one completely new concept. As an alternative to the perpetuity period based on lives in being, it is permissible to specify a fixed period of years not exceeding 80 as the perpetuity period.[3] The period must be expressly specified. It cannot be left to be implied, as in a gift by will to such of the testator's descendants are living 80 years after his death; but it suffices if two dates are specified from which the period between can be calculated.[4] The proper course is to use some expression such as "which I specify as the perpetuity period for this gift." It will be noted that this period can be used with much the same effect as the "royal lives" clauses at common law. However, nothing in the Act affects the validity of a "royal lives" or similar perpetuity clause where the gift must vest, if at all, within the specified period.

6. Separate application. Where a deed or will contains two or more limitations, the rule is applied to each limitation separately. Thus if there is a gift—

[99] For problems that arise when some children, if they live, will attain the requisite age within 21 years, and others will not, see M. & W. 269; [1969] C.L.J. 286 (M. J. Pritchard). For class gifts, see *post*, pp. 195 *et seq*.
[1] See s.4(2). This assumes that A was the last surviving statutory life in being.
[2] Act of 1964, s.5.
[3] *Ibid*. s.1.
[4] *Re Green's W.T.* [1985] 3 All E.R. 455.

"to A for life, remainder to his eldest son for life, remainder to B's eldest grandson in fee simple,"

the perpetuity rule must be applied to each of the three limitations separately. If all are valid, no difficulty arises; but if one or more are bad, the following rules must be applied.

(a) *Prior limitation.* No limitation is void merely because it is followed by a void limitation.[5] A gift "to A for life" standing by itself is clearly good, and it is not invalidated merely because a limitation which infringes the rule is added, *e.g.* "to A for life, remainder to be first of his descendants to marry a Latvian." In such a case, A takes a life interest, and after his death the property reverts to the grantor or passes under his will or intestacy, unless the remainder is saved by the Act of 1964.

(b) *Subsequent limitation.* A limitation which is subsequent to and dependent upon a void limitation is itself void.[6] A limitation is not void merely because it follows a void limitation; it is invalidated by the rule only if in addition to following the void limitation it is also dependent upon it.[7] Thus if a testator devises property in fee simple—

"to the first of X's sons to become a clergyman, but if X has no such son, to Y in fee simple,"

and when the testator dies X is alive, the first part of the gift is void since the requisite event might occur more than 21 years after the death of lives in being. The gift to Y is subsequent to and dependent upon this void limitation; not until X and all his sons have died without any son having become a clergyman could it be said that Y is entitled. Thus even though the gift to Y is in favour of a living person, at common law it failed as being dependent upon a void limitation.[8]

On the other hand, if property is given—

"to A for life, remainder for life to any wife he may marry, remainder for life to any husband whom such wife may marry, remainder to such of A's children as attain the age of 21,"

the gifts to A and his wife are both valid, for A is a life in being and his wife must be ascertained in his lifetime. But at common law the limitation to the wife's husband was void for perpetuity, since A's wife may not be alive at the time of the gift and may marry more than 21 years after A's death. Nevertheless, the gift to A's children is valid, for although it follows a void limitation, it has its own independent date of vesting which cannot exceed the perpetuity period.[9]

[5] *Garland* v. *Brown* (1864) 10 L.T. 292.
[6] *Re Abbott* [1893] 1 Ch. 54; *Re Hubbard's W.T.* [1963] Ch. 275.
[7] See *Re Coleman* [1936] Ch. 528.
[8] *Proctor* v. *Bishop of Bath and Wells* (1794) 2 Hy. Bl. 358.
[9] See *Re Coleman, supra.*

The precise meaning of "dependent" in this context is obscure. Some-times it seems to mean no more than "contingent," so that there is no special rule as to "dependence." But sometimes a remainder which seems plainly vested is struck down as being "dependent" upon a prior void limitation.[10] Such cases can be explained on the principle that if a testator intends the remainder not to take effect until the prior limitation ends, it would be contrary to that intention to allow the remainder to take immediate effect merely because the prior limitation is void for perpetuity. The remainder accordingly falls with the prior limitation. Thus if a testator gives property for life to the first son of A (a bachelor) to marry, and then to B, he may well have intended no immediate gift to B. Further, where a void limitation stands between two or more valid limitations, the limitation following the void limitation will be held dependent on it, and so invalid, unless it will "dovetail in and accord with" the prior limitations.[11]

(c) *Act of 1964.* The whole doctrine of "dependence" was so unsatis-factory and obscure that the Act of 1964 abolished it for gifts made after July 15, 1964. Such a gift is not void merely because it is "ulterior to and dependent upon" a void gift. It is only the doctrine of dependence which has been abolished. If the ultimate gift is contingent, the contingency must be satisfied before it can vest. Thus of the gifts mentioned above, that to B is dependent only; but the gift "but if X has no such son, to Y" is contingent as well as dependent. The Act further provides that the existence of the prior void gift will no longer prevent the acceleration of the vesting of the sub-sequent gift.[12]

7. Alternative contingencies. Where a gift expresses two alternative con-tingencies upon which the property may vest, and one contingency is too remote but the other is not, the gift is good if in fact the valid contingency occurs.[13] Thus in one case,[14] a testator gave property to his grandchildren and issue of his grandchildren living—

"on the decease of my last surviving child or on the death of the last surviving widow or widower of my children as the case may be whichever shall last happen."

It was held that this gift did not infringe the perpetuity rule as it stood, and that if in fact one of the testator's children outlived all the other children and their spouses, the gift would be valid. There were two alternatives:

(i) that one of the testator's children (a life in being) would be the last survivor, or
(ii) that the spouse of one of the testator's children (not necessarily a life in being) would be the last survivor;

[10] *Re Backhouse* [1921] 2 Ch. 51.
[11] *Monypenny* v. *Dering* (1852) 2 De G.M. & G. 145 at 182.
[12] s.6.
[13] *Hodgson* v. *Halford* (1879) 11 Ch.D. 959.
[14] *Re Curryer's W.T.* [1938] Ch. 952.

if the former actually occurred, the gift did not infringe the rule. To this extent, there is a "wait and see" in the perpetuity rule even at common law.

The foregoing applies only if the two alternative contingencies are expressed in the gift.[15] If only one contingency is expressed in the gift and that may be too remote, the gift fails even if there are in fact two contingencies. Thus in *Proctor* v. *Bishop of Bath and Wells*,[16] only one contingency was expressed, namely, that if no son of X became a clergyman, Y should be entitled. In fact, two contingencies were implicit in the gift, namely,

   (i) X might leave no son; this must be known at X's death, which would be within the period;

   (ii) X might leave one or more sons, who might become clergymen more than 21 years after X's death, which would be outside the period.

Nevertheless, the gift to Y was void *ab initio*, for the only contingency expressed was a void one. Had the gift over been worded—

"but if no son of X shall become a clergyman, or if X shall leave no son, to Y in fee simple,"

the gift to Y would have been valid if X had died leaving no son, *i.e.* if the valid contingency had occurred.[17]

The Act of 1964 has not specifically altered these rules, but its general "wait and see" provisions will apply if the unduly remote contingency occurs, or if there is only one composite contingent gift.

8. Class gifts. A class gift is a gift of property to all who come within some description, the property being divisible in shares varying according to the number of persons in the class.[18]

Thus gifts of property—

"to my children who shall live to be 25," or
"to all the nephews and nieces of my late husband who were living at his death, except A and B"

are class gifts. But gifts of property to be equally divided between—

"the five daughters of X," or
"my nine children,"

or a gift of £2,000—

"to each of my daughters,"

are not class gifts, for a distinct one-fifth or one-ninth share or the sum of £2,000 is given to each child, exactly as if he or she had been named.

---

[15] *Re Bence* [1891] 3 Ch. 242.
[16] *Ante*, p. 193.
[17] *Miles* v. *Harford* (1879) 12 Ch.D. 691 at 703.
[18] *Pearks* v. *Moseley* (1880) 5 App.Cas. 714 at 723; *Kingsbury* v. *Walter* [1901] A.C. 187 at 192.

(a) *At common law*. The perpetuity rule applies at common law to class gifts in the following way. If a single member of the class might possibly take a vested interest outside the period, the whole gift fails, even as regards those members of the class who have already satisfied any required contingency.[19] A class gift cannot be good as to part and void as to the rest: "the vice of remoteness affects the class as a whole, if it may affect an unascertained number of its members."[20] Until the total number of members of the class has been ascertained, it cannot be said what share any member of the class will take, and this state of affairs will continue as long as it is possible for any alteration in the number to be made.

Thus if before 1926 personalty was given—

"to A for life and after his death to be equally divided between all his children who shall attain the age of 25,"

an intent being shown to include every child of A, the remainder was void even as regards children alive at the time of the gift, who were thus lives in being.[21] This was so even if A was in fact many years past the age of child-bearing,[22] for in theory other children might be born, and since one of these might not be 25 until more than 21 years after the death of all lives in being at the time of the gift, the period might be exceeded.

(b) *The class-closing rules*. Sometimes a class gift is saved by the operation of the class-closing rules that have already been considered.[23] Subject always to a sufficient contrary intention, these rules close the class as soon as any member of it is entitled to claim his share, and exclude anyone who subsequently becomes a member of the class. Thus at common law a devise "equally between all my grandchildren who marry" would prima facie be void for perpetuity if any child of the testator survived him. But if one or more grandchildren married before the testator died, each of the grandchildren then living would become entitled to his share on marrying, with the prospect of that share being increased from the prospective shares of any of the other living grandchildren who died without marrying. The gift would thus take effect as a gift to lives in being, to the exclusion of grandchildren born after the testator's death.

Where there is no class gift but individual gifts to each member of a class,[24] such as £5,000 to each of X's children, or to each of Y's children to attain full age, the only persons who can take are children of X who are alive when the testator dies or the children of Y whose minorities had ended by then: for if other children could take, the estate could not be distributed, and so a rule of convenience excludes them.[25] But where A is given a life interest in the

[19] *Leake* v. *Robinson* (1817) 2 Mer. 363.
[20] *Pearks* v *Moseley, supra*, at p. 723.
[21] *Leake* v. *Robinson, supra*.
[22] Nowadays s.2 of the Act of 1964 lays down sensible child-bearing age presumptions: *ante* p. 185.
[23] *Ante*, p. 154.
[24] See *Storrs* v *Benbow* (1853) 3 De G.M. & G. 390.
[25] *Rogers* v. *Mutch* (1878) 10 Ch.D. 25.

estate prior to the gifts to the children, all children who qualify before A's death will be included,[26] for this causes no inconvenience.

(c) *Statutory class reduction.* Where the class closing rules do not save a gift at common law but the gift is made after July 15, 1964, the Act of 1964 may save the gift by excluding from the class those members whose presence makes the gift void for perpetuity. In such cases, the common law rule that a class gift cannot be partly good and partly bad does not apply. The Act provides that where it becomes apparent that the inclusion of potential members of the class would cause the gift to be void for remoteness, those members are to be excluded from the class, unless this would exhaust the class.[27] Thus under a devise "to A for life with remainder equally among his grandchildren whenever born," the last two words oust the class-closing rules, and at common law the gift is void for perpetuity unless A predeceased the testator. But under the Act, one must wait until the end of the perpetuity period to see how many grandchildren have been born, and then they alone will take, to the exclusion of any future-born grandchildren.

(d) *Age reduction under the Act of 1964.* If a class gift to which the Act of 1964 applies would be void at common law despite the class-closing rules and it is not saved by the "wait and see" principle, it may still be saved by age reduction under the Act of 1964.[28] If a will gives property "to all X's children who attain the age of 25," and X dies 10 years later leaving children aged three and one, the age will be reduced. The reduction seems to be to 22 for each child, but possibly it is to 24 for the younger child.[29]

(e) *Class and age reduction.* Under the Act of 1964, the provisions for class reduction may be combined with those for age reduction. If property is given to A (a bachelor) for life, with remainder—

"equally between all of A's children who attain 25 together with all the children of any child of A who dies under 25, such children taking their parents' share,"

the gift to the compound class is void at common law[30] and would not be saved by reducing the age to 21: for an unborn grandchild might attain 21 after the expiration of the perpetuity period. If the gift is not saved under the "wait and see" principle, the grandchildren will be excluded under the class reduction provisions, and under the age reduction provisions the age will be reduced so far as is necessary.[31]

9. Determinable and conditional interests[32]

(a) *Determinable interests.* "The rule against perpetuities is not dealing

[26] *A.-G.* v. *Crispin* (1784) 1 Bro.C.C. 386.
[27] Act of 1964, s.4(4).
[28] *Ante*, p. 191.
[29] A difficult question: see M. & W. 269.
[30] *Pearks* v. *Moseley* (1880) 5 App.Cas. 714.
[31] Act of 1964, s.4(3).
[32] See also *ante*, pp. 35 *et seq.*

with the duration of interests but with their commencement, and as long as the interest vests within lives in being and 21 years it does not matter how long that interest lasts."[33] Thus it can be said that the perpetuity rule does not invalidate a limitation merely because it provides that an interest shall cease at some future date outside the perpetuity period. Accordingly where property is given to an unborn person—

"for life or until she becomes a member of the Roman Catholic Church"

or—

"for life or until marriage,"

the specified event may occur outside the perpetuity period but the limitation is nevertheless valid.[34] The better view is that it is immaterial that the determinable interest is a fee simple and the event on which it will determine may not happen for centuries, *e.g.* where property is conveyed to the X Co. Ltd. in fee simple until the premises are used otherwise than as a biscuit factory. When the event occurs, no new estate arises; the X Co. Ltd.'s fee simple terminates, and the grantor's possibility of reverter (a vested interest which after 1925 can only be an equitable interest) takes effect.[35]

A similar rule applies to resulting trusts.[36] Where land is conveyed to trustees in trust for an orphans' home, and on failure of that trust, in trust for the then owner of other land, the initial gift is good but the gift over is plainly void for perpetuity; instead, there will be a resulting trust for the grantor's estate, and this will not be void for perpetuity.[37]

(b) *Conditional interests.* A condition may be either precedent or subsequent.[38] A condition precedent is one which must be fulfilled before the beneficiary is entitled to a vested interest, *e.g.*—

"to X and his heirs when he marries."

In such a case the perpetuity rule applies, for a new interest is limited to arise when the event occurs; consequently, if the condition might be fulfilled outside the perpetuity period the whole gift failed at common law,[39] though the "wait and see" principle may now save it if the Act of 1964 applies.

A condition subsequent is one which authorises the grantor or his representatives to determine an existing interest. Thus a gift of land to X in fee simple—

"on condition that he never sells it out of the family"

gives the grantor a right of re-entry if the condition is broken. If such a

---

[33] *Re Chardon* [1928] Ch. 464 at 468.
[34] *Wainwright* v. *Miller* [1897] 2 Ch. 255; *Re Gage* [1898] 1 Ch. 498.
[35] But see *Hopper* v. *Corporation of Liverpool* (1944) 88 S.J. 213; contrast 1945 Conv. Y.B. pp. 203–206. And see further M. & W. 275, 276.
[36] Any beneficial interest of which the settlor fails to dispose remains in him under a resulting trust: see *post*, p. 270.
[37] *Re Cooper's Conveyance Trusts* [1956] 1 W.L.R. 1096.
[38] *Ante*, p. 35.
[39] See, *e.g.* *Pickford* v. *Brown* (1856) 2 K. & J. 426.

condition infringes the perpetuity rule it is void, but the interest which it was to defeat is not invalidated. Thus at common law, if there was a valid gift by a testator to his grandchildren followed by a clause providing for the forfeiture of the interest of any grandchild who should forsake the Jewish faith or marry outside the faith, all the beneficiaries took absolute interests; the forfeiture clause was void since it might not take effect until the perpetuity period had expired, but there was nothing to invalidate the gift to the grandchildren.[40] Where the Act of 1964 applies, however, the "wait and see" principle may save the condition.

It will be noticed that a breach of a condition subsequent gives rise to a right of re-entry, so that some active step must be taken to determine the estate; a determinable limitation, on the other hand, requires no future activity, for the estate automatically determines by force of the original limitation.[40a]

(c) *Act of 1964.* Under the Act of 1964 the rules for determinable and conditional interests have been assimilated. The rule against perpetuities applies to possibilities of reverter and resulting trusts created by dispositions made after the Act as if they were in the form of conditions subsequent.[41] If after "waiting and seeing" the determining event has not occurred within the perpetuity period, then the interest subjected to the condition becomes absolute.

10. Powers. Settlements often authorise trustees, tenants for life and others to do things which they would not otherwise be entitled to do. One class of such powers may authorise acts of administration, such as the sale or leasing of the settled land.[42] Other powers, known as powers of appointment, may authorise an alteration of the beneficial interests. The application of the rule against perpetuities to powers is somewhat complicated.

(a) *Administrative powers*

(1) AT COMMON LAW. In general, an administrative power which was exercisable outside the perpetuity period was void, *e.g.* a power to lease or sell during the lifetime of an unborn person.[43]

(2) ACT OF 1964. It was generally thought that the extension of the rule to administrative powers was unwarranted, and that it ought to be confined to the invalidation of the remote vesting of beneficial interests. Accordingly the Act provides that the rule is not to operate to invalidate a power conferred on trustees and other persons "to sell, lease, exchange or otherwise dispose of any property for full consideration, or to do any other act in the administration (as opposed to the distribution) of any property."[44]

---

[40] *Re Spitzel's W.T.* [1939] 2 All E.R. 266.
[40a] See *ante*, pp. 35 *et seq.*
[41] s.12.
[42] See *post*, p. 241.
[43] *Re Allott* [1924] 2 Ch. 498.
[44] s.8(1).

Exceptionally, this provision is retrospective to the extent that it applies to the exercise of a power after July 15, 1964, even if the settlement or will which conferred the power took effect before then.[45]

(b) *Powers of appointment.* A power of appointment is a power for the person to whom it is given ("the donee of the power") to appoint property to such persons ("the objects of the power") as he may select.

(1) GENERAL AND SPECIAL POWERS. A power is a "special power" if the donee's choice is restricted to a limited class of objects, such as X's children, and a "general power" if his choice is unrestricted and so he himself could benefit.

(i) At common law. For the purposes of the perpetuity rule, the general test is whether or not the donee of the power is as free to dispose of the property as an absolute owner is. Thus for this purpose a joint power of appointment has been held special,[46] and so has a power to appoint with the consent of X,[47] unless, perhaps X's consent is a requisite merely to the exercise of the power and he has no control over the amounts appointed or the persons to benefit, in which case the power may be general. Whether a power to appoint "to anyone except Z" is general or special for this purpose is doubtful. An unrestricted power to appoint by will alone (where the donee, of course, is unable to appoint to himself) is treated as being special in determining whether the power itself is valid, but as being general in determining whether an appointment is valid.[48]

(ii) Act of 1964. The Act of 1964 has codified the distinction between general and special powers. It adopts the formulation worked out in the cases, and resolves the doubts which have been mentioned. In dispositions taking effect after July 15, 1964, a power is treated as a special power unless—

(a) it is expressed to be exercisable by one person only, and
(b) it could be exercised by him so as to transfer the property to himself without the consent of any other person or compliance with any condition (apart from a mere formal condition relating only to the mode of exercise of the power).[49]

Under this provision, a power to appoint "to anyone except X" is now general, but the exceptional position of general testamentary powers has been left unchanged.

(2) VALIDITY OF THE POWER. In the application of the perpetuity rule to powers of appointment, two separate points have to be considered:

(a) Does the power itself infringe the rule?

---

[45] s.8(2). For the general rule, see *ante*, p. 183.
[46] *Re Churston S.E.* [1954] Ch. 334; *Re Earl of Coventry's Indentures* [1974] Ch. 77.
[47] *Re Watts* [1931] 2 Ch. 302.
[48] *Morgan* v. *Gronow* (1873) L.R. 16 Eq. 1; *Rous* v. *Jackson* (1885) 29 Ch.D. 521.
[49] s.7.

(b) If it does not, does the appointment made under the power infringe the rule?

(i) A special power. A special power of appointment is subject to the ordinary rule relating to powers and is thus void if it could be exercised outside the period; time runs from the date when the instrument creating the power took effect[50] and the donor's bounty gave the objects their hope of benefit. Thus if the donee of the power will not necessarily be ascertained within the period (if at all) or is capable of exercising the power when the period has expired, the power is bad.[51] But a power exercisable only by a person living when it was created can never be void for remoteness.

If a power complies with these conditions, it is not void merely because an appointment which offends the rule might be made under it.[52] Thus where a living person is given power to appoint to his issue, he might make an appointment to his great-great-grandchildren, but this possibility does not invalidate either the power itself or an appointment which in fact complies with the rule.

The Act of 1964 applies the new "wait and see" principle to powers created by instruments taking effect after July 15, 1964. The power is to be treated as void only if and so far as it is not fully exercised within the perpetuity period.[53] If the objects of the power are in existence at the creation of the power and are reasonably ascertainable they are included among the lives in being.[54]

If a power is void for remoteness, a gift in default of appointment (*e.g.* "but if no appointment shall be made, to X and Y equally") is not thereby invalidated; provided it does not itself infringe the rule, it is valid.[55]

(ii) A general power. For the purposes of the perpetuity rule, a general power to appoint by deed is so nearly akin to absolute ownership that principles similar to those appropriate to absolute ownership are applied: the perpetuity rule is satisfied if the power must be acquired within the period, if at all, even if the power might be exercised outside the period.[56] But if the power is exercisable only by will, it is treated as a special power and so will be bad if it might be exercised outside the period.[57]

Here, too, the Act of 1964 applies the "wait and see" principle. A general power created by an instrument taking effect after July 15, 1964, will not be void on the ground that it might be acquired at too remote a time, but will be valid unless and until it becomes established that it will not be exercisable within the period.[58] Under the Act of 1964, a general testamentary power,

---

[50] *Re De Sommery* [1912] 2 Ch. 662.
[51] *Re Abbott* [1893] 1 Ch. 54.
[52] *Slark* v. *Dakyns* (1874) 10 Ch.App. 35.
[53] s.3(3).
[54] s.3(5)(b)(iii). For lives in being, see *ante*, p. 190.
[55] *Re Abbott, supra.*
[56] See *Re Fane* [1913] 1 Ch. 404.
[57] *Wollaston* v. *King* (1868) L.R. 8 Eq. 165.
[58] s.3(2).

being special, is treated as being void only if and so far as it is not fully exercised within the perpetuity period.[59]

(3) VALIDITY OF APPOINTMENTS. If the power itself is void, clearly no valid appointment can be made under it. But even if the power itself is valid, an appointment made under it may nevertheless be too remote.

(i) A special power. In the case of a special power of appointment, the property is fettered from the moment the power is created. It can be said at once that either an appointment will be made in favour of one or more of the designated class of persons or else it will pass to those nominated to take in default of appointment, or, if none, to the grantor. The perpetuity period therefore starts to run from the creation of the power.[60] However, as has been seen,[61] the mere fact that the power authorises the making of an appointment which may be too remote does not invalidate it, and until the appointment has been made, it cannot be seen if in fact it is too remote. Consequently, contrary to the general rule in matters of perpetuity, even at common law "the principle seems to be to wait and see."[62] When the appointment is ultimately made, it must be examined to see whether the interests appointed are bound to vest (if at all) within 21 years of the dropping of the lives of persons who were living or *en ventre sa mère*[63] at the time of the creation of the power and not at the time of the appointment. Further, the facts existing at the time of the appointment must be taken into account when deciding this point. In short, in ascertaining the *lives in being* the relevant time is that of the *creation of the power*; in ascertaining the *facts* of the case, the relevant time is that of the *making of the appointment*.

Some examples of the position apart from the Act of 1964 may make this clearer.

(i) Devise to A for life with power to appoint to his children: A appoints to his son B "when he is 23": B was unborn at the testator's death but aged three at the time of the appointment. A is the only life in being, but since the property is bound to vest (if at all) within 20 years of his death, the appointment is good. Had B been under the age of two at the time of the appointment, then if it had been made before 1926 it would have been void; if it was made after 1925, B would have taken when he was 21.[64]

(ii) Marriage settlement upon C for life, remainder as he should appoint among his issue: C appoints in favour of his daughter D, postponing the vesting of her interest until her marriage: D is unmarried at the date of the appointment. The appointment is void. A few years later, D marries and C then executes a document confirming the void

[59] See *ante*, p. 200.
[60] *Re Thompson* [1906] 2 Ch. 199.
[61] *Ante*, p. 201.
[62] *Re Witty* [1913] 2 Ch. 666 at 673, *per* Cozens-Hardy M.R.
[63] *Re Stern* [1962] Ch. 732.
[64] L.P.A. 1925, s.163; *ante*, p. 189.

appointment. D is entitled to the property, since the confirmation operates as a fresh appointment, and taking the facts existing at the time of the appointment, the property has vested during the lifetime of a person alive at the date of the settlement, namely, C.[65]

(iii) Deed giving property to F for life with power to appoint to his issue: F appoints by will in favour of his grandchildren G and H (neither of whom was alive at the date of the gift) for their joint lives as tenants in common, with remainder to the survivor. The interest for their joint lives is valid but the remainder is void.[66]

The Act of 1964 has enlarged the scope of "wait and see" in relation to the exercise of special powers, as well as providing for age reduction and class reduction. If the powers in the example given above are created after July 15, 1964,[67] the result will be as follows:

(i) If B is under two years old at the time of the appointment, he will take when he is 23 if in fact he attains that age within the period, *e.g.* if A lives until B is five. But if A dies before B is two, B will take at whatever age he is when 21 years have elapsed after A's death.[68]

(ii) The first appointment to D will be valid unless and until it appears that D will not marry within the perpetuity period, running from the date of the settlement.

(iii) The remainder is valid if it in fact vests within the period, *i.e.* 21 years after the death of the survivor of the donor, F, and any of F's children living at the date of the deed and any persons who were then their spouses.

(ii) A general power. Since the property is unfettered until the appointment has been made, the donee of the power being able to deal with it as he wishes, the perpetuity period does not begin to run until the date of the appointment. Thus for the purposes of the perpetuity rule there is no difference between the exercise of a general power and a conveyance by an absolute owner.

The difference between appointments under general and special powers may be summarised thus. In both cases, the relevant facts are those existing at the time of the appointment; but the time at which the lives in being must be ascertained is the creation of the power in the case of a special power, and the exercise of the power in the case of a general power.

11. Contracts, covenants and options The rule against perpetuities is essentially a rule relating to property, and so it has only a limited application to contracts, covenants and options.

---

[65] This is based on *Morgan* v. *Gronow* (1873) L.R. 16 Eq. 1.
[66] *Re Legh's S.T.* [1938] Ch. 39.
[67] The Act does not apply to appointments made after July 15, 1964, under a special power created earlier: s.15(5).
[68] See *ante*, pp. 191, 192.

(a) *At common law*

(1) PERSONAL OBLIGATIONS. The rule against remoteness does not apply to contracts in so far as they create mere personal obligations, *e.g.* to pay mining royalties.[69] The rule is directed against the vesting of interests in some specific property at too remote a date, and personal contracts do not do this. Further, even if a contract confers a right to an interest in some specific property exercisable at too remote a date, the rule did not prevent damages[70] or specific performance[71] being awarded against a party to the contract; for the court is merely enforcing his personal obligations and not any rights of property.

(2) PROPRIETARY INTERESTS. Where, however, the plaintiff's case depends not on a personal obligation but on the existence of an interest in specific property, the rule applies. Thus if a lease for 99 years confers on the lessee and his assigns an option to purchase a freehold at any time during the lease[72] (an option appurtenant to the lease), or a corporation is given an option to purchase or take a lease of land[73] (an option is gross), an action to enforce the option against a successor in title of the person who granted the option cannot be based on any personal obligation, and must depend on the burden of the option running with the land. The rule accordingly makes the option unenforceable against the successor unless its exercise is confined within the period.

(3) COVENANTS TO RENEW LEASE. Exceptionally, a covenant in a lease giving the tenant the right to an extension of the term is not void merely because it can be exercised outside the perpetuity period.[74] An option to renew a lease (unlike an option to purchase the reversion) "touches and concerns"[75] the land held under the lease so as to run with it and form part of the tenant's present interest. But a contract made after 1925 to renew a lease for more than 60 years from its termination is void.[76]

(b) *Statutory modifications*.

The Act of 1964 has made three changes in relation to dispositions in instruments taking effect after July 15, 1964.

(1) PERSONAL OBLIGATIONS. The Act reverses the rule that damages or specific performance may be obtained against an original contracting party even though the proprietary interest conferred by the contract is void for perpetuity. A disposition *inter vivos* which creates an interest in property is void between the original contracting parties wherever it would be void for perpetuity against a third party.[77]

---

[69] *Witham* v. *Vane* (1883) Challis R.P. 440; and see M. & W. 287–292.
[70] *Worthing Corporation* v. *Heather* [1906] 2 Ch. 532.
[71] *Hutton* v. *Watling* [1948] Ch. 26, 398.
[72] *Woodall* v. *Clifton* [1905] 2 Ch. 257.
[73] *London and South Western Ry.* v. *Gomm* (1882) 20 Ch.D. 562.
[74] *Woodall* v. *Clifton, supra,* at pp. 265, 268; *Weg Motors Ltd.* v. *Hales* [1962] Ch. 49.
[75] See *post,* p. 351.
[76] L.P.A. 1922, Sched. 15, para. 7; *post,* p. 321.
[77] s.10.

(2) OPTIONS APPURTENANT TO LEASES. The rule against remoteness does not apply to an option for a lessee to purchase the freehold or superior leasehold title which is exercisable only by the lessee or his successors in title and which ceases to be exercisable not later than a year after the end of the lease.[78]

(3) OPTIONS IN GROSS. An option to acquire for value any interest in land is subject to a specially short perpetuity period of 21 years only.[79] The "wait and see" principle applies, so that even if no time limit is specified in the instrument conferring the option, it will remain exercisable for 21 years.

Sect. 3. Exceptions from the Rule

The preceding section has indicated some cases to which the rule against perpetuities does not apply, namely—

(a) Personal obligations;
(b) Covenants for renewal of a lease; and
(c) Covenants in a lease for the purchase of the landlord's reversion.

There are certain other exceptions.

1. Certain limitations after entails. A limitation which is bound to take effect, if at all, during the continuance, or at the moment of the determination, of an entail is not rendered void by the rule, even though the entail may continue for longer than the perpetuity period.[80] Thus a gift to X in tail, with remainder to such of Y's issue as are alive when the entail determines, is valid, even though the persons entitled to take the remainder may not be ascertained for several hundred years.[81] The entail can always be barred by the tenant in tail, and so he is not fettered by the remainder.

This exception, however, does not protect limitations which can or must vest when an interval has elapsed after the determination of the entail.[82] If property is given to trustees in trust for A in tail, remainder to the first of the great-grandchildren of B to attain the age of 30, A's entail is valid but the remainder is void, for it might very well vest many years after the period has run and the entail has determined.

2. Certain gifts to charities. The general rule is that a gift to a charity is subject to the rule in the same way as any other gift.[83] However, if there is a gift to one charity followed by a gift over to another charity on a certain event, the gift over is not void merely because the event may occur outside

---

[78] s.9(1).
[79] s.9(2). But see *Governors of Peabody Donation Fund* v. *London Residuary Body* (1987) 55 P. & C.R. 355 (exemption from rule provided by statutory scheme).
[80] *Nicolls* v. *Sheffield* (1787) 2 Bro.C.C. 215.
[81] See *Heaseman* v. *Pearse* (1871) 7 Ch.App. 275 at 282, 283.
[82] See *Bristow* v. *Boothby* (1826) 2 Sim. & St. 465.
[83] *Chamberlayne* v. *Brockett* (1872) 8 Ch.App. 206.

the perpetuity period. Thus if property is given to Charity A with a proviso that it shall go to Charity B if Charity A fails to keep the testator's tomb in repair, the gift over is valid.[84] To this extent alone are charities exempted from the rule against remoteness.[85]

3. Certain rights of entry and re-entry. The right to re-enter and determine a lease if a covenant is broken, which most leases give to the landlord, is excepted from the perpetuity rule.[86] Again, the statutory remedies for enforcing payment of a rentcharge[87] or any like powers or remedies conferred by any instrument were expressly excepted from the rule in 1925[88]; for rentcharges created after July 15, 1964, the Act of 1964 extends the exemption to all powers and remedies for enforcing rentcharges.[89] Further, the Law of Property Act 1925[90] sets out a list of certain rights retrospectively excepted from the rule, such as a right to enter or use the surface of land in order to work minerals or execute repairs. A right of re-entry in respect of a fee simple is not within this exception and will accordingly be void if it is exercisable outside the perpetuity period.[91]

4. Mortgages. "The rule has never been applied to mortgages," and thus a clause postponing the mortgagor's right to redeem the property is not invalid merely because the right is postponed for longer than the perpetuity period.[92]

Part 3

THE RULE AGAINST INALIENABILITY

1. The rule. It is a fundamental principle of English law that property cannot be rendered inalienable. Thus a devise of land to be retained in perpetuity as a family burial ground is void.[93] This is not affected by the property being subject to powers to sell or otherwise dispose of it where the restrictions would apply to the purchase money, so that there would be a fund which in one form or another must be held indefinitely to order to provide income under the terms of the gift. A gift is bad if effect can be given to it only by holding the property for ever and applying the income for the purposes specified.[94] The rule is sometimes called "the rule against trusts of

---

[84] *Re Tyler* [1891] 3 Ch. 252; and see *post*, pp. 207, 208.
[85] See also the exemption from the rule against inalienability, *post*, p. 208.
[86] *Re Tyrell's Estate* [1907] 1 I.R. 292 at 298.
[87] *Post*, p. 364.
[88] L.P.A. 1925, s.121.
[89] s.11(1).
[90] s.162.
[91] *Re Trustees of Hollis' Hospital and Hague's Contract* [1899] 2 Ch. 540; L.P.A. 1925, s.4; and see *ante*, pp. 36, 198, 199.
[92] *Knightsbridge Estates Trust Ltd.* v. *Byrne* [1939] Ch. 441 at 463 *per* Greene M.R.; on appeal, [1940] A.C. 613.
[93] *Yeap Cheah Neo* v. *Ong Cheng Neo* (1875) L.R. 6 P.C. 381.
[94] See *Cocks* v. *Manners* (1871) L.R. 12 Eq. 574 at 585, 586.

perpetual duration," or "the rule that gifts which tend to a perpetuity" are void.

2. The period. Although property cannot be made inalienable for ever, or for a period to which no clear or definite limit is set,[95] it appears to be settled that a limitation making property inalienable is valid if it is limited to a maximum period of a life or lives in being at the time of the gift, with a further 21 years.[96] This period is borrowed from the rule against perpetuities, considered above.[97] It is not affected by the Perpetuities and Accumulations Act 1964[98]; thus the "wait and see" principle, the 80 years' period, and the statutory list of lives in being do not apply to the rule against inalienability.

3. Purpose trusts. The rule has no application to a trust for abstract or impersonal objects or purposes (as distinct from persons) where there is nobody who can enforce it; for such trusts are void.[99] Where there is a trust for some non-charitable purpose, such as preserving the independence and integrity of newspapers,[1] or pursuing inquiries into a new alphabet,[2] or providing "some useful memorial" of the testator,[3] the trust is void because there is no beneficiary or other person who can enforce it. Such trusts are sometimes called "trusts of imperfect obligation." There are a few cases of doubtful authority in which testamentary trusts for maintaining individual animals[4] or a tomb,[5] or for furthering fox hunting,[6] have been held valid, the duration in each case having been limited to the perpetuity period. Further, what at first appears to be merely a purpose trust may be enforceable by persons for whose benefit it was imposed, as where land is given on the terms that for the perpetuity period it is to be maintained as a sports ground for the benefit of identifiable employees of a company.[7] On the other hand, where the trust is wholly charitable in nature, it is not void for lack of anyone to enforce it, for the Attorney General can do this; and it is exempt from the rule against inalienability.[8] This may be employed to secure indirectly the carrying out of some purpose such as the maintenance of a tomb indefinitely.[9]

---

[95] *Re Wightwick's W.T.* [1950] Ch. 260.
[96] See *Re Dean* (1889) 41 Ch.D. 552 at 557.
[97] *Ante*, p. 187.
[98] See s.15(4), where the sense requires "remoteness" to mean "inalienability." And see M. & W. 269.
[99] *Re Denley's Trust Deed* [1969] 1 Ch. 373.
[1] *Re Astor's S.T.* [1952] Ch. 534.
[2] *Re Shaw* [1957] 1 W.L.R. 729 (G.B.S.).
[3] *Re Endacott* [1960] Ch. 232.
[4] *Re Dean* (1889) 41 Ch.D. 552 (horses and dogs).
[5] *Re Hooper* [1932] 1 Ch. 38.
[6] *Re Thompson* [1934] Ch. 342.
[7] *Re Denley's Trust Deed, supra.*
[8] *Chamberlayne* v. *Brockett* (1872) 8 Ch.App. 206; compare the rule against perpetuities: *ante*, p. 205.
[9] *Ante*, p. 206.

4. Immediate gifts. Where property is given to an unincorporated association, such as a members' club, it must be decided whether the gift is made to
all the members of the association, both present and future, or whether it is
an immediate gift to all the existing members of the association. This
depends on the terms of the gift and the rules of the association: either may
impose a trust or obligation to hold the property for the benefit of all present
and future members. If it does this, the gift is void for inalienability unless it
is confined to the perpetuity period.[10] Otherwise the gift will take effect as an
absolute gift to the existing members; and as each of them can call forthwith
for his distributive share, no question of inalienability arises.[11] The same
applies to a gift to the trustees of an association for its general purposes
where the trustees are free to alienate the property forthwith.[12] Further, an
immediate gift of income for an indefinite period to a company does not
infringe the rule merely because it is to cease at an indefinite future date (*e.g.*
when a tomb is no longer in good repair), for the company is always free to
assign the right to the future income, and nothing is inalienable.[13]

5. Charities. Charities are exempt from the rule against inalienability; no
gift for charitable purposes is void merely because it renders property
inalienable in perpetuity.[14]

Part 4

THE RULE AGAINST ACCUMULATIONS

The rule against accumulations resembles the rule against inalienability in
that it is directed against remoteness of control over a vested interest rather
than against interests which may vest at too distant a date. The rule was first
laid down by the ill-drafted Accumulations Act 1800, which was passed as a
result of *Thellusson* v. *Woodford*.[15] In that case, Mr. Thellusson by his will
directed that the income of his property should be accumulated during the
lives of his sons, grandsons and their issue who were living at his death, and
that on the death of the survivor, the accumulated fund should be divided
among certain of his descendants. This direction, being confined to lives in
being, was held valid, but as it was calculated that the accumulated fund
would amount to many millions of pounds, Parliament intervened to prevent further directions of this nature.

At common law, the rule was that a direction to accumulate was valid if it

---

[10] *Re Macaulay's Estate* (1933) [1943] Ch. 435n; *Re Grant's W.T.* [1980] 1 W.L.R. 360 ("the
Labour Party property committee").
[11] See *Re Ray's W.T.* [1936] 2 All E.R. 93 at 97, 98; and see *Leahy* v. *Attorney-General for New
South Wales* [1959] A.C. 457 at 477.
[12] *Re Prevost* [1930] 2 Ch. 383 (the London Library); *Re Recher's W.T.* [1972] Ch. 526.
[13] *Re Chardon* [1928] Ch. 464; *Re Wightwick's W.T.* [1950] Ch. 267.
[14] *Chamberlayne* v. *Brockett* (1872) 8 Ch.App. 206 at 211; contrast the rule against remoteness,
ante, p. 205.
[15] (1799) 4 Ves. 227; (1805) 11 Ves. 112; hence the Act is often called "the Thellusson Act."

was confined to the perpetuity period,[16] so that Mr. Thellusson might have effectively directed accumulation for a further 21 years; probably he did not do so because the permissibility of the extra period of 21 years after lives in being was not firmly established when he made his will.

Sect. 1. The Statutory Periods

1. The periods. The present law is contained in the Law of Property Act 1925,[17] and the Perpetuities and Accumulations Act 1964.[18] If the disposition took effect before July 16, 1964, a direction or power[19] to accumulate may be validly given for any one (but not more) of the following periods:

(1) The life of the grantor or settlor.
(2) 21 years from the death of the grantor, settlor or testator.
(3) The minority or respective minorities of any person or persons living or *en ventre sa mère* at the death of the grantor, settlor or testator.
(4) The minority or respective minorities only of any person or persons who under the limitations of the instrument directing accumulation would for the time being, if of full age, be entitled to the income directed to be accumulated.

For dispositions taking effect after July 15, 1964, two further periods have been added[20]:

(5) 21 years from the date of the making of the disposition.
(6) The minority or respective minorities of any person or persons in being at that date.

2. Choice of periods. The question which period has been chosen in each particular case is one of construction.[21] The first two and the fifth periods cause little difficulty. Of the first, it should be noted that it is the only period of a life available for accumulation, and that it must be the life of the grantor or settlor himself and not of some third person. The second period is a fixed term of years which starts to run at the beginning of the day after the testator's death and expires at the end of the twenty-first anniversary of his death.[22] Thus if a testator directs accumulations to start at the end of an interval after his death and continue for 21 years, he exceeds the second period. The second period was of little use save in wills. Now, the fifth period allows the 21 years to run from the date of the settlement.

---

[16] *Wilson* v. *Wilson* (1851) 1 Sim. (N.S.) 288 at 298.
[17] ss.164–166.
[18] ss.13, 14.
[19] *Re Robb* [1953] Ch. 459; Act of 1964, s.13(2). *Re Robb* was disapproved in *Re Earl of Berkeley* [1968] Ch. 744, but not so as to affect this point: *Baird* v. *Lord Advocate* [1979] A.C. 666 at 675.
[20] Act of 1964, s.13(1).
[21] *Jagger* v. *Jagger* (1883) 25 Ch.D. 729.
[22] *Gorst* v. *Lowndes* (1841) 11 Sim. 434.

The third, fourth and sixth periods are all minorities. Minority now ends at the age of 18.[23] The periods differ in the following respects:

(i) The third and sixth periods are confined to the minorities of persons alive or *en ventre sa mère* at the death of the grantor, settlor or testator, or at the date of the settlement, as the case may be. The fourth period is not.

(ii) The third and sixth periods are not restricted to the minorities of those who are prospectively entitled to any benefit under the gift, whereas the fourth period is confined to the minorities of those who can say "but for my minority I would be entitled to the income being accumulated."[24]

(iii) The third and sixth periods can never exceed a single minority; for even if accumulation is directed during a large number of minorities, the period is in effect merely the longest of these minorities. Under the fourth period, on the other hand, accumulation during successive minorities is possible.

An example may make this clear.[25] A testator devises the residue of his property between all the children of his sons, whether born before or after his death, the income of their shares to be accumulated during their respective minorities. At the testator's death, there is only one child of his sons alive, and she is a minor named D. The whole of the income must be accumulated during this minority, the direction to accumulate falling within the fourth period; for if she was of full age she would for the time being be entitled to the whole of the income. After D attains her majority, a child, C, is born to one of the testator's sons. C becomes entitled to one half of the estate, subject to the same liability, *i.e.* that his share may be partially divested by the birth of other children. During the minority of C, the income from his share must be accumulated, even though the income from the whole of the residuary estate has already been accumulated once.

If D had not been born until after the testator's death, there could have been no accumulation under the fourth period until her birth, for not until then would her minority have commenced.

3. Purchase of land. Where after June 27, 1892, accumulation is directed for the sole purpose of purchasing land, only the fourth period may be selected. But this restriction does not apply to accumulations to be held as capital money under the Settled Land Act 1925 or any of the Acts which it replaces.[26]

---

[23] Family Law Reform Act 1969, s.1. The period of 21 years in the second and fifth periods is not affected, nor is the validity of directions for accumulation in dispositions made before 1970 with reference to the previous period of minority ending at the age of 21.

[24] *Jagger* v. *Jagger*, *supra*, at p. 733, as corrected in *Re Cattell*, *infra*, at p. 189.

[25] See *Re Cattell* [1914] 1 Ch. 177.

[26] L.P.A. 1925, s.166; see *post*, p. 260.

4. Ambit of rules. These rules apply whether the limitations are contained in a deed or a will, whether the accumulation is at compound or, it seems, merely simple interest,[27] and whether it is the whole or merely part of the income of a fund that is to be accumulated.[28] Yet there is no accumulation if income is merely retained to meet possible future deficiencies in the income required for paying annuities, and is not added to capital.[29]

Sect. 2. Excessive Accumulation

1. Exceeding perpetuity period. If the period for which accumulation is directed may exceed the perpetuity period, the direction to accumulate is totally void, *e.g.* where accumulation was directed until a lease with over 60 years to run had "nearly expired."[30] This applies even to accumulations for the benefit of charities.[31] The "wait and see" provisions of the Act of 1964 apply to a power to accumulate, but not, it seems to a direction to accumulate, unless, perhaps, the direction can be treated as being a power that is subject to a duty to exercise it.[32]

2. Exceeding accumulation period. If the period for which accumulation is directed cannot exceed the perpetuity period but exceeds the relevant accumulation period, the direction to accumulate is good *pro tanto*, and only the excess over the appropriate accumulation period is void; the statutory provisions are merely restrictive of the wider powers formerly enjoyed.[33]

Which is the appropriate period depends on the circumstances.[34] Thus where accumulation is directed for the lifetime of any person (other than the settlor in the case of an *inter vivos* settlement), accumulation will take place for 21 years from the date of the settlement or, as the case may be, from the testator's death, if the named person so long lives.[35] This uses the second or fifth period, and these periods are also the most appropriate whenever accumulation is directed for a period of years. The same applies where accumulation is directed until X is 25,[36] or from the time Y remarries until her death,[37] or from the death of either A or B until the death of the survivor. In each of these cases, if accumulation is still continuing 21 years after the

---

[27] See *Re Garside* [1919] 1 Ch. 132.
[28] *Re Travis* [1900] 2 Ch. 541.
[29] *Re Earl of Berkeley* [1968] Ch. 744.
[30] *Curtis* v. *Lukin* (1842) 5 Beav. 147.
[31] *Re Bradwell* [1952] Ch. 575.
[32] s.3(3); M. & W. 305.
[33] *Leake* v. *Robinson* (1817) 2 Mer. 363 at 389.
[34] See *Re Ransome* [1957] Ch. 348 at 361.
[35] *Griffiths* v. *Vere* (1803) 9 Ves. 127. In the case of a settlement *inter vivos* made before July 16, 1964, the first period was the most appropriate, and accumulation continued during the period common to the lives of the settlor and the named person: *Re Lady Rosslyn's Trust* (1848) 16 Sim. 391.
[36] *Crawley* v. *Crawley* (1835) 7 Sim. 427.
[37] *Weatherell* v. *Thornburgh* (1878) 8 Ch.D. 261.

date of the settlement or the death of the testator, it must cease forthwith, even if it has been proceeding for only a short period, *e.g.* two years.[38]

Again, if property is given by will to all the children of X (a living person) who attain their majority, and accumulation of the whole fund is directed while any child of X is a minor, the first two periods are clearly not intended and the fourth is not appropriate, for the accumulation is directed to continue for as long as *any* child is a minor, even if some of the children are 18; the latter children, though of full age, are not entitled to the income to be accumulated within the wording of the fourth period. Consequently the third period is the most appropriate, and so far as it is exceeded the direction is void; accumulation will therefore cease as soon as all children living at the testator's death are 18.[39]

3. Surplus income. The income for any period during which accumulation is invalidly directed passes to the person who would have been entitled had no excessive accumulation been directed.[40] Thus if there is a gift of a vested interest subject only to an excessive trust for accumulation, the vested interest will carry any income not validly accumulated. For example, where property is given by will to X, subject to a direction that the income exceeding a certain figure is to be accumulated during X's life for the benefit of Y, the accumulation must cease 21 years after the testator's death, and the surplus income will go to X.[41] But otherwise, the income reverts to the settlor or his estate, or in the case of a gift by will, passes under any residuary gift, or, in default, to the persons entitled on intestacy.[42]

Sect. 3. The Rule in Saunders v. Vautier

Under the rule in *Saunders* v. *Vautier*,[43] a beneficiary of full age who has an absolute indefeasible interest in property may at any time, notwithstanding any direction to accumulate, require the transfer of the property to him and terminate any accumulation; a man may do as he likes with his own, and the same applies to a charity.[44] Thus if property is given to A with a direction to accumulate the income for his benefit until he is 24, A can demand payment of both the original property and the accumulations as soon as he is of full age.[45] The rule applies, however, only if the beneficiary or beneficiaries seeking to put an end to the accumulation together comprise every person who has any vested or contingent interest in the property.[46] Thus it will not apply if there is a gift to a class of persons or charities not yet determined, or

[38] *Shaw* v. *Rhodes* (1836) 1 My. & Cr. 135.
[39] *Re Watt's W.T.* [1936] 2 All E.R. 1555.
[40] L.P.A 1925, s.164.
[41] *Trickey* v. *Trickey* (1832) 3 My. & Cr. 560. See also *Brotherton* v. *I.R.C.* [1978] 1 W.L.R. 610.
[42] *Mathews* v. *Keble* (1867) L.R. 4 Eq. 467 at 473, 474 (affd. 3 Ch.App. 691).
[43] (1841) 4 Beav. 115; affd. Cr. & Ph. 240.
[44] *Wharton* v. *Masterman* [1895] A.C. 186; contrast *Re Levy* [1960] Ch. 346.
[45] *Josselyn* v. *Josselyn* (1837) 9 Sim. 63. A took at 21; today he would take at 18.
[46] *Berry* v *Geen* [1938] A.C. 575.

to beneficiaries whose interests are contingent or liable to be defeated by some event occurring.

Sect. 4. Exceptions from the Rule against Accumulations

The rule against accumulations does not apply in the following cases.[47]

1. Payment of debts: a provision for accumulation for the payment of the debts of any person,[48] whether the settlor, testator or anyone else.[49] An accumulation for the payment of the debts of the settlor or testator is valid even if it may exceed the perpetuity period[50]; such a direction can cause little mischief, for the creditors may terminate the accumulation at any time by demanding payment. But an accumulation to pay the debts of any other person must be confined within the perpetuity period.

This exception includes all debts, whether existing or contingent, provided the accumulation is directed bona fide for their payment; thus it extends to accumulations to discharge a mortgage or to provide for liability under a leasehold covenant not yet broken.[51] It does not extend to debts not in existence when the instrument directing accumulation took effect, such as estate duty or inheritance tax payable on the death of a tenant for life.[52]

2. Portions: a provision for accumulation for raising portions for any issue of the grantor, settlor or testator or any person to whom an interest is limited under the settlement.[53] This is an exception from the rule against accumulations only; such accumulations must be confined to the perpetuity period. The meaning of "portions" here is not clear. It is not confined to sums raised out of real estate, nor to provisions for the benefit of the younger children of a marriage.[54] It does not, however, apply where there is no existing obligation to use the fund for portions but a mere future discretionary power,[55] nor where the direction is to accumulate the income from the whole of a testator's estate, for "it is not raising a portion at all, it is giving everything."[56]

3. Timber or wood: a provision for accumulating the produce of timber or wood.[57] Although excepted from the accumulation rules, such a direction will be void if it exceeds the perpetuity period.[58]

[47] See L.P.A. 1925, ss.164, 165.
[48] *Ibid.* s.164.
[49] *Viscount Barrington* v. *Liddell* (1852) 2 De G.M. & G. 480.
[50] *Bateman* v. *Hotchkin* (1847) 10 Beav. 426.
[51] *Re Hurlbatt* [1910] 2 Ch. 553.
[52] *Re Rochford's S.T.* [1965] Ch. 111.
[53] L.P.A. 1925, s.164; see also *post*, p. 215.
[54] *Re Stephens* [1904] 1 Ch. 322.
[55] *Re Bourne's S.T.* [1946] 1 All E.R. 411.
[56] *Edwards* v. *Tuck* (1853) 3 De G.M. & G. 40 at 58, *per* Lord Cranworth L.C.
[57] L.P.A. 1925, s.164. This exception is said to be due to the need for naval timber in 1800.
[58] *Ferrand* v. *Wilson* (1845) 4 Hare 344.

4. Maintenance of property: a provision for maintaining property at its present value. Directions to devote surplus income to maintaining buildings in a proper state of repair, or to apply a fixed annual sum to keep up an insurance policy to replace the capital lost by not selling leaseholds, are outside the rule against accumulations; although income is added to capital, the payments are merely to keep up the property and not add to it, so that there is no true accumulation.[59] But they must be confined to the perpetuity period.[60]

5. Minority: accumulations made during a minority under the general law or any statutory power. While the person entitled to any trust property is a minor, a statutory power is given to the trustees to apply the income for his maintenance; subject thereto, they are bound to accumulate the residue of the income.[61] It is expressly provided that the period of such accumulation is to be disregarded when determining the period for which accumulations are permitted.[62] Thus if a testator directs accumulation for 21 years after his death and the beneficiary at the end of the period is a minor, the accumulations both for the 21 years and during the minority are valid.[63]

6. Certain commercial contracts: transactions which cannot fairly be described as settlements or dispositions. Many commercial transactions involve a measure of accumulation, such as partnership agreements which provide for the accumulation of certain profits, and investment trusts which capitalise part of their income. Such transactions are outside the Act,[64] which merely provides that no person may "settle or dispose" of property in breach of the Act[65]; and many of them are also outside the perpetuity rule as creating merely personal obligations.

7. Corporations: settlements made by a corporation. The statute applies only to natural persons and not to corporations.[66]

---

[59] *Vine* v. *Raleigh* [1891] 2 Ch. 13; *Re Gardiner* [1901] 1 Ch. 697.
[60] *Curtis* v. *Lukin* (1842) 5 Beav. 147.
[61] T.A. 1925, s.31.
[62] L.P.A. 1925, s.165.
[63] *Re Maber* [1928] Ch. 88.
[64] See *Bassil* v. *Lister* (1851) 9 Hare 177 at 184; *Re A.E.G. Unit Trust (Managers) Ltd.'s Deed* [1957] Ch. 415.
[65] L.P.A. 1925, s.164(1).
[66] *Re Dodwell & Co. Ltd.'s Trust* [1979] Ch. 301.

CHAPTER 7

SETTLED LAND AND TRUSTS FOR SALE

Part 1

BEFORE 1883

IT is now necessary to turn from matters of substance to matters of machinery. The last chapter discussed the rules regulating the various future interests in land which could be created, and this chapter will examine how land which is the subject of future interests is managed and disposed of. The starting point is to consider settlements.

The basic idea of a settlement is to make provision out of property for two or more persons in succession. Settlements were frequently made on marriage, providing for the spouses and issue by giving the property to the husband for life, with remainder to the children in tail, subject to paying the wife an annual sum. But not all settlements are marriage settlements, and for most purposes it can be taken that a settlement exists whenever future interests in property have been created.

By the middle of the nineteenth century two methods of settling land were firmly established: these were the strict settlement and the trust for sale.

Sect. 1. The Strict Settlement

1. Principal provisions. A strict settlement was the type of settlement employed "to keep land in the family." Provided the various rules of law and equity were observed, the settlor might create such limitations as he thought fit; but the type of settlement most frequently encountered has been the marriage settlement, giving a life interest to the husband and entails to the children. Provision was also made for the wife by giving her a jointure (an annual income during widowhood), and for the children who did not obtain the land under the entails by giving them portions (lump sums of money to assist them in their careers and in matrimony).[1] This form of settlement was adopted because it made provision for all members of the family and yet preserved the land as a unit. The device of giving the husband a mere life estate with remainder to his son in tail (the son, of course, being unborn at the time of the settlement, which was made shortly before the marriage) was adopted as being the best way of keeping the land in the family. If an entail had been given to the husband, he could at once have barred it; and under the rule in *Whitby* v. *Mitchell*,[2] a succession of life estates to the husband, his

---

[1] For details, see M. & W. 412 *et seq.*; and see generally Harvey, *Settlements of Land* (1973).
[2] *Ante*, p. 182.

son, the son's son and so on was invalid after the first gift to an unborn person.

2. Alienation

(a) *Settlement and resettlement.* The effect of such a settlement was to render the land substantially inalienable until the eldest son became able to bar the entail on attaining his majority. Shortly after the son's twenty-first birthday he was usually persuaded (often by some financial inducement) to bar the entail with his father's consent; the land was then resettled on the husband for life, remainder to the son for life, remainder to the son's son in tail. The land was thus tied up for another generation. This process of settlement and resettlement prevented any person of full age from having more than a life estate; and the tenant in possession of the land was always a tenant for life. The tenant for life could alienate his life estate, but that was all; no matter how desirable or necessary it was, he had no power to sell the fee simple in any part of the land, or to grant leases which would be binding after his death. If improvements to the property were required, he could effect them only if he paid for them out of his own pocket. Unless he was unimpeachable of waste,[3] the discovery of valuable minerals beneath the land was of little importance to him, for he could not open mines; and even if he was unimpeachable of waste, he could not grant mining leases with an adequate security of tenure for the lessee. In short, for many purposes the land was sterilised.

(b) *Powers in settlement.* These defects were frequently met by a series of provisions in the settlement. Many powers were given to the tenant for life, such as powers to grant specified leases which would be binding on his successors. He was also empowered to sell the fee simple provided the purchase money was paid to trustees to hold on the trusts of the settlement; his own rights and the rights of his son and the other beneficiaries were thus overreached.[4] Usually the bulk of the land would be retained and not sold, but a power of sale was useful for emergencies.

(c) *Legal estate.* The legal estate in settled land might be either split up between the beneficiaries or vested in trustees, according to the way in which the settlement was made. For example, a conveyance—

"to T and his heirs to the use of A for life, remainder to B and the heirs of his body, remainder to C and his heirs"

gave A a legal life estate, B a legal fee tail and C a legal fee simple. If the conveyance had been worded—

"unto and to the use of T and his heirs in trust for . . ."

the legal fee simple would have been in T, and A, B and C would have had

---

[3] *Ante,* p. 50.
[4] *Ante,* p. 5.

merely equitable interests. In the first case, the settlement conferred the desired powers upon A by means of legal powers operating under the Statute of Uses 1535; the settlement took effect as if the land had been given to A for life and then, subject to such sales, leases and other authorised dealings as A made, to B in tail with remainder to C in fee simple. In the second case, the powers conferred upon A would be merely equitable, but T was bound to give effect to any authorised disposition made by A, and the court would compel him to create or transfer the necessary legal estate.[5]

(d) *Absence of powers.* Although it was thus possible for a settlement to provide the necessary powers, in many cases this was not done, especially where the settlement was made by will. In such cases the land could not be dealt with unless the expense of obtaining a private Act of Parliament was incurred. Further, even if the powers were inserted, difficulties sometimes arose over the construction to be put upon them; and in any case the settlement became of formidable length.

3. Intervention of statute. This position was dealt with by a series of statutes passed in the nineteenth century. Starting with Acts such as the Settled Estates Drainage Acts 1840 and 1845 concerning certain limited improvements, the legislature proceeded to enact the Settled Estates Acts 1856 and 1877, which enabled the court to authorise a number of dealings, and even enabled the tenant for life to grant certain leases without application to the court. These comparatively timid measures remained the law until the Settled Land Act 1882, drafted by Mr. Wolstenholme, was piloted through Parliament by Lord Cairns.

Sect. 2. Trusts for Sale

1. Origin. Compared with strict settlements, settlements by way of trust for sale are of comparatively recent origin.[6] It is true that trusts for sale created by will can be traced back for some 500 years, but most of the earliest of these trusts seem to have been designed to raise sums of money, *e.g.* for the payment of debts, rather than to provide for persons by way of succession. Trusts for sale created *inter vivos* are more recent in origin; not until some 150 years ago do marriage settlements by way of trust for sale appear to have become at all common. The purpose of such trusts for sale usually differed greatly from that of a strict settlement. Where the property to be settled was a family estate on which the beneficiaries would reside and over which the tenant for life would wish to exercise direct control, the settlor usually employed a strict settlement which would keep the land in the family. Where, however, the property was in the nature of an investment, such as a row of shops, there would be no desire to keep it in the family in any particular form, nor would the tenant for life wish to live on it or manage it:

[5] See *Re Brown* (1886) 32 Ch.D. 597 at 601.
[6] See generally (1927) 3 Camb. L.J. 59 (J. M. Lightwood).

in such cases, a trust for sale would be employed, the primary object of such a settlement being to produce a regular income for the beneficiaries.

2. Retention unsold. For these reasons, in a trust for sale the legal estate was vested in the trustees upon trust to sell the land and hold the income until sale and the proceeds thereafter upon specified trusts for the beneficiaries. The trustees were usually given power to postpone sale in their discretion, and to manage the land until sale. Thus as long as the land produced a satisfactory income, it could be retained, and the trustees need not sell until market conditions made an advantageous sale possible. Often the consent of the beneficiaries entitled in possession was made requisite to a sale. The purchase-money arising on a sale was usually directed to be invested in stocks, shares and other securities.

3. Conversion. The effect of creating a trust for sale was that even before sale, the rights of the beneficiaries were deemed to be rights in personalty. Equity treated that as done which ought to be done, and since there was a binding obligation to sell the land sooner or later, the beneficiaries were treated as having forthwith interests in the purchase-money into which the land was to be converted: this is known as the equitable doctrine of conversion. For this reason, trusts for sale are often referred to as "personalty settlements," in common with settlements of stocks and shares and other personal property; and the doctrine has important consequences, not least in relation to wills.[7] They were also sometimes called "traders' settlements," since they are more appropriate to the urban property of business men than the rural estates of the landed gentry.

Part 2

THE SETTLED LAND ACT 1882

The Settled Land Act 1882, which was passed as the result of a period of agricultural depression, had as its paramount object the well-being of settled land. "The leading purpose of the Legislature was to prevent the decay of agricultural and other interests occasioned by the deterioration of lands and buildings in the possession of impecunious life-tenants."[8] The general scheme of the Act was to give the tenant for life under the settlement wide powers of dealing with the land free from the limitations of the settlement without making any application to the court, and to protect the rights of the beneficiaries in the case of a sale by shifting the settlement from the land to the purchase-money, which had to be paid into court or into the hands of the trustees. A purchaser was not concerned with the rights of the beneficiaries, even if he had full knowledge of them; those rights were not destroyed, but,

---

[7] *Post*, p. 257.
[8] *Bruce* v. *Marquess of Ailesbury* [1892] A.C. 356 at 363, *per* Lord Watson.

being overreached, were transformed from rights in the land to rights in the money paid for it.

In this legislation, the term "settlement" sometimes means the documents by which the land was settled, but more usually means the state of affairs resulting from them[9]; the context usually indicates which. The Act also applied in a somewhat unsatisfactory way to trusts for sale.[10] The following is a brief statement of the principal provisions of the Act.

Sect. 1. Settled Land

A. Definition of Settled Land

Any land, or any estate or interest therein, which was the subject of any document or documents whereby it stood for the time being limited to, or in trust for, any persons by way of succession, was deemed to be settled land and so subject to the Act, whether the settlement was made before or after the Act.[11] Thus if freehold land was conveyed or given by will—

"unto and to the use of A and B and their heirs in trust for X for life, remainder in trust for Y and his heirs,"

or freehold land was conveyed—

"to A for life, remainder to B and his heirs," or

"to X and his heirs to the use of Y and the heirs of his body,"

in each case the land was settled land, whether the legal estate was vested in trustees as in the first example or in the person currently beneficially entitled as in the other two examples. Leasehold land might similarly be settled. In the third case the requirement that there should be an element of succession was satisfied by the resulting use to the grantor in fee simple subject to Y's entail.

In one case, land was deemed settled land even if no element of succession was involved: this was where a minor was entitled to it in possession.[12]

B. Powers of the Tenant for Life

1. The powers. The object of the Act was to give to one person wide and unfettered powers of sale, exchange, leasing, mortgaging and otherwise dealing with the land.[13] That person was the tenant for life or other limited owner in possession, such as a tenant in tail, tenant in fee simple subject to a gift over, or person entitled to a base fee.[14] For convenience, the phrase "tenant for life" is used to include not only those who had an actual life estate, but any other person who had the powers of a tenant for life. If the

---

[9] See *Re Spencer's S.E.* [1903] 1 Ch. 75 at 79; *Re Ogle's S.E.* [1927] 1 Ch. 229 at 233.
[10] *Post*, p. 222.
[11] S.L.A. 1882, s.2.
[12] *Ibid.* s.59; and see M. & W. 318.
[13] *Ibid.* ss.3, 6, 18.
[14] *Ibid.* ss.2, 58.

tenant for life was a minor, the trustees of the settlement could exercise the statutory powers on the minor's behalf.[15]

2. Tenant for life a trustee. In relation to the exercise of his statutory powers, the tenant for life was deemed to be a trustee for the other beneficiaries, and was bound to consider their interests.[16] This enabled the court to intervene if he sought to sell at a price infinitely below the value of the property[17] or to make an investment which, although not outside his powers, was undesirable. Nevertheless, provided the transaction was a proper one, it would not be invalidated merely because the motive of the tenant for life was not very commendable, *e.g.* that "he is selling out of ill will or caprice, or because he does not like the remainderman, because he desires to be relieved from the trouble of attending to the management of land, or from any other such object, or with any such motive."[18]

3. Powers unfettered. Subject to this restriction, the tenant for life was in general unfettered in the exercise of his powers. They could not be taken away or cut down either directly or indirectly, nor could he curtail or divest himself of them or effectively contract not to exercise them.[19] Additional or larger powers could be conferred by the settlor on the tenant for life or the trustees, and the Act in no way restricted such powers.[20] However, so far as the settlement conferred on the trustees powers to do things which the Act already authorised the tenant for life to do, the terms of the Act prevailed, and the trustees were unable to exercise such powers without the consent of the tenant for life.[21] The tenant for life was thus normally in complete control of the land, even if he was "a spendthrift, who has ruined himself by his own extravagance and folly, who has brought disgrace on the family name, and who has exposed the family estate to destruction for the rest of his life."[22]

C. The Trustees of the Settlement

The Act contained an elaborate definition of the persons who were the trustees of the settlement, but in any settlement made after 1882 they normally consisted of those persons expressly appointed as trustees of the settlement for the purposes of the Act.[23] It is important to note that whether or not the legal estate was vested in the trustees, they had no real control over the land. Their most important function arose from the fact that capital money arising on any transaction, such as the sale of the land, had to be paid either to the trustees or into court; and unless the settlement otherwise

---

[15] S.L.A. 1882, s.60.
[16] *Ibid.* s.53; *Re Lord Stamford's S.E.* (1889) 43 Ch.D. 84 at 95.
[17] *Wheelwright* v. *Walker (No.* 1) (1883) 23 Ch.D. 752 at 762.
[18] *Cardigan* v. *Curzon-Howe* (1885) 30 Ch.D. 531 at 540, *per* Chitty J.
[19] S.L.A. 1882, ss.50–52.
[20] *Ibid.* ss.56, 57.
[21] *Ibid.* s.56.
[22] *Re Marquis of Ailesbury's S.E.* [1892] 1 Ch. 506 at 535, *per* Lindley L.J.
[23] S.L.A. 1882, s.2; S.L.A. 1890, s.16.

provided,[24] the trustees had to be two or more in number to give an effective receipt.[25] The tenant for life was also obliged to give them one month's notice in writing before selling or leasing the land, and to obtain their consent or an order of the court before selling the principal mansion house.[26] In short, the full control of the land was in the hands of the tenant for life, and the trustees merely had certain supervisory functions designed to protect the interests of the beneficiaries.

D. *Effect of a Sale or Other Dealing*

The effect of a dealing with the settled land such as a sale was that the rights of the beneficiaries under the settlement were overreached, provided that the money was paid to the trustees, being not less than two in number, or into court.[27] This was so whether the legal estate was vested in trustees or split up between the beneficiaries. A tenant for life had a statutory power to convey something not vested in him, namely, the whole legal estate. The capital money in the hands of the trustees, which had to be invested in accordance with the Act, was treated as being land.[28] "The effect of a sale under the Settled Land Act is merely to substitute money for land, and whatever rights persons had in the land are preserved to them in the money produced by its sale."[29] For example, if land was settled on "A for life, remainder to B for life, remainder to C and his heirs," the effect of a sale by A was to vest the legal fee simple in the purchaser, free from the legal rights of A, B and C, who took corresponding rights in the capital money. Thus C had a fee simple in remainder in the capital money, which, on his death, would pass with the rest of his realty under his will, or if he was intestate, to his heir. If the land had been conveyed "unto and to the use of" trustees on trust for the beneficiaries, the position was exactly the same: A's statutory power of sale enabled him to transfer to the purchaser the legal estate vested in the trustees.

This power of the tenant for life to defeat the expectations of those in remainder who wished to enjoy the settled land itself might seem to be unjust, but "what the statute intended to do was to release the land from the fetters of the settlement—to render it a marketable article notwithstanding the settlement."[30] It was more important in the public interest that land should be freely alienable despite any settlement than that "sentimental considerations"[31] should be allowed to sterilise it.

---

[24] Contrast *post*, p. 260.
[25] S.L.A. 1882, ss.22, 39.
[26] *Ibid.* ss.15, 45; S.L.A. 1890, s.10.
[27] S.L.A. 1882, ss.20, 22, 39.
[28] *Ibid.* s.22.
[29] *Hampden* v. *Earl of Buckinghamshire* [1893] 2 Ch. 531 at 544, *per* Lindley L.J.
[30] *Bruce* v. *Marquess of Ailesbury* [1892] A.C. 356 at 361, *per* Lord Halsbury L.C.
[31] *Ibid.* at p. 362, *per* Lord Halsbury L.C.

Sect. 2. Trusts for Sale

1. Application of the Act. The original draft of the Act did not apply to land held on trust for sale, but "the unprompted wisdom of Parliament" added a section, section 63, "drafted in a fine style of perplexed verbiage."[32] This provided that such land was to be deemed settled land (and thus within the Act) if the proceeds of sale or income were to be applied or disposed of for any person or persons for life or any other limited period. The effect of this was to defeat the main purpose of a trust for sale (namely, that the land should be sold as and when the trustees thought best); the hands of the trustees were tied by the prohibition in the Act against their exercising any power to sell given to them by the settlement unless the tenant for life gave his consent.[33] Under a trust for sale, the trustees were normally intended to have control. Yet in consequence of section 63, the wide powers given by the Act were all vested in the tenant for life.

2. Order of court. One solution of the difficulty would have been to repeal the section added by Parliament. Instead, the Settled Land Act 1884, s.7, provided that in the case of trusts for sale within the Settled Land Act 1882 the tenant for life should be unable to exercise his statutory powers unless he obtained an order of the court. Until such an order was made, the trustees were empowered to sell without the consent of the tenant for life.[34] A purchaser could safely deal with the trustees for sale unless such an order had been registered as a *lis pendens* (pending action).[35]

The result of this was substantially to restore the position as it was before 1883. Land subject to a trust for sale was nominally settled land, but unless the tenant for life had obtained an order from the court, he had none of the statutory powers and the trustees had the sole unfettered power of sale. However, they had no powers of leasing, mortgaging or otherwise dealing with the land except by way of sale unless the trust for sale conferred these powers on them expressly or by implication.[36]

3. Trust or power. A mere power of sale did not create a trust for sale. For a trust for sale, there had to be an obligation to sell. If there was, that sufficed, even if it was subject to a power to postpone sale indefinitely or a restriction against selling unless the tenant for life requested or consented to it.[37] A trust to "retain or sell" the land might or might not be a trust for sale, depending on whether the general intention of the settlement was that the land should be sold or that it should be retained as land.[38]

[32] 27 S.J. 113; 28 S.J. 322.
[33] *Ante*, p. 220.
[34] S.L.A. 1884, s.6.
[35] See *ante*, p. 82.
[36] *Walker* v. *Southall* (1887) 56 L.T. 882; *Re Bellinger* [1898] 2 Ch. 534.
[37] *Re Wagstaff's S.E.* [1909] 2 Ch. 201; contrast *Re Goodall's Settlement* [1909] 1 Ch. 440.
[38] *Re Johnson* [1915] 1 Ch. 435 (trust for sale); *Re White's Settlement* [1930] 1 Ch. 179 (no trust for sale).

4. Bare trusts. The Settled Land Acts never applied to a trust where one or more persons of full age were entitled in possession absolutely and there was no element of succession, whether there was a trust for sale or a mere trust. Thus a conveyance "to A in fee simple in trust for B in fee simple" creates a bare trust which is not within the Acts.

Part 3

THE SETTLED LAND ACT 1925

The Settled Land Act 1925 continued the policy of the Act of 1882, but important alterations were made in conformity with the simpler principles of the 1925 legislation as a whole. These alterations will be considered first, before dealing with the other provisions of the Act.

Sect. 1. Basic Alterations Made by the Act of 1925

A. Trusts for Sale are Excluded from the Act

Land subject to "an immediate binding trust for sale" is expressly excluded from the definition of settled land.[39] Trusts for sale are now governed by the Law of Property Act 1925 and are considered later under a separate head.[40]

B. The Legal Estate is Normally in the Tenant for Life

Before 1926, the legal estate in settled land was either vested in trustees or split up between the beneficiaries, depending upon how the settlement was made.[41] After 1925, the legal estate is always[42] vested in the tenant for life. Where a settlement is made after 1925, the legal estate must be conveyed to the tenant for life, unless, of course, it is already vested in him,[43] as is the case where the owner of property settles it upon himself as tenant for life, with remainders over: ("with remainders over" is a concise way of referring to the remainders following the life interest without setting them out in detail). In the case of a settlement made before 1926, the legal estate was automatically vested in the tenant for life at the first moment of 1926.[44]

Thus today the tenant for life has the legal estate as well as the statutory powers vested in him, and he holds both the estate and the powers on trust for himself and the other beneficiaries under the settlement.[45] This emphasises the dual capacity of a tenant for life: he holds two interests in the land, the legal estate as trustee and his own equitable interest beneficially.[46]

[39] S.L.A. 1925, s.1(7), added by L.P.(Am.)A. 1926, Sched.
[40] *Post*, pp. 251 *et seq.*
[41] *Ante*, p. 216.
[42] For the two exceptions, see below.
[43] S.L.A. 1925, s.4.
[44] L.P.A. 1925, Sched. 1, Pt. II, para. 6.
[45] S.L.A. 1925, ss.16, 107.
[46] See generally *Re Liberty's W.T.* [1937] Ch. 176.

In two cases, however, the legal estate and statutory powers are vested not in a tenant for life, but in the "statutory owner."[47] These two cases are as follows.

1. Tenant for life a minor. A legal estate cannot be vested in a minor after 1925 and it would be undesirable to give him the statutory powers. Consequently, where the tenant for life is a minor the legal estate and the statutory powers are vested in the statutory owner, consisting of—

   (i) a personal representative if the land is vested in him and no vesting instrument[48] has been executed, *e.g.* where the settlement has been made by the will of a testator who has just died; but otherwise

  (ii) the trustees of the settlement.

2. No tenant for life. Where under a settlement there is no tenant for life, the legal estate and statutory powers are vested in the statutory owner, consisting of—

   (i) any person of full age upon whom the settlement expressly confers the powers; if none,

  (ii) the trustees of the settlement.

The question who is a tenant for life and the cases where there is no tenant for life are dealt with below.[49] For the present, it is sufficient to say that there usually is a tenant for life, but that in those cases where there is not the Act of 1925 has effected a considerable improvement, for in such cases before 1926 the land could not be dealt with at all.

It will be seen from this that whereas before 1926 the legal estate and statutory powers might be vested in different persons (*e.g.* where land was conveyed "unto and to the use of T1 and T2 and their heirs in trust for A for life, remainder to B and his heirs"), the scheme of the Act of 1925 is to ensure that they will not be separated. It should be noted, however, that the legal estate is never vested in the trustees of the settlement as such, although they may hold it in some other capacity, such as statutory owner or special personal representatives.[50]

C. All Settlements Must be Made by Two Documents

1. Introduction. The reasons for the changes made in 1925 will be examined briefly before considering the changes.

(a) *Before 1926.* Before 1926, a settlement was usually made by one document. If the settlement was made by will, the will constituted the

---

[47] S.L.A. 1925, ss.4, 23, 26, 117; L.P.A. 1925, Sched. 1, Pt. II, paras. 3, 5, 6. And on the death of a tenant for life the legal estate normally vests temporarily in personal representatives: see *post*, p. 231.
[48] For vesting instruments, see *post*, p. 225.
[49] *Post*, p. 237.
[50] *Post*, pp. 231, 238.

settlement, whereas a settlement *inter vivos* was made by deed. The result was that if the land was sold, the purchaser had to examine the lengthy and, for this purpose, mainly irrelevant provisions of the settlement to discover the principal facts essential to his obtaining a good title; these were normally—

   (i) that the land he had agreed to buy was included in the settlement;

  (ii) that the person who had agreed to sell to him was the duly constituted tenant for life; and

 (iii) that the persons to whom he was proposing to pay the purchase-money were the duly appointed trustees of the settlement.

To discover these facts was often a tedious task, for the settlement was a long document setting out the trusts in full and a purchaser often had to waste time in reading clauses which were of no interest to him in order to ascertain the few simple facts he required. In addition, all the details of the family's arrangements were laid bare to a stranger's gaze. There was, of course, no question of the purchaser being prejudiced by the notice he had of the beneficiaries' interests, for whether they were legal or equitable and whether or not he knew what they were, statute had laid down that he took free from them, provided he paid his money to the trustees or into court.

(b) *After 1925.* The Settled Land Act 1925 avoids these disadvantages by providing that every settlement made after 1925 must be made by two documents, a vesting instrument and a trust instrument. The vesting instrument contains all the information to which a purchaser is entitled; it gives him, in effect, a short certificate of the few matters with which he is concerned. The trust instrument sets out the details of the settlement, and the purchaser is normally not concerned with them. The trusts are said to be "behind the curtain" formed by the vesting instrument, and the curtain is one behind which the purchaser is not entitled to peep. Settlements made before 1926 are brought into line by the provision that the document creating the settlement is to be treated as the trust instrument, and that before the land can be dealt with a vesting instrument must be executed. These provisions must now be examined in greater detail.

2. Settlements made after 1925

(a) *Settlements inter vivos.* Every settlement of a legal estate in land made *inter vivos* after 1925 must be made by two deeds, a principal vesting deed and a trust instrument.[51] The contents of these deeds are as follows:

TRUST INSTRUMENT

This—

   (i) Declares the trusts affecting the settled land.

  (ii) Bears any *ad valorem* stamp duty payable in respect of the settlement.

[51] S.L.A. 1925, ss.4, 5.

(iii) Appoints trustees of the settlement.
(iv) Contains the power, if any, to appoint new trustees of the settlement.
(v) Sets out, either expressly or by reference, any powers intended to be conferred by the settlement in extension of those conferred by the Act.

PRINCIPAL VESTING DEED

This—

(i) Describes the settled land, either specifically or generally.
(ii) Declares that the settled land is vested in the person or persons to whom it is conveyed, or in whom it is declared to be vested, upon the trusts from time to time affecting the settled land.
(iii) States the names of the trustees of the settlement.
(iv) States the names of any persons empowered to appoint new trustees of the settlement.
(v) States any additional or larger powers conferred by the trust instrument.

It will be noticed that the last three particulars in each document are similar, the only difference being that whereas the trust instrument actually makes the appointment and confers the powers, the vesting deed merely recites what has been done by the trust instrument. The first two particulars in each of the deeds are, of course, completely dissimilar. The second requirement of a vesting deed is worded so as to cover two cases: (i) where the vesting deed acts as a conveyance from the settlor to the tenant for life or statutory owner, as where X settles property on A for life with the remainders over; and (ii) where the same person is both settlor and tenant for life, so that there is no transfer of the legal estate, as where Z on his marriage settles property on himself for life with remainders over.

(b) *Settlements by will.* Where land is settled by the will of a testator dying after 1925, the will is treated as the trust instrument and the testator's personal representatives, after providing for debts and inheritance tax, hold the land on trust to execute a vesting instrument in favour of the tenant for life or statutory owner on being required to do so.[52] The vesting instrument may be either a vesting deed or a vesting assent. A vesting assent is a document merely in writing containing the same particulars as a vesting deed[53]; it attracts no stamp duty, whereas a vesting deed, being a deed, must carry a stamp. Personal representatives will thus use a vesting assent.

3. Settlements made before 1926. A deed creating a settlement existing at the beginning of 1926 is treated as a trust instrument. The Act provided that as soon as was practicable the trustees of the settlement might, and at the request of the tenant for life or statutory owner must, execute a vesting

[52] S.L.A. 1925, ss.6, 8.
[53] *Ibid.* s.8.

deed.[54] Normally this conveys no estate but merely declares that the legal estate in the settled land is vested in the tenant for life or statutory owner, for in nearly all cases the Law of Property Act 1925 automatically vested the legal estate in him at the beginning of 1926[55]; but if in fact the legal estate was outstanding, the vesting deed operates to convey it.

This provision is of little assistance to a purchaser, however, for this is one of the two important cases where the trust instrument is not kept behind the curtain.[56] Despite the existence of a vesting deed, a purchaser must verify from the settlement that the vesting deed includes the land in question and that the proper persons are tenant for life and trustees of the settlement.[57]

4. Section 13

(a) *The rule.* Some provision had to be made to prevent evasions of the requirement that there should be a vesting instrument. Whilst a vesting deed is not invalidated merely by some error in the statements required to be contained in it,[58] the absence of any vesting instrument at all usually makes it impossible to deal with the land.

First, a settlement *inter vivos* of a legal estate in land made otherwise than by two deeds cannot transfer or create a legal estate; the tenant for life or statutory owner, however, can require the trustees of the settlement to execute a vesting deed.[59] Thus if A purports to convey his fee simple to B in fee simple on trust for B for life with remainder to C in fee simple, no legal estate passes to B and so B cannot dispose of any legal estate.

Second, section 13 of the Settled Land Act 1925 (sometimes called the "paralysing section") in effect provides that where a tenant for life or statutory owner has become entitled to have a vesting instrument executed in his favour, no disposition of a legal estate can be made until a vesting instrument has been executed in accordance with the Act. Until this has been done, any purported disposition of the land *inter vivos* by any person operates only as a contract for valuable consideration to carry out the transaction after the requisite vesting instrument has been executed. This applies even if the legal estate is already vested in the tenant for life, as where he is the settlor, or where the transitional provisions have vested it in him automatically.

(b) *Exceptions.* There are four exceptions to this rule.

(1) DISPOSITION BY PERSONAL REPRESENTATIVE. The section does not apply where the disposition is made by a personal representative.[60] Thus if a settlement was made before 1926 and the tenant for life has just died without

---

[54] *Ibid.* Sched. 2, para. 1.
[55] L.P.A. 1925, Sched. 1, Pt. II, paras. 3, 5, 6.
[56] For the other case, see *post*, p. 229.
[57] S.L.A. 1925, s.110.
[58] *Ibid.* s.5.
[59] *Ibid.* ss.4, 9.
[60] *Ibid.* s.13.

a vesting deed having been executed, the legal estate (which was nevertheless automatically vested in the tenant for life at the beginning of 1926) duly passes to his personal representatives, who can dispose of the land without a vesting instrument being executed, *e.g.* if part of the land is sold to raise money for inheritance tax.

(2) PURCHASER WITHOUT NOTICE. The section does not apply where the disposition is made to a purchaser of a legal estate without notice of the tenant for life or statutory owner having become entitled to a vesting instrument.[61] For example, if by a deed A settles land on himself for life with remainders over, and then, suppressing the deed, sells the land to a purchaser who is ignorant of the settlement, the purchaser gets a good title even though no vesting deed has been executed.

(3) SETTLEMENT AT AN END. The section does not apply where the settlement has come to an end before a vesting instrument has been executed. Thus where at the end of 1925 X was a tenant in tail in possession free from any trusts or incumbrances, it has been held that if before any vesting instrument is executed he bars the entail and so terminates the settlement, it is unnecessary for a vesting instrument to be executed before he conveys the land to a purchaser.[62] When the land ceases to be settled, the fetters of section 13 drop off.

(4) SECTION 1 OF THE AMENDMENT ACT. Section 13 does not apply where advantage is taken of section 1 of the Law of Property (Amendment) Act 1926. In a limited class of cases, this allows settled land to be dealt with as if it were not settled; the section is dealt with below.[63]

(c) *Operation of the provisions.* An illustration of the operation of these provisions is given by the case of a settlor who attempts to make a settlement *inter vivos* after 1925 in favour of his son and family by a single document. In such a case—

   (i) The document is ineffective to transfer or create any legal estate, which thus remains vested in him.

  (ii) The document is treated as a trust instrument.

 (iii) As soon as it is practicable the trustees of the settlement may, and at the request of the tenant for life or statutory owner must, execute a principal vesting deed, which will operate to take the legal estate out of the settlor and vest it in the tenant for life or statutory owner.

 (iv) Until a vesting deed has been duly executed, section 13 prevents any disposition of the land being made. The deed must be executed by the trustees; the settlor cannot do so, and thus correct his error, even if the legal estate is still vested in him. If there are no trustees and no persons able and willing to appoint trustees, an application must be made to the court for the appointment of trustees.

---

[61] S.L.A. 1925, as amended by L.P.(Am.)A. 1926, Sched.
[62] *Re Alefounder's W.T.* [1927] 1 Ch. 360.
[63] *Post*, p. 237.

(v) Even after a vesting deed has been executed the settlement is not so satisfactory as one made in the proper manner, for the document creating the settlement, although treated as the trust instrument, is not behind the curtain. This is the other of the two important exceptions to the rule that a purchaser is not concerned with the trust instrument.[64] A purchaser must examine the document creating the settlement to see that it includes the land in question and that the proper persons are tenant for life and trustees of the settlement.

5. Dispositions under settlements: section 18

(a) *Unauthorised transactions.* Once a vesting instrument has been duly executed, section 13 ceases to apply, but the land is subject to section 18. Under this, until the trustees of the settlement have been duly discharged, any disposition by the tenant for life or statutory owner is void if it is not authorised by the Act, any other statute, or any additional or larger powers mentioned in the vesting instrument, except so far as it binds the tenant for life's own beneficial interest.[65] Further, where any capital money is payable, a conveyance to a purchaser takes effect only if the capital money is paid to (or by the direction of) the trustees of the settlement, being at least two in number or a trust corporation, or into court.[66] Thus if a tenant for life, dishonestly concealing the fact that the land is settled land, mortgages it to raise money for his personal purposes, the mortgage is void against other beneficiaries under the settlement both because it is not authorised by the Act and because the money is not paid to the trustees of the settlement[67]; and unlike section 13, section 18 makes no exception for a purchaser without notice. Such concealment is possible where the tenant for life, having previously bought the land, sells it to somebody else (*e.g.* his father) who then makes the settlement; the tenant for life may afterwards mortgage the land by suppressing all the transactions subsequent to his purchase.[68]

(b) *Protection against irregularity.* On any disposition, a purchaser dealing in good faith[69] with a tenant for life or statutory owner is to be conclusively taken, as against all persons entitled under the settlement, to have given the best price, consideration or rent that could reasonably be obtained by the tenant for life or statutory owner "and to have complied with all the requisitions of this Act."[70] Although this provision has been held to apply only where the purchaser knew that he was dealing with a tenant for life,[71] the better view is that such knowledge is immaterial,[72] and that the remedy of the beneficiaries is not against the mortgagee or other purchaser but against

---

[64] For the first exception, see *ante*, p. 227.
[65] S.L.A. 1925, s.18(1)(a).
[66] *Ibid.* s.18(1)(b), (c).
[67] *Weston* v. *Henshaw* [1950] Ch. 510.
[68] *Ibid.*
[69] See *Chandler* v. *Bradley* [1897] 1 Ch. 315.
[70] S.L.A. 1925, s.110(1).
[71] *Weston* v. *Henshaw, supra.*
[72] *Re Morgan's Lease* [1972] Ch. 1.

the tenant for life for breach of his fiduciary duties.[73] In any case, the language of the statutory protection seems to be confined to irregularities in authorised transactions,[74] and not as extending to transactions that are wholly unauthorised, such as the grant of an oral tenancy by a tenant for life.[75]

6. Subsidiary vesting deed. Where a settlement of land is already in existence and other land is brought into the settlement, a subsidiary vesting deed is required to convey the land to the tenant for life or statutory owner. The contents of a subsidiary vesting deed are as follows[76]:

   (i) particulars of the last or only principal vesting deed affecting land subject to the settlement;
  (ii) a statement that the land conveyed is to be held upon and subject to the same trusts and powers as the land comprised in the principal vesting deed;
 (iii) the names of the trustees of the settlement;
 (iv) the name of any person entitled to appoint new trustees of the settlement.

There is no need to refer to the trust instrument or any additional powers conferred by it.

7. The "curtain" principle

(a) *The curtain.* The purpose of a vesting instrument is to provide a purchaser with all that he needs to know. It is therefore provided that "a purchaser of a legal estate in settled land" is not entitled to see the trust instrument,[77] and he is also bound and entitled to assume that the particulars required to be set out in the vesting instrument are correct,[78] such as the persons who are the tenant for life and the trustees. Further, a vesting deed is not invalidated merely by any error in the particulars required to be contained in it.[79]

(b) *Errors.* No statutory provision is made for cases in which there is some error in the vesting instrument. Thus if land is settled on W for life or until remarriage, with remainder to X in fee simple, W ceases to be a tenant for life on remarriage and so has no power to sell the land. If she nevertheless purports to sell it, the purchaser cannot discover from the vesting instrument that she is no longer tenant for life, and is bound to assume from the vesting instrument that she still is. While the legal estate remains vested in her, she

---

[73] *Mogridge* v. *Clapp* [1892] 3 Ch. 382 (on S.L.A. 1882, s.54, the predecessor of S.L.A. 1925, s.110(1)).
[74] See, *e.g. Hurrell* v. *Littlejohn* [1904] 1 Ch. 689 (rent under proper lease).
[75] See *Bevan* v. *Johnston* [1990] 2 E.G.L.R. 33 (tenancy held void under s.18(1) without mention of s.110(1)).
[76] S.L.A. 1925, s.10.
[77] *Ibid.* s.110(2).
[78] *Ibid.*
[79] *Ibid.* s.5(3).

probably can still convey it; but she cannot overreach the equitable interests, and these will bind the purchaser. Such problems are unlikely to occur in practice, for truth will out when the purchaser seeks to pay the purchase money to the trustees. If such a case did arise, the Act[80] and case law[81] give some support to the view that the protection given to a purchaser of a legal estate "in settled land"[82] would probably apply to land which merely appears to be settled land. In any case, the purchaser might also be treated as being a purchaser without notice of the interests under the trust instrument which statute precludes him from inspecting.[83]

(c) *Exceptions.* In four cases a purchaser may and should inspect the trust instrument.[84] Two cases are where the principal vesting instrument gives effect to a settlement made before 1926, or to an imperfect settlement made after 1925.[85] The other two, less important, are cases of "deemed" settlements, where land is held on trust for charitable, ecclesiastical or public purposes,[86] or where a minor became entitled under an intestacy.[87] All four are cases with the increased risk of error that comes from vesting instruments being executed after the settlement arose.

8. Duration and determination of settlements. When a tenant for life dies, or his interest comes to an end in some other way (*e.g.* by forfeiture or surrender), the settlement may still continue or it may come to an end. In each case, provision has been made for the execution of a document that will reveal to a purchaser which has occurred, without looking behind the curtain. Provision has also been made for the devolution of the legal estate vested in the tenant for life. If the settlement continues, the document will be a vesting deed or vesting assent (a document containing all the particulars required in a vesting deed[88]), and this will vest the legal estate in the next tenant for life. If the settlement ends, the document will usually be an ordinary conveyance or an ordinary assent, vesting the legal estate in the person entitled. Such a conveyance or assent does not state the names of the trustees of the settlement, and this entitles and binds a bona fide purchaser for value of a legal estate to assume that the person in whom the land was thereby vested holds the land free from all rights under the settlement.[89] The court has wide powers to make an appropriate order if there is any difficulty in obtaining the execution of the requisite document.[90] Occasionally the

---

[80] See s.110(2)(e), which requires a purchaser of a legal estate "in settled land" to assume the correctness of statements in a "deed of discharge," which *ex hypothesi* shows that the land is no longer settled: see *post*, p. 233.
[81] See *Re Cugny's W.T.* [1931] 1 Ch. 305 (on S.L.A. 1925, s.36; *post*, p. 232).
[82] S.L.A. 1925, s.110(2); see above.
[83] See [1984] Conv. 354 (P. A. Stone), and compare [1985] Conv. 377 (R. Warrington).
[84] S.L.A. 1925, s.110(2), proviso.
[85] *Ante*, pp. 227, 229.
[86] S.L.A. 1925, s.29; *ante*, p. 173.
[87] *Ibid.* s.1(2).
[88] *Ibid.* s.8(4).
[89] *Ibid.* s.110(4).
[90] *Ibid.* s.12.

document required will not be a vesting instrument, conveyance or assent but a deed of discharge, which transfers no legal estate. The two main categories will be considered in turn.

(a) *Settlement continuing.* Land once settled remains settled so long as—

   (i) any limitation, charge or power of charging under the settlement still exists or is capable of being exercised, or
   (ii) the person beneficially entitled in possession is an infant,

unless in either case the land is held on trust for sale.[91] Once land is either held on trust for sale or else vested in a person of full age free from all actual or possible rights under the settlement, the settlement is at an end.

If the tenant for life dies, but the land remains settled land, the legal estate will vest in the trustees of the settlement who, as his special personal representatives, will take out probate or letters of administration to his estate, limited to the settled land.[92] They will then vest the legal estate in the next tenant for life by means of a vesting assent.[93] Where the tenant for life is still alive but has ceased to be tenant for life (as where his life interest has been determined by forfeiture or surrender), he must vest the legal estate in the next tenant for life by a vesting deed.[94] Where a minor who is entitled in possession attains his majority, the legal estate must be vested in him (normally by the statutory owner[95]) by a vesting deed if the settlement is continuing and by an ordinary conveyance if it is not.[96]

(b) *Settlement ended.* Where the settlement comes to an end on the death of the tenant for life, the legal estate vests in his ordinary personal representatives, who will take out a grant of probate or letters of administration.[97] They will then vest the legal estate in the person absolutely entitled, or in trustees for sale, by means of an ordinary (and not vesting) assent. If those entitled are tenants in common of full age, the personal representatives should vest the legal estate in them on trust for sale by an ordinary assent[98]; but if one of them is a minor, the personal representatives should instead vest it in the former trustees of the settlement on trust for sale for the tenants in common by an ordinary assent, even if they are the same persons as those former trustees.[99] If the settlement comes to an end for some reason other than the death of the tenant for life, as where another person has become absolutely entitled, the tenant for life must convey the legal estate to that other person by an ordinary conveyance.[1] But if it is the tenant for life who

---

[91] S.L.A. 1925, s.3; L.P.(Am.)A. 1926, Sched.
[92] S.L.A. 1925, s.7(1); A.E.A. 1925, s.22; Supreme Court Act 1981, s.113.
[93] S.L.A. 1925, s.8.
[94] *Ibid.* ss.7(4), 8(4)(a).
[95] See *ante*, p. 224.
[96] S.L.A. 1925, s.7(2), (5).
[97] *Re Bridgett and Hayes' Contract* [1928] Ch. 163.
[98] L.P.A. 1925, s.3(1)(b)(ii), proviso.
[99] S.L.A. 1925, s.36; *Re Cugny's W.T.* [1931] 1 Ch. 305; the word "vesting" at p. 309 is an obvious slip.
[1] S.L.A. 1925, s.7(5).

has become absolutely entitled, as where he has purchased the interests of all the other beneficiaries, or the last remaining interest under the settlement is that of an annuitant who has died, the former trustees of the settlement must execute a deed of discharge, declaring that they are discharged from the trust so far as the land is concerned.[2] This entitles a purchaser to assume that the land has ceased to be settled land and is subject to no trust for sale.[3] But if a settlement comes to an end before any vesting instrument has been executed,[4] no deed of discharge is required.[5]

Sect. 2. Continuing Provisions Relating to Settled Land

Now that the basic alterations in the law laid down by the Act of 1882 have been considered, it is possible to turn to provisions in the Act of 1925 which in the main correspond to similar provisions in the Act of 1882; but in some cases important extensions and additions have been made.

A. Essentials of Settled Land

The three essential points to consider are—

(1) whether the land is settled land;
(2) who is the tenant for life; and
(3) who are the trustees.

I. DEFINITION OF SETTLED LAND

1. "Settlement." Land is settled land if "it is or is deemed to be the subject of a settlement."[6] A settlement is any deed, will, agreement, Act of Parliament[7] or other instrument (including, it seems, an order of the court[8]) or any number of instruments whereby one of the following requirements is satisfied.[9]

(a) *Succession*: the land stands limited in trust for any persons by way of succession.

In addition to cases such as limitations "to A for life, remainder to B in fee simple," this definition seems to be wide enough to cover the following cases which are somewhat superfluously set out in the section as independent heads, namely, where land is limited in trust for any person in possession—

(i) for an entailed interest, whether or not capable of being barred or defeated;

---

[2] *Ibid.* s.17.
[3] *Ibid.*; and see s.110(2)(e).
[4] As in *Re Alefounder's W.T.* [1927] 1 Ch. 360; *ante*, p. 228.
[5] See S.L.A. 1925, s.17.
[6] *Ibid.* s.2.
[7] See, *e.g. Re Lord Hereford's S.E.* [1932] W.N. 34.
[8] See *post*, p. 236.
[9] S.L.A. 1925, s.1.

    (ii) for an estate in fee simple or for a term of years absolute subject to an executory gift over (*e.g.* a devise to trustees in trust for "A in fee simple but for B in fee simple when B marries");

    (iii) for a base or determinable fee, including a fee determinable by condition, or any corresponding interest in leasehold land;

or where—

    (iv) land is limited in trust for any person for an estate in fee simple or for a term of years absolute contingently on the happening of an event (*e.g.* a devise to trustees in trust for X in fee simple if his brothers die under the age of 21 years).

In all these cases there is an element of succession sufficient to satisfy the definition in (a). Thus if S settles land upon trust for X in tail, the land stands limited in trust for persons by way of succession and the limitations arise under the settlement; for any estate or interest not disposed of under the settlement and remaining in or reverting to the settlor or anyone deriving title under him is deemed to arise under the settlement, with the consequence that S's fee simple reversion upon X's entail is deemed to arise under the settlement.[10]

    (b) *Minors:* the land stands limited in trust for a minor in possession for an estate in fee simple or for a term of years absolute.

    (c) *Family charges:* the land stands charged, whether voluntarily or in consideration of marriage or by way of family arrangement, with the payment of any sums for the benefit of any persons.

    2. "Limited in trust." It will be seen that under heads (a) (succession) and (b) (minors), but not (c) (family charges), it is necessary for the land to be "limited in trust" if it is to fall within the definition; if there is no trust, or if the trust is an immediate binding trust for sale,[11] the land is not settled land. In all cases where property is given by will, there is necessarily a trust for the beneficiaries by reason of the legal estate first vesting in the testator's personal representatives. Where the disposition is made *inter vivos* it will be made either—

    (i) by a proper vesting deed and trust instrument, whereupon the legal estate vests in the tenant for life as trustee, or

    (ii) by a single instrument, in which case the legal estate will remain in the settlor and only an equitable interest will be transferred; for none of the interests mentioned in (a) is capable of existing at law (except, it seems, a fee simple determinable by condition[12] where the right of entry is legal[13]), and in (b), by reason of a minor's inability after 1925 to hold a legal estate in land, no legal estate passes. Consequently, on the principle

---

[10] See *Re Hunter and Hewlett's Contract* [1907] 1 Ch. 46.
[11] See *post*, p. 251.
[12] See *ante*, p. 35.
[13] See M. & W. 345.

that there is a trust if the legal estate is in one person and the equitable interest in another, the grantor will hold the land in trust even without any express limitation in trust.[14]

Under head (c), no limitation by way of trust is required. Whether the estate which is subject to family charges is conveyed directly to the beneficiary or whether it is held in trust for the beneficiary, the land is nevertheless settled land.

3. Licences and equities. Sometimes a person is given the right to occupy or reside in property rent free for his life. If this gives him a life interest, and it has been given to him under a "settlement," he will be tenant for life under the Settled Land Act 1925 and have the extensive powers that it confers. But if the gift is construed as giving him a mere licence or permission to reside not amounting to an interest in land, he will not be tenant for life or have those powers.[15] At one time distinctions were made between a mere permission to reside in a house for life and the grant of a right to occupy it for life; and only in the latter case was there a life interest.[16] As will be seen,[17] the border-line between licence and tenancy is far from clear, and the modern policy is not to restrict the class of persons who constitute tenants for life within the Act.[18] The tendency is thus to construe such limitations as creating tenancies for life within the Act.[19] Thus when V conveyed a cottage to P on the oral understanding (duly reflected in the price) that V could occupy the cottage rent free for life, V was held to be a tenant for life under a constructive trust who fell within the Settled Land Act 1925.[20] The result was similar when under an agreement in writing an employer permitted an employee's widow to occupy a cottage rent free for life, a purchaser from the employer agreeing (at a reduced price) to take the cottage subject to the widow's right of occupation.[21]

In these cases little or no attention appears to have been given to whether there was a "settlement," nor whether an oral "agreement" could be one.[22] An order of the court may suffice as evidence of a binding agreement which constitutes a "settlement,"[23] but it is not clear whether in cases of proprietary estoppel[24] the order itself can be a "settlement" if it gives the plaintiff a life

---

[14] See *Griffiths* v. *Williams* [1978] E.G.D. 919 at 926.

[15] *Griffiths* v. *Williams* [1978] E.G.D. 919; see *esp.* at pp. 925, 926.

[16] See *Parker* v. *Parker* (1863) 1 N.R. 508; *May* v. *May* (1881) 44 L.T. 412.

[17] See *post*, pp. 309, 427.

[18] See *Re Baroness Llanover's Will* [1903] 2 Ch. 16 at 24.

[19] *Re Carne's S.E.* [1899] 1 Ch. 324; *Re Baroness Llanover's Will* [1903] 2 Ch. 16; and see *Re Boyer's S.E.* [1916] 2 Ch. 404; *Re Gibbons* [1920] 1 Ch. 372 at 377. Contrast *Morss* v. *Morss* [1972] Fam. 204; and see Harvey 82–88.

[20] *Bannister* v. *Bannister* [1948] 2 All E.R. 133; and see *Ungurian* v. *Lesnoff* [1990] Ch. 206.

[21] *Binions* v. *Evans* [1972] Ch. 359, a case that "stretched to the very limit" the application of the Act: *Ivory* v. *Palmer* [1975] I.C.R. 340 at 347, *per* Cairns L.J. On these cases, see generally (1977) 93 L.Q.R. 561 (J. A. Hornby).

[22] See *Griffiths* v. *Williams* [1978] E.G.D. 919 at 925, 926. The words "agreement . . . or other instrument" in S.L.A. 1925, s.1(1) look unpromising.

[23] *Bacon* v. *Bacon* [1947] P. 151 at 158.

[24] See *ante*, p. 67; *post*, p. 436.

interest as the resolution of his claim.[25] A fear that to give the plaintiff a life interest would confer on him all the powers of a tenant for life as well, and so give him more extensive rights than the court considered just, has induced the court to give him some other relief instead.[26] Yet the proposed life interest would have conferred those powers only if it arose under a "settlement," a point that was not considered; unless the order of the court declaring the life interest constituted a "settlement," there was none, and the fears were groundless.[27] When the point is properly considered, it seems probable that the definition of a "settlement" will be held to include an order of the court.

4. Extended scope of settled land. Before 1926 even if settled land had become vested in one person in fee simple, it continued to be settled land if there still existed a jointure or provisions for portions or annuities under a settlement, provided in each case that they were not merely sums presently payable but were limited to arise in the future, thus satisfying the requirement that the land should be limited to persons by way of succession.[28] The provision in the Act of 1925 is wider than this, and contains no requirement of futurity. It is essential that the sum of money should have been charged on the land either voluntarily, or in consideration of marriage, or by way of family arrangement; the Act does not apply if the charge was created for money or money's worth, as where a tenant in fee simple sells his land and takes a charge on it as part of the price. But subject to this requirement, it is immaterial whether the provision is present or future, whether it is for capital or annual sums, or whether it is for a limited period (*e.g.* for life) or in perpetuity. Thus if a testator devises land to trustees on trust to pay a perpetual annuity to X, and subject thereto on trust for A in fee simple, the land becomes settled land.[29]

(a) *Resulting inconvenience.* The effect of this provision was that at the beginning of 1926 much land which had previously not been settled land was forthwith converted into settled land. In a number of cases this caused hardship to those who had purchased such land before 1926. The practice in such cases was that unless the land could be freed from the charges (as by the owners of the charges all releasing them in return for a share of the purchase-money) the vendor conveyed the land to the purchaser subject to the charges but with an indemnity against them, *i.e.* the vendor agreed to pay the charges himself and so ensure that they would not be enforced against the land. In cases where this had been done, the astonished purchaser found (if, indeed, he could understand the matter at all) that at the beginning of 1926

[25] Consider *Morss* v. *Morss* [1972] Fam. 264.
[26] *Dodsworth* v. *Dodsworth* [1973] E.G.D. 233.
[27] See *Griffiths* v. *Williams* [1978] E.G.D. 919 at 925, 926; and see *post,* p. 436.
[28] *Re Mundy and Roper's Contract* [1899] 1 Ch. 275.
[29] *Re Austen* [1929] 2 Ch. 155.

his land had become settled land and that it could be sold only after compliance with the troublesome Settled Land Act procedure, *e.g.* as to the appointing of trustees and the execution of a vesting deed.

(b) *Means of escape.* To meet this situation, the Law of Property (Amendment) Act 1926, s.1, provides that where a person of full age is beneficially entitled in possession to land in fee simple or for a term of years absolute subject to charges of this kind, he can nevertheless create or convey a legal estate subject to the charges in the same way as if the land were not settled land. This applies whether the charges arose before 1926 or after 1925, and whether the person entitled to the land is the tenant under the settlement or a purchaser from him; but it applies only if the sole reason for the land being deemed settled land is that it is subject to the charges and not, for example, when it is also entailed. Where the Amendment Act applies, a vendor may thus sell the land either (i) free from the charges, by making use of the Settled Land Act procedure, or (ii) subject to the charges, by virtue of the Amendment Act.

II. DEFINITION OF TENANT FOR LIFE

1. Tenant for life. The Settled Land Act 1925[30] gives an elaborate definition of "tenant for life." The definition includes not only a person entitled to a life interest but also a tenant in tail, a tenant in fee simple subject to a gift over or to family charges, a tenant for years terminable on life (unless at a rent[31]), a tenant *pur autre vie*, and a person entitled to the income of land for his own or any other life.

In addition to falling within the above category a person must also be of full age and beneficially entitled in possession[32]; thus a trustee for another person, or somebody who is entitled only to a future interest in the land, cannot be a tenant for life under the Act. The practical effect of the definition is that where there is some person of full age beneficially entitled to either the possession of settled land or the whole of the income from it, that person will be the tenant for life. The position where two or more persons are thus entitled jointly or in common is dealt with later.[33]

2. Cases where there is no tenant for life. Although there will normally be a tenant for life under the above provisions, there are some cases where there is no tenant for life, as where land is given to trustees on trust to pay X a fixed annuity[34] or a definite fraction of the income,[35] with a direction to accumulate the balance, or where there is an immediate discretionary trust, such as a direction to trustees to pay the income to such one or more members of a class of persons as they think fit, no member being entitled as of right to any

---

[30] ss.19, 20; and see M. & W. 350–353.
[31] *Re Catling* [1931] 2 Ch. 359.
[32] *Re Morgan* (1883) 24 Ch.D. 114 at 116; *Re Jemmett and Guest's Contract* [1907] 1 Ch. 629.
[33] *Post*, p. 296.
[34] *Re Jefferys* (*No.* 2) [1939] Ch. 205.
[35] *Re Frewen* [1926] Ch. 580.

of the income.[36] In these cases the legal estate and statutory powers are in the statutory owner.[37]

The position where the tenant for life is a minor has already been considered.[38]

III. DEFINITION OF TRUSTEES OF THE SETTLEMENT

The trustees of the settlement are defined by section 30 of the Settled Land Act 1925. There are five heads, which must be applied in turn; thus if there are any trustees under one head, they exclude any under a subsequent head. The definition is as follows:

   (i) The persons who, under the settlement, are trustees with power to sell the land (even if this power is subject to the consent of anyone) or with power of consenting to or approving the exercise of a power of sale.

For example, if in a settlement on A for life, with remainders over, there is a trust giving X and Y a general[39] power to sell the land, this will make them trustees of the settlement, in preference even to any other persons expressly appointed Settled Land Act trustees. X and Y will in fact have no power to sell the land for, as will be seen,[40] this power is taken away from them and given to the tenant for life; nevertheless, the attempt to give them the power suffices to make them trustees of the settlement.

   (ii) The persons declared by the settlement to be trustees thereof for the purposes of the Settled Land Acts 1882 to 1890, or 1925, or any of them.

This is the head under which the trustees of the settlement will usually be found, for cases under head (i) are rare. It is not sufficient to appoint X and Y "trustees of the settlement"[41]: the appointment will be ineffective unless words such as "for the purposes of the Settled Land Act 1925" are added.

   (iii) Persons who, under the settlement, are trustees with power of sale or of consenting to or approving a sale, or upon trust for sale, of *other* land held under the same settlement and upon the same trusts.

   (iv) Persons who, under the settlement, are trustees with a *future* power of sale, or under a *future* trust for sale, or with a power of consenting to or approving the exercise of such a future power of sale, even if the power or trust does not take effect in all events.

Thus if there is a settlement of Greenacre and Brownacre which gives trustees a power of sale over Greenacre alone, clause (iii) makes those

---

[36] *Re Gallenga W.T.* [1938] 1 All E.R. 106.
[37] *Ante*, p. 224.
[38] *Ante*, p. 224.
[39] See *Re Carne's S.E.* [1899] 1 Ch. 324.
[40] *Post*, p. 248.
[41] Consider *Re Bentley* (1885) 54 L.J. Ch. 782.

trustees Settled Land Act trustees of both properties.[42] Again, if Redacre is settled on A for life with remainder to X and Y on trust for sale, clause (iv) makes X and Y Settled Land Act trustees.[43]

(v) The persons appointed by deed by those able to dispose of the whole equitable interest in the settled land.

For example, if land is settled on A for life, remainder to B in tail, remainder to C in fee simple, A and B between them could dispose of the whole equitable interest in the land by barring the entail, and so they can appoint trustees of the settlement.[44]

Where a settlement arises under a will or intestacy and there are no trustees under any other provisions, the personal representatives of the deceased are trustees of the settlement until other trustees are appointed.[45] This useful provision deals with the most frequent cause of a lack of trustees, namely, a will made without proper legal advice. Where even this provision fails (*e.g.* where there is a home-made settlement created *inter vivos*) the court has power to appoint trustees on the application of any person interested under the settlement.[46]

B. Compound Settlements

1. Definition. Before 1926, difficulties sometimes arose in the case of compound settlements. "Compound settlement" is the term used to describe the state of affairs when the trusts affecting the land in question are created by two or more instruments. The most usual example of a compound settlement arises where land has been settled on A for life with remainder (subject to provisions for others of the family) to his son in tail; on the son attaining his majority, A and the son bar the entail and resettle the property on A for life, remainder to the son for life, with remainders over. Where such a process takes place there are three distinct settlements to consider—

(1) the original settlement;
(2) the resettlement; and
(3) the compound settlement, which is a separate entity.[47]

2. Position of tenant for life. The position of a tenant for life under a compound settlement was formerly as follows.

(i) He could exercise his powers as tenant for life under the original settlement, and provided there were trustees under that settlement, he could, on disposing of the land, overreach the rights of the beneficiaries under both the settlement and the resettlement[48]; but while

---

[42] *Re Moore* [1906] 1 Ch. 789.
[43] *Re Johnson's S.E.* [1913] W.N. 222.
[44] *Re Spearman S.E.* [1906] 2 Ch. 502.
[45] S.L.A. 1925, s.30. This rarely applies on intestacies since trusts for sale then normally arise: *ante*, p. 157.
[46] S.L.A. 1925, s.34.
[47] See *Re Coull's S.E.* [1905] 1 Ch. 712 at 720.
[48] *Re Lord Wimborne and Browne's Contract* [1904] 1 Ch. 537.

acting under the settlement he could not avail himself of any additional powers conferred by the resettlement.

(ii) He could act as tenant for life under the resettlement, availing himself of any additional powers conferred by it, but in this case he could not, on disposing of the land, overreach the rights of beneficiaries under the original settlement.[49]

(iii) He could act as tenant for life under the compound settlement, exercising any additional powers conferred by either settlement; and provided there were trustees of the compound settlement, he could overreach the rights of the beneficiaries under both the settlement and the resettlement.[50]

3. Tenant for life and trustees of compound settlement. As the third method combined the advantages of the first two methods, it was important to know in any given case whether there were any trustees of the compound settlement and whether the tenant for life could act under the compound settlement. Except where trustees of the compound settlement were appointed by the persons together able to dispose of the whole equitable interest, they could be appointed only by the court; for on making a settlement, the settlor probably had no power to declare who should be the trustees of any resettlement, and on a resettlement being made, an appointment of trustees thereof could not bind beneficiaries under the original settlement.[51] As regards the tenant for life, it was settled law that where one person was tenant for life under both settlements, or under the resettlement alone, he could act as tenant for life under the compound settlement.[52] In the example given above, A could exercise the powers of a tenant for life under either settlement or under the compound settlement.

4. Need for trustees of compound settlement. In most cases the comparative rarity of trustees of the compound settlement caused no difficulty, as, for example, where the tenant for life wished to sell free from the rights of the beneficiaries under both settlements, and he held under the original settlement of which there were properly appointed trustees, or where he held under the resettlement and merely wished to exercise additional powers conferred thereby. But in one case, trustees of the compound settlement were needed in order to achieve the desired object: this was where there was no tenant for life under the original settlement and the tenant for life under the resettlement wished to overreach the rights of beneficiaries under the original settlement. In this case it was impossible to avoid the expense of an application to the court if no such trustee existed.[53]

5. After 1925. After 1925, this difficulty no longer exists. Where before

[49] See *Re Mundy and Roper's Contract* [1899] 1 Ch. 275 at 295.
[50] *Re Phillimore's Estate* [1904] 2 Ch. 460.
[51] *Re Spencer's S.E.* [1903] 1 Ch. 75.
[52] *Re Phillimore's Estate, supra.*
[53] *Re Trafford's S.E.* [1915] 1 Ch. 9.

1926 the court had appointed trustees of the compound settlement, they continue in office. In other cases, it has been provided in effect that even in the case of settlements made before 1926, the trustees of the original settlement, or in default, the trustees of the resettlement shall be trustees of the compound settlement.[54]

C. Powers of the Tenant for Life

The powers and position of a tenant for life remain substantially the same as under the Act of 1882, although a number of important details have been modified. Such changes as have been made mainly give the tenant for life wider powers. In general, what follows applies to statutory owners as well as to tenants for life. As was the case under the Act of 1882, a tenant for life is normally subject to no control in the exercise of his powers. The chief safeguards against the abuse of his powers are—

  (1) his position as a trustee for the beneficiaries;
  (2) the provision that in the case of the most important powers he must give notice to the trustees of his intention to exercise them; and
  (3) the provision that in a few exceptional cases he must not exercise his powers without the leave of the trustees or an order of the court.

The position of the tenant for life as trustee has already been mentioned, and will be further considered later.[55] His powers are considered below.

I. POWERS EXERCISABLE UPON GIVING NOTICE[56]

If the tenant for life intends to make a sale, exchange, lease, mortgage or charge, or to grant an option, he must give written notice to the trustees of the settlement, and, if known, to their solicitor. The notice must be given by registered letter or recorded delivery posted at least one month before the transaction or the contract therefor, and is invalid unless when it is given the trustees consist of two or more persons or a trust corporation; thus if there are no trustees, a tenant for life is not entitled to exercise these powers. The object of this provision for giving notice seems to be to enable the trustees to prevent any fraudulent dealing by applying to the court for an injunction.[57] In fact, however, it affords comparatively little protection, for—

  (i) the trustees are apparently under no obligation to interfere with an improper transaction[58];
  (ii) except in the case of a mortgage or charge, a general notice suffices, *e.g.* "take notice that I intend from time to time to exercise any or all of my powers under the Settled Land Act 1925." In such cases, however, the tenant for life must, at the request of a trustee of the

[54] S.L.A. 1925, s.31.
[55] See *ante*, pp. 220, 223; *post*, p. 248.
[56] S.L.A. 1925, ss.38–48, 51, 71, 101.
[57] *Wheelwright* v. *Walker* (*No.* 1) (1883) 23 Ch.D. 752.
[58] S.L.A. 1925, s.97.

settlement, give reasonable information as to any sales, exchanges or leases effected, in progress or immediately intended[59];

(iii) any trustee may by writing accept less than one month's notice or waive it altogether[60]; and

(iv) a person dealing in good faith with the tenant for life is not concerned to inquire whether notice has been given.[61] Even if there are no trustees, a bona fide purchaser for value of a legal estate gets a good title if the transaction is one on which no capital money is payable, *e.g.* the grant of a lease for which no premium is payable.[62]

Each of the powers in respect of which notice is normally required must now be examined.

1. Power to sell. A tenant for life may sell the settled land or any part thereof, or any easement, right or privilege of any kind over the land.[63] He may, for example, sell to a railway company the right to tunnel under the land. With certain qualifications, he must obtain the best consideration in money that can reasonably be obtained. In one case[64] a tenant for life was made an offer by another beneficiary, but being unwilling to sell to him, proposed to sell to a third party for a lower price; the court restrained the tenant for life from selling for less than the price offered by the beneficiary, or from selling at all without informing the beneficiary of the proposed price and giving him two days in which to increase his offer. But there is no need for the sale to be by auction. Further, a purchaser is protected by the provision that if he deals in good faith with the tenant for life, he is to be conclusively taken, as against all the beneficiaries, to have given the best consideration reasonably obtainable and to have complied with all the requirements of the Act; this applies both to sales and other dealings such as leases,[65] and applies whether the transaction has been completed or is still the subject of an executory contract.[66] Thus a purchaser who made a good bargain and bought for £2,000 property which he forthwith resold for £3,000 was held to be protected.[67]

2. Power to exchange. Settled land, or any part of it, or any easement, right or privilege over it, may be exchanged for other land or any easement, right or privilege.[68] For "equality of exchange" (*i.e.* to adjust any difference in value) capital money may be paid or received.

---

[59] S.L.A. 1925, s.101.
[60] *Ibid.*
[61] *Ibid.*
[62] *Mogridge* v. *Clapp* [1892] 3 Ch. 382; *Re Morgan's Lease* [1972] Ch. 1.
[63] S.L.A. 1925, ss.38, 39. See *post*, p. 296, for joint tenants for life.
[64] *Wheelwright* v. *Walker* (*No. 2*) (1883) 31 W.R. 912.
[65] S.L.A. 1925, s.110; *ante*, p. 229.
[66] *Re Morgan's Lease* [1972] Ch. 1.
[67] *Hurrell* v. *Littlejohn* [1904] 1 Ch. 689.
[68] S.L.A. 1925, ss.38, 40.

3. Power to lease

(a) *The power.* The settled land, or any part of it, or any easement, right or privilege over it, may be leased for any period not exceeding—

(i) 999 years for building or forestry;
(ii) 100 years for mining;
(iii) 50 years for any other purpose.[69]

Before 1926 the periods were 99, 60 and 21 years respectively, and there was no special provision for forestry leases. After 1925, however, the new periods apply even if the settlement was made before 1926. A building lease is one made partly in consideration of erecting, improving, adding to or repairing buildings, or an agreement to do this[70]; the advantage to the settled land is that in return for a reduced rent the lessee must leave on the land at the end of his lease the new or improved buildings. By the Forestry Act 1967, a forestry lease means a lease to the Minister of Agriculture, Fisheries and Food for purposes authorised by the Act.

(b) *Conditions of lease.* Every lease of settled land must comply with the following conditions.[71]

(i) It must be made by deed.
(ii) It must be made to take effect in possession not more than one year after its date, or in reversion after an existing lease with not more than seven years to run at the date of the new lease. Thus if a tenant for life grants a lease to commence in 14 months' time, it is invalid unless it is to commence after the determination of an existing lease.
(iii) It must reserve the best rent reasonably obtainable in the circumstances, regard being had to any fine (*i.e.* a premium or lump sum) taken, and to any money laid out or to be laid out for the benefit of the land. Any fine is capital money. A lease granted by a tenant for life in return for a bribe or the release from a claim for damages against him personally has accordingly been held not to comply with the statutory requirements.[72] A nominal or reduced rent may be reserved for not longer than the first five years of a building lease or the first 10 years of a forestry lease; and in the case of mining or forestry leases, there are wide powers to vary the rent, *e.g.* according to the value of the minerals or trees taken.[73]
(iv) It must contain a covenant by the lessee for payment of rent and a condition of re-entry (*i.e.* a provision for forfeiture of the lease) on rent not being paid within a specified time not exceeding 30 days.
(v) A counterpart (*i.e.* copy) of the lease must be executed by the lessee

---

[69] *Ibid.* s.41.
[70] *Ibid.* s.44.
[71] *Ibid.* s.42. For defective leases, see M. & W. 364, 365; (1971) 87 L.Q.R. 338 (D. W. Elliott).
[72] *Re Handman and Wilcox's Contract* [1902] 1 Ch. 599.
[73] S.L.A. 1925, ss.44, 45, 48.

and delivered to the tenant for life; it is sufficient evidence that this has been done if the tenant for life duly executes the lease.

It will be seen that normally a lease must be by deed and notice must be given to the trustees. In certain cases, however, these requirements are relaxed. A lease at the best rent reasonably obtainable without a fine and not exempting the lessee from liability for waste has two privileges:

(i) if it is for not more than 21 years, it may be made without giving notice to the trustees; and

(ii) if it is for not more than three years, it may also be made merely in writing and not by deed,[74] though not orally.[75]

As a corollary to his power to grant leases, a tenant for life has wide powers of accepting surrenders of leases and of varying or waiving the terms of any lease.[76] These powers are exercisable without notice to the trustees.

(c) *Rent from leases.* The normal rule is that the tenant for life is entitled to the whole of the rent from leases of the settled land.[77] But as seen above,[78] this does not apply to mining leases, where the capital value of the land is being diminished. The general rule as to rent from mining leases granted under the Act is that, subject to any contrary intention in the settlement, the tenant for life is entitled to three-quarters of the rent unless he is impeachable of waste and the mine is an unopened one, when he is entitled to only one-quarter of the rent; the balance in each case is capital.[79] These provisions, however, apply only to rent from leases granted under the Act, so that if the lease is granted under an express power in the settlement,[80] or if the lease or a contract therefor[81] was made before the land was settled or resettled,[81a] the tenant for life is entitled to the whole of the income. As has been seen, the rules as to the tenant for life working the minerals himself are different from the rules as to leases.[82] Where the tenant for life has not a life interest but some interest such as a fee simple subject to a gift over, he may be unimpeachable of waste even if the settlement is silent on the subject; the owner of a mere life interest, on the other hand is impeachable unless the settlement exempts him from liability for waste.[83]

4. Power to mortgage or charge. In the absence of a contrary provision in the settlement, a tenant for life has no power to mortgage or charge the legal

---

[74] S.L.A. 1925, s.42.
[75] *Bevan* v. *Johnston* [1990] 2 E.G.L.R. 33.
[76] S.L.A. 1925, ss.52, 59.
[77] See, *e.g. Re Wix* [1916] 1 Ch. 279.
[78] *Ante*, p. 50.
[79] S.L.A. 1925, s.47; *Re Fitzwalter* [1943] Ch. 285.
[80] *Earl of Lonsdale* v. *Lowther* [1900] 2 Ch. 687.
[81] *Re Kemeys-Tynte* [1892] 2 Ch. 211.
[81a] *Re Arkwright's Settlement* [1945] Ch. 195.
[82] He can keep the whole of the profits unless he is impeachable of waste and the mine is unopened, when he cannot work it at all: *ante*, p. 50.
[83] *Ante*, pp. 39, 42, 48.

estate for his own benefit. If he wishes to raise money for his own use, he can of course do so by mortgaging his beneficial interest, consisting of his life interest, entail or whatever interest he has. The legal estate, on the other hand, can be mortgaged only for certain specified purposes for the benefit of the settled land or those entitled under the settlement, *e.g.* to pay for improvements, discharge incumbrances or provide money which is required to be raised under the provisions of the settlement, such as portions.[84]

5. Power to grant options. A tenant for life may grant an option in writing to purchase or take a lease of all or any part of the settled land or of any easement, right or privilege over it. But—

(i) the price or rent must be the best reasonably obtainable and must be fixed at the time of granting the option[85]; a tenant for life thus has no power to agree to sell at a price to be fixed by arbitration;

(ii) the option must be made exercisable within an agreed number of years not exceeding 10; and

(iii) the option may be granted with or without any consideration being paid, but if any is paid, it is capital money.[86]

II. POWERS EXERCISABLE ONLY WITH CONSENT

In the following cases, the tenant for life can exercise his powers only with the consent of the trustees of the settlement or under an order of the court.

1. Power to dispose of the principal mansion house. If the tenant for life wishes to make a disposition (whether by sale, lease, exchange or otherwise[87]) of the principal mansion house, if any, and the pleasure-grounds and park,[88] and the lands, if any, usually occupied therewith, the consent of the trustees or an order of the court is required—

(i) if the settlement was made before 1926 and does not expressly provide to the contrary; or

(ii) if the settlement was made after 1925 and expressly requires such consent or order to be obtained.[89]

In other cases, no consent is required, but the usual notice must be given.

If a house is usually occupied as a farmhouse, or if the site of a house and the pleasure-grounds and park and lands, if any, usually occupied therewith do not together exceed 25 acres, the house is not deemed a principal mansion house.[90] In other cases, it is a question of fact whether at a given moment a house is a principal mansion house. Where two separate establishments are comprised in the same settlement, there may be two principal

[84] S.L.A. 1925, ss.16, 71; and see M. & W. 366. For portions, see *ante*, pp. 213, 215.
[85] See *Re Morgan's Lease* [1972] Ch. 1, where the option was contained in an existing lease.
[86] S.L.A. 1925, s.51.
[87] *Ibid.* s.117.
[88] See *Pease* v. *Courtney* [1904] 2 Ch. 503.
[89] S.L.A. 1925, s.65.
[90] *Ibid.*

mansion houses, or one may be subsidiary to the other, as where one is used as the main residence and the other as a shooting-box.[91] Again, a house may cease to be a principal mansion house, as where it is let as a school; and if the tenant for life then uses a smaller house on the estate as his home, that may become a principal mansion house.[92]

2. Power to cut and sell timber. This has already been dealt with.[93] It is only if the tenant for life is impeachable of waste that he requires the consent of the trustees or an order of the court and three-quarters of the proceeds are capital money; if he is unimpeachable, he needs no consent or order and may keep all the proceeds.

3. Power to compromise claims. Subject to the consent in writing of the trustees, the tenant for life has a wide power to compromise and settle disputes relating to the settled land or any part thereof.[94]

4. Power to sell settled chattels. With the leave of the court the tenant for life may sell any chattels settled to devolve with the land,[95] as furniture, pictures and the like sometimes are.

5. Power to effect any proper transaction. The court has a statutory jurisdiction to authorise the tenant for life to effect any transaction not otherwise authorised by the Act or the settlement if it is for the benefit of the land or the beneficiaries and is a transaction which an absolute owner could validly effect.[96] This power even permits the court to sanction alterations in the beneficial interests under the settlement.[97]

III. OTHER POWERS OF A TENANT FOR LIFE

1. Power to effect improvements. The power to effect improvements is complex.[98]

(a) *Making the improvements.* A tenant for life may of course effect improvements to the land at his own expense, but if he wishes the cost to be borne either temporarily or permanently by capital money, or to be raised by a mortgage or charge of the settled land, he must comply with the Act. He no longer needs prior approval of a scheme,[99] but he must first ascertain that the proposed improvements are within the list of those authorised by the

---

[91] *Gilbey* v. *Rush* [1906] 1 Ch. 11 at 21.
[92] *Re Feversham S.E.* [1938] 2 All E.R. 210.
[93] *Ante*, p. 48.
[94] S.L.A. 1925, s.58.
[95] *Ibid.* s.67; and see M. & W. 370, 371 for the complexities.
[96] S.L.A. 1925, s.64; Settled Land and Trustee Acts (Court's General Powers) Act 1943, s.2.
[97] *Re Simmons* [1956] Ch. 125.
[98] S.L.A. 1925, ss.83–87; and see M. & W. 372–377.
[99] As he did under S.L.A. 1882, s.26.

Act. He must then obtain the appointment of a surveyor or engineer, for capital money cannot be applied in paying for improvements unless—

(1) if the money is in the hands of the trustees,
- (a) a certificate is furnished by a competent engineer or able practical surveyor employed independently of the tenant for life, certifying—
  - (i) that the work or some specific part thereof has been properly executed; and
  - (ii) the amount properly payable in respect thereof; or
- (b) an order of the court directs or authorises payment:
(2) if the money is in court,
- (a) a report or certificate of the Minister of Agriculture, Fisheries and Food is given; or
- (b) a report of a competent engineer or able practical surveyor approved by the court is given; or
- (c) such other evidence as the court thinks fit is given.

(b) *Repayment.* When the improvements are paid for out of capital, the question arises whether or not the tenant for life must repay the money. This depends on the nature of the improvements. A long list is set out in the Third Schedule to the Act, which is divided into three parts:

(i) If the improvement falls within Part I (*e.g.* drainage or erection of bridges) or is authorised by the settlement, repayment cannot be ordered. In the case of agricultural land, ordinary repairs reasonably required for proper farming are somewhat surprisingly included under this head if effected after April 1948.[1]
(ii) If the improvement falls within Part II (*e.g.* the restoration or reconstruction of buildings damaged or destroyed by dry rot), the trustees or the court have a discretion to order repayment by instalments.
(iii) If the improvement falls within Part III (*e.g.* the installation of artificial light in a building), the trustees or the court must order repayment by instalments.

The number of the instalments is within the discretion of the court or the trustees, except that the trustees may not order more than 50 half-yearly instalments.

2. Power to select investments for capital money. Capital money must be applied in one or more of the 21 methods specified in the Act.[2] These include investment in trustee securities, paying for improvements, and the purchase of land held in fee simple or on a lease with 60 years or more unexpired.[3] The tenant for life may select which of these methods of application is to be employed, in default of which the trustees make the choice.

---

[1] See the cases cited in *Re Lord Brougham and Vaux's S.E.* [1954] Ch. 24; [1954] Camb.L.J. 63 (H. W. R. Wade).
[2] S.L.A. 1925, s.73.
[3] See *Re Wellsted's W.T.* [1949] Ch. 296.

D. Position of the Tenant for Life

1. The tenant for life as trustee. As already seen,[4] the tenant for life is a trustee both of the land and of his powers. This has consequences if he wishes to acquire any or all of the settled land for himself. It is a settled rule of equity that any acquisition of trust property by a trustee, either directly or indirectly, is voidable by any beneficiary, no matter how fair the transaction may be, for otherwise the trustee might be in a position where his interest conflicts with his duty.[5] To avoid this difficulty, the Settled Land Act 1925[6] authorises the trustees of the settlement to exercise all the powers of a tenant for life in carrying out any transaction whereby the tenant for life acquires any interest in the settled land.[7]

Where any question arises as to the exercise of any of the powers of the tenant for life, the court, on the application of anyone interested, may make such order as it thinks fit.[8] But the court will not intervene where joint tenants for life are in honest disagreement.[9]

2. No powers can be given to anyone else. Any power, other than a power of revocation or appointment, which the settlement purports to give to anyone except the tenant for life, is exercisable not by that person but by the tenant for life as if it were an additional power conferred by the settlement.[10] Thus if land is devised "to X and Y in fee simple with power to sell, on trust for A for life and then for B absolutely" the power of sale purported to be given to X and Y is divested from them and given to A; this is so even though A already has a statutory power of sale. But the abortive attempt to give a power of sale to X and Y may not be wholly ineffective, for it may make them Settled Land Act trustees.[11]

3. The statutory powers cannot be ousted, curtailed or hampered

(a) *The Act prevails.* The settlor may confer additional powers on the tenant for life, and such powers are exercisable in the same way as if they were conferred by the Act.[12] Further, nothing in the Act in any way restricts powers which the settlement gives to the tenant for life or purports to give to the trustees to be exercised with the approval of the tenant for life: the powers given by the Act and the settlement are cumulative. But in other respects, so far as the settlement and the Act conflict in relation to powers exercisable under the Act, the Act prevails.[13] Thus if the settlement provides

---

[4] *Ante*, p. 223.
[5] Snell 249.
[6] s.68.
[7] See *Re Pennant's W.T.* [1970] Ch. 75. If the tenant for life is also one of the trustees, he should join in the conveyance to himself as one of the conveying parties: *ibid.*
[8] S.L.A. 1925, s.93.
[9] *Re 90 Thornhill Road, Tolworth, Surrey* [1970] Ch. 261.
[10] S.L.A. 1925, s.108.
[11] *Ante*, p. 238.
[12] S.L.A. 1925, s.109.
[13] *Ibid.* s.108.

that no sale shall be made without the consent of some specified person, this provision is inconsistent with the unfettered power of sale given by the Act, and the latter prevails.[14]

In particular, it is enacted that any provision in any document is void to the extent to which it purports or tends to prevent or discourage the tenant for life from exercising his statutory powers or from requiring the land to be vested in him.[15] This applies even when the attempt to restrain the exercise of the powers is made by way of determinable limitation, as where land is settled on "Y for life until he ceases permanently to reside in the property." Notwithstanding anything in a settlement, the exercise of a statutory power can never cause a forfeiture.

(b) *Conditions of residence.* These provisions are most frequently invoked by conditions of residence, *e.g.* a proviso in the settlement that the tenant for life shall forfeit his interest on ceasing to reside on the settled land. In such cases, if the tenant for life ceases to reside for some reason other than the exercise of his statutory powers (as where he moves out to allow a relation to live there rent-free), the proviso for forfeiture is operative and he loses his interest.[16] But if the reason for his ceasing to reside is that he has exercised his statutory powers, as by leasing or selling the land, there is no forfeiture and he continues to be entitled as tenant for life, receiving the rent from the lease or the income from the purchase-money.[17] These provisions may also apply where the settlement provides a fund for the payment of outgoings while the tenant for life occupies the land. If his occupation ceases because he has exercised his statutory power of leasing, the payments from the fund will still continue.[18] If instead he sells the land, thus taking it out of the settlement, he has no claim to any of the income of the fund, for none has been given to him[19]; but if the settlement had given him any surplus income not required for the outgoings until the land is sold, he would have been entitled to the whole of the income for life, for it had all become surplus and the provision for the income to cease on sale is void.[20]

4. The tenant for life cannot assign, release or contract not to exercise his powers[21]

(a) *Exercise of powers.* Once a person has become a tenant for life, he is incapable of divesting himself of his powers, even if he parts with his entire beneficial interest, as he is entitled to do; it is he, and not the assignee of his beneficial interest, who alone can exercise the statutory powers.[22] However,

---

[14] *Re Jefferys (No. 2)* [1939] Ch. 205. Contrast trusts for sale: *post,* p. 255.
[15] S.L.A. 1925, s.106.
[16] *Re Trenchard* [1902] 1 Ch. 378.
[17] *Re Orlebar* [1936] Ch. 147.
[18] *Re Patten* [1929] 2 Ch. 276.
[19] *Ibid.*; contrast *Re Aberconway's S.T.* [1953] Ch. 647.
[20] *Re Herbert* [1946] 1 All E.R. 421.
[21] S.L.A. 1925, s.104.
[22] *Re Earl of Carnarvon's Chesterfield S.E.* [1927] 1 Ch. 138 at 145, 146.

in three cases the statutory powers may become exercisable by someone other than the tenant for life.

(1) EXTINGUISHMENT OF INTEREST. Where the interest of the tenant for life has been assured, with intent to extinguish it, to the person next entitled under the settlement, the statutory powers cease to be exercisable by the tenant for life and become exercisable as if he were dead.[23] Thus if land is settled on A for life, remainder to B for life, remainder to C in fee simple, the effect of A surrendering his life interest to B is to make the statutory powers exercisable by B instead of A, and A must forthwith convey the legal estate to B by a vesting deed. If B then surrenders his life interest to C, he must convey the legal estate to C, but by an ordinary conveyance, for the land ceases to be settled land.[24] This exception does not apply if there is an intervening limitation which might take effect, *e.g.* to D for life, remainder to the sons of D, remainder to E for life, and D, aged 80 and childless, surrenders to E.[25]

(2) ORDER OF COURT. If the tenant for life—

(i) has ceased to have a substantial interest in the land, whether by bankruptcy, assignment or otherwise, and
(ii) either consents to an order being made or else has unreasonably refused to exercise his statutory powers,

any person interested in the land may apply to the court for an order authorising the trustees to exercise any or all of the statutory powers in the name and on behalf of the tenant for life.[26] Such an order prevents the tenant for life from exercising any of the powers affected by the order, but until it has been registered[27] the order does not affect those dealing with the tenant for life. Such an order vests neither the legal estate nor the statutory powers in the trustees, who do not become the statutory owner; the order merely authorises the trustees to exercise the powers on behalf of the tenant for life and in his name.

(3) MENTAL PATIENTS. Where the tenant for life is a mental patient, his receiver may, in his name and on his behalf under an order of the Court of Protection, exercise his statutory powers.[28]

(b) *Position of assignees.* Where an assignment of the beneficial interest of a tenant for life is made after 1925, the consent of the assignee is not required for the exercise of the statutory powers by the tenant for life, even if the assignment is made for money or money's worth.[29] But for the application of

[23] S.L.A. 1925, s.105.
[24] See *ante*, p. 231.
[25] *Re Maryon-Wilson's Instruments* [1971] Ch. 789.
[26] S.L.A. 1925, s.24.
[27] As "an order affecting land": *ante*, p. 83.
[28] Mental Health Act 1983, s.96(1). For mental patients, see *ante*, p. 170.
[29] S.L.A. 1925, s.104.

capital money affected by the assignment for any purpose other than for investment in trustee securities, the consent of the assignee is necessary if the assignment so provides or takes effect by operation of the law of bankruptcy, and the trustees have notice of this. Further, unless the assignment otherwise provides, notice of any intended transaction must be given to the assignee. If the land is sold the rights of the assignee are transferred to the capital money which represents the land; and provision is made for obtaining consents in any cases of difficulty.

E. Functions of Settled Land Act Trustees

It may be useful to collect together the principal functions of Settled Land Act trustees. They are—

    (i) to receive and hold capital money[30];

    (ii) to receive notice from the tenant for life of his intention to effect certain transactions[31];

   (iii) to give consent to certain transactions[32];

   (iv) to act as special personal representatives on the death of a tenant for life[33];

    (v) to act as statutory owner if the tenant for life is an infant or there is no tenant for life[34];

   (vi) to exercise the powers of the tenant for life if he wishes to acquire the settled land for his own benefit[35];

  (vii) to exercise the powers of the tenant for life where he has no substantial beneficial interest and either consents to such exercise or unreasonably refuses to exercise his powers[36]; and

 (viii) to exercise a general supervision over the well-being of the settled land.[37]

Part 4

TRUSTS FOR SALE AFTER 1925

1. What is a trust for sale. It has been seen[38] that after 1925 land cannot be settled land if it is subject to an "immediate binding trust for sale." Whenever land is limited in trust for persons by way of succession or for some other reason falls within the definition of settled land, it will be governed by the Settled Land Act 1925 unless it can be shown that it is subject to a trust

---

[30] *Ante*, p. 220; *post*, p. 260.
[31] *Ante*, p. 241.
[32] *Ante*, p. 245.
[33] *Ante*, p. 232.
[34] *Ante*, p. 224.
[35] *Ante*, p. 248.
[36] *Ante*, p. 250.
[37] See *Re Boston's W.T.* [1956] Ch. 395 at 405.
[38] *Ante*, p. 223.

for sale of this nature. The meaning of the phrase is thus of great importance and must be examined closely.

(a) *There must be a "trust" for sale.* As before 1926, there must be a true trust to sell and not a mere power of sale.[39] Thus a conveyance to trustees on trust for persons in succession, giving the trustees a power of sale, makes the land settled land; the conveyance operates as an imperfect settlement and the trustees cannot sell.[40] Some of the difficulties which arose from trusts "to retain or sell the land"[41] are solved by the provision that in a disposition or settlement coming into operation after 1925, such a trust shall be construed as a trust for sale with power to postpone sale.[42]

(b) *The trust for sale must be "immediate."* Here again, the position is substantially the same as before 1926[43]; a trust to sell at some future date, *e.g.* when X attains the age of 25, does not prevent land from being settled land.[44] But if there is a trust for sale which is immediately operative, this takes the land out of the Settled Land Act 1925, even if the trustees have power to postpone the sale and even if a sale cannot be made without the request or consent of some person.[45]

(c) *The trust for sale must be "binding."* The interpretation of the word "binding" has given rise to considerable difficulty, especially in cases where the land is first subject to the Settled Land Act 1925 and then to a trust for sale, as where it is limited to A for life with remainder to trustees for sale. Three views have been put forward:

  (i) That it means a trust for sale capable of binding, in the sense of overreaching, as many interests as possible. Thus if an equitable interest created under the earlier settlement cannot be overreached by the trustees for sale then the trust for sale is not "binding."[46]
 (ii) That the word "binding" was inserted to emphasise that a revocable trust for sale is excluded, or else that the word is mere surplusage.[47]
(iii) That a "binding" trust for sale is one which is capable of binding the whole legal estate which has been settled.[48] If the legal estate is vested in the trustees for sale as such, the trust for sale is "binding," even if equitable interests such as charges under a former settlement are still outstanding. But where such equitable charges are outstanding when the tenant for life dies, this will normally prevent the trustees for sale

---

[39] See M. & W. 323.
[40] *Ante*, pp. 227, 248.
[41] *Ante*, p. 222.
[42] L.P.A. 1925, s.25.
[43] See M. & W. 324.
[44] *Re Hanson* [1928] Ch. 96; and see *Bevan* v. *Johnston* [1990] 2 E.G.L.R. 33.
[45] L.P.A. 1925, s.205(1)(xxix).
[46] *Re Leigh's S.E.* (*No.* 1) [1926] Ch. 852. See *post*, p. 263, for *ad hoc* trusts for sale with wider overreaching powers.
[47] *Re Parker's S.E.* [1928] Ch. 247 at 261.
[48] See *Re Beaumont S.E.* [1937] 2 All E.R. 353; *Re Sharpe's Deed of Release* [1939] Ch. 51.

from requiring the special personal representatives to vest the legal estate in them,[49] so that the trust for sale will not be "binding."[50]

It seems safe to say that the first alternative is now generally recognised as being wrong,[51] and that although the second view is innocuous, the third is probably correct. The issue is largely technical: there is clearly a power of sale and the sole question is who is to exercise it.[52]

2. How a trust for sale comes into being. A trust for sale may arise—

(a) expressly, by land being deliberately limited on trust for sale, or
(b) by operation of statute.

(a) *Express trusts for sale.* With a view to keeping the trusts off the title, the general practice for many years has been to employ two documents, namely, a conveyance on trust for sale and a trust instrument; it was this practice which suggested the vesting deed and trust instrument of the Settled Land Act 1925. Although today two documents are almost invariably employed to create a trust for sale *inter vivos*, there is nothing in the 1925 legislation to make this essential. In the case of testamentary trusts for sale, the usual position before 1926 was that the will was the sole document concerned. After 1925, a written assent is required to vest the legal estate in the trustees for sale, so that now there will usually be two documents in such cases. But even if a trust for sale is created by a single document, it is now provided that a purchaser of the legal estate from the trustees for sale is not concerned with the trusts affecting the rents and profits of the land until sale and the proceeds of sale thereafter, whether or not the trusts are declared by the same instrument as that by which the trust for sale is created.[53]

Where a trust for sale was created before 1926, the legal estate remains vested in trustees for sale if it was already vested in them; if not, it automatically vested in them at the beginning of 1926.[54]

(b) *Statutory trusts for sale.* A trust for sale is imposed by statute in a number of cases. For example—

(i) if two or more persons are entitled to land as joint tenants or tenants in common, a trust for sale is normally imposed by the Law of Property Act 1925[55];
(ii) the Administration of Estates Act 1925 imposes a trust for sale on the property of a person dying intestate[56];
(iii) if trustees lend money on mortgage and the property becomes vested in them free from the right of repayment (*e.g.* by foreclosure), they

---

[49] S.L.A. 1925, s.7(5).
[50] *Re Norton* [1929] 1 Ch. 84; and see *Re Parker's S.E.*, *supra*.
[51] *Ibid.*
[52] See further M. & W. 387–389.
[53] L.P.A. 1925, s.27; and see *post*, p. 278.
[54] *Ibid.* Sched. 1, Pt. II, paras. 3, 6.
[55] *Post*, p. 279.
[56] *Ante*, p. 157.

hold it upon trust for sale.[57] This preserves the character of the trust property; the money was pure personalty, and under the doctrine of conversion, the rights of the beneficiaries under a trust for sale are treated as being interests in pure personalty, even if the subject-matter of the trust is land; and

(iv) if the trustees of a personalty settlement invest trust funds in the purchase of land, they hold it on trust for sale unless the settlement otherwise provides.[58]

3. Position of trustees for sale

(a) *Power of postponement.* Unless a contrary intention appears, a power to postpone sale is implied after 1925 in every trust for sale of land, even if it was created before 1926.[59] In the absence of an express provision to the contrary, the trustees are not liable in any way if they postpone sale indefinitely in the exercise of their discretion, nor is a purchaser of legal estate concerned with directions respecting the postponement of sale.[60] If the trustees cannot agree whether to sell the land, normally it must be sold: the land is subject to a trust for sale, and the power to postpone sale cannot be exercised unless the trustees are unanimous.[61] But this does not apply where a sale would defeat the spirit or object of the trust or amount to a breach of contract,[62] an aspect which has become important in cases of co-ownership.[63] Many trusts for sale are created with the intention that the land shall be retained for a long time before being sold, an intention which is effectuated by the trustees duly concurring in exercising their power to postpone any sale. As a means of making a settlement, the trust for sale has long been a recognised alternative to settled land.[64]

(b) *Continuance of trust.* Once a trust for sale has been created, the trust is, for the protection of any purchaser thereunder, deemed to be subsisting until the land has been conveyed either to the beneficiaries themselves or to some other person under their direction.[65] This meets the difficulty that if all the possible beneficiaries were of full age and subject to no disability, they could put an end to the trust for sale by electing to have the land retained as land. For this reason, purchasers who knew that all the possible beneficiaries were *sui juris* sometimes raised objections to a sale without the concurrence of the beneficiaries; formerly this difficulty was overcome by requiring one

[57] L.P.A. 1925, s.31.
[58] *Ibid.* s.32; see *Re Hanson* [1928] Ch. 96.
[59] L.P.A. 1925, s.25.
[60] *Ibid.*
[61] *Re Mayo* [1943] Ch. 302. Contrast joint tenants for life of settled land: *post*, p. 297.
[62] See *Re Buchanan-Wollaston's Conveyance* [1939] Ch. 738; *Re Hyde's Conveyance* (1952) 102 L.J. News. 58; *Jones* v. *Challenger* [1961] 1 Q.B. 176.
[63] *Post*, p. 295.
[64] For a comparison of the two methods, see *post*, pp. 265 *et seq.* For the application of income, see M. & W. 393.
[65] L.P.A. 1925, s.23; and see *post*, p. 266.

of the beneficiaries to concur in the conveyance, thus showing that there had not been a unanimous election to terminate the trust for sale.[66]

(c) *Powers of trustees*. The powers of trustees for sale have been considerably extended by the Law of Property Act 1925. Before 1926, they normally had no powers of leasing, mortgaging or otherwise dealing with the land except by sale[67]; after 1925 they have all the powers both of a tenant for life of settled land and of Settled Land Act trustees.[68] Thus trustees for sale can exercise even those powers which are exercisable by a tenant for life only with the consent of the trustees of the settlement. Further, where settled land becomes vested in the Settled Land Act trustees in the form of trust for sale known as the "statutory trusts,"[69] the trustees have all the additional powers (if any) conferred by the settlement on the tenant for life, statutory owner or trustees of the settlement.[70] If trustees for sale refuse to exercise their powers a beneficiary can apply to the court for the court to make such order as it thinks fit.[71]

(d) *Curtailment of powers*. The extent to which the powers of trustees for sale can be curtailed by the settlement is uncertain. It is clear that the Law of Property Act 1925 contemplates the exercise of their power of sale or any other of their powers being made subject to the requirement that the consent of specified persons should be first obtained[72]; for if the consent of more than two persons is required, the Act provides that a bona fide purchaser for value is protected if the consent of any two such persons is obtained, and further, that he need not concern himself with the consents of any persons under disability.[73] But this provision applies only to a purchaser: the trustees will be guilty of a breach of trust if they do not obtain the full number of consents stipulated. Any consent required from a minor, however, may be given by his parent or guardian, and that of a mental patient by his receiver; and the court has power to dispense with consents which cannot be obtained,[74] as where they are refused.[75] The requirement of a consent need not be explicit but may be inferred, as where the trusts give a beneficiary a right to the land itself at a future date.[76] Yet although it is clear that consents may be made requisite to the trustees exercising their powers, it is by no means clear whether the powers can be taken away or curtailed in any other way. It is arguable that as the trustees have all the powers of a tenant for life,

[66] See *Re Jenkins and H. E. Randall & Co.'s Contract* [1903] 2 Ch. 362.
[67] *Ante*, p. 222.
[68] L.P.A. 1925, s.28; see *Re Wellsted's W.T.* [1949] Ch. 296.
[69] See *post*, p. 297.
[70] L.P.A. 1925, s.28; L.P.(Am.)A. 1926, Sched.
[71] L.P.A. 1925, s.30.
[72] Contrast settled land: *ante*, p. 249.
[73] L.P.A. 1925, s.26.
[74] *Ibid.* ss.26, 30; Mental Health Act 1983, s.96(1)(k).
[75] *Re Beale's S.T.* [1932] 2 Ch. 15.
[76] *Re Herklots' W.T.* [1964] 1 W.L.R. 583, considered in *Dodsworth* v. *Dodsworth* [1973] E.G.D. 233.

and as the powers of a tenant for life cannot be restricted in any way,[77] so the powers of trustees for sale cannot be hampered except so far as is provided by statute: and perhaps this argument[78] will ultimately be accepted by the courts.

4. Rights of the beneficiaries. After 1925, the person for the time being entitled to the income under a trust for sale has none of the powers of a tenant for life of settled land, for all the powers are vested in the trustees for sale. However, this rule is subject to four qualifications.

(a) *Delegation*. The trustees may revocably and in writing delegate certain powers to the person of full age (not being merely an annuitant) who for the time being is beneficially entitled in possession to the net rents and profits of the land for his life or any less period.[79] The powers which may be so delegated are the powers of, and incidental to, leasing, accepting surrenders of leases and management. The powers thus delegated must be exercised in the names and on behalf of the trustees. If they are misused, the liability rests not on the trustees but on the person exercising the powers, who is deemed to be in the position of a trustee[80]; yet the trustees themselves may also be liable if they have erred in not revoking the delegated powers. If the trustees refuse to delegate these powers, an application may be made to the court to compel them to do so.[81]

(b) *Consents*. As seen above,[82] a person may restrain the exercise of the powers of trustees for sale if his consent to this has been made requisite.

(c) *Consultation*. In some cases the trustees are under an obligation, so far as is practicable, to consult the persons of full age for the time being beneficially entitled in possession in the rents and profits of the land until sale, and must, so far as is consistent with the general interests of the trust, give effect to their wishes, or to the wishes of the majority in value.[83] However, there are many express trusts for sale to which this provision does not apply, for it is confined to trusts for sale which either are created by statute or show an intention that this provision is to apply. Further, the trustees are not bound to follow the wishes of the beneficiaries, nor is a purchaser concerned to see that the trustees have complied with this requirement.[84]

(d) *Inaction by trustees*. If trustees for sale refuse to sell or to exercise any of their statutory powers, "any person interested" may apply to the court for an order giving effect to the proposed transaction, or directing the trustees

---

[77] *Ante*, p. 248.
[78] Urged but not decided in *Re Davies' W.T.* [1932] 1 Ch. 530; see at pp. 532, 533. See M. & W. 394.
[79] L.P.A. 1925, s.29.
[80] *Ibid.*
[81] *Ibid.* s.30.
[82] *Ante*, p. 255.
[83] L.P.A. 1925, s.26; L.P.(Am.)A. 1926, Sched.
[84] *Ibid.*

for sale to do so, and the court may make such order as it thinks fit.[85] "Person interested" includes a creditor with a charging order against the interest of a co-owner.[86]

5. The doctrine of conversion

(a) *The doctrine.* It has long been settled that the rights of a beneficiary under a trust for sale are to be regarded as being rights not in the land itself but in the proceeds of sale; for equity looks on that as done which ought to be done. The trustees are bound by a trust to convert the land into money, sooner or later; and so, on the simple principle that it would be wrong that the precise moment when the trustees carried out their administrative duty of selling should alter the devolution of the beneficial interests,[87] the nature of those interests remain unchanged throughout.[88]

This doctrine has many important effects. Before 1926, interests under a trust for sale of land devolved on intestacy on the next of kin and not the heir; and if a testator dies today leaving all his realty to R and all his personalty to P, it is P who will take the testator's interests under a trust for sale[89] but R if the trust for sale had ended by the testator becoming solely entitled before his death.[90] Indeed, when a tenant in common died after 1925 leaving a will made before 1926 which gave his share in Greenacre to R, R took nothing; for the testator no longer had any share in Greenacre but only a share under the trust for sale which statute imposed in 1926.[91] Again, where before 1926 two or more persons were entitled to land as tenants in common in tail, the trust for sale imposed in 1926 converted the entails into absolute interests, since before 1926 no entail could exist in personalty[92]; but statute has now retrospectively provided that an entail should be deemed to exist in the proceeds of sale.[93] Further, although by statute a charging order may now be made against an interest under a trust for sale of land, such an order still does not seem to be registrable as a writ or order affecting land.[94]

(b) *Limits to the doctrine.* The doctrine still remains in full force, but in recent years it has not been applied relentlessly, particularly in relation to modern statutes drafted without overt regard to the impact of the doctrine. Under certain statutory provisions, beneficiaries under a trust for sale of land have been held to be "interested in land"[95] and to own "an interest in

[85] L.P.A. 1925, s.30.
[86] *Midland Bank Plc.* v. *Pike* [1988] 2 All E.R. 434.
[87] See *Re Richerson* [1892] 1 Ch. 379 at 383.
[88] See *Fletcher* v. *Ashburner* (1779) 1 Bro.C.C. 497; M. & W. 315–317.
[89] *Re Kempthorne* [1930] 1 Ch. 268.
[90] *Re Cook* [1948] Ch. 212.
[91] *Re Newman* [1930] 2 Ch. 409; contrast *Re Warren* [1932] 1 Ch. 42 (confirmatory codicil after 1925); and for the trust for sale, see *post*, p. 289.
[92] *Re Price* [1928] Ch. 579; see *ante*, p. 43.
[93] Law of Property (Entailed Interests) Act 1932, s.1.
[94] See *ante*, p. 83.
[95] *Elias* v. *Mitchell* [1972] Ch. 652.

real estate"[96] or an "interest in land."[97] There has also been some judicial reluctance to apply the doctrine where the real concern of the beneficiaries is with the land itself (as where it is their home) and not merely with the proceeds of sale under a trust for sale imposed by statute.[98] An interest under a trust for sale of the land is not the same as an interest only in the proceeds of sale after it has been sold.[99] Today, the doctrine is more likely to be confined than extended.[1]

Part 5

OVERREACHING EFFECT OF DISPOSITIONS

Sect. 1. Under the Settled Land Act 1925

As already explained,[2] an interest in land is said to be overreached if it is transferred from land to the purchase-money on a sale or other disposition being made. The Settled Land Act 1925, after first authorising a tenant for life to effect a sale or other transaction by deed, goes on to state the overreaching effect of such a deed.

1. Rights under the settlement.[3] The deed is effectual to pass the land or other interest concerned "discharged from all the limitations, powers, and provisions of the settlement, and from all estates, interests, and charges subsisting or to arise thereunder"; it is immaterial whether or not a purchaser has notice of these rights. In short, the purchaser takes the land free from all the rights under the settlement. The Act then makes certain qualifications to this rule: the land is to pass to the purchaser discharged from the above rights, "but subject to and with the exception of"[4]—

(a) All legal estates and charges by way of legal mortgage having priority to the settlement.

In nearly every case this provision is mere surplusage, for no power is given to overreach rights prior to the settlement and so the qualification is unnecessary. If X makes a legal mortgage of land and later settles the land, the tenant for life has no power to overreach the mortgage, which continues to bind the land.

[96] *Re Bradshaw* [1950] Ch. 78.
[97] *Cooper* v. *Critchley* [1955] Ch. 431; but see *City of London B.S.* v. *Flegg* [1988] A.C. 54 at 82, 83, criticised in [1988] Conv. 108 at 117, 118 (M. P. Thompson).
[98] *Barclay* v. *Barclay* [1970] 2 Q.B. 677 at 684, 685; *Williams & Glyn's Bank Ltd.* v. *Boland* [1979] Ch. 312 at 329, 336; [1981] A.C. 487 at 507.
[99] *Barclay* v. *Barclay, supra.*
[1] See generally the historical survey at (1984) 100 L.Q.R. 86 (S. Anderson); and see [1986] Conv. 415 (J. Warburton).
[2] *Ante*, pp. 6, 92.
[3] S.L.A. 1925, s.72.
[4] See *Re Dickin and Kelsall's Contract* [1908] 1 Ch. 213 at 221.

(b) All legal estates and charges by way of legal mortgage which have been conveyed or created for securing money actually raised at the date of the deed.

This is a true exception, for it excludes something which otherwise would have been included in the overreaching provision. Thus if a tenant for life creates a legal mortgage to pay for improvements or raise portions, and the mortgagee has actually paid the money, the mortgage cannot be over-reached even though it is an interest arising under the settlement. "Mort-gagees who have actually lent their money on the security of the land are regarded as strangers to the settlement, and are not to have the security which they bargained for on the land itself transferred to the purchase-money at the will of the tenant for life."[5] If the money has not in fact been paid (*e.g.* where a legal term of years has been created to secure portions which have not been raised[6]) the right is overreached.[7]

(c) All leases and grants of other rights (except annuities, limited owner's charges and general equitable charges[8]) which at the date of the deed are—
  (i) binding on the successors in title of the tenant for life, and
  (ii) duly registered if capable of registration.

This also is a true exception, but unlike the previous provisions it is not confined to legal rights. It thus apparently applies to a restrictive covenant creating a mere equitable burden on the land.

2. Rights prior to the settlement. Having dealt with the exceptions to the rule that all rights arising under the settlement can be overreached, the Act proceeds to the converse case, namely, the exceptions to the rule that rights prior to the settlement cannot be overreached. The Act[9] provides that—

(1) an annuity,
(2) a limited owner's charge, and
(3) a general equitable charge

will be overreached on a disposition under the Act even if they have been duly protected by registration; these rights are treated as if they had been created by the settlement even if in fact they arose before it came into existence. They are all rights which can be represented in terms of money and so will not suffer from being transferred to the purchase-money.

3. Summary. It cannot be said that the overreaching provisions, which in the main reproduce corresponding provisions in the Settled Land Act 1882, are very happily drawn. For those who wish to have a bird's eye view of their

---

[5] *Re Mundy and Roper's Contract* [1899] 1 Ch. 275 at 289, *per* Chitty L.J.
[6] For this device, virtually obsolete, see M. & W. 413, 414.
[7] See *Re Du Cane and Nettlefold's Contract* [1898] 2 Ch. 96 at 108.
[8] For these rights, see *ante*, pp. 78, 81.
[9] S.L.A. 1925, s.72.

effect (necessarily at the expense of some accuracy) the position may be represented as follows:

(i) There is in general no power to overreach legal rights.
(ii) Subject to the three exceptions set out above, there is no power to overreach equitable rights already existing when the settlement was made.
(iii) There is power to overreach all the equitable rights of the beneficiaries under the settlement, including derivative rights, *e.g.* the rights of a mortgagee of the beneficial interest of a tenant for life.

4. Payment of capital money. There is one important condition which must be observed if a deed is to take effect under the Act and so have an overreaching effect. This is the rule that, notwithstanding anything to the contrary in the settlement, any capital money payable in respect of the transaction must be paid either—

(i) to, or by the direction of, all the trustees of the settlement, who must be either two or more in number or a trust corporation (the definition of "trust corporation" includes certain officials such as the Public Trustee and certain companies with a large paid-up capital[10]), or
(ii) into court.[11]

It lies with the tenant for life to decide which of the two methods of payment is to be adopted.[12] If a purchaser fails to pay his money in accordance with these provisions, and pays it, for example, to the tenant for life, he will not get a good discharge and will be unable to make a good title to a subsequent purchaser.[13] Where no capital money arises on a transaction (as where a lease is granted without taking a fine), a disposition in favour of a bona fide purchaser for value of a legal estate takes effect under the Act and thus has an overreaching effect even though there are no trustees.[14]

5. Capital money as land. The capital money and any investments representing it are for all purposes of disposition, transmission and devolution (but not otherwise, *e.g.* for fiscal purposes[15]) treated as land, and are held for and go to the same persons, in the same manner and for the same estates, interests and trusts, as the land wherefrom they arise would have been held and have gone under the settlement.[16] Thus where a tenant for life had become absolutely entitled to the land, a will of his that effectively disposed of personalty alone could not carry any capital money[17]; whereas an option

---

[10] See Snell 579, 580.
[11] S.L.A. 1925, s.18.
[12] *Ibid.* s.75; *Hatten* v. *Russell* (1888) 38 Ch.D. 334 at 345.
[13] *Re Norton and Las Casas' Contract* [1909] 2 Ch. 59. For purchases made without knowing that the land is settled, see *ante*, p. 229.
[14] S.L.A. 1925, s.110(4).
[15] *Earl of Midleton* v. *Baron Cottesloe* [1949] A.C. 418.
[16] S.L.A. 1925, s.75.
[17] *Re Cartwright* [1939] Ch. 90.

under the settlement to purchase the land can be exercised so as to obtain the capital money.[18] In short, the state in which the settled property happens to be at any given moment, whether it is land, investments or money, cannot affect the rights of the beneficiaries or those claiming under them.

Sect. 2. Under a Trust for Sale

In one sense, it can be said that a trust for sale has no overreaching effect; for by the equitable doctrine of conversion, so long as the land remains unsold, the rights of the beneficiaries are already deemed to be rights in the purchase-money into which it will ultimately be converted. It can thus be said that a sale or other transaction does not transfer the rights of the beneficiaries from the land to the purchase-money, for strictly they never were attached to the land. This view rather overstates the impact of the doctrine of conversion, particularly when the beneficiaries are in possession of the land.[19] It is therefore both convenient and less misleading to use the term "overreaching" as including the process by which the beneficiaries have their rights in what is money in theory but land in fact transferred to what is money both in theory and in fact.

A disposition under a trust for sale is effective to overreach the equitable rights of the beneficiaries thereunder; there is no power to overreach legal estates, nor, apparently, to overreach rights already existing when the trust for sale was created. As already seen, a purchaser of a legal estate from the trustees for sale is not concerned with the rents and profits of the land until sale and the proceeds of sale thereafter, even if the trusts are declared by the instrument which created the trust for sale.[20]

For beneficial interests to be overreached,[21] the proceeds of sale or other capital money must be paid to or applied by the direction of not less than two persons as trustees for sale except where the trustee is a trust corporation or a sole personal representative.[22] A beneficiary may obtain an injunction to restrain a sale if there is only one trustee,[23] though one trustee suffices if no capital money arises.[24] There is no provision for payment into court. Where capital money is paid to only one trustee, there is no overreaching; but if the land is registered land a beneficiary in actual occupation will have an overriding interest binding upon the purchaser.[25] For unregistered land, a purchaser will be bound by the beneficial interest unless he is a bona fide purchaser for value of a legal estate without notice.[26]

---

[18] *Re Armstrong's W.T.* [1943] Ch. 400.
[19] (1984) 100 L.Q.R. 86 (S. Anderson); and see *post*, p. 295.
[20] L.P.A. 1925, s.27; *ante*, p. 253.
[21] *City of London B.S.* v. *Flegg* [1988] A.C. 54.
[22] L.P.A. 1925, ss.2, 27; L.P.(Am.)A. 1926, Sched.
[23] *Waller* v. *Waller* [1967] 1 W.L.R. 451; for the appointment of additional trustees, see *post*, p. 275.
[24] L.P.A. 1925, s.27(2); L.P.(Am.)A. 1926, Sched.
[25] *Williams & Glyn's Bank Ltd.* v. *Boland* [1981] A.C. 487; *ante*, p. 103.
[26] *Kingsnorth Finance Co. Ltd.* v. *Tizard* [1986] 1 W.L.R. 783; *ante*, p. 61.

Proceeds of sale or other capital money arising under a trust for sale may be applied in the same way as capital money arising from settled land.[27] This does not, however, effect a conversion into realty, and the rights of the beneficiaries remain rights in personalty.[28] Any land acquired under this provision must be conveyed to the trustees for sale to hold on trust for sale.[29]

Sect. 3. Under *Ad Hoc* Settlements and Trusts for Sale

The original intention of the 1925 legislation was that a conveyance under a settlement or trust for sale should overreach not only the interests of the beneficiaries but also prior equities as well. This provision was attacked in Parliament, and ultimately a workable scheme was produced and duly embodied in the 1925 legislation. Clearly some equities cannot be over-reached; thus a restrictive covenant (*e.g.* against building) and an equitable easement (*e.g.* an equitable right of way) cannot become corresponding rights in the purchase-money. The present scheme is that dispositions under ordinary settlements and trusts for sale have the overreaching effect considered above, and that those under certain special settlements and trusts for sale have a special wider overreaching effect. To obtain this wider effect the settlement or trust for sale must have "guaranteed" trustees, *i.e.* either trustees appointed or approved by the court, or a trust corporation. The idea is that such trustees are likely to be particularly trustworthy and that this will console those whose rights are overreached but would not have been over-reached under an ordinary settlement or trust for sale. That is the theory; in practice, little use is made of such settlements and trusts for sale, for the additional overreaching powers are meagre. The details of such settlements and trusts for sale are as follows.

1. Creation

(a) *Ad hoc settlements.* If a person of full age is beneficially entitled in possession to a legal estate subject to any equitable interests or powers then, for the purpose of overreaching these rights, he may by deed declare that the legal estate is vested in him on trust to give effect to all equitable interests and powers affecting the legal estate.[30] Such a deed is treated as a vesting deed and must be executed either by two or more individuals approved or appointed by the court, or by a trust corporation, who must be stated to be Settled Land Act trustees. Thereupon the land is deemed to be settled land and the estate owner becomes a tenant for life: the instruments which create his estate and the equitable interests or powers are deemed to be the trust instrument, in default of which a trust instrument must be executed contemporaneously with the vesting deed. It will be seen that these provisions are

---

[27] L.P.A. 1925, s.28; *Re Wellsted's W.T.* [1949] Ch. 296. *Cf. Re Wakeman* [1945] Ch. 177. See Thompson, *Co-ownership*, pp. 7, 8.
[28] *Re Kempthorne* [1930] 1 Ch. 268.
[29] L.P.A. 1925, s.28.
[30] S.L.A. 1925, s.21.

inappropriate to land which is already settled, for normally there will be no person *beneficially* entitled in possession to a *legal* estate: the provisions contemplate only settlements set up *ad hoc* (expressly for the purpose).

(b) *Ad hoc trusts for sale.* If a legal estate is subject to a trust for sale and the trustees thereof are either—

(i) two or more individuals approved or appointed by the court, or their successors in office, or
(ii) a trust corporation,

then the effect of a conveyance is to overreach equities having priority to the trust for sale, with the exceptions set out below.[31] It will be noticed that this provision is not confined to trusts for sale created *ad hoc*, but extends to any trusts for sale, whether already in existence or set up expressly for the purpose of overreaching equities: provided the conditions as to trustees are satisfied, the wider overreaching powers exist.[32] Nevertheless, "*ad hoc* trusts for sale" is a convenient name for such trusts even if they have not in fact been set up *ad hoc*.

2. Overreaching effect of dispositions

(a) *Equities prior to settlement.* As regards the overreaching effect of a conveyance or other disposition, the provisions as to *ad hoc* settlements and *ad hoc* trusts for sale are in similar terms.[33] Equitable rights having priority to the settlement or trust for sale are overreached with the exception of—

(a) equitable interests protected by a deposit of documents relating to the legal estate affected;
(b) restrictive covenants;
(c) equitable easements;
(d) estate contracts;
(e) equitable interests protected by registration under the Land Charges Act 1972,[34] other than—
  (i) annuities,
  (ii) limited owner's charges and
  (iii) general equitable charges.

It will be observed that the last three rights can be overreached under an *ad hoc* settlement or an *ad hoc* trust for sale. Such rights can, indeed, be overreached under an ordinary settlement, so that no wider powers are given in this case; but probably they cannot be overreached under an ordinary trust for sale, so that in this respect an *ad hoc* trust for sale has marked advantages over an ordinary trust for sale. Apart from these three rights, however, the list of exceptions given above covers all the important

[31] L.P.A. 1925, s.2.
[32] *Re Leigh's S.E. (No.* 2) [1927] 2 Ch. 13.
[33] S.L.A. 1925, s.21; L.P.A. 1925, s.2.
[34] Replacing Land Charges Act 1925.

equitable rights likely to be encountered in practice. The first exception is designed to cover temporary equitable mortgages and charges where the lender has secured himself by obtaining the title deeds. Heads (b), (c) and (d) could not, from their very nature, be overreached. Head (e) adds little to the previous provisions, for apart from one spouse's right to occupy a house owned by the other,[35] the only rights it includes are included under (b), (c) and (d). These rights are, in general, capable of registration only if created after 1925,[36] so that, for example, a restrictive covenant is protected by head (b) if created in 1920 and by heads (b) and (e) if created in 1930.

(b) *Limited advantages.* Although in general *ad hoc* settlements and trusts for sale may justly be said to be both complicated and ineffective, there are certain equitable rights which will be overreached by an *ad hoc*, but not by an ordinary, settlement or trust for sale. A prior equitable right which is not in the catalogue of registrable interests, and is not comprised in heads (a) to (d), will, it seems, be overreached under an *ad hoc* settlement or trust for sale, but not under an ordinary settlement or trust for sale. Some pre-1926 family interests would qualify, *e.g.* a widow's right of dower, or a rentcharge for life created by a marriage settlement.[37] Recently, however, certain commercial interests have been established as being equitable rights which are not registrable; and they do not fall within heads (a) to (d). These rights include an inchoate right of way arising by proprietary estoppel,[38] and certain rights of entry to secure performance of a covenant.[39] But from their very nature such rights could not sensibly be "overreached," and despite the statutory language they seem unlikely to be held overreachable under the *ad hoc* provisions. It is fortunate that these provisions are of so little practical importance.

Sect. 4. Summary of Overreaching Provisions

In broad outline, the position may be summarised as follows:

(a) A conveyance under an ordinary trust for sale overreaches the rights of the beneficiaries thereunder.

(b) A conveyance under an ordinary settlement overreaches—
  (i) the rights of the beneficiaries thereunder, and
  (ii) annuities, limited owner's charges and general equitable charges.

(c) A conveyance under an *ad hoc* settlement or trust for sale overreaches—
  (i) the rights of the beneficiaries thereunder;

---

[35] See *ante*, p. 81.
[36] *Ante*, p. 80.
[37] See Wolstenholme & Cherry, *Conveyancing Statutes* (13th ed. 1972), vol. 3, pp. 30, 82.
[38] *E. R. Ives Investment Ltd.* v. *High* [1967] 2 Q.B. 379; *post*, p. 432.
[39] *Shiloh Spinners Ltd.* v. *Harding* [1973] A.C. 80; *ante*, p. 77.

(ii) annuities, limited owner's charges and general equitable charges; and

(iii) certain other equities, such as a widow's right of dower.

Part 6

COMPARISON OF SETTLED LAND WITH TRUSTS FOR SALE

A person proposing to settle land can do so either by making the land settled land or by creating a trust for sale. The 1925 legislation has endowed trusts for sale with all the advantages of settled land. Thus trustees for sale have all the powers of a tenant for life and trustees under the Settled Land Act 1925, and entails can now be created under a trust for sale.[40] In deciding which method to employ, important points to be considered are as follows.

1. Control of the land, subject to the powers of the court, is in the hands of the trustees under a trust for sale, but in the hands of the tenant for life in the case of settled land.[41] Thus if the land is a family estate on which the tenant for life will reside, it may be better for the land to be made settled land; but if it consists of a row of shops, a trust for sale may be created so as to free the beneficiaries from the burden of managing the property. Again, if the proposed tenant for life is not a good businessman it may be better to create a trust for sale.

2. Restrictions on dealings. Although it is now impossible to create a settlement which will effectively prevent the land from being sold or otherwise dealt with, some measure of restraint can be imposed under a trust for sale by requiring the trustees, before dealing with the land, to obtain the consent of a specified person who is unlikely to give it. Paradoxically, in this way, the trust for sale is now a more effective method of keeping land in the family than settled land. But the power of the court to override a refusal of consent prevents the land being made totally unmarketable.[42]

3. Economy. The trust for sale is usually less complicated and expensive than settled land, and so is the more suitable alternative for small estates. The difficulty of discovering in whom the legal estate and statutory powers are vested occurs not infrequently in the case of settled land, but rarely in the case of trusts for sale. A testator who makes his own will leaving his house to his widow during widowhood, then to his daughter until she marries, and then to his children equally, is unwittingly invoking most of the provisions designed by the legislature for large estates. The whole creaking structure of Settled Land Act trustees, special personal representatives, vesting assents, deeds of discharge and so on may be involved for a house or cottage worth

[40] *Ante*, p. 43.
[41] See *ante*, pp. 241, 255, 256.
[42] *Ante*, pp. 248, 255.

only a relatively small sum. If instead the testator had devised his land to trustees on trust for sale, all these difficulties would have been avoided. The trouble is that the words "on trust for sale" or their equivalent are required to take land out of the Settled Land Act 1925, and these words have not reached the consciousness of the average testator who makes his own will.

4. Preservation of a unit. A trust for sale is more convenient than a strict settlement where a testator wishes to provide for his children equally. A strict settlement, on the other hand, is normally used "to make an eldest son," *i.e.* to give the principal benefit to the eldest son and make provision for the younger children a subsidiary matter. Before 1926, the doctrine of conversion and the impossibility of creating entails in personalty combined to make trusts for sale unsuitable for this purpose. This difficulty no longer exists, although the doctrine of conversion must still be considered, *e.g.* when drafting a will for a beneficiary under a trust for sale.

5. Termination of trusts. Under the Settled Land Act 1925, when a settlement comes to an end, there will always be a document on the legal title that discloses this, whether an ordinary assent or conveyance or a deed of discharge.[43] For trusts for sale there is no corresponding provision. If all the beneficial interests become vested in X absolutely, the trust for sale is at an end,[44] but a purchaser could confirm this only by investigating the equitable interests. In order to avoid this, X may leave the legal estate vested in the trustees for sale. If he does so, then for the safety and protection of a purchaser from the trustees the trust for sale is "deemed to be subsisting"; and this deeming continues until the land has been conveyed to X or under his direction,[45] so that a purchaser need not investigate the equitable interests.

6. Flexibility. There are many types of beneficial interests where the flexibility of trusts for sale makes them more suitable than settled land. Today, discretionary trusts have become popular. In addition to some fiscal advantages, they enable a settlor to provide for classes of persons, such as his descendants or the employees of a company, according to their needs as they arise in the future. The land is given to trustees for sale to hold it (and the income and proceeds of sale) on trust for such members of the designated class as the trustees shall from time to time select, duly confining the trust within the perpetuity period. The complexity of settled land and the flexibility and comparative simplicity of trusts for sale have also led to various suggestions for reform. Thus all settlements could be made to take effect as modified trusts for sale.[46] More radically, both settled land and trusts for sale could be replaced by a new form of trust. Under this, the trustees would have

---

[43] *Ante*, pp. 231, 232.
[44] *Re Cook* [1948] Ch. 212.
[45] L.P.A. 1925, s.23; *ante*, p. 254.
[46] See (1961) 24 Mod.L.R. 123 (G. A. Grove).

power (but not a trust) to sell or retain the land, and to exercise all the powers of an absolute owner.[47] But despite all faults, the present dual system is workable.

Part 7

TRUSTS AND TRUSTEES

Much of the law of trusts and trustees is more appropriate to text-books on equity than to a book on real property. But some account must be given here of the general points that most concern the law of land, in addition to the special provisions for settled land and land held on trust for sale.

1. TRUSTS

Sect. 1. Classification

A. Conveyancing Classification

From the point of view of a conveyancer, a trust of land may fall under one of three heads:

(1) Settled land.
(2) Trust for sale.
(3) Bare trust.

The first two have already been dealt with. A bare, or simple, trust arises when a trustee or trustees hold property (whether legal or equitable) on trust for a person who is of full age and absolutely beneficially entitled, the nature of the trust not being prescribed by the settlor but being left to the construction of the law, as where X conveys land—

"to T in fee simple on trust for A in fee simple."

In such a case, the position of the parties is similar to that under a simple use before 1535[48]: T is bound to permit A to occupy the land or receive the rents and profits and must obey A's instructions about the disposition of the land. A bare trust may also arise where on a purchase of land the money is provided by one person but the conveyance is made to another. Thus where P, wishing to keep his name out of the transaction, provides N with the money to buy the land, N holds on a bare trust for P.[49]

Bare trusts of land existing at the end of 1925 have ceased to exist, for by the Law of Property Act 1925, where at the end of 1925 a person was entitled to require a legal estate (not vested in trustees for sale) to be vested in him, the legal estate automatically vested in him at the beginning of 1926.[50] But there is nothing to prevent bare trusts from being created after 1925.

[47] See Law Com. No. 181 (1989).
[48] See *ante*, p. 64; and see *post*, p. 270.
[49] See *Dyer* v. *Dyer* (1788) 2 Cox Eq. 92 at 93.
[50] Sched. 1, Pt. II, paras. 3, 6(d).

B. Equity's Classification

In equity, trusts may be classified as trusts imposed by statute, and express, implied, resulting or constructive trusts.

1. Trusts imposed by statute. Various trusts are imposed by statute. Thus—

(i) A statutory trust for sale is imposed in the case of joint tenancies and tenancies in common.[51]

(ii) Where a person dies intestate, in certain cases his personal representatives hold his property on statutory trusts for his relatives.[52]

(iii) By virtue of the Settled Land Act 1925, an attempted conveyance of a legal estate in land to a minor operates as a contract to make a settlement upon the minor and in the meantime to hold the land on trust for him.[53]

(iv) A statutory trust for sale is created when property on the security of which trustees have lent money becomes vested in them by foreclosure, or where trustees of a personalty settlement exercise a power conferred thereby to invest money in the purchase of land.[54]

Both (i) and (ii) are referred to in the 1925 legislation as "the statutory trusts." Although other trusts imposed by statute are in a sense "statutory" trusts, they are usually not thus referred to, and to avoid confusion they are perhaps better called "trusts imposed by statute."

2. Express trusts. Express trusts are those expressly declared by the settlor. For such a trust the "three certainties" are required.[55]

(a) *The three certainties.* The first certainty is that there must be imperative words of trust. At one time merely precatory words, expressing only a hope or request, were sometimes held to suffice. But today precatory words are no longer enough unless the instrument as a whole shows an intention to create a trust. The word "trust" need not be used, but there must be language showing an imperative obligation. Second, there must be certainty of subject-matter, both as to the property to be held on trust and as to the beneficial interest to be taken by each beneficiary. Third, there must be certainty of objects. It must be possible to ascertain who are the beneficiaries. A trust for "my old friends" is uncertain as to the concept of the persons who are to be regarded as the donor's "old friends."[56]

The result of the absence of any of the certainties is as follows. If there is no certainty as to the subject-matter to be held on trust, the transaction is wholly ineffective. If that certainty is present, but there is no certainty of words, the person entitled to the property holds it beneficially, free from any

[51] *Post*, p. 289.
[52] *Ante*, p. 160.
[53] *Ante*, p. 168.
[54] *Ante*, pp. 253, 254; *post*, p. 449.
[55] See Snell 113–117.
[56] See *Brown* v. *Gould* [1972] Ch. 53 at 57.

trust. If both these certainties are present, but there is uncertainty of objects, there is a resulting trust for the settlor. The same applies where there is uncertainty of subject-matter as regards the beneficial interest, unless any beneficiary can establish a claim to the whole.

(b) *Completely and incompletely constituted trusts.* A trust is completely constituted as soon as the trust property is vested in the trustee upon the trusts; until then it is incompletely constituted. The importance of the distinction is that a completely constituted trust may be enforced by any of the beneficiaries, even if they are merely volunteers, whereas if the trust is incompletely constituted it cannot be enforced by volunteers but only by beneficiaries who have given valuable consideration. A trust may be completely constituted either by the trust property being effectually vested in the trustees upon the requisite trusts, or else by a "present irrevocable declaration of trust" being made by the settlor. In the latter case the settlor need not expressly declare that he holds the property on trust, but he must do something equivalent to this. An ineffective gift will not be construed as being a declaration of trust, and so there is no equity to perfect an imperfect gift.[57]

(c) *Formalities*. The formalities required for the creation of a trust and for the transfer of an interest under a trust are considered below.[58]

3. Implied trusts. An implied trust is said to arise where, without any conveyance of the property in question having been made, two people enter into such a relationship with each other that equity implies therefrom that one holds on trust for the other. Thus if one person agrees for value to make a settlement or conveyance of his estate, equity forthwith deems him to be a trustee of that estate for the beneficiaries or the purchaser. Again, under a contract for the sale of land the vendor holds it on an implied trust for the purchaser, subject to certain important rights which protect the vendor.[59]

4. Constructive trusts. In their origin, constructive trusts are trusts arising by operation of equity out of some existing fiduciary relationship. Thus if a person receives property knowing that it is subject to a trust and that the transfer to him is in breach of trust, he will hold it subject to the trusts as a constructive trustee. If instead he receives the property innocently but later, after getting knowledge of the trusts, he deals with it inconsistently with the trusts, he will similarly be a constructive trustee. Again, a trustee who profits from his trusts will hold the profit on a constructive trust. Further, a person who knowingly assists a trustee in a fraudulent design will be liable as a constructive trustee even if he receives none of the trust property. But although constructive trusts are primarily extensions of existing trusts, they

---

[57] *Richards* v. *Delbridge* (1874) L.R. 18 Eq. 11 (attempted gift of lease by indorsement). For a statutory exception, see *ante*, p. 169.
[58] *Post*, pp. 271, 272.
[59] *Ante*, p. 122.

have expanded into other fields, including cases of fraud; and today there is a tendency for the courts to hold that a constructive trust exists in a variety of other cases where equity and good conscience require it.[60] Some jurisdictions now treat constructive trusts as being a general remedy in cases of inequitable conduct,[61] but English law has yet to adopt this approach.[62]

5. Resulting trusts. A resulting trust is said to exist where, on a conveyance of property, a trust arises by operation of equity.[63] Three cases must be considered.

(a) *Trusts not exhaustive.* Where a disposition of property is made by the owner and all or part of the equitable interest is not effectively disposed of, there is a resulting trust for the owner. If the property is conveyed expressly on trust, *e.g.*

"to X on trust,"

there is no difficulty; a trustee can take no benefit from the fact that the declared trusts do not exhaust the beneficial interest, and so much of the equitable interest as is not disposed of results to the grantor. Thus if G conveys property to X on trust for a beneficiary who is dead, there is a resulting trust of the entire beneficial interest in favour of G. What a person fails effectually to dispose of remains automatically vested in him.[64]

(b) *Voluntary conveyance.* Before 1926, on a conveyance by G to X made without any consideration and without expressing any use, there was a resulting use to G in fee simple which the Statute of Uses 1535 promptly executed, thereby making the conveyance totally ineffective. The Law of Property Act 1925[65] prevents any corresponding resulting trust arising after 1925. It provides that in a voluntary conveyance executed after 1925, no resulting trust for the grantor is to be implied merely by reason that the property is not expressed to be conveyed for the use or benefit of the grantee. But this does not prevent a resulting trust for the grantor from arising where it appears that the grantee was intended to take as a trustee, as where the property is conveyed on express trusts which fails to exhaust the entire beneficial interest; and in other cases there will be presumed to be a resulting trust, though the presumption is easily rebutted.[66]

(c) *Purchase in the name of another.* Where a conveyance is made to one person, but the purchase-money is provided by another as purchaser, there is a resulting trust in favour of the person providing the purchase-money. If V conveys land to P, A being the real purchaser and as such providing the purchase-money, prima facie P holds on a resulting trust for A.[67] Neverthe-

---

[60] See generally Snell 192–197.
[61] Snell 196, 197.
[62] *Ibid.*; see *Re Sharpe* [1980] 1 W.L.R. 219 at 225.
[63] See generally Snell 175–192.
[64] See *Re Vandervell's Trusts (No. 2)* [1974] Ch. 269 at 288, 289, 294 (not affected on appeal).
[65] s.60(3), (4).
[66] See *Re Vandervell's Trusts (No. 2)*, *supra.*
[67] See *Dyer* v. *Dyer* (1788) 2 Cox Eq. 92 at 93.

less, this is only a presumption which can be rebutted by evidence that P was intended to benefit.[68] It may also be displaced by the presumption of advancement. That presumption arises if P is the wife or child of A. It is itself rebuttable, and it does not apply to other relationships, as where A is the wife, mother, stepmother or aunt of P.[69]

6. Uncertainties of classification. The foregoing equitable classification of trusts is not uniformly observed. Some authorities include trusts imposed by statute under the head of express trusts, and treat "constructive trusts" as including all except express trusts. In practice, the category into which a trust falls is often of minor importance. Except for the distinction between express trusts and other trusts, the division is frequently little more than a convenient way of setting out the nature of the different forms of trust.

Sect. 2. Formalities for the Creation of a Trust

A. Pure Personalty

An enforceable trust of pure personalty can be validly created by word of mouth, whether the owner is declaring himself a trustee of the property or is transferring it to a third party on trust for the beneficiaries.[70]

B. Land

1. Evidenced by writing. Before 1677, a trust of land could be created by word of mouth, but thereafter the Statute of Frauds 1677[71] and now the Law of Property Act 1925[72] provided that a declaration of trust respecting any land or any interest therein must be evidenced either by writing signed by some person able to declare the trust, or else by his will. The chief points to note on this provision are as follows:

(a) "*Any land.*" This includes leaseholds, and included copyholds before they were abolished.

(b) "*Evidenced.*" The actual words in both statutes are "manifested and proved." It is settled that this does not require that the declaration should actually be made in writing, but that it suffices if an oral declaration is supported by some signed acknowledgement or declaration in existence when the action is begun, such as a letter,[73] or a recital in a deed, even if this was made some time after the trust was declared.[74] The writing must show not only that there is a trust but also what its terms are.[75]

---

[68] *Fowkes* v. *Pascoe* (1875) 10 Ch.App. 343.
[69] See generally Snell 178–182.
[70] See *M'Fadden* v. *Jenkyns* (1842) 1 Ph. 153.
[71] ss.7, 8.
[72] s.53(1)(*b*).
[73] *Childers* v. *Childers* (1857) 1 De G. & J. 482.
[74] *Rochefoucauld* v. *Boustead* [1897] 1 Ch. 196 at 206.
[75] *Smith* v. *Matthews* (1861) 3 De G.F. & J. 139; and see *ante*, p. 117.

(c) *"Some person able to declare the trust."* This means the owner of the beneficial interest, so that if a trust is declared of an equitable interest held under an existing trust, the writing must be signed by the beneficiary; the signature of the trustees is not sufficient.[76] There is no provision for signature by an agent.[77]

2. Exceptions. To these requirements, there are two important exceptions:

(a) *Resulting, implied or constructive trusts.* They do not affect the creation or operation of resulting, implied or constructive trusts.[78]

(b) *Fraud.* The court will not permit them to be used as an engine of fraud. "It is a fraud on the part of a person to whom land is conveyed as a trustee, and who knows it was so conveyed, to deny the trust and claim the land himself. Consequently, notwithstanding the statute, it is competent for a person claiming land conveyed to another to prove by parol evidence that it was so conveyed upon trust for the claimant, and that the grantee, knowing the facts, is denying the trust and relying upon the form of conveyance and the statute, in order to keep the land himself."[79]

Sect. 3. Formalities for Transferring an Interest Under a Trust

By the Law of Property Act 1925,[80] a disposition[81] of an existing equitable interest or trust must either be in writing signed by the person disposing of it or his agent authorised in writing, or else be made by will. On this, the following points should be noted.

(a) *"In writing."* A parol assignment supported by evidence thereof in writing is not enough. Unlike the rule for the creation of trusts, the rule here requires the assignment itself to be written, and is thus not a mere rule of evidence.

(b) *"Signed by the person disposing of it or his agent authorised in writing."* This should be contrasted with—

    (i) the rule for the creation of a trust of land, where the signature of an agent is not enough[82]; and

    (ii) the rule for contracts for the disposition of land, where the signature of an agent suffices even if his authority was given only by word of mouth.[83]

---

[76] *Kronheim* v. *Johnson* (1877) 7 Ch.D. 60.
[77] Contrast transfers, *infra.*
[78] L.P.A. 1925, s.53(2), replacing Statute of Frauds 1677, s.8.
[79] *Rochefoucauld* v. *Boustead, supra,* at p. 206, *per* Lindley L.J.
[80] s.53(1)(c), replacing Statute of Frauds 1677, s.9.
[81] See *Grey* v. *I.R.C.* [1960] A.C. 1 (oral direction); *Oughtred* v. *I.R.C.* [1960] A.C. 206 (oral agreement); but see *Vandervell* v. *I.R.C.* [1967] 2 A.C. 291 (oral directions extended to legal estate).
[82] *Supra.*
[83] *Ante,* p. 121.

(c) *Pure personalty*. The rule applies to pure personalty as well as land. Although a trust of pure personalty is enforceable even if it is not evidenced in writing, once the trust has been created, a disposition of any interest under it is void unless it is in writing.

2. TRUSTEES

The Trustee Act 1925, replacing earlier legislation, makes general provision for the appointment, replacement, retirement and removal of trustees, and also for the vesting of the trust property when a change is made. These heads will be taken in turn.

Sect. 1. Appointment of Trustees

A. Original Appointment

1. Appointment. Trustees are usually appointed by the settlor when creating the trust. If he neither makes an appointment nor makes any provision for one, the court may appoint trustees; once the trust has been created, the settlor has no power of making an appointment unless he has reserved such a power. A person appointed trustee need not accept the trust even if he had agreed to do so before it was created, provided he disclaims the trust before he has accepted it either expressly or by acting as trustee.[84] A disclaimer should preferably be express but it may be inferred from conduct[85]; and although the presumption is in favour of acceptance, a person appointed a trustee who maintains a complete inactivity in relation to the trust for a long period may be held thereby to have disclaimed the trust.[86] Disclaimer retrospectively divests the person appointed both of his office and of the trust property.[87]

2. Maximum number. Not more than four trustees of settled land or land held on trust for sale can be appointed if the settlement or trust for sale is created after 1925. If more than four are named as trustees, the first four who are able and willing to act become trustees to the exclusion of the others.[88] Where, at the beginning of 1926, there were more than four trustees of settled land or land held on trust for sale, all the trustees continued to act but no new trustees could be appointed until the number dropped below four.[89] These provisions apply only to land; and in general there is no limit to the number of trustees of pure personalty.

3. Minimum number. There is no minimum number of trustees even in the

---

[84] See *Noble* v. *Meymott* (1851) 14 Beav. 471.
[85] *Re Birchall* (1889) 40 Ch.D. 436.
[86] *Re Clout and Frewer's Contract* [1924] 2 Ch. 230 (29 years' inactivity).
[87] *Re Martinez' Trusts* (1870) 22 L.T. 403.
[88] T.A. 1925, s.34(2).
[89] *Ibid.* s.34(1).

case of land. But in the case of settled land or land held on trust for sale, notwithstanding any contrary provision, a sole trustee cannot give a valid receipt for capital money unless that trustee is a trust corporation.[91] This restriction, however, does not affect the right of a sole personal representative acting as such to give valid receipts for purchase-money,[92] *e.g.* where a sole administrator sells under the trust for sale which is imposed on all the property of an intestate.[93]

B. Replacement

1. The power. Even if there are properly appointed trustees when the trust is created, it may later become necessary to appoint new trustees, *e.g.* owing to the death of trustees. The events upon which new trustees can be appointed may be specified in the trust instrument. This is not usual, however, and reliance is normally placed on the statutory provisions, which apply notwithstanding any such express provision[94] unless a contrary intention is shown.[95] By the Trustee Act 1925[96] a new trustee or trustees may be appointed if a trustee—

is dead; or remains outside the United Kingdom for a continuous period exceeding 12 months; or desires to be discharged from all or any of his trusts or powers; or refuses to act; or is unfit to act; or is incapable of acting; or is a minor; or is removed under a power in the trust instrument.

2. Mode of appointment. The appointment must be in writing and must be made[97]—

(1) by the person or persons nominated by the trust instrument for the purpose of appointing new trustees; in default of there being any such person able and willing to act,
(2) by the remaining trustees; in default,
(3) by the personal representatives of the last remaining trustee; in default,
(4) by the court.

3. Who may be appointed. It is expressly provided that the person making the appointment may appoint himself.[98] Even if he appoints a person whom the court would not normally appoint, such as a beneficiary, or the husband of a beneficiary, or the solicitor to the trustees or beneficiaries, the appointment will not thereby be rendered invalid[99]; but an appointment of a minor

[91] S.L.A. 1925, s.18(1); L.P.A. 1925, s.27(2); see *ante*, pp. 260, 261.
[92] L.P.A. 1925, s.27(2).
[93] *Ante*, p. 157.
[94] See *Re Wheeler and De Rochow* [1896] 1 Ch. 315.
[95] T.A. 1925, s.69(2).
[96] s.36(1), replacing earlier provisions.
[97] *Ibid.*, ss.36(1), 41, replacing earlier provisions.
[98] *Ibid.* s.36(1).
[99] *Re Earl of Stamford* [1896] 1 Ch. 288.

as trustee, whether of realty or personalty, is void.[1] Where a single trustee was originally appointed, the appointment of a single trustee in his place is valid,[2] except that in the case of settled land or land held on trust for sale, a sole trustee (not being a trust corporation) cannot be appointed under the statutory power if, after his appointment, he would be unable to give receipts for capital money,[3] as would be the case if there were no other trustee. There is never any obligation to appoint more than two trustees even if originally more than two were appointed.[4] The appointment may increase the number of trustees, provided that in the case of settled land, or land held on trust for sale, the number is not increased above four.[5]

C. Additional Trustees

Even though no occasion has arisen for the appointment of new trustees, if there are not more than three trustees and none of them is a trust corporation, one or more additional trustees may be appointed, provided the effect of the appointment is not to increase the number above four. The appointment must be made by the same persons and in the same way as an appointment of new trustees, except that there is no provision for an appointment by the personal representatives of the last remaining trustee, or for the appointor to appoint himself.[6]

Sect. 2. Retirement and Removal of Trustees

1. Retirement. A trustee may retire—

(i) If another trustee is appointed in his place; this has already been considered.[7]
(ii) If no new trustee is being appointed in his place, provided that after his discharge there will be left either two or more individuals or a trust corporation to act in the trust. The retirement is effected by a deed declaring the trustee's desire to retire; this is executed by the retiring trustee, the continuing trustees and the person entitled to appoint new trustees, all of whom must concur in the retirement.[8]
(iii) If authorised to do so by an express power in the trust instrument.
(iv) With the consent of all the beneficiaries if they are all *sui juris* and between them absolutely entitled to the trust property.
(v) With the leave of the court; this method should be employed only in cases of difficulty, for if the trustee applies to the court without good cause he may have to pay his own costs.[9]

[1] L.P.A. 1925, s.20.
[2] T.A. 1925, s.37(1)(c), replacing earlier provisions.
[3] *Ibid.* s.37(2).
[4] *Ibid.* s.37(1)(c), replacing earlier provisions.
[5] *Ibid.* s.34(2).
[6] *Ibid.* s.36(6); *Re Power's S.T.* [1951] Ch. 1074.
[7] *Ante,* p. 274.
[8] T.A. 1925, s.39(1), replacing earlier provisions.
[9] *Porter* v. *Watts* (1852) 21 L.J.Ch. 211.

2. Removal. A trustee may be removed—

(i) Under the power to appoint new trustees considered above.[10]

(ii) Under any express power to do so contained in the trust instrument.

(iii) Under the court's inherent jurisdiction to remove a trustee where it is necessary for the safety of the trust property or the welfare of the beneficiaries,[11] as where the trustee has been inactive for a long while, or his interests conflict with those of the beneficiaries, or there has been friction with the beneficiaries on the mode of administering the trust.[12]

Sect. 3. Vesting of Trust Property

Some trustees have no property vested in them, as is often the case with trustees of settled land; in such cases, no question of the devolution of trust property arises. But where property is vested in trustees, questions of the transfer of the trust property arise on their death, retirement or removal, or on the appointment of new trustees.

A. On Death

Trustees are always made joint tenants or joint owners of the trust property, whether it is real or personal. The advantage of this is that on the death of one trustee the estate or interest vested in him passes to the surviving trustees by the doctrine of survivorship.[13] If a sole surviving trustee dies the estate or interest held on trust vests in his personal representatives notwithstanding any provision in his will.[14] Until new trustees are appointed, the personal representatives may exercise any power or trust exercisable by the former trustee, without being obliged to do so[15]; and they may appoint new trustees.[16]

B. On Appointment of New Trustees

1. Vesting declaration. On an appointment of new trustees, the trust property has to be vested in the new trustees jointly with any continuing trustees. Formerly, a formal conveyance of the trust property by the persons in whom it was vested was necessary; if A and B were trustees and C was appointed a new trustee on A's death, B had to convey the trust property to himself and C jointly.[17] But by section 40 of the Trustee Act 1925,[18] if an

---

[10] *Ante*, p. 274.
[11] *Re Wrightson* [1908] 1 Ch. 789 at 803.
[12] *Letterstedt* v. *Broers* (1884) 9 App.Cas. 371.
[13] *Ante*, p. 4; *post*, p. 282.
[14] A.E.A. 1925, s.1.
[15] T.A. 1925, s.18(2).
[16] *Ibid.* s.36(1).
[17] See M. & W. (4th ed.) 458.
[18] Replacing earlier provisions.

appointment of new trustees is made by deed, a declaration therein by the appointor that the property shall vest in the trustees (a "vesting declaration") is sufficient to vest the property in them. This applies to all deeds executed after 1881[19]; and if the deed is executed after 1925, a vesting declaration is implied in the absence of an express provision to the contrary.[20]

These provisions apply even if the trust property is not vested in the appointor. He has a statutory power to transfer what he has not got. Thus where A and B are the trustees and X has the power to appoint new trustees, if A dies and X appoints C a trustee in his place, the deed of appointment will vest the property in B and C jointly.

2. Exceptions. In certain cases the trust property cannot be transferred by a vesting declaration, either express or implied. These cases are when the property consists of—

(1) land which the trustees hold by way of mortgage for securing trust money;
(2) land held under a lease with a provision against assigning or disposing of the land without consent, unless—
   (i) the requisite consent has first been obtained, or
   (ii) the vesting declaration would not be a breach of covenant or give rise to a forfeiture;
(3) any share, stock or other property which is transferable only in books kept by a company or other body, or in a way directed by statute[21]; or
(4) registered land.

In these excepted cases the trust property must be transferred by the method appropriate to the subject-matter, *e.g.* in the case of shares and registered land, by a duly registered transfer.[22] The reason for the inclusion of (1) is to avoid bringing the trusts on to the title, for otherwise, when the borrower sought to repay the loan, he would have to investigate the trust documents to see that he was paying the right persons; and (2) is included to avoid accidental breaches of the terms of the lease.

3. Vesting orders. The court has a wide jurisdiction to make vesting orders where this is desirable.[23]

C. On Retirement or Removal

Where a trustee retires or is discharged from a trust without a new trustee being appointed, and the transaction is effected by deed, the trust property can be divested from the former trustee and vested solely in the continuing

---

[19] T.A. 1925, s.40(6).
[20] *Ibid.* s.40(1).
[21] *Ibid.* s.40(4), replacing earlier provisions.
[22] See Ruoff & Roper 32–13.
[23] T.A. 1925, ss.44–56.

trustees by means of a vesting declaration. This applies only if the deed is executed by the retiring trustee, the continuing trustees and any person with power to appoint new trustees; if the deed is executed after 1925, a vesting declaration is implied.[24] There are the same exceptions as in the case of vesting declarations on the appointment of new trustees. This special provision is necessary since the *jus accrescendi* operates only on death and not on retirement.

Sect. 4. Procedure for Settled Land and Trusts for Sale

1. One document. Although it is undesirable, a trust for sale may be created by only one instrument. In this case, when a new trustee is appointed, the appointment may be made by a single document. This may be merely in writing, but it should be by deed so that the legal estate may be vested in the new and continuing trustees by virtue of section 40 of the Trustee Act 1925,[25] thus avoiding the necessity of a separate conveyance. In addition, a memorandum must be indorsed on or annexed to the instrument creating the trust for sale, stating the names of those who are the trustees after the appointment is made,[26] and not merely the names of the new trustees.

2. Two documents. Normally, however, a trust for sale is created by two documents. In this case, and in the case of settled land, the procedure is more complicated. There must be[27]—

  (i) An instrument to go with the conveyance on trust for sale or the vesting instrument, which purchasers can see.

  (ii) An appointment to go with the trust instrument.

  (iii) An indorsement on the conveyance on trust for sale or on the vesting instrument, stating the names of those who are the trustees after the appointment.

In the case of settled land, the first document must be a deed; it merely states who are now the trustees. In the case of a trust for sale, it may be merely in writing, but, as above, should be by deed in order to take advantage of section 40 of the Trustee Act 1925; in either case it effects the actual appointment of the persons named in it as trustees for sale. A similar procedure applies if a trustee of settled land is discharged without a new trustee being appointed. The second document, both for settled land and trusts for sale, is an appointment which may be either in writing or by deed.[28]

---

[24] T.A. 1925, s.40(2), replacing earlier provisions.
[25] *Ante*, p. 276.
[26] T.A. 1925, s.35(3).
[27] *Ibid.* 35; S.L.A. 1925, s.35(1); and see *ante*, p. 253.
[28] T.A. 1925, s.35; S.L.A. 1925, s.35.

Part 8

REGISTERED LAND

The provisions for settled land and trusts for sale that have been considered above apply to registered land with appropriate modifications. The Settled Land Act 1925 expressly provides that it takes effect subject to the provisions of the Land Registration Act 1925.[29]

Sect. 1. Settled Land

1. Registration. The legal estate in settled land is registered in the name of the tenant for life, statutory owner or personal representatives as the case may be.[30] The interests of the beneficiaries are merely minor interests,[31] but they will be protected by the entry of a restriction on the register.[32] On the registration of the tenant for life, the restriction will provide that except under an order of the registrar, no disposition will be registered unless it is authorised by the Settled Land Act 1925,[33] and that no disposition under which capital money arises is to be registered unless the money is paid to the trustees of the settlement (being not less than two nor more than four in number, or a trust corporation), or into court.[34]

2. Vesting. Vesting assents and ordinary assents are used for registered land as they are used for unregistered land, and so are deeds of discharge.[35] But vesting transfers replace vesting deeds, and ordinary transfers replace ordinary conveyances.[36] Where there is a deed of discharge, the restriction will, on application, be removed from the register.[37]

3. Failure to comply. Where these requirements are not satisfied, the result will often depend upon the principle that in registered land the register is paramount. If a registered proprietor creates trusts that make the land settled land, he ought to secure the registration of the appropriate restriction. If he omits to do this, the register will continue to show him as the registered proprietor, subject to no restriction. If he then sells the land, the purchaser will take free from the interests of the beneficiaries, for they are merely minor interests. Again, if the restriction has been duly registered but the tenant for life secures its deletion by means of a forged deed of discharge, a purchaser from him would obtain a good title on registration of the

[29] S.L.A. 1925, s.119(3).
[30] *Ibid.* ss.41, 86(1), (5), 91.
[31] *Ibid.* s.86(2); *ante*, p. 105.
[32] *Ibid.* s.86(3).
[33] Or by any extended power under the settlement: L.R.R. 1925, r. 58(2).
[34] See L.R.R. 1925, r. 58(1); Sched., Form 9.
[35] See *ante*, pp. 226, 233.
[36] L.R.R. 1925, Sched., Forms 21, 23, 56, 57.
[37] L.R.A. 1925, s.87(4); L.R.R. 1925, Sched., Form 77.

transfer. But in such cases there might well be a valid claim to rectification of the register.[38]

Sect. 2. Trusts for Sale

Where land is subject to a trust for sale, whether express, implied or statutory, the title must be registered in the name of the trustees for sale, not being more than four.[39] The interests of the beneficiaries will be minor interests, but they will be protected by the entry of a restriction on the register. This will provide that no disposition by the sole surviving proprietor (not being a trust corporation) under which capital money arises is to be registered except under an order of the registrar or the court.[40] A purchaser will take free from the interests of the beneficiaries, which are minor interests, except for any of them which is also an overriding interest, as where the beneficiary is in "actual occupation" of the land[41] under a trust for sale of the land.[42]

---

[38] See *ante*, p. 112.
[39] L.R.A. 1925, ss.94, 95.
[40] *Ibid.* s.58(3); L.R.R. 1925, r. 213, Sched., Form 62, as varied.
[41] See *ante*, p. 104.
[42] See *ante*, p. 258.

CHAPTER 8

CO-OWNERSHIP

LITTLE has so far been said about cases where two or more persons are
entitled to the simultaneous enjoyment of land. Formerly, there were four
types of such ownership: joint tenancy; tenancy in common; co-parcenary;
and tenancy by entireties. The two latter types need only brief mention.
Co-parcenary formerly arose on intestacy when two or more persons
together constituted the heir, as where an intestate left three daughters and
no son. It resembled a tenancy in common in that each co-parcener had a
separate share, and there was no *jus accrescendi*. Normally no co-parcenary
can arise on deaths after 1925, for there is no descent to the heir.[1] A tenancy
by entireties was virtually an unseverable joint tenancy which before 1883[2]
arose at common law on a conveyance to husband and wife.[3] Both co-
parcenary and tenancy by entireties are obsolete; but joint tenancies and
tenancies in common are important, and must be considered in some detail.
The terms "co-ownership," "concurrent interests," and "estates and interests in community" may each be used to include these forms of co-ownership. The main provisions are those governing joint tenancies and tenancies
in common, and they will be considered together; but party walls fall into a
different category, and they will be considered separately.

Part 1

JOINT TENANCY AND TENANCY IN COMMON

Sect. 1. Nature of the Tenancies

A. Joint Tenancy

"A gift of lands to two or more persons in joint tenancy is such a gift as
imparts to them, with respect to all other persons than themselves, the
properties of one single owner."[4] Although as between themselves joint
tenants have separate rights, as against everyone else they are in a position
of a single owner. The intimate nature of joint tenancy is shown by the two
principal features, the right of survivorship and the "four unities."

1. The right of survivorship

(a) *The right.* The right of survivorship is the distinguishing feature of a

---

[1] *Ante*, p. 156; and see M. & W. 456–460.
[2] Married Women's Property Act 1882, ss.1, 5.
[3] See M. & W. 460–462.
[4] Williams R.P. 143.

281

joint tenancy. On the death of one joint tenant, his interest in the land passes to the other joint tenants by the *jus accrescendi* (right of survivorship), and this process continues until there is but one survivor, who then holds the land as sole owner.[5] This *jus accrescendi* takes precedence over any disposition made by a joint tenant's will, and the same principle applies if a joint tenant dies intestate; a joint tenancy cannot pass under a will or intestacy.[6] For this reason it has been said that each joint tenant holds nothing and yet holds the whole[7]: he will become entitled to nothing or to all, according to whether or not he survives his fellows. But if he acts in his lifetime he may convert his interest into a tenancy in common.[8]

(b) *Corporations*. The common law held that although a corporation could be a tenant in common, no joint tenancy could exist between a corporation and a natural person. A corporation never died, and the natural person would thus have no effective right of survivorship. However, Parliament provided in 1899 that a corporation should be able to acquire and hold any property in joint tenancy in the same manner as if it were an individual.[9] This provision became necessary as banks and other corporations were taking up the work of acting as trustees.

(c) *Trustees*. Trustees are always made joint tenants because of the convenience of the trust property passing automatically by the *jus accrescendi* to the surviving trustees when one trustee dies; if trustees were made tenants in common, a conveyance of the trust property to the surviving trustees by the personal representatives of the deceased trustee would be necessary. Although the *jus accrescendi* of a joint tenancy is often unsuitable for beneficial owners because it introduces an element of chance, it is ideal for trustees.

2. The four unities must be present. The four unities of a joint tenancy are the unities of possession, interest, title and time.[10]

(a) *Unity of possession*. Each joint tenant is as much entitled to possession of any part of the land as the others.[11] No tenant can point to any part of the land as his own to the exclusion of the others; if he could, there would be separate ownership and not joint tenancy. In this respect, the position is similar to that of partners; no partner can point to any particular asset of the business as being his, for each is entitled to possession of all the assets.

Unity of possession is common to all forms of co-ownership. If one co-owner of land under a trust for sale (as distinct from a co-owner whose

---

[5] Litt. 280.
[6] Litt. 287.
[7] *Murray* v. *Hall* (1849) 7 C.B. 441 at 455n.: he holds "*per mie* [nothing] *et per tout*."
[8] *Post*, p. 299.
[9] Bodies Corporate (Joint Tenancy) Act 1899.
[10] See *A.G. Securities* v. *Vaughan* [1990] 1 A.C. 417 at 474. Their initial letters form the convenient mnemonic P.I.T.T.
[11] Litt. 288: *Bull* v. *Bull* [1955] 1 Q.B. 234.

only right is in the proceeds of sale when it has been sold[12]) is in sole occupation of any or all of the land, the others cannot evict him[13]; and he is not liable to pay any rent or compensation to them[14] unless he excludes them from possession.[15] But if he lets the land, he must account to the others if he receives more than his just share.[16] If he is not in occupation, he appears to have no right to insist on being let into possession, though the trustees may in their discretion permit beneficiaries entitled in possession to occupy the land in lieu of receiving the rents and profits.[17]

(b) *Unity of interest.* The interest of each joint tenant is the same in extent, nature and duration, for in theory of law they hold but one estate. This means—[18]

(i) that although in theory of law each tenant has the whole of the property, the rents and profits of the land are divided equally between the tenants;

(ii) that there can be no joint tenancy between those with interests of a different nature, *e.g.* a freeholder and a tenant for years;

(iii) that there can be no joint tenancy between those whose interests are similar but of different duration. Thus before 1926, a tenant in fee simple and a tenant in tail both owned freeholds, but the differing durations of the estates prevented them from being held in joint tenancy; and

(iv) that any legal act, such as surrendering a lease or giving notice under a contractual power to determine it,[19] or giving a statutory notice,[20] can be done only by all the tenants jointly: one alone cannot effectually bind the estate, for the whole estate is not his. In the case of periodic tenancies (*e.g.* weekly or yearly) this rule somewhat paradoxically means that a notice to quit may be valid even if given by only one of the joint tenants; for such tenancies expire at the end of each period unless all concerned, either expressly or tacitly, concur in their continuation,[21] and so a notice given by one of joint landlords[22] or one of joint tenants[23] shows that there is no unanimity in a continuation.

---

[12] *Barclay* v. *Barclay* [1970] 2 Q.B. 677. See also *Irani Finance Ltd.* v. *Singh* [1971] Ch. 59 at 80, and consider Thompson, *Co-ownership*, 120, 121.

[13] *Bull* v. *Bull* [1955] 1 Q.B. 234, criticised at [1955] C.L.J. 155, but accepted in *Williams & Glyn's Bank Ltd.* v. *Boland* [1981] A.C. 487.

[14] *Jones* v. *Jones* [1977] 1 W.L.R. 438.

[15] *Dennis* v. *McDonald* [1982] Fam. 63.

[16] *Henderson* v. *Eason* (1851) 17 Q.B. 701.

[17] See *Re Bagot's Settlement* [1894] 1 Ch. 177; *Re Landi* [1939] Ch. 828 at 836; (1955) 19 Conv. 146 (F. R. Crane).

[18] See Co.Litt. 188a; 2 Bl.Com. 181.

[19] *Leek and Moorlands B.S.* v. *Clark* [1952] 2 Q.B. 788.

[20] *Newman* v. *Keedwell* (1977) 35 P. & C.R. 393 (counter-notice under A.H.A. 1948, s.24: *post*, p. 528).

[21] *Post*, p. 316.

[22] *Doe* d. *Aslin* v. *Summersett* (1830) 1 B. & Ad. 135; *Parson* v. *Parsons* [1983] 1 W.L.R. 1390.

[23] *Hammersmith and Fulham L.B.C.* v. *Monk* [1992] 1 A.C. 478.

(c) *Unity of title*. Each joint tenant must claim his title to the land under the same act or document.[24] This requirement is satisfied if all the tenants acquired their rights by the same conveyance or if they simultaneously took possession of land and acquired title to it by adverse possession.[25]

(d) *Unity of time*. The interest of each tenant must vest at the same time. This does not necessarily follow from the existence of unity of title. For example, if land was conveyed before 1926 "to A for life, remainder to the heirs of B and C," and B and C died at different times in A's lifetime, B's heir and C's heir took the fee simple remainder as tenants in common; the heirs could not take as joint tenants, for although there was unity of title, there was no unity of time.[26]

Two exceptions to the necessity for unity of time grew up: neither in a conveyance to uses nor in a gift by will was the rule applied. Thus if a bachelor conveyed land to the use of himself and any wife he might marry, when he married he held as a joint tenant with his wife. Again, if land was devised or conveyed to the use of A for life with remainder to the use of the children of B, each child of B born in A's lifetime acquired a vested interest at birth, yet the disparity of time did not prevent them from taking as joint tenants.[27]

B. Tenancy in Common

A tenancy in common differs greatly from a joint tenancy.

1. The tenants hold in undivided shares. Unlike joint tenants, tenants in common hold in undivided shares: each tenant in common has a distinct fixed share in property which has not yet been divided among the co-tenants.[28] There is no *jus accrescendi*; the share of each tenant is fixed once and for all and is not affected by the death of one of his fellows. When a tenant in common dies, his interest passes under his will or intestacy, for his undivided share is his to dispose of as he wishes.[29]

2. Only the unity of possession is essential. Although the four unities of a joint tenancy may be present in a tenancy in common, the only unity which is essential is the unity of possession. In particular, it should be noted that the unity of interest may be absent and the tenants may hold unequal interests, so that one tenant in common may be entitled to a one-fifth share and the other to four-fifths, or one may be entitled for life and the other in fee simple.[30]

[24] Co. Litt. 189a, 299b.
[25] *Ward* v. *Ward* (1871) 6 Ch.App. 789; *post*, p. 493.
[26] Co. Litt. 188a; 2 Bl.Com. 181.
[27] *Ruck* v. *Barwise* (1865) 2 Dr. & Sm. 510; *Doe* d. *Hallen* v. *Ironmonger* (1803) 3 East 533.
[28] *Fisher* v. *Wiggs* (1700) 12 Mod. 296 at 302.
[29] Challis R.P. 368.
[30] Co.Litt. 189a; Williams R.P. 148; 2 Bl.Com. 191.

Sect. 2. Estates in which the Tenancies Can Exist

In general, before 1926 joint tenancies and tenancies in common could exist at law or in equity (*i.e.* as legal estates or as equitable interests), and in possession or in remainder, in any of the estates of freehold or in lease-holds.[31] Thus if land was given to A and B as joint tenants for their lives, they enjoyed it jointly for their joint life, and the survivor enjoyed the whole for the rest of his life.[32] If A and B had converted their joint tenancy into a tenancy in common, the survivor would have been entitled only to half for the rest of his life. Again, if X and Y were joint tenants for the life of X, if X survived he became sole tenant of the whole for the rest of his life, whereas if Y were the survivor he took nothing, for the estate which he acquired by survivorship was one which determined at the moment he received it.

After 1925, the position is substantially the same except that a tenancy in common can no longer exist at law; this is dealt with below.[33] Further, since life estates and entails can exist only in equity,[34] even a joint tenancy in these must also be equitable.

Sect. 3. Mode of Creating the Tenancies

The key to a proper understanding of joint tenancies and tenancies in common is always to consider the legal estate separately from the equitable interest.[35] Thus it may be found that at law A and B are joint tenants, while in equity they are tenants in common. The effect of A's death on the legal joint tenancy is that B is solely entitled; in equity, on the other hand, A's share passes under his will or intestacy. In the result, B holds the legal estate on trust for himself as to his share, and for A's personal representatives as to A's share.

The mode of creating joint tenancies and tenancies in common must now be considered.

A. Before 1926

I. AT LAW

At law, the presumption was in favour of a joint tenancy,[36] for it had advantages for feudal lords, for tenants, and for conveyancers.[37] The rule was thus that if land was conveyed to two or more persons a joint tenancy of the legal estate was created unless either—

---

[31] Williams R.P. 143.
[32] *Moffat* v. *Burnie* (1853) 18 Beav. 211.
[33] *Post*, p. 288.
[34] *Ante*, p. 71.
[35] Despite *Re Selous* [1901] 1 Ch. 921, criticised in Williams V. & P. 501, 502.
[36] *Morley* v. *Bird* (1798) 3 Ves. 628.
[37] See M. & W. 424.

(i) one of the unities was absent; or
(ii) words of severance were employed.

1. Absence of unities. The four unities have already been considered. If there was unity of possession but one or more of the other unities were missing, the parties took as tenants in common; if there was no unity of possession, the parties took as separate owners.

2. Words of severance. Any words in the grant showing that the tenants were each to take a distinct share in the property amounted to words of severance and thus created a tenancy in common. Words which have been held to have this effect include—

"share and share alike"
"to be divided amongst"
"equally"
"between."

Further, words showing that the tenants were to take unequal interests (such as "two-thirds to A and one-third to B") sufficed to create a tenancy in common; and even if there were no clear words of severance, the gift taken as a whole might show that a tenancy in common was intended.[38] Thus, if under a settlement on children there was provision for making advances out of capital, any advance to a child would have to be debited against that child's share, and this could not be done unless the child was a tenant in common and so had a distinct share.[39]

II. IN EQUITY

Despite the feudal and conveyancing advantages of a joint tenancy, equity did not favour it. Equity looked to the beneficial interests of the co-tenants, and preferred the certainty and equality of a tenancy in common to the element of chance which the *jus accrescendi* of a joint tenancy introduced. "Survivorship is looked upon as odious in equity,"[40] and none the less because few laymen contemplate that a gift to two or more persons gives rise to such a right.[41] This preference for a tenancy in common was manifested by equity holding that a tenancy in common would exist in equity not only in those cases where it existed at law, but also in certain other cases where an intention to create a tenancy in common could be discerned. In short, there was a tenancy in common in equity in the following five cases.

1. Tenancy in common at law. There was a tenancy in common in equity whenever there was a tenancy in common at law.[42]

---

[38] See, *e.g. Surtees* v. *Surtees* (1871) L.R. 12 Eq. 400.
[39] See *L'Estrange* v. *L'Estrange* [1902] 1 I.R. 467 at 468, 469; *Re Dunn* [1916] 1 Ch. 97.
[40] *R.* v. *Williams* (1735) Bunb. 342 at 343.
[41] See *Re Woolley* [1903] 2 Ch. 206 at 211.
[42] *Supra.*

2. Purchase-money provided in unequal shares. If two or more persons together purchased property and provided the money in unequal shares, the purchasers were presumed to take as tenants in common in shares proportionate to the sums advanced.[43] Thus if A found one-third and B two-thirds of the price, they were presumed tenants in common as to one-third and two-thirds respectively. If, on the other hand, the purchasers provided the money in equal shares, they were presumed joint tenants. These presumptions could be rebutted by evidence of circumstances showing that those providing the purchase-money equally intended to take as tenants in common or *vice versa*.

3. Loan on mortgage. Where two or more persons advanced money on mortgage, whether in equal or unequal shares, equity presumed a tenancy in common in the land between the mortgagees. "If two people join in lending money upon a mortgage, equity says, it could not be the intention, that the interest in that should survive. Though they take a joint security, each means to lend his own and take back his own."[44] "It is obvious, however, that this proposition cannot be put higher than a presumption capable of being rebutted."[45] Yet it should be noted that the "joint account clause" which is normally inserted in mortgages to make the mortgagees appear as joint tenants to the outside world and so simplify the mechanism of discharging the mortgage[46] does not affect this presumption of a tenancy in common in the relationship of the mortgagees *inter se*.[47]

4. Partnership assets. Where partners acquired land as part of their partnership assets, they were presumed to hold it as tenants in common.[48] "*Jus accrescendi inter mercatores locum non habet*": the right of survivorship has no place between merchants. The rule extended to any joint undertaking with a view to a profit, even if there was no formal partnership between the parties; the legal estate might be held on a joint tenancy, but in equity the partners were presumed to be entitled in undivided shares, so that the surviving partners (or whoever held the legal estate) would be compelled to hold the legal estate on trust for those entitled to the property of a deceased partner as far as his share was concerned.[49] The same applies where a tenancy of business premises is granted to tenants for each to occupy separate but unequal areas.[50]

5. Executory trusts. Executory trusts are trusts where the details have not been set out but a further document is to be drawn up to give effect to the

---

[43] *Lake* v. *Gibson* (1729) 1 Eq.Ca.Abr. 290 at 291; and see *post*, p. 293.
[44] *Morley* v. *Bird* (1798) 3 Ves. 628 at 631, *per* Arden M.R.
[45] *Steeds* v. *Steeds* (1889) 22 Q.B.D. 537 at 541, *per* Wills J.
[46] *Post*, p. 474.
[47] *Re Jackson* (1887) 34 Ch.D. 732.
[48] *Lake* v. *Craddock* (1732) 3 P.Wms. 158.
[49] See *Re Fuller's Contract* [1933] Ch. 652.
[50] *Malayan Credit Ltd.* v. *Jack Chia-MPH Ltd.* [1986] A.C. 549.

settlor's intention. Thus "marriage articles," which are the preliminary agreement for a marriage settlement, create executory trusts, and the marriage settlement itself creates executed trusts. In such cases there was a tenancy in common where any intention to create such a tenancy could be found or presumed. "Joint tenancy as a provision for the children of a marriage, is an inconvenient mode of settlement,"[51] for no child could rely upon having a distinct share for his family until he had severed his joint tenancy (*i.e.* converted it into a tenancy in common) nor could any advance to a child be set against his share until this had been done.[52] Accordingly the court would readily infer that a provision in marriage articles or other executory trusts for the benefit of a class of children was intended to be a provision for them as tenants in common, despite the absence of words of severance.[53]

B. After 1925

I. AT LAW

For the benefit of purchasers,[54] substantial changes in the law have been made by the Law of Property Act 1925.

1. A legal tenancy in common cannot exist after 1925. Even if there are clear words of severance, after 1925 the legal estate cannot be held on a tenancy in common[55]; and correspondingly a legal joint tenancy cannot be severed and converted into a legal tenancy in common.[56] As explained below, a tenancy in common can still exist in equity, but at law the only form of co-ownership possible after 1925 is a joint tenancy. Thus a conveyance today "to A, B and C in fee simple as tenants in common" (all being of full age) will vest the legal estate in A, B and C as joint tenants, although in equity they will be tenants in common.[57] If A had been a minor, his rights in equity would not have been affected, but no legal estate would have vested in him.[58] If A, B and C had all been minors, the legal estate would have remained in the grantor, though it is not clear whether the grantor would be deemed to have made an agreement for value to execute a settlement in their favour and in the meantime to hold the land in trust for them, or whether the transaction would be void.[59]

---

[51] *Taggart* v. *Taggart* (1803) 1 Sch. & Lef. 84 at 88.
[52] *Ante*, p. 286.
[53] See *Mayn* v. *Mayn* (1867) L.R. 5 Eq. 150.
[54] *Ante*, p. 4; *post*, p. 291.
[55] L.P.A. 1925, ss.1(6), 34(1), 36(2); S.L.A. 1925, s.36(4).
[56] *Post*, p. 301.
[57] L.P.A. 1925, s.34(2).
[58] *Ibid.* s.19(2).
[59] See *ante*, p. 168; M. & W. 435.

2. The legal estate is held upon trust for sale[60]

(a) *The statutory trusts.* After 1925, subject to the special provisions relating to settled land,[61] land is held upon the "statutory trusts" whenever it is conveyed to or held by two or more persons beneficially, whether as tenants in common[62] or joint tenants, *i.e.* wherever there is beneficial co-ownership.[63] The "statutory trusts" may be summarised thus:

> upon trust to sell the land, and stand possessed of the net proceeds of sale and of the net rents and profits until sale upon such trusts and subject to such powers and provisions as may be requisite for giving effect to the rights of those interested in the land,[64] whether beneficially or as trustees.[65]

This applies only where the co-ownership is beneficial and not merely fiduciary. Thus it applies where land is conveyed to A and B to hold jointly, or to hold on trust for C and D jointly, but not where they are to hold on trust for E absolutely, for then the only co-ownership is not beneficial.

The statutory trusts apply not only when land is "expressed" to be conveyed to persons in undivided shares,[66] but also where the undivided shares arise extraneously, as where land is conveyed to A alone but he and B are beneficially entitled as tenants in common because they contributed to the purchase price in unequal shares.[67] There are considerable theoretical difficulties in the statutory language,[68] but without paying undue attention to them the courts have managed to carry out the evident general intention of the legislation; and it is now generally accepted that whenever there is beneficial co-ownership, however it arose, the land will be held on the statutory trusts[69] unless it is settled land.[70]

(b) *Overreaching.* The trusts for sale created by the statutory trusts take effect in the same way as the trusts for sale already considered.[71] In particular, the land must be sold unless either all trustees concur in postponing sale (as they often do)[72] or a sale would defeat the object of the trust or be a breach of the contractual obligations of the trustee who seeks to sell.[73]

---

[60] See M. & W. 436–439.
[61] *Post*, p. 296.
[62] L.P.A. 1925, s.34(2), Sched. 1, Pt. IV.
[63] *Ibid.* s.36(1).
[64] *Ibid.* s.35.
[65] *Re Hayward* [1928] Ch. 367.
[66] L.P.A. 1925, s.34(2).
[67] *Bull* v. *Bull* [1955] 1 Q.B. 234.
[68] See (1963) 27 Conv.(N.S.) 51 (B. Rudden); [1986] Conv. 379, [1987] Conv. 451 at 454–457 (W. J. Swadling). For this and other cases of difficulty, see M. & W. 437, 438.
[69] *Bull* v. *Bull*, *supra* (relying on S.L.A. 1925, s.36(4)); *Re Buchanan-Wollaston's Conveyance* [1939] Ch. 217 at 222, *ibid.* 738 at 744 (relying on L.P.A. 1925, s.36(1)); *Williams & Glyn's Bank Ltd.* v. *Boland* [1981] A.C. 487; *City of London B.S.* v. *Flegg* [1988] A.C. 54 at 77, 78.
[70] *Post*, p. 296.
[71] *Ante*, pp. 251 *et seq.*
[72] *Ante*, p. 254.
[73] *Re Buchanan-Wollaston's Conveyance*, *supra*; *Jones* v. *Challenger* [1961] 1 Q.B. 176. See *post*, p. 295.

Further, the overreaching provisions apply. Consequently, provided that the purchaser pays his purchase-money to the trustees for sale (being at least two in number or a trust corporation) he takes free from the rights of the beneficiaries, irrespective of whether or not they are in occupation of the land.[74] To a purchaser who does this, it is immaterial whether in equity there are three or thirty people entitled, or whether they are joint tenants or tenants in common. In practice, on a conveyance to joint tenant or tenants in common, it is usual for the conveyance to be made on an express trust for sale.

(c) *Union in sole tenant.* If the whole legal estate and equitable interest become vested in one person, the trust for sale is at an end,[75] as where A and B were joint tenants at law and in equity, and A dies; B's interest is thereupon reconverted into realty. Further, the Schedule to the Law of Property (Amendment) Act 1926 provides that nothing in the Law of Property Act 1925 is to affect the right of a survivor of joint tenants who is solely and beneficially interested to deal with his legal estate as if it were not held on trust for sale. Thus B, as the sole beneficial owner, can make title by himself despite the fact that a sole trustee for sale is unable to give a proper receipt for purchase-money.

Formerly there was a practical difficulty in satisfying a purchaser that B was in fact solely beneficially entitled. An act of severance might have occurred in A's lifetime,[76] causing A and B to become tenants in common, so that the trust for sale continued to exist after A's death. Because B could not prove that this had not happened, a purchaser would insist upon the appointment of a second trustee to receive the purchase money together with B. This difficulty has been overcome by the Law of Property (Joint Tenants) Act 1964, which is retrospective to January 1, 1926.[77] It provides that in favour of a purchaser of a legal estate, a survivor of two or more joint tenants is "deemed to be solely and beneficially interested if he conveys as beneficial owner[78] or the conveyance includes a statement that he is so interested."[79] Where the survivor has himself died, his personal representatives have similar powers. The Act does not apply if, before the conveyance by the survivor, a memorandum recording the severance is indorsed on or annexed to the conveyance which vested the land in the joint tenants.[80] Nor does it apply where a bankruptcy petition or bankruptcy order has been registered,[81] or where the title to the land is registered.[82]

---

[74] *City of London B.S.* v. *Flegg* [1988] A.C. 54.
[75] *Re Cook* [1948] Ch. 212.
[76] See *post*, pp. 299 *et seq.*
[77] s.2.
[78] *Ante*, p. 130.
[79] s.1.
[80] *Ibid.*
[81] *Ante*, pp. 82, 84.
[82] s.3, assuming (incorrectly: see *ante*, p. 103) that an interest under a trust for sale could not be an overriding interest but only a minor interest requiring protection on the register.

3. The legal estate cannot be vested in more than four persons. The position here is clear in the case of tenancies in common and rather less clear in the case of joint tenancies; each type of tenancy will be dealt with separately.[83]

(a) *Tenancies in common*. If land is conveyed to trustees for sale on trust for tenants in common, the general prohibition against the number of trustees exceeding four applies.[84] If the conveyance is expressed to be made to the tenants in common themselves, and they are of full age, statute provides for it to operate as a conveyance "to the grantees, or, if there are more than four grantees, to the four first named in the conveyance, as joint tenants upon the statutory trusts."[85] Further, a gift of land by will to, or in trust for,[86] tenants in common operates as a gift to the Settled Land Act trustees of the will, or, if none, to the testator's personal representatives, upon the statutory trusts[87]; and the number of Settled Land Act trustees or personal representatives cannot exceed four. If all the beneficiaries are of full age and absolutely entitled, they can instead require the legal estate to be vested in themselves (or not more than four of them) as joint tenants on trust for sale for themselves as tenants in common.[88]

(b) *Joint tenancies*. There are no provisions dealing expressly with the number of persons in whom the legal estate can be vested when two or more persons are beneficially entitled as joint tenants. But the trust for sale arising in such cases involves the general provision that, in a trust for sale of land made or coming into operation after 1925, the number of trustees must not exceed four,[89] and "where more than four persons are named as such trustees, the first four named (who are able and willing to act) shall alone be the trustees."[90] In the case of a devise to joint tenants, the general prohibition against more than four trustees of land coupled with the fact that there is a trust for sale prevents the personal representatives from vesting the legal estate in more than four persons.

4. Benefit to purchaser. It will be noticed that the three main changes introduced by the 1925 legislation all assist the purchaser. The prohibition of a legal tenancy in common and the limitation of the number of tenants of the legal estate to four means that purchasers are no longer exposed to the burden of having to investigate the titles of each of, say, 30 legal tenants in common, some of whom might own a sixty-eighth share, and who might be so scattered about the world that it took six months to get all their signatures

---

[83] Elaborate transitional provisions were enacted with the object of ensuring that the legal estate should vest in suitable persons on January 1, 1926. For these, see M. & W. 447–449.
[84] Trustee Act 1925, s.34.
[85] L.P.A. 1925, s.34(2); for minors, see *ante* p. 167.
[86] *Re House* [1929] 2 Ch. 166.
[87] L.P.A. 1925, s.34(3).
[88] *Saunders* v. *Vautier* (1841) Cr. & Ph. 240; L.P.A. 1925, s.3(1)(b)(ii).
[89] T.A. 1925, s.34.
[90] *Ibid*. s.34(2).

to the conveyance.[91] Further, the overreaching effect of a trust for sale enables a purchaser to ignore the equitable rights of the beneficiaries.

II. IN EQUITY

On the position in equity after 1925, there is little to be added to the foregoing. Strictly there can be no "tenancy" in common after 1925 because those interested hold no estate or interest in the land but are entitled merely as beneficiaries under a trust for sale; the 1925 legislation throughout refers not to "tenancies in common" but to "undivided shares." In general, however, the rights of these beneficiaries correspond to the rights of tenants in common before 1926, and the same applies to those entitled in equity as joint tenants.

Sect. 4. Position of the Beneficiaries

A. *Extent of the Beneficial Interests*

1. Express trusts. In many cases of co-ownership there is an express trust, declared in the will or in the conveyance to the co-owners or trustees for them. If this states that the parties are to be beneficial joint tenants, or to be tenants in common, showing the size of their shares, it will conclusively determine the matter, subject to any question of rescission or rectification[92]; and for this the burden of proof is heavy.[93] Thus a conveyance to two or more persons expressly as joint tenants makes them joint tenants, each with an equal potential share, even if they contributed unequally to the purchase money.[94] As an express trust of land must at least be evidenced in writing,[95] the question will normally be merely[96] one of construing the document or documents. Contradictory expressions such as "as beneficial joint tenants in equal shares"[97] can usually be resolved without resort to the quaint rule that, if all else fails, the first words prevail in a deed but the last in a will.[98]

2. Resulting and constructive trusts. In the absence of any express trust, a resulting or constructive trust may nevertheless arise; and these are exempt from the statutory requirement of writing.[99] In the cases the division between these two categories is sometimes blurred.

---

[91] See (1929) 15 Conv. (o.s.) 83 (A. H. Cosway); and see *City of London B.S.* v. *Flegg* [1988] A.C. 54 at 77.

[92] *Pettitt* v. *Pettitt* [1970] A.C. 777 at 813; *Pink* v. *Lawrence* (1977) 36 P. & C.R. 98; *Goodman* v. *Gallant* [1986] Fam. 106; *Turton* v. *Turton* [1988] Ch. 542.

[93] See *Thames Guarantee Ltd.* v. *Campbell* [1985] Q.B. 210; Snell 626 *et seq.*

[94] *Goodman* v. *Gallant*, *supra*.

[95] *Ante*, p. 271.

[96] "Merely" is sometimes an overstatement.

[97] *Martin* v. *Martin* (1987) 54 P. & C.R. 238 ("in equal shares" prevailed).

[98] *Slingsby's Case* (1587) 5 Co.Rep. 18b at 19a; M. & W. 426; and see *ante*, p. 152.

[99] See *ante*, p. 272.

(a) *Resulting trusts*. The presumption of a resulting trust depends on any common intention and on the making of contributions.

(1) PRESUMPTION. When property is purchased with money provided by A and B, and there is a common intention (whether expressed or, more usually, to be inferred[1]) that each of them is to have a beneficial interest in it, there will be presumed to be a resulting trust for them in shares proportionate to their contributions, whether the property is conveyed to one or both of them or to some third party. Thus if a house is conveyed to A alone, but the price is provided as to nine-tenths by A under a mortgage for which he is solely liable and as to one-tenth by B, A will be presumed to hold the house at to nine-tenths for himself and one-tenth for B.[2] The two elements in cases of this kind are the intention and the contributions.

(2) COMMON INTENTION. The common intention must be established by the evidence as a whole, whether or not it is in writing. Often it has to be inferred from the contributions and the circumstances in which they were made, for clear agreements are unlikely to have been made, especially as between husband and wife[3]; the main weight is thus on the contributions. The question is what in fact the common intention was, and not what the court considers it might or ought to have been.[4] Many of the cases arise where the parties, whether married or not, are purchasing a house on mortgage for use as their home; and in the absence of any expression of a common intention, that intention has to be inferred from the facts surrounding the purchase. It is doubtful whether such an intention can be inferred from anything less than direct contributions to the purchase price.[5] No resulting trust will be inferred where money is provided by way of gift or loan[6]; and the presumption of a resulting trust may be rebutted where there is a presumption of advancement,[7] though in this field that presumption is of little weight today.[8]

(3) CONTRIBUTIONS. Contributions to the purchase price are sometimes made in money (*e.g.* in paying a deposit) but often they take the form of regularly bearing a share of the mortgage repayments on the property; merely occasional payments are not enough.[9] Indirect contributions suffice. Thus where A purchased property out of the profits of a family business to which B's unpaid work in the business had substantially contributed, B was

---

[1] See *Gissing* v. *Gissing* [1971] A.C. 886 at 902.
[2] *Re Rogers' Question* [1948] 1 All E.R. 328; *Walker* v. *Hall* [1984] F.L.R. 126 (purchase in joint names).
[3] See *Bernard* v. *Josephs* [1982] Ch. 391 at 402, 403; *Burns* v. *Burns* [1984] Ch. 317 at 335, 336.
[4] *Gissing* v. *Gissing* [1971] A.C. 886, esp. at p. 898; and see *Pettitt* v. *Pettitt* [1970] A.C. 777.
[5] See *Lloyds Bank Plc* v. *Rosset* [1991] A.C. 107 at 133, where "constructive" seems to be used in the sense of "resulting."
[6] See *Re Sharpe* [1980] 1 W.L.R. 219; contrast *Risch* v. *McFee* (1990) 61 P. & C.R. 42 (loan becoming a contribution).
[7] *Ante*, p. 271.
[8] *Pettitt* v. *Pettitt*, *supra*, at pp. 793, 811, 824; cp. 813, 815.
[9] *Gissing* v. *Gissing*, *supra*, at pp. 900, 906. For endowment mortgages, see Thompson, *Co-ownership*, 52.

entitled to a beneficial interest.[10] At one time the court sometimes considered that other contributions sufficed, such as bearing some of the household expenses, purchasing chattels for use in the house and looking after
children.[11] But it is now settled that nothing will do except contributions to
the purchase of the property, whether direct or indirect.[12] Thus money spent
or renovating, improving and redecorating the property, or paying the rates,
is not enough by itself.[13] Yet an arrangement that one party should bear all
the household expenses in order to enable the other party to pay the
mortgage instalments is sufficiently related to the acquisition of the property
for the inference to be drawn that each party was intended to have a
beneficial interest.[14]

By statute,[15] subsequent contributions towards improvements (as distinct
from the original acquisition) may now be invoked[16] in order to alter the
balance of beneficial ownership as between husband and wife, but not
others. Any substantial contribution in money or money's worth made by a
husband or wife to the improvement of real or personal property in which
either or both of them have a beneficial interest will entitle the contributor to
such a share or enlarged share as is agreed or, in default, as seems "just" in
all the circumstances.

(b) *Constructive trusts.* Where there is an agreement or common intention
that land is to be held on trust, a beneficiary cannot enforce any trust if the
statutory requirement of evidence in writing[17] is not satisfied. But if a
beneficiary, in reliance on the trust, acts to his detriment in relation to the
property in the reasonable belief that he is entitled to a beneficial interest
under the trust, it would be inequitable to allow the legal owner to rely on
the statute as defeating the claim of the beneficiary[18]: the statute cannot be
used as an instrument of fraud.[19] The court will accordingly give effect to the
intended trust by imposing a constructive trust on the property to the same
effect.[20] This process has much in common with the doctrine of proprietary
estoppel.[21] In such cases, the size of the interest taken by the beneficiary

---

[10] *Re Cummins* [1972] Ch. 62; *Bothe* v. *Amos* [1976] Fam. 46.
[11] *Hazell* v. *Hazell* [1972] 1 W.L.R. 301; *Hussey* v. *Palmer* [1972] 1 W.L.R. 1286 at 1289, 1290
(constructive trust); *Hall* v. *Hall* [1982] 3 F.L.R. 379 at 381. See generally (1976) 92 L.Q.R.
489 (F. Webb).
[12] *Gissing* v. *Gissing* [1971] A.C. 886; *Burns* v. *Burns* [1984] Ch. 317.
[13] *Pettitt* v. *Pettitt* [1970] A.C. 777; *Burns* v. *Burns, supra*; *Lloyds Bank Plc* v. *Rosset* [1991]
A.C. 107; and see [1990] Conv. 314 (M.P. Thompson). See also *Savage* v. *Dunningham*
[1974] Ch. 181 (tenancy: rent).
[14] See *Gissing* v. *Gissing, supra*, at p. 903; and see at p. 909.
[15] Matrimonial Proceedings and Property Act 1970, s.37.
[16] See *Suttill* v. *Graham* [1977] 1 W.L.R. 819 at 824.
[17] *Ante*, p. 271.
[18] *Gissing* v. *Gissing* [1971] A.C. 886 at 905; *Midland Bank Plc* v. *Dobson* [1986] 1 F.L.R. 171.
[19] *Rochefoucauld* v. *Boustead* [1897] 1 Ch. 196; *Bannister* v. *Bannister* [1948] 2 All E.R. 133.
See (1985) 36 N.I.L.Q. 358 at 364–370 (M.P. Thompson).
[20] *Gissing* v. *Gissing* [1971] A.C. 886; *Midland Bank Plc* v. *Dobson, supra*; and see *Maharaj* v.
Chand [1986] A.C. 898 at 907.
[21] See *Grant* v. *Edwards* [1986] Ch. 638 at 656, 657; *Stokes* v. *Anderson* [1991] 1 F.L.R. 391 at
398–400. For proprietary estoppel, see *post*, pp. 434 *et seq.*

depends on what was agreed, either in fact or by inference, rather than on the size of any contribution to the purchase made by him in reliance on the agreement.[22] The acts of reliance are not, as for resulting trusts, confined to direct or indirect payments towards the purchase price, but include other acts carried out in reliance on the trust, such as doing heavy work to the house and grounds[23] and even making substantial contributions to the general household expenses.[24]

B. Sale

1. Occupation trusts. The purpose of many trusts for sale is to provide financial benefits for the beneficiaries, giving them income until sale and holding the capital for them after sale. But since 1925, the imposition of a trust for sale in cases of co-ownership has meant that there are many other trusts for sale where the main purpose is not the provision of financial benefits but to provide the means of occupying the property, usually a house. For brevity, such trusts may be called "occupation trusts", in contrast with "financial trusts." There is no formal classification of this kind, but the distinction is useful in relation to selling the property and orders for sale.[25]

2. Sale. Under a financial trust, there is usually no reason why the trustees should not carry out their duty to sell the property when they no longer concur in exercising their power to postpone sale[26]; the sale will merely convert one form of financial asset into another. But where there is an occupation trust, a sale would often defeat the purpose of the trust by making one or more of the co-owners homeless, and so the occupying co-owner cannot be evicted by the others.[27] Where the purpose of the trust is the provision of a family or matrimonial home for a married or unmarried couple, that purpose ends when the couple separate, and so it will no longer prevent a sale[28]; and a sale will usually, but not always, be ordered unless the occupying co-owner pays a proper rent or compensation[29] for his occupation.[30] But where the purpose or the trust is to provide a family home for a man and woman and their children, the house will not cease to be occupied as a family home merely because the man leaves it, and so he will be refused an order for sale.[31] On a divorce, disputes of this kind should normally be

---

[22] See *Re Densham* [1975] 1 W.L.R. 1519 at 1524; *Eves* v. *Eves* [1975] 1 W.L.R. 1338; and see *Ungarian* v. *Lesnoff* [1990] Ch. 206 (life interest).
[23] *Eves* v. *Eves, supra.*
[24] *Grant* v. *Edwards* [1986] Ch. 638; and see the wide language at p. 657. See also *Hammond* v. *Mitchell* [1991] 1 W.L.R. 1127.
[25] Under L.P.A. 1925, s.30, *ante*, p. 257.
[26] *Ante*, p. 254.
[27] *Bull* v. *Bull* [1955] 1 Q.B. 234; *ante*, p. 254.
[28] *Jones* v. *Challenger* [1961] 1 Q.B. 176; *Bernard* v. *Josephs* [1982] Ch. 391.
[29] *Ante*, p. 283.
[30] *Dennis* v. *McDonald* [1982] Fam. 63; contrast *Stott* v. *Ratcliffe* (1982) 126 S.J. 310 (no order).
[31] *Re Evers' Trust* [1980] 1 W.L.R. 1327; and see *Chhokar* v. *Chhokar* [1984] F.L.R. 313 at 327.

resolved under the wide-ranging and discretionary matrimonial jurisdiction[32] rather than under the general law[33]; yet for the unmarried it is often possible to achieve similar results under the general law.[34]

3. Bankruptcy. Where a co-owner has been adjudicated bankrupt and his trustee in bankruptcy seeks an order for the sale of the property,[35] the court has a discretion whether to make the order, and must balance the conflicting interests. However, the interests of the creditors will usually prevail over those of any other co-owners or occupants of the property, and so an order for sale will normally be made.[36] A man must be just (to his creditors) before he can be generous (to his family).[37] Only rarely will the circumstances justify refusing an immediate order for sale, as by postponing the sale of a house for five years while children are being educated.[38] Statute has now supplemented the authorities.[39] Where a bankrupt and his spouse or former spouse hold a dwelling-house on trust for sale, and the trustee in bankruptcy applies for an order for sale at least a year after the dwelling vested in him, the court must assume (unless the circumstances of the case are exceptional) that the interests of the bankrupt's creditors outweigh all other considerations.[40]

Sect. 5. Position of Settled Land

Before 1926, where land fell within the definition of settled land but two or more persons were together entitled in possession, they together formed a composite tenant for life, whether they held as joint tenants, tenants in common or otherwise.[41] After 1925, their position depends upon whether in equity they are entitled as joint tenants or in undivided shares.

A. Joint Tenants

If two or more persons of full age are entitled as joint tenants of settled land, they together constitute the tenant for life.[42] If any of them are minors, such one or more of them as for the time being is or are of full age constitute the tenant for life[43]; if they are all minors, the legal estate and statutory powers are vested in the statutory owner[44] until one of them is of full age.[45] The land

[32] See Matrimonial Causes Act 1973, ss.23–25.
[33] *Williams* v. *Williams* [1976] Ch. 278.
[34] See [1984] Conv. 103 (M.P. Thompson).
[35] *e.g.* under L.P.A. 1925, s.30: see *ante* p. 257.
[36] *Re Bailey* [1977] 1 W.L.R. 278; *Re Lowrie* [1981] 3 All E.R. 353; *Re Citro* [1991] Ch. 142. See generally Thompson, *Co-ownership* 108–112.
[37] See *Re Bailey*, *supra*, at pp. 283, 284.
[38] *Re Holliday* [1981] Ch. 405 (bankrupt's own petition: creditors not pressing for payment); contrast *Re Lowrie*, *supra* (immediate sale, completion only postponed for three months).
[39] Insolvency Act 1986, s.336.
[40] *Ibid.* s.336(5).
[41] S.L.A. 1882, s.2(6).
[42] S.L.A. 1925, s.19(2).
[43] *Ibid.* s.19(3).
[44] *Ante*, p. 224.
[45] L.P.A. 1925, s.26(4), (5).

thus remains settled land and there is no trust for sale. All the joint tenants in whom the land is vested must concur in exercising the power of sale and other statutory powers. The court will not compel a dissident tenant to concur unless he is acting in bad faith.[46]

B. Undivided Shares[47]

1. Trust for sale. If after 1925 two or more tenants in common become entitled in possession to settled land, the land forthwith ceases to be settled land and becomes subject to a trust for sale. The Settled Land Act trustees can require the legal estate to be conveyed to them if it is not already vested in them[48]; they will hold it on the statutory trusts, namely, on trust for sale, with power to postpone sale, holding the income until sale and the proceeds thereafter upon such trusts and subject to such provisions are as requisite for giving effect to the rights of the persons interested in the land.[49] Thus if land is settled on A for life, remainder to B and C in equal shares as tenants in common for life, remainder to the children of B and C in fee simple, when A dies the land will be held upon trust for sale and must be vested in the Settled Land Act trustees.

2. Land ceasing to be settled. This provision that the legal estate shall be vested in the Settled Land Act trustees and not in the persons beneficially entitled applies even if the land ceases to be settled at the moment when the tenants in common become entitled in possession. Thus if land is settled on A for life, remainder to his children in fee simple in equal shares as tenants in common, the land ceases to be settled land on the death of A, for it becomes subject to an immediate binding trust for sale. Nevertheless, A's personal representatives must convey the legal estate to the Settled Land Act trustees as joint tenants upon trust for sale, and not to the children[50]; to this extent the land retains traces of its former status as settled land. But the children may instead, if they are *sui juris*, require the legal estate to be vested in themselves on trust for sale.[51]

3. Overreaching powers. The Settled Land Act trustees hold on a special form of trust for sale which enables them to overreach not only the rights under the trust for sale but also any other rights existing under a former settlement and not protected by a legal mortgage, even if these rights are prior to the trust for sale.[52] For example, if land is settled on A for life, subject to an equitable rentcharge for B, with remainder to C and D as

---

[46] *Re 90 Thornhill Road, Tolworth, Surrey* [1970] Ch. 261. Contrast trusts for sale, *ante*, p. 254.
[47] See M. & W. 451–454.
[48] S.L.A. 1925, s.36(1); L.P.A. 1925, Sched. 1, Pt. IV, para. 2.
[49] S.L.A. 1925, s.36(2), (6).
[50] *Re Thomas* [1939] Ch. 513.
[51] *Ante*, p. 291.
[52] S.L.A. 1925, s.36(2); L.P.A. 1925, Sched. 1, Pt. IV, para. 1(3), as amended by L.P.(Am.)A. 1926, Sched.

tenants in common, on the death of A the Settled Land Act trustees will hold
the land on trust for sale with power to overreach B's rentcharge even
though it has priority to the trust for sale.

Sect. 6. Determination of Joint Tenancies and Tenancies in Common

Joint tenancies and tenancies in common may be determined by partition or
by union in a sole tenant; joint tenancies may also be determined by
severance, which converts them into tenancies in common.

A. Partition

1. No power at common law. Joint tenants and tenants in common have
always been able to make a voluntary partition of the land concerned if all
agreed; their co-ownership thus came to an end by each of them becoming
sole tenant of the piece of land allotted to him. But at common law there was
no right to compel a partition.

2. Partition Acts. By the Partition Acts 1539 and 1540, a statutory right to
compel partition was conferred upon joint tenants and tenants in common,
one tenant being entitled to insist upon a partition, however inconvenient it
might be. It was not until the Partition Act 1868 that the court was empowered to decree a sale instead of partition, an order which might be highly
desirable where, for example, the cost of partition proceedings would
exceed the value of the property, or where a single house had to be parti-
tioned into thirds, and the owner of two-thirds was given all the chimneys
and fireplaces and the only stairs.[53]

3. Sale. The Partition Acts have now been repealed. Instead, subject to
certain qualifications, a power is given to the trustees for sale in whom the
legal estate is vested to effect a partition with the consent of the beneficiaries.[54] If the trustees or any of the beneficiaries refuse to agree to a
partition, any person interested may apply to the court, which may make
such order as it thinks fit,[55] such as an order for sale.[56]

B. Union in a Sole Tenant

Joint tenancies and tenancies in common may be determined by the entirety
of the land becoming vested in a sole tenant. Thus where one of two
surviving joint tenants dies, the other becomes sole tenant and the joint

[53] See *Turner* v. *Morgan* (1803) 8 Ves. 143, 11 Ves. 157n.; but if there had been three houses,
each share would have consisted of one house and not one-third of each house: *Earl of
Clarendon* v. *Hornby* (1718) 1 P.Wms. 446.
[54] L.P.A. 1925, s.28(3).
[55] *Ibid*. s.30.
[56] See *Re Solomon* [1967] Ch. 573.

tenancy is at an end. Similarly if one joint tenant or tenant in common acquires the interests of all his fellows, as by purchase, the co-ownership is at an end.

Because in theory each joint tenant is seised of the whole of the land, the appropriate way for one joint tenant to transfer his rights to another is by a release operating to extinguish rather than to convey any rights, and so requiring no words of limitation; but any sort of conveyance will be construed as a release,[57] and it has now been retrospectively provided that the transaction can also be effected by grant.[58] A tenant in common, on the other hand, cannot release his share to his fellows, but has to convey it by some assurance by which a sole tenant could have conveyed his land, for "a release supposes the party to have the thing in demand."[59]

Co-ownership in land is also extinguished if the land is sold to a purchaser, for the co-ownership is transferred from the land to the proceeds of sale.

C. Severance

The common law mitigated the uncertainty of the *jus accrescendi* by enabling a joint tenant to destroy the joint tenancy by severance, thereby becoming a tenant in common. "The duration of all lives being uncertain, if either party has an ill opinion of his own life, he may sever the joint tenancy by a deed granting over a moiety [*i.e.* conveying one half] in trust for himself; so that survivorship can be no hardship, where either side may at pleasure prevent it."[60] "Severance" strictly includes partition, but the word is normally used to describe the process whereby a joint tenancy is converted into a tenancy in common, and it is used in this sense here. Although no joint tenant owned any distinct share in the land, yet each had a potential share equal in size to that of his companions, and so depending upon the number of joint tenants at the time in question. Thus if there were five joint tenants, each had the right to sever his joint tenancy and become tenant in common of one undivided fifth share; if one joint tenant died before the severance each of the survivors had a potential quarter share, and so on. The potential shares in land conveyed to two or more persons as beneficial joint tenants will always be equal, even if they contributed unequally to the purchase price.[61]

I. BEFORE 1926

Before 1926, a joint tenancy could be severed both at law and in equity. Severance was effected by destroying one of the unities. Unity of time could not be severed, and severance of the unity of possession meant partition; but severance of the unity either of title or of interest converted a joint tenancy

[57] See *Re Schär* [1951] Ch. 280.
[58] L.P.A. 1925, s.72(4).
[59] Litt. s.304, n. 1.
[60] *Cray* v. *Willis* (1729) 2 P.Wms. 529, *per* Verney M.R.
[61] *Goodman* v. *Gallant* [1986] Fam. 106.

into a tenancy in common. A joint tenancy could be severed in the following ways.

1. By acquiring another estate in the land. Although it was not fatal to a joint tenancy that one of the tenants was initially given some further estate in the land than his joint tenancy, the subsequent acquisition of an additional estate in the land destroyed the unity of interest and severed the joint tenancy.[62] Thus if land was limited to A, B and C as joint tenants for life, with remainder to C in fee simple, the mere existence of C's fee simple remainder did not destroy his tenancy for life; however, if A acquired C's fee simple, A's life estate merged in the fee simple and severed his joint tenancy for life. It should be noted, however, that this method of severance required that some estate different from the estate held in joint tenancy should be acquired. Thus in the above example if A released his interest to B, B took A's one-third share as tenant in common, but his joint tenancy with C in the remaining two-thirds was not affected.

2. By alienation. If a joint tenant alienated his interest *inter vivos*,[63] his joint tenancy was severed and the person to whom the interest was conveyed took it as tenant in common with the other joint tenants, for he had no unity of title with them.[64] Such a severance did not affect the other joint tenants, who remained joint tenants *inter se*. Thus if A, B and C were joint tenants, and A sold his interest to X, X became tenant in common of one-third and B and C joint tenants of two-thirds. If B then died, C alone profited by the *jus acrescendi*, X and C being left as tenants in common as to one-third and two-thirds respectively.

An involuntary alienation sufficed, as where a joint tenant became bankrupt and his interest vested in his trustee in bankruptcy.[65] Again, partial alienation was enough, as where a joint tenant mortgaged his interest or (probably) leased it[66]; and a purported conveyance[67] or mortgage[68] of the entire property, effected by one joint tenant forging the signature of the other, severed the forger's joint tenancy and took effect only as to his interest. In equity, an agreement by a joint tenant to alienate his interest severed his equitable joint tenancy if the agreement was specifically enforceable,[69] and even if it was not, where it was made with another of the joint tenants instead of a third party.[70] But mere negotiations for an agreement

---

[62] *Wiscot's Case* (1599) 2 Co.Rep. 60b.
[63] *Ante*, p. 281.
[64] *Partriche* v. *Powlet* (1740) 2 Atk. 54; and see *Goddard* v. *Lewis* (1909) 101 L.T. 528, collecting many of the authorities.
[65] *Re Dennis* [1992] 3 W.L.R. 204.
[66] See M. & W. 431.
[67] *Ahmed* v. *Kendrick* (1987) 56 P. & C.R. 121.
[68] *First National Securities Ltd.* v. *Hegerty* [1985] Q.B. 850.
[69] *Brown* v. *Raindle* (1796) 3 Ves. 256.
[70] *Burgess* v. *Rawnsley* [1975] Ch. 429. See [1976] C.L.J. 20 (D.J. Hayton).

were not enough,[71] nor was a mere unilateral declaration of a desire to sever.[72]

3. By a mutual course of dealing. A severance could be made by means of any course of dealing between joint tenants which sufficiently indicated an intention that they were to become tenants in common.[73] There had to be a course of dealing which showed that all concerned were treating their interests as being tenancies in common, as where some of the tenants authorised the trustees to make a particular investment or to pay one of the tenants his share.[74] The burden of proof lay on the person seeking to establish a severance,[75] and it was not enough merely to show that the joint tenants of a house had converted it into maisonettes so that each could live separately,[76] or that partners had included the farmhouse and land which they held as joint tenants in their partnership accounts.[77]

4. By homicide. Nobody can benefit in law by his crime.[78] Hence if one joint tenant was guilty of the murder or deliberate and violent manslaughter[79] of another joint tenant, the criminal was treated as having severed the joint tenancy and so he took nothing by survivorship,[80] though in 1982 this became subject to the power of the court to grant relief.[81] In other jurisdictions, where constructive trusts are more freely used, a doctrine emerged that homicide worked no severance, but that anything which passed to the criminal by survivorship would be held by him on a constructive trust.[82] If A, B and C are beneficial joint tenants, and A murders B, the doctrine of severance would leave A with his one-third and give C two-thirds, whereas the constructive trust would give B's estate and C half each.

II. AFTER 1925

After 1925, a legal joint tenancy can never be severed so as to create a legal tenancy in common; but this does not prevent one joint tenant from releasing his interest to the others, nor does it affect the right to sever a joint tenancy in equity.[83]

In equity, a severance can be effected by any of the former methods, and also by a new method. There is nothing to prevent the severance of an

---

[71] *Gore* v. *Carpenter* (1990) 60 P. & C.R. 456; but see *Burgess* v. *Rawnsley, supra.*
[72] See *Nielson-Jones* v. *Fedden* [1975] Ch. 222, and contrast *Burgess* v. *Rawnsley, supra.* See now *post*, p. 302.
[73] *Williams* v. *Hensman* (1861) 1 J. & H. 546 at 557.
[74] *Williams* v. *Hensman* (1861) 1 J. & H. 546.
[75] *Re Denny* [1947] L.J.R. 1029.
[76] *Greenfield* v. *Greenfield* (1979) 38 P. & C.R. 570.
[77] *Barton* v. *Morris* [1985] 1 W.L.R. 1257.
[78] See *ante*, p. 149.
[79] *Ibid.*
[80] *Re K.* [1986] Ch.180.
[81] *Ibid.*; *ante*, p. 149.
[82] See (1973) 89 L.Q.R. 235 (T.G. Youdan); (1974) 37 M.L.R. 481 (T.K. Earnshaw & P.J. Pace).
[83] L.P.A. 1925, s.36(2).

equitable joint tenancy in a dwelling-house merely because the joint tenants are married and live in it.[84]

1. Methods available before 1926. A joint tenancy may be severed in equity by doing any acts or things which would have been effective in equity in the case of personalty[85]; and this includes all the methods considered above.

2. Notice in writing. "Where a legal estate (not being settled land) is vested in joint tenants beneficially, and any tenant desires to sever the joint tenancy in equity, he shall give to the other joint tenants a notice in writing of such desire," whereupon the parties concerned are to be treated in equity as if there had been an actual severance.[86] This provision is limited in its operation. Settled land is expressly excluded, thus preventing it becoming subject to a trust for sale,[87] and it appears to be confined to land, thus excluding pure personalty.[88] It plainly applies where A and B hold the legal estate on trust for themselves jointly, but, read literally, not where they hold it on trust for themselves and others, or where other trustees hold it on trust for them. But the court may be able to read "vested in joint tenants beneficially" as being "vested in any persons for joint tenants beneficially," and so cure this strange omission. A notice given to one but not all of the other joint tenants seems to be ineffective as having been given not to "the other joint tenants" but only to one of them.

No form for such a notice is prescribed, and a notice duly posted is effective even if it not received.[89] A writ or originating summons commencing legal proceedings, or an affidavit in the proceedings, may suffice if a claim to an immediate interest in the property is asserted, even if the proceedings are not pursued[90]; yet a divorce petition which makes no immediate claim but prays for a property adjustment order to be made in the future is not enough.[91]

D. Operation of the Present Law

An example illustrating the present position may be useful. In 1960 X purported to convey land to A, B, C, D, and E in fee simple; all were of full age. The legal estate vested in A, B, C, and D on the statutory trusts; in

[84] In *Bedson* v. *Bedson* [1965] 2 Q.B. 666, p. 690 is plainly preferable to p. 678. See *Radziej* v. *Radziej* [1967] 1 W.L.R. 659; *Re Draper's Conveyance* [1969] 1 Ch. 486; *Harris* v. *Goddard* [1983] 1 W.L.R. 1203 at 1208.
[85] L.P.A. 1925, s.36(2).
[86] *Ibid.*
[87] See *ante*, p. 296.
[88] See *Nielson-Jones* v. *Fedden* [1975] Ch. 222; but see *Burgess* v. *Rawnsley* [1975] Ch. 429 at 440.
[89] *Re 88 Berkeley Road, N.W.9* [1971] Ch. 648; and see *McDowell* v. *Hirschfield, Lipson & Rumney* [1992] *The Times*, Feb. 13 (notice in a letter sent "without prejudice").
[90] *Burgess* v. *Rawnsley* [1975] Ch. 429 at 447.
[91] *Harris* v. *Goddard* [1983] 1 W.L.R. 1203.

equity, A, B, C, D and E were tenants in common if there were words of severance or if it was one of equity's special cases, but otherwise joint tenants. If they were joint tenants and A died, B, C, and D would then hold the legal estate on the statutory trusts for B, C, D and E as joint tenants; E would not automatically fill the vacancy at law, but could, of course, be appointed by the remaining trustees to be a new trustee in place of A. If B afterwards sold his interest to P, then B, C and D would hold the legal estate on the statutory trusts for P as tenant in common of a quarter and C, D and E as joint tenants of three-quarters. If C then severed his joint tenancy (*e.g.* by agreement with D and E), the legal estate would remain in B, C and D as before, on the statutory trusts for P and C as tenants in common of one-quarter each, and D and E as joint tenants of half. On D's death, B and C would hold on the statutory trusts for P, C and E as tenants in common as to one-quarter, one-quarter and one-half respectively.

Sect. 7. Registered Land

Where there is co-ownership of registered land, the interests of the bene-ficial co-owners will normally be protected by the entry of a restriction on the register.[92] This will ensure that on a sale the purchase money will be properly paid to the trustees (whether the co-owners themselves or others), and the beneficial interests of the co-owners will be overreached and become corresponding rights in the proceeds of sale.[93] This is so even as to any of the beneficiaries who are in "actual occupation" of the land; for their interests, having been overreached, are no longer "subsisting" in the land, and so cannot be overriding interests.[94] They can be no more than minor interests.[95]

Part 2

PARTY WALLS

Sect. 1. Before 1926

1. Categories. Where a wall separates land owned by A from land owned by B, the wall may either be in the sole ownership of one party, free from any rights of the other, or else be a party wall. There appears to be no precise legal definition of the term "party wall." Four possible meanings are as follows.[96]

    (a) *Tenancy in common*: the two adjoining owners are tenants in com-mon of the wall.

---

[92] *Ante*, p. 280.
[93] See *City of London B.S.* v. *Flegg* [1988] A.C. 54.
[94] *Ibid.*; *ante*, pp. 102, 103.
[95] See *Elias* v. *Mitchell* [1972] Ch. 652; *ante*, p. 280.
[96] See *Watson* v. *Gray* (1880) 14 Ch.D. 192 at 194, 195.

(b) *Divided*: the wall is divided longitudinally into two strips, one belonging to each of the neighbouring owners.

(c) *Divided with easements*: the wall is divided as in (b), but each half is subject to an easement of support in favour of the owner of the other half.

(d) *Ownership subject to easement*: the wall belongs entirely to one of the adjoining owners, but is subject to an easement or right in the other to have it maintained as a dividing wall.

2. Presumption. The presumption was in favour of a party wall falling within the first category, at all events if evidence was given that each owner had exercised dominion over the entire wall.[97] The first category had the disadvantage that either owner could insist upon a partition, but it was less unsatisfactory than the second category, where either owner, acting with reasonable care, could remove his half of the wall and leave a structure which was perhaps incapable of standing alone.[98] Neither owner could pull down a wall of the first kind except for the purpose of rebuilding it with all reasonable dispatch,[99] nor could either prevent the other from enjoying any part of the wall, as by covering the top with broken glass or replacing it with part of a shed.[1] There was no presumption in favour of the third or fourth categories because these could be established only on proof that the appropriate easements existed.

3. Ownership of soil. The presumption in favour of the first category applied only where the exact situation of the boundary could not be shown, or where the site of the wall could be shown to have been owned in common.[2] Where the wall was built entirely on A's land, the presumption was that the wall was A's; and where the wall was built on the boundary, so that substantially half the soil on which it stood was A's and half B's, the case usually fell into the second or third category, the wall being regarded as divided into two walls each of half the thickness.[3] The principle in these cases was that "as a matter of law, the property in the wall followed the property in the land upon which it stood."[4] Subject to this, the ownership of the wall was a question of fact for the jury. A wall might even be in sole ownership for part of its height and a party wall for the rest.[5]

In some parts of the country, particularly London, these rules have been modified to some extent by statute.[6]

---

[97] *Watson* v. *Gray* (1880) 14 Ch.D. 192 at 194, 195.
[98] See *Cubitt* v. *Porter* (1828) 8 B. & C. 257 at 264.
[99] *Cubitt* v. *Porter* (1828) 8 B. & C. 257.
[1] *Stedman* v. *Smith* (1857) 8 E. & B. 1 at 6, 7.
[2] See *Wiltshire* v. *Sidford* (1827) 1 Man. & Ry. 404 at 407, 409.
[3] *Murly* v. *M'Dermott* (1838) 8 A. & E. 138 at 142.
[4] *Jones* v. *Read* (1876) 10 Ir.R.C.L. 315 at 320, *per* Palles C.B.
[5] *Weston* v. *Arnold* (1873) 8 Ch.App. 1084.
[6] *e.g.* the London Building Acts 1930 to 1982: see Greater London (General Powers) Act 1982, s.3(6).

Sect. 2. After 1925

Unless special provision had been made, all party walls in the first category would have become subject to a trust for sale after 1925. It was consequently provided that after 1925 all party walls in this category should be deemed to be severed vertically, and that the owner of each part should have such rights of support and user over the rest of the wall as were requisite for giving the parties rights similar to those which they would have enjoyed had they been tenants in common of the wall.[7] The practical effect of this provision is to translate all party walls in the first category into the third. Apart from this, the law of party walls remains unchanged.

[7] L.P.A. 1925, s.38(2), Sched. 1, Pt. V.

CHAPTER 9

LANDLORD AND TENANT

Part 1

INTRODUCTORY

BEFORE considering leases and tenancies in detail, some mention will be made of their history and terminology.

Sect. 1. History

1. Leases. A lease, as generally understood today, is a document creating an interest in land for a fixed period of certain duration,[1] usually in consideration of the payment of rent. This has not always been so.

2. Leases for lives. The owner of a life estate in land was able to recover the land itself if he was dispossessed, whereas until the end of the fifteenth century a tenant for a term of years could not do so. One result of this was that in early times it was a common practice for a lessee to take a lease of land for the duration of a specified number of lives, instead of for a specified term of years. Thus, instead of a lease for 99 years, a tenant would take a lease for the life of the survivor of X, Y and Z. The tenant had an estate *pur autre vie*, which, being an estate of freehold and classified as real property,[2] entitled him to recover the land if he was dispossessed. The disadvantage of the uncertainty of the period was outweighed by the advantages it gave to the tenant and sometimes to the lord. The rent payable was usually fairly small, but a fine was paid when the lease was granted; a further fine was payable when, on the dropping of the lives, the tenant exercised the right the lease gave him to replace them and so extend the lease. If the lessor was a corporation such as a monastery or college, the fines were treated as income by the then members of the corporation, to the disadvantage of their successors. Leases for life finally lost their popularity when legislation in the first half of the nineteenth century compelled corporations to add such fines to their capital.[3] Nowadays a lease for life is converted into a 90 year determinable term.[4]

3. Leases for fixed terms of years. Leases for fixed terms of years are used today for more purposes than one.

[1] See *ante*, p. 26.
[2] *Weigall* v. *Brome* (1833) 6 Sim. 99; *ante*, pp. 15, 25.
[3] See Radcliffe, *Real Property* (2nd ed., 1928), p. 28.
[4] *Post*, p. 319.

(1) The usual type of lease is the occupational lease, where the tenant holds at a rent or in consideration of a fine, or both, and occupies the property himself, or sub-lets it. This type is dealt with in this chapter.

(2) Sometimes leases are granted as a mere conveyancing device. Such leases are granted without a fine and at no rent, in order to provide security for the payment of money. The most important modern example is the lease granted by a mortgagor to the mortgagee as security for the money lent. In this case it is unusual for the lessee to take possession of the land. Such leases are dealt with under mortgages.[5]

Sect. 2. Terminology

It is important to be familiar with the terms used in the law of leases. A lease is sometimes referred to as a "demise" and the premises in question as the "premises demised." The term "tenancy" is normally used for interests lasting for a relatively short period only, while "lease" usually indicates a more enduring interest; there is no hard-and-fast division, and in this chapter "lease" normally includes "tenancy." "Lease" and "term of years" are virtually synonymous terms today; before 1926 a term of years could only be regarded as one kind of lease, since leases for lives were by no means unknown. Today, leases for lives have nearly all disappeared.[6] "Lease" is often used interchangeably for the document and the "term of years" or "leasehold interest" created by it, although strictly it merely means the document.

The grantor of a lease is known as the lessor, the person to whom it is granted as the lessee. On the grant of a lease, the lessor retains a reversion, which he may assign; similarly, the lessee may assign the lease. Instead of assigning the lease (*i.e.* transferring the property for the whole of the period for which it is held), the owner of the lease may grant a sub-lease (or underlease) for some shorter period, the parties to this sub-lease being known as the sub-lessor and sub-lessee respectively. Where the original lessor and original lessee have both assigned their interests, the new owners of the reversion and the lease are sometimes called the lessor and lessee, although it is better to keep these expressions for the original parties to the lease, and refer to the owners for the time being, whether original or by assignment, as the landlord and the tenant.

These expressions may be illustrated as follows:

$$
\begin{array}{ccc}
X & \longrightarrow & Y \\
\downarrow\ 99 & & \\
A & \longrightarrow & B \\
& \downarrow\ 21 & \\
& C & \longrightarrow\ D
\end{array}
$$

---

[5] See *post*, p. 441.
[6] *Post*, p. 319.

This diagram is the usual way of representing the following events. X grants a 99 years' lease to A and then assigns the reversion to Y. B takes an assignment of A's lease and grants a sub-lease to C for 21 years, C assigning his sub-lease to D. As to the 99 years' lease, X is the "lessor," Y is the "assignee of the reversion" or "landlord," and A the "lessee." B is in a dual position; as to the 99 years' lease, he is the "assignee" or "tenant" and as to the 21 years' lease he is the "sub-lessor" or "landlord." C is the "sub-lessee," and D the "assignee" of the sub-lease, or the "sub-tenant."

For the purpose of enforcing covenants it is important to note that "privity of contract" exists between X and A and between B and C, whilst "privity of estate" exists between Y and A, and then Y and B (having the same estates as were originally vested in X and A), and between B and D.[7]

Part 2

CREATION OF LEASES AND TENANCIES

Sect. 1. Essentials of a Lease or Tenancy

No lease or tenancy can be created unless four conditions are satisfied. They are (a) that the premises are sufficiently defined; (b) that the tenant has the right to exclusive possession of the premises during the term; (c) that the requirements as to duration are satisfied; and (d) that the proper formalities have been observed. Under a tenancy there is nearly always a requirement to pay rent, but this is not essential.[8] In recent years there has been much litigation on whether or not a tenancy has been created, for whereas a tenancy of a dwelling-house can be protected by the Rent Acts,[9] a mere licence to occupy the dwelling cannot. Many landlords have therefore sought to grant licences in lieu of tenancies, with varying success.

The four heads will be considered in turn.

A. Premises Sufficiently Defined

A lease or tenancy can exist only in relation to defined premises. Thus a contract by the owner of a building to store goods in them, though with liberty to change the rooms in which they are stored, at his convenience, can create no tenancy since no rights are given over any particular area.[10] But where the premises are clearly defined, the mere imposition of severe restrictions on the use that can be made of them will not negative a tenancy.[11]

---

[7] See *post*, pp. 348, 349.
[8] *Ashburn Anstalt* v. *Arnold* [1989] Ch. 1; and see L.P.A. 1925, s.205(1)(xxvii).
[9] For these, see *post*, pp. 531 *et seq.*
[10] *Interoven Stove Co. Ltd.* v. *Hibbard* [1936] 1 All E.R. 263; and see *Wells* v. *Kingston-upon-Hull Corporation* (1875) L.R. 10 C.P. 402.
[11] *Joel* v. *International Circus and Christmas Fair* (1920) 124 L.T. 459.

B. Right to Exclusive Possession

In determining whether a tenancy has been granted, the essential question is whether there has been the grant of a right to the exclusive possession of the premises. If there has, then provided the other requirements for a tenancy are satisfied, a tenancy will have been created.[12]

1. Right. The question is not whether it was intended to confer a right to exclusive possession, nor whether exclusive possession is in fact enjoyed, but whether a right to exclusive possession has in fact been given[13]; and this has to be determined from the substance of the transaction as a whole, though disregarding any provisions which are mere pretences or shams.[14] A pronged instrument for digging is a fork even if its maker insists that he intended to make a spade, and has done so.[15] What must be considered is what the parties have in fact done, and not what they intended, or pretended, to do. Their intention is important, however, in deciding whether or not they intended to enter into legal relations, or whether the transaction was a mere family arrangement or act of friendship or generosity.[16]

2. Exclusive possession. The right must be to "exclusive" possession, entitling the tenant to exclude all others (including the landlord) from the premises during the term.[17] Lodgers are not tenants, because the owner and his staff have unrestricted access to the room or rooms to provide attendance or services, and although the lodger has the right to be there he cannot call the place his own.[18] The same applies to occupants of old people's homes,[19] a local authority's hostel for homeless men,[20] and hotel rooms and bed-sitting rooms.[21]

3. Pretences or shams. In determining whether or not a tenancy has been granted, the court will ignore any provisions in the agreement which are mere pretences or shams seeking to negative a tenancy.[22] Thus provisions in a "licence" to occupy a small room which negated any right to exclusive possession, allowed the licensor (who retained a set of keys) to use and authorise others to use the room, and conferred no right to occupy the room from 10.30 until noon each day have been held to be mere pretences which

---

[12] *Street* v. *Mountford* [1985] A.C. 809. The authorities are fully considered in Megarry's *Rent Acts* (11th ed., 1989) and Second Supp. 1991.

[13] *Street* v. *Mountford, supra.*

[14] *Infra.*

[15] See *Street* v. *Mountford, supra*, at p. 819.

[16] See *Facchini* v. *Bryson* [1952] 1 T.L.R. 1386 at 1389; and see *Marcroft Wagons Ltd.* v. *Smith* [1951] 2 K.B. 496. See also *Street* v. *Mountford, supra*, at p. 826 as to other relationships.

[17] *Street* v. *Mountford* [1985] A.C. 809.

[18] *Ibid.* at p. 818.

[19] *Abbeyfield (Harpenden) Society Ltd.* v. *Woods* [1968] 1 W.L.R. 374.

[20] *Westminster City Council* v. *Clarke* [1992] 2 W.L.R. 229.

[21] *Luganda* v. *Service Hotels Ltd.* [1969] 2 Ch. 209 (see at p. 219).

[22] *Street* v. *Mountford* [1985] A.C. 809 at 825; *A.G. Securities* v. *Vaughan* [1990] 1 A.C. 417 at 462.

did not prevent a tenancy arising.[23] Again, where a cohabiting couple simultaneously made separate agreements to occupy a small flat on terms that they had no exclusive possession and that the use of the flat was to be in common with the landlord and others authorised by him, the two agreements, being interdependent, were held to make the couple joint tenants.[24] But independent agreements made at different times and on different terms which gave four persons the exclusive right to use a flat in common with each other made them mere licensees; and, lacking the four unities,[25] they could not in any case have been joint tenants.[26]

C. Requirements as to Duration

The general nature of an estate less than freehold has already been considered,[27] and details of the requisite duration of each particular type of lease or tenancy are set out below.[28] A lease cannot be for an uncertain period such as the duration of a war.[29]

D. Requisite Formalities

I. LEGAL LEASES

To create a legal estate after 1925, a lease or tenancy must not only grant a term of years absolute within section 1(1) of the Law of Property Act 1925[30] but also be made with the proper formalities.

1. Leases and tenancies. A lease cannot create a legal estate unless it is made by deed.[31] But there is an exception for a lease which—

  (i) takes effect in possession (*i.e.* starts forthwith),
 (ii) is for a term not exceeding three years, whether or not the lessee is given power to extend the term, and
(iii) is at the best rent reasonably obtainable without taking a fine.[32]

If all three conditions are complied with, a legal lease or tenancy can be created orally or in writing.

2. Contracts for leases and tenancies. Even if a lease or tenancy fell within the above exception, a contract to grant a lease or tenancy was formerly unenforceable by action unless it was sufficiently evidenced in writing or

---

[23] *Aslan* v. *Murphy (No.* 1) [1990] 1 W.L.R. 766; and see *Street* v. *Mountford, supra*, at p. 825.
[24] *Antoniades* v. *Villiers* [1990] 1 A.C. 417. But consider *Mikeover Ltd.* v. *Brady* (1989) 21 H.L.R. 513 (no joint tenancy as no joint obligation to pay the rent: *sed quaere*).
[25] See *ante*, p. 282.
[26] *A.G. Securities* v. *Vaughan* [1990] 1 A.C. 417.
[27] *Ante*, p. 26.
[28] *Post*, pp. 314–318.
[29] *Post*, p. 314.
[30] *Ante*, p. 74.
[31] L.P.A. 1925, ss.52(1), 205(1)(ii), (xxiii).
[32] *Ibid.* ss.52(1), (2)(d), 54(2); but see *post*, p. 322 (assignment).

supported by part performance.[33] But statute[34] has made two changes for contracts made after September 26, 1989. First, the contract is void unless it is actually made in writing[35]; and second, contracts for leases or tenancies within the above exception are exempt from this requirement,[36] and so may be made orally.

II. EQUITABLE LEASES

1. Informal lease void at law. A lease which did not satisfy the above requirements was void at law and passed no legal estate. However, although at law the lease was ineffective to create any tenancy, a tenancy at law might arise independently of the lease. For if the tenant took possession with the landlord's consent, a tenancy at will arose; and as soon as rent was paid and accepted, the tenancy at will was converted into a yearly or other periodic tenancy (depending on the way the rent was paid[37]), on such of the terms of the lease as were consistent with the periodic tenancy created. Thus if in 1890 a lease for 99 years was granted orally or merely in writing, the largest estate which the tenant could claim in a court of law was usually a yearly tenancy; and his claim to this depended not on the lease but upon his possession and the payment and acceptance of rent.

2. Effect as contract. Although such a lease itself failed to create any legal estate, it was not entirely ineffective, for it might be treated as a contract to grant the lease. A lease is clearly distinct from a contract to grant a lease: the difference is between "I hereby grant you a lease" and "I hereby agree that I will grant you a lease." Nevertheless, both law and equity concurred in treating an imperfect lease as a contract to grant a lease, provided it was made for value and was sufficiently evidenced in writing, or, so far as equity was concerned, was supported by a sufficient act of part performance.[38] Today, the requirements of evidence in writing or part performance have been replaced by a requirement that the lease should actually be in writing.[39] The attitude of equity was particularly important, for under the doctrine of *Parker* v. *Taswell*[40] equity would first treat an imperfect lease as a contract to grant the lease, and then order specific performance of the contract.[41] Once the actual lease had been granted in pursuance of the decree of specific performance, the position of the parties was the same for the future as if the lease had been a legal lease granted by deed in the first place.

3. Walsh v. Lonsdale.[42] The rights of the parties under an imperfect lease

[33] *Ante*, p. 116.
[34] L.P.(M.P.)A. 1989.
[35] *Ante*, p. 117.
[36] L.P.(M.P.)A. 1989, s.2(5)(a).
[37] *Martin* v. *Smith* (1874) L.R. 9 Ex. 50; *post*, p. 317.
[38] See *Tidey* v. *Mollett* (1864) 16 C.B.(N.S.) 298; but see *Harte* v. *Williams* [1934] 1 K.B. 201.
[39] L.P.(M.P.)A. 1989, s.2, applying to contracts made after September 26, 1989: see *ante*, p. 117.
[40] (1858) 2 De G. & J. 559.
[41] *Zimbler* v. *Abrahams* [1903] 1 K.B. 577.
[42] (1882) 21 Ch.D.9.

were thus clear whenever specific performance had been decreed. What was not so clear was the position if, as was far more often the case, no decree of specific performance had been granted but the parties were entitled to obtain one. In equity, the principle is "Equity looks on that as done which ought to be done," so that the parties were treated as if the lease had been granted. But there was no such principle at law, and, indeed, it would have been strange if the positive requirements of statute could have been so easily circumvented. Yet equity might intervene to restrain the parties from exercising their legal rights in opposition to their equitable obligations, and the Judicature Act 1873[43] provided that where the rules of law and equity conflicted, the rules of equity should prevail. Accordingly, in *Walsh* v. *Lonsdale*[44] it was held that the relationship of the parties was the same as if the lease had actually been granted.

In that case L agreed in writing to grant by a deed a lease of a mill to T for seven years, one of the terms being that T should on demand pay a year's rent in advance. No deed was executed, but T was let into possession and for a year and a half paid rent quarterly, although not in advance. L then demanded a year's rent in advance, and on T's refusal to pay, distrained for it. T then brought an action for damages for wrongful distress, and for specific performance of the agreement.

T contended that distress was a legal, and not an equitable, remedy, and that as at law he was only a yearly tenant with no obligation to pay rent in advance, L could not distrain for the rent.[45] It was held, however, that since the distress would have been legal had the lease agreed upon been granted by deed, and since equity treated the parties as if this had been done, the distress was lawful in equity; the equitable rule prevailed over the rule at law and so even at law T could not complain of the distress. This principle applies even if the lease to T was granted while L had no legal estate in the land but only a contract to purchase it; for equity would enforce both contracts.[46]

4. Differences between legal and equitable leases. The effect of *Walsh* v. *Lonsdale* is to render an enforceable agreement for a lease very nearly as good as a legal lease, and the same applies to an imperfect lease which is enforceable as an agreement for lease. There are still, however, some points of difference.[47]

(a) *Specific performance.* The rule depends upon the willingness of equity to grant the discretionary remedy of specific performance, so that if an agreement for a lease is one of which the court will not grant specific performance (as where the tenant is in breach of his obligations to the

[43] s.25(11), then J.A. 1925, s.44, now Supreme Court Act 1981, s.49.
[44] *Supra.*
[45] See *Manchester Brewery Co.* v. *Coombs* [1901] 2 Ch. 608 at 617, 618.
[46] *Industrial Properties (Barton Hill) Ltd.* v. *Associated Electrical Industries Ltd.* [1977] Q.B. 580.
[47] See M. & W. 642–644.

landlord and so does not come to equity with clean hands),[48] the position under it will be precarious. Further, if the court lacks jurisdiction to order specific performance,[49] a tenant will not be able to enforce the agreement in that court,[50] though he could defend proceedings by the landlord which ignored the agreement, as the court can give effect to an equitable defence.[51] In any case, a tenant who has gone into possession and paid rent may rely on his yearly or other periodic tenancy.[52]

(b) *Easements*. Certain easements and similar rights may be created on a grant of a legal estate which will not be created by a mere contract.[53]

(c) *The burden of covenants*. The doctrine of *Walsh* v. *Lonsdale* does not treat an enforceable agreement for a lease as being as good as a lease as regards third parties, but only as regards the actual parties to the agreement. As between them, there is privity of contract; and as the benefit of a contract is assignable, an assignee from either of them can take the benefit of the covenants in the lease. But assignees will not be bound by the covenants, for the burden of a contract does not bind assignees, and there is no privity of estate which can make the burden run with the estate, as it would if a lease (and so an estate) had been granted.[54] However, where a yearly or other periodic tenancy has arisen from the tenant taking possession and paying rent, the burden of any covenants that are consistent with such a tenancy will run with it.[55]

(d) *Third parties*. The rights of a tenant under an agreement for a lease, being merely equitable, are subject to the same frailty as all equitable interests, namely, they are void against a bona fide purchaser for value of a legal estate without notice of them. Thus if L agrees to grant a lease for seven years to T and then grants a legal lease or a legal mortgage to X, or conveys the legal fee simple to him, T's rights will be unenforceable against X if X took his estate in good faith and for value without notice of T's rights. Before 1926, the usual rules of actual, constructive and imputed notice applied[56]; and if T was in possession of the land, that would normally suffice to give notice of his rights to X.[57] The same rules apply after 1925, save that if T's agreement was made after 1925, it must be registered as a land charge. Registration is deemed to be notice to the whole world; but if the agreement should have been registered and has not, it will be void

---

[48] *Coatsworth* v. *Johnson* (1886) 55 L.J.Q.B. 220 at 222. But see (1987) 7 Oxf. J.L.S. 60 (S. Gardner).
[49] See *e.g.* County Courts Act 1984, s.23(d).
[50] *Foster* v. *Reeves* [1892] 2 Q.B. 255; contrast *Cornish* v. *Brook Green Laundry Ltd.* [1959] 1 Q.B. 394.
[51] *Kingswood Estate Co. Ltd.* v. *Anderson* [1963] 2 Q.B. 169.
[52] *Bell Street Investments Ltd.* v. *Wood* [1970] E.G.D. 812.
[53] Under L.P.A. 1925, s.62: see *post*, p. 381.
[54] See *post*, p. 353.
[55] *Doe* d. *Thomson* v. *Amey* (1840) 12 A. & E. 476.
[56] *Ante*, p. 60.
[57] See *Hunt* v. *Luck* [1902] 1 Ch. 428 at 432, 433.

against a purchaser for money or money's worth of a legal estate in the land.[58] Actual knowledge by the purchaser is immaterial in these cases.[59]

In practice, a written agreement for a lease is virtually as secure as an actual lease, especially if it has been registered, thus ensuring that the whole world has notice of it and so curing the principal defect to which equitable interests are subject. In the case of tenancies for a relatively short period at a rack rent it is usual to accept a mere agreement and not to register it, relying upon the tenant's evident possession of the land to put any prudent purchaser on inquiry; and a purchaser will be bound by any periodic tenancy at common law arising from the payment and acceptance of rent.[60] In the case of registered land, any tenant in actual occupation or in receipt of the rents and profits will be protected as holding an overriding interest.[61]

Sect. 2. Types of Leases and Tenancies

A. Classification

Leases and tenancies may be classified under the five following heads.

1. Leases for a fixed period

(a) *Certainty of term.* A lease may be granted for any certain period of certain duration, no matter how long or short. Leases for a week or for 3,000 years are equally valid. Both the commencement and the duration of the term must either be certain or else be rendered certain before the lease takes effect.[62] Thus a lease for 99 years from January 1 next complies with this rule, and so does a lease from the determination of an existing tenancy for as many years as X shall name, once X has named the period; but a tenancy granted during wartime "for the duration of the war" does not.[63] An Act of 1944[64] converted tenancies for the duration of the current war or emergency into valid tenancies for 10 years determinable after the war or emergency by (usually) one month's notice; but there is nothing in the Act to rescue tenancies for other uncertain periods, *e.g.* until the landlord requires the land for road widening,[65] or "so long as the company is trading,"[66] from the rule that makes them void. The rule applies even if each party has been given power to determine the tenancy during the uncertain period,[67] and even

---

[58] L.C.A. 1972, s.4(6), (7), replacing L.C.A. 1925, s.13(2); *Hollington Bros. Ltd.* v. *Rhodes* [1951] 2 T.L.R. 691; for land charges, see *ante,* pp. 77 *et seq.*
[59] *Ante,* p. 88.
[60] *Ante,* p. 311.
[61] *Ante,* pp. 103 *et seq.*
[62] *Harvey* v. *Pratt* [1965] 1 W.L.R. 1025.
[63] *Lace* v. *Chantler* [1944] K.B. 368.
[64] Validation of War-Time Leases Act 1944.
[65] *Prudential Assurance Co. Ltd.* v. *London Residuary Body* [1992] 3 W.L.R. 279.
[66] *Birrell* v. *Carey* (1989) 58 P. & C.R. 184.
[67] *Prudential Assurance Co. Ltd.* v. *London Residuary Body, supra,* overruling *Ashburn Anstalt* v. *Arnold* [1989] Ch. 1.

though the tenancy is a yearly or other periodic tenancy granted subject to a provision negating the power of determination[68] for an uncertain period.[69] Where the rule invalidates a lease but a periodic tenancy arises from the payment and acceptance of rent, that tenancy will not incorporate any provisions for determination in the void lease that are inconsistent with the periodic tenancy.[70]

(b) *Reversionary leases.* Before 1926, there was no restriction upon the length of time that might elapse before the term began; a lease could thus be granted in 1917 to commence in 1946,[71] such a lease being known as a reversionary lease. The perpetuity rule was not infringed by such a grant, for the lessee took a vested interest forthwith; only the vesting in possession was postponed.[71A] However, the grant of a term to take effect more than 21 years from the instrument creating it is void if made after 1925 at a rent or in consideration of a fine, and the same applies to any contract made after 1925 to create such a term.[72] Thus the grant of a lease in 1992 to commence in 2020, or a contract made in 1992 to grant in 1993 a lease to commence in 2020 is void; but there is nothing to invalidate a contract made in 1992 to grant in 2020 a lease to commence forthwith, for the lease is not reversionary.[73] An option in a lease for 35 years to renew it on its determination is similarly not invalidated,[74] and grants or contracts made before 1926 and leases taking effect in equity under a settlement (*e.g.* as portions terms[75]) are not affected.

(c) *Interesse termini.* Before 1926, there was a common law rule that a lessee acquired no actual estate in the land until he had taken possession during the term of the lease. Until he had exercised his right to take possession, he had a mere *interesse termini* (an interest in the term), and not an actual lease. This troublesome doctrine has been abolished in respect of all leases, whether made before or after 1925.[76]

(d) *Determination.* The general rule is that a lease for a fixed period automatically determines when the fixed period expires; but there are statutory exceptions to this rule.[77]

2. Yearly tenancies

(a) *Creation.* A yearly tenancy is one which continues from year to year

---

[68] See *post*, p. 317.
[69] *Prudential Assurance Co. Ltd.* v. *London Residuary Body, supra,* overruling *Re Midland Railway Co.'s Agreement* [1971] Ch. 725.
[70] *Prudential Assurance Co. Ltd.* v. *London Residuary Body, supra.*
[71] *Mann, Crossman & Paulin Ltd.* v. *Registrar of Land Registry* [1918] 1 Ch. 202.
[71A] *Ibid.*
[72] L.P.A. 1925, s.149(3).
[73] (1947) 63 L.Q.R. 20; *Re Strand and Savoy Properties Ltd.* [1960] Ch. 582; *Weg Motors Ltd.* v. *Hales* [1962] Ch. 49.
[74] *Re Strand and Savoy Properties Ltd., supra.*
[75] See M. & W. 413, 647.
[76] L.P.A. 1925, s.149(1), (2). See M. & W. 647, 648.
[77] See *post*, pp. 524 *et seq.*

indefinitely until determined by proper notice, notwithstanding the death of either party or the assignment of his interest. Continuation each year depends on the will of the parties as shown by their omission to serve a notice to quit; and in retrospect it is considered a single tenancy and not a succession of tenancies.[78] Such a tenancy may be created either expressly or by implication. Thus an express grant to A "from year to year" or "as a yearly tenant" will create a yearly tenancy. It should be noted, however, that a grant "to X for one year and thereafter from year to year" will give X a tenancy for at least two years; for he has been given a definite term of one year followed by a yearly tenancy which can be determined only at the end of the first year thereof.[79]

A yearly tenancy arises by implication whenever a person occupies land with the owner's consent in circumstances indicating a tenancy, and rent measured with reference to a year is paid and accepted, unless there is sufficient evidence to show that some other kind of tenancy was intended.[80] A yearly tenancy also arises when a tenant under a lease for a fixed term holds over (*i.e.* remains in possession at the end of his term) and, in circumstances indicating a tenancy,[81] rent is paid and accepted on a yearly basis. In this case, the tenant will hold under such of the terms of the expired lease as are not inconsistent with a yearly holding.[82] Thus covenants to repair,[83] or to carry on some specified trade on the premises[84] and provisos for re-entry by the landlord on non-payment of rent[85] may be implied in a yearly tenancy. But a covenant to paint every three years[86] and a provision for two years' notice to quit[87] are inconsistent with a yearly tenancy and cannot be implied in this way.

The payment of rent at more frequent intervals than a year will not prevent a yearly tenancy from arising by implication. The test is the period by reference to which the parties calculated the rent. Thus an agreement for "£1040 per annum payable weekly" prima facie creates a yearly tenancy; had the agreement been for "£20 per week," a weekly tenancy would be presumed, despite the fact that in each case the tenant would in fact have made the same payments, namely, £20 every week.[88]

(b) *Determination.* A yearly tenancy may be determined by such notice and at such time as the parties agree.[89] Different periods for the landlord and

---

[78] *Hammersmith and Fulham L.B.C.* v. *Monk* [1992] 1 A.C. 478; for joint tenants, see *ante*, p. 283.
[79] *Re Searle* [1912] 1 Ch. 610.
[80] *Kemp* v. *Derrett* (1814) 3 Camp. 510; *Javad* v. *Aqil* [1991] 1 W.L.R. 1007.
[81] *Clarke* v. *Grant* [1950] 1 K.B. 104; *Longrigg, Burrough & Trounson* v. *Smith* [1979] E.G.D. 472.
[82] *Dougal* v. *McCarthy* [1893] 1 Q.B. 736.
[83] *Wyatt* v. *Cole* (1877) 36 L.T. 613.
[84] *Sanders* v. *Karnell* (1858) 1 F. & F. 356.
[85] *Thomas* v. *Packer* (1857) 1 H. & N. 669.
[86] *Pinero* v. *Judson* (1829) 6 Bing. 206.
[87] *Tooker* v. *Smith* (1857) 1 H. & N. 732.
[88] See *Adler* v. *Blackman* [1953] 1 Q.B. 146.
[89] *Re Threlfall* (1880) 16 Ch.D. 274 at 281, 282.

tenant may be agreed, and it may be provided that the landlord should be entitled to give notice only in certain circumstances,[90] *e.g.* if he requires the premises for his own occupation.[91] But a term that one party should not be entitled to give notice at all is void as repugnant to the nature of a periodic tenancy.[92] In default of such agreement, the tenancy can be determined by at least half a year's notice expiring at the end of a completed year of the tenancy. The meaning of "half a year" depends on the day upon which the tenancy began. If the tenancy began on one of the usual quarter-days (Lady Day (March 25), Midsummer Day (June 24), Michaelmas (September 29)[93] or Christmas (December 25)), "half a year" means "two quarters"; otherwise "half a year" means 182 days.[94] Thus if a yearly tenancy began on March 25, notice to quit given on or before September 29 is good, although it is less than 182 days[95]; and if a yearly tenancy began on September 29, notice must be given on or before March 25, even though it is more than 182 days. In each of these cases, the tenancy began on a quarter-day[96]; had it started on some other day, *e.g.* March 26, at least 182 days' notice would have been required.[97] It will be noted that in neither case is the period of the notice necessarily six months, although of course the parties may agree that such shall be the notice required.

As has been seen,[98] a notice to quit for a periodic tenancy is not invalid merely because it has been given by only one of joint landlords or joint tenants.

3. Weekly, monthly and other periodic tenancies. A tenancy from week to week, month to month, quarter to quarter, and the like (including a tenancy for some artificial period, such as for successive periods of 364 days[99]) can be created in a similar way to a yearly tenancy, namely, either by express agreement, or by inference, such as that arising from the payment and acceptance of rent measured with reference to a week, month or quarter, as the case may be, in circumstances indicating a tenancy.[1] In general, the position of the parties under such a tenancy is similar to that under a yearly tenancy, save that notice of termination is not half a period, but a full period, expiring at the end of a completed period, subject to any contrary agreement between the parties.[2] This is the "corresponding date" rule, under which

[90] *Re Midland Railway Co.'s Agreement* [1971] Ch. 725.
[91] As in *Breams Property Investment Co. Ltd.* v. *Stroulger* [1948] 2 K.B. 1.
[92] *Centaploy Ltd.* v. *Matlodge Ltd.* [1974] Ch. 1.
[93] A mnemonic is that for these three the last digit is the same as the number of letters in the month.
[94] *Anon.* (1575) 3 Dy. 345a.
[95] *Doe* d. *Durant* v. *Doe* (1830) 6 Bing. 574.
[96] *Morgan* v. *Davies* (1878) 3 C.P.D. 260.
[97] Co.Litt. 135b.
[98] *Ante*, p. 283.
[99] *Land Settlement Association Ltd.* v. *Carr* [1944] K.B. 657.
[1] *Cole* v. *Kelly* [1920] 2 K.B. 106 at 132; *Clarke* v. *Grant* [1950] 1 K.B. 104; *Longrigg, Burrough & Trounson* v. *Smith* [1979] E.G.D. 472.
[2] *Queen's Club Gardens Estates Ltd.* v. *Bignell* [1924] 1 K.B. 117; *Lemon* v. *Lardeur* [1946] K.B. 613.

"month" normally means calendar month, despite the differing lengths.[3] Thus in the absence of any contrary agreement, a weekly tenancy commencing on a Monday can be determined either by notice given on or before one Monday to expire on the following Monday,[4] or, since a week starting on a Monday is complete at midnight on the following Sunday, by notice given on or before one Sunday to expire on the following Sunday.[5] But for dwellings, not less than four weeks' notice in writing must be given, containing (if given by the landlord) prescribed information relating to orders for possession and legal advice; and this now extends to residential licences, with certain exceptions, such as rent free or family sharing licences.[6]

4. Tenancies at will. A tenancy at will arises whenever a tenant, with the consent of the landlord, occupies *qua* tenant (and not merely as a servant or agent) on the terms that either party may determine the tenancy at any time. In some cases the tenant holds rent free, as where the vendor of a fee simple, owing to some delay in completion, lets the purchaser into possession of the property before the conveyance has been executed.[7] But unless the parties agree that the tenancy shall be rent free, the landlord is entitled to compensation for the use and occupation of the land[8]; and if a rent is fixed the landlord may distrain for it in the usual way.

A tenancy at will comes to an end when either party does any act incompatible with the continuance of the tenancy, as where the tenant commits voluntary waste,[9] or the landlord enters the land and cuts trees or carries away stone,[10] or either party gives notice to the other determining the tenancy. The tenancy is also determined if either party dies or assigns his interest in the land.[11] Essentially, the tenancy is a personal relation between the landlord and his tenant.[12]

If a tenancy at will is created without any agreement as to payment of rent, and rent is subsequently paid and accepted upon some regular periodical basis, a yearly, monthly or other periodical tenancy will normally arise under the rules set out under heads 2 and 3 above, unless the circumstances indicate otherwise.[13]

5. Tenancies at sufferance. A tenancy at sufferance arises where a tenant, having entered upon land under a valid tenancy, holds over without the

[3] See *Dodds* v. *Walker* [1981] 1 W.L.R. 1027; *E. J. Riley Investments Ltd.* v. *Eurostile Holdings Ltd.* [1985] 1 W.L.R. 1139.
[4] *Newman* v. *Slade* [1926] 2 K.B. 328.
[5] *Bathavon R.D.C.* v. *Carlile* [1958] 1 Q.B. 461.
[6] Protection from Eviction Act 1977, ss.3A, 5; H.A. 1988, ss.31, 32; S.I. 1988 No. 2201; *Schnabel* v. *Allard* [1967] 1 Q.B. 627.
[7] *Howard* v. *Shaw* (1841) 8 M. & W. 118. See also *Hagee (London) Ltd.* v. *A. B. Erikson & Larson* [1976] Q.B. 209.
[8] Distress for Rent Act 1737, s.11; *Howard* v. *Shaw, supra.*
[9] *Countess of Shrewsbury's Case* (1600) 5 Co.Rep. 13b.
[10] *Turner* v. *Doe* d. *Bennett* (1842) 9 M. & W. 643.
[11] See *Pinhorn* v. *Souster* (1853) 8 Exch. 763 at 772.
[12] *Wheeler* v. *Mercer* [1957] A.C. 416 at 427, 428.
[13] *Javad* v. *Aqil* [1991] 1 W.L.R. 1007.

landlord's assent or dissent.[14] Such a tenant differs from a trespasser in that his original entry was lawful, and from a tenant at will in that his tenancy exists without the landlord's assent. No rent, as such, is payable, but the tenant is liable to pay compensation for his use and occupation of the land.[15] The tenancy may be determined at any time, and may be converted into a yearly or other periodic tenancy in the usual way, *e.g.* if rent is paid and accepted with reference to a year in circumstances where the parties intended there to be a tenancy.

There are statutory penalties for tenants who hold over after giving or receiving notice to quit:

(a) *Double annual value.* If the landlord gives the tenant written notice to quit and the tenant·is a tenant for life or for years, the tenant is liable to pay the landlord a sum calculated at double the annual value of the land in respect of the period for which he holds over after the notice expired; this can be enforced by action but not otherwise, *e.g.* not by distress.[16] This provision applies to tenancies from year to year as well as to tenancies for fixed terms of years or for a year certain, but not to weekly,[17] or, no doubt, other periodic tenancies.

(b) *Double rent.* If the tenant gives the landlord written or oral notice to quit, then, whatever the type of tenancy, the tenant is liable to pay double rent in respect of the period for which he holds over after the notice expired; payment can be enforced by action or distress.[18]

The curiously differing terms of these aged provisions will be noticed. The rent and the annual value may be the same, but they often differ, as where premises have been let at a reduced rent in consideration of a fine.

B. Statutory Modifications

Although the parties to a lease can in general create a lease for such periods as they think fit, statute has made some modifications to this position.

1. Leases for lives. By the Law of Property Act 1925,[19] a lease at a rent or a fine for life or lives, or for a term of years determinable with a life or lives or on the marriage of the lessee, is converted into a term of 90 years, whether it was granted before or after 1925; a contract for such a lease is treated in a similar way. The lease continues even after the death or marriage, as the case may be, although either party may determine it thereafter (but not before) by serving on the other one month's written notice to expire on one of the quarter-days applicable to the tenancy, or, if no special quarter-days

[14] See *Remon* v. *City of London Real Property Co. Ltd.* [1921] 1 K.B. 49 at 58.
[15] *Leigh* v. *Dickeson* (1884) 15 Q.B.D. 60.
[16] L. & T.A. 1730, s.1.
[17] *Lloyd* v. *Rosbee* (1810) 2 Camp. 453.
[18] Distress for Rent Act 1737, s.18.
[19] s.149(6).

are applicable, on one of the usual quarter-days. Thus leases at a rent or fine granted—

"to A for life,"
"to B for 10 years if he so long lives," and
"to C for 99 years if he so long remains a bachelor"

are all converted into terms which will continue for 90 years unless by the proper notice they are determined on any quarter-day (not necessarily the first) after the event has occurred. But these provisions do not apply to a lease which takes effect in equity under a settlement.[20]

2. Perpetually renewable leases. A perpetually renewable lease was a lease which gave the tenant the right to renew it for another period as often as it expired; usually the tenant had to make some payment on exercising this right. A lease will be perpetually renewable if there is a covenant to renew it on the terms of the existing lease "including this covenant for renewal,"[21] but not if the inclusion of the covenant for renewal is part of a separate obligation.[22] By the Law of Property Act 1922,[23] all such leases existing at the end of 1925 were converted into terms of 2000 years, calculated from the beginning of the existing terms; and perpetually renewable leases granted after 1925 take effect as terms of 2000 years from the date fixed for the commencement of the term. Any perpetually renewable sub-lease created out of a perpetually renewable lease is converted into a term of 2000 years less one day. The 2000-year lease is subject to the same terms as the original lease, with the following modifications.

(a) *Termination.* The tenant for the time being (but not the landlord) may terminate the lease on any date upon which, but for the conversion by the Act, the lease would have expired if it had not been renewed, provided he gives at least 10 days' written notice to the landlord.

(b) *Assignment.* Every assignment or devolution of the lease must be registered with the landlord or his solicitor or agent within six months, and a fee of one guinea paid.

(c) *Breach of covenant.* A tenant who assigns the lease is not liable for breaches of covenant committed after the assignment. The general rule is that the original lessee is liable for all breaches occurring during the term, even if they occur after he has assigned the lease[24]; perpetually renewable leases are a statutory exception to this rule.

(d) *Fine.* Any fine or other payment for renewal for which the lease provides is converted into additional rent and spread over the period be-

[20] L.P.A. 1925 ss.149(6)(a), 205(1)(xxvi); S.L.A. 1925 s.117(1)(xxiv).
[21] *Parkus* v. *Greenwood* [1950] Ch. 644; *Caerphilly Concrete Products Ltd.* v. *Owen* [1972] 1 W.L.R. 372.
[22] *Marjorie Burnett Ltd.* v. *Barclay* (1980) 258 E.G. 642.
[23] s.145 and 15th Sched.
[24] See *post*, p. 350.

tween the renewal dates, except where the lease is granted after 1925, when the obligation for payment is void.

It should be noted that the landlord has no right to determine the lease at the renewal dates. Before 1926, if L granted T a lease for 21 years with a perpetual right of renewal, it was T alone who had the right to decide each 21 years whether or not to renew the lease. This position is preserved, save that now the lease continues unless determined, instead of requiring renewal.

3. Over-lengthy renewals. A contract made after 1925 to renew a lease for over 60 years from its termination is void.[25] This is aimed at single renewals, not perpetual renewals, and does not affect contracts made before 1926.

4. Reversionary leases. A lease at a rent or a fine cannot be granted after 1925 to commence at too distant a future date. This has already been dealt with.[26]

C. Estoppel

1. Estoppel. On the grant of a lease or tenancy, both landlord and tenant and their successors in title are in general mutually estopped from denying the validity of the transaction. Neither landlord nor tenant will be permitted to assert that the tenancy which they have purported to create is invalid,[27] and this is so even if the tenancy is merely oral.[28] The tenant is still estopped from denying his landlord's title after going out of possession and so can still be sued on repairing covenants, unless evicted by title paramount.[29] But except in the case of companies within the Companies Acts,[30] this doctrine does not prevent a corporation from contending that it had no power to grant or receive a tenancy, for estoppel cannot validate an *ultra vires* act.[31]

2. Tenancy by estoppel. One consequence of this rule is that if the landlord in fact has no estate in the land, then although the lease or tenancy can confer no actual estate on the tenant, and cannot be effective against third parties,[32] it is good between the parties to it and their successors in title.[33] Both landlord and tenant will be estopped from denying the validity of their lease or tenancy; they cannot "blow hot and cold" by claiming that the transaction was valid when entered into, and yet asserting subsequently that it was a nullity.

[25] L.P.A. 1922, 15th Sched.
[26] *Ante*, p. 315.
[27] See *Cuthbertson* v. *Irving* (1859) 4 H. & N. 742; (1860) 6 H. & N. 135.
[28] *E. H. Lewis & Son Ltd.* v. *Morelli* [1948] 2 All E.R. 1021.
[29] *Industrial Properties (Barton Hill) Ltd.* v. *Associated Electrical Industries Ltd.* [1977] Q.B. 580.
[30] Companies Act 1985, s.35, as substituted by Companies Act 1989, s.108.
[31] *Rhyl U.D.C.* v. *Rhyl Amusements Ltd.* [1959] 1 W.L.R. 465.
[32] *Tadman* v. *Henman* [1893] 2 Q.B. 168.
[33] See *E. H. Lewis & Son Ltd.* v. *Morelli, supra.*

No tenancy by estoppel arises, however, if the lessor had a legal interest (as distinct from an equitable interest[34]) in the land when he granted the lease. If his interest was greater than the tenancy, the lease takes effect in the ordinary way; if it was equal to or smaller than the tenancy, the grant of the lease operates as an assignment of the lessor's interest.[35] Thus if L grants T a lease for 99 years, T will take a lease for 99 years by estoppel if L had no interest in the land when the lease was granted. But if L had a lease for 10 years at that time, the lease for 99 years will operate as an assignment to T of L's lease for 10 years.

3. Feeding the estoppel. If there is a tenancy by estoppel, and subsequently the landlord acquires an interest in the land out of which the tenancy could have been created (*e.g.* the fee simple), this is said to "feed the estoppel." From that moment the lease becomes fully effective, giving the tenant an actual estate in the land.[36] This formerly created difficulties if the landlord purchased the land on mortgage. Theoretically, the legal estate vested in the landlord an instant before he mortgaged the land; and in that instant the estoppel was fed, and so the tenancy would bind the mortgagee.[37] But theory has yielded to convenience, and now the transactions are treated as being simultaneous, so that the mortgagee takes free from the tenancy.[38]

Part 3

ASSIGNMENT OF LEASES AND TENANCIES

In order to effect a legal assignment of a lease, a deed must be employed,[39] even if the lease has been created by word of mouth, *e.g.* a yearly tenancy in possession at a rack rent.[40] However, on principles similar to those applicable to the creation of leases,[41] an assignment in writing will be effective in equity, though only as between assignor and assignee. Thus, unless estopped from so doing, the assignee may deny liability to the landlord on the covenants of the lease since there will be no privity of estate between them save in respect of any periodic tenancy that arises from the payment and acceptance of rent.[42] On an assignment the assignor can reserve a right of entry to ensure compliance by the assignee and his successors with

[34] *Universal Permanent B.S.* v. *Cooke* [1952] Ch. 95 at 102 (tenancy by estoppel on letting by purchaser before completion).
[35] *Beardman* v. *Wilson* (1868) L.R. 4 C.P. 57; *Wollaston* v. *Hakewill* (1841) 3 Man. & G. 297 at 323.
[36] *Macley* v. *Nutting* [1949] 2 K.B. 55.
[37] *Church of England B.S.* v. *Piskor* [1954] Ch. 553.
[38] *Abbey National B.S.* v. *Cann* [1991] 1 A.C. 56.
[39] L.P.A. 1925, s.52(1), replacing R.P.A. 1845, s.3.
[40] *Crago* v. *Julian* [1992] 1 W.L.R. 372.
[41] *Ante*, p. 311.
[42] *Rodenhurst Estates Ltd.* v. *W. H. Barnes Ltd.* [1936] 2 All E.R. 3.

covenants in the assignment.[43] Other matters concerning assignments are dealt with below.[44]

The grant of sub-leases is governed by the rules relating to the grant of leases.[45]

Part 4

DETERMINATION OF TENANCIES

A lease or tenancy may come to an end in the following ways.

(1) By expiry.
(2) By notice.
(3) By forfeiture.
(4) By surrender.
(5) By merger.
(6) By becoming a satisfied term.
(7) By enlargement.
(8) By disclaimer.
(9) By frustration.

Sect. 1. By Expiry

As has been seen,[46] a lease or tenancy for a fixed period automatically determines when the fixed period expires, with certain exceptions. In some cases the tenant may be entitled to be granted a new lease or to remain in possession as a statutory tenant.[47]

Sect. 2. By Notice

A lease or tenancy for a fixed period cannot be determined by notice unless this is expressly agreed upon. Thus a lease for a substantial term such as 21 years often contains provisions enabling the tenant to determine it at the end of the seventh or fourteenth year, in which case the length of the notice required, the time when it is to be given, and other matters of this kind, depend on the terms of the lease. In the absence of any such provision the lease will continue for the full period.

Yearly, weekly, monthly and other periodical tenancies can be determined by notice. These provisions, and the determination of tenancies at will and at sufferance, have already been considered.[48]

Many periodic tenants have statutory protection against eviction.[49]

---

[43] *Shiloh Spinners Ltd.* v. *Harding* [1973] A.C. 691.
[44] *Post*, pp. 343, 350, 354, 355.
[45] *Ante*, pp. 308 *et seq.*
[46] *Ante*, p. 315.
[47] *Post*, pp. 523 *et seq.*
[48] *Ante*, pp. 315–318.
[49] See *post*, pp. 522 *et seq*

Sect. 3. By Forfeiture

A. Right to Forfeit

A landlord's right to forfeit a lease (*i.e.* enforce a forfeiture of it) may arise under three heads.

1. Forfeiture clause. Nearly every lease contains a list of things which the tenant shall and shall not do, and these may be framed as conditions or as covenants. If, as is normally the case, they are framed as covenants (*e.g.* "The tenant hereby covenants with the landlord as follows . . ."), the landlord has no right to forfeit the lease if they are broken unless the lease contains an express provision for forfeiture on breach of a covenant.[50] There is no necessary connection between the tenant failing to perform a covenant made by him and the determination of the lease; every well-drawn lease consequently contains a forfeiture clause which in a legal lease creates a legal right of re-entry,[51] making the lease voidable at the landlord's option if a covenant is broken.

2. Breach of condition. If the tenant's obligations are worded as conditions, however (*e.g.* if the lease is granted "upon condition that" or "provided always that" certain things are done or not done), the lease may be forfeited on breach of condition even if there is no forfeiture clause.[52] In such a case, the continuance of the lease has been made conditional upon the tenant performing his obligations, and upon breach of one of them the lease becomes voidable at the landlord's option; but if the landlord does not treat the lease as forfeited, the tenant cannot set up his breach in order to avoid his liability under the lease.[53]

3. Denial of title. If a tenant clearly and unambiguously denies his landlord's title to the whole (and not merely part) of the land,[54] as by asserting (even orally) that he or some third party is the true owner, the landlord is forthwith entitled to forfeit the tenancy.[55] But a mere denial of title in a pleading in an action merely puts the other party to proof of his case and so works no forfeiture, especially if it is withdrawn before the landlord elects to take advantage of it.[56]

---

[50] *Doe* d. *Willson* v. *Phillips* (1824) 2 Bing. 13. For proposals for reforming the law of forfeiture, see (1985) Law Com. No. 142.

[51] See *ante*, p. 76.

[52] See *Doe* d. *Lockwood* v. *Clarke* (1807) 8 East 185.

[53] See *Doe* d. *Bryan* v. *Bancks* (1821) 4 B. & Ald. 401; *Roberts* v. *Davey* (1833) 4 B. & Ad. 664.

[54] *W. G. Clark* (*Properties*) *Ltd.* v. *Dupre Properties Ltd.* [1992] Ch. 297.

[55] *Wisbech St. Mary Parish Council* v. *Lilley* [1956] 1 W.L.R. 121. *Quaere* whether the provisions as to notice and relief apply: see *post*, p. 330.

[56] *Warner* v. *Sampson* [1959] 1 Q.B. 297; and see *post*, p. 330.

B. Waiver of Breach

Even if the landlord has shown that he is treating the lease as forfeited, he may subsequently prevent himself from proceeding with the forfeiture if he waives the breach of covenant; and *a fortiori* a waiver of the breach may take place before the landlord has shown that he is treating the lease as forfeited. Waiver may be express or implied. It will be implied if—

(i) the landlord is aware of the acts or omissions of the tenant giving rise to the right of forfeiture, and
(ii) the landlord does some unequivocal act recognising the continued existence of the lease.[57]

To constitute a waiver, both elements must be present. The landlord will be treated as having the knowledge of his managing agents or of porters who are under a duty to inform him[58]; but mere suspicion is not knowledge.[59] A waiver will be implied where a landlord, with knowledge of the breach, distrains for rent, whether due before or after the breach,[60] or demands or sues for or accepts rent falling due after the breach,[61] even if the rent is accepted "without prejudice"[62] or by the mistake of a clerk of the landlord's agents.[63] Waiver is a matter of law, not intention.[64] Other acts, such as negotiating a variation of terms of the lease and so recognising its continuance, may amount to a waiver, though not against a background of threatened proceedings for forfeiture[65]; and there can be no waiver once the landlord has shown his final decision to treat the lease as forfeited, as by commencing an action for possession.[66]

As would be expected, a waiver extends only to the particular breach in question, and does not operate as a general waiver of all future breaches, although the law was once different; and the same applies to a licence granted to the tenant to do any act.[67] All that is waived is the right of forfeiture for the breach, and not the breach itself.[68] A waiver is no bar to an action for damages for breach of the covenant.[69]

---

[57] *Matthews* v. *Smallwood* [1910] 1 Ch. 777 at 786.
[58] *Metropolitan Properties Co. Ltd.* v. *Cordery* (1979) 39 P. & C.R. 10.
[59] *Chrisdell Ltd.* v. *Johnson* (1987) 54 P. & C.R. 257. Compare *Van Haarlam* v. *Kasner* [1992] 36 E.G. 135 (knowledge of tenant's arrest enough).
[60] *Ward* v. *Day* (1863) 4 B. & S. 337 at 353; 5 B. & S. 364.
[61] *Goodright* d. *Charter* v. *Cordwent* (1795) 6 T.R. 219; *David Blackstone* v. *Burnetts (West End) Ltd.* [1973] 1 W.L.R. 1487 (rent payable in advance).
[62] *Davenport* v. *R.* (1877) 3 App.Cas. 115; *Segal Securities Ltd.* v. *Thoseby* [1963] 1 Q.B. 887.
[63] *Central Estates (Belgravia) Ltd.* v. *Woolgar (No. 2)* [1972] 1 W.L.R. 1048.
[64] See *Matthews* v. *Smallwood, supra,* at p. 786.
[65] *Expert Clothing Service & Sales Ltd.* v. *Hillgate House Ltd.* [1986] Ch. 340; and see *Church Commissioners for England* v. *Nodjoumi* (1985) 51 P. & C.R. 155.
[66] *Grimwood* v. *Moss* (1872) L.R. 7 C.P. 360.
[67] L.P.A. 1925, ss.143, 148, replacing earlier provisions which altered the law laid down in *Dumpor's Case* (1603) 4 Co.Rep. 119b.
[68] See *Greenwich L.B.C.* v. *Discreet Selling Estates Ltd.* (1990) 61 P. & C.R. 405.
[69] *Stephens* v. *Junior Army and Navy Stores Ltd.* [1914] 2 Ch. 516.

C. Mode of Forfeiture

The normal method of enforcing a forfeiture is by issuing and serving a writ claiming possession; such a writ usually contains an unequivocal demand for possession, so that the mere service of the writ operates to determine the lease.[70] Alternatively, unless the premises are let as a dwelling and some person is lawfully residing in it or in any part of it,[71] the landlord can enforce his right of forfeiture by making peaceable entry on the land.[72] It is usually inadvisable for a landlord to adopt this method, for it is an offence if any violence is used or threatened and the landlord knows that there is someone on the premises who is opposed to the entry[73]; but unless made unlawfully,[74] such an entry does not give the tenant any remedy in damages.[75]

D. Conditions for Forfeiture

The conditions under which a right of forfeiture can be enforced depend upon whether the right arises from breach of the covenant or condition to pay rent or from breach of any other provision. Moreover, in each case, first, equity, and later, statute, have intervened so as to allow tenants to obtain relief from forfeiture in certain circumstances.[76]

I. FORFEITURE FOR NON-PAYMENT OF RENT

Where a landlord has the right to forfeit a lease for non-payment of rent, two important points to be considered are the landlord's formal demand for the rent and the tenant's right to relief.

1. Landlord's formal demand: the landlord must either have made a formal demand for the rent, or else be exempted from making such a demand.

(a) *Formal demand.* To make a formal demand, the landlord or his authorised agent must demand the exact sum due on the day when it falls due at such convenient hour before sunset as will give time to count out the money, the demand being made upon the demised premises and continuing until sunset.[77]

(b) *Exemption from formal demand.* To avoid the technicalities of a formal demand, every well-drawn lease provides that the lease may be

---

[70] *Elliott* v. *Boynton* [1924] 1 Ch. 236, as explained in *Canas Property Co. Ltd.* v. *K.L. Television Services Ltd.* [1970] 1 Q.B. 433.

[71] Protection from Eviction Act 1977, s.2; and see *post*, p. 553.

[72] See, *e.g. Billson* v. *Residential Apartments Ltd.* [1992] 2 W.L.R. 15.

[73] Criminal Law Act 1977, s.6, replacing statutes from 1381 onwards. For another disadvantage, see *R.* v. *Hussey* (1924) 18 Cr.App.R. 160 (getting shot).

[74] See Housing Act 1988, s.27.

[75] *Hemmings* v. *Stoke Poges Golf Club* [1920] 1 K.B. 720.

[76] For the equitable jurisdiction, see *Shiloh Spinners Ltd.* v. *Harding* [1973] A.C. 691; *Billson* v. *Residential Apartments Ltd.*, *supra*.

[77] See 1 Wms. Saund. (1871) 434 *et seq.*

forfeited if the rent is a specified number of days in arrear, "whether formally demanded or not." The words quoted exempt the landlord from making a formal demand. However, even if a lease contains no such clause, the Common Law Procedure Act 1852[78] dispenses with a formal demand in any action for forfeiture if—

(i) half a year's rent is in arrear, and
(ii) no sufficient distress (*i.e.* goods available for distraint) can be found[79] upon the premises to satisfy all the arrears due.[80]

2. Tenant's right to relief: the tenant may be able to claim relief against the forfeiture. Equity considered that a right of forfeiture was merely security for payment of the rent, so that if—

(i) the tenant paid the rent due; and
(ii) the tenant paid any expenses to which the landlord had been put; and
(iii) it was just and equitable to grant relief,

equity would restore the tenant to his position despite the forfeiture of the lease.[81] Originally, there was no limit to the time within which application for relief had to be made, apart from the general principle that equity would give no assistance to stale claims.[82] But the Common Law Procedure Act 1852[83] provides that if, before trial, the tenant pays the arrears and costs,[84] the proceedings must be stayed. Furthermore, where the landlord has obtained and procured the execution of a judgment for possession, an application for relief must be made within six months of the execution.[85] If the landlord re-enters without an order, the statute does not apply, and the old equitable jurisdiction remains.[86] While the court will tend to adopt the same time limit, it will not "boggle at a matter of days."[87] If relief is granted, the tenant holds under the old lease[88] and execution of a new document is not required.

Where a lease is forfeited, any underleases created out of it automatically come to an end.[89] However, an underlessee (or mortgagee) has the same

---

[78] s.210, re-enacting L. & T.A. 1730, s.2; County Courts Act 1984, s.139(1).
[79] See *Hammond* v. *Mather* (1862) 3 F. & F. 151 (no distress can be "found" if the outer doors are locked).
[80] See *Cross* v. *Jordan* (1853) 8 Exch. 149.
[81] See *Howard* v. *Fanshawe* [1895] 2 Ch. 581.
[82] See *Hill* v. *Barclay* (1811) 18 Ves. 56 at 59, 60.
[83] ss.210–212, replacing L. & T.A. 1730, ss.2, 4. And see County Courts Act 1984, s.138.
[84] *Standard Pattern Co. Ltd.* v. *Ivey* [1962] Ch. 432, criticised in (1962) 78 L.Q.R. 168 (R.E.M.).
[85] Common Law Procedure Act 1852, s.210; similarly in county courts (County Courts Act 1984, s.138, as amended by Administration of Justice Act 1985, s.55). Yet in the High Court the six months' limit does not apply to a mortgagee of the lease who was not party to the proceedings for forfeiture: *United Dominions Trust Ltd.* v. *Shellpoint Trustees* [1992] 39 E.G. 144, examining the turgid statutory drafting.
[86] *Thatcher* v. *C. H. Pearce & Sons (Contractors) Ltd.* [1968] 1 W.L.R. 748.
[87] *Ibid.* at p. 756, *per* Simon P.
[88] Common Law Procedure Act 1852, s.212; J.A. 1925, s.46; and see County Courts Acts 1984, s.139(2).
[89] *Great Western Ry.* v. *Smith* (1876) 2 Ch.D. 235 at 253.

right of applying for relief against forfeiture as the tenant under the head lease.[90]

II. FORFEITURE FOR BREACH OF OTHER COVENANTS OR CONDITIONS

The general rule is that forfeiture for breach of a covenant or condition other than for payment of rent is subject to the landlord's obligation to serve a notice in the statutory form and the tenant's right to relief; and this perhaps applies to forfeiture for denial of title.[91] There are some exceptions to this rule, however, and there are special provisions for sub-tenants. The right to receive a notice and to apply for relief prevails over any stipulation to the contrary.[92] Hence a device such as an undated surrender executed by the tenant as a guarantee against breaches of covenant is void.[93]

1. General rule

(a) *Service of notice.* Before proceeding to enforce a forfeiture either by action or re-entry, the landlord must serve on the tenant a statutory notice in writing under the Law of Property Act 1925, section 146.[94] The notice must—

   (i) specify the breach complained of; and
  (ii) require it to be remedied, if this is possible; and
 (iii) require the tenant to make compensation in money for the breach,[95] if the landlord requires such compensation.[96]

(b) *"Capable of remedy."* A breach of a positive covenant (*i.e.* to do something) is normally capable of remedy by doing what has been left undone, such as carrying out building work[97] or painting,[98] even though this is done belatedly. However, if the covenant is negative (*i.e.* not to do something) it has been said that it can never be remedied,[99] for "that which was done cannot be undone."[1] This seems to give "remedy" an unduly narrow meaning, and it now appears that at least some breaches of negative covenants are capable of remedy,[2] though not all. Thus a breach of a

---

[90] Common Law Procedure Act 1852, s.210; L.P.A. 1925, s.146(4); *Belgravia Insurance Co.* v. *Meah* [1964] 1 Q.B. 436.
[91] *W. G. Clark (Properties) Ltd.* v. *Dupre Properties Ltd.* [1992] Ch. 297; *sed quaere.*
[92] L.P.A. 1925, s.146(12).
[93] *Plymouth Corporation* v. *Harvey* [1971] 1 W.L.R. 549; and see *Richard Clarke & Co. Ltd.* v. *Widnall* [1976] 1 W.L.R. 845.
[94] Replacing C.A. 1881, s.14, and C.A. 1982, ss.2, 4.
[95] L.P.A. 1925, s.146(1); and see *post*, p. 346 (repairs).
[96] *Lock* v. *Pearce* [1893] 2 Ch. 271 (despite the words "in any case").
[97] *Expert Clothing Service & Sales Ltd.* v. *Hillgate House Ltd.* [1986] Ch. 340.
[98] See *Hoffmann* v. *Fineberg* [1949] Ch. 245 at 257.
[99] *Rugby School (Governors)* v. *Tannahill* [1934] 1 K.B. 695 at 701 (in C.A. [1935] 1 K.B. 87); and see *Scala House & District Property Co. Ltd.* v. *Forbes* [1974] Q.B. 575 at 585.
[1] *Rugby School (Governors)* v. *Tannahill* [1934] 1 K.B. 695 at 701, *per* MacKinnon J.
[2] *Rugby School (Governors)* v. *Tannahill* [1935] 1 K.B. 87.

covenant against assigning or sub-letting the premises is incapable of remedy[3]; an assignment is valid despite having been made in breach of covenant, and so it is on the assignee that the statutory notice must be served.[4] Again, the use of the premises for prostitution in breach of a covenant against permitting them to be used for any illegal or immoral purpose cannot be remedied merely by ceasing the prohibited use, for this will not remove the stigma attached to the premises.[5] But the breach is remediable where there is no notoriety and the immoral use by the sub-tenant can be suppressed by the tenant taking prompt action as soon as he discovers the breach.[6] The question seems to be whether the harm to the landlord done by the breach is for practical purposes capable of being retrieved.[7] The path of safety is for the statutory notice to require the specified breach to be remedied "if it is capable of remedy."[8] A notice may be valid even if it does no more than specify the breach, as where the breach is irremediable and the landlord seeks no compensation, perhaps to avoid soiling his hands with the fruits of prostitution, or other illegal or immoral activities.[9]

(c) *Time for compliance.* After serving the notice, the landlord must allow the tenant a reasonable time for compliance with it. The Act does not define what is a reasonable time, but it will be measured by the time that it would take to perform the covenant, as by doing the requisite building work or decoration, or, if the covenant is negative, by terminating the breach.[10] For many positive covenants a period of three months is usually considered to be enough in normal circumstances. Even if the breach is irremediable, reasonable notice must be given so as to enable the tenant to consider his position; in such cases, two days' notice has been held to be insufficient[11] although fourteen days may be enough.[12]

(d) *Relief.* If within a reasonable time the notice has not been complied with, the landlord may proceed to enforce the forfeiture. This he may do either in person or by action. But while he "is proceeding" to enforce the forfeiture by action or otherwise, the tenant may apply to the court for relief, either in any action by the landlord to enforce the forfeiture or by making a

---

[3] *Scala House & District Property Co. Ltd.* v. *Forbes* [1974] Q.B. 575; and see *Horsey Estates Ltd.* v. *Steiger* [1899] 2 Q.B. 79 (tenant in liquidation).

[4] *Old Grovebury Manor Farm Ltd.* v. *W. Seymour Plant Sales and Hire Ltd.* [1979] 1 W.L.R. 1397.

[5] *Rugby School (Governors)* v. *Tannahill, supra*; *British Petroleum Pension Trust Ltd.* v. *Behrendt* (1985) 52 P. & C.R. 117; and see *Hoffmann* v. *Fineberg* [1949] Ch. 245 (illicit gaming); *Van Haarlam* v. *Kasner* [1992] 36 E.G. 135 (using premises for spying).

[6] *Glass* v. *Kencakes Ltd.* [1966] 1 Q.B. 611.

[7] *Expert Clothing Service & Sales Ltd.* v. *Hillgate House Ltd., supra.*

[8] See *Glass* v. *Kencakes Ltd., supra*, at p. 629.

[9] *Rugby School (Governors)* v. *Tannahill, supra.*

[10] *Expert Clothing Service & Sales Ltd.* v. *Hillgate House Ltd., supra*, at p. 357.

[11] *Horsey Estate Ltd.* v. *Steiger* [1899] 2 Q.B. 79.

[12] *Scala House & District Property Co. Ltd.* v. *Forbes, supra.*

separate application.[13] "Is proceeding" is here used in the sense of "proceeds,"[14] or "has proceeded"[15]; and a tenant may seek relief as soon as the
landlord has served the statutory notice,[16] though usually it will be better to
wait as the landlord may decide not to proceed to forfeiture. Where the
forfeiture is being enforced by action, the right to apply for relief is exercisable at any time before the landlord has taken possession under a judgment
in his favour[17]; thereafter no relief can be granted, even within six months of
the forfeiture.[18] Where the forfeiture is enforced in person, the right to apply
for relief continues for an indefinite period after the landlord's entry, though
in deciding whether to grant relief the court will take into account all the
circumstances, including any delay by the tenant in applying.[19]

The court may grant relief on such terms as it thinks fit[20]; and if relief is
granted the effect is as if the lease had never been forfeited.[21] Relief is
usually granted where the breach has been remedied, though it may be
refused if the tenant's personal qualifications are important and he has
proved unsatisfactory.[22] But where the breach involves immoral use, relief
will be refused except in very exceptional circumstances.[23] Where premises
are physically divided and separately occupied, and the breaches are confined to one part only, relief may be granted in respect of the other part.[24]
Relief takes effect subject to any legal lease granted by the landlord after the
forfeiture to a lessee who takes without notice of the previous tenant's equity
to seek relief.[25]

2. Exceptional cases. The above provisions concerning the necessity for
serving a notice and the tenant's right to apply for relief probably do not
affect forfeiture for denial of title,[26] but they govern all covenants and
conditions (other than those for payment of rent) with two exceptions.
These two exceptions are as follows.

(a) *Mining lease*: cases where there has been a breach of a covenant in a
mining lease providing for inspection of the books, accounts, weighing

---

[13] L.P.A. 1925, s.146(2).
[14] *Billson* v. *Residential Apartments Ltd.* [1992] 1 A.C. 494.
[15] *Ibid.*; see at p. 539.
[16] *Ibid.* at pp. 539, 540, 544.
[17] *Ibid.* at p. 540.
[18] Contrast non-payment of rent: *ante*, p. 327.
[19] *Billson* v. *Residential Apartments Ltd.*, *supra*, at pp. 540, 543.
[20] L.P.A. 1925, s.146(2).
[21] *Dendy* v. *Evans* [1909] 2 K.B. 894.
[22] *Bathurst (Earl)* v. *Fine* [1974] 1 W.L.R. 905 (stately home); and see L.P.A. 1925, s.146(9): *post*, p. 331.
[23] *Central Estates (Belgravia) Ltd.* v. *Woolgar (No. 2)* [1972] 1 W.L.R. 1048 (short-lived homosexual brothel: tenant aged and sick: value of premises not diminished); *Ropemaker Properties Ltd.* v. *Noonhaven Ltd.* [1989] 2 E.G.L.R. 50 (valuable lease of West End clip joints); *Van Haarlam* v. *Kasner* [1992] 36 E.G. 135.
[24] *G.M.S. Syndicate Ltd.* v. *Gary Elliott Ltd.* [1982] Ch. 1 (ground floor shop; immoral "club" in basement).
[25] *Fuller* v. *Judy Properties Ltd.* [1992] 14 E.G. 106.
[26] *Warner* v. *Sampson* [1958] 1 Q.B. 404; revsd. on other grounds [1959] 1 Q.B. 297. Contrast *W.G. Clark (Properties) Ltd.* v. *Dupre Properties Ltd.* [1992] Ch. 297, *obiter*.

machines or other things, or of the mine itself.[27] Since the rent reserved on such a lease usually varies with the quantity of minerals got, such a covenant is most important to the landlord. There is consequently no restriction upon the landlord forfeiting the lease without serving a notice, and no provision enabling the tenant to obtain relief.

(b) *Bankruptcy or execution*: cases where there has been a breach of a condition against the tenant's bankruptcy (or, for a corporation, winding up[28]) or the taking of the lease in execution[29]; the bankruptcy of a surety for the tenant is outside this provision.[30] This head must be divided into two.

(1) NO PROTECTION. In five specified cases, on breach of such a condition, section 146 has no application at all; the lease can thus be forfeited at once without service of a notice and without possibility of relief.[31] These cases are those where the lease is of—

   (i) agricultural or pastoral land, or
  (ii) mines or minerals, or
 (iii) a public house or beershop, or
  (iv) a furnished house, or
   (v) property with respect to which the personal qualifications of the tenant are of importance for the preservation of the value or character of the property,[31a] or on the ground of neighbourhood to the landlord or to any person holding under him.

(2) PROTECTION FOR ONE YEAR AND AFTER. In all other cases, on breach of such a condition, the protection of section 146 applies for one year from the bankruptcy or taking in execution; if during that year the landlord wishes to forfeit the lease, he must serve the notice and the tenant can apply for relief. But once the year has elapsed, the tenant is no longer protected; the landlord can forfeit the lease without serving notice and the court has no power to grant relief.[32] Yet if the tenant's lease is sold during the year, the protection of section 146 continues indefinitely.[33] This allows the trustee in bankruptcy or sheriff to dispose of the lease to a purchaser at a reasonable price, for if the lease were liable to be forfeited after the year, without the service of notice or the chance of relief, it would be difficult to find a purchaser.

3. Sub-tenants. Under section 146, as amended by the Law of Property (Amendment) Act 1929,[34] a sub-tenant may apply for relief against the forfeiture of his landlord's lease on whatever ground that forfeiture is being

[27] L.P.A. 1925, s.146(8).
[28] *Ibid.* s.205(1)(i).
[29] *Ibid.* s.146(9).
[30] *Halliard Property Co. Ltd.* v. *Jack Segal Ltd.* [1978] 1 W.L.R. 377.
[31] L.P.A. 1925, s.146(9).
[31a] See *Bathurst (Earl)* v. *Fine* [1974] 1 W.L.R. 905.
[32] L.P.A. 1925, s.146(10)(b).
[33] *Ibid.* s.146(10)(a).
[34] s.1.

enforced; and a mere mortgagee or chargee is a "sub-tenant" for these purposes.[35] A sub-tenant has this right whether the head lease is being forfeited for non-payment of rent, for one of the exceptional cases mentioned above or for any other reason, irrespective of whether the tenant himself can claim relief. If relief is granted, the court will grant the sub-tenant a term not longer than the term he held under his sub-lease,[36] and will normally impose terms that will restore the landlord to his former position.[37] The sub-tenant usually enters into a new lease direct with the reversioner of the forfeited lease on terms similar to (though not necessarily the same as) those of the old sub-lease.

Sect. 4. By Surrender

If a tenant surrenders his lease to his immediate landlord, who accepts the surrender, the lease merges in the landlord's reversion and is extinguished. The surrender must be to the immediate landlord; a transfer of the lease to a superior landlord does not work a surrender but operates merely as an assignment of the lease. Thus if L leases land to T for 99 years and T sub-leases to S for 21 years, S's sub-lease will be extinguished by surrender if he transfers it to T but not if he transfers it to L. A surrender by an assignee which releases him from all liabilities under the lease will also release prior assignees, even if liable under direct covenants with the landlord.[38] But a surrender takes effect subject to the rights of others in the lease surrendered, and so they will be binding for as long as it would have lasted.[39]

Surrender may be either express or by operation of law. For an express surrender, a deed is required,[40] although probably a surrender in writing made for value would suffice in equity. There will be surrender by operation of law if the parties do some act showing an intention to terminate the lease, and the circumstances are such that it would be inequitable for them to rely on the fact that there has been no surrender by deed.[41] Surrender by operation of law will take place if the tenant accepts a fresh lease from his immediate reversioner, even though the new lease is for a shorter term than the old one or starts at a future date[42]; and if a lease is varied by extending the term, this operates by way of surrender and regrant.[43] Other variations, *e.g.* an agreed increase of rent, do not necessarily bring about a surrender and regrant.[44] There will also be a surrender by operation of law if the tenant

---

[35] *Grand Junction Co. Ltd.* v. *Bates* [1954] 2 Q.B. 160; and see *post*, p. 443.
[36] L.P.A. 1925, s.146(4); and see *Ewart* v. *Fryer* [1901] 1 Ch. 499 at 515.
[37] *Chatham Empire Theatre Ltd.* v. *Ultrans Ltd.* [1961] 1 W.L.R. 817; *Belgravia Insurance Co. Ltd.* v. *Meah* [1964] 1 Q.B. 436.
[38] *Deanplan Ltd.* v. *Mahmoud* [1992] 3 W.L.R. 467.
[39] *E. S. Schwab & Co. Ltd.* v. *McCarthy* (1975) 31 P. & C.R. 196.
[40] L.P.A. 1925, s.52, replacing R.P.A. 1845, s.3.
[41] See *Glynn* v. *Coghlan* [1918] 1 I.R. 482 at 485.
[42] *Ive's Case* (1597) 5 Co.Rep. 11a.
[43] *Baker* v. *Merckel* [1960] 1 Q.B. 657.
[44] *Jenkin R. Lewis & Son Ltd.* v. *Kerman* [1971] Ch. 477.

gives up possession of the premises and the landlord accepts it,[45] but not if there is a mere uncompleted contract by the tenant to purchase the reversion.[46]

Sect. 5. By Merger

Merger is the counterpart of surrender. Under a surrender, the landlord acquires the lease, whereas merger is the consequence of the tenant retaining the lease and acquiring the reversion, or of a third party acquiring both lease and reversion. The principle is the same in both surrender and merger: the lease is absorbed by the reversion and destroyed.

For merger to be effective, the lease and the reversion must be vested in the same person in the same right with no vested estate intervening.[47] Merger may take place even if the immediate reversion consists of a lease shorter than the lease merged.[48] Thus if A, a tenant in fee simple, leases land to B for 1000 years and a few years later leases the same land to C for 400 years, the result is to give C for 400 years the reversion on B's lease. If X then acquires both C's reversion and B's lease, the 1000 years' lease will merge in the 400 years' reversion and leave X with but 400 years.[49] But there is now no merger if the person in whom the two interests vest intends that there shall be none.[50]

Sect. 6. By Becoming a Satisfied Term

If a lease is granted as security for the payment of money, the term becomes satisfied and the lease automatically ceases when all the money has been paid.[51]

Sect. 7. By Enlargement

Under certain conditions, not frequently encountered in practice, a lease may be enlarged into a fee simple by the tenant executing a deed of enlargement. Under the Law of Property Act 1925[52] this can be done only if—

 (i) there is not less than 200 years of the lease unexpired; and
 (ii) the lease was originally granted for at least 300 years; and

---

[45] See *Oastler* v. *Henderson* (1877) 2 Q.B.D. 575; but see *Chamberlaine* v. *Scally* [1992] E.G.C.S. 90 (no unequivocal conduct by the parties).
[46] *Nightingale* v. *Courtney* [1954] 1 Q.B. 399.
[47] See *Chambers* v. *Kingham* (1878) 10 Ch.D. 743.
[48] *Hughes* v. *Robotham* (1593) Cro.Eliz. 302.
[49] *Stephens* v. *Bridges* (1821) 6 Madd. 66.
[50] See L.P.A. 1925, s.185; *post*, p. 366.
[51] See *post*, pp. 441, 476.
[52] s.153, replacing C.A. 1881, s.65 and C.A. 1882, s.11.

(iii) no trust or right of redemption[53] exists in favour of the reversioner; and

(iv) the lease is not liable to be determined by re-entry for condition broken; and

(v) no rent of any money value is payable. A rent of "one silver penny if lawfully demanded" is a rent of no money value, but a rent of three shillings is not.[54] A rent under such a lease which does not exceed £1 per annum and which has not been paid for a continuous period of 20 years (five having elapsed since 1925) is deemed to have ceased to be payable and can no longer be recovered.

For a sub-lease to be capable of enlargement under the section, it must be derived out of a lease which is itself capable of enlargement. A fee simple acquired by enlargement is subject to all the provisions which affected the term of years out of which it arose. This seems to be a way of making positive covenants run with freehold land.[55]

Sect. 8. By Disclaimer

A right to disclaim a lease can arise only by statute. Thus tenants whose premises were rendered unfit by war damage were given a statutory power to disclaim their tenancies; the effect of a valid disclaimer is the same as if there had been a surrender.[56] Similar rights were given to certain tenants of premises which were requisitioned under emergency powers.[57] But not all statutory provisions for disclaimer take effect as if there had been a surrender; thus a trustee in bankruptcy may disclaim an onerous lease, but by so doing he only terminates any liability of himself and the bankrupt and does not destroy the lease.[58]

Sect. 9. By Frustration

Leases are more than mere contracts in that they create estates in land. Nevertheless, the doctrine of frustration of contracts applies in principle to leases, though only rarely will it operate.[59] Thus a lease of a warehouse for 10 years will not be frustrated by the closure of the only means of access to it for 20 months when some five years of the term has elapsed.[60] But a lease might perhaps be ended by frustration[61] if the land is physically destroyed (*e.g.* by being engulfed by the sea), or if the lease is merely incidental to a commer-

---

[53] *e.g.* a right of redemption under a mortgage; see *post*, p. 441.
[54] *Re Chapman and Hobbs* (1885) 29 Ch.D. 1007; *Re Smith and Stott* (1883) 29 Ch.D. 1009n.
[55] See *post*, p. 419.
[56] Landlord and Tenant (War Damage) Acts 1939 and 1941.
[57] Landlord and Tenant (Requisitioned Land) Acts 1942 and 1944.
[58] Insolvency Act 1986, s.315; *Re Thompson and Cottrell's Contract* [1943] Ch. 97 at 99.
[59] *National Carriers Ltd.* v. *Panalpina (Northern) Ltd.* [1981] A.C. 675.
[60] *Ibid.*
[61] *Ibid.*; *Cricklewood Property and Investment Trust Ltd.* v. *Leighton's Investment Trust Ltd.* [1945] A.C. 675; see the various dicta.

cial contract that has been frustrated, or where the lease is a short lease of a holiday villa which is totally destroyed by lightning before the term begins. Agreements for a lease and covenants in a lease may similarly, but not readily, be held to have been frustrated.[62]

Similarly, a tenancy will normally not be determined by repudiation, *i.e.* by one party accepting a breach of a fundamental term of the tenancy by the other as being a repudiation of the tenancy.[62a] But this may not apply in extreme cases.[62b]

Part 5

RIGHTS AND DUTIES OF THE PARTIES UNDER A LEASE OR TENANCY

The rights and duties of the landlord and tenant under a lease or tenancy fall under five heads. First, the lease may be silent as to everything except the essential terms as to parties, premises, rent and duration. This is not infrequently the case with weekly and other periodic tenancies. Second, the parties may have agreed to be bound by the "usual covenants." Third, the lease may provide in the orthodox way not only for the matters dealt with by the "usual covenants" but also for a number of other matters. Fourth, there are a number of statutory provisions relating to the rights and duties of the parties to a lease. Last, there are fixtures: these have already been considered.[63]

The question how far covenants in a lease can be enforced between persons other than the original lessor and original lessee is considered separately.[64]

Sect. 1. Position in the Absence of Express Provision

Except so far as the lease or tenancy agreement otherwise provides, the position of the parties is as set out below.

A. Position of the Landlord

1. Quiet enjoyment. A covenant by the landlord for quiet enjoyment (or a corresponding agreement if the tenancy is not created by deed[65]) is automatically inferred from the mere relationship of landlord and tenant,[66] unless it

---

[62] *Ibid.*; M. & W. 689–691.

[62a] *Total Oil Great Britain Ltd.* v. *Thompson Garages (Biggin Hill) Ltd.* [1972] 1 Q.B. 318, not citing *Wilson* v. *Finch Hatton* (1877) 2 Ex.D. 336; *post*, p. 337.

[62b] See *Hussein* v. *Mehlman* [1992] 32 E.G. 59 (landlord's wilful and persistent refusal to repair defects making premises unfit for habitation). Yet consider a tenant's prolonged refusal to pay rent.

[63] *Ante*, pp. 15 *et seq.*

[64] *Post*, pp. 351 *et seq.*

[65] *Baynes & Co.* v. *Lloyd & Sons* [1895] 1 Q.B. 820 at 826 (in C.A. [1895] 2 Q.B. 610); *Budd-Scott* v. *Daniell* [1902] 2 K.B. 351.

[66] *Budd-Scott* v. *Daniell, supra*; *Markham* v. *Paget* [1908] 1 Ch. 697; *Kenny* v. *Preen* [1963] 1 Q.B. 499; and see *ante*, pp. 130, 131.

is displaced by the presence of an express covenant for quiet enjoyment,[67] which may differ in its terms. The implied covenant extends to all acts of the landlord and any *lawful* acts of those claiming under him, but not the acts of others, such as someone claiming by title paramount (*e.g.* a superior land-lord),[68] nor to acts of the landlord himself if he is acting under statutory authority.[69] The covenant is not one for "quiet" enjoyment in the acoustic sense; the landlord undertakes not that the tenant will be free from the nuisance of noise, but that he will be free from disturbance by adverse claimants to the property.[70] The covenant is broken if a person to whose acts it extends causes subsidence to the land by working minerals under it,[71] or in some other way physically and substantially interferes with the tenant's enjoyment of the land[72]; and this includes persistent intimidation of the tenant to induce her to leave.[73] No exemplary damages can be awarded merely for breach of the covenant,[74] though they can be if the tort of trespass has been committed.[75] In addition, a residential occupier now has a right to statutory damages if he is unlawfully evicted from his premises, whether directly or indirectly.[76]

When granting a lease, the lessor does not use the words "as beneficial owner"; even if he did, the words would not import the four covenants for title (including a covenant for quiet enjoyment) which arise from using this phrase in a conveyance.[77]

2. No derogation from grant. It is a principle of general application that a grantor must not derogate from his grant[78]; he must not seek to take away with one hand what he has given with the other. In the case of leases, the covenant for quiet enjoyment will extend to many of the acts which might be construed as a derogation from the lessor's grant; but acts not amounting to a breach of the covenant may nevertheless be restrained as being in deroga-tion of the grant. Thus if land is leased for the express purpose of storing explosives, the lessor and those claiming under him will be restrained from using adjoining land so as to endanger the statutory licence necessary for storing explosives.[79]

There must, however, be some act making the premises substantially less fit for the purposes for which they were let. No action will lie if the landlord, having let the premises for some particular trade, *e.g.* for a wool shop only,

---

[67] *Miller* v. *Emcer Products Ltd.* [1956] Ch. 304.
[68] *Baynes & Co.* v. *Lloyd & Sons* [1895] 2 Q.B. 610; *Jones* v. *Lavington* [1903] 1 K.B. 253.
[69] *Commissioners of Crown Lands* v. *Page* [1960] 2 Q.B. 274 (requisitioning).
[70] *Hudson* v. *Cripps* [1896] 1 Ch. 265 at 268.
[71] *Markham* v. *Paget, supra.*
[72] *Owen* v. *Gadd* [1956] 2 Q.B. 99 (adjacent scaffolding).
[73] *Kenny* v. *Preen, supra.*
[74] *Perera* v. *Vandiyah* [1953] 1 W.L.R. 672; *Branchett* v. *Beaney* [1992] 3 All E.R. 910.
[75] *Drane* v. *Evangelou* [1978] 1 W.L.R. 455.
[76] *Post*, p. 554.
[77] See *ante*, p. 131.
[78] *Palmer* v. *Fletcher* (1663) 1 Lev. 122; and see (1964) 80 L.Q.R. 244 (D. W. Elliott).
[79] *Harmer* v. *Jumbil (Nigeria) Tin Areas Ltd.* [1921] 1 Ch. 200.

lets adjoining premises for purposes which offer trade competition; for the original premises are still fit for use as a wool shop even if the profits will be diminished.[80] Nor will mere invasion of privacy, as by erecting an external staircase passing the windows of the flat demised, amount to a breach of the obligation,[81] although interference with the stability of the house by vibrations caused by powerful engines on adjoining land may suffice, and so may excessive noise, such as that caused in altering another flat in the same building.[82]

3. In certain cases, obligations as to fitness and repair. In general, the landlord gives no implied undertaking that the premises will be fit for habitation,[83] nor is he liable to repair them. But this rule is subject to five qualifications, which to some extent overlap.

(a) *Furnished lettings.* Where a house is let furnished, the landlord impliedly undertakes that it is fit for human habitation when let.[84] If this is not the case, the tenant may repudiate the tenancy and recover damages for any loss he has suffered.[85] But if the premises are fit for human habitation when let, the landlord need do no more; he is under no obligation to keep them in this condition.[86] And the tenant is not deemed to warrant his fitness to occupy the premises, *e.g.* that he is free from contagious diseases.[87]

(b) *Houses let at a low rent.* Under the Landlord and Tenant Act 1985,[88] if a house is let for human habitation at a low rent, then, notwithstanding any stipulation to the contrary, there is—

   (i) an implied condition that it is fit for human habitation at the beginning of the tenancy, and
   (ii) an implied undertaking by the landlord that he will keep it in this condition throughout the tenancy.

This liability applies only to defects of which the landlord has notice,[89] though it extends to minor matters such as a broken sash-cord, for the question is not how difficult it is to repair the defect but whether by ordinary use of the premises damage may be naturally caused to the occupier.[90] Yet these provisions are of limited importance today as they still apply only if the rent does not exceed £80 a year in London and £52 elsewhere.[91]

---

[80] *Port* v. *Griffith* [1938] 1 All E.R. 295.
[81] *Browne* v. *Flower* [1911] 1 Ch. 219.
[82] *Newman* v. *Real Estate Debenture Corporation Ltd.* [1940] 1 All E.R. 131.
[83] *Hart* v. *Windsor* (1844) 12 M. & W. 68.
[84] *Smith* v. *Marrable* (1843) 11 M. & W. 5 (bugs).
[85] *Wilson* v. *Finch Hatton* (1877) 2 Ex.D. 336; *Charsley* v. *Jones* (1889) 53 J.P. 280; cp. *ante*, p. 335.
[86] *Sarson* v. *Roberts* [1895] 2 Q.B. 395.
[87] *Humphreys* v. *Miller* [1917] 2 K.B. 122.
[88] s.8, replacing earlier legislation.
[89] *McCarrick* v. *Liverpool Corporation* [1947] A.C. 219.
[90] *Summers* v. *Salford Corporation* [1943] A.C. 283 (tenant injured when other sash-cord broke).
[91] L. & T.A. 1985, s.8; and see ss.8(5), 10. See *Quick* v. *Taff Ely B.C.* [1986] Q.B. 809 at 817, 821, for unsurprising judicial surprise.

(c) *Short leases of dwellings.* In any lease or agreement for a lease[92] of a dwelling house granted on or after October 24, 1961, whatever the rent or rateable value, a covenant by the landlord to do certain repairs is implied if the term is less than seven years (unless the tenant can extend it to seven years or more) or if the landlord can determine it within seven years.[93] The covenant cannot be excluded or limited by any agreement to the contrary unless the county court has authorised this as being reasonable; and any covenant by the tenant to repair or pay money in lieu thereof is of no effect so far as it is covered by the landlord's covenant.

The obligations of the landlord under the implied covenant are as follows.

(1) STRUCTURE AND EXTERIOR: to keep the structure and exterior of the dwelling in repair.[94] This includes the drains, gutters and external pipes,[95] and also the outside walls (even if excluded from the demise[96]) and any outside steps which form an essential part of the means of access to the dwelling,[97] but not a backyard.[98] The obligation does not extend to defects such as condensation which arise from faulty design rather than disrepair.[99]

(2) INSTALLATIONS: to keep in repair and proper working order the installations in the dwelling—

   (i) for the supply of water, gas and electricity, and for sanitation, includ-
       ing basins, sinks, baths and sanitary conveniences, but not other
       appliances for making use of water, gas and electricity; and
   (ii) for space heating and heating water.[1]

This head does not apply to a central heating boiler not within the dwelling.[2] An ill-designed water closet cistern in a maisonette which floods the floor whenever used is not in "proper working order."[3]

There are two main limitations on these obligations of the landlord. First, they do not apply to works or repairs for which the tenant is liable by virtue of his duty to use the premises in a tenant-like manner,[4] such as his duty to take reasonable precautions against burst pipes when leaving the premises unoccupied during winter.[5] Second, the obligations do not apply to any defect in the demised premises unless the landlord has notice or knowledge

---

[92] *Brikom Investments Ltd.* v. *Seaford* [1981] 1 W.L.R. 863.
[93] L. & T.A. 1985 ss.11 (as amended by H.A. 1988, s.116), 12–14, 36, 38.
[94] L. & T.A. 1985, s.11(1)(a).
[95] *Ibid.*
[96] *Campden Hill Towers Ltd.* v. *Gardner* [1977] Q.B. 823.
[97] *Brown* v. *Liverpool Corporation* [1969] 3 All E.R. 1345.
[98] *Hopwood* v. *Cannock Chase D.C.* [1975] 1 W.L.R. 373. See further *Re Irvine's Estate* v. *Moran* (1990) 24 H.L.R. 1.
[99] *Quick* v. *Taff Ely B.C.* [1986] Q.B. 809; contrast *Stent* v. *Monmouth D.C.* (1987) 19 H.L.R. 269.
[1] L. & T.A. 1985, s.11(1)(b).
[2] *Campden Hill Towers Ltd.* v. *Gardner, supra.*
[3] *Liverpool C.C.* v. *Irwin* [1977] A.C. 239.
[4] L. & T.A. 1985, s.11(2)(a); and see (b), (c). For the tenant's duty, see *post*, p. 340.
[5] *Wycombe Health Authority* v. *Barnett* (1982) 47 P. & C.R. 394 (two days' absence: not liable); criticised (1984) 81 L.S.G. 3408 (M. P. Thompson), discussing lagging.

of the defect, either specifically or from facts that would put a reasonable man on inquiry.[6]

Where the statutory covenant applies to the landlord, there is an implied covenant by the tenant to permit the landlord to enter and view the premises at reasonable times of the day on 24 hours' prior notice in writing to the occupier.[7]

Where a lease is granted after January 14, 1989, and the dwelling forms part only of a building, the landlord's statutory covenant is extended so as to apply to any part of the building in which he has an estate or interest. It also applies to any installations which directly or indirectly serve the dwelling if they are owned by him or are under his control, or if they are part of any part of the building in which he has an estate or interest. But it is a defence if he shows that he made reasonable endeavours to obtain adequate access to do the works, and failed.[8]

(d) *Duty of care.* In some cases a landlord owes to all persons who might reasonably be expected to be affected by defects in the state of any part of the premises let[9] a statutory duty to take reasonable care to see that they and their property are reasonably safe from injury or damage. This duty arises where the landlord is under an obligation to the tenant for the maintenance or repair of the premises, or has a right to enter the premises to maintain and repair them, and he knows or ought to have known of the defect.[10] The landlord cannot contract out of his liability under this provision.[11]

(e) *Implied terms.* In some cases the court may imply a covenant or obligation by the landlord as to the physical condition of the premises. Thus where a flat in a tower block is let on terms which impose obligations on the tenant but not on the landlord, the landlord will be held to be under an implied obligation to take reasonable care to maintain the common parts of the block (*i.e.* the lifts, the stairs and the lighting on the stairs) in a state of reasonable repair and efficiency, thereby supplementing the incomplete terms of the tenancy.[12] Again, where a tenant has covenanted to keep the interior of a house in good repair, the landlord may be subject to an implied covenant to keep the exterior in good repair, thus giving the tenant's covenant business efficacy by imposing a correlative obligation that will preserve the interior from the elements.[13] But where the lease sets out the

---

[6] *O'Brien* v. *Robinson* [1973] A.C. 912; *Dinefwr B.C.* v. *Jones* (1987) 19 H.L.R. 445; *Hall* v. *Howard* (1988) 20 H.L.R. 566.

[7] L. & T.A. 1985, s.11(6).

[8] *Ibid.* s.11(1A), (3A), inserted by Housing Act 1988, s.116.

[9] *Smith* v. *Bradford Metropolitan Council* (1982) 44 P. & C.R. 171 (patio).

[10] Defective Premises Act 1972, s.4. See, *e.g. McAuley* v. *Bristol C.C.* [1992] 1 Q.B. 134 (defective garden step). See also *Targett* v. *Torfaen B.C.* [1992] 3 All E.R. 27 (liability of builder at common law for negligent design or construction).

[11] Defective Premises Act 1972, s.6(3).

[12] *Liverpool C.C.* v. *Irwin* [1977] A.C. 239; and see *King* v. *South Northamptonshire D.C.* (1991) 64 P. & C.R. 35 (access to rear entrance).

[13] *Barrett* v. *Lounova* (1982) *Ltd.* [1990] 1 Q.B. 348. Contrast *Demetriou* v. *Poolaction Ltd.* [1991] 1 E.G.L.R. 100, where there was no such obligation.

full obligations of both parties, terms will be implied in it only if it is
necessary to do so in order to give the lease business efficacy, and not merely
because they seem reasonable.[14]

(f) *Local housing authorities.* Local housing authorities have extensive
powers of compelling the person who has control of a house (usually the
owner or his agent) to make it fit for human habitation.[15] Many tenants avoid
the burden of directly enforcing their rights by setting the local housing
authority in motion.

B. Position of the Tenant

1. Obligation to pay rent. This is discussed below.[16]

2. Obligation to pay rates and taxes. The tenant is under an obligation to
pay all rates and taxes except those for which the landlord is liable. Under
Schedule A the landlord is liable to income tax on the rent.[17] If he fails to pay
it, the tenant may be required to pay it up to the amount of his rent, and he
may deduct any such payment from any subsequent rent due from him.[18]

3. Obligation not to commit waste. A tenant's liability for waste depends
upon the nature of his tenancy. A tenant for a fixed term of years is liable for
both voluntary and permissive waste, and must therefore keep the premises
in proper repair.[19] A yearly tenant is similarly liable save that his liability for
permissive waste is limited to keeping the premises wind- and water-tight.[20]
A weekly tenant, on the other hand, is not liable for permissive waste as
such, though he must use the premises in a tenant-like manner, and so must
take proper care of them, *e.g.* by keeping the chimneys swept and the drain
pipes unblocked.[21] The same rule probably applies to monthly and quarterly
tenants. A tenant at will is not liable for permissive waste,[22] although if he
commits voluntary waste his tenancy is thereby terminated and he is liable
to an action for damages.[23] A tenant at sufferance is liable for voluntary
waste,[24] though probably not for permissive waste.

4. Landlord's right to view. A landlord may by statute or by the terms of

---

[14] *Liverpool C.C.* v. *Irwin, supra; Duke of Westminster* v. *Guild* [1985] Q.B. 688.
[15] Housing Act 1985, Pt. VI, replacing earlier legislation. See generally Evans and Smith, *The
     Law of Landlord and Tenant* (3rd ed., 1989), pp. 199, 200.
[16] *Post*, p. 343.
[17] Income and Corporation Taxes Act 1988, s.15. This Schedule A is distinct from the former
     Schedule A tax on the annual value of land ("landlord's property tax") which was discon-
     tinued as from 1963–64; see Finance Act 1963, ss.14, 68.
[18] Income and Corporation Taxes Act 1988, s.23.
[19] *Yellowly* v. *Gower* (1855) 11 Exch. 274; for waste, see *ante*, p. 47.
[20] *Wedd* v. *Porter* [1916] 2 K.B. 91.
[21] *Warren* v. *Keen* [1954] 1 Q.B. 15.
[22] *Harnett* v. *Maitland* (1847) 16 M. & W. 257.
[23] *Countess of Shrewsbury's Case* (1600) 5 Co.Rep. 13b.
[24] *Burchell* v. *Hornsby* (1808) 1 Camp. 360.

the tenancy be expressly authorised to enter the premises; and if he is liable to repair the premises he has an implied right to enter them for this purpose.[25] Otherwise, he has no right to enter the premises so long as the tenancy endures.[26]

5. Right to take emblements. The nature of emblements has already been considered.[27] A tenant at sufferance has no right to emblements, but at common law a tenant at will, a yearly tenant or a tenant for years determinable with lives was entitled to them, provided the determination of the tenancy was not caused by his own act.[28] A tenant for a fixed term of years could also claim emblements if his lease came to a premature end without his fault, *e.g.* if the landlord had only a life estate and his death brought the lease to an end. However, the importance of these rules has been greatly diminished by statute. By the Landlord and Tenant Act 1851,[29] a tenant at a rack rent whose tenancy determined by the death of the landlord or cesser of his interest was given the right to continue his tenancy on the existing terms until the expiration of the current year of the tenancy, in lieu of any right to emblements. In the case of agricultural holdings, the Agricultural Holdings Act 1986[30] provides that in such a case the tenancy continues until determined at the end of a year of the tenancy by 12 months' notice to quit. These provisions, coupled with the conversion of most leases for lives into terms of 90 years,[31] have made this subject of little consequence.

6. Right to estovers. A tenant for years has the same right to estovers and botes as a tenant for life.[32]

Sect. 2. Position under a Lease Containing the Usual Covenants

1. Effect of agreement. If a lease has actually been granted, the obligations of the parties in the absence of any contrary provision in the lease are as set out above. If, on the other hand, the parties have merely agreed that a lease containing the "usual covenants" shall be granted, or if there is an agreement that a lease shall be granted, no reference being made to the covenants it should contain, then, subject to any contrary agreement by the parties, the lease must contain whatever covenants and conditions may be "usual" in the circumstances, and if it does not, it may be rectified to accord with the agreement. Except in so far that they cover the same ground, the obligations imposed by the "usual" covenants and conditions are additional to those set out under Sect. 1 above.[33]

[25] *Saner* v. *Bilton* (1878) 7 Ch.D. 815.
[26] *Stocker* v. *Planet Building Society* (1879) 27 W.R. 877.
[27] *Ante*, p. 51.
[28] See, *e.g. Haines* v. *Welch* (1868) L.R. 4 C.P. 91.
[29] s.1.
[30] s.21; for agricultural holdings generally, see *post*, pp. 526 *et seq.*
[31] *Ante*, p. 319.
[32] Co.Litt. 41b; and see *ante*, p. 48.
[33] *Ante*, pp. 335 *et seq.*

2. The usual covenants. The following covenants and conditions are always "usual."[34]

   1. On the part of the landlord—
      a covenant for quiet enjoyment in the usual qualified form, *i.e.* extending only to the acts of the lessor or the rightful acts of any person claiming from or under him.

   2. On the part of the tenant—
     (a) a covenant to pay rent;
     (b) a covenant to pay tenant's rates and taxes, *i.e.* all rates and taxes except those which statute requires the landlord to bear;
     (c) a covenant to keep the premises in repair and deliver them up at the end of the term in this condition;
     (d) a covenant to permit the landlord to enter and view the state of repair, if he is liable to repair; and
     (e) a condition of re-entry for non-payment of rent, but not for breach of any other covenant.

3. Usual by custom or usage. In addition to the above provisions, which are always "usual," other covenants may be "usual" in the circumstances of the case, by virtue, for example, of the custom of the neighbourhood or trade usage; in each case, this is a question of fact for the court, taking into account the nature of the premises, their situation, the purpose for which they are being let, the length of the term, the evidence of conveyancers and the contents of books of precedents.[35] Today, a right of re-entry for breach of *any* covenant will normally be "usual."[36] In the absence of such special circumstances, however, many covenants which in practice are usually inserted in leases and are therefore literally "usual" are nevertheless not deemed to be "usual" in the technical sense of the word. Examples are covenants against assignment, covenants against carrying on specified trades, and provisos for forfeiture if the tenant has a bankruptcy order made against him or enters into liquidation or suffers any distress or process of execution to be levied upon his goods or makes any assignment or composition for the benefit of his creditors. Such provisions are frequently inserted when (as is usually the case) no contract to take a lease has been made and the terms of the lease are a matter for negotiation between the parties. But if a contract for a lease has been made, no covenant can be inserted in the lease without the concurrence of both parties unless either the contract provides for it or the covenant is technically a "usual" covenant.

Sect. 3. Position under Certain Covenants Usually Found in Leases

A number of covenants have already been considered, but certain other covenants must be mentioned as well.

[34] See *Hampshire* v. *Wickens* (1878) 7 Ch.D. 555.
[35] See *Flexman* v. *Corbett* [1930] 1 Ch. 672.
[36] *Chester* v. *Buckingham Travel Ltd.* [1981] 1 W.L.R. 96. See [1992] Conv. 18 (L. Crabb).

1. Covenant to pay rent. Unless the lease provides for payment in advance, rent is normally payable in arrear.[37] It continues to be payable even if the premises cannot be used, *e.g.* owing to destruction by fire[38] or other calamity, or seizure by military authorities for the occupation of troops,[39] save in the exceptional case of the lease being frustrated.[40] However, this stern common law rule is frequently mitigated by an express provision in the lease, and in the case of war damage and requisitioning (but not other events) the tenant has been given a statutory right to disclaim his tenancy.[41]

The landlord may enforce payment of the rent—

(a) directly, by—
   (i) an action for the money, or
   (ii) distress;
(b) indirectly, by the threat of forfeiture if the lease contains a forfeiture clause.

Forfeiture has already been dealt with,[42] and there is no need to discuss an action for the money. The subject of distress is extremely intricate,[43] and all that need be said here is that in essence it consists of the right of the landlord, exercisable without application to the court but ordinarily exercised by a court certificated bailiff, to enter the premises[44] and enforce payment by seizing and selling enough of any goods that are found there.

2. Covenant against assigning, underletting or parting with possession

(a) *The tenant's rights.* If the lease is silent on the matter the tenant is entitled to assign, underlet or part with possession of the premises without the landlord's consent; for during the term the property is the tenant's. However, a covenant against assignment, underletting or parting with possession of all or any part of the premises is often inserted in leases; and although an assignment or sub-lease made in breach of covenant is valid,[45] the breach will usually give rise to forfeiture or a claim for damages.

(b) *Unreasonable withholding of consent.* If the covenant is absolute, the landlord can enforce it if he wishes; and although he may waive a breach in any particular instance, he cannot be compelled to do so, even if his attitude is entirely unreasonable. But if the covenant is one against assigning or

---

[37] *Coomber* v. *Howard* (1845) 1 C.B. 440.
[38] *Belfour* v. *Weston* (1786) 1 T.R. 310.
[39] *Whitehall Court Ltd.* v. *Ettlinger* [1920] 1 K.B. 680.
[40] See *ante*, p. 334.
[41] *Ante*, p. 334.
[42] *Ante*, pp. 324 *et seq.*
[43] See M. & W. 709–712, and (1991) Law Com. (No. 194), which advocates the abolition of distress.
[44] See *Evans* v. *South Ribble B.C.* [1992] 2 W.L.R. 429 (no entry merely by inserting documents through letter-box).
[45] *Old Grovebury Manor Farm Ltd.* v. *W. Seymour Plant and Hire Ltd.* (*No.* 2) [1979] 1 W.L.R. 1397.

sub-letting "without licence or consent" (often called a "qualified covenant") the Landlord and Tenant Act 1927[46] provides that notwithstanding
any provision to the contrary the covenant is deemed to be subject to a
proviso that the licence or consent is not to be unreasonably withheld. This
does not permit the tenant to assign or sublet without seeking the landlord's
consent: if he does so, he is in breach of covenant even if the landlord, if
asked, could not properly have withheld his consent.[47] But if he seeks
consent and it is unreasonably withheld he may forthwith assign or sublet
without the consent,[48] or else pursue the safer but slower course of seeking a
declaration from the court of his right to do so.[49]

The Landlord and Tenant Act 1988 has now strengthened the position of
the tenant, particularly against dilatory or evasive landlords.[50] If the tenant
serves a written application for consent on the landlord, the landlord is
under a duty to give his consent unless it is reasonable not to do so; and, if
consent is withheld or is granted subject to conditions, he must give written
notice of the reasons for withholding the consent or imposing the conditions,
and this notice must be given within a reasonable time.[51] The burden of
proof on these matters now lies on the landlord,[52] and any breach of duty
under the Act now sounds in damages.[53]

These provisions do not apply to a term in a lease requiring that before
seeking to assign the lease the tenant must offer to surrender it to the
landlord *gratis*; for in effect this is a condition precedent to there being any
right to assign, rather than the withholding of consent under an existing
right.[54] Such a term is registrable as an estate contract.[55]

(c) *Reasonableness.* In determining whether the withholding of consent is
reasonable, the question is whether, having regard to the purpose of the
covenant, the landlord can show[56] that the withholding was reasonable.[57] He
cannot rely on matters unconnected with the relationship of landlord and
tenant, and although he need consider only his own relevant interests, it is
unreasonable to withhold consent where the detriment to the tenant would
be extreme, and disproportionate to the benefit to the landlord[58]; and
contra, if *vice versa*.[59] The landlord now appears to be confined to the
reasons given in response to the tenant's application,[60] and in any event he

---

[46] s.19(1).
[47] *Eastern Telegraph Co. Ltd.* v. *Dent* [1899] 1 Q.B. 835.
[48] *Treloar* v. *Bigge* (1874) L.R. 9 Ex. 151.
[49] *Young* v. *Ashley Gardens Properties Ltd.* [1903] 2 Ch. 112.
[50] See *29 Equities Ltd.* v. *Bank Leumi (U.K.) Ltd.* [1986] 1 W.L.R. 1490 at 1494.
[51] L. & T.A. 1988, s.1(3), (4). See, *e.g. Midland Bank Plc* v. *Chart Enterprises Inc.* [1990] 2 E.G.L.R. 59 (delay).
[52] L. & T.A. 1988, s.1(5).
[53] *Ibid.* s.4.
[54] *Bocardo S.A.* v. *S. & M. Hotels Ltd.* [1980] 1 W.L.R. 17.
[55] *Ante*, p. 79.
[56] L. & T.A. 1988, s.1(5).
[57] *Leeward Securities Ltd.* v. *Lilyheath Properties Ltd.* (1983) 17 H.L.R. 35.
[58] *International Drilling Fluids Ltd.* v. *Louisville Investments (Uxbridge) Ltd.* [1986] Ch. 513.
[59] *Deverall* v. *Wyndham* [1989] 1 E.G.L.R. 57.
[60] See L. & T.A. 1988, s.1(3), (5).

cannot rely on any reason which did not in fact influence his mind when withholding consent.[61] If any of the reasons given is plainly bad, this may establish unreasonableness.[62] Usually no withholding of consent will be reasonable unless it is based on the person of the assignee or the proposed use of the premises,[63] and this includes the impact of supervening statutes which would confer additional protection on the tenant.[64] Moreover, statute has provided that it is unreasonable to withhold consent on the ground of "colour, race, nationality or ethnic or national origins"; but this does not apply to "small premises" where the landlord or a near relative shares some of the accommodation with others.[65] Unless the lease provides for it, the landlord may not require the payment of a fine or other valuable consideration for giving his consent.[66]

(d) *Breach.* To amount to a breach of covenant against assignment on underletting, there must in general be some voluntary dealing with the property *inter vivos.* Thus a bequest of the lease is no breach,[67] nor is the involuntary vesting of the lease in the trustee in bankruptcy upon the tenant's bankruptcy,[68] or the compulsory sale of the lease under statutory provisions,[69] as distinct from a voluntary sale by the tenant's trustee in bankruptcy.[70] A mortgage made by the grant of a sub-lease is a breach, but one made by a mere deposit of the title deeds is not, nor is a declaration of trust made by the tenant for the benefit of his creditors.[71] A covenant merely against underletting is perhaps not broken by an assignment or by letting lodgings.

3. Covenant to repair

(a) *Construction of covenant.* In long leases, the tenant usually covenants to do all repairs; in short leases, the landlord frequently assumes liability for external and structural repairs, and in some cases is compelled by statute to do so.[72] Subject to this, in every case, the matter is one for negotiation. If no provision is made for repairs, neither party is liable for them, apart from statute and the general law relating to waste.[73] The extent of the liability of any party under a repairing covenant depends, of course, upon the wording of the covenant, but expressions such as "tenantable repair," "sufficient

---

[61] *Bromley Park Garden Estates Ltd.* v. *Moss* [1982] 1 W.L.R. 1019.
[62] See *Berenyi* v. *Watford B.C.* (1980) 256 E.G. 271.
[63] See *Viscount Tredegar* v. *Harwood* [1929] A.C. 72.
[64] *West Layton Ltd.* v. *Ford* [1979] Q.B. 593. Consider, *e.g.* the Leasehold Reform Act 1967 and the Rent Act 1974: see *post,* pp. 534, 549, 552.
[65] Race Relations Act 1976, s.24; see ss.1–3, 22.
[66] L.P.A. 1925, s.144, replacing C.A. 1892, s.3.
[67] *Fox* v. *Swann* (1655) Sty. 482.
[68] *Re Riggs* [1901] 2 K.B. 16.
[69] *Slipper* v. *Tottenham & Hampstead Junction Ry.* (1867) L.R. 4 Eq. 112.
[70] *Re Wright* [1949] Ch. 729.
[71] *Gentle* v. *Faulkner* [1900] 2 K.B. 267.
[72] *Ante,* pp. 337 *et seq.* See the general survey of the responsibility for the state and condition of property in Law Com. Consultation Paper No. 123 (1992).
[73] *Ante,* pp. 47 *et seq.*

repair," or "good and substantial repair" seem to add little to the meaning of the word "repair."[74] On a letting of premises that are out of repair, a covenant to "keep" them in good repair requires them to be put into good repair.[75] If the covenant is qualified by words such as "fair wear and tear excepted," they exclude liability for defects due to reasonable use of the premises or the action of the elements, but not for consequential damage caused, *e.g.* by rain entering through an unrepaired skylight.[76]

(b) *Repair.* "Repair" is not confined to restoring the original structure but extends to replacing subsidiary parts of the building which can no longer be repaired, as by rebuilding a wall,[77] replacing the roof,[78] or providing new drainpipes for old. It is often difficult to draw the line between "repair" and "renewal" or "improvement." The matter is essentially one of degree, and in particular whether the works will so change the character of the building as to restore to the landlord a building that is wholly different from that demised.[79] The basic question is whether in all the circumstances of the case the requisite work as a whole can fairly be called a repair; it may be so substantial as to be beyond anything that a reasonable person could con-template as being a repair.[80] The circumstances to be considered include the terms of the lease; the nature of the building; its state when let; the nature and extent of the repair; the nature, extent and cost of the works to be done, and who is to do them; the value and life-span of the building, and the effect of the works on them; and the comparative cost of alternative remedial works, their effect on the occupants and the likelihood of a recurrence in each case: and the weight to be attached to these factors will vary from case to case.[81] Thus to remedy an inherent defect may or may not be repair. Curing dampness in a modern high-class flat by inserting a silicone damp course will be a repair,[82] whereas it is not a repair where the damp in an aged cellar with porous bricks can be cured only by constructing new walls.[83] Premises that are still in the same physical condition as they were when first let are not out of repair merely because through some inherent structural defect the basement has been flooded, though without doing any harm.[84]

(c) *Measure of damages.* The measure of damages recoverable by a landlord for the breach of a repairing covenant formerly varied according to the time of the breach. If the breach occurred during the term, damages

---

[74] *Anstruther-Gough-Calthorpe* v. *McOscar* [1924] 1 K.B. 716 at 722, 723.
[75] *Proudfoot* v. *Hart* (1890) 25 Q.B.D. 42 at 50.
[76] *Regis Property Co. Ltd.* v. *Dudley* [1959] A.C. 370.
[77] *Lurcott* v. *Wakely* [1911] 1 K.B. 905.
[78] *Elite Investments Ltd.* v. *T. I. Bainbridge Silencers Ltd.* [1986] 2 E.G.L.R. 43.
[79] *Ravenseft Properties Ltd.* v. *Davstone (Holdings) Ltd.* [1980] Q.B. 12.
[80] *Brew Brothers Ltd.* v. *Snax (Ross) Ltd.* [1970] 1 Q.B. 612.
[81] *Holding and Management Ltd.* v. *Property Holding Plc* [1990] 1 All E.R. 938 at 945 (omitted from [1989] 1 W.L.R. 1313).
[82] *Elmcroft Developments Ltd.* v. *Tankersley-Sawyer* (1984) 15 H.L.R. 63.
[83] *Pembery* v. *Lamdin* [1940] 2 All E.R. 434.
[84] *Post Office* v. *Aquarius Properties Ltd.* [1987] 1 All E.R. 1055.

were calculated on the decrease in the value of the reversion caused by the breach,[85] *i.e.* on the difference between the value of the landlord's interest with the repairs done and its value without. Thus the longer the lease had to run, the less would be the damages. But if the breach occurred at the end of the term, the cost of repairing the premises was recoverable by the landlord[86] even if he did not propose to spend the money in making the repairs but intended to demolish the premises instead. Now, however, by the Landlord and Tenant Act 1927,[87] damages for breach of a repairing covenant are not to exceed the diminution in the value of the reversion, though if the repairs are going to be done, that diminution will usually be measured by the cost of the repairs.[88] Further, no damages are recoverable if the premises are to be demolished, or structurally altered in such a way as to make the repairs valueless, at or soon after the end of the term. There are special provisions enabling the court in certain cases to relieve the tenant from liability for internal decorative repairs.[89]

(d) *Leave to sue.* There are also provisions which protect the tenant of any property (except agricultural holdings) let for a term of years certain of not less than seven years which has at least three years unexpired.[90] The lack of any provision for relief against claims for damages for non-repair often enabled landlords to force tenants to surrender their leases prematurely, and so the Leasehold Property (Repairs) Act 1938[91] provides that no action for damages for breach of a covenant to repair the property can be brought unless the landlord has first served on the tenant a notice in the form required by the Law of Property Act 1925, s.146,[92] and one month has elapsed thereafter. Further, whether the landlord is claiming damages or forfeiture, he cannot proceed without the leave of the court in such cases if within 28 days the tenant serves on the landlord a counter-notice claiming the protection of the Act; and the notice served by the landlord must inform the tenant of his right to serve a counter-notice. The court can grant leave only on certain specified grounds, *e.g.* that the cost of immediate repair would be small compared with the cost of repair in the future. An application for leave as a preliminary to proceedings for forfeiture is registrable as a pending land action.[93] The Act does not apply where the landlord, under a power in the lease, enters and carries out the repairs, and sues the tenant for the cost, for his claim against the tenant is for a debt, and not for "damages" within the Act.[94]

---

[85] *Ebbetts* v. *Conquest* [1895] 2 Ch. 377 (affd. [1896] A.C. 490).
[86] *Joyner* v. *Weeks* [1891] 2 Q.B. 31.
[87] s.18(1).
[88] *Smiley* v. *Townshend* [1950] 2 K.B. 311.
[89] L.P.A. 1925, s.147.
[90] Leasehold Property (Repairs) Act 1938, as extended by L. & T.A. 1954, s.51.
[91] s.1.
[92] See *ante*, p. 328.
[93] *Ante*, p. 83.
[94] *Hamilton* v. *Martell Securities Ltd.* [1984] Ch. 266; *Colchester Estates (Cardiff)* v. *Carlton Industries Plc* [1986] Ch. 80.

(e) *Deducting cost of repairs from rent.* A tenant who does repairs for which the landlord is liable is entitled to deduct the cost from the present or future rent,[95] though this should not be done without prior notification to the landlord.[96]

4. Covenant to insure. A covenant to insure against fire is broken if the premises are uninsured for any period, however short, even if no fire occurs.[97]

Sect. 4. Statutory Protection for Tenants

Three important classes of property are subject to special statutory codes designed to protect the tenant, particularly by giving him security of tenure and restricting the rent. The three classes are most agricultural holdings, most business premises, and many dwelling-houses. They will be dealt with in due course.[98]

Part 6

LEASEHOLD COVENANTS

Sect. 1. General Principles

Usually, a covenant is a promise under seal, *i.e.* contained in a deed; but in the law of landlord and tenant "covenant" includes other enforceable agreements.[99] It is necessary to consider how far covenants in leases are enforceable; and enforcement may be direct or indirect.

A. Direct Enforcement

1. If there is privity of contract, all covenants are enforceable. There is said to be privity of contract when the parties concerned have made a legally enforceable agreement.[1] Clearly, if two people have agreed to do or not to do certain things, their obligations bind them, whether or not their contract has anything to do with land, and whether the covenant is negative or positive. The covenants can be enforced both at law, by an action for damages, and in equity, by an injunction or specific performance.

---

[95] *Lee-Parker* v. *Izzet* [1971] 1 W.L.R. 1688; *Asco Developments Ltd.* v. *Gordon* [1978] E.G.D. 376.
[96] See [1981] Conv. 199 (A. Waite) for this and other precautions.
[97] *Penniall* v. *Harborne* (1848) 11 Q.B. 386.
[98] *Post*, pp. 522 *et seq.*
[99] See *Weg Motors Ltd.* v. *Hales* [1961] Ch. 176 at 193; [1962] Ch. 49 at 73.
[1] See the example *ante*, p. 307.

2. If there is merely privity of estate, only covenants which touch and concern the land are enforceable. There is said to be privity of estate between the parties when the relationship of landlord and tenant exists between them under the lease which contains the covenant in question.[2] In this case, any covenants in the lease which touch and concern the land, such as repairing covenants, are enforceable both at law and in equity. But covenants which do not relate to the land are not enforceable under this head.

3. If there is privity neither of contract nor of estate, then with two exceptions, no covenants are directly enforceable. There is privity neither of contract nor of estate between a lessor and a sub-lessee, or between the vendor of freehold land and a person who buys it from the purchaser. In such cases, the general rule is that covenants concerning the land are not enforceable. To this rule there are two exceptions, the second of which is of great importance.

(a) *Benefit.* First, even the common law allowed the *benefit* of certain covenants (*i.e.* the right to sue on the covenant) to be assigned with land; and equity followed the law. One example already mentioned[3] is that of covenants for title, the benefit of which runs with the land, so that whoever is entitled to the land is entitled to the benefit of the covenants. But the *burden* of a covenant (*i.e.* the liability to be sued upon it) cannot be assigned; at law, if there is no privity of estate the covenantor alone can be sued on a covenant.

(b) *Restrictive covenants in equity.* Second, equity allows the transmission of the burden (as well as the benefit) of restrictive covenants affecting the land, *i.e.* covenants which are negative in nature, restraining the doing of some act, such as building on the land. As usual, however, a purchaser of a legal estate takes free from such burdens if he takes without notice or if the covenants are void against him for want of registration.[4]

These three principles should be borne in mind whenever considering questions of the enforceability of covenants. They should be applied in the given order: if there is privity of contract, there is no need to look further, and if there is privity of estate, there is no need to consider the third head. Little more need be said about privity of contract, but the other heads must be considered in some detail.

B. Indirect Enforcement

Where a leasehold covenant cannot be enforced directly because there is privity neither of contract nor of estate, it may sometimes be enforced indirectly by virtue of a forfeiture clause in the lease. Thus if L leases land to T, and T sub-lets it to S, there is no privity between L and S; and similarly if T

---

[2] *Ibid.*
[3] *Ante*, p. 131.
[4] See *ante*, pp. 80, 87; and see *post*, p. 360.

makes a merely equitable assignment to A. Yet although L cannot directly enforce the covenants in the lease against S or A, proceedings for forfeiture of the lease will normally impel S or A to comply with the covenant (*e.g.* by doing the requisite repairs), and so avoid losing their interests; for if a lease is forfeited, the assignee loses it, and a sub-tenancy falls with it. Unlike direct enforcement, this indirect enforcement is subject to the important powers of the court to grant relief against forfeiture[5]; yet often it will be better to perform the covenant than to face the uncertainty, delay and cost of seeking relief. There seems to be nothing to confine this type of enforcement to covenants which touch and concern the land; and forfeiture clauses may be imposed on the assignment of a lease or on the grant of a fee simple.[6]

Sect. 2. Position of the Original Parties

If a lease is granted by L to T, there is privity of contract between them. The effect of this is not only that L may enforce all the covenants in the lease against T while he retains it, but also that T remains liable on the covenants for the whole term, notwithstanding any assignment of the lease.[7] Thus if T takes a lease for 99 years, he makes himself liable for 99 years, even if he assigns the lease after only one year has run; L may accordingly sue T for unpaid rent or for damages if the covenant to repair is not observed by the assignee. Similarly L remains liable on his covenants for the whole term, notwithstanding any assignment of the reversion by him.[8]

The rule is strict. An original lessee remains liable on covenants which, after assigning the lease, he is powerless to perform,[9] unless by apt wording in the lease he has limited his liability to the time while the lease is vested in him.[10] Otherwise he must rely on his rights to indemnity from subsequent assignees,[11] and these may prove to be little worth.[12] If the lease contains a rent review clause, he will be liable for any increased rent that has been properly fixed under the clause, even though he has had no say in the increase.[13] A lessor correspondingly remains liable on his covenants even after assigning his reversion.[14] The stringency of the rule, ill-understood by many lessees, has led to proposals for its abolition, for both lessor and lessee.[15]

---

[5] *Ante*, p. 329.
[6] See *ante*, pp. 76, 322.
[7] *Thursby* v. *Plant* (1670) 1 Wms.Saund. 230. Exceptions are few: see *ante*, p. 320 (perpetually renewable leases); and see Matrimonial Homes Act 1983, Sched. 1.
[8] *Stuart* v. *Joy* [1904] 1 K.B. 368; L.P.A. 1925, s.142(2).
[9] *Thames Manufacturing Co. Ltd.* v. *Perrotts* (*Nichol & Peyton*) *Ltd.* (1984) 50 P. & C.R. 1.
[10] See *Johnsey Estates Ltd.* v. *Webb* [1990] 1 E.G.L.R. 80 (sureties).
[11] See *post*, p. 356.
[12] See, *e.g. Weaver* v. *Mogford* [1988] 2 E.G.L.R. 48.
[13] *Centrovincial Estates Plc* v. *Bulk Storage Ltd.* (1983) 46 P. & C.R. 393; *Selous Street Properties Ltd.* v. *Oronel Fabrics Ltd.* (1984) 270 E.G. 643.
[14] See *Hua Chiao Commercial Bank Ltd.* v. *Chiaphua Industries Ltd.* [1987] A.C. 99.
[15] (1988) Law Com. No. 174; and see at p. 15 (large retail company's theoretical exposure to £50m.).

Sect. 3. Legal Leases: Position of Assignees

Where a lease is legal and not merely equitable[16] the benefit and burden of a covenant in it will usually pass to assignees of the lease or of the reversion. Yet the liability of such assignees depends on many factors, including the following.

(a) Whether the covenants "touch and concern" the land.

(b) Whether the burden of the covenants has passed to the assignee of the lease or of the reversion, as the case may be.

(c) Whether the benefit of the covenants has passed to the assignee of the reversion or of the lease, as the case may be.

(d) How far the personal representatives of a deceased lessee or assignee are liable for previous breaches.

(e) How far an assignee of a lease is liable to indemnify the original lessee.

(f) What effect a severance of the reversion has.

(g) What rights an assignee of the reversion has in respect of previous breaches.

These factors will now be considered.

A. Covenants Touching and Concerning the Land

The rights and liabilities of assignees, either of the lease or of the reversion, depend on whether or not the covenant in question "touches and concerns the land" or, to use more modern phraseology, has "reference to the subject-matter" of the lease.[17] Any covenant which affects the landlord *qua* landlord or the tenant *qua* tenant may be said to touch and concern the land.[18] A covenant by a tenant touches and concerns the land if (i) it is beneficial only to the reversioner for the time being; (ii) it affects the nature, quality, mode of user or value of the reversioner's land; and (iii) it is not expressed to be personal in nature[19]; and correspondingly for covenants by a landlord. Yet the rules have been assailed as being "purely arbitrary" and the distinctions as mostly being "quite illogical,"[20] and there have been proposals for the test to be abandoned.[21] Some examples of the operation of the test may be helpful: covenants in the left-hand column overleaf have been held to touch and concern the land, while those in the right-hand column have been held not to do so.[22]

---

[16] *Ante*, pp. 310 *et seq.* For covenants in equitable leases, see *post*, p. 359.

[17] L.P.A. 1925, ss.141(1), 142(1).

[18] *Breams Property Investment Co. Ltd.* v. *Strougler* [1948] 2 K.B. 1.

[19] *P. & A. Swift Investments* v. *Combined English Stores Group Plc* [1989] A.C. 632 at 642; and see *Horsey Estates Ltd.* v. *Steiger* [1899] 2 Q.B. 79 at 89.

[20] See *Grant* v. *Edmondson* [1931] 1 Ch. 1 at 29, *per* Romer L.J.

[21] (1988) Law Com. No. 174 at p. 17.

[22] For a fuller citation of authorities and further examples, see M. & W. 744, 745.

1. Covenants by a lessee

To pay rent.

To repair.

To pay the landlord £40 towards redecoration.[25]

To use as a private dwelling-house only.

Not to assign the lease without the lessor's consent.

To pay an annual sum to a third party.[23]

To repair and renew the tools of a smithy standing on the land.[24]

Not to employ persons living in other parishes to work in the demised mill.[26]

2. Covenants by a lessor

To renew the lease.[27]

To supply the demised premises with water.

Not to build on certain parts of the adjoining land.

To give the lessee the first refusal if adjoining land is sold.[28]

To pay at the end of the lease for chattels not amounting to fixtures.

To pay the tenant £500 at the end of the lease unless a new lease is granted.[29]

To repay to the tenant money deposited as security against breaches of covenant.[30]

B. *Principles of Transmission*

Having considered which covenants touch and concern the land, the rights and liabilities of assignees must next be examined.[31] As in every case when the question of enforcing legal liabilities arises, two separate points must be considered:

(i) Is the defendant liable? and

[23] *Mayho* v. *Buckhurst* (1617) Cro.Jac. 438.
[24] *Williams* v. *Earle* (1868) L.R. 3 Q.B. 739.
[25] *Boyer* v. *Warbey* [1953] 1 Q.B. 234.
[26] *Congleton Corporation* v. *Pattison* (1808) 10 East 130.
[27] *Richards* v. *Sydenham* (1703) 2 Vern. 447. The inclusion of this is regarded as somewhat anomalous: *Woodall* v. *Clifton* [1905] 2 Ch. 257 at 279.
[28] *Collison* v. *Lettsom* (1815) 6 Taunt. 224.
[29] *Re Hunter's Lease* [1942] Ch. 124.
[30] *Hua Chiao Commercial Bank Ltd.* v. *Chiaphua Industries Ltd.* [1987] A.C. 99.
[31] See generally (1991) 11 Leg.Stud. 47 (R. Thornton).

(ii) Is the plaintiff entitled to sue?

In the case of the rights and liabilities of assignees under covenants concerning land, this may be expressed in the form of—

(i) Has the burden of the covenant passed? and
(ii) Has the benefit of the covenant passed?

These questions are governed by the common law where the lessee assigns his lease, but by statute where the lessor assigns his reversion.

I. WHERE THE LESSEE ASSIGNS HIS LEASE

If L grants a legal lease to T, and T assigns it by deed to A, the common law rule laid down in *Spencer's Case*[32] is that A is entitled to the benefit, and subject to the burden, of all covenants and conditions touching and concerning the land; for there is privity of estate. In short, both the benefit and the burden of the covenants run with the land.

In applying this rule, the following points should be noted.

1. The lease must be in due form. Originally, the benefit and burden of covenants ran only with a lease by deed, but it can now run with a lease for three years or less made by unsealed writing.[33] A legal oral tenancy for less than three years has been held not to suffice,[34] but this rule may no longer be law.[35]

2. There must be a legal assignment of the whole term

(a) *Legal assignment.* The benefit and burden of covenants run with the lease only in the case of a legal assignment of the whole of the remainder of the term.[36] Where instead of an assignment there has been a sub-lease, the sub-lessee takes neither the benefit nor the burden of the covenants in the lease, even if his sub-lease is only one day shorter than the head lease. Thus if L leases land to X for 99 years, X assigns the lease to T, and T sub-leases the land to S for the residue of the term of 99 years less one day, S is not an assignee and there is privity neither of contract nor of estate between L and S. T is still the tenant under the lease for 99 years, and until he assigns it, he remains liable upon it. Consequently if S does some act which is contrary to a covenant in the 99 years' lease, L cannot sue S but can sue T. In practice, the covenants inserted in a sub-lease are always at least as stringent as those in the head lease, so that if a sub-tenant does some act forbidden by the head lease, this will constitute a breach of the covenants in the sub-lease and thus make the sub-tenant liable to the tenant, though not to the head lessor.

---

[32] (1583) 5 Co.Rep. 16a.
[33] See *Boyer* v. *Warbey* [1953] 1 Q.B. 234.
[34] *Elliot* v. *Johnson* (1866) L.R. 2 Q.B. 120.
[35] See *Boyer* v. *Warbey, supra,* at p. 246; and see *ante,* p. 310, for the tenancies which can be created orally; see also *post,* p. 357.
[36] *West* v. *Dobb* (1869) L.R. 4 Q.B. 634; *ante,* p. 322.

(b) *No legal assignment.* If there is no legal assignment, the benefit and burden of covenants in a lease do not run with it. Thus as a legal assignment can be made only by deed,[37] the covenants will not run where the assignment is made in some other way (*e.g.* by a contract to assign) and so takes effect only in equity.[38] Again, a squatter on leasehold land is not even an assignee of the lease, and so he can neither sue nor be sued on the covenants.[39] But an equitable assignee or a squatter may each be estopped from denying liability on the covenants in the lease,[40] and in any case the *benefit* of the covenants may be assigned.[41] In the case of registered land, privity of estate may perhaps be established if the squatter is registered as proprietor of the lease.[42]

(c) *Things in posse.* The burden of a covenant relating to a thing *in posse*, requiring the lessee to do something entirely new (such as to erect a building) formerly ran with the land only if the lessee had expressly covenanted for himself *and his assigns* that the covenant would be performed.[43] This still applies to leases granted before 1926; but it does not apply to leases granted after 1925,[44] and it has never applied to covenants relating to things *in esse* (in existence).

3. Liability of assignees. Although the original lessee is liable for all breaches of covenant throughout the term of the lease, an assignee is liable only for breaches committed while the lease is vested in him. He is under no liability for breaches committed either before the lease was assigned to him[45] or after he has assigned it[46]; but if a covenant is broken while the lease is vested in him, his liability for this breach continues despite any assignment.[47] Thus while the original lessee of an onerous lease cannot divest himself of liability for future breaches, an assignee can do so by assigning the lease, *e.g.* to a pauper,[48] though he will remain liable to indemnify the tenant who assigned the lease to him.[49]

[37] *Ante*, p. 322.
[38] *Cox* v. *Bishop* (1857) 8 De G.M. & G. 815; *Friary Holroyd and Healey's Breweries Ltd.* v. *Singleton* [1899] 1 Ch. 86 (revsd. on other grounds [1899] 2 Ch. 261).
[39] *Tichborne* v. *Weir* (1892) 67 L.T. 735; *post*, p. 503.
[40] See *Rodenhurst Estates Ltd.* v. *W. H. Barnes Ltd.* [1936] 2 All E.R. 3 (equitable assignee); *Ashe* v. *Hogan* [1920] 1 I.R. 159 (squatter); and see *ante*, p. 321.
[41] *Ante*, p. 349.
[42] See L.R.A. 1925, ss.9, 11, 75. The point was left open in *Spectrum Investment Co.* v. *Holmes* [1981] 1 W.L.R. 221: see at pp. 229, 230.
[43] *Spencer's Case, supra*; but see *Minshull* v. *Oakes* (1858) 2 H. & N. 793 (conditionally *in posse*).
[44] L.P.A. 1925, s.79.
[45] *Granada Theatres Ltd.* v. *Freehold Investment (Leytonstone) Ltd.* [1959] Ch. 592.
[46] *Paul* v. *Nurse* (1828) 8 B. & C. 486; but see L. & T.A. 1985, s.3(3)(a), inserted by L. & T.A. 1987, s.50 (dwellings: liability continues until tenant is notified of new landlord).
[47] *Harley* v. *King* (1835) 2 Cr.M. & R. 18.
[48] *Hopkinson* v. *Lovering* (1883) 11 Q.B.D. 92.
[49] See *post*, p. 356.

4. Liability of personal representatives

(a) *Liability.* Personal representatives may incur personal as well as representative liability.

(1) PERSONAL LIABILITY. If a lessee or assignee dies and his personal representatives take possession of the demised premises, the personal representatives occupy the position of assignees of the lease and so become personally liable on the covenants.[50] However, as regards the payment of rent (but not as regards other covenants) a personal representative may by proper pleading limit his liability to the yearly value of the premises.[51] Further, a personal representative who does not take possession of the premises incurs no personal liability upon any covenant.[52]

(2) REPRESENTATIVE LIABILITY. Upon the death of the original lessee, his personal representatives become liable upon the covenants of the lease for the rest of the term, but only to the extent of the assets of the deceased in their hands.[53] Similarly, if the deceased was an assignee, his personal representatives succeed to his liabilities (*e.g.* for breaches of covenant committed while the lease was vested in him), but only to the extent of his assets.[54] It is irrelevant to this head whether or not the personal representatives take possession of the premises.

(b) *Protection.* If the deceased was the original lessee, the personal representatives are in a difficult position since they cannot tell what breaches of covenant may occur in the future. Although it was settled that they need not put aside part of the estate as an indemnity fund for future breaches,[55] their position was precarious in other respects. In order to make it unnecessary for personal representatives to seek the protection of the court in such cases, the Trustee Act 1925[56] provides that if personal representatives in whom a lease is vested—

  (i) satisfy any existing liabilities which have been claimed,
 (ii) set aside any *fixed* sum agreed to be laid out on the premises, and
(iii) assign the lease to the person entitled under the will or intestacy, or to a purchaser,

they cease to have representative liability in respect of the assets which came to their hands. This does not render the assets immune from liability, for they may be followed into the hands of the beneficiaries; but the personal representatives need not concern themselves with this. These provisions apply equally whether the deceased was a lessee or an assignee. They do not, however, protect personal representatives from their personal liability if

[50] *Tilney* v. *Norris* (1700) 1 Ld.Raym. 553.
[51] *Rendall* v. *Andreae* (1892) 61 L.J.Q.B. 630.
[52] *Wollaston* v. *Hakewill* (1841) 3 Man. & G. 297 at 320.
[53] *Helier* v. *Casebert* (1665) 1 Lev. 127; *Youngmin* v. *Heath* [1974] 1 W.L.R. 135 (weekly tenancy).
[54] See *Re Lewis* [1939] Ch. 232.
[55] *King* v. *Malcott* (1852) 9 Hare 692.
[56] s.26, replacing L.P.Am.A. 1859, s.27.

they have taken possession of the premises, though they may set aside a fund from the estate by way of indemnity,[57] to be distributed when no longer needed.[58]

5. Indemnities by assignees

(a) *Implied indemnity.* If a covenant has been broken, the lessee and the assignee entitled to the lease at the time of the breach are each liable to be sued by the lessor. But although the lessor may sue either or both, he can only have one satisfaction: he has no right to recover twice.[59] The primary liability is that of the assignee, and if the lessee is sued, he may claim indemnity from the assignee in whom the lease was vested at the time of the breach, whether that assignee obtained the lease from the lessee or from some other assignee.[60]

(b) *Express indemnity.* In addition to this implied obligation to indemnify the lessee, it is usual for each assignee to enter into an express covenant to indemnify his assignor against future breaches of covenant; and by the Law of Property Act 1925,[61] in any assignment for value made after 1925 such a covenant is implied.

(c) *Effect.* The effect of these rights of indemnity may be illustrated thus:

```
A
| 99 years
B ——— C ——— D ——— E
                    | 21 years
                    F
```

A has leased land to B for 99 years; by successive assignments E has become entitled to the lease and has granted a sub-lease to F for 21 years. If F does some act which is contrary to a covenant in the head lease, A can sue either B (privity of contract) or E (privity of estate). If A sues B, B has an implied right to indemnity against E. Alternatively, if on the assignment to C a covenant of indemnity was given to B, he may claim indemnity from C. C in turn may claim indemnity from D, and D from E, provided in each case that a covenant for indemnity was given on the assignment. The importance of these various rights is emphasised if one of the parties is insolvent or has disappeared. Apart from the rules relating to restrictive covenants,[62] F incurs no liability to anyone except so far as his act was a breach of a covenant in the sub-lease and so makes him liable to E.

II. WHERE THE LESSOR ASSIGNS HIS REVERSION

If L, a tenant in fee simple, leased his land to T, and then L conveyed his

[57] *Re Owers* [1941] Ch. 389.
[58] *Re Lewis* [1939] Ch. 232.
[59] *Brett* v. *Cumberland* (1619) Cro.Jac. 521.
[60] *Wolveridge* v. *Steward* (1833) 1 Cr. & M. 644; *Moule* v. *Garrett* (1872) L.R. 7 Ex. 101.
[61] s.77(1)(c); Sched. 2, Pt. IX.
[62] *Post*, pp. 409 *et seq.*

fee simple, subject to the lease, to R, the common law rule was that with the exception of "implied covenants" (*i.e.* certain covenants which the law implied, such as to pay rent),[63] neither the benefit nor the burden of the covenants in the lease ran with the reversion: R was neither able to sue nor liable to be sued. But by the Grantees of Reversions Act 1540, sections 1 and 2, the benefit and burden of all covenants and provisions contained in a lease which touched and concerned the land (or had reference to the subject-matter of the lease, to use the modern phrase) passed with the reversion. These provisions were subsequently replaced and extended by statute, and are now contained in the Law of Property Act 1925, sections 141 and 142.

The following points should be noted.

1. The lease must be in due form. The Act of 1540 applied only to leases under seal,[64] but under the doctrine of *Walsh* v. *Lonsdale*[65] a specifically enforceable agreement is now treated as a lease by deed for this purpose,[66] and it suffices if the provisions are contained in a signed document.[67] After 1925, probably even a mere oral tenancy is sufficient, for by section 154 of the Law of Property Act 1925, sections 141 and 142 extend to an underlease "or other tenancy."[68]

2. The reversion may have been assigned by deed in whole or in part. The assignee of the entire reversion takes the benefit and burden of the provisions in the lease. Where the reversion is not assigned in its entirety, the position is not so simple. Two separate cases must be considered.

(a) *Severance as regards the estate.* Where the assignee has part of the reversion, as where a fee simple reversioner grants a lease of his reversion to X, the reversion is severed as regards the estate. In this case, X, as the person entitled to part of the reversion, falls within the statutory provisions, so that the benefit and burden of both covenants and conditions pass to him as the immediate reversioner.[69]

(b) *Severance as regards the land.* Where the assignee has the reversion of part, as where a fee simple reversioner conveys the fee simple in half the land to X, the reversion is severed as regards the land. In this case, under the Act of 1540 the covenants ran with the reversion.[70] But conditions[71] (*e.g.* a condition for forfeiture on non-payment of rent) did not, unless the severance took place by operation of law, *e.g.* on a compulsory acquisition.[72]

---

[63] See *Vyvyan* v. *Arthur* (1823) 1 B. & C. 410.
[64] *Smith* v. *Egginton* (1874) L.R. 9 C.P. 145.
[65] *Ante*, p. 311.
[66] *Rickett* v. *Green* [1910] 1 K.B. 253.
[67] *Rye* v. *Purcell* [1926] 1 K.B. 446; *Weg Motors Ltd.* v. *Hales* [1962] Ch. 49; see *ante*, pp. 117 *et seq.* for the requirements for contracts made after September 26, 1989.
[68] Contrast *ante*, p. 353.
[69] *Wright* v. *Burroughes* (1846) 3 C.B. 685.
[70] *Twynam* v. *Pickard* (1818) 2 B. & Ald. 105.
[71] See *ante*, p. 324.
[72] *Piggott* v. *Middlesex County Council* [1909] 1 Ch. 134.

However, by the Law of Property Act 1925,[73] all conditions and rights of re-entry became severable on the severance of the reversion. The tenancy itself, however, continues as one tenancy.[74]

3. Rights of an assignee of the reversion to sue and forfeit for previous breaches. At common law, a right to sue for damages or to forfeit the lease for breach of covenant could not be assigned, so that if a reversion was assigned after a covenant had been broken, the new reversioner could not sue[75] or forfeit[76] the lease. Now, after an assignment of the reversion, the assignee is alone entitled to sue the tenant for rent or for breaches of covenant, whether such rent accrued or such breaches occurred before or after the assignment.[77] This is brought about by the Law of Property Act 1925,[78] which also provides that rights of re-entry are enforceable by the new reversioner, provided they have not been waived. Waiver may be express or implied.[79] Waiver will not be implied merely because the reversion is assigned "subject to and with the benefit of" the lease[80]; it is "the merest *res inter alios acta*", without any impact on the tenant.[81]

4. Enforcement after assignment. The liability of the original parties to a lease during the whole term of the lease[82] is not destroyed by assignment. Thus for covenants touching and concerning the land an original lessor remains liable even after he has assigned the reversion[83]; and an original lessee who assigns his term remains liable even to a subsequent assignee of the reversion with whom he has never had any privity of estate.[84] Further, a tenant's right to sue his landlord for existing breaches of covenant continues to exist after he has assigned the lease.[85]

Sect. 4. Equitable Tenancies: Position of Assignees

Where a lease or tenancy is merely equitable (*e.g.* through the lack of a deed[86]), the original parties are of course bound by privity of contract[87]; but

---

[73] s.140(1), replacing L.P.Am.A. 1859, s.3, as extended by C.A. 1881, s.12. The old law continues to apply if the lease was made before 1882 and the reversion was severed before 1926.
[74] *Jelley* v. *Buckman* [1974] Q.B. 488.
[75] *Flight* v. *Bentley* (1835) 7 Sim. 149.
[76] *Hunt* v. *Remnant* (1854) 9 Exch. 635.
[77] *Re King* [1963] Ch. 459; *London and County (A. & D.) Ltd.* v. *Wilfred Sportsman Ltd.* [1971] Ch. 764.
[78] s.141, replacing C.A. 1911, s.2.
[79] For waiver, see *ante*, p. 325.
[80] *London and County (A. & D.) Ltd.* v. *Wilfred Sportsman Ltd.*, *supra*.
[81] *Ibid.* at p. 782, *per* Russell L.J.
[82] *Ante*, p. 350.
[83] *Celsteel Ltd.* v. *Alton House Holdings Ltd. (No. 2)* [1986] 1 W.L.R. 666 at 672, 673; [1987] 1 W.L.R. 291 at 296.
[84] *Arlesford Trading Co. Ltd.* v. *Servansingh* [1971] 1 W.L.R. 1080.
[85] *City and Metropolitan Properties Ltd.* v. *Greycroft* (1987) 54 P. & C.R. 266.
[86] See *ante*, pp. 311–314.
[87] *Ante*, p. 350.

the rules for the running of the benefit and burden of covenants which touch and concern the land, as considered above, are only partly applicable.

1. Running with the land. The common law rule in *Spencer's Case*[88] under which an assignee of the tenancy takes the benefit and burden of such covenants does not appear to apply.[89] Thus if L grants an equitable tenancy to X, and X assigns it to Y, L cannot enforce the covenants against Y,[90] for there is no privity of estate which will carry the burden to Y. It would be convenient if equity were to follow the law and make the burden of the covenants run with the land, and there are dicta supporting the view that it does.[91] There is also a broad principle that he who takes the benefit must also bear the burden.[92] But authorities to the contrary[93] have yet to be disposed of satisfactorily.[94]

The *benefit* of such covenants is less confined. If L grants an equitable tenancy to X, who then assigns it to Y, Y may be able to enforce the covenants against L, since the benefit of the covenants, being assignable,[95] can be passed to Y.[96]

2. Running with the reversion. Where the reversion on an equitable tenancy is assigned, the position is substantially the same as where the tenancy is legal: for the statutory provisions[97] for the running of the benefit and burden with the reversion are applicable. "Lease" in the statute is defined as including an underlease "or any other tenancy," and this makes the benefit and burden run with the reversion in the same way as if the tenancy were legal.[98]

Sect. 5. No Privity: Restrictive Covenants

Where there is privity neither of contract nor of estate, the rule at law is that no covenants can be enforced. Thus if L grants a lease to T, who grants a sublease to S, there is no privity of contract or estate between L and S, and so the covenants in the lease and sub-lease cannot be enforced between them. Again, when V sells his freehold land to P, and P then sells it to Q, there is no privity of contract or estate between V and Q. Yet although in such cases covenants are not enforceable at law, in equity a doctrine grew up in the last

[88] (1583) 5 Co.Rep. 16a; *ante*, p. 353.
[89] *Marquis Camden* v. *Batterbury* (1860) 7 C.B.N.S. 864; *Elliott* v. *Johnson* (1866) L.R. 2 Q.B. 120.
[90] See *Austerberry* v. *Corporation of Oldham* (1885) 29 Ch.D. 750.
[91] See *Boyer* v. *Warbey* [1953] 1 Q.B. 234 at 246, 247.
[92] *Tito* v. *Waddell* (*No.* 2) [1977] Ch. 106 at 299–302.
[93] See, *e.g. Elliott* v. *Johnson, supra*; and see the authorities on equitable assignments, *ante*, p. 354.
[94] See the general survey of equitable leases and equitable assignments at [1978] C.L.J. 98 (R. J. Smith).
[95] *Ante*, pp. 349, 351.
[96] See *Griffith* v. *Pelton* [1958] Ch. 205, where, however, the lease was legal.
[97] L.P.A. 1925, ss.141, 142, replacing C.A. 1881, ss.10, 11; *ante*, p. 357.
[98] *Rickett* v. *Green* [1910] 1 K.B. 253; *Rye* v. *Purcell* [1926] 1 K.B. 446.

century which made restrictive covenants relating to land (*i.e.* covenants prohibiting certain acts on the land) enforceable in equity despite the lack of any privity. Various conditions evolved, mainly in relation to freehold land, which regulated the application and operation of the doctrine; and in some important respects these conditions resemble those governing easements.[99] Restrictive covenants will accordingly be discussed after easements have been considered.[1] For the present, it need only be said that restrictive covenants in a head lease that comply with the relevant rules may usually be enforced in equity against sub-tenants. In addition, covenants in a head lease, whether restrictive or not, may be indirectly enforceable against sub-tenants by virtue of a forfeiture clause in the lease.[2]

---

[99] See *post*, p. 374.
[1] See *post*, pp. 409 *et seq.*; and see *ante*, p. 349.
[2] See *ante*, p. 349.

CHAPTER 10

INCORPOREAL HEREDITAMENTS

IT has already been seen that incorporeal hereditaments are rights in land which do not give the owner present physical possession of the land.[1] There are two quite distinct classes of incorporeal hereditaments:

1. Those which may ripen into corporeal hereditaments. Thus a grant to A for life with remainder to B in fee simple gave B an incorporeal hereditament which became corporeal after A's death.
2. Those which can never become corporeal hereditaments but are merely rights over the land of another, *e.g.* rentcharges.

The first class has already been dealt with.[2] It is with incorporeal hereditaments in the latter class that this chapter is concerned. Most are either obsolete or of little importance in connection with the modern law of real property, *e.g.* titles of honour, advowsons[3] and tithes.[4] The only incorporeal hereditaments which need be considered at length are rentcharges, easements and profits. They do not form a homogeneous class. Some, such as easements, can exist only for the benefit of other land, while others, such as rentcharges, lead an independent existence. In one sense, those in the former category are not hereditaments at all, for they cannot be inherited or dealt with except as appendages to the land which they benefit.

Part 1

RENTCHARGES

Sect. 1. Nature of Rentcharges

1. Rentcharges and rent services. Periodical payments in respect of land fall under the two main heads of rentcharges and rent services. Where the relationship of lord and tenant exists between the parties, any rent payable by virtue of that relationship by the tenant to the lord is a rent service. If there is no relationship of lord and tenant, the rent is a rentcharge. Thus if L grants a lease to T at £5,000 per annum and X charges his fee simple estate with the payment of £2,000 per annum to Y, L has a rent service and Y a rentcharge. Since the Statute *Quia Emptores* 1290 it has been impossible for a grantor to reserve any services on a conveyance of freehold land in fee

---

[1] *Ante*, p. 66; and see generally M. & W. 813–818.
[2] *Ante*, pp. 174 *et seq.*
[3] See *ante*, p. 72.
[4] See *ante*, p. 76.

simple, for the grantee holds of the grantor's lord, and not of the grantor. Consequently, no rent reserved on a conveyance of freehold land in fee simple after 1290 can be a rent service. Although at law services could be reserved when an owner in fee simple granted a life estate[5] or a fee tail, it was most unusual to do so. The only rent service now met with in practice is the rent reserved upon the grant of a lease for a term of years. A rent service is annexed to a reversion, while a rentcharge stands on its own. In some parts of the country (including Manchester, Bath and Bristol) rentcharges were for long used wholly or partly instead of paying a capital sum on the purchase of property.[6]

2. Legal and equitable rentcharges. A rentcharge is real property, so that both at law and in equity it could be held for any of the usual estates or interests.[7] However, since 1925 an interest in a rentcharge can be legal only if it is—

(a) in possession, and
(b) either perpetual or for a term of years absolute.[8]

Further, a rentcharge cannot exist at law unless the proper formalities have been employed for its creation.[9]

3. Rentcharge on a rentcharge. At common law, a rentcharge could be charged only upon a corporeal hereditament. There could be no rentcharge charged upon another rentcharge or other incorporeal hereditament[10]; a right of distress would clearly be inappropriate in such cases. However, since 1925 a rentcharge charged upon another rentcharge is valid, even if created before 1926; and special provisions have been made for enforcing payment.[11]

4. Restrictions on rentcharges. The Rentcharges Act 1977 severely curtailed most rentcharges, excepting those types which still performed a useful service. Apart from the exceptions, the Act—

(i) prevented the creation of any rentcharge after August 21, 1977; and
(ii) provided for the extinguishment of existing rentcharges after 60 years.

These provisions will be considered below.

---

[5] A grant for life at a rent now creates a term of 90 years: see *ante*, p. 319.
[6] See generally (1975) Law.Com. No. 68.
[7] See, *e.g. Chaplin* v. *Chaplin* (1733) 3 P.Wms. 229 (entail); *Re Fraser* [1904] 1 Ch. 726 (term of years).
[8] *Ante*, p. 75.
[9] *Infra*.
[10] *Re The Alms Corn Charity* [1901] 2 Ch. 750 at 759.
[11] L.P.A. 1925, s.122: *post*, p. 365.

Sect. 2. Creation and Transfer of Rentcharges

Subject to the Rentcharges Act 1977, a rentcharge can be created only as follows.

1. Form

(a) *By statute.* A rentcharge may be created either by statute, or by virtue of powers conferred thereby.[12]

(b) *By instrument inter vivos.* Apart from statute, a legal rentcharge can be created *inter vivos* only by a deed[13]; but a document merely in writing may create an equitable rentcharge.[14]

(c) *By will.* A will now operates only in equity,[15] so that if a rentcharge is created or devised by will, the beneficiary gets no legal interest until the personal representatives have assented to the gift.[16]

2. Words of limitation. If an existing rentcharge is being transferred by deed or will, the normal rule for corporeal hereditaments applies and the whole interest in the rentcharge passes without words of limitation unless a contrary intention is shown.[17] But if a rentcharge is being created by will or (perhaps) by deed, only a life interest will be created unless an intention is shown to create some larger interest.[18]

3. Restrictions on creation. By the Rentcharges Act 1977,[19] no new rentcharge can, with certain exceptions, be created either at law or in equity after August 21, 1977. The exceptions are as follows.[20]

(a) *Family charges:* a rentcharge which makes the land settled land, or would do so if it were not already settled or held on trust for sale.[21]

(b) *Court or statute:* a rentcharge imposed under an order of the court or a statutory rentcharge for works on land.

(c) *Estate rentcharges:* an "estate rentcharge," *i.e.* a rentcharge for a nominal amount which is subject to a right of re-entry imposed as a means of enforcing covenants or other obligations relating to land.[22]

---

[12] See, *e.g.* Improvement of Land Act 1864.
[13] See *Hewlins* v. *Shippam* (1826) 5 B. & C. 221 at 229.
[14] *Jackson* v. *Lever* (1792) 3 Bro.C.C. 605; L.P.A. 1925, s.53.
[15] See L.P.A.(Am.)A. 1924, Sched. IX.
[16] For assents, see *ante*, p. 165.
[17] *Ante*, p. 31.
[18] See *Nichols* v. *Hawkes* (1853) 10 Hare 342; *Grant* v. *Edmondson* [1930] 2 Ch. 245 at 254; [1931] 1 Ch. 1; *ante*, pp. 31, 32; M. & W. 822, 823.
[19] s.2(1), (2).
[20] s.2(3), (4), (5).
[21] See *ante*, p. 234.
[22] See *post*, p. 419.

Sect. 3. Means of Enforcing Payment

A. Rentcharge Charged on Land

There are four remedies available to the owner of a rentcharge charged on land if it is not paid. The first remedy, namely, an action for the money, is given by the common law; the other three are created by statute,[23] and replace remedies formerly expressly conferred by most instruments creating rentcharges.

1. Action for the money. A personal action for the rent will lie against the "terre tenant" (the freehold tenant in possession of the land upon which the rent is charged) even if the rent was not created by him[24] and exceeds the value of the land.[25] If the land has been divided, the terre tenant of any part is liable for the full amount[26]; but a mere lessee for a term of years is not liable,[27] for the action lies only against the freeholder.

Although the right to sue and the liability to be sued run with the rentcharge and the land respectively, the benefit of an express covenant for payment does not run with the rentcharge without express assignment.[28] Thus if a rentcharge created by A in favour of X is conveyed to Y and the land to B, Y cannot sue A on his covenant for payment if B fails to pay.

2. Distress. If an express power of distress is given by the instrument creating the rentcharge, the extent of the right is a question of construction. If there is no such express power, and the rentcharge was created before 1882, the rentcharge owner can distrain upon the land as soon as the rent or any part of it is in arrear.[29] If the rentcharge was created after 1881, then, subject to any contrary intention, the rentcharge owner can distrain as soon as the rent or any part of it is 21 days in arrear.[30]

3. Entry into possession. If a rentcharge was created after 1881 and shows no contrary intention, the rentcharge owner may, when the rent or any part of it is 40 days in arrear, enter and take possession of the land without impeachment of waste and take the income until he has paid himself all rent due with costs.[31]

4. Demise to a trustee. If the rentcharge was created after 1881 and shows no contrary intention, the rentcharge owner may, if the rent or any part of it is 40 days in arrear, demise the land to a trustee for a term of years, with or

---

[23] L.P.A. 1925, s.121, replacing C.A. 1881, s.44.
[24] *Thomas* v. *Sylvester* (1873) L.R. 8 Q.B. 368.
[25] *Pertwee* v. *Townsend* [1896] 2 Q.B. 129.
[26] *Christie* v. *Barker* (1884) 53 L.J.Q.B. 537.
[27] *Re Herbage Rents* [1896] 2 Ch. 811.
[28] See *Grant* v. *Edmondson* [1931] 1 Ch. 1, criticised (1931) 47 L.Q.R. 380 (W. Strachan).
[29] L. & T.A. 1730, s.5.
[30] L.P.A. 1925, s.121(2).
[31] *Ibid.* s.121(3).

without impeachment of waste, on trust to raise the money due, with all costs and expenses, by creating a mortgage, receiving the income or any other reasonable means.[32] If a rentcharge owner has only an equitable interest, he can grant only an equitable lease to the trustee, but the estate owner can be compelled to clothe the equitable lease with the legal estate.[33]

If the rentcharge is created after July 15, 1964, the rule against perpetuities does not apply to any powers or remedies for enforcing it.[34] If the rentcharge was created before that date the last three statutory remedies were expressly excepted from the rule, together with similar express powers conferred by an instrument.[35] Other, wider, provisions were not considered to be excepted from the rule, *e.g.* a clause which is sometimes inserted entitling the rentcharge owner to effect a permanent forfeiture of the land if the rent is unpaid for a specified period.[36]

B. Rentcharge Charged on Another Rentcharge

Instead of the statutory remedies of distress, entry into possession and demise to a trustee, the owner of a rentcharge charged upon another rentcharge may appoint a receiver if the rent or any part of it is 21 days in arrear.[37] The receiver has all the powers of a receiver appointed by a mortgagee.[38] Thus if Greenacre is charged with a rent of £100 per annum and that rentcharge is charged with a rent of £25 per annum in favour of X, a receiver of the £100 can be appointed by X if the £25 is unpaid for 21 days.

Sect. 4. Extinguishment of Rentcharges

A rentcharge may be extinguished by release, statutory discharge, merger, limitation or the expiry of the 60-year period under the Rentcharges Act 1977.

1. Release. The owner of a rentcharge may by deed release the land from the rent, either wholly or in part. A partial release may take the form of releasing all the land from part of the rent,[39] or releasing part of the land from the whole of the rent.[40] An informal release may be valid in equity.

2. Statutory redemption. Land will be discharged from a rentcharge if the landowner obtains a "redemption certificate" from the Secretary of State for

[32] *Ibid.* s.121(4).
[33] *Ibid.* ss.3(1), 8(2).
[34] Perpetuities and Accumulations Act 1964, s.11, amending L.P.A. 1925, s.121(6); *ante,* p. 206.
[35] L.P.A. 1925, s.121(6).
[36] See *Re Trustees of Hollis' Hospital and Hague's Contract* [1899] 2 Ch. 540, criticised in Challis R.P. 190.
[37] L.P.A. 1925, s.122(2), (3).
[38] *Ibid.* s.122(2); *post,* p. 457.
[39] Co.Litt. 148a.
[40] L.P.A 1925, s.70.

the Environment (or Wales) certifying that he has paid the owner of the rentcharge a sum representing the capital value as certified by the Secretary of State.[41]

3. Merger. At common law, if a rentcharge became vested in the same person as the land upon which it was charged, the rentcharge became extinguished by merger, even if this was not the intention.[42] For this to occur, both the rent and the land must have been vested in the same person at the same time and in the same right.[43] This automatic rule of the common law no longer applies, for, by the Law of Property Act 1925,[44] there is to be no merger at law except in cases where there would have been a merger in equity, and the equitable rule is that merger depends upon the intention of the parties.[45] Even if an intention that there should be no merger cannot be shown, there will be a presumption against merger if it is to the interest of the person concerned to prevent it.[46]

4. Limitation. If a rentcharge is not paid for 12 years and no sufficient acknowledgement of the owner's title is made, it is extinguished under the Limitation Act 1980.[47]

5. Elapse of 60 years. With certain exceptions, every rentcharge will be extinguished, without compensation, when 60 years have elapsed since it was first payable or since July 21, 1977 (*i.e.* on July 21, 2037), whichever is the later.[48] But this does not apply to variable rentcharges, nor to any rentcharge, whenever created, that is of the kind excluded from the prohibition against creation.[49]

Sect. 5. Types of Rent

A summary of the various kinds of rent may be useful.

1. Rent service: this is rent due from a tenant to his lord by reason of tenure; it is now encountered only in the case of rent due under a lease or tenancy.

2. Rentcharge: this is a periodical sum charged on land independently of any relationship of lord and tenant, supported by a power of distress.

3. Rent seck: this was a rentcharge with no power of distress. It is now obsolete.

[41] Rentcharges Act 1977, ss.8–10, replacing L.P.A. 1925, s.191.
[42] *Capital and Counties Bank Ltd.* v. *Rhodes* [1903] 1 Ch. 631 at 652.
[43] *Re Radcliffe* [1892] 1 Ch. 227.
[44] s.185, replacing J.A. 1873, s.25(4).
[45] *Ingle* v. *Vaughan Jenkins* [1900] 2 Ch. 368.
[46] *Re Fletcher* [1917] 1 Ch. 339.
[47] See *post*, p. 498.
[48] Rentcharges Act 1977, s.3(1).
[49] *Ibid.* s.3(3), (4), (5); *ante*, p. 363.

4. Chief rent: this was a rent service reserved on the subinfeudation of freehold land in fee simple. The Statute *Quia Emptores* 1290 for the most part prevented such rents being created.[50] Any chief rents existing in 1925 were extinguished by the end of 1935.[51] In some parts of the country, *e.g.* Manchester, rentcharges are sometimes called chief rents.

5. Fee farm rent: this was the name originally used for chief rents; latterly, it has been applied to rentcharges reserved on a conveyance in fee simple.

6. Quit rent: this was a rent service payable by a copyholder to his lord, whereby he went quit of his obligation to perform agricultural services; and chief rents were sometimes called quit rents. Quit rents existing in 1925 were extinguished by the end of 1935.[52]

7. Rents of assize: this term is rarely encountered today; it was applied both to chief rents and quit rents.

Part 2

EASEMENTS AND PROFITS

Sect. 1. Nature of Easements

An easement may be defined as a right to use, or restrict the use of, the land of another person in some way. This definition is neither exact nor particularly helpful, for it includes certain rights which are not easements, such as restrictive covenants, and it fails to illustrate what sort of a right an easement is. Examples of easements are rights of way, rights of light and rights of water. The best way in which to amplify this imperfect definition is to examine—

   (a) the essentials of an easement, and
   (b) the distinction between easements and certain analogous rights.

A. *Essentials of an Easement*

1. There must be a dominant and a servient tenement.[53] If X owns Greenacre and grants a right to use a path across it to the owner for the time being of the neighbouring plot of Whiteacre, Greenacre is the servient tenement and Whiteacre the dominant tenement. Had X granted the right to A who owned no land at all, A would have acquired a licence to walk over Greenacre, but his right could not exist as an easement, for a dominant tenement is

---

[50] *Ante*, p. 361.
[51] See *ante*, p. 22.
[52] *Ibid.*
[53] *Hawkins* v. *Rutter* [1892] 1 Q.B. 668.

lacking. Put technically, an easement cannot exist in gross[54] (independently of the ownership of land) but only as appurtenant (attached) to a dominant tenement.[55] On any transfer of the dominant tenement, the easement will pass with the land, so that the occupier for the time being can enjoy it,[56] even if he is a mere lessee.[57]

2. The easement must accommodate the dominant tenement. A right cannot exist as an easement unless it confers a benefit on the dominant tenement as a tenement. It is not enough that the right should give the owner for the time being some personal advantage unconnected with his land, such as a right to use a wall on the servient tenement for advertising generally and not merely in connection with a business carried on upon the dominant tenement.[58] The test is whether the right makes the dominant tenement a better and more convenient tenement, *e.g.* a right to affix to adjoining premises a signboard for a public house.[59] There has to be some nexus between the enjoyment of the right and the use of the dominant tenement, so that the grant to a purchaser of the right free of charge to attend a nearby zoo or cricket ground cannot create an easement.[60]

Again, if X owns land in Northumberland, he cannot burden it with an easement of way in favour of land in Kent, for although it may be very convenient for the owner of the Kentish land to walk across X's Northumberland estate when he goes north, the right of way does not improve the Kentish land as a tenement.[61] This does not mean that a right cannot exist as an easement unless the dominant and servient tenements are contiguous; even if they are separated by other land, an easement can still exist, provided it in fact confers some benefit upon the dominant tenement as such,[62] as does a right for the dominant owner to enjoy an adjacent pleasure ground.[63] Nor will a right be any the less an easement merely because it benefits other land as well as the dominant tenement.[64]

In *Ackroyd* v. *Smith*[65] it was held that a right of way granted "for all purposes" to the tenant of Whiteacre and his successors in title was not an easement, for the grant permitted the way to be used for purposes not connected with Whiteacre. Had the grant been worded "for all purposes

---

[54] *Rangeley* v. *Midland Ry.* (1868) 3 Ch.App. 306 at 310. See (1980) 96 L.Q.R. 557 (M. F. Sturley).

[55] See *Re Salvin's Indenture* [1938] 2 All E.R. 498 (dominant tenement partly incorporeal).

[56] L.P.A. 1925, s.187(1); *Leech* v. *Schweder* (1874) 9 Ch.App. 463 at 474, 475.

[57] *Thorpe* v. *Brumfitt* (1873) 8 Ch.App. 650.

[58] *Clapman* v. *Edwards* [1938] 2 All E.R. 507.

[59] *Moody* v. *Steggles* (1879) 12 Ch.D. 261.

[60] *Re Ellenborough Park* [1956] Ch. 131 at 174.

[61] See *Bailey* v. *Stephens* (1862) 12 C.B. (N.S.) 91 at 115.

[62] *Todrick* v. *Western National Omnibus Co. Ltd.* [1934] Ch. 561; *Pugh* v. *Savage* [1970] 2 Q.B. 373.

[63] *Re Ellenborough Park* [1956] Ch. 131 (park in a square).

[64] *Simpson* v. *Mayor of Godmanchester* [1897] A.C. 696.

[65] (1850) 10 C.B. 164.

connected with Whiteacre" it could have created an easement. Probably the words used would be construed in this sense if the case arose today.[66]

In *Hill* v. *Tupper*[67] the owner of a canal leased land on the bank of the canal to Hill, and granted him the sole and exclusive right of putting pleasure boats on the canal. Tupper, without any authority, put rival pleasure boats on the canal. The question was whether Hill could successfully sue Tupper. If Hill's right amounted to an easement, he could sue anyone who interfered with it, for it was a right in land. If it was not an easement, then it could only be a licence,[68] *i.e.* a mere personal arrangement between Hill and the canal owner not amounting to an interest in land, so that Hill would have no right to sue those interfering with it. It was held that since the right did not improve Hill's land *qua* land, but gave him a mere personal advantage, it was not an easement and so he could not sue Tupper. The result would have been different if the right granted had been to cross and recross the canal to get to and from Hill's land. The canal owner, of course, could have sued Tupper for trespassing on the canal.[69]

3. The dominant and servient tenements must be owned or occupied by different persons. An easement is essentially a right in *alieno solo* (in the soil of another): a man cannot have an easement over his own land. "When the owner of Whiteacre and Blackacre passes over the former to Blackacre, he is not exercising a right of way in respect of Blackacre; he is merely making use of his own land to get from one part of it to another."[70]

It should be noted, however, that the same person must not only own both tenements but also occupy both of them before the existence of an easement is rendered impossible. Thus if an easement over Greenacre is appurtenant to Whiteacre, it will not be affected by the fee simple in each plot becoming vested in one person if the plots are occupied by different lessees[71]; unity of ownership without unity of possession is not fatal to an easement. Similarly, if the fee simple in each plot is owned by different persons, the easement will not be destroyed if the plots are leased to the same tenant, creating unity of possession without unity of ownership; during the currency of the lease the easement is suspended but it will revive when the lease ends.[72]

The name "quasi-easements" is often used to describe rights habitually exercised by a man over part of his own land which, if the part in question were owned and occupied by another, would be easements. These are of some importance, for in certain circumstances they may become true easements.[73]

[66] See *Todrick* v. *Western National Omnibus Co. Ltd.* [1934] Ch. 561 at 583–585; and see *Clapman* v. *Edwards*, *supra*.
[67] (1863) 2 H. & C. 121.
[68] See *post*, pp. 374, 427.
[69] See *Lord Chesterfield* v. *Harris* [1908] 2 Ch. 397 at 412 (affd. [1911] A.C. 623).
[70] *Roe* v. *Siddons* (1888) 22 Q.B.D. 224 at 236, *per* Fry L.J.
[71] *Richardson* v. *Graham* [1908] 1 K.B. 39; and see *Buckby* v. *Coles* (1814) 5 Taunt. 311 at 315.
[72] *Thomas* v. *Thomas* (1835) 2 Cr.M. & R. 34 (see especially at p. 40).
[73] *Post*, pp. 384 *et seq.*

4. The easement must be capable of forming the subject-matter of a grant.
No right can exist as an easement unless it could have been granted by deed.
This involves the following points.

(a) *There must be a capable grantor.* There can be no claim to an easement
if at the relevant times the servient tenement was owned by someone
incapable of granting an easement, *e.g.* a statutory corporation with no
power to grant easements.[74]

(b) *There must be a capable grantee.* An easement can be claimed only by a
legal person capable of receiving a grant. Thus a claim by a company with no
power to acquire easements must fail[75]; similarly, a fluctuating body of
persons, such as "the inhabitants for the time being of the village of X,"
cannot claim an easement, for no grant could be made to them. But such
bodies may claim similar rights by showing that there is a custom to that
effect, such as a customary right of way across land to reach the parish
church,[76] or a customary right to play games[77] or dry nets on certain land.[78]
There may also be a customary duty, such as a duty binding the frontagers to
a common to fence against cattle grazing the common.[79]

(c) *The right must be sufficiently definite.* The extent of the right claimed
must be capable of reasonable definition. Thus although there can be an
easement of light where a defined window receives a defined amount of
light, there can be no easement of privacy,[80] nor of prospect (the right to a
view), for "the law does not give an action for such things of delight."[81]
Again, an easement for the passage of air through a defined channel may
exist, but there can be no easement for the general flow of air over land to a
windmill or chimney.[82] But sometimes such rights may be obtained by
restrictive covenants or under the rule against derogation from grant.[83]

(d) *The right must be within the general nature of rights capable of existing
as easements.* Although most easements fall under one of the well-known
heads of easements, such as way, light, support and so on, the list of
easements is not closed. "The category of servitudes and easements must
alter and expand with the changes that take place in the circumstances of
mankind."[84] But there are limits. "It must not therefore be supposed that
incidents of a novel kind can be devised and attached to property, at the
fancy or caprice of any owner."[85] Today, new rights are unlikely to be

[74] See *Re Salvin's Indenture* [1938] 2 All E.R. 498.
[75] *National Guaranteed Manure Co.* v. *Donald* (1859) 4 H. & N. 8.
[76] *Brocklebank* v. *Thompson* [1903] 2 Ch. 344.
[77] *New Windsor Corporation* v. *Mellor* [1974] 1 W.L.R. 1504.
[78] *Mercer* v. *Denne* [1905] 2 Ch. 538; *post*, p. 375.
[79] *Egerton* v. *Harding* [1975] Q.B. 62.
[80] *Browne* v. *Flower* [1911] 1 Ch. 219.
[81] *William Aldred's Case* (1610) 9 Co.Rep. 57b at 58b, *per* Wray C.J.
[82] *Webb* v. *Bird* (1862) 13 C.B. (N.S.) 841; *Bryant* v. *Lefever* (1879) 4 C.P.D. 172.
[83] *Post*, pp. 375, 409 *et seq.*
[84] *Dyce* v. *Hay* (1852) 1 Macq. 205 at 312, *per* Lord St. Leonards L.C.
[85] *Keppell* v. *Bailey* (1833) 2 My. & K. 517 at 535, *per* Lord Brougham L.C.

recognised as easements if they prevent the servient owner from doing things on his land, in the way that rights of light do, as distinct from requiring him merely to suffer something to be done on his land.[86] Nor are rights likely to be accepted as easements if they involve the servient owner in the expenditure of money, for no recognised easement does this.[87] An exception is the obligation to fence land in order to keep out cattle.[88] This has been described as "in the nature of a spurious easement,"[89] or, more kindly, as "in the nature of an easement"[90]; and it may also arise by custom.[91] But new rights which do not involve the servient owner in expenditure have from time to time been recognised as easements. Thus in 1896 the right to go upon the land of another to open sluice gates,[92] in 1915 a right to store casks and trade produce on land,[93] in 1955 the right to use a neighbour's lavatory,[94] in 1956 the right to enjoy a park[95] and in 1973 the right to use an airfield[96] were all recognised as being capable of existing as easements.

An easement is a right over the land of another, and not a right to it. Thus the continuous occupation of the whole of a strip of land for the storage and repair of vehicles cannot be an easement, for it amounts to virtually the whole beneficial use of the land.[97] But the ordinary parking of cars is a discontinuous process,[98] and the right to park a car intermittently anywhere in a defined area can be an easement[99]; and so may the right of the tenant of part of a house to store coal in a shed in the garden.[1]

B. Distinction between Easements and Certain Analogous Rights

The nature of easements may be further indicated by contrasting them with certain other rights.

I. QUASI-EASEMENTS

As already explained,[2] rights exercised by a landowner over his own land

---

[86] See *Phipps* v. *Pears* [1965] 1 Q.B. 76 (protection of wall from weather by adjoining house: no easement); contrast *Sedgwick Forbes Bland Payne Group Ltd.* v. *Regional Properties Ltd.* (1979) 257 E.G. 64 at 70 (building divided horizontally).

[87] See *Pomfret* v. *Ricroft* (1669) 1 Wms.Saund. 321; *Rance* v. *Elvin* (1985) 50 P. & C.R. 9 (right to passage of water through pipe but not to a supply of water).

[88] *Crow* v. *Wood* [1971] 1 Q.B. 77; *Egerton* v. *Harding* [1975] Q.B. 62.

[89] *Lawrence* v. *Jenkins* (1873) L.R. 8 Q.B. 274 at 279, *per* Archibald J.

[90] *Crow* v. *Wood, supra,* at p. 85, *per* Lord Denning M.R.

[91] *Egerton* v. *Harding, supra.*

[92] *Simpson* v. *Mayor of Godmanchester* [1896] 1 Ch. 214; [1897] A.C. 696.

[93] *Att.-Gen. of Southern Nigeria* v. *Holt* [1915] A.C. 599. The headnote calls the right an irrevocable licence, but it was clearly recognised as an easement: see at p. 617.

[94] *Miller* v. *Emcer Products Ltd.* [1956] Ch. 304.

[95] *Re Ellenborough Park* [1956] Ch. 131.

[96] *Dowty Boulton Paul Ltd.* v. *Wolverhampton Corporation (No. 2)* [1976] Ch. 13.

[97] *Copeland* v. *Greenhalf* [1952] Ch. 488, in which *Wright* v. *Macadam, infra,* was not cited.

[98] *Williams* v. *Usherwood* (1981) 45 P. & C.R. 235 at 251; and see *Pavledes* v. *Ryesbridge Properties Ltd.* (1989) 58 P. & C.R. 459 (car park for factory).

[99] *Newman* v. *Jones* [1982] March 22, *unrep.* (Megarry V.-C.); and see *Patel* v. *W. H. Smith (Eziot) Ltd.* [1987] 1 W.L.R. 853 at 859.

[1] *Wright* v. *Macadam* [1949] 2 K.B. 744; contrast *Copeland* v. *Greenhalf, supra.*

[2] *Ante,* p. 369.

which, if he did not own that land, could exist as easements, are sometimes called quasi-easements.

II. NATURAL RIGHTS

In addition to his rights over his own land, every landowner has a natural right to support, *i.e.* a right that the support for his land provided by his neighbour's land should not be removed,[3] whether directly or by causing the subsoil to liquefy.[4] A similar right exists in cases where the surface of the land and the soil underneath are owned by different persons; the owner of the surface has a natural right to have it supported by the subjacent soil[5] unless this right is excluded by clear words or necessary implication in some statute or agreement.

This natural right, however, extends only to land in its natural state; there is no natural right to support for buildings or for the additional burden on land which they cause.[6] But if support is withdrawn, and the land would have fallen even it had not been built upon, an action lies in respect of any damage to the buildings.[7]

Similarly, there is no natural right to have buildings supported by neighbouring buildings.[8] If no more damage is done than is necessary, a man may pull down his house without having to provide support for his neighbour's house. The right to have buildings supported by land or by other buildings can, however, be acquired as an easement.[9]

III. PUBLIC RIGHTS

An easement must always be appurtenant to land; it is a right exercisable by the owner for the time being by virtue of his estate in the land. A public right, on the other hand, is a right exercisable by anyone, whether he owns land or not, merely by virtue of being a member of the public.

The public rights which most closely resemble easements are public rights of way. The land over which a public right of way exists is known as a highway, and although most highways have been made up into roads, and most easements of way exist over footpaths, the presence or absence of a made road has nothing to do with the distinction. There may be a highway over a footpath, while a well-made road may be subject only to an easement of way, or may exist only for the landowner's benefit and be subject to no easement at all.

1. Creation. A public right of way may be created in the following ways.

(a) *By statute.* This needs no explanation.

(b) *By dedication and acceptance.*

---

[3] *Backhouse* v. *Bonomi* (1861) 9 H.L.C. 503.
[4] *Lotus Ltd.* v. *British Soda Co. Ltd.* [1972] Ch. 123.
[5] *London & North Western Ry.* v. *Evans* [1893] 1 Ch. 16 at 30.
[6] *Wyatt* v. *Harrison* (1823) 3 B. & Ad. 871.
[7] *Stroyan* v. *Knowles* (1861) 6 H. & N. 454; *Lotus Ltd.* v. *British Soda Co. Ltd.*, *supra.*
[8] *Peyton* v. *Mayor of London* (1829) 9 B. & C. 725.
[9] *Post*, p. 383.

(1) AT COMMON LAW. To establish a highway at common law by dedication and acceptance, it must be shown—

(i) that the owner of the land dedicated the way to the public, and also
(ii) that the public accepted that dedication, the acceptance normally being shown by user by the public.[10]

Dedication may be formal, although this is comparatively infrequent. It is usually inferred from long user by the public, the user thus being effective to prove both dedication and acceptance. But to raise a presumption of dedication, there must have been open use as of right for so long a time that it must have come to the notice of the landowner that the public were using the way as of right, thus justifying the inference that the landowner consented to this user.[11] User with the landowner's licence is not user as of right,[12] for it acknowledges that the way is being used not because the public has a right to do so but because the landowner has agreed not to treat it as a trespass in the particular case in question. Further, the use must have been without interruption by the owner. A practice frequently adopted to disprove any intention to dedicate is to close the way for one day in each year, for this openly asserts the landowner's right to exclude the public at will.[13]

The length of the enjoyment to be shown depends on the circumstances of the case. Where the circumstances have pointed to an intention to dedicate, 18 months have been held to be enough,[14] while where the circumstances are against dedication, a substantially greater period may be insufficient.

(2) UNDER THE HIGHWAYS ACT 1980. The Rights of Way Act 1932 (now replaced by provisions in the Highways Act 1980) simplified the position to some extent by laying down a definite period of use that will suffice to show that a right of way exists. The public can still claim a right of way based on use for a shorter period than that laid down by the Act if an intent to dedicate can be inferred.

The Act of 1980 provides that a way over land (not including a river[15]) is to be deemed to have been dedicated as a highway if it "has been actually enjoyed by the public as of right and without interruption for a full period of 20 years," unless "there is sufficient evidence that there was no intention during that period to dedicate it."[16] "Interruption" means interruption in fact, and not, *e.g.* the mere closing of the way only at times when nobody used it or was likely to do so.[17] The absence of any intention to dedicate can be shown either in one of the usual ways, as by closing the way for one day in

---

[10] See *Cubitt* v. *Lady Caroline Maxse* (1873) L.R. 8 C.P. 704 at 715.
[11] *Greenwich District Board of Works* v. *Maudslay* (1870) L.R. 5 Q.B. 397 at 404.
[12] *R.* v. *Broke* (1859) 1 F. & F. 514.
[13] See *British Museum Trustees* v. *Finnis* (1833) 5 C. & P. 460; and see [1986] Conv. 161 (A. Samuels).
[14] *North London Ry.* v. *The Vestry of St. Mary, Islington* (1872) 27 L.T. 672.
[15] *A.-G. ex rel. Yorkshire Derwent Trust Ltd.* v. *Brotherton* [1992] 1 A.C. 425 (right of navigation cannot be acquired under the Act).
[16] Highways Act 1980, s.31(1).
[17] *Lewis* v. *Thomas* [1950] 1 K.B. 438.

each year, or in one of the special ways provided by the Act, namely, by exhibiting a notice visible to those using the way, or by depositing a map with the local council with a statement of what ways the landowner admits to be highways and lodging statutory declarations at intervals of not more than six years, stating whether any other ways have been dedicated. A reversioner or remainderman upon an interest for life or *pur autre vie* is entitled to the same remedies against the public as if he were in possession.[18]

The 20-years' period is to be calculated as that next before the time when the right to use the way was brought into question by a notice exhibited to the public negativing the dedication or otherwise.[19]

2. Extinguishment. When a highway has been established, it can be stopped up or diverted only by an order made under certain statutory provisions[20]; the mere obstruction of the highway or the failure by the public to use it will not destroy the rights of the public, for "once a highway always a highway."[21] And a mere closing order for a highway leaves unaffected any easement over the route of the highway.[22]

IV. LICENCES

Licences resemble easements in that they authorise the use of the land of another in some way. But licences, which cannot exist as legal estates or interests or, probably, as equitable interests, are far more flexible and less restricted than easements. Thus they may be created without formality; they require no dominant tenement; and they may authorise the occupation of land.[23]

V. RESTRICTIVE COVENANTS

Easements and restrictive covenants are similar in that an easement, like a restrictive covenant, may entitle a landowner to restrict the use that his neighbour makes of his land; thus the owner of an easement of light may prevent the servient owner from obstructing his light by erecting a building on the adjoining land.[24] There are other resemblances, such as the need for dominant and servient tenements, and in general the law of restrictive covenants may be regarded as being an equitable extension of the law of easements. However, certain points of difference should be mentioned.

1. Scope: restrictive covenants are wider in scope and more flexible than easements. As has been seen, there can be no easement entitling the dominant owner to a view or the general flow of air.[25] But by means of

[18] Highways Act 1980, s.33.
[19] *Ibid.* s.31(2).
[20] *e.g.* Highways Act 1980, ss.116–123; Town and Country Planning Act 1990, ss.247–260.
[21] *Dawes* v. *Hawkins* (1860) 8 C.B. (N.S.) 848 at 858, *per* Byles J.
[22] *Walsh* v. *Oates* [1953] 1 Q.B. 578.
[23] For licences, see *post*, pp. 427 *et seq.*
[24] For restrictive covenants, see *post*, pp. 409 *et seq.*
[25] *Ante*, p. 370.

suitable restrictive covenants preventing his neighbour from building, a landowner can enjoy both the view and a general flow of air.

2. Visibility: an inspection of the land will suggest the existence of many easements, but it is otherwise with restrictive covenants. Thus footpaths suggest an easement of way and pipes an easement of drainage, but no inspection of the land will reveal the existence of a covenant against trading upon it.

3. Existence at law: an easement may be legal or equitable, whereas the burden of a restrictive covenant runs only in equity.

4. Prescription: an easement may be acquired by prescription; not so a restrictive covenant.

5. Positive nature: a restrictive covenant is entirely negative; it neither entitles the dominant owner nor binds the servient owner to do any positive act. Easements similarly do not bind the servient owner to do any positive act,[26] but as regards the dominant owner certain easements (called "positive easements") entitle the owner to do positive acts, *e.g.* easements of way, while others (called "negative easements") do not, *e.g.* easements of light. Certain easements thus contain a positive element which is lacking in restrictive covenants.

VI. RIGHTS UNDER THE RULE AGAINST DEROGATION FROM GRANT

A grantor may not derogate from his grant: where he sells or leases land, knowing that the grantee intends to use it for a particular purpose, neither he nor his successors in title may do anything to impede such purposed use, and the grantee obtains corresponding rights.[27] Thus, where a lease was granted to a timber merchant who needed a free general flow of air to dry his timber, a purchaser of the lessor's adjoining land could not build upon it so as to obstruct the ventilation required by the lessee.[28]

VII. CUSTOMARY RIGHTS OF FLUCTUATING BODIES

These have been considered above.[29] They differ from easements in that they are exercisable by all who are included within the custom, independently of ownership of a dominant tenement. Thus the custom may extend to all the inhabitants of a particular locality, whether or not they own land.[30]

Sect. 2. Nature of a Profit à Prendre

A profit *à prendre* has been described as "a right to take something off

---

[26] But see the obligation to fence: *ante,* p. 371.
[27] See M. & W. 848; (1964) 80 L.Q.R. 244 (D. W. Elliott).
[28] *Aldin* v. *Latimer Clark, Muirhead & Co.* [1894] 2 Ch. 437.
[29] *Ante,* p. 370; see also *post,* p. 378.
[30] *Race* v. *Ward* (1855) 4 E. & B. 702.

another person's land."[31] This is too wide. The thing taken must be some-thing taken out of the soil,[32] *i.e.* it must be either the soil, the natural produce thereof, or the wild animals existing on it; and the thing taken must at the time of taking be susceptible of ownership.[33] A right to "hawk, hunt, fish and fowl" may thus exist as a profit,[34] for this gives the right to take creatures living on the soil which, when killed, are capable of being owned. But a right to take water from a spring or a pump, or the right to water cattle at a pond, may be an easement though it cannot be a profit; for the water, when taken, was not owned by anyone nor was it part of the soil.[35] A right to take water stored in an artificial receptacle, *e.g.* a cistern, is not an easement but may perhaps exist either as a profit or a mere licence, probably the latter.[36]

A. *Classification of Profits à Prendre*

I. AS TO OWNERSHIP

A profit *à prendre* may be enjoyed—

 (i) by one person to the exclusion of all others; this is known as a several profit; or
 (ii) by one person in common with others; this is known as a profit in common, or a common.

II. IN RELATION TO LAND

A profit is not necessarily appurtenant to land, as is the case with easements. It may exist in the following forms.

1. A profit appurtenant. This is a profit, whether several or in common, attached to land by act of parties. A profit appurtenant may be acquired either by grant or by prescription. In general, there must be compliance with the four conditions necessary for the existence of an easement, which can exist only as appurtenant to land.[37] Thus a profit of piscary appurtenant cannot be exploited for commercial purposes; the number of fish taken must be limited to the needs of the dominant tenement.[38]

2. A profit appendant. This is a profit annexed to land by operation of law; probably it exists only in the form of a common of pasture.[39] If before the Statute *Quia Emptores* 1290 the lord of a manor sub-infeudated arable land to a freeholder, the freeholder obtained, as appendant to the arable lands, the right to pasture, on the waste land of the manor, animals to plough and

---

[31] *Duke of Sutherland* v. *Heathcote* [1892] 1 Ch. 475 at 484, *per* Lindley L.J.
[32] *Manning* v. *Wasdale* (1836) 5 A. & E. 758 at 764.
[33] *Race* v. *Ward, supra*, at p. 709; *Lowe* v. *J. W. Ashmore Ltd.* [1971] Ch. 545 at 557.
[34] *Wickham* v. *Hawker* (1840) 7 M. & W. 63.
[35] See *Mason* v. *Hill* (1833) 5 B. & Ad. 1 at 24; *Manning* v. *Wasdale, supra*, at p. 764.
[36] See (1938) 2 Conv. (N.S.) 203. (J. S. Fiennes).
[37] *Ante*, p. 368.
[38] *Harris* v. *Earl of Chesterfield* [1911] A.C. 623.
[39] See 6 Halsbury, (4th ed.), pp. 199, 220; but see Tudor L.C.R.P., pp. 713–716.

manure the land granted to him.[40] This right was known as a common of pasture appendant and was limited both as to the kind and number of animals which could be depastured. It extended only to horses and oxen (to plough the land) and cows and sheep (to manure it),[41] and only to the number of these "levant and couchant" on the land to which the right was appendant, *i.e.* the number which the dominant tenement was capable of maintaining during the winter.[42] It was immaterial that the land was at any particular time used for purposes temporarily rendering the maintenance of cattle impossible, for the test was not the number actually supported but the number which the land could be made to support.

No common appendant could be created after 1290,[43] for a conveyance of freehold land in a manor after that date resulted in the feoffee holding of the feoffor's lord, and the land passed out of the manor altogether.

3. A profit pur cause de vicinage. This exists only in the form of a common of pasture. If two adjoining commons are open to each other, there is a common *pur cause de vicinage* if the cattle put on one common by the commoners have always been allowed to stray to the other common, and *vice versa*.[44] The claim fails if in the past the cattle have been driven off one common by the commoners thereof,[45] or if the commons have been fenced off,[46] or if the two commons are not contiguous to each other, even if they are separated only by a third common.[47]

4. A profit in gross. This is a profit, whether several or in common, exercisable by the owner independently of his ownership of land; there is no dominant tenement. Thus a right to take fish from a canal without stint (*i.e.* without limit) can exist as a profit in gross,[48] but not, as already seen, as a profit appurtenant.[49] A profit in gross is an interest in land which will pass under the owner's will or intestacy or can be sold or dealt with in any of the usual ways.

B. Distinctions between Profits à Prendre and Certain Analogous Rights

I. QUASI-PROFITS

The principles that apply to quasi-profits are similar to those that govern quasi-easements.[50]

---

[40] *Earl of Dunraven* v. *Llewellyn* (1850) 15 Q.B. 791 at 810.
[41] *Tyrringham's Case* (1584) 4 Co.Rep. 36b at 37a.
[42] *Robertson* v. *Hartopp* (1889) 43 Ch.D. 484 at 516.
[43] See *ante*, pp. 22, 361.
[44] *Pritchard* v. *Powell* (1845) 10 Q.B. 589 at 603.
[45] *Heath* v. *Elliott* (1838) 4 Bing.N.C. 388.
[46] *Tyrringham's Case* (1584) 4 Co.Rep. 36b.
[47] *Commissioners of Sewers* v. *Glasse* (1874) L.R. 19 Eq. 134.
[48] *Staffordshire & Worcestershire Canal Navigation* v. *Bradley* [1912] 1 Ch. 91.
[49] *Ante*, p. 376.
[50] *Ante*, pp. 369, 371.

II. OTHER NATURAL RIGHTS

The same applies.[51] An example is the right of a riparian owner to the unimpeded passage of fish from neighbouring portions of the stream.[52]

III. PUBLIC RIGHTS

The public right which most closely resembles a profit is the right of the public to fish in the sea and all tidal waters. However, since in theory the right is the Crown's, it was formerly possible for the Crown to grant to an individual the exclusive right to fish in a specified part of the sea or tidal waters; such a franchise was known as a free fishery.[53] In short, the public may fish in all tidal waters except a free fishery. But it has been held that the effect of *Magna Carta* 1215 was to prevent the Crown from creating any new free fisheries,[54] although any already existing remain valid and transferable to this day.

The right to fish in non-tidal water is dealt with below.[55]

IV. RIGHTS OF FLUCTUATING BODIES

There can be no custom for a fluctuating body of persons to take a profit.[56] The reason is said to be that otherwise the subject-matter would be destroyed.[57] However, if in fact such a right has been enjoyed for a long time as of right the courts will endeavour to find a legal origin for it. Two methods have been evolved.

1. Presumed incorporation by Crown grant. The reason why a fluctuating body cannot own a profit is that the body is not a legal person to which a grant could be made.[58] However, the Crown is able to incorporate any body of persons (*i.e.* make them into a corporation), and so could, for example, grant a charter to a village making it a city or borough. Consequently there is nothing to prevent the Crown from making a grant of a profit to the inhabitants of a district and providing therein that for the purposes of the grant they should be treated as a corporation, though for other purposes they remain unincorporated. In fact, such grants have been made but rarely.[59] Their chief importance is that the court will presume that a grant of rights of this kind owned by the Crown at the time of the supposed grant has been made, provided—

    (a) long enjoyment is proved, and

---

[51] *Ante*, p. 372.

[52] See *Barker* v. *Faulkner* (1898) 79 L.T. 24.

[53] 3 Cru.Dig. 261; see, *e.g. Stephens* v. *Snell* [1939] 3 All E.R. 622.

[54] *Malcolmson* v. *O'Dea* (1863) 10 H.L.C. 593 at 618; but see Theobald, *Land*, pp. 58 *et seq.*

[55] *Post*, p. 406.

[56] *Alfred F. Beckett Ltd.* v. *Lyons* [1967] Ch. 449.

[57] *Race* v. *Ward* (1855) 4 E. & B. 702 at 705, 709.

[58] *Fowler* v. *Dale* (1594) Cro.Eliz. 362.

[59] See, *e.g. Willingdale* v. *Maitland* (1866) L.R. 3 Eq. 103.

(b) those claiming the grant, and their predecessors, have always regarded themselves as a corporation and have acted as such as regards the right, as by holding meetings or appointing some officer to supervise the right.[60]

2. Presumed charitable trust. Even when the court cannot presume incorporation by Crown grant because the claimants have not acted as a corporation, if long enjoyment is shown the court may be able to find a legal origin for the right by presuming a grant of the profit to some corporation, subject to a trust or condition that the corporation should allow the claimants to exercise the rights claimed. Thus in *Goodman* v. *Mayor of Saltash*[61] the free inhabitants of certain ancient tenements had for 200 years enjoyed an oyster fishery from Candlemas (February 2) to Easter Eve each year. This right had been shared by the local corporation, which had enjoyed the right all the year round from time immemorial. The House of Lords refused to presume a grant incorporating the inhabitants for the purpose of the grant, but held that the corporation was entitled to a profit subject to a trust or condition in favour of the free inhabitants. Such a trust is charitable and so is not subject to the rule against inalienability.[62]

Sect. 3. Acquisition of Easements and Profits

An easement or profit can exist as a legal interest in land only if—

(i) it is held for an interest equivalent to a fee simple absolute in possession or term of years absolute[63]; and
(ii) it is created either by statute, deed or prescription.

A legal easement or profit can be created only by deed,[64] although other documents may create a valid equitable easement or profit if made for value. Oral agreements for value could formerly do the same if they were supported by sufficient evidence in writing or part performance,[65] though now only an agreement in writing signed by both parties will suffice.[66] But in cases of part performance there may be an estoppel under which similar rights may arise.[67]

The various methods of acquisition must now be considered.

A. By Statute

Easements created by statute are most frequently found in the case of local

---

[60] See *Re Free Fishermen of Faversham* (1887) 36 Ch.D. 329; *Lord Rivers* v. *Adams* (1878) 3 Ex.D. 361.
[61] (1882) 7 App.Cas. 633.
[62] *Ibid.*; and see *ante*, p. 208.
[63] *Ante*, p. 75.
[64] *Duke of Somerset* v. *Fogwell* (1826) 5 B. & A. 875.
[65] See, *e.g. Mason* v. *Clarke* [1955] A.C. 778.
[66] *Ante*, pp. 116 *et seq.*
[67] *Ante*, p. 120; see *e.g. Crabb* v. *Arun D.C.* [1976] Ch. 179.

Acts of Parliament, such as an Act giving a right of support to a canal constructed under statutory powers.

B. By Express Reservation or Grant

When a landowner sells part of his land and retains the rest, he may reserve easements or profits over the land sold, and grant the purchaser rights over the land retained. Today these transactions can be achieved quite simply, but this has not always been so.

1. Express reservation. Before 1926, a legal easement or profit could not be created by a simple reservation in favour of the grantor. Being a new right it had to be granted by someone, and a person could not grant to himself. If, however, the conveyance reserved the right to the grantor, and the grantee also executed the conveyance, it operated as a conveyance to the grantee followed by the re-grant of the easement or profit by the grantee to the grantor.[68] The effect of a simple reservation not executed by the grantee was merely to create an equitable easement or profit.[69]

Since 1925 it has not been necessary for the grantee to execute the conveyance, as statute has provided that the reservation of a legal estate or interest shall be effective at law without any execution of the conveyance by the grantee "or any regrant by him."[70] It seems, however, that despite these words, the change merely goes to formalities.[71] The so-called reservation is still deemed to operate as a grant by the purchaser, which may have significant consequences. Where land held on trust was sold, and conveyed to the purchaser by the legal and equitable owners, a reservation by the equitable owners took effect as a grant of an legal easement by the purchaser and not as a reservation of a mere equitable easement by the vendor of the equitable interest.[72] Another consequence lies in the operation of the rule that where grants are ambiguous they are construed against the grantor.[73]

2. Express grant. The ordinary case of an easement or profit created by the express words of a deed needs little discussion. The word "grant," though usual, is no longer essential; but not even the "grant" of a mere "licence" will create an easement.[74] The dominant tenement, if not sufficiently identified, may be inferred from the circumstances.[75] Further, an

---

[68] *Durham & Sunderland Ry.* v. *Walker* (1842) 2 Q.B. 940 at 967; and see M. & W. 857 (Statute of Uses, 1535).
[69] *May* v. *Bellville* [1905] 2 Ch. 605.
[70] L.P.A. 1925, s.65; see also *Wiles* v. *Banks* (1984) 50 P. & C.R. 80 (conveying "subject to" a right may make it an easement; and see *post*, p. 434).
[71] *St. Edmundsbury and Ipswich Diocesan Board of Finance* v. *Clark (No. 2)* [1975] 1 W.L.R. 468 at 478–480, commenting on *ibid.* [1973] 1 W.L.R. 1572 at 1587–1591, where the view that the change is one of substance was maintained.
[72] *Johnstone* v. *Holdway* [1963] 1 Q.B. 601.
[73] *Bulstrode* v. *Lambert* [1953] 1 W.L.R. 1064 at 1068; *St. Edmundsbury and Ipswich Diocesan Board of Finance* v. *Clark (No. 2)* [1975] 1 W.L.R. 468 at 477–480; but see *Cordell* v. *Second Clanfield Properties Ltd.* [1969] 2 Ch. 9. See also *post*, p. 401.
[74] L.P.A. 1925, s.51(1); *I.D.C. Group Ltd.* v. *Clark* [1992] *The Times*, July 23.
[75] *The Shannon Ltd.* v. *Venner Ltd.* [1965] Ch. 682.

easement or profit may be created by express grant even though it is not mentioned in any deed. The Law of Property Act 1925, s.62(1),[76] provides that any conveyance made after 1881 shall, subject to any contrary intention expressed in the conveyance,[77] operate to convey with the land a wide range of things and rights, including all privileges, easements, rights and advantages appertaining or reputed to appertain to the land or any part of it.[78] Thus, if a landlord grants his tenant a mere licence to use a coal shed for domestic purposes,[79] or to go through the landlord's house to reach the premises demised,[80] a subsequent conveyance to the tenant will operate to grant him the right as an easement. A right to require a neighbour to maintain fences may similarly arise.[81]

(a) *Nature of rights*. The section will not elevate into easements or profits rights which the grantor has no power to create by express grant,[82] or rights which cannot exist as legal easements or profits.[83] Thus it will not apply to a "right" to have a house protected from the weather by a contiguous house,[84] or to have central heating and hot water,[85] nor to a "right" of way over a courtyard during business hours when not inconvenient to the landlord,[86] or to use the landlord's passage-way only while he is in occupation.[87] Nor will it apply where it is apparent that the "right" is merely temporary. Thus the first purchaser of a house in a housing development will not have the access of light to his windows transformed into an easement of light that would prevent adjoining plots of land from being built upon.[88]

(b) *Diversity of occupation or continuous and apparent*. Section 62 will apply only where at the time of the grant either the two tenements are in different occupation or else the "right" is continuous and apparent.[89] What a landowner does on his own land he does as owner and not by virtue of any "right" in respect of one part of it over another.[90] But where one part is occupied by a tenant and he has been enjoying "rights" over the other part while it was occupied by the landlord, section 62 can apply to make those "rights" into easements if the landlord then grants the tenant a formal

---

[76] Replacing C.A. 1881, s.6(1): see also L.P.A. 1925, s.62(2).
[77] L.P.A. 1925, s.62(4).
[78] See *Graham* v. *Philcox* [1984] Q.B. 747 (enlarged dominant tenement).
[79] *Wright* v. *Macadam* [1949] 2 K.B. 744.
[80] *Goldberg* v. *Edwards* [1950] Ch. 247.
[81] *Crow* v. *Wood* [1971] 1 Q.B. 77. For this "spurious easement," see *ante*, p. 371.
[82] *Quicke* v. *Chapman* [1903] 1 Ch. 659 (grantor a mere licensee); *M.R.A. Engineering Ltd.* v. *Trimster Co. Ltd.* (1987) 56 P. & C.R. 1 (land previously sold by grantor).
[83] *International Tea Stores Co.* v. *Hobbs* [1903] 2 Ch. 165 at 172.
[84] *Phipps* v. *Pears* [1965] 1 Q.B. 76.
[85] *Regis Property Co. Ltd.* v. *Redman* [1956] 2 Q.B. 612.
[86] *Green* v. *Ashco Horticulturist Ltd.* [1966] 1 W.L.R. 889.
[87] *Goldberg* v. *Edwards*, *supra*.
[88] *Godwin* v. *Schweppes Ltd.* [1902] 1 Ch. 926; and see *Green* v. *Ashco Horticulturist Ltd.*, *supra*.
[89] *Long* v. *Gowlett* [1923] 2 Ch. 177; [1979] Conv. 113 (C. Harpum).
[90] See *Sovmots Investments Ltd.* v. *Secretary of State for the Environment* [1979] A.C. 144 at 169, 176.

lease.[91] The section may also apply to a right which is reputed to appertain to the land as being continuous and apparent, such as windows enjoying a "right" of light,[92] a watercourse through visible pipes,[93] or a hard-beaten road.[94]

(c) *Operation of the section.* The section applies to any "conveyance of land,"[95] and this includes any assurance of property by an instrument, including leases, mortgages and assents,[96] but not a will or contract, nor an oral tenancy.[97] Where the section applies, the "right" in question becomes a legal easement or profit. Sometimes the section operates unexpectedly. A landlord who renews a lease[98] or sells the reversion to the tenant[99] may find that he has transformed into easements "rights" over his adjoining land which he has merely permitted the tenant to enjoy. Again, a vendor who lets the purchaser into possession before completion may find that "rights" over his adjoining land which the purchaser has enjoyed on sufferance have become easements on completion.[1] These unintended grants may be avoided by the insertion of suitable provisions into contracts, conveyances and leases, excluding the operation of the section; and most standard forms of contract do this,[2] though sometimes the subsequent conveyance inadvertently fails to do so.[3]

The relationship of the section with implied grants will be considered later.[4]

C. By Implied Reservation or Grant

1. Implied reservation. A grant is normally construed against the grantor and in favour of the grantee. Further, a grantor must not derogate from his grant. Consequently the general rule is that no easements will be implied in favour of a grantor; if he wishes to reserve any easements he must do so expressly.[5] To this rule there are two exceptions.

(a) *Easements of necessity.* If a grantor conveys the whole of a plot of land except a piece in the middle which, being completely surrounded by the part conveyed, is inaccessible, a way of necessity over the part conveyed will be

---

[91] *Wright* v. *Macadam, supra; Goldberg* v. *Edwards, supra.*
[92] *Broomfield* v. *Williams* [1897] 1 Ch. 602.
[93] *Watts* v. *Kelson* (1970) 6 Ch.App. 166.
[94] *Bayley* v. *G.W.R.* (1884) 26 Ch.D. 434.
[95] L.P.A. 1925, s.62(1).
[96] *Ibid.* s.205(1)(ii).
[97] *Rye* v. *Rye* [1962] A.C. 496.
[98] *Wright* v. *Macadam* [1949] 2 K.B. 744.
[99] *International Tea Stores Co.* v. *Hobbs* [1903] 2 Ch. 165.
[1] See *Lyme Valley Squash Club Ltd.* v. *Newcastle under Lyme B.C.* [1985] 2 All E.R. 405.
[2] See *Squarey* v. *Harris-Smith* (1981) 42 P. & C.R. 119; and see the Standard Conditions of Sale 1990 (*ante*, p. 124), Condition 3.4 (*Encyclopedia of Forms and Precedents* (5th ed.), Service Volume C (vol. 35), Form 21.1, para. 442.7).
[3] See *Lyme Valley Squash Club Ltd.* v. *Newcastle under Lyme B.C., supra.*
[4] *Post*, p. 385.
[5] *Wheeldon* v. *Burrows* (1879) 12 Ch.D. 31 at 49.

implied in favour of the part retained.[6] This is so even if some of the surrounding land belongs to third parties, though it is essential that the necessity should exist at the time of the conveyance and not merely arise later.[7] The question is not whether the way is necessary for the reasonable enjoyment of the land retained, but whether the land cannot be used at all without the way.[8] Thus no such way will be inferred if there is some other means of access (*e.g.* by water[9]), even if it is difficult and inconvenient.[10] The right is based on the inference that unless otherwise provided the parties did not intend to make the land inaccessible.[11] The former owner of both plots may select the particular way to be enjoyed, provided it is convenient[12]; but, once selected, it cannot be changed except by agreement.[13]

(b) *Intended easements.* Easements required to carry out the common intention of the parties will be implied in favour of the grantor even though not expressed in the conveyance. Thus on the grant of one of two houses supported by each other, the mutual grant and reservation of easements of support will be implied if (as is usual) such an intention can be inferred.[14] A grantor who wishes to show that a reservation was mutually intended has a heavy onus of proof to discharge.[15]

2. Implied grant. If the owner of two plots conveys one of them, certain easements over the land retained are implied in favour of the land conveyed. The express grant of the land is said to be accompanied by the implied grant of the easements. Rights which will arise by implied grant are as follows:

(a) *Easements of necessity* and

(b) *Intended easements.* The rules which apply in these two cases are similar to those in the case of implied reservation. Thus where a landlord let his basement for use as a restaurant, and from the outset such a use was not lawful unless a proper ventilation system was installed, the tenant was held to be entitled to instal and use a ventilation duct attached to the outside of the landlord's premises as an easement of necessity.[16]

(c) *Ancillary easements.* These are easements necessary for the enjoyment of some right expressly granted. Thus if there is a grant of an easement of the

---

[6] *Pinnington* v. *Galland* (1853) 9 Exch. 1.
[7] *Midland Ry.* v. *Miles* (1886) 33 Ch.D. 632.
[8] *Union Lighterage Co.* v. *London Graving Dock Co.* [1902] 2 Ch. 557 at 573; contrast *post*, p. 384.
[9] *Manjang* v. *Drammeh* (1990) 61 P. & C.R. 194.
[10] *M.R.A. Engineering Ltd.* v. *Trimster Co. Ltd.* (1987) 56 P. & C.R. 1 (public footpath but no road).
[11] *Nickerson* v. *Barraclough* [1981] Ch. 426, rejecting public policy.
[12] See *Pearson* v. *Spencer* (1861) 1 B. & S. 571 at 585; affd. (1863) 3 B. & S. 761.
[13] *Deacon* v. *South Eastern Ry.* (1889) 61 L.T. 377.
[14] *Richards* v. *Rose* (1853) 9 Exch. 221.
[15] *Re Webb's Lease* [1951] Ch. 808 (no implied reservation of right to advertise on tenant's outside walls).
[16] *Wong* v. *Beaumont Property Trust Ltd.* [1965] 1 Q.B. 173.

right to draw water from a spring, a right of way to the spring will be implied.[17]

(d) *Easements within the Rule in Wheeldon* v. *Burrows.* In *Wheeldon* v. *Burrows*[18] it was laid down that upon the grant of part of a tenement, there would pass to the grantee as easements all quasi-easements over the land retained which—

  (i) were continuous and apparent,
 (ii) were necessary to the reasonable enjoyment of the land granted, and
(iii) had been, and were at the time of the grant, used by the grantor for the benefit of the part granted.

A "continuous" easement is one giving the right to do some act of a continuous and constant nature. An "apparent" easement is one which is evidenced by some sign on the servient tenement discoverable on a careful inspection by a person ordinarily conversant with the subject.[19] Thus a drain into which water from the eaves of a house runs,[20] a watercourse through visible pipes,[21] and windows enjoying light,[22] all indicate the existence of continuous and apparent easements. On the other hand, a right to take water from a neighbour's pump from time to time[23] or a right to project the bowsprit of ships when in dock over the land of another[24] have been held to be outside the meaning of "continuous and apparent"[25] easements. Rights of way do not in general fall within the definition, but a way over a made road, or one which betrays its presence by some indication such as a worn track, will pass under the rule in *Wheeldon* v. *Burrows.*[26]

An easement is "necessary to the reasonable enjoyment of the land" if the land cannot be reasonably enjoyed without it; the test is much less stringent than for an easement of necessity.[27] It is still not clear whether this requirement and the requirement of "continuous and apparent" user are alternatives[28] or, probably, cumulative, with the first requirement being based on conveyancing convenience and the second on the rule against derogation from grant.[29]

These rules apply to contracts to make a grant[30] as well as to grants. They also apply where the grantor, instead of retaining any land himself, makes

---

[17] *Pwlbach Colliery Co. Ltd.* v. *Woodman* [1915] A.C. 634 at 646.
[18] (1879) 12 Ch.D. 31; see M. & W. 861–864.
[19] *Pyer* v. *Carter* (1857) 1 H. & N. 916 at 922.
[20] *Pyer* v. *Carter* (1857) 1 H. & N. 916.
[21] *Watts* v. *Kelson* (1870) 6 Ch.App. 166.
[22] *Phillips* v. *Low* [1892] 1 Ch. 47 at 53.
[23] *Polden* v. *Bastard* (1865) L.R. 1 Q.B. 156.
[24] *Suffield* v. *Brown* (1864) 4 De G.J. & S. 185.
[25] On the origin of the phrase, see (1967) 83 L.Q.R. 240 (A. W. B. Simpson).
[26] See *Hansford* v. *Jago* [1921] 1 Ch. 322.
[27] *Ante*, p. 383.
[28] See M. & W. 862.
[29] See *Sovmots Investments Ltd.* v. *Secretary of State for the Environment* [1979] A.C. 144 at 168, 169, 175; (1977) 41 Conv. 415 at 422 (C. Harpum).
[30] *Borman* v. *Griffith* [1930] 1 Ch. 493.

simultaneous grants to two or more grantees. Each grantee obtains the same easements over the land of the other as he would have obtained if the grantor had retained it[31]; and similarly for two or more gifts that are made by the same will.[32]

3. Relation to section 62. The importance of the rules relating to implied grant[33] has been considerably reduced by the operation of section 62 of the Law of Property Act 1925.[34] Yet implied grants have not been superseded by the section: the provisions overlap but are by no means identical in their operation. They may be compared as follows.

(a) *Width.* The section is wider than the rules for implied grant. The section applies to "all . . . rights . . . appertaining or reputed to appertain" to the land, and is not limited to rights that are necessary for the reasonable enjoyment of the land.[35] Further, unlike implied grants, the section can apply to profits *à prendre.*

(b) *Contracts.* The rules for implied grants apply not only to conveyances but also to contracts and wills.[36] The section applies only to a "conveyance," and widely though that word is defined,[37] it does not include contracts[38] or wills. Nor does it apply to a lease in writing for over three years, for, not being by deed, the lease can take effect only as a contract to grant a lease, which is no conveyance.[39]

(c) *Restriction and rectification.* It will be seen that a conveyance will sometimes convey more than the purchaser is entitled to under the contract. If both contract and conveyance are silent as to easements, the narrower rules for implied grant will limit the purchaser's rights under the contract, while the more ample operation of the section may give him wider rights. Thus a non-apparent way may be outside the doctrine of implied grant but within the section.[40] In such cases the vendor can insist on the conveyance being worded so as to restrict it to the rights which the contract gives the purchaser.[41] If the conveyance has been executed, a vendor who acts promptly may seek to have it rectified,[42] except as against a purchaser without notice of the equity of rectification.

---

[31] *Swansborough* v. *Coventry* (1832) 2 M. & S. 362.
[32] *Schwann* v. *Cotton* [1916] 2 Ch. 459.
[33] *Ante*, p. 383.
[34] *Ante*, p. 381.
[35] *Ante*, p. 383.
[36] *Supra.*
[37] *Ante*, p. 382.
[38] *Re Peck and the School Board for London* [1893] 2 Ch. 315.
[39] *Borman* v. *Griffith, supra*; and see *ante*, p. 310.
[40] See *Ward* v. *Kirkland* [1967] Ch. 194.
[41] *Re Walmsley and Shaw's Contract* [1917] 1 Ch. 93.
[42] See *Clark* v. *Barnes* [1929] 2 Ch. 368.

D. By Presumed Grant, or Prescription

I. GENERAL PRINCIPLES

The basis of prescription is that if long enjoyment of a lawful right is shown, the court will uphold the right by presuming that it had a lawful origin, *i.e.* that there once was an actual grant of the right, even though it is impossible to produce any evidence of such a grant. However, it is not enough to show long user by itself: user of a particular kind is required. There are three types of prescription, namely, prescription at common law, prescription under the doctrine of lost modern grant, and prescription under the Prescription Act 1832, an unsatisfactory system that calls for simplification by Parliament.[43] Except so far as the Act otherwise provides, a claim to an easement or profit under any head must be supported by user complying with the following conditions.

1. User as of right: the user must be as of right, which means that it must have been enjoyed *nec vi*, *nec clam*, *nec precario* (without force, without secrecy, without permission).[44] The claimant must show that he has used the right as if he were entitled to it. Forcible user (*vi*) occurs not only where the dominant owner breaks down barriers or commits other acts of violence, but also where the user is continued despite the servient owner making continuous and unmistakable protests.[45] Secret user (*clam*) occurred where a dock had been supported by invisible rods sunk under the servient tenement,[46] or where there had been intermittent and secret discharges of injurious chemicals into a sewer.[47] So, too, no easement can be established against an owner who, owing to absence or other reason, is able to prove that he had no knowledge of the user.[48] The whole law of prescription rests upon acquiescence[49]; and mere toleration is enough.[50]

If the servient owner has given the claimant the right to use the easement or profit claimed, so that there has been an actual grant of such a right, the user is not *precario*, and the claimant can rely upon his grant without resorting to prescription. But if the claimant has been given permission to use the right claimed "until further notice," or has had to seek permission anew each year, the user is *precario* and no easement or profit can rise from it by prescription. Similarly, if applications for permission to use a

---

[43] See *Tehidy Minerals Ltd.* v. *Norman* [1971] 2 Q.B. 528 at 543.

[44] *Solomon* v. *Mystery of Vintners* (1859) 4 H. & N. 585 at 602 (common law prescription); *Sturges* v. *Bridgman* (1879) 11 Ch.D. 852 at 863 (lost modern grant); Prescription Act 1832, ss.1, 2 and *Tickle* v. *Brown* (1836) 4 A. & E. 369 at 382 (prescription under the Act); and see M. & W. 870–872.

[45] *Dalton* v. *Angus & Co.* (1881) 6 App.Cas. 740 at 786. See, *e.g. Newnham* v. *Willison* (1987) 56 P. & C.R. 8.

[46] *Union Lighterage Co.* v. *London Graving Dock Co.* [1902] 2 Ch. 557.

[47] *Liverpool Corporation* v. *H. Coghill & Son Ltd.* [1918] 1 Ch. 307.

[48] *Diment* v. *N. H. Foot Ltd.* [1974] 1 W.L.R. 1427.

[49] *Dalton* v. *Angus & Co.* (1881) 6 App.Cas. 740 at 773, 803.

[50] *Mills* v. *Silver* [1991] Ch. 271.

way have been made by the claimant from time to time,[51] or he has made annual payments for his enjoyment, there is evidence that the user was *precario*, for such acts are inconsistent with the claimant having a right to the easement or profit claimed.

User during unity of possession, *i.e.* while the claimant was in possession of both dominant and servient tenements, is not user as of right,[52] and the same applies to user under the mistaken belief that the claimant was entitled to the servient tenement[53] or that he had the temporary permission of the landlord. But proof that the claimant exercised his right under the mistaken belief that a valid easement or profit had already been granted to him will not prevent the user from being as of right.[54] The principle involved is that the right must have been exercised *qua* easement or profit and not, for example, under any actual or supposed right of an occupant of both tenements.

2. User in fee simple: the user must be by or on behalf of a fee simple owner against a fee simple owner who both knows of the user and is able to resist it. In general, only easements or profits in fee simple can be acquired by prescription.[55] An easement or profit for life or for years, for example, may be expressly granted but cannot be acquired by prescription, for the basis of prescription is a presumed grant by the owner of the servient tenement, and only a grant in fee simple will be presumed. Consequently the claimant must show either that he is the fee simple owner himself or that he claims on behalf of the fee simple owner. A tenant under a lease must thus prescribe on behalf of the fee simple owner and not merely on his own behalf.[56]

As prescription rests on acquiescence,[57] a claim will fail if user can be proved only when the servient land was occupied by a tenant for life[58] or for years,[59] for the fee simple owner may be unable to contest the user. But if the user began against the fee simple owner it will not become ineffective because the land is later settled or let.[60] Further, if A leases two plots of his land to two tenants, one tenant cannot prescribe for an easement against the other, for otherwise the result would be that A would acquire an easement over his own land.[61]

There are certain modifications of this rule. First, profits in gross may be acquired by prescription at common law,[62] or under the doctrine of lost

[51] *Monmouth Canal Co.* v. *Harford* (1834) 1 Cr.M. & R. 614.
[52] *Bright* v. *Walker* (1834) 1 Cr.M. & R. 211 at 219.
[53] *Lyell* v. *Lord Hothfield* [1914] 3 K.B. 911.
[54] *Earl de la Warr* v. *Miles* (1881) 17 Ch.D. 535; *Bridle* v. *Ruby* (1987) 56 P. & C.R. 155; but see [1989] Conv. 261 (G. Kodilinye).
[55] See, *e.g. Kilgour* v. *Gaddes* [1904] 1 K.B. 457 at 460.
[56] *Gateward's Case* (1607) 6 Co.Rep. 59b; *Dawnay* v. *Cashford* (1697) Carth. 432.
[57] *Dalton* v. *Angus & Co.* (1881) 6 App.Cas. 740 at 773, 774.
[58] *Roberts* v. *James* (1903) 89 L.T. 282.
[59] *Daniel* v. *North* (1809) 11 East 372.
[60] *Pugh* v. *Savage* [1970] 2 Q.B. 373.
[61] *Kilgour* v. *Gaddes* [1904] 1 K.B. 457; *Simmons* v. *Dobson* [1991] 1 W.L.R. 720.
[62] *Johnson* v. *Barnes* (1873) L.R. 8 C.P. 527.

modern grant. In this case, the right is claimed not in respect of any estate but on behalf of the claimant personally. Such prescription is known as prescription in gross. The claimant must show that he and his predecessors in title to the profit (often his ancestors) have enjoyed the right,[63] instead of showing that he and his predecessors in title to the dominant tenement have enjoyed it.[64] There can be no prescription in gross for easements (which cannot exist in gross), nor can a profit in gross be claimed under the Prescription Act 1832.[65] Second, certain modifications are made in claims under the Prescription Act 1832. Thus under the Act easements of light can be acquired by one tenant against another tenant of the same landlord.[66] This is anomalous; it applies only to light and only to claims under the Act. Other modifications under the Act will be noted later.

3. Continuous user: the claimants must show a continuity of enjoyment. This is interpreted reasonably; in the case of easements of way it is clearly not necessary to show ceaseless user by day and night. User whenever circumstances require it is normally sufficient,[67] provided the intervals are not excessive; but merely casual use, dependent on tolerance, is not enough.[68] Continuity is not broken if the user is varied by agreement, as where the parties vary the line of a way for convenience.[69]

The three types of prescription must now be considered in turn.

II. PRESCRIPTION AT COMMON LAW

1. Length of user. User of the nature discussed above must be shown to have continued since time immemorial, namely, since 1189. If this is shown, the court presumes that a grant was made prior to that date. The reason for 1189 being adopted is that from time to time limits were fixed within which actions for the recovery of land were to be brought. Instead of adopting a specified period of years, events such as the beginning of the reign of Henry I or the last voyage of Henry II to Normandy were periodically selected. The last choice to be made was the beginning of the reign of Richard I, namely, 1189. These periods originally had nothing to do with prescription, but the courts adopted the last date as the period of time immemorial upon which all claims based on custom or prescription depended. Modern legislation has altered the rule for claims to land, but 1189 remained the essential date for custom and prescription.[70]

2. Presumption. It is clearly impossible in most cases to show continuous

[63] *Welcome* v. *Upton* (1840) 6 M. & W. 536.
[64] Such prescription is "in the *que* estate": the user is by the claimant and "*ceux que estate il ad*" (those whose estate he has). See Litt. 183.
[65] *Shuttleworth* v. *Le Fleming* (1865) 19 C.B. (N.S.) 687.
[66] See *post*, p. 397.
[67] *Dare* v. *Heathcote* (1856) 25 L.J. Ex. 245.
[68] *Ironside* v. *Cook* (1978) 41 P. & C.R. 326 (way over roadside verge).
[69] *Davis* v. *Whitby* [1974] Ch. 186.
[70] See generally *Bryant* v. *Foot* (1867) L.R. 2 Q.B. 161 at 180, 181.

user since 1189, and so the courts adopted the rule that if unexplained user for 20 years or more is shown, the court would presume that that user has continued since 1189; user for less than 20 years requires supporting circumstances to raise the presumption.[71] However, this presumption may be met by showing that at some time since 1189 the right could not or did not exist.[72] Thus an easement of light cannot be claimed by prescription at common law for a building which is shown to have been erected since 1189.[73] Consequently it was virtually impossible to establish a claim to light at common law, and many claims based on enjoyment lasting for centuries were liable to be defeated by evidence that there could have been no enjoyment of the right in 1189. Again, if it could be shown that any time since 1189 the dominant and servient tenements had been in the same ownership and occupation, any easement or profit would have been extinguished and so any claim at common law would fail.[74] To meet this state of affairs, the courts invented what has been called the "revolting fiction"[75] of the lost modern grant.

III. LOST MODERN GRANT

1. The presumption. The weakness of common law prescription was the liability to failure if it was shown that user had begun at some date after 1189. The doctrine of lost modern grant avoided this by presuming from long user that an actual grant of the easement or profit had been made at some time subsequent to 1189 but prior to the user supporting the claim, and that unfortunately this grant had been lost.[76] "Juries were first told that from user, during living memory, or even during 20 years, they might presume a lost grant or deed; next they were recommended to make such presumption; and lastly, as the final consummation of judicial legislation, it was held that a jury should be told, not only that they might, but also that they were bound to presume the existence of such a lost grant, although neither judge nor jury, nor anyone else, had the shadow of a belief that any such instrument had ever really existed."[77] In their anxiety to find a legal origin for a right of which there had been open and uninterrupted enjoyment for a long period, unexplained in any other way, the courts presumed that a grant had been made, and so made it immaterial that enjoyment had not continued since 1189. User for 20 years normally sufficed to raise the presumption[78]; and unlike prescription under the Act, once the period has run, the easement comes into existence and is not affected by any subsequent cessation of the user.[79]

---

[71] *Bealey* v. *Shaw* (1805) 6 East 208 at 215.
[72] *Hulbert* v. *Dale* [1909] 2 Ch. 570 at 577.
[73] *Duke of Norfolk* v. *Arbuthnot* (1880) 5 C.P.D. 390.
[74] See *post*, p. 400.
[75] *Angus & Co.* v. *Dalton* (1877) 3 Q.B.D. 85 at 94, *per* Lush J.
[76] See, *e.g. Dalton* v. *Angus & Co.* (1881) 6 App.Cas. 740 at 813.
[77] *Bryant* v. *Foot* (1867) L.R. 2 Q.B. 161 at 181, *per* Cockburn C.J.
[78] *Penwarden* v. *Ching* (1829) Moo. & M. 400.
[79] *Mills* v. *Silver* [1991] Ch. 271; *post*, p. 391.

2. Evidence. Rather stronger evidence of user is required to induce the court to presume a lost modern grant than is required for prescription at common law.[80] Further, the doctrine can be invoked only if something prevents the application of common law prescription.[81] Since the doctrine is admittedly a fiction, the claimant will not be ordered to furnish particulars of the fictitious grant (*e.g.* as to the parties), but he must plead whether the grant is alleged to have been made before or after a particular date.[82] The presumption cannot be rebutted by evidence that no grant was in fact made.[83] But the claim is defeated by proof that during the entire period when the grant would have been made there was nobody who could lawfully have made it.[84] Thus the court has refused to presume a lost grant of a way where the land had been in strict settlement (under which there was no power to make a grant) from the time when the user began down to the time of action.[85]

IV. PRESCRIPTION ACT 1832

The Prescription Act 1832 was passed to meet the difficulties and uncertainties mentioned above, and in particular the difficulty of persuading juries to presume grants to have been made when they knew this was not the case. It is ill-drafted, but in many cases it has substituted certainty for uncertainty. The Act makes special provision for easements of light, so that the other rights under the Act will be dealt with first, and then easements of light.

(a) Easements (except light) and profits

The Act is perhaps best dealt with by giving a summary of the effect of each section and then annotating the sections in groups.

1. Sections 1 to 4

Section 1: profits. No claim to a profit is to be defeasible by showing that user commenced after 1189 if 30 years' uninterrupted enjoyment as of right is shown. If 60 years' uninterrupted enjoyment as of right is shown, the right is deemed to be absolute unless it has been enjoyed by written consent or agreement.

Section 2: easements except light. The section makes exactly similar provisions for all easements except the easement of light, though the periods are 20 and 40 years respectively instead of 30 and 60.

---

[80] *Tilbury* v. *Silva* (1890) 45 Ch.D. 98 at 123.
[81] *Bryant* v. *Lefever* (1879) 4 C.P.D. 172 at 177.
[82] *Tremayne* v. *English Clays Lovering Pochin & Co. Ltd.* [1972] 1 W.L.R. 657, not following *Gabriel Wade & English Ltd.* v. *Dixon & Cardus Ltd.* [1937] 3 All E.R. 900.
[83] *Tehidy Minerals Ltd.* v. *Norman* [1971] 2 Q.B. 528.
[84] *Neaverson* v. *Peterborough R.D.C.* [1902] 1 Ch. 557.
[85] *Roberts* v. *James* (1903) 89 L.T. 282. See now S.L.A. 1925, s.49(1).

Section 3: light. Easements of light are dealt with below.[86]

Section 4: periods and interruptions. All periods of enjoyment under the Act are those periods next before some action in which the claim is brought into question. Further, no act is to be deemed an interruption until it has been submitted to or acquiesced in for one year after the party interrupted had notice both of the interruption and of the person making it.

The chief points to note on this group of sections are as follows.

(a) *"Next before some action."* The Act does not say that an easement or profit comes into existence after 20, 30, 40 or 60 years' user in the abstract; all periods under the Act are those next before some action in which the right is questioned. Thus until some action is brought, there is a mere inchoate right to an easement or profit, however long the user.[87] Further, even if there has been user for longer than the statutory periods, the vital period is always that period (*e.g.* of 20 years) next before some action. Thus if user commenced 50 years ago but ceased five years ago, a claim will fail if the action is commenced today, for there has not been continuous user during the 20 or 40 years next before the action.[88] Similarly a claim under the Act will fail if there has been unity of possession for a substantial period immediately before the action, for there has not been user *as an easement* during the whole of the vital period.[89]

(b) *"Without interruption."* The user must be "without interruption"; but a special meaning is given to "interruption." If D has used a way over S's land for over 20 years, and then a barrier is erected barring his way, D can still succeed in establishing an easement, provided that at the time an action is brought he has not acquiesced in the obstruction for one year after he has known both of the obstruction and of the person responsible for it.[90] "Interruption" means some hostile obstruction and not mere non-user.[91] A complaint or protest against an interruption suffices to negative acquiescence if it is communicated to the servient owner; and its effect normally endures for some time after it has been made, so that there is no acquiescence in an interruption for a year merely because a year has elapsed since the last protest was made.[92]

User for 19 years and a day followed by 364 days' interruption is thus, for the purposes of the Act, 20 years' user upon which a claim will succeed. But this does not mean that 364 days is in fact deducted from the periods in the

---

[86] *Post*, pp. 396 *et seq.*
[87] *Hyman* v. *Van den Bergh* [1908] 1 Ch. 167.
[88] *Parker* v. *Mitchell* (1840) 11 A. & E. 788; contrast lost modern grant: *ante*, p. 389.
[89] *Aynsley* v. *Glover* (1875) 10 Ch.App. 283.
[90] *Seddon* v. *Bank of Bolton* (1882) 19 Ch.D. 462.
[91] *Smith* v. *Baxter* [1900] 2 Ch. 138 at 143. For commons, see *post*, p. 395.
[92] *Davies* v. *Du Paver* [1953] 1 Q.B. 184; *Dance* v. *Triplow* (1991) 64 P. & C.R. 1 (2½ years too much).

Act. To say that user for 19 years and a day is as good as user for 20 years is inaccurate, for—

(i) no action can be brought to establish an easement if only 19 years and a fraction have elapsed since the user began,[93] whereas after 20 years' user, an action can be started forthwith; and

(ii) if an interruption commences after user for 19 years and a day, not until it has lasted for 364 days can the dominant owner commence an action to establish his easement, for not until then is there a period of 20 years.[94] If he waits another day, the interruption will have lasted for a year and his claim must fail. Thus he has only one day on which to issue his writ, whereas if he has enjoyed user for 20 years when an interruption commences, he may issue his writ on any of the next 364 days.

(c) *User "as of right."* Sections 1 and 2 provide that the enjoyment must be by a "person claiming right thereto," and section 5 provides that it is sufficient to plead enjoyment "as of right." The effect is that claims under the Act must be based on user which would have sufficed at common law, *i.e. nec vi, nec clam, nec precario.*[95]

At common law, any consent or agreement by the servient owner, whether oral or written, rendered the user *precario*. Under the Act, this rule applies to the shorter periods (20 years for easements, 30 years for profits); but in the case of the longer periods (40 years for easements, 60 years for profits) a special meaning is given to *precario* by providing that the right is to be absolute unless enjoyed by written consent or agreement. A mere oral consent given at the beginning of the period and not renewed will thus not defeat a claim based on one of the longer periods, although it would be fatal at common law. However, oral consents repeatedly given during a period will defeat a claim based even on the longer periods.[96]

(d) *Effect of consents.* The effect of consents may be summarised thus[97]:

(i) Any consents, whether oral or written, which have been given intermittently during the period make the user *precario* and defeat a claim based on either the shorter or longer periods.

(ii) A written consent given at the beginning of the user (and extending throughout) defeats a claim based on either the shorter or longer periods.

(iii) An oral consent given at the beginning of the user (and extending throughout) defeats a claim based on the shorter periods but not a claim based on the longer periods.

If user commences by consent, the question whether it continues by consent

---

[93] *Lord Battersea* v. *Commissioners of Sewers for the City of London* [1895] 2 Ch. 708.
[94] *Reilly* v. *Orange* [1955] 1 W.L.R. 616.
[95] *Gardner* v. *Hodgson's Kingston Brewery Co. Ltd.* [1903] A.C. 229 at 238, 239.
[96] *Gardner* v. *Hodgson's Kingston Brewery Co. Ltd.* [1903] A.C. 229.
[97] See *Tickle* v. *Brown* (1836) 4 A. & E. 369; *Healey* v. *Hawkins* [1968] 1 W.L.R. 1967.

is one of fact.[98] In the case of a written consent or agreement, signature by the servient owner is not essential; a document signed by the dominant owner or his leasehold tenant may suffice.[99]

The remaining sections of the Act must now be dealt with.

2. Sections 5 to 8

Section 5 deals with pleadings.

Section 6 provides that enjoyment for less than the statutory periods shall give rise to no claim. This does not prevent a lost grant being presumed from user for less than a statutory period if there is some evidence to support it in addition to the enjoyment.[1]

Section 7 provides that any period during which the servient tenant has been a minor, mental patient or tenant for life shall automatically be deducted from the shorter periods; further, the period during which an action is pending and actively prosecuted is also to be deducted.

Section 8 provides that if the servient tenement has been held under a "term of life, or any term of years exceeding three years from the granting thereof," the term shall be excluded in computing the period of 40 years in the case of a "way or other convenient [*sic*] watercourse or use of water," provided the claim is resisted by a reversioner upon the term within three years of its determination.

No more need be said about sections 5 and 6. Sections 7 and 8 are complicated and can conveniently be dealt with together.

(a) *Deduction*. Where either section applies, the period deducted is excluded altogether when calculating the period next before action. Thus if there has been enjoyment of a profit for 45 years in all, consisting of 25 years' user against the fee simple owner, then 19 years against the life tenant, and then a further year against the fee simple owner, the claim fails; for by section 7 the period of the life tenancy is deducted when calculating the period next before action brought, and thus less than 30 years' user is left. But if the user continues for another four years, the claim would succeed, for there is 30 years' user consisting of 25 years before and five years after the life tenancy; since the period of the life tenancy is disregarded, the 30 years' period is, for the purposes of the Act, next before action within section 4.[2] The sections in effect connect the periods immediately before and after the period deducted, but they will not connect two periods separated in any other way, *e.g.* by a period of unity of possession.[3]

---

[98] *Gaved* v. *Martyn* (1865) 19 C.B. (N.S.) 732; *Healey* v. *Hawkins, supra.*
[99] *Hyman* v. *Van den Bergh* [1908] 1 Ch. 167.
[1] *Hanmer* v. *Chance* (1865) 4 De G.J. & S. 626 at 631.
[2] *Clayton* v. *Corby* (1842) 2 Q.B. 813.
[3] *Onley* v. *Gardiner* (1838) 4 M. & W. 496.

(b) *Application.* Section 7 applies to the shorter periods both for easements and profits; but section 8 does not apply to profits at all, and applies to
the longer period only in the case of easements of way "or other convenient
watercourse or use of water." Probably "convenient" is a misprint for
"easement," and the phrase should read "or other easement, watercourse or
use of water" as in section 2. If so, section 8 applies to all easements (except
light): but the point is unsettled.[4]

(c) *Ambit.* Section 7 applies to the servient owner being a minor, mental
patient or tenant for life: section 8 applies where the servient tenement has
been held under a term for over three years, or for life. Thus a life tenancy
can be deducted under both sections, but infancy or mental illness affect
only the shorter periods. If D has enjoyed a way against S's land for 25 years,
but S has been mentally ill for the last 15 of those years, section 7 defeats D's
claim. If D continues his user for another 15 years, however, his claim
succeeds even though S's mental illness continues throughout.

Further, it will be observed that the only provision for deduction of
leasehold terms is in section 8. Thus, where there had been user of a way for
20 years, the servient land being under lease for 15 of the 20 years, but free
from any lease at the beginning and end of the period, an easement was
established[5]: for section 7 makes no mention of leaseholds, and section 8
does not apply to the 20 years' period. It will be noted that here the user
commenced against the fee simple owner who, by leasing the land, voluntarily put it out of his power to resist the user: had the lease been granted
before the user commenced and continued throughout, the position would
have been different, for no user as against a fee simple owner able to resist it
could be shown.[6] In short, a lease may affect a claim in two ways:

   (i) by showing that there has been no user against a fee simple owner
        who knows of it and can resist it; and
   (ii) by falling within the provisions of section 8 allowing deduction.

The first of these is a common law rule not affected by the Act; the second is
a creature of the statute and can apply only to claims under the Act based on
the 40 years' period.

(d) *Right to deduct.* In section 7, the provision for deduction is absolute: in
section 8, it is conditional, the condition being that the reversioner resists the
claim within three years of the determination of the term of years or life.
Thus if the reversioner fails to resist the claim within three years, he has no
right of deduction. Further section 8 extends only to a reversioner and not to
a remainderman,[7] so that it will rarely apply to the usual kind of settlement.

It will be seen from this that section 7 is wide in its scope, giving an
absolute right of deduction from the shorter periods for both easements and

---

[4] See *Laird* v. *Briggs* (1881) 19 Ch.D. 22 at 33.
[5] *Palk* v. *Shinner* (1852) 18 Q.B. 568; *Pugh* v. *Savage* [1970] 2 Q.B. 373; *ante*, p. 387.
[6] *Bright* v. *Walker* (1834) 1 Cr.M. & R. 211.
[7] *Symons* v. *Leaker* (1885) 15 Q.B.D. 629. But see *Holman* v. *Exton* (1692) Carth. 246
(remainderman "within the equity" of a statute applicable to reversioners).

profits; section 8, on the other hand, is very narrow, giving only a reversioner a conditional right of deduction from the 40 years' period in the case
of (possibly) only two classes of easements.

(e) *Commons.* An additional right to deduct from both longer and shorter
periods is available in the case of commons. Where during the period a right
to graze animals could not be exercised for reasons of animal health or
because the common was requisitioned by a government department, the
time of non-user is to be left out of account both in computing the periods
and in determining whether there was an interruption.[8]

(f) *Difference between longer and shorter periods.* In the case of the
shorter periods, the only benefits which the Act confers upon a claimant are
that the period for which he must show user is clearly laid down, and that he
cannot be defeated by proof that his enjoyment began after 1189. The nature
of the user required is still substantially the same, so that the claimant must
show continuous, uninterrupted user as of right by or on behalf of a fee
simple owner against a fee simple owner who both knew of the user and
could resist it.

In the case of the longer periods, however, although uninterrupted user as
of right is expressly required, and easements can be acquired only on behalf
of a fee simple owner, the Act provides that the right becomes absolute after
the required period next before action has elapsed. User against a fee simple
owner who both knew of it and was able to resist it is therefore not required[9];
the only exceptions to this are those provided by section 8. Thus user of a
way for 20 years against land held under a life tenancy will give no claim
under the Act,[10] but user for 40 years will suffice, subject to section 8.[11] It
seems, therefore, that although all prescription is, in general, founded upon
the presumption of a grant, there is no need to presume a grant in the case of
claims based on the longer periods under the Act, *e.g.* where the servient
owner is a corporation with no power of grant. This is clearly so in the case of
claims to light under the Act,[12] and in the case of other easements "forty
years' user has the same effect which (under the third section) twenty years'
user has as to light."[13] But the point cannot be regarded as settled,[14] and the
fact that *actual* enjoyment confers an easement of light, whereas user *as of
right* is required for other easements, is some indication that it is light alone
which requires no presumption of a grant.

The difference between the longer and the shorter periods may be summarised thus:

---

[8] Commons Registration Act 1965, s.16.
[9] *Wright* v. *Williams* (1836) 1 M. & W. 77.
[10] *Bright* v. *Walker* (1834) 1 Cr.M. & R. 211.
[11] *Wright* v. *Williams*, *supra*, not cited in *Davies* v. *Du Paver* [1953] 1 Q.B. 184.
[12] *Tapling* v. *Jones* (1865) 11 H.L.C. 290 at 304.
[13] *Dalton* v. *Angus & Co.* (1881) 6 App.Cas. 740 at 800, *per* Lord Selborne L.C.
[14] See M. & W. 887.

(i) A presumption of a grant is required in the case of the shorter periods, though possibly not in the case of the longer periods.

(ii) An oral consent given at the beginning of the period defeats a claim based on one of the shorter periods, but not one based on one of the longer periods.

(iii) The shorter periods are subject to the provisions of section 7 but not section 8: the 40 years' period is subject to section 8 in the case of easements of way and water alone, it seems, but otherwise the longer periods are subject to neither section.

(b) Easements of light

Easements of light are in some respects on a footing different from that of other rights under the Act. Section 3 provides in effect that after the actual enjoyment of the access of light to a "dwelling house, workshop, or other building" (which includes a greenhouse[15]) has continued for 20 years without interruption, the right is deemed absolute unless enjoyed by written consent or agreement. On the effect of this, the main points to note are the following.

1. Resemblances. Light resembles other rights claimed under the Act in two respects.

(a) *Section 4 applies*, so that the period in question is that next before action,[16] and, with the modification noted below, "interruption" has the same meaning as in other cases[17]; and

(b) *Written consent*: the rules relating to written consent are the same as for other claims under the Act.

2. Differences. Light differs from other rights claimed under the Act in six respects.

(a) *Only one period*. There is only one period for light, namely, 20 years.

(b) *Disabilities*. Sections 7 and 8 do not apply.

(c) *Obstruction*. Wartime restrictions and later planning control made it difficult to interrupt the enjoyment of inchoate rights of light with screens or other erections. Instead, a servient owner may now provide a notional obstruction. He must first obtain from the Lands Tribunal a certificate either of exceptional urgency or that due notice has been given to those likely to be affected. He may then register as a local land charge a notice identifying the dominant and servient tenements and specifying the size and position of the notional obstruction; and for a year this notice takes effect as an obstruction known to and acquiesced in by all concerned. While the notice is in force, the

---

[15] *Clifford* v. *Holt* [1899] 1 Ch. 698.

[16] *Hyman* v. *Van den Burgh* [1908] 1 Ch. 167.

[17] *Smith* v. *Baxter* [1900] 2 Ch. 138.

dominant owner may sue for a declaration as if his light actually had been obstructed, and for the cancellation or variation of the registration. Further, for this purpose he may treat his enjoyment as having begun a year earlier than it did; this avoids the "19 years and a day" type of problem.[18]

(d) *Actual user suffices.* User as of right is not required[19]: actual enjoyment suffices, provided there has been no written consent. Thus the provision that written consent defeats the claim is the only fragment of *nec vi, nec clam, nec precario* which is left in claims to light under the Act; oral consent is no bar, even though evidenced by annual payments.[20] But there must be enjoyment of the light *qua* easement: enjoyment during unity of possession is not enough.[21]

(e) *No grant.* There is no need to presume a grant, because the Act provides that 20 years' actual enjoyment confers an absolute right[22]; in other words, it is not necessary to show user by or on behalf of one tenant in fee simple against another. Thus the mere fact that the servient tenement has been under lease for the whole period does not prevent the acquisition under the Act of an easement of light valid against the reversioner.[23] This has been taken to its logical conclusion, so that under the Act one tenant can acquire an easement of light over land occupied by another tenant of the same landlord,[24] or by the landlord himself.[25] In the former case, on the expiration of the lease of the servient tenement, the easement is effective against the landlord and all subsequent owners of the land.[26]

(f) *Crown not bound.* Sections 1 and 2 mention the Crown: section 3 does not. A statute does not bind the Crown unless it so provides either expressly or by necessary implication,[27] and so an easement of light cannot be acquired under the Act against the Crown[28]; but other easements and profits can.

(c) Limits to the Act

The Prescription Act 1832 does not enable claimants to establish as easements or profits rights which could not be established as such at common law. Thus a claim by the freemen and citizens of a town to enter land and hold races thereon on Ascension Day cannot be established under the Act.[29] Nor has the Act abolished the other methods of prescription. Consequently, it is usual to plead all three methods of prescription, although the claimant

---

[18] Rights of Light Act 1959, ss.2, 3; and see *ante*, pp. 91, 392.
[19] *Colls* v. *Home & Colonial Stores Ltd.* [1904] A.C. 179 at 205.
[20] *Plasterers' Co.* v. *Parish Clerk's Co.* (1851) 6 Exch. 630.
[21] *Ladyman* v. *Grave* (1871) 6 Ch.App. 763.
[22] *Tapling* v. *Jones* (1865) 11 H.L.C. 290 at 304, 318.
[23] *Simper* v. *Foley* (1862) 2 J. & H. 564.
[24] *Morgan* v. *Fear* [1907] A.C. 429.
[25] *Foster* v. *Lyons & Co. Ltd.* [1927] 1 Ch. 219 at 227.
[26] *Morgan* v. *Fear, supra.*
[27] *Perry* v. *Eames* [1891] 1 Ch. 658 at 665.
[28] *Wheaton* v. *Maple & Co.* [1893] 3 Ch. 48.
[29] *Mounsey* v. *Ismay* (1865) 3 H. & C. 486.

does this at his own risk as to costs, *e.g.* if this form of pleading needlessly increases the other party's expenses.[30] If a claim is made solely under the Act, it is liable to be defeated by showing unity of possession at any time during the period[31]; this is not so under the doctrine of lost modern grant[32] or at common law.[33] Again, if the claim is made solely at common law, it will be defeated if it is shown that the enjoyment started after 1189. But as seen already, this would not defeat a claim by lost modern grant or under the Act. Nor should a claim be based on lost modern grant alone, for the court will not presume a modern grant if the right can be established in any other way.[34] However, a method of prescription under which it is legally impossible for a claim to succeed should never be pleaded. Thus a profit in gross should not be claimed under the Act,[35] although it may be claimed by prescription at common law.[36]

Sect. 4. Extinguishment of Easements and Profits

A. By Statute

An Act of Parliament may extinguish an easement or profit expressly or by implication. Under this head must be considered the extinguishment of commons by approvement, by inclosure, and by failure to register the right of common.

1. Approvement. The lord of a manor had a common law right to "approve" the manorial waste over which the tenants exercised rights of pasture. Approvement was effected by the lord taking part of the waste for his separate enjoyment. The Statutes of Merton 1236[37] and Westminster II 1285[38] confirmed this practice, but obliged the lord to leave sufficient land for the commoners. The onus of proving sufficiency was on the lord, and there had to be enough pasture for all the animals which the commoners were entitled to turn out, and not merely for those in fact turned out in recent years.[39] Since the Commons Act 1876, a person seeking to approve a common otherwise than in accordance with the strict procedure for inclosures under that Act must advertise his intention in the local Press on three successive occasions[40]; and the consent of the Secretary of State for the

---

[30] *Harris* v. *Jenkins* (1882) 22 Ch.D. 481 at 482.
[31] *Damper* v. *Bassett* [1901] 2 Ch. 350.
[32] *Hulbert* v. *Dale* [1909] 2 Ch. 570; and see *Mills* v. *Silver* [1991] Ch. 271 (cessation of user: *ante*, p. 389).
[33] *Dalton* v. *Angus & Co.* (1881) 6 App.Cas. 740 at 814.
[34] *Gardner* v. *Hodgson's Kingston Brewery Co. Ltd.* [1903] A.C. 229 at 240.
[35] *Shuttleworth* v. *Le Fleming* (1865) 19 C.B. (N.S.) 687.
[36] *Johnson* v. *Barnes* (1873) L.R. 8 C.P. 527.
[37] c. 4, now called the Commons Act 1236: Statute Law Revision Act 1948, Sched.2.
[38] c. 46, now called the Commons Act 1285: Statute Law Revision Act 1948, Sched. 2.
[39] *Robertson* v. *Hartopp* (1889) 43 Ch.D. 484.
[40] s.31.

Environment (or Wales), given after holding a local inquiry[41] is required to validate the approvement.[42]

2. Inclosure. Inclosure involves the discharge of the whole manorial waste from all rights of common, whereas approvement applies only to commons of pasture appendant or appurtenant, and discharges only part of the land. From the middle of the eighteenth century, a large number of private inclosure Acts were passed. The policy of Parliament was to encourage the efficient production of food, which was hardly possible under the relics of the feudal system. The Inclosure (Consolidation) Act 1801 and the Inclosure Act 1845 facilitated inclosures, but public opinion was aroused by the disappearance of open spaces, and the Inclosure Act 1852 prevented inclosures being made without the consent of Parliament. The procedure is now governed by the Commons Act 1876. An application must first be made to the Secretary of State for the Environment (or Wales), and if a prima facie case is made out, regard being had to the benefit of the neighbourhood, a local inquiry is held. A provisional order is then submitted to Parliament for confirmation.[43]

3. Non-registration. Rights of common could be lost by failure to register them under the complex provisions of the Commons Registration Act 1965.[44] The Act came into force on January 2, 1967, and it required applications to the appropriate local authority for the registration of all rights of common (except those held for a term of years or from year to year) to be made before January 3, 1970.[45] Rights of common, however created, were extinguished if they were not duly registered.[46] Registration was merely provisional, pending the determination of any objections; and these had to be lodged before August 1972.[47] Objections were investigated by Commons Commissioners appointed under the Act.[48] Their jurisdiction is subject to a right of appeal to the High Court on a point of law, but otherwise the courts have no jurisdiction to investigate rights of common save in cases of bad faith.[49] New rights of common may be created and registered in respect of land over which no rights had been previously registered.[50]

B. By Release

1. Express release. At law, a deed is required for an express release.[51] In

[41] As in the case of inclosure, *infra*.
[42] Law of Commons Amendment Act 1893, ss.2, 3; S.I. 1970 No. 1681.
[43] Commons Act 1876, ss.10–12.
[44] See also Common Land (Rectification of Registers) Act 1989 (dwellings).
[45] Commons Registration Act 1965, ss.1(1), 2(1), 4(6), 22(1); S.I. 1966 No. 1470.
[46] Commons Registration Act 1965, s.1(2); *Re Turnworth Down, Dorset* [1978] Ch. 251.
[47] Commons Registration Act 1965, s.5(2); S.I. 1968 No. 989, 1970 No. 384.
[48] For procedure, see S.I. 1971 No. 1727.
[49] *Wilkes* v. *Gee* [1973] 1 W.L.R. 742.
[50] S.I. 1969 No. 1843.
[51] Co.Litt. 264b.

equity, however, an informal release will be effective provided it would be inequitable for the dominant tenant to claim that the right still exists, as where he has orally consented to his light being obstructed and the servient tenant has spent money on erecting the obstruction.[52]

2. Implied release. If the dominant owner shows an intention to release an easement or profit, it will be extinguished by implied release. Mere non-user is never enough by itself: an intention to abandon the right must be shown.[53] Abandonment may be presumed from non-user for over 20 years, but not where there has been no occasion for any user.[54]

It is a question of fact whether an act was intended as an abandonment. Alterations to the dominant tenement which make the enjoyment of an easement or profit impossible or unnecessary may show an intent to abandon the right. Thus if a mill to which an easement of water is appurtenant is demolished without any intent to replace it, the easement is released.[55] Similarly the demolition of a house to which an easement of light is appurtenant may amount to an implied release, unless it is intended to replace the house by another building.[56] It is not essential that the new windows should occupy exactly the same positions as the old, provided they receive substantially the same light[57]; the test is identity of light, not identity of aperture. Further, if the dominant tenement is so altered that the burden of the easement is substantially increased, the right may be extinguished altogether.[58] Acquiescence in obstructions in the servient land may show an intent to abandon, but not if it can be explained, *e.g.* by the use of an alternative but precarious way.[59]

Extinguishment by frustration seems to be possible but improbable.[60]

C. By Unity of Ownership and Possession

If the dominant and servient tenements come into the ownership and possession of the same person, any easement[61] or profit[62] is extinguished. Unity of possession without unity of ownership is not enough[63]: the right is merely suspended until the unity of possession ceases. Similarly, unity of ownership without unity of possession effects no extinguishment[64]: the right continues

[52] *Waterlow* v. *Bacon* (1866) L.R. 2 Eq. 514.
[53] *Swan* v. *Sinclair* [1924] 1 Ch. 254; affd. [1925] A.C. 227; and see *Tehidy Minerals Ltd.* v. *Norman* [1971] 2 Q.B. 528.
[54] *Moore* v. *Rawson* (1824) 3 B. & C. 332 at 339; *Benn* v. *Hardinge* [1992] *The Times*, Oct. 13 (175 years).
[55] *Liggins* v. *Inge* (1831) 7 Bing. 682 at 693.
[56] *Ecclesiastical Commissioners for England* v. *Kino* (1880) 14 Ch.D. 213.
[57] *Scott* v. *Pape* (1886) 31 Ch.D. 554.
[58] *Ankerson* v. *Connelly* [1906] 2 Ch. 544; affd. [1907] 1 Ch. 678; and see *Ray* v. *Fairway Motors (Barnstaple) Ltd.* (1968) 20 P. & C.R. 261 (extra burden insufficient).
[59] *Treweeke* v. *36 Wolseley Road Pty. Ltd.* (1973) 128 C.L.R. 274; and see *Ward* v. *Ward* (1852) 7 Exch. 838.
[60] See *Huckvale* v. *Aegean Hotels Ltd.* (1989) 58 P. & C.R. 163.
[61] *Buckby* v. *Coles* (1814) 5 Taunt. 311.
[62] *Tyrringham's Case* (1584) 4 Co.Rep. 36b at 38a; *White* v. *Taylor* [1969] 1 Ch. 150.
[63] *Canham* v. *Fisk* (1831) 2 Cr. & J. 126.
[64] *Richardson* v. *Graham* [1908] 1 K.B. 39.

until there is also unity of possession. Thus if both dominant and servient tenements are under lease, the easement or profit will not be extinguished merely by both leases being assigned to X, not will it be extinguished merely by Y purchasing both reversions; but if both leases and both reversions become vested in Z, the right is gone.

Sect. 5. Species of Easements

A. Rights of Way

1. Extent of easements of way. An easement of way may be either general or limited. A general right of way is one which may be used by the owner of the dominant tenement at any time and in any manner. A limited right of way is one which is subject to some restriction. The restriction may be as to time, *e.g.* a way which can be used only in the daytime[65] or in case of fire,[65a] or it may be as to the mode in which the way can be used, *e.g.* a way limited to foot passengers, or to cattle and other animals in the charge of a drover, or to wheeled traffic,[66] and the like.

A right of way can normally be used only as a means of access to the dominant tenement. A right to pass over Plot A to reach Plot B cannot be used as a means of access to Plot C lying beyond Plot B.[67]

In the absence of a contrary agreement or special circumstances,[68] it is for the grantee of a way, not the grantor, to construct the way and to repair it when constructed[69]; the grantee may enter the servient tenement for these purposes.[70] If the way becomes impassable, there is no right to deviate from it unless the servient owner has obstructed it.[71]

2. Effect of mode of acquisition. The extent of an easement of way depends upon how it was acquired.

(a) *Express grant or reservation.* Here the question is primarily one of construction. If the intention is not made clear, a grant is construed most strongly against the person making it, in accordance with the general rule, while a reservation is construed in his favour, for it takes effect as a regrant by the other party.[72] Thus an easement granted in general terms is not confined to the purpose for which the land is used at the time of the grant.[73] A right of way for general purposes granted as appurtenant to a house can

---

[65] *Collins* v. *Slade* (1874) 23 W.R. 199.
[65a] *I.D.C. Group Ltd.* v. *Clark* [1992] *The Times*, July 23.
[66] *Ballard* v. *Dyson* (1808) 1 Taunt. 279.
[67] *Harris* v. *Flower* (1904) 74 L.J. Ch. 127; *Bracewell* v. *Appleby* [1975] Ch. 408.
[68] See *Saint* v. *Jenner* [1973] Ch. 275 (failure to repair results in obstruction).
[69] See *Miller* v. *Hancock* [1893] 2 Q.B. 177 (not affected by *Fairman* v. *Perpetual Investment Building Society* [1923] A.C. 74 on the duty to the dominant owner).
[70] *Newcomen* v. *Coulson* (1877) 5 Ch.D. 133.
[71] *Selby* v. *Nettlefold* (1873) 9 Ch.App. 111.
[72] For this rule, see *ante*, p. 380.
[73] *South Eastern Ry.* v. *Cooper* [1924] 1 Ch. 211.

accordingly be used for the business of an hotel if that house is subsequently converted into an hotel.[74]

If a way is granted "as at present enjoyed," *prima facie* these words refer to the quality of the user (*e.g.* on foot or with vehicles) and do not limit the quantity of the user to that existing at the time of the grant.[75] In cases of difficulty, the surrounding circumstances must be considered: thus both the condition of the way (*e.g.* whether it is a footpath or a metalled road) and the nature of the dominant tenement (*e.g.* whether it is a dwelling-house or a factory) may be of assistance.[76]

(b) *Implied grant or reservation.* A way of necessity is limited to the necessity existing at the time the right arose; thus if an encircled plot is used for agricultural purposes at the time of the grant, the way of necessity over the surrounding land is limited to agricultural purposes and cannot be used for carting building materials.[77]

In other cases of implied grant, the circumstances of the case must be considered. Thus where a testator devised adjoining plots of land to different persons and one plot was bought by a railway company for conversion into a railway station, it was held that a way which had been used in the testator's lifetime for domestic purposes and for the purposes of warehouses on the land could not be used as a public approach to the station.[78]

(c) *Prescription.* Where an easement of way is acquired by long user, the extent of the way is limited by the nature of the user. Thus a way acquired by long user for farming purposes cannot be used for mineral purposes or for the cartage of building materials.[79] It has been held that user during the prescriptive period as a carriageway does not authorise user for cattle,[80] although it covers use as a footway[81] (since *prima facie* the greater includes the less) and it extends to use for motor traffic even if the user proved was for horse-drawn vehicles alone.[82] Moreover, unless there is a radical change in the nature of the dominant tenement, the user is not limited to the number or frequency of vehicles or pedestrians using the way during the prescriptive period.[83]

B. Rights of Light

1. No natural right. There is no natural right of light; a landowner may so

---

[74] *White* v. *Grand Hotel, Eastbourne Ltd.* [1913] 1 Ch. 113 (affd. on another point, 84 L.J. Ch. 938); and see *Alvis* v. *Harrison* (1990) 62 P. & C.R. 10.

[75] *Hurt* v. *Bowmer* [1937] 1 All E.R. 797.

[76] *Cannon* v. *Villars* (1878) 8 Ch.D. 415 at 420, 421; *St. Edmundsbury & Ipswich Diocesan Board of Finance* v. *Clark* (*No.* 2) [1973] 1 W.L.R. 1572 at 1591–1596; affd. [1975] 1 W.L.R. 468.

[77] *Corporation of London* v. *Riggs* (1880) 13 Ch.D. 798.

[78] *Milner's Safe Co. Ltd.* v. *Great Northern and City Ry.* [1907] 1 Ch. 208.

[79] *Wimbledon Conservators* v. *Dixon* (1875) 1 Ch.D. 362.

[80] *Ballard* v. *Dyson* (1808) 1 Taunt. 279.

[81] *Davies* v. *Stephens* (1836) 7 C. & P. 570.

[82] *Lock* v. *Abercester Ltd.* [1939] Ch. 861.

[83] *British Railways Board* v. *Glass* [1965] Ch. 538; *Woodhouse & Co. Ltd.* v. *Kirkland (Derby) Ltd.* [1970] 1 W.L.R. 1185.

build on his land as to prevent any light from reaching his neighbour's windows,[84] unless his neighbour has an easement of light or some other right such as a restrictive covenant against building. The access of light to windows is sometimes deliberately obstructed in order to prevent an easement of light being acquired by prescription.[85]

2. Quantum of light. The amount of light to which the dominant owner is entitled was finally settled in *Colls* v. *Home and Colonial Stores Ltd.*[86]: this amount is enough light according to the ordinary notions of mankind for the comfortable use of the premises as a dwelling, or, in the case of business premises, for the beneficial use of the premises for ordinary shop or other business purposes. The quantum of light is greater where it is needed for the ordinary beneficial use of the particular building, and for a greenhouse it includes the direct access of the sun's rays.[87] In each case the test is that of the ordinary use of the dominant tenement: the dominant owner is not entitled to object even to a substantial diminution in his light, provided enough is left for the ordinary purposes. The test is not "How much light has been taken away?" but "How much light is left?"[88] An easement for more light than is required for ordinary purposes may be acquired by enjoyment of it for 20 years for purposes known by the servient owner to require it.[89] But the quantum of light to which the dominant owner is entitled is not affected by the fact that he has used the room in question for purposes requiring but little light,[90] for a right of light is a right to have the access of light for all ordinary purposes to which the room may be put,[91] including any subdivision of it that might reasonably be expected.[92]

3. Alteration of apertures. An easement of light can exist only in respect of a window or other aperture in a building, such as a skylight.[93] If the dominant owner alters the size or position of the window, the burden on the servient owner cannot be increased; an obstruction which would not have been actionable before the alteration will not be actionable even if it deprives the altered window of most of its light.[94] But if it is established that an obstruction is an infringement of an easement of light for one set of windows, and another set of windows (for which no easement exists) is also obstructed by it, the dominant owner can recover damages in respect of both sets of windows; for the obstruction is illegal and the damage to both sets of windows is the direct and foreseeable consequence of it.[95]

---

[84] *Tapling* v. *Jones* (1865) 11 H.L.C. 290.
[85] See *ante*, p. 396.
[86] [1904] A.C. 179.
[87] *Allen* v. *Greenwood* [1980] Ch. 119.
[88] *Higgins* v. *Betts* [1905] 2 Ch. 210 at 215.
[89] *Allen* v. *Greenwood, supra.*
[90] *Price* v. *Hilditch* [1930] 1 Ch. 500.
[91] *Yates* v. *Jack* (1866) 1 Ch.App. 295.
[92] *Carr-Saunders* v. *Dick McNeil Associates Ltd.* [1986] 1 W.L.R. 922.
[93] *Easton* v. *Isted* [1903] 1 Ch. 405.
[94] *Ankerson* v. *Connelly* [1907] 1 Ch. 678.
[95] *Re London, Tilbury & Southend Ry., etc.* (1889) 24 Q.B.D. 326.

4. Standard of light. The standard of light varies to some extent from neighbourhood to neighbourhood,[96] the test in each case being that laid down in *Colls'* case. There is no "45 degrees" rule, *i.e.* no rule that an interference with light is actionable only if the obstruction rises above a line drawn upwards and outwards from the centre of the window at an angle of 45 degrees; at most, the test provides a very slight presumption.[97] Modern standards of lighting have risen, too.[98]

5. Other sources. In considering whether an easement of light has been obstructed, other sources of light of which the dominant owner cannot be deprived must be taken into account, such as vertical light through a sky-light.[99] In one case[1] a room was lit though two sets of windows, one set facing A's land and the other facing B's land. It was held that the light received by both sets of windows had to be considered, but that A could not obscure the greater part of the light passing over his land in reliance upon B supplying a large quantity of light. Neither servient owner could build to a greater extent than, assuming a building of like height on the other servient tenement, would still leave the dominant tenement with sufficient light according to the test in *Colls'* case.

C. Rights of Water

A variety of easements may exist in connection with water, such as rights—

to take water from a pump, spring or river, though this is now subject to statutory restrictions[2];

to water cattle at a pond;

to pollute the waters of a stream or river[3];

to discharge water on to the land of another;

to enter the land of another to open sluice gates; and

to permit rain water to drop from a roof on to a neighbour's land ("easement of eavesdrop").

D. Rights of Support

These have already been considered.[4]

---

[96] *Fishenden* v. *Higgs & Hill Ltd.* (1935) 153 L.T. 128.
[97] *Ibid.* For scientific tests as to "sill ratio," "grumble points" and 50 per cent. adequacy, see *Charles Semon & Co. Ltd.* v. *Bradford Corporation* [1922] 2 Ch. 737; *Fishenden* v. *Higgs & Hill Ltd.*, *supra*; *Ough* v. *King* [1967] 1 W.L.R. 1547.
[98] *Ough* v. *King, supra.*
[99] *Smith* v. *Evangelisation Society (Incorporated) Trust* [1933] Ch. 515.
[1] *Sheffield Masonic Hall Co. Ltd.* v. *Sheffield Corporation* [1932] 2 Ch. 17.
[2] See *Cargill* v. *Gotts* [1981] 1 W.L.R. 441; *post*, p. 508.
[3] See *Scott-Whitehead* v. *National Coal Board* (1985) 53 P. & C.R. 263, considered [1987] Conv. 368 (S. Tromans).
[4] *Ante*, p. 372.

E. Rights of Air

These have already been considered.[5]

F. Miscellaneous Easements

There are a variety of miscellaneous easements, such as rights—

to create a nuisance by the discharge of gases, fluids or smoke, or by making noises or vibrations;

to hang clothes on a line passing over another's land[6];

to mix manure on the servient tenement for the benefit of the adjoining farm;

to use a wall for nailing trees thereto or for supporting a creeper;

to extend the bowsprits of ships over a wharf[7];

to use a coal shed for domestic purposes[8];

to store casks and trade produce on the servient tenement;

to let down the surface of land by mining operations under it;

to use an airfield[9];

to enter the servient tenement to repair buildings on the dominant tenement[10]; and

to enjoy a garden or park (a "*jus spatiandi*").[11]

Certain rights are not easements but resemble them. A right to use a pew in a church has been described as not being an interest in land but an interest of a peculiar nature in the nature of an easement created by Act of Parliament[12]; and the right to require a neighbouring landowner to repair his fences exists as a spurious easement.[13]

Sect. 6. Species of Profits à Prendre

The following are the main types of profit *à prendre*. Some are usually met with as commons, and some as several profits.

A. Profit of Pasture

A profit of pasture may exist in the following forms.

1. Appendant. A profit of pasture appendant is limited to horses, oxen, cows and sheep, the numerical test being levancy and couchancy.[14]

---

[5] *Ante*, p. 370.
[6] *Drewell* v. *Towler* (1832) 3 B. & Ad. 735.
[7] *Suffield* v. *Brown* (1864) 4 De G.J. & Sm. 185.
[8] *Wright* v. *Macadam* [1949] 2 K.B. 744.
[9] *Dowty Boulton Paul Ltd.* v. *Wolverhampton Corporation (No. 2)* [1976] Ch. 13.
[10] *Ward* v. *Kirkland* [1967] Ch. 194.
[11] *Re Ellenborough Park* [1956] Ch. 131.
[12] *Brumfitt* v. *Roberts* (1870) L.R. 5 C.P. 224 at 233.
[13] *Ante*, p. 371.
[14] *Ante*, p. 377.

2. Appurtenant. A profit of pasture appurtenant is not confined to any particular animals, but depends on the terms of the grant or, in the case of prescription, the animals habitually turned out to pasture. The number of animals may either be tested by levancy and couchancy, or be fixed; it cannot be unlimited.[15]

3. Pur cause de vicinage. Under a common of pasture *pur cause de vicinage*, the commoners of one common may not put more cattle upon it than it will maintain; thus if Common A is 50 acres in extent and Common B 100 acres, the commoners of A must not put more cattle on A than the 50 acres will support, in reliance on their cattle straying to B.[16]

4. In gross. A profit of pasture in gross may exist for a fixed number of animals or *sans nombre*. The last phrase means literally "without number" (an alternative form is "without stint"), but such a right is limited to not more cattle than the servient tenement will maintain in addition to any existing burdens.

5. Limitation of numbers. Rights of common registrable under the Commons Registration Act 1965[17] must be registered for a definite number of animals. After registration has become final, the right is exercisable only in relation to the number so registered.[18]

B. Profit of Turbary

A profit of turbary is the right to dig and take from the servient tenement peat or turf for use as fuel in a house on the dominant tenement. It may exist as appurtenant, or, where it is limited to some specified quantity, in gross.[19] Where it is appurtenant, the turves can be used only for the benefit of the dominant tenement and not, *e.g.* for sale, even if the dominant owner is entitled to a fixed quantity.[20]

C. Profit of Estovers

A profit of estovers is the right to take wood from the land of another as house-bote, plough-bote or hay-bote.[21] It may exist as appurtenant, or, if limited to a specified quantity, in gross.

D. Profit of Piscary and Other Sporting Rights

A profit of piscary is a right to catch and take away fish. It can exist in gross

---

[15] *Benson* v. *Chester* (1799) 8 T.R. 396 at 401.
[16] *Corbet's Case* (1585) 7 Co.Rep. 5a.
[17] See *ante*, p. 399, for registration.
[18] Commons Registration Act 1965, s.15.
[19] *Mellor* v. *Spateman* (1669) 1 Wms.Saund. 339 at 346.
[20] *Hayward* v. *Cunnington* (1668) 1 Lev. 231.
[21] *Ante*, pp. 48, 49.

(when it may be unlimited) or as appurtenant (when it must be limited to the needs of the dominant tenement). Other sporting rights, such as a right of hunting, shooting, fowling and the like, may also exist as profits *à prendre*.[22] It is no infringement of such a right for the servient owner merely to cut timber in the ordinary way, even if he thereby drives away game[23]; but it is otherwise if fundamental changes in the land are made, as where the whole or a substantial part of the land is built upon or converted into racing stables.[24]

E. Profit in the Soil

A profit in the soil is the right to enter the servient tenement and take sand, stone, gravel and the like.[25] It may exist as appurtenant or in gross.

Sect. 7. Registered Land

Easements and profits relating to registered land fall into two categories, namely, those existing prior to first registration, and those arising on or after first registration.

A. Existing Prior to First Registration

1. Servient land. Any easement, right, privilege or benefit created by an instrument must be noted on the register if it appears on the title at the time of first registration and adversely affects the land.[26] Other rights of this kind, such as those not created by an instrument or not appearing on the title, may be noted against the title if admitted or proved to the registrar's satisfaction.[27] Even though omitted from the register, such rights will usually, if legal, be overriding interests,[28] and as such will bind the servient owner.

2. Dominant land. On first registration of the dominant land, any easement, right or privilege that has been acquired for its benefit automatically becomes appurtenant to the land as if it had been granted to the registered proprietor, subject to any entry to the contrary on the register.[29] The benefit of such rights can be registered only if they are appurtenant to the land and capable of existing as legal estates.[30]

B. Arising on or after First Registration

1. Express grant or reservation. Any express grant of a legal easement or

[22] *Ewart* v. *Graham* (1859) 7 H.L.C. 331 at 345.
[23] *Gearns* v. *Baker* (1875) 10 Ch.App. 355.
[24] *Peech* v. *Best* [1931] 1 K.B. 1.
[25] Co.Litt. 122a.
[26] L.R.A. 1925, s.70(2); *Re Dances Way, West Town, Hayling Island* [1962] Ch. 490 at 508.
[27] L.R.A. 1925, s.70(3).
[28] *Ante*, p. 102.
[29] L.R.A. 1925, s.72; and see *Re Evans' Contract* [1970] 1 W.L.R. 583.
[30] L.R.R. 1925, r. 257.

profit must be completed by registration.[31] A notice must be entered in the charges register of the servient title, and the right must be entered in the property register of the dominant title. If no notice appears on the servient title, the right may nevertheless take effect as an overriding interest if it appertains or is reputed to appertain to the dominant tenement, or is enjoyed therewith or is known or reputed to be appurtenant to it.[32]

2. Implied grant or reservation

(a) *Grant*. Easements and profits may be acquired under section 62 of the Law of Property Act 1925, or, it seems, by implied grant, in the same way as if the land were unregistered.[33] They are overriding interests[34] until they are registered as appurtenant to the dominant title and noted against the servient title.[35]

(b) *Reservation*. There is no express provision for implied reservations. As an implied reservation ranks as a disposition by the purchaser,[36] it seems to require completion by registration if it is to be legal.[37]

3. Prescription. Easements and profits may be acquired by prescription as

for unregistered land, and they take effect as overriding interests.[38] The registrar, if satisfied, may enter notice of them on the charges register of the servient title,[39] and may enter them in the property register as appurtenant to the dominant title.[40]

Sect. 8. Rights of Access

Under the Access to Neighbouring Land Act 1992, the court can make an "access order," giving a landowner the right of access to adjoining or adjacent land. This can be done so as to enable the landowner to do works that are reasonably necessary for the preservation of his land (or part of it), but only if the works cannot be carried out (or would be substantially more difficult to carry out) without entering the servient land.[41] An access order binds successors in title to the servient land, subject to registration as a writ or order affecting land, or, for registered land, protection by a notice or caution, since the order is not an overriding interest; and both for unregistered and registered land, an application for an order is a pending land action.[42]

---

[31] L.R.A. 1925, ss.19(2), 22(2).
[32] *Ibid.* s.70(1)(a); L.R.R. 1925, r.258; *Celsteel Ltd.* v. *Alton House Holdings Ltd.* [1985] 1 W.L.R. 205 (in C.A. [1986] 1 W.L.R. 512); and see Ruoff & Roper 6–07.
[33] L.R.A. 1925, ss.20(1), 23(1); L.R.R. 1925, r. 251; Ruoff & Roper 6–07; *ante*, pp. 380–384.
[34] L.R.R. 1925, r. 258.
[35] *Ibid.* rr. 252–254.
[36] *Ante*, p. 380.
[37] L.R.A. 1925, ss.18(5), 19(2).
[38] L.R.R. 1925, r. 250; *ante*, p. 102.
[39] L.R.A. 1925, s.70(3).
[40] L.R.R. 1925, rr. 250(2), 254(1).
[41] Access to Neighbouring Land Act 1992, s.1.
[42] *Ibid.*, ss.4, 5, inserting s.6(1)(d) into L.C.A. 1972 and s.49(1)(j) into L.R.A. 1925; *ante*, pp. 82, 106. The Act will probably be brought into force in January 1993.

CHAPTER 11

RESTRICTIVE COVENANTS

1. No privity. As has been seen,[1] where there is privity of contract, all lawful covenants are enforceable, whether or not they concern land, and whether they are positive or negative. It has also been seen[2] that where there is privity of estate, all covenants which touch and concern the land are enforceable, again whether they are positive or negative. What must be considered in this chapter is the position where there is no privity either of contract or of estate. Thus if V conveys part of his land to P, and P enters into covenants with V relating to the rest of V's land, V can of course enforce those covenants against P. But if V then sells his remaining land to W, and P sells his land to Q, there is no privity between W and Q. Whether W can enforce P's covenants against Q depends on two different questions, namely—

(i) Whether the benefit of P's covenants has passed to W, and
(ii) Whether the burden of P's covenants has passed to Q.

Only if both questions are answered Yes can the covenants be enforced: the plaintiff must be entitled to sue, and the defendant must be liable to be sued. If either of them is an original party to the covenant, then obviously only one of these questions will arise. If V had not conveyed the rest of his land to W, the question whether the benefit of the covenant had passed to him would not arise; and similarly if P is the defendant.

2. Law and equity. In answering these questions, equity has partly followed the law and partly diverged sharply from it. In broad terms, the benefit of a covenant, whether positive or negative, will run with land if it touches and concerns it, and has been annexed to it. This is the rule at law, and equity has followed the law, though with some relaxations and considerable complexity in the details. But the burden of the covenant is another matter. At law, the burden of the covenant would not pass with the land affected, though this rule can be mitigated by certain devices.[3] On the other hand, equity developed a doctrine known as the rule in *Tulk* v. *Moxhay*[4] under which the burden of a covenant attached to the covenantor's land would run with it, provided the covenant was negative in nature and not positive. The law of covenants where there was no privity thus came to be the equitable law of restrictive covenants. This law grew up soon after the

---

[1] *Ante*, p. 348.
[2] *Ante*, p. 349.
[3] See *post*, p. 418.
[4] (1848) 2 Ph. 774; *post*, p. 421.

outburst of building and increase of population associated with the Industrial Revolution. Restrictive covenants became analogous to negative equitable easements[5]; and, like them,[6] they are extinguished when there is unity of seisin and possession for both plots of land,[7] with one important exception.[8] Most easements (except light) entitle a landowner to do positive acts affecting neighbouring land; but restrictive covenants, like easements of light, enable him to prohibit certain acts on that land. Throughout the subject, two questions must always be asked:

   (i) Benefit: has the plaintiff the benefit of the covenant so that he is entitled to sue? and
   (ii) Burden: is the defendant subject to the burden of the covenant so that he is liable to be sued?

These questions will be considered separately, first at law and then in equity. For completeness, the position of the original parties to the covenant will also be considered, although they, of course, have privity of contract.

Part 1

BENEFIT

Sect. 1. The Benefit at Law

A. The Original Covenantee

A covenant taken for the benefit of land may of course be worded so as to apply only so long as the covenantee owns the land. But otherwise an original covenantee who has not assigned the benefit of the covenant can always enforce it against the original covenantor, even if the covenantee has parted with the dominant tenement.[9] Normally the original covenantee will be a party to the deed creating the covenant, but by statute this is not now essential. Under section 56 of the Law of Property Act 1925[10] a person may now take a benefit under a deed even if he is not named as a party to it. For this, the deed must purport to be made with him,[11] and not merely to be made for his benefit.[12] Where A and B are the only parties to a deed, the difference is between A covenanting with B for the benefit of C, and A

---

[5] See *Re Nisbet and Potts' Contract* [1906] 1 Ch. 386 at 409; *Kelly* v. *Barrett* [1924] 2 Ch. 379 at 405; *Newton Abbot Co-operative Society Ltd.* v. *Williamson & Treadgold Ltd.* [1952] Ch. 286 at 293.
[6] *Ante*, p. 400.
[7] *Re Tiltwood, Sussex* [1978] Ch. 269.
[8] *Post*, p. 418.
[9] See *L.C.C.* v. *Allen* [1914] 3 K.B. 642 at 664. Damages will be only nominal.
[10] Replacing R.P.A. 1845, s.5; see *Beswick* v. *Beswick* [1968] A.C. 58 at 102–107.
[11] *White* v. *Bijou Mansions Ltd.* [1937] Ch. 610 at 625; [1938] Ch. 351 at 365; *Lyus* v. *Prowsa Developments Ltd.* [1982] 1 W.L.R. 1044 at 1049.
[12] See *Re Miller's Agreement* [1947] Ch. 615.

covenanting directly with C: only in the latter case is C within the section. Thus if V sells land to P, and P binds his land by a covenant expressed to be with V and the owners for the time being of certain adjoining plots of land, these adjoining owners can sue on the covenant as original covenantees, even though they were not parties to the conveyance creating the covenant.[13] In such a case, the adjoining owners are clearly identifiable persons in existence at the time of the conveyance. But if the covenant was expressed to be made with their successors in title as well, those successors would not be original covenantees, for at the date of the conveyance they were not ascertained or ascertainable.[14] Similarly, if a covenant is made expressly for the benefit of the present owner of a plot of land and his successors in title, the owner at the time of the conveyance is an original covenantee but future owners are not; they can enforce the covenant only under the rules relating to assignees.

B. Assignees

If V sells part of his land to P in fee simple and P enters into covenants binding the land he buys, the benefit of P's covenant may run at law with V's fee simple estate in the land he retains, so that a subsequent purchaser of V's land can enforce the covenant against P. It is immaterial whether the covenant is negative (not to do something) or positive (to do something). Thus the common law doctrine applies equally to a covenant not to build on the land purchased by P or a covenant to supply pure water to the land retained by V.[15] It is also immaterial that the covenant has nothing to do with P's land or, indeed, that the covenantor has no land.[16] For a covenant to be enforceable in this way, the following conditions must be satisfied.

1. The covenant must touch and concern land of the covenantee.[17] It is essential that the covenant should be made for the benefit of land owned by the covenantee (*i.e.* V in the above examples) at the time of the covenant. In general, the test for determining whether a covenant touches and concerns the land is similar to that applicable to covenants in a lease.[18] Thus if in a lease a surety enters into a covenant with the landlord which touches and concerns the land, the benefit of the covenant will run with the reversion.[19]

2. Annexation of covenant: the benefit of the covenant must be annexed to a legal estate in the land of the covenantee. Where the covenant benefits the

---

[13] *Dyson* v. *Forster* [1909] A.C. 98. See also Re *Ecclesiastical Commissioners for England's Conveyance* [1936] Ch. 430 (where liability was equitable: *post*, p. 412).
[14] *Westhoughton U.D.C.* v. *Wigan Coal and Iron Co. Ltd.* [1919] 1 Ch. 159 at 169, 170.
[15] See *Shayler* v. *Woolf* [1946] 1 All E.R. 464 at 467 (affd. [1946] 2 All E.R. 320).
[16] *Smith* v. *River Douglas Catchment Board* [1949] 2 K.B. 500. See, *e.g. The Prior's Case*, Y.B. 42 Edw. 3, Hil., pl. 14 (1368) (covenant to sing).
[17] *Rogers* v. *Hosegood* [1900] 2 Ch. 388.
[18] *Ante*, pp. 351 *et seq.*
[19] *P. & A. Swift Investments* v. *Combined English Stores Group Plc.* [1989] A.C. 632; *Coronation Street Industrial Properties Ltd.* v. *Ingall Industries Plc.* [1989] 1 W.L.R. 304.

land, no formal words of annexation are needed.[20] But at law, it is not enough to show that the covenantee has an equitable interest in the land retained. It must be shown that the covenant was made for the benefit of some legal estate into whomsoever's hands it might come, and not for the mere personal advantage of the covenantee.[21]

3. Ownership of the land: an assignee who seeks to enforce a covenant made before 1926 must show that he has the legal estate to which the benefit of the covenant was attached.[22] But a covenant made after 1925 is deemed to be made with the covenantee and his successors in title, and the persons deriving title under him or them,[23] and so is enforceable by those claiming under the covenantee. Thus whether a mere tenant under a lease can enforce a covenant annexed to the legal fee simple depends on the date of the covenant. It is immaterial whether the person enforcing the covenant knew of its existence when he obtained the land[24]: what is annexed to the land passes with the land.

Sect. 2. The Benefit in Equity

As mentioned above,[25] the rules in equity for the passing of the benefit of a covenant are similar to those at law. Yet although they are rather less strict, they are considerably more complicated.[26]

A. The Original Covenantee

The position of the original covenantee in equity is similar to that at law. In particular, section 56 of the Law of Property Act 1925 applies.[27] However, if the original covenantee parts with the land for the benefit of which it was taken, equity will not enforce it against the covenantor's successor in title, since enforcement would no longer be for the protection of land.[28]

B. Assignees

For anyone except an original covenantee to be entitled to enforce a covenant in equity he must show, first, that the covenant touches and concerns land, and, second, that the benefit of the covenant has passed to him.

I. TOUCHING AND CONCERNING LAND

The covenant must touch and concern land of the covenantee. Equity

---

[20] See *Westhoughton U.D.C.* v. *Wigan Coal and Iron Co. Ltd.* [1919] 1 Ch. 159 at 170.
[21] *Rogers* v. *Hosegood, supra.*
[22] *Westhoughton U.D.C.* v. *Wigan Coal and Iron Co. Ltd.* [1919] 1 Ch. 159.
[23] L.P.A. 1925, s.78.
[24] *Rogers* v. *Hosegood, supra.*
[25] *Ante,* p. 409.
[26] For a general survey, see (1938) 6 C.L.J. 339 (S.J. Bailey); and see (1971) 87 L.Q.R. 539 (D.J. Hayton); [1972B] C.L.J. 157 (H.W.R. Wade).
[27] *Ante,* p. 410.
[28] *Chambers* v. *Randall* [1923] 1 Ch. 149 at 157, 158.

follows the law, and the legal rules apply.[29] By analogy with easements,[30] it may be said that the covenant must accommodate the dominant tenement.

II. ENTITLED TO BENEFIT OF COVENANT

The plaintiff must establish that he is entitled to the benefit of the covenant. He may do this by showing either—

(1) ANNEXATION TO LAND: that the benefit of the covenant has been annexed to land and that he owns some interest in that land; or

(2) ASSIGNMENT WITH LAND: that the benefit of the covenant has been assigned to him and that he owns some interest in the land for the benefit of which the covenant was made; or

(3) SCHEME OF DEVELOPMENT: that there is a building scheme or other scheme of development.

1. Annexation to land. The rules developed by equity have two requirements: first, that the benefit of the covenant has been annexed to land, and, second, that the plaintiff owns some interest in that land. Equity's rules for annexation have now been supplemented by statute.

(a) *Annexation in equity.* A landowner who obtains a covenant from another landowner may do so merely for his own personal advantage, or he may do so for the benefit of his land, enjoying the advantage so long as the land is his. Covenants of the first kind will not automatically run with the covenantee's land, but those of the second type normally will. The question is whether the covenant sufficiently indicates the land with which the benefit is to run, and also whether it shows that it is made either for the benefit of that land or else with the covenantee in his capacity of owner of it.[31] A covenant with the vendors "their heirs, executors, administrators, and assigns" will not suffice, for it indicates no land.[32] A classic formulation is "with intent that the covenant may enure to the benefit of the vendors their successors and assigns and others claiming under them to all or any of their lands adjoining or near to" the land conveyed.[33] Where the precise land is not identified, it may be ascertained by extrinsic evidence.[34] Express words of annexation are desirable, but they are not required if from the words of the covenant and the surrounding circumstances it appears that annexation was intended.[35]

(b) *Annexation by statute.* By section 78 of the Law of Property Act 1925,[36]

---

[29] *Re Union of London and Smith's Bank Ltd.'s Conveyance* [1933] Ch. 611.
[30] See *ante*, p. 368.
[31] See *Drake* v. *Gray* [1936] Ch. 451 at 466.
[32] *Renals* v. *Cowlishaw* (1878) 9 Ch.D. 125; affd. (1879) 11 Ch.D. 866.
[33] See *Rogers* v. *Hosegood* [1900] 2 Ch. 388 at 389.
[34] See [1972B] C.L.J. 157 at 166–168 (H.W.R. Wade).
[35] *Shropshire C.C.* v. *Edwards* (1982) 46 P. & C.R. 270; *J. Sainsbury Plc.* v. *Enfield L.B.* [1989] 1 W.L.R. 590; and see *ante*, p. 412 (position at law).
[36] Replacing C.A. 1881, s.58, where the wording was different.

a covenant made after 1925 "relating to any land of the covenantee shall be deemed to be made with the covenantee and his successors in title and the persons deriving title under him or them, and shall have effect as if such successors and other persons were expressed." For restrictive covenants, the words "successors in title" include the owners and occupiers for the time being of the covenantee's land intended to be benefited.[37] This provision, and in particular the phrase "successors in title," is plainly apt to show that the covenant is intended to be for the benefit of the covenantee's land rather than himself personally, and so is to be annexed to the land. Yet for over 50 years the section remained in obscurity until in 1979 the *Federated Homes* case[38] gave it full effect. For covenants made after 1925 it is no longer necessary to show from other sources that it was intended to annex the benefit of the covenant to the covenantee's land: instead, it will be automatically annexed by virtue of section 78 unless a contrary intention appears, as where the benefit is expressly made transmissible only by express assignment.[39] Though much criticised,[40] the decision seems sound; and it is plainly convenient. As at law, the benefit of a covenant duly annexed to land passes to successors in title even if they know nothing of it; and the successors in title take only by succession and not as original covenantees.[41]

It is improbable that the benefit of a covenant not annexed to land could pass under section 62 of the Law of Property Act 1925,[42] for it is difficult to see how it could be a right "appertaining or reputed to appertain" to land.[43]

(c) *Area.* The benefit of a covenant may be annexed to the covenantee's land only as a whole, so that it will not pass with parts of that land.[44] But indications to the contrary are readily found,[45] and now the rule is that the benefit of a covenant annexed to land will *prima facie* run both with the land as a whole and also with each part of it separately.[46] But if a covenant is made for the benefit of an area of land too great to be reasonably benefited (*e.g.*, "the Childwickbury estate," of some 1,700 acres), the benefit will not be annexed to it.[47] Nevertheless, if the covenant is expressed to be for the benefit of the land "or any part" of it, the benefit can run with the parts which it benefits.[48]

(d) *Ownership of land.* In addition to showing that the benefit of the

---

[37] L.P.A. 1925, s.78(1).
[38] *Federated Homes Ltd.* v. *Mill Lodge Properties Ltd.* [1980] 1 W.L.R. 594.
[39] *Roake* v. *Chadha* [1984] 1 W.L.R. 40.
[40] See (1980) 43 M.L.R. 445 (D.J. Hayton); (1981) 97 L.Q.R. 32 (G.H. Newsom); [1982] Legal Studies 53 (D.J. Hurst).
[41] *Ante,* p. 412.
[42] Considered *ante,* p. 381.
[43] See *Roake* v. *Chadha, supra,* at p. 47.
[44] *Re Union of London and Smith's Bank Ltd.'s Conveyance* [1933] Ch. 611 at 628; *Re Jeff's Transfer (No. 2)* [1966] 1 W.L.R. 841.
[45] *Drake* v. *Gray* [1936] Ch. 451; *Re Selwyn's Conveyance* [1967] Ch. 674.
[46] *Federated Homes Ltd.* v. *Mill Lodge Properties Ltd., supra.* So also at law: *Williams* v. *Unit Construction Co. Ltd.* (1951) 19 Conv.N.S. 262.
[47] *Re Ballard's Conveyance* [1937] Ch. 473.
[48] *Marquess of Zetland* v. *Driver* [1939] Ch. 1.

covenant has been annexed to land, the plaintiff must establish that he owns some interest in that land. He need not show that he has succeeded to the covenantee's estate in the land, nor that he has the whole of it.[49]

2. Assignment with land

(a) *Express assignment.* Where the benefit of a covenant has not been annexed to land, it can nevertheless be expressly assigned.[50] Such an assignment, like other assignments of rights under a contract, enables the assignee to enforce the covenant against the original covenantor. But successors in title to the covenantor are liable only in equity under the rule in *Tulk* v. *Moxhay*,[51] and equity will permit an assignee of the covenantee to enforce the covenant only if the benefit of it has been assigned to him together with some or all of the land protected by it. That land must be properly identified, if not from the wording of the deed,[52] then from the surrounding circumstances.[53] Although at law the benefit of the covenant cannot be assigned in pieces, yet in equity this can be done if the proper conditions are observed.[54]

(b) *Time of assignment.* The assignment must, it seems, be made at the time of the conveyance of the land which is to be protected.[55] An express assignment is not required if the circumstances show that the benefit of the covenant was intended to be included in the sale.[56] But once the land has been sold, the benefit of the covenant cannot be assigned: one purpose of the covenant is to make the covenantee's land more readily saleable, and if he has succeeded in disposing of the whole of his land without assigning the benefit of the covenant, it ceases to be assignable.[57] If only part of his land has been disposed of, he can assign the benefit of the covenant when he sells any of the parts still retained, but he cannot assign it to those who have already purchased parts of the land.[58]

(c) *Subsequent assignment.* The assignment need not necessarily be made by the original covenantee. If, for example, the original covenantee dies, both the covenant and the land that it benefits will devolve on his personal representatives, who may hold it as bare trustees for a devisee under the covenantee's will or for some other successor to the land. As owner in equity, the successor can sue on the covenant without joining the personal representatives,[59] and can assign it to a purchaser.[60] Subsequent owners of

---

[49] *Formby* v. *Barker* [1903] 2 Ch. 539.
[50] *Re Union of London and Smith's Bank Ltd.'s Conveyance* [1933] Ch. 611.
[51] (1848) 2 Ph. 744; *ante*, p. 409; *post*, p. 420.
[52] *Re Union of London and Smith's Bank Ltd.'s Conveyance, supra*, at pp. 625, 631.
[53] *Newton Abbot Co-operative Society Ltd.* v. *Williamson & Treadgold Ltd.* [1952] Ch. 286; *Marten* v. *Flight Refuelling Ltd.* [1962] Ch. 115.
[54] *Re Union of London and Smith's Bank Ltd.'s Conveyance, supra*, at p. 630.
[55] *Chambers* v. *Randall* [1923] 1 Ch. 149.
[56] *Renals* v. *Cowlishaw* (1878) 9 Ch.D. 125 at 129.
[57] *Re Rutherford's Conveyance* [1938] Ch. 396.
[58] *Re Union of London and Smith's Bank Ltd.'s Conveyance, supra*, at p. 632.
[59] *Earl of Leicester* v. *Wells-next-the-Sea U.D.C.* [1973] Ch. 110.
[60] *Newton Abbot Co-operative Society Ltd.* v. *Williamson & Treadgold Ltd.* [1952] Ch. 286.

the land have been held to be entitled only if there is a complete chain of assignments of the benefit of the covenant to them[61]; but the better view is that the first assignment of the benefit together with the land operates as a "delayed annexation" of the benefit, so that it will thereafter run with the land without further assignment.[62]

3. Schemes of development

(a) *Mutual enforceability*. Where land has been laid out in lots which are to be sold to purchasers and built upon, restrictions are often imposed on the purchasers of each lot for the benefit of the estate generally, such as covenants restraining trading on the estate, prohibiting the erection of cheap buildings and the like. In the ordinary way, these covenants would be enforceable only by the vendor. But much of the purpose of the covenants given by a purchaser of one lot would be lost if they could not be enforced—

    (i) by those who have previously bought lots, and
    (ii) by those who subsequently buy the unsold lots.

Each of these results could be achieved without any special rules for schemes of development. The first would be achieved if the purchaser's covenants were expressly made with those who had previously bought lots as well as with the vendor. The second could be achieved by the covenant being expressed to be for the benefit of the whole or any part of the land retained by the vendor, and so attaching the benefit of them to each lot sold in the future, or by the vendor expressly assigning the benefit of the covenants with each lot sold.[63]

(b) *Principle of schemes*. It is, however, unnecessary for these arrangements to be made. There is a wide principle that where an owner of a defined[64] area of land deals with it on the footing of imposing restrictive obligations on the use of various parts of it as and when he sells them off, for the common benefit of himself (insofar as he retains any land) and of the various purchasers *inter se*, and the purchasers buy on this footing, then the common intention gives rise to an independent equity which binds each owner (including the vendor) as soon as the first part is sold[65]; at that point, the scheme crystallises.[66] This common intention may appear either expressly from the terms of a deed of mutual covenant[67] or of a series of conveyances, or else impliedly from extrinsic evidence which satisfies the

---

[61] *Re Pinewood Estate, Farnborough* [1958] Ch. 280.
[62] See (1968) 84 L.Q.R. 22 at 31, 32 (P.V. Baker).
[63] See *ante*, pp. 412–414.
[64] *Lund* v. *Taylor* (1975) 31 P. & C.R. 167.
[65] *Baxter* v. *Four Oaks Properties Ltd.* [1965] Ch. 816 at 825; *Re Dolphin's Conveyance* [1970] Ch. 654; *Brunner* v. *Greenslade* [1971] Ch. 993 at 1003–1005, stating the principles.
[66] *Brunner* v. *Greenslade, supra*, at p. 1003.
[67] *Baxter* v. *Four Oaks Properties Ltd., supra*.

conditions for a building scheme.[68] "Building schemes," though important, are but a species of the genus "scheme of development."[69]

(c) *Building schemes*. The conditions of a building scheme were for most part laid down in *Elliston* v. *Reacher*.[70] These are as follows:

(i) The plaintiff and defendant must each have derived title from a common vendor or a successor in title who is bound in equity by the obligations of the common vendor.[71]

(ii) Previously to the sale of the plaintiff's and defendant's plots, the common vendor must have laid out or intended to lay out the estate in lots subject to restrictions which were intended to be imposed on all of them and were consistent only with some general scheme of development.

(iii) The common vendor must have intended the restrictions to be for the benefit not merely of himself but of all lots sold.[72]

(iv) The plaintiff's and defendant's plots must both have been bought from the common vendor on the footing that the restrictions were to be for the benefit of the other lots.

(v) The area to which the scheme extends must be clearly defined.[73]

The whole essence of a building scheme is that each purchaser should know when he buys his plot from the common vendor that the covenants given by him are to be enforceable by the owners of all the other lots.[74] It is not necessary to prove an express undertaking by him that this should be so, provided the circumstances show that he must have realised it. If before his purchase he saw some plan of the estate with the restrictions endorsed thereon, as in *Elliston* v. *Reacher*, this suffices; but the absence of a proper plan may be fatal.[75] A scheme establishes a "local law" for a defined area, and the landowners within it have both community of interest and reciprocity of obligation.[76] The reservation by the common vendor of a power to release all or part of the land from the restrictions does not negative a building scheme, nor is it essential that the restrictions imposed on each plot should be identical: it suffices if there is some general scheme of development.[77]

(d) *Sub-schemes*. Where a lot has been divided into sub-lots, the scheme

---

[68] See *Re Dolphin's Conveyance, supra*, at pp. 662, 663; (1971) 87 L.Q.R. 539 at 546–551 (D.J. Hayton).

[69] See *Brunner* v. *Greenslade, supra*, at p. 999.

[70] [1908] 2 Ch. 374 at 384; affd. [1908] 2 Ch. 665. The first real hint of the doctrine was in *Western* v. *MacDermott* (1866) L.R. 1 Eq. 499; but see *Re Pinewood Estate, Farnborough* [1958] Ch. 280 at 286, 287.

[71] *Re Dolphin's Conveyance* [1970] Ch. 654.

[72] Which may be hard to prove: see, *e.g. Tucker* v. *Vowles* [1893] 1 Ch. 195.

[73] This last condition was added by *Reid* v. *Bickerstaff* [1909] 2 Ch. 305: see *Kelly* v. *Barrett* [1924] 2 Ch. 379 at 401.

[74] See *Jamaica Mutual Life Assurance Society* v. *Hillsborough Ltd.* [1989] 1 W.L.R. 1101.

[75] *e.g. Osborne* v. *Bradley* [1903] 2 Ch. 446; *Harlow* v. *Hartog* (1977) 245 E.G. 140.

[76] *Reid* v. *Bickerstaff, supra*, at pp. 319, 323.

[77] *Pearce* v. *Maryon-Wilson* [1935] Ch. 188; *Reid* v. *Bickerstaff* [1909] 2 Ch. 305 at 319.

may be enforceable by and between the purchasers of the sub-lots.[78] Furthermore, one result of the "local law" established by a scheme is that where two or more lots come into the same hands, the covenants are not *pro tanto* extinguished but become enforceable between the owners of the lots if and when they are again separated.[79]

(e) *Buildings already erected.* If a fully-built upon estate is disposed of in sections, and conditions analogous to those laid down for building schemes are satisfied, the covenants will be enforceable as in building schemes.[80] Again, the principle of a building scheme has been applied to a block of residential flats, preventing the landlord from letting or using any of them otherwise than for residential purposes[81]; but the court will be slow to infer a letting scheme from the mere similarity of the covenants when each floor of a large house is sub-let separately.[82]

Part 2

BURDEN

Sect. 1. The Burden at Law

A. The Rule

As already mentioned,[83] the rule at law is that the burden of a covenant will not pass with freehold land.[84] This contrasts with the rule for leaseholds, where the benefit and burden of covenants run at law with the lease and the reversion,[85] and also with the rule in equity, where the burden of restrictive covenants can run with freehold land.[86] Nevertheless, there are certain means whereby what cannot be achieved directly can be accomplished indirectly. There are four heads.

1. Chain of covenants. If V sells land to P, and P covenants, for example, to erect and maintain a fence, P will remain liable to V on the covenant by virtue of privity of contract even if P sells the land to Q. P will accordingly protect himself by extracting from Q a covenant of indemnity against future breaches of the covenant to fence. If Q then fails to maintain the fence, V cannot sue Q, but he can sue P, and P can then sue Q on the covenant for

---

[78] *Brunner* v. *Greenslade* [1971] Ch. 993.
[79] *Texaco Antilles Ltd.* v. *Kernochan* [1973] A.C. 609. Contrast other restrictive covenants: *ante*, p. 410.
[80] *Torbay Hotel Ltd.* v. *Jenkins* [1927] 2 Ch. 225 at 241.
[81] See *Hudson* v. *Cripps* [1896] 1 Ch. 265.
[82] *Kelly* v. *Battershell* [1949] 2 All E.R. 830.
[83] *Ante*, p. 409.
[84] *Austerberry* v. *Corporation of Oldham* (1885) 29 Ch.D. 750 at 781–785; *E. & G.C. Ltd.* v. *Bate* (1935) 79 L.J. News. 203; *Cator* v. *Newton* [1940] 1 K.B. 415 (registered land).
[85] *Ante*, pp. 351 *et seq.*
[86] *Post*, p. 420.

indemnity. In theory, liability can be maintained indefinitely in this way; but with each sale of the land the chain of covenants of indemnity becomes longer, and more liable to be broken by the insolvency or disappearance of one of the parties to it. This indirect enforcement of covenants by means of indemnities is thus an imperfect substitute for the direct enforcement which the common law refuses to allow.

2. Enlarged long lease. A more effective but artificial method is to insert the covenant in a lease which can be enlarged into a fee simple, and then to enlarge the lease.[87]

3. Right of entry annexed to rentcharge. A right of entry annexed "for any purpose" to a legal rentcharge is a legal interest in the land.[88] It is possible, therefore, to secure the performance of covenants to build, repair, and so on, by reserving a rentcharge and annexing to it a right of entry, allowing the proprietor to enter and make good any default in the observance of the covenants, and to charge the cost to the owner in possession.[89] Such rentcharges may still be created despite the Rentcharges Act 1977.[90]

4. Conditional benefit. A man who claims the benefit of a conveyance or other deed must submit to its burdens. Thus if a conveyance of land on a housing estate gives the purchaser the right to use the estate roads but imposes on him a liability to contribute to the cost of their upkeep, a successor in title cannot use the roads without paying the contributions.[91] The liability is thus not absolute but conditional; he who does not enjoy need not submit. Yet often there will be little choice. The principle has been extended to a case in which grants of mining rights were made to a company in return for covenants to replant the land, and the company's successors in title were held liable on the covenants as having taken the benefit of the grants of mining rights.[92] If it becomes established, this "pure principle of benefit and burden" (as distinct from conditional benefit and burden) will leave little of the common law rule against the burden of covenants running with land.

B. Summary of the Position at Law

1. Enforcement. It will be observed that only within narrow limits does the common law enforce covenants outside the confines of privity of contract or privity of estate. As will be seen shortly, equity became far more flexible and would enforce covenants in many cases where the common law would not.

---

[87] See *ante*, p. 333; *Re M'Naul's Estate* [1902] 1 I.R. 114; (1958) 22 Conv.N.S. 101 (T.P.D. Taylor).
[88] *Ante*, p. 76.
[89] See Law Com. No. 68 (1975), para. 49; M. & W. 767, 768.
[90] *Ante*, p. 363.
[91] *Halsall* v. *Brizell* [1957] Ch. 169; *E.R. Ives Investment Ltd.* v. *High* [1967] 2 Q.B. 379.
[92] *Tito* v. *Waddell (No. 2)* [1977] Ch. 106 (the "*Ocean Island*" case); see esp. at pp. 289–311.

This does not, however, render the rules at law obsolete, for if a covenant is enforceable at law, the plaintiff, on proving his case, is entitled as of right to a judgment for damages (even though they may be nominal), whereas if a covenant is enforceable only in equity the court has a discretion in deciding whether to give any remedy. However, since the equitable remedy of an injunction is the one usually desired, this point is not of great practical importance. Yet it should be remembered that at law it is quite immaterial whether the covenantor has any land or whether the covenant is negative or positive, and that in the case of a positive covenant, damages will usually be the most suitable remedy.

2. Reform. The present rule against the burden of covenants running with the land at law still creates many problems. The indirect enforcement of such covenants, considered above,[93] is unsatisfactory, and although the burden of covenants will run with land in equity if they are negative, the burden of positive covenants will not. Various proposals have been made for enabling the burden of positive covenants to run with land,[94] including a new form of land-holding termed "commonhold."[95] But the proposals themselves are controversial, and they have not so far been implemented.

Sect. 2. The Burden in Equity

A. Liability

It has been seen[96] that the rules in equity as to the benefit of a covenant are in the main merely a more relaxed and detailed version of the rules at law. As to the burden of the covenant, however, the rules in equity came to be completely different. Until *Tulk* v. *Moxhay*[97] was decided in 1848 (a time when the full effects of the vast expansion in industrial and building activities were being felt), equity had gone no further than the common law.[98] In that case it was decided that a covenant to maintain Leicester Square garden uncovered with any buildings would be enforced by injunction against a purchaser of the land who bought with notice of the covenant.

For some while the question was thought to be one of notice: a person who took land with notice that it had been bound by some restriction could not disregard that restriction. On this footing, it was immaterial whether the restriction had been imposed to benefit other land or merely the covenantee personally: it sufficed that there was some contractual restriction on the use of the land and that the land had been acquired with notice of it.[99] But since

---

[93] *Ante*, p. 418.
[94] See Law Com. No. 11 (1967); Law Com. No. 127 (1984).
[95] See (1987) Cmnd. 179 (the Aldridge Committee).
[96] *Ante*, pp. 412 *et seq.*
[97] (1848) 2 Ph. 774.
[98] Despite *Whatman* v. *Gibson* (1838) 9 Sim. 196, the question was regarded as still being open in *Bristow* v. *Wood* (1844) 1 Coll.C.C. 480.
[99] See *Luker* v. *Dennis* (1877) 7 Ch.D. 227.

1882[1] it has been accepted that equity will enforce a restrictive covenant against a purchaser only if it was made for the protection of other land. Restrictive covenants came to resemble easements as being rights over one plot of land ("the servient tenement") existing for the benefit of another plot of land ("the dominant tenement"). In short, at a leap, the law of restrictive covenants passed from the sphere of contract to the sphere of property.

I. THE ORIGINAL COVENANTOR

The original covenantor usually remains liable on the covenant, even if he has parted with the servient tenement, for the common form of covenant extends to the acts of persons claiming under him[2]; but today, words limiting its ambit are often inserted.

II. ASSIGNEES

An assignee of land of the original covenantor is bound by the covenant only if three conditions are fulfilled.

1. The covenant must be negative in nature. After a few cases in which the court was prepared to enforce positive covenants, the rule was settled in 1881 that none except negative covenants would be enforced by equity.[3] The question is whether in substance[4] the covenant is negative in nature: it is immaterial whether the wording is positive or negative. Thus the covenant in *Tulk* v. *Moxhay*[5] itself was positive in wording, but part of it was negative in nature (to keep land in Leicester Square "in an open state, uncovered with any buildings"), so that this part merely bound the covenantor to refrain from building, without requiring him to do any positive act.

The test is whether the covenant requires expenditure of money for its proper performance; if the covenant requires the covenantee to put his hand in his pocket, it is not negative in nature.[6] A covenant to give the first refusal of a plot of land is negative in nature, for in effect it is a covenant not to sell to anyone else until the covenantee has had an opportunity of buying; but a covenant "not to let the premises get into disrepair," despite its apparently negative form, is in substance positive, for it can be performed only by the expenditure of money on repairs. Among the restrictive covenants most frequently met with in practice are covenants against building on land, and against carrying on any trade or business (or certain specified trades or businesses[7]) on the premises concerned.

---

[1] See *London & South Western Ry.* v. *Gomm* (1882) 20 Ch.D. 562 at 583.

[2] *L.C.C.* v. *Allen* [1914] 3 K.B. 642 at 660, 673; and see L.P.A. 1925, s.79(1).

[3] *Haywood* v. *Brunswick Permanent Benefit B.S.* (1881) 8 Q.B.D. 403. See [1981] Conv. 55 (C.D. Bell); [1983] Conv. 29 (R. Griffith).

[4] *Shepherd Homes Ltd.* v. *Sandham (No. 2)* [1971] 1 W.L.R. 1062.

[5] *Supra.*

[6] *Haywood* v. *Brunswick Permanent Benefit B.S.*, *supra*, at pp. 409, 410.

[7] Such covenants are apparently not subject to the doctrine of restraint of trade when given on the acquisition of property: *Esso Petroleum Co. Ltd.* v. *Harper's Garage (Stourport) Ltd.* [1968] A.C. 269 at 298, 309, 316, 325, 334; and see *Cleveland Petroleum Co. Ltd.* v. *Dartstone Ltd.* [1969] 1 W.L.R. 116 (covenant in lease).

2. At the date of the covenant, the covenantee must own land that will benefit therefrom. Here again, as mentioned above, the rule was not settled at first. It is now accepted, however, that with statutory exceptions in favour of local authorities,[8] a restrictive covenant is similar to an equitable easement, and that the burden of the covenant will run with land only if the covenant was made for the protection of land belonging to the covenantee; as with easements,[9] there must be a dominant tenement which the covenant will benefit (or accommodate).[10] Thus covenants binding land in Hampstead will be too remote to benefit land in Clapham,[11] and if the covenantee retains no other land, a purchaser of the Hampstead land will take free from the covenant. Yet a landlord's reversion on a lease is a sufficient interest to entitle him to enforce the covenant against a sub-tenant, even though he has no other adjoining land.[12]

3. The burden of the covenant must have been intended to run with the covenantor's land. A covenant may be confined, either expressly or by implication, so as to bind the covenantor alone.[13] In this case, assignees of the covenantor's land are not bound by the covenant. But if the covenant was made by the covenantor for himself, his heirs and assigns, the burden will normally be attached to his land. Covenants relating to the covenantor's land which are made after 1925 are deemed to have been made by the covenantor on behalf of himself, his successors in title, and the persons deriving title under him or them, unless a contrary intention appears.[14]

B. Effect

If these conditions are satisfied, the effect is that the burden of the covenant runs *in equity*. There are two main consequences of this.

1. Equitable remedies. Only equitable remedies are available, and these are discretionary remedies. However, since the Chancery Amendment Act 1858,[15] equity has been entitled to award damages in any case where an injunction or specific performance could have been awarded, although the plaintiff is not, as in an action at law, entitled to insist upon some damages being awarded if he makes out his case.

2. Purchaser without notice. The covenant suffers from the infirmity of all

---

[8] See, *e.g.* Housing Act 1985, s.609; Town and Country Planning Act 1990, s.106(3).
[9] *Ante*, p. 368.
[10] See *Formby* v. *Barker* [1903] 2 Ch. 539; *L.C.C.* v. *Allen* [1914] 3 K.B. 642; (1971) 87 L.Q.R. 539 at 545 (D.J. Hayton).
[11] *Kelly* v. *Barrett* [1924] 2 Ch. 379 at 404.
[12] *Regent Oil Co. Ltd.* v. *J. A. Gregory* (*Hatch End*) *Ltd.* [1966] Ch. 402 at 433.
[13] See *Re Fawcett and Holmes' Contract* (1889) 42 Ch.D. 150; *Re Royal Victoria Pavilion, Ramsgate* [1961] Ch. 581.
[14] L.P.A. 1925, s.79(1).
[15] Supreme Court Act 1981, s.50. The jurisdiction survived the repeal of the Act of 1858: *Leeds Industrial Co-operative Society Ltd.* v. *Slack* [1924] A.C. 851.

equitable interests, namely, that it will not be enforced against a bona fide purchaser for value of a legal estate without notice of the covenant, or someone claiming through such a person.[16] But as has been seen,[17] the doctrine of notice has been significantly affected by the Land Charges Act 1925 (now the Land Charges Act 1972). Covenants made before 1926, and covenants in leases, whenever made, are still subject to the old rules as to notice and are not registrable; but a restrictive covenant made after 1925 otherwise than between a lessor and a lessee must be registered as a land charge.[18] If not registered, it will be void against a subsequent purchaser for money or money's worth of a legal estate in the land. A registered restrictive covenant will bind everyone.[19]

Part 3

ENFORCEMENT

Sect. 1. Determination

The enforceability of a restrictive covenant may be decided in any of three ways:

(1) In an action to enforce the covenant;
(2) On application to the court for a declaration; or
(3) On application to the Lands Tribunal for the discharge or modification of the covenant.

1. Action to enforce the covenant. *Prima facie*, a restrictive covenant remains enforceable indefinitely.[20] In certain cases, however, the court may refuse to enforce an action brought by the person entitled to the benefit of a covenant. Thus if the person entitled to enforce the covenant has remained inactive in the face of open breaches for so long and in such circumstances that a reasonable person would believe that the covenant no longer applies, the court will not enforce it[21]; and the same applies if the neighbourhood is so completely changed (as from a residential to a shopping area) that an action to enforce the covenant would be unmeritorious, not *bona fide* and brought with some ulterior motive.[22]

2. Declaration by the court. Sometimes a landowner will be content to break a covenant and rely upon being able to establish one of the above defences if an action is brought. This, however, will not always be satisfactory, as where it is desired to sell or lease the land and the purchaser or

---

[16] *Wilkes* v. *Spooner* [1911] 2 K.B. 473; *ante,* p. 58.
[17] *Ante,* p. 85.
[18] *Ante,* p. 80. For lessees who cannot investigate the lessor's title, see *ante,* p. 86.
[19] *White* v. *Bijou Mansions Ltd.* [1937] Ch. 610.
[20] See *Mackenzie* v. *Childers* (1889) 43 Ch.D. 265 at 279.
[21] *Chatsworth Estates Co.* v. *Fewell* [1931] 1 Ch. 224.
[22] *Ibid.*; *Westripp* v. *Baldock* [1939] 1 All E.R. 279.

lessee wishes to be assured that he is in no danger from the covenant. Consequently, provision has now been made permitting an application to the court for a declaration whether any freehold land is affected by any restriction, and if so, the nature, extent and enforceability of it.[23] This provision is often used in respect of the many nineteenth-century covenants which are today unenforceable through non-compliance with the rules governing the transfer of the benefit of the covenants. There is no power under this head to modify or discharge a valid covenant.

3. Discharge or modification by the Lands Tribunal. In some cases a covenant may still be enforceable, but it may be undesirable for this state of affairs to continue. Consequently, a discretionary[24] power has been given to the Lands Tribunal[25] to modify or discharge the restrictive covenant, with or without the payment of compensation; and an order may be refused unless the applicant accepts reasonable alternative restrictions.[26] An applicant is not disqualified merely because he recently bound himself by the covenant, though this is a factor to be considered.[27] He must bring his case within one of four heads.

(a) *Obsolete.* By reason of changes in the character of the property or neighbourhood or other material circumstances the restriction ought to be deemed obsolete.

(b) *Obstructive.* The continued existence of the restriction would impede some reasonable use of the land for public or private purposes, and either it confers no practical benefit[28] of substantial value or advantage, or it is contrary to the public interest, and (in either case) any loss can be adequately compensated in money.[29]

(c) *Agreement.* The persons of full age and capacity entitled to the benefit of the restrictions have agreed, either expressly or by implication, by their acts and omissions, to the discharge or modification sought.

(d) *No injury.* The discharge or modification would not injure the persons entitled to the benefit of the covenant.

Both for the court and the Lands Tribunal, these powers apply to restrictions whenever made, but do not apply to restrictions imposed on a disposition made either gratuitously or for a nominal consideration for public purposes.[30] They apply to restrictions on freehold land, and to restrictions

---

[23] L.P.A. 1925, s.84(2). See s.84(7), *infra.*
[24] *Driscoll* v. *Church Commissioners for England* [1957] 1 Q.B. 330.
[25] Lands Tribunal Act 1949, s.1(4).
[26] *Jones* v. *Rhys-Jones* (1974) 30 P. & C.R. 451.
[27] L.P.A. 1925, s.84(1), (1C); L.P.A. 1969, s.28.
[28] *Gilbert* v. *Spoor* [1983] Ch. 27 (a view).
[29] See the questions as formulated in *Re Bass Ltd.'s Application* (1973) 26 P. & C.R. 156 and discussed in (1979) 129 N.L.J. 523 (H.W. Wilkinson).
[30] L.P.A. 1925, s.84(7).

on leasehold land if the lease was made for more than 40 years and at least 25 have expired[31]; but they do not apply to mining leases.[32]

There is also provision for the county court to authorise the conversion of a house into two or more tenements in contravention of a restrictive covenant or a provision in a lease if owing to changes in the neighbourhood the house cannot readily be let as a whole, or if planning permission for the conversion has been granted.[33]

Sect. 2. Town Planning

In recent years, the extension of town and country planning control[34] has to some extent reduced the importance of restrictive covenants. If planning control imposes restrictions which will preserve the amenities of a neighbourhood, landowners have little incentive to impose or enforce restrictive covenants with the same object. Nevertheless, restrictive covenants have not been superseded by planning control. A landowner must see that what he proposes to do will contravene neither the private system of restrictive covenants nor the public system of planning control; and restrictive covenants sometimes extend to matters not usually dealt with by planning law. Further, a covenantee has the enforcement of the covenant under his control, whereas a landowner may be disappointed in the way in which the local planning authority imposes or enforces planning control against his neighbours. Nevertheless, the practical advice to give a landowner whose neighbour's activities are objectionable is often not to launch proceedings to enforce any apposite restrictive covenant, with consequent delay, expense and uncertainty, but to encourage the local planning authority to exercise its powers of enforcing planning control.[35]

Sect. 3. Registered Land

1. Benefit. Except in the case of schemes of development, it is usually difficult for an applicant for registration to establish that he is entitled to the benefit of a restrictive covenant, and so it is unusual for the benefit of such covenants to be entered on the register. But sometimes the registrar will enter a notice that the applicant claims to be entitled to their benefit.[36]

2. Burden. Restrictive covenants over registered land (not being made between a lessor and lessee) are protected by a notice in the charges register of the land,[37] or, in case of difficulty, by a caution.[38] Such covenants rank as

---

[31] *Ridley* v. *Taylor* [1965] 1 W.L.R. 611.
[32] L.P.A. 1925, s.84(12), as amended by L. & T.A. 1954, s.52.
[33] H.A. 1985, s.610. See *Josephine Trust Ltd.* v. *Champagne* [1963] 2 Q.B. 160.
[34] *Post*, pp. 510 *et seq.*
[35] For these powers, see *post*, pp. 515–517.
[36] See Ruoff & Roper 3–07, 17–49, 35–23, 24.
[37] L.R.A. 1925, s.50; L.R.R. 1925, r. 212; Ruoff & Roper 3–12, 35–21.
[38] See *ante*, p. 106.

minor interests, and unless duly protected on the register will not bind a purchaser.[39] Such protection confers no additional validity on a covenant and so will not make it run with the land if it is positive and not negative,[40] or if the benefit of the covenant cannot be shown to have passed to the plaintiff.

3. Discharge or modification. Any release, waiver, discharge or modification of a restrictive covenant will be noted on the register. Where this has been effected by the court or the Lands Tribunal, or the court has refused to enforce the covenant by injunction,[41] the entry on the register will be cancelled or otherwise dealt with.[42]

---

[39] L.R.A. 1925, ss.20(1), 23(1). See *Hodges* v. *Jones* [1935] Ch. 657.
[40] L.R.A. 1925, s.52(2); *Cator* v. *Newton* [1940] 1 K.B. 415.
[41] *Ante*, p. 423.
[42] L.R.A. 1925, s.50(3); L.P.(Am.) A. 1969, s.28(7); L.R.R. 1925, r. 212; Ruoff & Roper 35–25.

CHAPTER 12

LICENCES AND PROPRIETARY ESTOPPEL

SOMETHING has already been said about licences as contrasted with tenancies,[1] but they must now be considered in greater detail.[2] In addition, something must be said about proprietary estoppel, not only as affecting licences but also in its own right.

Sect. 1. Nature of Licences

In essence, a licence is a mere permission given by the occupier of land to a person to do something on that land which would otherwise be a trespass.[3] The scope of licences is great. They range from a simple oral permission given to a boy to fetch his ball from the garden to an elaborate deed granting exclusive possession of a large building for an indefinite period which would have been a lease if the period has been definite.[4] At common law, most licences could be revoked at any time, though if the licensor did this in breach of contract he would be liable in damages. A licence created no interest in the land, so that if V sold his lodging house to P, the lodgers could not resist eviction by P, and their only remedy was to sue V for damages. Normally a licence gave no right to the exclusive possession of the land. In recent years, there has been much activity in the law of licences, and as will be seen, some basic concepts have been modified.

Sect. 2. Types of Licences

Some licences give the licensee the right to the exclusive occupation of the land. This has become increasingly common for flats and other dwellings, where the owner seeks to avoid the application of the Rent Acts, which apply only to tenancies.[5] Other licences confer a right of occupation but not exclusive possession, as with lodgers and guests in a hotel.[6] There is also a wide range of miscellaneous licences, such as leave to use a concert hall for a few days[7]; permission to put pleasure boats on a canal[8]; permission to erect an advertisement hoarding or electrical sign[9]; the grant of the "front of the

---

[1] *Ante*, pp. 309, 310.
[2] See generally Dawson and Pearce's *Licences relating to the Occupation or Use of Land* (1979).
[3] See *Thomas* v. *Sorrell* (1673) Vaugh. 330 at 351.
[4] See *ante*, pp. 309, 310, 314, 315.
[5] *Ante*, p. 309; *post*, p.533.
[6] *Ante*, pp. 309, 310.
[7] See *Taylor* v. *Caldwell* (1863) 3 B. & S. 826.
[8] *Hill* v. *Tupper* (1863) 2 H. & C. 121; *ante*, p. 369.
[9] *Wilson* v. *Tavener* [1901] 1 Ch. 578; *Walton Harvey Ltd.* v. *Walker and Homfrays Ltd.* [1931] 1 Ch. 274.

427

house rights" in a theatre, *i.e.* the exclusive right to supply refreshments and to use the refreshment rooms[10]; and permission to see a race or cinema performance.[11]

Four main categories of licence[12] require consideration: the first two are relatively straightforward, but the other two are more complex, especially as regards revocability, and whether successors in title will be bound.

1. Bare licence. A bare licence is the simplest form of licence. It is a licence not granted for valuable consideration, such as a gratuitous permission to enter a house or cross a field. Even if it is granted by deed, the licensor can revoke it at any time without being liable in damages,[13] though the licensee will not become a trespasser until he has been given a reasonable time to withdraw.[14] He cannot resist the licensor's claim by denying his title, as he will be estopped from doing this as long as he is in possession[15]; but thereafter he is free to do so.[16] A revocable licence is automatically revoked by the death of the licensor or by a disposition of the land.[17]

2. Licence coupled with an interest. A licence may be coupled with an interest in the land or chattels thereon. Thus the right to enter another man's land to hunt and take away the deer killed, or to cut down a tree and remove it, involves the grant of an interest in the deer or tree and also a licence annexed to it to come on the land.[18] The interest must be a recognised interest in property,[19] and it must have been validly created. Thus at law a right to take game or minerals, being a profit *à prendre*,[20] must have been created by deed or prescription,[21] whereas no formalities are required for the grant of a right to take away chattels, such as felled timber or cut hay. Equity will give effect to a specifically enforceable agreement to grant an interest, so that a licence coupled with a profit *à prendre* granted merely in writing but for value may be protected by injunction.[22]

A licence[23] coupled with an interest is irrevocable[24] and also assignable, though only with the interest with which it is coupled. It binds successors in title to the land in the same way as that interest.

---

[10] *Frank Warr & Co. Ltd.* v. *L.C.C.* [1904] 1 K.B. 713.
[11] *Wood* v. *Leadbitter* (1845) 13 M. & W. 838; *Hurst* v. *Picture Theatres Ltd.* [1915] 1 K.B.1.
[12] This classification may not be exhaustive.
[13] *Wood* v. *Leadbitter, supra*, at p.845; *Aldin* v. *Latimer Clark, Muirhead & Co.* [1894] 2 Ch. 437.
[14] *Minister of Health* v. *Bellotti* [1944] K.B. 298.
[15] *Terunnanse* v. *Terunnanse* [1968] A.C. 1086; and see *ante*, p. 321.
[16] *Government of the State of Penang* v. *Beng Hong Oon* [1972] A.C. 425.
[17] *Terunnanse* v. *Terunnanse, supra*, at p. 1095
[18] See *Thomas* v. *Sorrell* (1673) Vaugh. 331 at 351; *Wood* v. *Leadbitter* (1845) 13 M. & W. 838 at 845.
[19] See *Hounslow L.B.C* v. *Twickenham Garden Developments Ltd.* [1971] Ch. 233 at 244, 254, doubting *Vaughan* v. *Hampson* (1875) 33 L.T.15 ("interest" in attending a meeting).
[20] *Ante*, pp. 406, 407.
[21] *Duke of Somerset* v. *Fogwell* (1826) 5 B. & C. 875.
[22] *Frogley* v. *Earl of Lovelace* (1859) Johns. 333.
[23] *James Jones & Sons Ltd.* v. *Earl of Tankerville* [1909] 2 Ch. 440 at 442.
[24] *Muskett* v. *Hill* (1839) 5 Bing. N.C. 694 at 707, 708.

3. Contractual licence. A contractual licence is a licence granted for value, such as tickets for the theatre or a cricket match, or an agreement to house lodgers or hotel guests. The rights under such licences primarily depend on the terms of the contract. At common law, such licences were inherently revocable even where revocation would be a breach of contract: the power of revocation was not taken away by a contract not to exercise it. At common law, such licences created no interest in the land, and like other personal contracts they did not bind successors in title to that land. As will be seen below, each of these propositions has now been substantially modified. A contractual licence is not a separate entity from the contract conferring it but takes effect as part of it, according to its terms.[25]

4. Licence by estoppel. A licence by estoppel[26] is a licence which the licensor is precluded by estoppel from revoking or otherwise failing to put into effect. Thus where at a licensor's request the licensee extended a jetty and erected a warehouse on the licensor's land, the licensor was estopped from revoking the licence.[27] Estoppel is a broad principle that applies not only to express or implied licences but also to a wide variety of cases concerning land. Thus if A builds on B's land, believing it to be his own, and B knowingly stands silently by, B will be estopped from contending that the house is on his land.[28] Again, if there is an uncertain boundary between two plots of land, and X, who owns one plot, gets the agreement of his neighbour, Y, to X's garage being erected on a particular site near the boundary, Y will be estopped from later contending that the true boundary shows that part of the garage stands on his land.[29] Estoppel may apply not only to express or implied licences but also to a wide variety of cases concerning land. It will therefore be considered in a separate section at the end of this chapter.[30] The broad principle that has emerged is that an estoppel will arise when it would be unconscionable for the licensor to rely on his legal rights.[31]

Sect. 3. Creation of Licences

No formalities are required for the creation of a licence. It may arise not only from a document but also from the spoken word or the tacit acceptance of a state of affairs. But when a licence is coupled with an interest, such as a profit *à prendre*, that interest must comply with any requirements for its creation[32]; otherwise the creation of licences is free from formalities.

[25] *Millenium Productions Ltd.* v. *Winter Garden Theatre (London) Ltd.* [1946] 1 All E.R. 678, not affected in H.L. [1948] A.C. 173.
[26] See also *ante*, p. 67.
[27] *Plimmer* v. *Mayor etc. of the City of Wellington* (1884) 9 App.Cas. 699.
[28] *Ramsden* v. *Dyson* (1865) L.R.1 H.L. 129.
[29] *Hopgood* v. *Brown* [1955] 1 W.L.R. 213.
[30] *Post*, p. 434.
[31] See *Taylors Fashions Ltd.* v. *Liverpool Victoria Trustees Co. Ltd.* [1982] Q.B. 133n. at 154, 155; *post*, p. 435.
[32] *Ante*, p. 428.

Sect. 4. Revocation of Licences

As seen above,[33] a bare licence is revocable at any time, either expressly or by the death of the licensor or by a disposition of the land. On the other hand, a licence coupled with an interest is irrevocable.[34] Contractual licences and licences by estoppel are more complex, and require detailed consideration.

1. Contractual licences

(a) *At law.* By the common law, a contractual licence could be revoked at any time, even if it had been granted for a fixed period which had not expired.[35] On revocation, the licensee became a trespasser if he entered the land, or remained on it after the elapse of a reasonable time to remove himself and his belongings from it.[36] His only redress for a wrongful revocation was to sue for damages for breach of contract,[37] and in such an action he would merely recover the price of his ticket or other consideration.

(b) *In equity.* The rule at law has been modified by equity, if not reversed. Where a contractual licence is specifically enforceable, an injunction will be granted to restrain a threatened revocation of the licence or the enforcement of a wrongful revocation,[38] and specific performance of the licence may be decreed.[39] Thus a ticket-holder wrongly ejected from a cinema may now recover substantial damages for assault[40]: even though no injunction could be obtained in time, it seems that he will be treated as if he had what he was entitled to obtain. The common law rule emerged again in one case, but it has not prevailed. In that case,[41] the owner of a school agreed to share the use of his premises with the owner of another school. Disputes arose, and after the licensor had revoked the licence and had removed the licensee's property, the licensee forcibly re-entered the premises. An injunction was granted ordering him to leave the premises as his licence had been revoked and he had no specifically enforceable right to remain: the court cannot order two people to share premises peaceably. The actual decision can be supported as preserving the *status quo* by evicting a person who has forcibly

[33] *Ante*, p. 428.
[34] *Ante*, p. 428.
[35] *Wood* v. *Leadbitter* (1845) 13 M. & W. 838 (ejection from racecourse), not considering *Feltham* v. *Cartwright* (1839) 5 Bing. N.C. 569 (licence irrevocable once acted upon); and contrast *Butler* v. *Manchester, Sheffield and Lincolnshire Ry.* (1888) 21 Q.B.D. 207 (ejection of ticket-holder from railway carriage).
[36] See *Cornish* v. *Stubbs* (1870) L.R. 5 C.P. 334.
[37] *Kerrison* v. *Smith* [1897] 2 Q.B. 445.
[38] *Millenium Productions Ltd.* v. *Winter Garden Theatre (London) Ltd.* [1946] 1 All E.R. 678 at 485, not affected in H.L. [1948] A.C. 173.
[39] *Verrall* v. *Great Yarmouth B.C.* [1981] Q.B. 202.
[40] *Hurst* v. *Picture Theatres Ltd.* [1915] 1 K.B. 1.
[41] *Thompson* v. *Park* [1944] K.B. 408.

entered premises[42]; but the reasoning has been disapproved,[43] and it now seems that there is no right to eject a licensee in breach of contract, whether or not the contract is specifically enforceable.[44] In any case, the grant of an injunction to restrain a breach of contract is not confined to specifically enforceable contracts.

In the absence of an express contract, the courts sometimes infer the existence of a contract restricting the revocation of a licence, particularly where there is some informal family arrangement. Thus where a man brought a house as a home for himself, his mistress and their children, and the mistress gave up a rent controlled flat in order to move into the house, it was held that she had been given an implied contractual licence to remain in the house as long as the children were of school age and the house was reasonably needed to house her and them.[45] Again, where a mother bought a house for her son and his wife to occupy for £7 a week, and the son later left his wife, the court inferred that the couple had been granted a joint contractual licence determinable only for good reason, such as the wife taking another man to live with her in the house.[46] Yet in these cases it is often difficult to say whether any contract can really be inferred, and if it is, what its terms are.[47] It is sometimes better to rely on the more flexible doctrine of estoppel.[48]

2. Licence by estoppel. Whether a licence by estoppel is revocable depends on the interest arising from the estoppel; and this usually cannot be known until the court has spoken. If the licence is perpetual,[49] there is no question of revocation. If the licence is determinable on certain events,[50] it can be determined only on the occurrence of one or more of those particular events.

3. Determination by licensee. A licensee may determine his licence in accordance with its terms, or by abandoning it. No formalities are required for abandonment: it suffices if the licensee so conducts himself as to justify the licensor in acting on the assumption that the licence has been abandoned.[51]

---

[42] *Hounslow L.B.C.* v. *Twickenham Garden Developments Ltd.* [1971] Ch. 233 at 250, approved in *Verrall* v. *Great Yarmouth B.C.*, *supra*. There is a full review of the authorities in the *Hounslow* case.

[43] *Verrall* v. *Great Yarmouth B.C.*, *supra*.

[44] See *Verrall* v. *Great Yarmouth B.C.*, *supra*, where, however, the contract was specifically enforceable.

[45] *Tanner* v. *Tanner* [1975] 1 W.L.R. 1346; contrast *Horrocks* v. *Forray* [1976] 1 W.L.R. 230 (no licence).

[46] *Hardwick* v. *Johnson* [1978] 1 W.L.R. 683; and see *Chandler* v. *Kerley* [1978] 1 W.L.R. 693 (implied contractual licence determinable on reasonable notice: 12 months).

[47] See *Horrocks* v. *Forray, supra*; *Chandler* v. *Kerley, supra*

[48] See, *e.g. Maharaj* v. *Chand* [1986] A.C. 898; *post*, p. 436.

[49] *Plimmer* v. *Mayor etc. of the City of Wellington* (1884) 9 App.Cas. 699.

[50] See *Inwards* v. *Baker* [1965] 2 Q.B. 29 (as long as the licensee desires).

[51] *Bone* v. *Bone* [1992] E.G.C.S. 81.

Sect. 5. Transmission of Benefit

In general, the benefit of a licence is assignable unless the contrary appears from its nature or some provision in it. This is so even for bare licences,[52] though these may more readily indicate that they are not assignable (*e.g.* an invitation to tea, or to play tennis) than will most contractual licences or licences coupled with an interest.[53] A bare licensee probably cannot grant a sub-licence[54]; but for other licences this seems to depend on the nature and terms of the licence.

Sect. 6. Transmission of Burden

1. In general. The burden of a bare licence does not pass with the land.[55] On the other hand, the burden of a licence coupled with an interest will pass with the land in the same way as the burden of the interest will pass with it. Thus the burden of a licence coupled with a profit *à prendre* will pass with the land unless the profit, being merely equitable, is void for want of registration.[56] In the case of registered land, the burden of such licences will be entered in the register of the servient land.[57]

The burden of a licence by estoppel will run with the land, for estoppels bind successors in title.[58] Such rights are not registrable as land charges, and so if the estoppel is merely equitable it will not bind a purchaser without notice.[59] For registered land, such estoppels may constitute overriding interests[60] if the licensee is in actual occupation,[61] or if the right is in the nature of an easement.[62]

2. Contractual licences. The position of contractual licences is more complex, and must be considered in greater detail.

(a) *Principle.* In principle, a contractual licence, like other contracts, will bind the parties to it but will not bind third parties; the burden of the licence will not run with the land. Thus where A contracted to give B the right to fix posters to the flank walls of A's cinema for four years, but then sold the cinema to P before the four years had run, P took free from the licence, though A was liable to B for breach of his contract.[63]

---

[52] See *Mellor* v. *Watkins* (1874) L.R. 9 Q.B. 400.
[53] See *Shayler* v. *Woolf* [1946] Ch. 320.
[54] See *Goldsack* v. *Shore* [1950] 1 K.B. 708 at 714.
[55] *Wallis* v. *Harrison* (1838) 4 M. & W. 538; and see *Terunnanse* v. *Terunnanse* [1968] A.C. 1086 at 1095.
[56] See *ante*, pp. 80, 88.
[57] Ruoff & Roper 12–35.
[58] *Hopgood* v. *Brown* [1955] 1 W.L.R. 213; *Inwards* v. *Baker* [1965] 2 Q.B. 29; *E.R. Ives Investment Ltd.* v. *High* [1967] 2 Q.B. 379.
[59] *E.R. Ives Investment Ltd.* v. *High, supra.*
[60] *Ante*, pp. 102, 103.
[61] L.R.A. 1925, s.70(1)(g): see *Blacklocks* v. *J.B. Developments (Godalming) Ltd.* [1982] Ch. 183; [1983] Conv. 99 (T. Bailey).
[62] L.R.A. 1925, s.70(1)(a); [1986] Conv. 31 at 35 (M.P. Thompson).
[63] *King* v. *David Allen & Sons, Billposting, Ltd.* [1916] 2 A.C. 54; and see *Clore* v. *Theatrical Properties Ltd.* [1936] 3 All E.R. 483 ("front of the house" rights: *ante*, p. 428).

(b) *Binding successors in title*. For a time this basic position was altered by a line of cases beginning with *Errington* v. *Errington*,[64] in which contractual licences were held to be binding on successors in title. In that case a father bought a house on mortgage, and allowed his son and daughter-in-law to live in it, promising to convey the house to them if they remained in occupation and paid all the instalments under the mortgage. Before they had done this the father died, leaving all his property (including the house) to his widow. She was held to be bound by the licence on the basis that it constituted an equitable interest in the land that would bind everyone except a purchaser without notice.[65]

(c) *No interest in land*. It is now accepted that while it was right to hold that the licence bound the widow, it was wrong to hold this on the ground that the licence was an interest in land.[66] Yet although the burden of a mere contractual licence does not, as such, run with the land or bind successors in title, it may be accompanied by circumstances which produce that effect. Thus a licence may be binding on successors in title—

(a) because it constitutes an enforceable estate contract;
(b) because it is supported by an estoppel;
(c) because a constructive trust arises; or
(d) by virtue of the tort of interfering with contractual rights.[67]

The result in *Errington* v. *Erringon*,[68] holding that the licence was enforceable against the widow, could have been achieved on any of these grounds, without asserting that it created an interest in land; and that assertion, made without regard to binding authorities to the contrary, now has the status of a heresy that has received its *quietus*,[69] like the so-called deserted wife's equity.[70]

(d) *Bases for binding successors*. As stated above, there are four bases on which a contractual licence may be held to bind successors in title.

(1) ESTATE CONTRACT. As already seen, a specifically enforceable contract creates an equitable interest in the land that will bind successors in title, subject to registration.[71]

(2) ESTOPPEL. If a contractual licence is fortified by an estoppel, the burden will run with the land as in the case of a licence by estoppel.[72]

(3) CONSTRUCTIVE TRUST. If a contractual licence is supported by a

---

[64] [1952] 1 K.B. 290. See (1952) 68 L.Q.R. 337 (H.W.R. Wade).
[65] *Errington* v. *Errington, supra*, at pp. 294, 298, 299.
[66] *Ashburn Anstalt* v. *Arnold* [1989] Ch. 1. See [1988] Conv. 201 (M.P. Thompson).
[67] For (a) to (c), see *Ashburn Anstalt* v. *Arnold, supra*, at p. 17; for (d), see *Binions* v. *Evans* [1972] Ch. 359 at 371, *ante*, pp. 68, 69, and *infra*.
[68] *Supra*.
[69] *Ashburn Anstalt* v. *Arnold* [1989] Ch.1; *I. D. C. Group Ltd*. v. *Clark* [1992] 8 E.G. 108 at 110; affd. [1992] *The Times*, July 23.
[70] See *ante*, p. 81.
[71] *Ante*, pp. 79, 122.
[72] *Ante*, p. 431.

constructive trust it will bind successors in title in the same way as the trust. Such a trust will not arise unless the court is satisfied that the conscience of the estate owner is affected, so that it would be inequitable to allow him to deny the claimant's interest in the property.[73] In relation to the title to land, certainty is of prime importance, and neither inferences from slender material nor bare assertions will suffice to establish such a trust.[74] A licence is not given any greater efficacy, or made binding on a purchaser, merely because the land is sold "subject to" it; but where these words are not needed merely to protect the vendor, because the licence is in any case not binding on him, the circumstances of the sale, coupled with these words, may establish a constructive trust that binds the purchaser to give effect to the licence.[75] Thus where the trustees of an estate agreed to allow the widow of an employee to occupy her cottage rent free for her life, repairing it and cultivating the garden, and the trustees then sold it subject to her rights, and at a reduced price because of them, it was held that the purchaser was bound by a constructive trust to give effect to her rights, so that they could not evict her.[76]

(4) TORT. The tort of wrongfully interfering with the contractual rights of another has already been considered as part of the borderline between personal and proprietary rights.[77] Though little-explored in relation to licences, the decision in the case last considered, preventing the eviction of the rent-free licensee, could probably have been based on the tort.[78]

Sect. 7. Proprietary Estoppel

Proprietary estoppel is a form of equitable estoppel which affects or creates rights of property. At common law, estoppel became a somewhat strict and narrow doctrine which precluded a person from denying the existence of a state of affairs that he had previously asserted. Equity both extended the doctrine and relaxed the requirements; and today it is usually equitable estoppel that is in issue.[79] It is in the form known as proprietary estoppel that it is mainly relevant to rights of property.

1. Creation of estoppel. The general rule is that for an estoppel to arise in favour of C (the claimant) against O (the owner), certain requirements must be satisfied.[80] These are not rigid requirements, but guide-lines for deter-

---

[73] *Ashburn Anstalt* v. *Arnold, supra,* at pp. 22, 25.
[74] *Ibid.* at p. 24 (commenting on *D.H.N. Food Distributors Ltd.* v. *Tower Hamlets L.B.C.* [1976] 1 W.L.R. 852), 26.
[75] *Lyus* v. *Prowsa Developments Ltd.* [1982] 1 W.L.R. 1044; *Ashburn Anstalt* v. *Arnold, supra,* at pp. 24, 25, disapproving *Binions* v. *Evans* [1972] Ch. 359 at 368; and see *ante,* p. 380.
[76] *Binions* v. *Evans* [1972] Ch. 359; *Ashburn Anstalt* v. *Arnold, supra,* at p. 23.
[77] *Ante,* p. 68.
[78] See *Binions* v. *Evans, supra,* at p. 371.
[79] See generally Snell 568–579.
[80] See *e.g. Willmott* v. *Barber* (1880) 15 Ch.D. 96 at 105, 106.

mining the central question, namely, whether it would be unconscionable for O to rely on his legal rights.[81] The requirements are as follows.

(a) *Detriment.* C must have prejudiced himself by incurring expenditure or otherwise acting to his detriment,[82] as by spending money on improving property which in fact belongs to O. Thus he may have built a house on O's land,[83] or he may have built a mill on his own land in the belief that he would be able to take water for it from O's canal.[84] Again, C may have sold part of his land, making the rest land-locked, in the belief that he would have an easement of way over O's land to the land-locked land[85]; or he may have given up his job and his council house to go and live near his father in a house provided by the father, believing that it would be his.[86]

(b) *Expectation or belief.* C must have acted in the mistaken belief that he had or would obtain a sufficient interest in O's property to justify his expenditure or detriment.[87]

(c) *Reliance on encouragement.* C must have acted in reliance on some encouragement by O (or by a predecessor in title of his[88]), given either actively or else passively with knowledge of his own rights, as by standing silently by while C acted on it to his detriment, *e.g.* in building on land not knowing that it was O's, or that O had a mortgage on it.[89] Where C acts to his detriment after receiving the encouragement, he will be presumed to have done so in reliance on it, and so the burden will be on O to establish the opposite.[90]

(d) *No bar to the equity.* There must be no bar to the equity, as where it would contravene a statute or fetter the statutory discretion or statutory duty of a statutory body.[91] And C's own misconduct may make it inequitable for him to be given relief,[92] as where he supports his claim by putting forward what he knows to be wholly false particulars of his expenditure on the property.[93]

---

[81] *Taylors Fashions Ltd.* v. *Liverpool Victoria Trustees Co. Ltd.* [1982] Q.B. 133n. at 154, 155 (reliance on option void for want of registration); *Habib Bank Ltd.* v. *Habib Bank A.G. Zurich* [1981] 1 W.L.R. 1265.
[82] *Greasley* v. *Cooke* [1980] 1 W.L.R. 1306 at 1313; contrast p. 1311, which seems either too wide, or else wrong: he who is not prejudiced but instead obtains a benefit has slender claims to an equity.
[83] *Inwards* v. *Baker* [1965] 2 Q.B. 29.
[84] *Rochdale Canal Co.* v. *King (No. 2)* (1853) 16 Beav. 630.
[85] *Crabb* v. *Arun D.C.* [1976] Ch. 179.
[86] *Jones* v. *Jones* [1977] 1 W.L.R. 438; and see *Pascoe* v. *Turner* [1979] 1 W.L.R. 431.
[87] *Ramsden* v. *Dyson* (1866) L.R.1 H.L. 129 at 160, 168, 170; *Inwards* v. *Baker, supra.*
[88] *Hopgood* v. *Brown* [1955] 1 W.L.R. 213.
[89] *Ramsden* v. *Dyson, supra; Steed* v. *Whitaker* (1740) Barn.Ch. 220; *Inwards* v. *Baker, supra.*
[90] *Coombes* v. *Smith* [1986] 1 W.L.R. 808 at 821, explaining *Greasley* v. *Cooke* [1980] 1 W.L.R. 1306.
[91] *Chalmers* v. *Pardoe* [1963] 1 W.L.R. 677; *Western Fish Products Ltd.* v. *Penwith D.C.* [1981] 2 All E.R. 204 (town planning).
[92] See *Williams* v. *Staite* [1979] Ch. 291 at 299, 300; and see [1986] Conv. 406 (M.P. Thompson).
[93] *J. Willis & Son* v. *Willis* [1986] 1 E.G.L.R. 62.

2. Extent of the equity. The maximum extent of the equity arising from proprietary estoppel is that of the belief or expectation of C that O encouraged: C will not be given more than that.[94] Thus a right for C to live in a house for his life will not arise by estoppel if it would make C a tenant for life with all the powers (including sale) conferred by the Settled Land Act 1925,[95] though the parties could avoid any risk of this by substituting a lease at a nominal rent determinable on death.[96]

3. Satisfaction of the equity. If the equity is established, the court will give effect to it in whatever is the most appropriate way.[97] In some cases the equity defines itself, as where the terms of a proposed lease or contract have been agreed, and the only question is whether or not there is an estoppel that will give effect to them.[98] It may suffice simply to dismiss any proceedings by O for possession,[99] or to make an order for possession conditionally on O repaying to C the cost of his improvements.[1] Sometimes an injunction will be granted, *e.g.* to restrain O from obstructing C's improved ancient lights,[2] or C may be given a lien on O's property for his outlay.[3] In some cases O will be ordered to convey his land to C gratuitously, as where C has built a house[4] or carried out improvements[5] on land which O had ineffectually given to him; and where there is no intended gift, O may be ordered to convey the land to C on payment of its unimproved value.[6] There are also instances of easements, licences or other interests being created. The equity has also been applied to interlinked transactions. Thus where C and O arranged that O would buy C's building and the C would erect a new building on O's land, which he duly did, O was compelled to purchase C's building.[7]

In deciding how the equity should be satisfied, the court exercises a wide discretion. The court does not restrict itself to the circumstances initially giving rise to the equity or to the amount of C's expenditure, but considers the whole of the circumstances down to the time of the action. Thus where C would otherwise be entitled by estoppel to an easement on paying a reasonable sum for it, O's prolonged obstructive conduct may result in C being

---

[94] *Dodsworth* v. *Dodsworth* [1973] E.G.D. 233.

[95] *Dodsworth* v. *Dodsworth, supra*, pointing out (at p. 236) that this had been overlooked in *Inwards* v. *Baker, supra*. See *ante*, p. 235, for the Act.

[96] *Griffiths* v. *Williams* [1978] E.G.D. 919, pointing out (at p. 925) what had been overlooked in *Dodsworth* v. *Dodsworth, supra*: see *ante*, p. 236.

[97] *Plimmer* v. *Mayor etc. of the City of Wellington* (1884) 9 App. Cas. 699 at 713, 714. See [1986] Conv. 406 (M.P. Thompson).

[98] *A.–G. of Hong Kong* v. *Humphreys Estate* (*Queen's Gardens*) *Ltd.* [1987] A.C. 114; *J.D. Developments Ltd.* v. *Quinn* (1990) 62 P. & C.R. 33.

[99] *Williams* v. *Staite, supra*.

[1] *Dodsworth* v. *Dodsworth, supra*.

[2] *Cotching* v. *Bassett* (1862) 32 Beav. 101.

[3] *Unity Joint Stock Mutual Banking Association* v. *King* (1858) 25 Beav. 72.

[4] *Dillwyn* v. *Llewelyn* (1862) 4 De G.F. & J. 517, where O had died.

[5] *Pascoe* v. *Turner* [1979] 1 W.L.R. 431.

[6] *Duke of Beaufort* v. *Patrick* (1853) 17 Beav. 60.

[7] *Salvation Army Trustee Co. Ltd.* v. *West Yorkshire Metropolitan C.C.* (1980) 41 P. & C.R. 179.

awarded the easement without payment.[8] Again, where O knew that C's improvements to the house in which she lived were being made in the belief that O had given it to her, the circumstances justified an order that O should convey the house to C gratuitously, even though C's expenditure had been relatively modest.[9] In this field, equity is both inventive and flexible.

[8] *Crabb* v. *Arun D.C.* [1976] Ch. 179.
[9] *Pascoe* v. *Turner, supra.*

CHAPTER 13

MORTGAGES

Part 1

NATURE OF A MORTGAGE

1. Security. When one person lends money to another he may be content to make the loan without security, or he may demand some security for the payment of the money. In the former case, the lender has a right to sue for the money if it is not duly paid, but that is all; if the borrower becomes insolvent, the lender may lose part or all of his money. But if some security of adequate value is given for the loan, the lender is protected even if the borrower becomes insolvent, for the lender has a claim to the security which takes precedence over the claims of other creditors.

The most important kind of security is the mortgage. The essential nature of a mortgage is that it is a conveyance of a legal or equitable interest in property, with a provision for redemption, *i.e.* that upon repayment of a loan or the performance of some other obligation the conveyance shall become void or the interest shall be reconveyed.[1] The borrower is known as the "mortgagor," the lender as the "mortgagee."[2]

2. Other transactions. A mortgage must be distinguished from a lien, a pledge and a charge.

(a) *Lien.* A lien may arise at common law, in equity or under certain statutes. A common law lien is the right to retain possession of the property of another until a debt is paid; thus a garage proprietor has a common law lien upon a motor-car repaired by him. This lien is a mere passive right of retention, giving no right to sell or otherwise deal with the property,[3] and is extinguished if the creditor parts with possession to the debtor or his agent.[4]

An equitable lien is not dependent upon a continued possession of the property[5] and in this respect resembles a mortgage. But it differs from a mortgage (*inter alia*) in that a mortgage is a right founded on contract whereas an equitable lien arises from general principles of equity which do not permit a man who has acquired property under a contract to keep it without payment.[6] Thus a vendor of land who has conveyed it without

---

[1] See *Santley* v. *Wilde* [1899] 2 Ch. 474.
[2] The Law Commission has recommended fundamental changes in the law of mortgages: see (1986) Law Com.W.P. No. 99; (1991) Law Com. No. 204.
[3] But see Torts (Interference with Goods) Act 1977, ss.12, 13, Sched. 1, replacing Disposal of Uncollected Goods Act 1952.
[4] *Pennington* v. *Reliance Motor Works Ltd.* [1923] 1 K.B. 127.
[5] *Wrout* v. *Dawes* (1858) 25 Beav. 369.
[6] See *Mackreth* v. *Symmons* (1808) 15 Ves. 329 at 340.

438

receiving the full purchase price has an equitable lien upon it for the balance unpaid.[7]

A statutory lien is the creature of the statute under which it arises, and the rights which it confers depend on the terms of that statute. Railways, shipowners and solicitors have been given such rights.

(b) *Pledge.* A pledge or pawn consists of the loan of money in return for the delivery of possession of chattels to the lender. Although the lender has certain powers of sale, the general property in the goods remains in the borrower and the lender has possession; in a mortgage, on the other hand, the lender acquires ownership and the borrower usually retains possession.

(c) *Charge.* For most practical purposes, a charge is regarded as a species of mortgage, and is dealt with accordingly in this chapter. Nevertheless, there is an essential difference between a mortgage and a charge. A mortgage is a conveyance of property subject to a right of redemption, whereas a charge conveys nothing and merely gives the chargee certain rights over the property concerned as security for the loan.[8]

Part 2

CREATION OF MORTGAGES

Sect. 1. Legal Mortgages and Charges of Unregistered Land

The methods of creating a legal mortgage differ for freeholds and leaseholds. In each case, some mention must be made of the history of the subject before considering the position before 1926 and after 1925.

A. Freeholds

I. HISTORY

1. Twelfth and thirteenth centuries. In the twelfth and thirteenth centuries, the mortgagor leased the land to the mortgagee, who went into possession. This, as seen above, resembled a pledge. If the income from the land was used to discharge the mortgage debt, the transaction was known as *vivum vadium* (a live pledge), since it was self-redeeming. If the mortgagee kept the income, it was known as *mortuum vadium* (a dead pledge). This latter form was not unlawful, but the Church regarded it as sinful for a Christian to take the income. In either case, if the money was not repaid by the time the lease expired, the mortgagee could enlarge his lease into a fee simple.

2. Fifteenth century. By the middle of the fifteenth century, the usual form

---

[7] *Chapman* v. *Tanner* (1684) 1 Vern. 267.
[8] See *London County and Westminster Bank Ltd.* v. *Tompkins* [1918] 1 K.B. 515.

of mortgage had changed. Even in the thirteenth century, a form of mortgage by conveyance of the fee simple had been known, and this form gradually ousted the others, for it gave the mortgagee seisin. The mortgagor conveyed the land to the mortgagee in fee simple, subject to a condition that the mortgagor might re-enter and determine the mortgagee's estate if the money lent was repaid on a named date. The mortgagee still took possession forthwith. The condition was construed strictly; if the mortgagor was a single day late in offering to repay the money, he lost his land for ever and yet remained liable for the debt.

3. Seventeenth century. By the beginning of the seventeenth century two changes had taken place. First, the form of a mortgage was usually a conveyance in fee simple with a covenant to reconvey the property if the money was paid on the fixed date. This is the modern form, and it simplified proof of title: whether the fee simple was vested in the mortgagor or not no longer depended merely upon whether the money had been paid within the fixed time, but depended upon whether a reconveyance had been executed.[9]

Second, a far more important change had been made by the intervention of equity. Equity took the view that the property mortgaged was merely a security for the money lent, and that it was unjust that the mortgagor should lose his property merely because he was late in repaying the loan. At first, equity intervened in the cases of accident, mistake, special hardship and the like, but soon relief was given in all cases. Even if the date fixed for repayment had long passed, equity compelled the mortgagee to reconvey the property to the mortgagor on payment of the principal with interest and costs. The mortgagor was thus given an equitable right to redeem at a time when the agreement between the parties had provided that the mortgagee was to be the absolute owner.[10] In short, for 300 years a mortgagor has had two separate rights of redemption:

(a) *Legal right to redeem on the fixed day.* At law, a mortgagor has no right to redeem either before or after the date fixed by the mortgage for redemption, but on that one day alone.

(b) *Equitable right to redeem thereafter.* Equity allowed the mortgagor an equitable right to redeem on any day after the date fixed for redemption by the mortgage. This is a right which can be exercised only on equitable terms.

This equitable right to redeem revolutionised mortgages, and probably lies at the root of Lord Macnaghten's statement that "No one . . . by the light of nature ever understood an English mortgage of real estate."[11] The sum total of the mortgagor's rights in equity is known as his equity of redemption. This must be distinguished from his equitable right to redeem: the latter

---

[9] See *Durham Brothers* v. *Robertson* [1898] 1 Q.B. 765 at 772.

[10] See *Salt* v. *Marquess of Northampton* [1892] A.C. 1 at 18, 19; and see M. & W. 916–919.

[11] *Samuel* v. *Jarrah Timber and Wood Paving Corporation Ltd.* [1904] A.C. 323 at 326; and Maitland remarked that a mortgage is "one long *suppressio veri* and *suggesto falsi*" (*Equity,* p. 182).

does not exist until the legal date for redemption is past, whereas the equity of redemption exists as soon as the mortgage is made.[12] The equity of redemption is the mortgagor's right of ownership of the property subject to the mortgage,[13] and is an interest in land which can be granted, devised, entailed and, in short, dealt with like any other interest in land.[14] The equitable right to redeem, on the other hand, is but one of the adjuncts of the equity of redemption: it is not the equity of redemption itself.

II. BEFORE 1926

As seen above, the usual method of creating a mortgage of freeholds before 1926 was by a conveyance of the fee simple subject to a proviso for redemption, namely, a covenant by the mortgagee that he would reconvey the property if the money was repaid on a fixed date. That date was usually six months after the date of the mortgage, even though there was no real expectation by either party that the money would be repaid then.

Although a mortgage in this form left the mortgagor with a mere equity of redemption, this might be of considerable value (*e.g.* if the loan was £25,000 and the property worth £75,000), and it could itself be mortgaged. But since it was merely equitable, any mortgage of it would also be equitable, for there could be no legal mortgage of something which existed only in equity. Thus before 1926 there could be only one legal mortgage of this kind on any property; all other mortgages were necessarily equitable.

III. AFTER 1925

By the Law of Property Act 1925,[15] freeholds can no longer be mortgaged by conveyance of the fee simple. Two methods only are possible:

(i) by a demise for a term of years absolute, subject to a provision for cesser on redemption; or
(ii) by a charge by deed expressed to be by way of legal mortgage.

1. Demise for a term of years absolute

(a) *Mortgages made after 1925.* The term of years granted to the mortgagee is usually a long term, *e.g.* 3,000 years. The provision for cesser on redemption is a clause providing that the term of years shall cease when the loan is repaid; it is really unnecessary, for on repayment the term becomes a satisfied term and automatically ceases.[16] In other respects, the position is much as it was before 1926. A fixed redemption date is still named, and it is still usually six months after the date of the mortgage; thereafter the mortgagor has an equitable right to redeem in lieu of his legal right. The difficulty

---

[12] *Brown* v. *Cole* (1845) 14 Sim. 427; *Kreglinger* v. *New Patagonia Meat and Cold Storage Co. Ltd.* [1914] A.C. 25 at 48.
[13] *Re Wells* [1933] Ch. 29 at 52.
[14] See *Casborne* v. *Scarfe* (1738) 1 Atk. 603 at 605.
[15] s.85(1).
[16] See *ante*, p. 333.

that a mortgagee by demise has no right to the title deeds is obviated by an express provision giving a first mortgagee the same right to the deeds as if he had the fee simple.[17]

The principal change brought about by the new legislation is that the mortgagor now retains the legal fee simple. This does not mean that the equity of redemption has lost its importance; a fee simple giving the right to possession of land only when a lease for 3,000 years has expired is of little value compared with the right to insist that the fee simple shall forthwith be freed from the term of 3,000 years on payment of the money due. Indeed, the term "equity of redemption" is sometimes used as including the mortgagor's legal estate. But the change means that the mortgagor has, in addition to his equity of redemption, a legal fee simple out of which a further term of years may be granted. Consequently, second, third and subsequent mortgages may all be legal after 1925. Thus A, the fee simple owner of Blackacre, may create successive legal mortgages in favour of X, Y and Z. The term he grants to each mortgagee is usually at least one day longer than the term under the previous mortgage. Thus X may be given 2,000 years, Y 2,000 years and a day, and Z 2,000 years and two days, so that each mortgagee has a reversion upon the prior mortgage term.

The rights of Y and Z, though seemingly rather nebulous, are in fact quite substantial. Thus if A defaults and the property is sold by X under his power of sale,[18] the money is paid first to X to discharge his mortgage, the balance to Y to discharge his, the balance to discharge Z's mortgage, and any surplus to A; in short, the parties rank in the order X, Y, Z, A. Further, any mortgagee always has the right, upon giving proper notice, to insist upon redeeming any prior mortgage[19]; thus Y might insist upon buying up X's mortgage and so succeeding to X's position.

An attempt to create a first mortgage by conveyance of the fee simple now operates as the grant of a term of 3,000 years without impeachment of waste but subject to cesser on redemption.[20] An attempt to create a second or subsequent mortgage in the same way takes effect as the grant of a term one day longer than the preceding term.[21] The system is thus foolproof.

(b) *Transitional provisions.* Mortgages made before 1926 were automatically brought into line with the new scheme by being converted into mortgages by subdemise, subject to cesser on redemption.[22]

2. Charge by deed expressed to be by way of legal mortgage. This is a new creation of the Law of Property Act 1925,[23] which is usually for brevity called a "legal charge." To be effective, it must be—

[17] L.P.A. 1925, s.85(1).
[18] *Post*, pp. 451 *et seq.*
[19] *Post*, p. 469.
[20] L.P.A. 1925, s.85(2).
[21] *Ibid.*
[22] *Ibid.* Sched. 1, Pt. VII.
[23] s.87.

(i) made by deed: a charge merely in writing will have no effect at law; and
(ii) expressed to be by way of legal mortgage: the deed must contain a statement that the charge is made by way of legal mortgage, unless the title to the land is registered.[24]

The effect of such a charge of freeholds is that the chargee (whether first or subsequent) gets the same protection, powers and remedies as if he had a term of 3,000 years without impeachment of waste.[25] Although he gets no actual legal term of years, he is as fully protected as if he had one.[26] The name "charge" is thus a little misleading because although a legal charge is by nature a charge and not a mortgage,[27] for all practical purposes it is indistinguishable from a mortgage.

The advantages of a legal charge are considered below.[28]

B. Leaseholds

I. HISTORY

The intervention of equity in the case of mortgages of leaseholds closely resembles that in the case of freeholds.[29]

II. BEFORE 1926

A legal mortgage of leaseholds could be made before 1926 in either of two ways:

(i) By assignment of the lease to the mortgagee with a covenant for reassignment on redemption; or
(ii) By the grant to the mortgagee of a sub-lease at least one day shorter than the lease, with a proviso for cesser on redemption.

The first method was rarely employed, for it meant that the mortgagee became liable on such of the covenants in the lease as touched and concerned the land. This was not so if the second method was employed, for then the mortgagee was only an underlessee and there was privity neither of contract nor of estate between him and the lessor.[30] Whichever form was employed, the mortgage normally contained the usual provision for redemption on a fixed date six months ahead, and thereafter the mortgagor had an equitable right to redeem.

Where a mortgage had been made by assignment, second and subsequent mortgages were made by a mortgage of the mortgagor's equity of redemption. Where the prior mortgage had been made by sub-lease, subsequent

[24] *Cityland and Property (Holdings) Ltd.* v. *Dabrah* [1968] Ch. 166; Ruoff & Roper, 23.07.
[25] L.P.A. 1925, s.87(1).
[26] See *Regent Oil Co. Ltd.* v. *J.A. Gregory (Hatch End) Ltd.* [1966] Ch. 402.
[27] *Ante*, p. 439.
[28] *Post*, p. 445.
[29] *Ante*, pp. 440, 441.
[30] *Ante*, p. 349.

mortgages were made by the grant of other sub-leases, each normally being longer than the previous one.

III. AFTER 1925

By the Law of Property Act 1925,[31] leaseholds can no longer be mortgaged by assignment. Two methods only are possible:

  (i) By a subdemise for a term of years absolute, subject to a provision for cesser on redemption, the term being at least one day shorter than the term vested in the mortgagor; or

 (ii) By a charge by deed expressed to be by way of legal mortgage.

1. Subdemise for a term of years absolute

(a) *Mortgages made after 1925.* The term of the sub-lease must be at least one day shorter than the term of the lease which is being mortgaged, otherwise it would operate as an assignment.[32] If the lease requires the tenant to obtain the landlord's licence before a subdemise by way of mortgage is made, the licence cannot be unreasonably refused.[33] The first mortgagee has the same rights to the deeds as if his mortgage had been made by assignment.[34] It is usual to make the sub-term 10 days shorter than the lease, so as to allow room for second and subsequent mortgages. Thus if T's 50 years' lease is mortgaged, the first mortgage will be secured by a lease for 50 years less 10 days, the second by 50 years less 9 days, and so on. But this is not essential, for the old rule[35] that a lease may take effect in reversion upon another lease of the same or greater length has been confirmed by the Law of Property Act 1925.[36] Thus if the first mortgage was made by a sub-term of 50 years less one day, the second mortgage would be secured by a sub-term of the same length and so on; each mortgage would take effect in its proper order.

An attempted mortgage by way of assignment after 1925 operates as a subdemise for a term of years absolute subject to cesser on redemption. A first or only mortgagee takes a term 10 days shorter than the lease mortgaged. Second and subsequent mortgages take terms one day longer than under the previous mortgage, if this is possible; in every case, however, the sub-term must be at least one day shorter than the term mortgaged.[37]

(b) *Transitional provisions.* On January 1, 1926, mortgages made by assignment before 1926 were automatically converted into mortgages by subdemise, subject to cesser on redemption.[38]

---

[31] s.86(1).
[32] *Beardman* v. *Wilson* (1868) L.R. 4 C.P. 57; *ante*, p. 322.
[33] L.P.A. 1925, s.86(1).
[34] *Ibid.*
[35] *Re Moore & Hulme's Contract* [1912] 2 Ch. 105.
[36] s.149(5).
[37] L.P.A. 1925, s.86(2). See *Grangeside Properties Ltd.* v. *Collingwoods Securities Ltd.* [1964] 1 W.L.R. 139.
[38] L.P.A. 1925, Sched. 1, Pt. VIII.

2. Charge by deed expressed to be by way of legal mortgage

(a) *Rights and remedies.* A charge by deed expressed to be by way of legal mortgage gives the mortgagee (whether first or subsequent) the same rights and remedies as if he had a sub-term one day shorter than the term vested in the mortgagor.[39] As in the case of freeholds,[40] he gets no actual term of years but is as fully protected as if he had one, so that he may seek relief against forfeiture in the same way as a sub-lessee.[41]

(b) *Advantages of a legal charge.* There is nothing in the Law of Property Act 1925 to suggest any reason why a legal charge, either of freeholds or leaseholds, should be preferred to an ordinary mortgage. But there seem to be three practical advantages in using a legal charge.

(i)   It is a convenient way of mortgaging freeholds and leaseholds together; the deed is shortened by stating that all the properties specified in the schedule are charged by way of legal mortgage, instead of setting out the length of the mortgage terms in each case.

(ii) Probably the granting of a legal charge on a lease does not amount to a breach of any covenant in that lease against sub-letting, for the charge creates no actual sub-lease in favour of the mortgagee but merely gives him the same rights as if he had a sub-lease.

(iii) The form of a legal charge is short and simple.

Sect. 2. Equitable Mortgages and Charges of Unregistered Land

A. Equitable Mortgages

1. Mortgage of an equitable interest. If the mortgagor has no legal estate but only an equitable interest, any mortgage he effects must necessarily be equitable. Thus before 1926, once a legal mortgage by conveyance had been created, the mortgagor retained only an equity of redemption, and all subsequent mortgages would be equitable. Again, beneficiaries under a trust have mere equitable interests and so can create only equitable mortgages.

The 1925 legislation has not affected the form of equitable mortgages of equitable interests. Such mortgages are still made by a conveyance of the equitable interest with a proviso for reconveyance. The actual form of words employed is immaterial provided the meaning is plain.[42] Nor need the mortgage be made by deed, as is essential for a legal mortgage; but it must either be in writing signed by the mortgagor or his agent authorised in writing, or else be made by will.[43] The mortgagee should give notice to the trustees to secure priority under the Rule in *Dearle* v. *Hull*.[44]

[39] *Ibid.* s.87(1).
[40] *Ante*, p. 443.
[41] *Ante*, p. 332.
[42] See *William Brandt's Sons & Co.* v. *Dunlop Rubber Co. Ltd.* [1905] A.C. 454 at 462.
[43] L.P.A. 1925, s.53(1).
[44] (1828) 3 Russ. 1; *post*, p. 484.

2. Informal mortgages. Under the same principles as apply to leaseholds,[45] equity treated an enforceable contract to create a legal mortgage,[46] or an imperfect legal mortgage,[47] as being an actual mortgage. To be enforceable, the transaction was formerly required to be supported either by sufficient evidence in writing or by a sufficient act of part performance. For transactions after September 26, 1989, neither evidence in writing nor part performance will suffice; instead, the contract will be valid only if it is made in writing, containing all the terms, and is signed by all parties to it.[48]

This change in the law gives rise to difficulties in respect of mortgages by deposit of title deeds. Since 1783,[49] the rule has been that a mere deposit of the title deeds which cannot be accounted for in any other way would be taken as part performance of a contract to create a mortgage, even if not a word about such a contract had been uttered,[50] so that an equitable mortgage was created by such a deposit.[51] The deposit must have been made for the purpose of giving a security, so that delivery of the deeds by mistake, or to enable a mortgage to be drawn up, created no mortgage.[52] But it was not essential that all the deeds should have been deposited, provided that those that were delivered were material evidence of title.[53] The mortgagee had no lien on the deeds apart from his right to retain them under the mortgage, so that if the mortgage contract was void, the deeds had to be given up.[54]

Today, in the absence of any contract in writing signed by all parties, the contractual basis of such mortgages seems impossible to support. In practice, nearly all mortgages by deposit of title deeds have for long been accompanied by a deed setting out the terms of the mortgage, or requiring the mortgagor to execute a legal mortgage on request, thereby preventing disputes; and execution of the deed gives the mortgagee additional powers.[55] Such a deed will meet the present statutory requirement for a contract made in writing. But in other cases the disappearance of any theoretical contract appears to invalidate the mortgage, though it is possible that the courts will take the view that the concept of mortgages by deposit of title deeds is so well-established that they should continue to be accepted as valid, theory notwithstanding.[56]

B. Equitable Charges

An equitable charge is created where certain property is appropriated to the

[45] *Ante*, p. 311.
[46] See *Ex p. Wright* (1812) 19 Ves. 255 at 258.
[47] *Parker* v. *Housefield* (1834) 2 My. & K. 419 at 420.
[48] *Ante*, p. 117.
[49] *Russel* v. *Russel* (1783) 1 Bro.C.C. 269.
[50] *Bozon* v. *Williams* (1829) 3 Y. & J. 151 at 161.
[51] *Bank of New South Wales* v. *O'Connor* (1889) 14 App.Cas. 273 at 282; *Re Wallis & Simmonds (Builders) Ltd.* [1974] 1 W.L.R. 391.
[52] *Norris* v. *Wilkinson* (1806) 12 Ves. 192.
[53] *Lacon* v. *Allen* (1856) 3 Drew. 579.
[54] *Re Molton Finance Ltd.* [1968] Ch. 325.
[55] *Post*, pp. 451, 454, 457, 458.
[56] And see *ante*, pp. 121, 122.

discharge of some debt or other obligation without there being any change in ownership either at law or in equity.[57] Thus if a man signs a written contract agreeing that he thereby charges his real estate with the payment of £500 to A, an equitable charge is created[58]; the same applies where a will or voluntary settlement charges money on land.[59] An enforceable contract to create a legal charge creates an equitable charge.[60]

Sect. 3. Mortgages and Charges of Registered Land

Subject to any restriction on the power of mortgaging which is entered on the register, a mortgage of registered land may be effected in three ways.

1. Registered charge. A registered charge is the formal way in which to mortgage registered land. As seen above,[61] a registered charge is not an overriding interest, a minor interest or a registered estate, but is *sui generis*,[62] in some ways resembling a registered estate in that it is supported by a document of title in the form of a charge certificate. A registered charge may be effected by any deed charging the land by reference to its registration number or in any other identifiable way.[63] No legal estate arises until the charge has been registered,[64] though the mortgage will not be affected by overriding interests which arise after the creation of the charge but before its registration.[65] The expression "by way of legal mortgage" is not essential to the creation of a valid charge of registered land,[66] though charges registered under this head are necessarily legal. On registration, an entry is made in the charges register giving the name of the person in whose favour the charge is made, together with particulars of it. The land certificate must be deposited at the Registry for as long as a registered charge exists, and a charge certificate is issued to the chargee as his document of title.[67]

A registered chargee has all the powers of a legal mortgagee, unless the register otherwise provides.[68] The priority of registered charges is governed by the order of entry in the register, unless it otherwise provides.[69] As regards tacking, section 94 of the Law of Property Act 1925 does not apply to registered land; but further advances may be tacked only if made by a chargee under an obligation to do so which has been entered on the register,

---

[57] *London County and Westminster Bank Ltd.* v. *Tompkins* [1918] 1 K.B. 515 at 528.
[58] *Matthews* v. *Goodday* (1861) 31 L.J. Ch. 282 at 282, 283.
[59] *Re Owen* [1894] 3 Ch. 220.
[60] *Swiss Bank Corporation* v. *Lloyds Bank Ltd.* [1979] Ch. 548; on appeal, [1982] A.C. 584; and see *ante*, p. 311.
[61] *Ante*, p. 101.
[62] See L.R.A. 1925, s.3(xv), (xvi), (xxiii); and see ss.18(4), 21(4).
[63] *Ibid*. s.25.
[64] *Grace Rymer Investments Ltd.* v. *Waite* [1958] Ch. 831; and see *Lever Finance Ltd.* v. *Needleman's Trustee* [1956] Ch. 375.
[65] *Abbey National B.S.* v. *Cann* [1991] 1 A.C. 56.
[66] *Cityland and Property (Holdings) Ltd.* v. *Dabrah* [1968] Ch. 166; *ante*, p. 443.
[67] L.R.A. 1925, ss.25, 26, 65; L.R.R. 1925, r. 262.
[68] L.R.A. 1925, ss.27, 34.
[69] *Ibid*. s.29.

or, in the case of charges expressly for securing further advances, if made
before notice of the intervening incumbrance sent by the registrar ought, in
due course of post, to have reached the chargee making the advance.[70]

2. Unregistered mortgage. Registered land may be mortgaged in the same
way as if it were unregistered. Such a mortgage takes effect only in equity,
and it is liable to be overridden as a minor interest until it is protected on the
register by a notice or a caution.[71]

3. Deposit of the land certificate. Since the land certificate takes the place
of the title deeds, a lien may be created by deposit of the land certificate. A
chargee can similarly create a lien on his charge by deposit of his charge
certificate.[72] The mere possession of the certificate provides some protection,[73] though not against transactions for which production of the certificate
is not requisite, such as certain leases.[74] The lender, however, may have a
caution[75] or a notice of the deposit entered on the charges register of the
interest affected; the latter operates as a caution.[76]

A lien may also be created by giving the registrar a notice of intention to
deposit the land certificate.[77] This procedure is useful where a loan is made
in connection with the purchase of the land. Naturally the certificate is not
available until the transfer has been registered after completion of the
purchase. The certificate is delivered by the registrar to the person named in
the notice.

Part 3

RIGHTS OF THE PARTIES UNDER A MORTGAGE OR CHARGE

The rights of the parties under a mortgage or charge will be considered
under three heads:

(1) The rights of the mortgagee or chargee;
(2) Rights common to both parties; and
(3) The rights of the mortgagor or chargor.

Sect. 1. Rights of the Mortgagee or Chargee

A. Remedies for Enforcing Payment

Unless the parties have otherwise agreed, a mortgagee or chargee has five

[70] *Ibid.* s.30; L.P.(Am.)A. 1926, s.5. For tacking, see *post*, pp. 487 *et seq.*
[71] L.R.A. 1925, s.106, as substituted by Administration of Justice Act 1977, s.26.
[72] L.R.A. 1925, s.66.
[73] *Barclays Bank Ltd.* v. *Taylor* [1974] Ch. 137.
[74] See *Strand Securities Ltd.* v. *Caswell* [1965] Ch. 958.
[75] See *Re White Rose Cottage* [1965] Ch. 940.
[76] L.R.R. 1925, r. 239.
[77] *Ibid.* rr. 240–242.

remedies available for enforcing payment. Three of the remedies are primarily directed to recovering the capital due and putting an end to the security: these are an action for the money, foreclosure, and sale. The other two remedies are taking possession and appointing a receiver. These primarily seek merely to recover the interest due, though possession is now usually sought so as to facilitate sale with vacant possession. Sale and appointing a receiver are rights which used to be conferred by the mortgage deed but are now given by statute; the other remedies are inherent in the nature of the transaction. Today, actions for foreclosure have become rare.[77a] A mortgagee will not be restrained from enforcing payment merely because the mortgagor has some large cross-claim against him.[78] The remedies available differ according to whether the mortgage or charge is legal or equitable.

I. LEGAL MORTGAGEE OR LEGAL CHARGEE

A legal mortgagee or legal chargee has the following remedies for enforcing his security.

1. To sue for the money due. At any time after the date fixed for payment the mortgagee may sue for the money lent.[79] This remedy is, of course, in no way peculiar to mortgages.

2. To foreclose

(a) *The right of foreclosure.* By giving the mortgagor an equitable right to redeem after he had lost his legal right of redemption, equity interfered with the bargain made between the parties. But equity prescribed limits to the equity of redemption which it created. Thus before 1926, a legal first mortgagee of freeholds had the fee simple vested in him, and once the legal date for redemption had passed, the mortgagor's right to redeem was merely equitable.[80] "Foreclosure" was the name given to the process whereby the mortgagor's equitable right to redeem was extinguished and the mortgagee was left as owner of the property, both at law and in equity. Equity had interfered to prevent the conveyance of the legal fee simple from having its full effect, and on foreclosure "the court simply removes the stop it has itself put on."[81] From the first the mortgagee was absolute owner at law, and foreclosure, for which an order of the court is essential, made him an absolute owner in equity as well.

After 1925, a mortgagee does not have the whole legal estate of the mortgagor vested in him, but only a long term of years in the case of freeholds and an underlease in the case of leaseholds. Consequently it is no

---

[77a] See *Palk* v. *Mortgage Services Funding Plc.* [1992] *The Times* Aug. 7.

[78] *Samuel Keller (Holdings) Ltd.* v. *Martins Bank Ltd.* [1971] 1 W.L.R. 43; *Inglis* v. *Commonwealth Trading Bank of Australia* (1972) 126 C.L.R. 161.

[79] See *Bolton* v. *Buckenham* [1891] 1 Q.B. 278; but see *post*, p. 475.

[80] See *ante*, p. 440.

[81] *Carter* v. *Wake* (1877) 4 Ch.D. 605 at 606, *per* Jessel M.R.

longer sufficient for a decree of foreclosure merely to destroy the mortgagor's equity of redemption, and so the Law of Property Act 1925[82] provides that a foreclosure decree absolute shall vest the mortgagor's fee simple or term of years in the mortgagee, both for mortgages and for legal charges.

The right to foreclose does not rise until the legal right to redeem has ceased to exist, *i.e.* until the legal date for redemption has passed[83] or until there is a breach of a condition required for keeping the legal right of redemption alive.[84] Once this has happened, the mortgagee may commence foreclosure proceedings unless he has agreed not to do so[85]; for sometimes he contracts not to enforce the security by foreclosure or other means until he has given some specified notice or until the mortgagor has broken one of his covenants in the mortgage. If no redemption date is fixed or if the loan is repayable on demand, the right to foreclose arises when a demand for repayment has been made and a reasonable time thereafter has elapsed.[86]

(b) *Parties to a foreclosure action.* An action for foreclosure can be brought by any mortgagee of property, whether he is the original mortgagee or an assignee, and whether he is a first or subsequent mortgagee. The effect of a foreclosure order absolute in an action brought by the first mortgagee is to make him the sole owner both at law and in equity, free from any subsequent mortgages; if the action is brought by a second or subsequent mortgagee, he will hold the property subject to prior incumbrances, but free from all subsequent incumbrances. Where trustees foreclose, they hold the land on trust for sale.[87]

As will be seen shortly,[88] a foreclosure action gives the mortgagor and all others interested in the equity of redemption an opportunity of redeeming the mortgage. Consequently, all persons interested in the equity of redemption must be made parties to the action. Thus if X has made successive mortgages of his property to A, B and C, and B starts foreclosure proceedings, A will not be affected by them and so need not be made a party to the action. But if the action is successful, C will lose his mortgage and X his equity of redemption, and so both must be made parties to the action.

(c) *Procedure.* The first step in a foreclosure is to obtain from the court a foreclosure order *nisi.* This provides that if the mortgagor repays the money lent on a fixed day (usually six months from the accounts being settled by the master), the mortgage shall be discharged, but that if this is not done, the mortgagor shall be foreclosed. If there are several mortgagees and the first mortgagee is foreclosing, each mortgagee is given the alternative of either losing his security or else redeeming (paying off) the first mortgage. Sometimes the court will give the mortgagees successive periods to effect this

---

[82] ss.88(2), 89(2).
[83] *Williams* v. *Morgan* [1906] 1 Ch. 804.
[84] *Twentieth Century Banking Corporation Ltd.* v. *Wilkinson* [1977] Ch. 99.
[85] *Ramsbottom* v. *Wallis* (1835) 5 L.J.Ch. 92.
[86] *Toms* v. *Wilson* (1862) 4 B. & S. 442.
[87] L.P.A. 1925, s.31; *ante*, pp. 253, 254.
[88] *Infra.*

redemption, but usually there will be only one period between them.[89] At the request of the mortgagee or of any person interested (*e.g.* the mortgagor) the court may order a sale of the property instead of foreclosure.[90]

(d) *Opening a foreclosure absolute.* If no order for sale is made and the property is not redeemed on the date fixed, a foreclosure order absolute is made. This destroys the mortgagor's equity of redemption and transfers his fee simple or term of years to the mortgagee,[91] who thus becomes sole owner at law and in equity, subject only to prior incumbrances. For registered land, the mortgagee is registered as proprietor of the land and his charge is cancelled. Yet although the order of foreclosure absolute appears to be final, it is not necessarily so, for the court will sometimes open a foreclosure absolute. Circumstances which may influence the court to do this are an accident at the last moment preventing the mortgagor from raising the money, any special value which the property had to the mortgagor (*e.g.* if it was an old family estate), a marked disparity between the value of the property and the amount lent, and the promptness of the application. Even if the mortgagee has sold the property after foreclosure absolute, the court may still open the foreclosure; this is unlikely, however, if the purchaser bought the property some time after foreclosure and without notice of circumstances which might induce the court to interfere.[92]

3. To sell

(a) *History.* There is no right, either at common law or in equity, for a mortgagee to sell the mortgaged property free from the equity of redemption, although of course he can freely transfer the estate which is vested in him subject to the equity of redemption. Consequently, an express power was usually inserted in mortgage deeds enabling the mortgagee to sell the property free from the equity of redemption if certain specified events occurred. Lord Cranworth's Act 1860 gave a limited power of sale in the case of mortgages made after 1860, but this was usually thought too narrow to be relied upon. The Conveyancing Act 1881, however, gave a satisfactory power of sale which is now contained in the Law of Property Act 1925.[93]

(b) *The power.* Every mortgagee whose mortgage shows no contrary intention has a power of sale, provided—

(a) the mortgage was made by deed (and all legal mortgages must be made thus); and
(b) the mortgage money is due, *i.e.* the legal date for redemption has

---

[89] *Platt* v. *Mendel* (1884) 27 Ch.D. 246.
[90] L.P.A. 1925, s.91(2); *Twentieth Century Banking Corporation Ltd.* v. *Wilkinson* [1977] Ch. 99.
[91] L.P.A. 1925, ss.88(2), 89(2); L.R.A. 1925, s.34(3).
[92] *Campbell* v. *Holyland* (1877) 7 Ch.D. 166 at 172, 173.
[93] ss.101–107, applicable to mortgages made after 1881.

passed[94]; if the mortgage money is payable by instalments, the power of sale arises as soon as any instalment is in arrear.[95]

When these conditions have been fulfilled, the statutory power of sale *arises*; nevertheless, the power does not become *exercisable* unless one of the three following conditions has been satisfied[96]—

(i) notice requiring payment of the mortgage money has been served on the mortgagor and default has been made in payment of part or all of it for three months thereafter; or

(ii) some interest under the mortgage is two months or more in arrear; or

(iii) there has been a breach of some provision contained in the Act or in the mortgage deed (other than the covenant for payment of the mortgage money or interest) which should have been observed or performed by the mortgagor or by someone who concurred in making the mortgage.

(c) *Protection of purchaser.* The difference between the power of sale arising and becoming exercisable is as follows. If the power has not arisen, the mortgagee has no statutory power of sale at all; the most he can do is to transfer his mortgage. But if the power of sale has arisen, he can make a good title to a purchaser free from the equity of redemption even if the power has not become exercisable; the title of a purchaser in good faith is not impeachable merely because none of the three specified events has occurred or the power of sale has in some way been irregularly or improperly exercised. Any person injured by an unauthorised, improper or irregular exercise of the power has a remedy in damages against the person exercising it.[97] Thus while a purchaser from a mortgagee must satisfy himself that the power of sale has arisen, he need not inquire whether it has become exercisable. However, if he has actual or Nelsonian[98] knowledge (as distinct from merely constructive notice) that the power is not exercisable, or that there is some impropriety in the sale, he will not take free from the mortgagor's interest.[99]

(d) *Mode of sale.* In general, the statutory power of sale is exercisable without any order of the court being required. The mortgagee may sell by public auction or private contract, and has a wide discretion as to the terms and conditions upon which the sale is made.[1] The power is unaffected by any disposition by the mortgagor, so that a contract of sale entered into by the mortgagee will prevail over an earlier contract of sale made by the mortgagor.[2] The power becomes exercised as soon as a contract, albeit condi-

[94] L.P.A. 1925, s.101.
[95] *Payne* v. *Cardiff R.D.C.* [1932] 1 K.B. 241.
[96] L.P.A. 1925, s.103.
[97] *Ibid.* s.104(2).
[98] *i.e.* turning a blind eye to suspicious circumstances: see *Belmont Finance Corporation Ltd.* v. *Williams Furniture Ltd.* [1979] Ch. 250 at 267, 275.
[99] *Bailey* v. *Barnes* [1894] 1 Ch. 25 at 30; *Lord Waring* v. *London & Manchester Assurance Co. Ltd.* [1935] Ch. 310 at 318.
[1] L.P.A. 1925, s.101(1), (2).
[2] *Duke* v. *Robson* [1973] 1 W.L.R. 267.

tional, is made, so that thereupon the equity of redemption is suspended unless and until the contract goes off.[3] To prevent the mortgagee entering into a contract, the mortgagor must tender the redemption moneys in full.[4]

The mortgagee is not a trustee for the mortgagor of his power of sale,[5] for the power is given to the mortgagee for his own benefit to enable him the better to realise his security. Thus he need not delay the sale in the hope of obtaining a better price,[6] nor does he have to attempt to sell by auction before selling by private contract.[7] Moreover, his motive for selling, such as spite against the mortgagor, is immaterial.[8] But the sale must be a true sale: a "sale" by the mortgagee to himself, either directly or through an agent, is no true sale and may be set aside or declared void.[9]

The mortgagee is under a duty to take reasonable care to obtain a proper price,[10] so that he will be liable to the mortgagor if he advertises the property for sale by auction without mentioning a valuable planning permission,[11] or if he sells the property on a "crash sale" basis without exposing it to the market for a proper period of time.[12] The duty to obtain a proper price for the property, which may be excluded by an appropriately drafted term in the mortgage,[13] is owed not merely to the mortgagor but also to a surety for the loan,[14] though not to an equitable co-owner of the land.[15] If the mortgagee sells to an associated person or company, the onus is on him to show that a proper price was obtained.[16]

(e) *Proceeds of sale.* Although the mortgagee is not a trustee of his power of sale, he is a trustee of the proceeds of sale. After discharging any payments properly due, any balance must be paid to the next subsequent incumbrancer,[17] or, if none, to the mortgagor.[18] A mortgagee who has a surplus should therefore search in the registers of land charges[19] or the register of title,[20] as the case may be, to discover the existence of any

---

[3] *Property & Bloodstock Ltd.* v. *Emerton* [1968] Ch. 94.
[4] *Payne* v. *Cardiff R.D.C.* [1932] 1 K.B. 241.
[5] *Kennedy* v. *De Trafford* [1897] A.C. 180.
[6] *Bank of Cyprus (London) Ltd.* v. *Gill* [1980] 2 Ll.Rep. 51; and see *China & South Sea Bank Ltd.* v. *Tan Soon Gin* [1990] 1 A.C. 531.
[7] *Davey* v. *Durrant* (1857) 1 De G. & J. 535 at 553, 560.
[8] *Nash* v. *Eads* (1880) 25 S.J. 95.
[9] *Downes* v. *Grazebrook* (1871) 3 Mer. 200; *Williams* v. *Wellingborough B.C.* [1975] 1 W.L.R. 1327.
[10] For building societies the duty is statutory: Building Societies Act 1986, Sched. 4, replacing earlier legislation.
[11] *Cuckmere Brick Co. Ltd.* v. *Mutual Finance Ltd.* [1971] Ch. 949.
[12] *Predeth* v. *Castle Phillips Finance Co. Ltd.* [1986] 2 E.G.L.R. 144; [1986] Conv. 442 (M.P. Thompson).
[13] *Bishop* v. *Bonham* [1988] 1 W.L.R. 742 at 752.
[14] *Standard Chartered Bank Ltd.* v. *Walker* [1982] 1 W.L.R. 1410.
[15] *Parker-Tweedale* v. *Dunbar Bank Plc.* [1991] Ch. 12.
[16] *Tse Kwok Lam* v. *Wong Chit Sen* [1983] 1 W.L.R. 1349.
[17] See *Samuel Keller (Holdings) Ltd.* v. *Martin's Bank Ltd.* [1971] 1 W.L.R. 43.
[18] L.P.A. 1925, s.105; see *Thorne* v. *Heard* [1895] A.C. 495. And see *post*, pp. 498, 505, for the effect of the Limitation Act 1980.
[19] See *ante*, p. 78.
[20] Ruoff & Roper 23–15.

subsequent mortgages, since if he pays the money to the mortgagor he will be liable to any mortgagee of whom he had actual or constructive notice who is thereby prejudiced.[21] But a sale by a mortgagee does not affect any prior mortgage: the purchaser takes the property subject to any such mortgage, though free from the rights of the vendor, subsequent mortgagees, and the mortgagor.[22]

4. To take possession

(a) *The right.* Since a legal mortgage gives the mortgagee a term of years, he is entitled, subject to any contrary indication in the mortgage, to take possession of the mortgaged property as soon as the mortgage is made, even if the mortgagor is guilty of no default[23]; a legal chargee has a corresponding statutory right.[24] If the property is already lawfully let to tenants, the mortgagee cannot take physical possession, but instead takes possession by directing the tenants to pay their rents to him instead of to the mortgagor.[25] The mortgagee's right to possession may also be affected by the rights of co-owners, considered below.[26]

(b) *Strict account.* In practice, unless he plans to sell the property or it is already fully let, a mortgagee is slow to take possession, because if he does he is liable to account strictly on the footing of wilful default; this means that he must account not only for all that he receives but also for all that he ought to have received.[27] Thus where the mortgagee was a brewer and the mortgaged property a "free" house, a mortgagee who took possession and let the property as a "tied" house was held liable for the additional rent he would have obtained if he had let the property as a "free" house.[28] Again, if the mortgagee occupies the property himself instead of letting it he is liable for a fair occupation rent,[29] though he need pay no rent if through decay or otherwise the land is incapable of being beneficially occupied.[30] Where the property is already let, there is little risk in his taking possession.

(c) *Powers while in possession.* While in possession, a mortgagee whose mortgage was made by deed may cut and sell timber and other trees ripe for cutting which were not planted or left standing for shelter or ornament, or contract for this to be done within 12 months of the contract.[31] Although he is not liable for waste, he will be liable if he improperly cuts timber; and

[21] *West London Commercial Bank* v. *Reliance Permanent B.S.* (1885) 29 Ch.D. 954.
[22] L.P.A. 1925, s.104(1); L.R.A. 1925, s.34(4).
[23] *Birch* v. *Wright* (1786) 1 T.R. 378 at 383; *Four-Maids Ltd.* v. *Dudley Marshall (Properties) Ltd.* [1957] Ch. 317 at 320.
[24] L.P.A. 1925, s.87(1).
[25] *Horlock* v. *Smith* (1842) 6 Jur. 478.
[26] *Post*, p. 483.
[27] *Chaplin* v. *Young (No. 1)* (1863) 33 Beav. 330 at 337, 338.
[28] *White* v. *City of London Brewery Co.* (1889) 42 Ch.D. 237.
[29] *Marriott* v. *Anchor Reversionary Co.* (1861) 3 De G.F. & J. 177 at 193.
[30] *Marshall* v. *Cave* (1824) 3 L.J. (o.s.) Ch. 57, not cited in *Fyfe* v. *Smith* [1975] 2 N.S.W.L.R. 408 (hotel: occupation so as to preserve its business).
[31] L.P.A. 1925, s.101(1).

despite his right to work mines already opened, he may not open new mines. However, if the property becomes insufficient security for the money due, the court will not interfere if he cuts timber and opens mines, provided he is not guilty of wanton destruction.[32]

A mortgagee in possession must effect reasonable repairs,[33] and may without the mortgagor's consent effect reasonable but not excessive improvements; the cost will be charged to the mortgagor in the accounts.[34]

(d) *Relief of mortgagor*

(1) INHERENT JURISDICTION. The court has a very limited inherent jurisdiction to grant a short adjournment of proceedings for possession in order to give the mortgagor a chance of paying off the mortgage in full or otherwise satisfying the mortgagee, unless there is no reasonable prospect of this occurring.[35] An order for possession may be refused if the mortgagee is not acting as such but is merely an agent for the landlord.[36]

(2) DWELLING-HOUSES. Where the property mortgaged consists of or includes a dwelling-house, the court now has a wide statutory jurisdiction in claims for possession, not being proceedings for foreclosure in which possession is also claimed. The court may adjourn the proceedings, or stay or suspend execution of any judgment or order for possession for a defined or ascertainable period,[37] or postpone the date for delivery of possession.[38] This appears to apply whether or not the mortgagor is in arrear with his payments or otherwise in default[39]; but where he is, the jurisdiction is exercisable where it appears to the court that "the mortgagor is likely to be able within a reasonable period to pay any sums due under the mortgage," or to remedy any other default under it.[40] In the case of instalment mortgages (as most mortgages of dwelling-houses are), or mortgages which otherwise permit deferred payment,[41] the "sums due" are merely the instalments or payments in arrear, and not the whole capital sum, even if (as is usual) the mortgage makes this payable on any default by the mortgagor.[42] In deciding whether the mortgagor is likely to be able to pay the sums due within a reasonable time, the court must take into account not only the arrears[42a] but also the sums accruing.[43] The court will have regard to probabilities such as

---

[32] *Millett* v. *Davey* (1863) 31 Beav. 470 at 475, 476.
[33] *Richards* v. *Morgan* (1853) 4 Y. & C.Ex. 570.
[34] *Shepard* v. *Jones* (1882) 21 Ch.D. 469.
[35] *Birmingham Citizens Permanent B.S.* v. *Caunt* [1962] Ch. 883; contrast *Quennell* v. *Maltby* [1979] 1 W.L.R. 318 at 322, *obiter*.
[36] *Quennell* v. *Maltby* [1979] 1 W.L.R. 318.
[37] *Royal Trust Co. of Canada* v. *Markham* [1975] 1 W.L.R. 1416.
[38] Administration of Justice Act 1970, s.36.
[39] This was the majority view in *Western Bank Ltd.* v. *Schindler* [1977] Ch. 1.
[40] Administration of Justice Act 1970, s.36(1).
[41] See *Bank of Scotland* v. *Grimes* [1986] Q.B. 1179 (endowment mortgage included); *Habib Bank Ltd.* v. *Tailor* [1982] 1 W.L.R. 1218. See [1984] Conv. 91 (S. Tromans).
[42] Administration of Justice Act 1973, s.8(1); *First Middlesbrough Trading and Mortgage Co. Ltd.* v. *Cunningham* (1974) 28 P. & C.R. 69.
[42a] See *Town & Country B.S.* v. *Julien* (1991) 24 H.L.R. 312 (arrears over £190,000).
[43] Administration of Justice Act 1973, s.8(2).

an impending sale of the property,[44] but not to remote possibilities such as hoped-for legacies or winnings from the pools,[45] or the fruits of a counter-claim against the mortgagee.[46] The court will usually exercise its power of imposing conditions as to paying arrears and current sums or remedying defaults.[47]

(e) *Spouses.* Where the spouse of a mortgagor is entitled to occupy a dwelling-house by virtue of the Matrimonial Homes Act 1983,[48] the Act makes any payment by that spouse in respect of mortgage payments as good as if made by the mortgagor.[49] The spouse, often a deserted wife, can thus avert proceedings for possession by the mortgagee. The spouse is entitled to be made party to any proceedings by the mortgagee if the court sees no special reason against it and is satisfied that the spouse may be expected to make such payments or do such things as might affect the exercise of the court's statutory jurisdiction to grant relief.[50] If the spouse's statutory right of occupation has been registered,[51] the mortgagee must serve notice of any proceedings on the spouse.[52]

(f) *Attornment clause.* Many legal mortgages still contain an attornment clause, which is a clause where the mortgagor attorns, or acknowledges himself to be, a tenant at will or from year to year of the mortgagee, usually at a nominal rent such as a peppercorn or five pence. Formerly this was inserted because a speedy procedure in the High Court was available to enable landlords to recover possession of the demised property from their tenants, and no such procedure was available for mere mortgagees; the attornment clause enabled mortgagees to sue for possession *qua* landlords. But changes in the rules of court in 1933, 1936 and 1937 made the speedy procedure available to mortgagees as such, so that this reason for its use has gone. A surviving advantage of the clause is that covenants by the mortgagor in the mortgage relating to the premises will be enforceable against an assignee of the mortgagor under the doctrine that covenants in a lease which touch and concern the land will run with the lease and the reversion.[53] Unless otherwise provided, the tenancy must be determined by notice to quit before commencing proceedings for possession[54]; but neither the Rent Acts nor the

---

[44] *Royal Trust Co. of Canada* v. *Markham* [1975] 1 W.L.R. 1416; and see *Target Home Loans* v. *Clothier* [1992] *The Times* Aug. 7 (three months, to permit speedier sale by mortgagor).
[45] See *Hastings & Thanet B.S.* v. *Goddard* [1970] 1 W.L.R. 1544 at 1548.
[46] *Citibank Trust Ltd.* v. *Ayivor* [1987] 1 W.L.R. 1157.
[47] Administration of Justice Act 1970, s.36(3).
[48] See *ante*, p. 81.
[49] Matrimonial Homes Act 1983, s.1(5).
[50] *Ibid.* s.8(2). See above.
[51] *Ante*, p. 81.
[52] Matrimonial Homes Act 1983, s.8(3).
[53] *Regent Oil Co. Ltd.* v. *J.A. Gregory (Hatch End) Ltd.* [1966] Ch. 402. For the doctrine, see *ante*, pp. 349 *et seq.*
[54] *Hinckley & Country B.S.* v. *Henny* [1953] 1 W.L.R. 352.

Agricultural Holdings Act 1986 confer any protection on the tenant-mortgagor, for they are concerned only with true tenancies.[55]

5. To appoint a receiver

(a) *History*. In order to avoid the dangers of taking possession and yet achieve much the same result, mortgages used to provide for the appointment of a receiver with extensive powers of management of the mortgaged property. At first, the appointment was made by the mortgagor at the request of the mortgagee, but later, mortgagees began to reserve a power for themselves, acting in theory as agents for the mortgagor, to appoint a receiver. In such circumstances the receiver was deemed the agent of the mortgagor, and the mortgagee was not liable to account strictly[56] in the same way as would have been the case if he had taken possession or the receiver had been his agent.

Lord Cranworth's Act 1860 gave a somewhat unsatisfactory statutory power to appoint a receiver, but where the mortgage is made by deed the Conveyancing Act 1881, and now the Law of Property Act 1925,[57] confers a power which satisfies most mortgagees. For registered land, it cannot be exercised until the mortgagee has been registered as proprietor of the charge.[58]

(b) *The power*. The statutory power to appoint a receiver arises and becomes exercisable in the same circumstances as the power of sale.[59] The mortgagee makes the appointment by writing, and may remove or replace the receiver in the same way. The receiver is deemed the agent of the mortgagor, who is solely responsible for his acts unless the mortgage otherwise provides,[60] or unless the mortgagee represents him as being the mortgagee's agent.[61] The receiver has power to recover the income of the property by action, distress or otherwise, and to give valid receipts for it. The money received by the receiver, after discharging outgoings, interest on prior incumbrances and payment of the receiver's commission and other expenses, is used to pay the interest due under the mortgage. If the mortgagee so directs in writing, any surplus may be applied towards discharge of the principal money lent on mortgage; otherwise, it is payable to the person who would have been entitled to it had the receiver not been appointed, normally the mortgagor.[62] Unlike a mortgagee in possession,[63] a receiver can obtain no title against the mortgagor under the Limitation Act 1980, for he is the mortgagor's agent.

[55] *Steyning and Littlehampton B.S.* v. *Wilson* [1951] Ch. 1018; *Alliance B.S.* v. *Pinwill* [1958] Ch. 788.
[56] *Ante*, p. 454.
[57] s.101.
[58] *Lever Finance Ltd.* v. *Needleman's Trustees* [1956] Ch. 375.
[59] L.P.A. 1925, ss.101(1), 109(1).
[60] *Ibid*. s.109(2); *White* v. *Metcalf* [1903] 2 Ch. 567.
[61] *Chatsworth Properties Ltd.* v. *Effiom* [1971] 1 W.L.R. 144.
[62] L.P.A. 1925, s.109.
[63] *Young* v. *Clarey* [1948] Ch. 191.

6. The mortgagee's remedies are cumulative. A mortgagee is not bound to select one of the above remedies and pursue that and no other: subject to his not recovering more than is due to him, he may employ any or all of the remedies to enforce payment.[64] Thus if he sells the property for less than the mortgage debt, he may then sue the mortgagor upon the personal covenant for payment[65]; and this is so even if the sale was by the court and the mortgagee, bidding by leave of the court, has purchased the property.[66]

However, if he wishes to sue after foreclosure, he can do so only on condition that he opens the foreclosure[67]; for despite the foreclosure he is treating the mortgage as being still alive. Consequently, if by disposing of the property after foreclosure the mortgagee has put it out of his power to open the foreclosure, he cannot sue upon the personal covenant.[68]

It may be noted that two of the mortgagee's remedies are derived from the common law (an action on the covenant, and the right to take possession), one is equitable (foreclosure) and two were formerly contractual and are now statutory (sale, and the appointment of a receiver).

II. EQUITABLE MORTGAGEE OR CHARGEE

The extent to which the foregoing remedies are exercisable by an equitable mortgagee or chargee is as follows.

1. To sue for the money due. The position is the same as for a legal mortgage.

2. To foreclose. An equitable mortgagee may foreclose in the same way as a legal mortgagee, save that the court order will direct the mortgagor to convey the legal title to the mortgagee.[69] An equitable chargee, however, has no right of foreclosure,[70] for a charge effects no conveyance of a legal or equitable interest.

3. To sell

(a) *Unregistered land.* For unregistered land, the statutory power of sale[71] applies wherever the mortgage or charge was made by deed; other mortgagees or chargees have no power of sale, though they may apply to the court for an order for sale.[72] Although an equitable mortgagee or chargee by deed has the statutory power of sale, this probably does not enable him to

---

[64] *Palmer* v. *Hendrie* (1859) 27 Beav. 349 at 351.
[65] *Rudge* v. *Richens* (1873) L.R. 8 C.P. 358.
[66] *Gordon Grant & Co. Ltd.* v. *Boos* [1926] A.C. 781.
[67] *Perry* v. *Barker* (1806) 13 Ves. 198; and see *ante*, p. 451.
[68] *Palmer* v. *Hendrie* (1859) 27 Beav. 349.
[69] *James* v. *James* (1873) L.R. 16 Eq. 153.
[70] *Re Lloyd* [1903] 1 Ch. 385.
[71] *Ante*, pp. 451 *et seq.*
[72] L.P.A. 1925, s.91(2).

convey the legal estate to the purchaser.[73] To overcome this defect, either or both of two conveyancing devices are employed.

(1) *Power of attorney*: an irrevocable power of attorney is inserted in the deed empowering the mortgagee or his assigns to convey the legal estate.[74]

(2) *Declaration of trust*: a clause is inserted in the deed whereby the mortgagor declares that he holds the legal estate on trust for the mortgagee, and empowers the mortgagee to appoint himself or his nominee as trustee in place of the mortgagor. The mortgagee can thus vest the legal estate in himself or the purchaser.

(b) *Registered land*. For registered land, only a registered chargee has the statutory power of sale[75]; but equitable mortgagees may use the above conveyancing devices to sell the legal estate.[76]

4. Possible right to take possession. Although it is usually said that an equitable mortgagee, having no legal estate, has no right to possession, on principle there seems no reason why, like a tenant under an equitable lease, he should not be entitled to it[77]; and a provision in the mortgage may give him the right to it. If the land is let, he cannot collect the rent from the tenant, for that is payable to the legal reversioner[78] with whom there is privity of estate. An equitable chargee, who has not even the benefit of a contract to create a legal mortgage, cannot even claim possession.

5. To appoint a receiver. As in the case of the power of sale, the statutory power to appoint a receiver[79] exists only if the mortgage or charge was made by deed and, in the case of registered land, only if it is a registered charge.[80] In other cases, a receiver can be obtained only by applying to the court.

B. *Other Rights of a Mortgagee*

Certain other rights of a mortgagee must now be considered. The position of these and other matters is in general the same for both mortgages and charges, whether legal or equitable, and "mortgage" will accordingly be used hereafter to include all such incumbrances unless the contrary is indicated.

1. Right to fixtures. It is a question of construction to determine what property is included in a mortgage. However, subject to any contrary

---

[73] See *Re Hodson and Howes' Contract* (1887) 35 Ch.D. 668; contrast *Re White Rose Cottage* [1965] Ch. 940 at 951.

[74] These powers are now regulated by the Powers of Attorney Act 1971, ss.4(1), 5(3).

[75] L.R.A. 1925, s.34(1); *Lever Finance Ltd.* v. *Needleman's Trustee* [1956] Ch. 375.

[76] See, *e.g. Re White Rose Cottage* [1964] Ch. 483 at 495, 496; [1965] Ch. 940 at 955, 956.

[77] See M. & W. 951, 952; *ante*, p. 312.

[78] *Finck* v. *Tranter* [1905] 1 K.B. 427.

[79] *Ante*, p. 457.

[80] *Lever Finance Ltd.* v. *Needleman's Trustee* [1956] Ch. 375.

intention, a mortgage includes all fixtures attached to the land either at the date of the mortgage or thereafter; the exceptions as between landlord and tenant do not apply.[81]

2. Right to possession of the title deeds. A first mortgagee has the same right to the title deeds as if he had the fee simple or an assignment of the lease which has been mortgaged, as the case may be[82]; but under all mortgages made since 1881, the mortgagor is entitled to inspect and make copies of the deeds, despite any contrary agreement.[83] If the mortgage is redeemed by the mortgagor, the mortgagee must deliver the deeds to him, unless he has notice of some subsequent incumbrance, in which case the deeds should be delivered to the incumbrancer next in order of priority of whom the mortgagee has notice. Contrary to the general rule that registration is notice, registration under the Land Charges Act 1972 is not notice for this purpose,[84] although as has been seen a mortgagee is bound to search before he distributes any surplus after a sale.[85] If a mortgage becomes statute-barred by lapse of time,[86] the mortgagee must return the deeds even if no part of the mortgage debt has been or will be paid.[87] In the case of registered land the land certificate must be deposited at the Land Registry for the duration of any registered charge.[88]

3. Right to insure against fire at the mortgagor's expense. Under the Law of Property Act 1925[89] a mortgagee or registered chargee may insure the mortgaged property against fire and charge the premiums on the property in the same way as the money lent; this power, which is given only where the mortgage was made by deed, is exercisable as soon as the mortgage is made. The amount of the insurance must not exceed the amount specified in the deed, or, if none, two-thirds of the amount required to restore the property in case of total destruction. But the mortgagee cannot exercise his power if—

(i) the mortgage deed declares that no insurance is required; or
(ii) the mortgagor keeps up an insurance in accordance with the mortgage deed; or
(iii) the mortgage deed is silent as to insurance and the mortgagor keeps up an insurance to the amount authorised by the Act with the mortgagee's consent.

4. Right to consolidate

(a) *The right.* Consolidation may be described as the right of a person in

[81] *Ante*, p. 19.
[82] L.P.A. 1925, ss.85(1), 86(1).
[83] *Ibid.* s.96(1).
[84] *Ibid.* s.96(2), added by L.P.(Am.)A. 1926, Sched.
[85] *Ante*, p. 453.
[86] *Post*, p. 495.
[87] *Lewis* v. *Plunket* [1937] Ch. 306; and see *ante*, p. 446.
[88] L.R.A. 1925, s.65.
[89] ss.101(1), 108, replacing C.A. 1881, ss.19(1), 23.

whom two or more mortgages are vested to refuse to allow one mortgage to be redeemed unless the other or others are also redeemed. In its basic form, the principle is simple. If A has mortgaged both Greenacre and Whiteacre to X, each property being worth £50,000 and each loan being £40,000, it would be unfair, if the value of Greenacre subsequently sinks to £35,000 and the value of Whiteacre doubles, to allow A to redeem Whiteacre and leave Greenacre unredeemed. In such a case, equity permits X to consolidate, and so to oblige A to redeem both mortgages or neither. In seeking redemption, A is asking for the assistance of equity, and equity puts its own price upon its interference, saying that he who seeks equity must do equity.

This simple concept has been elaborated to some extent; different considerations may arise where third parties are concerned, *e.g.* by transfer of a mortgage. The rules on the subject may be stated as follows.

(b) *Conditions.* There can be no consolidation unless the following four conditions are satisfied.

(1) RESERVATION OF RIGHT: either both the mortgages were made before 1882, or at least one of the mortgages shows an intent to allow consolidation. Before 1882, the right existed automatically, provided the other conditions were satisfied; but after 1881, the Conveyancing Act 1881 made it necessary to reserve the right. The Law of Property Act 1925, s.93, now provides that with the two exceptions stated above there is no right to consolidate. It is common practice for a mortgage to contain a clause excluding the operation of section 93, so permitting consolidation.

(2) REDEMPTION DATES PASSED: in the case of both mortgages, the legal dates for redemption have passed.[90] Consolidation is an equitable doctrine and does not come into play unless only the equitable rights to redeem are concerned.

(3) SAME MORTGAGOR: both mortgages were made by the same mortgagor.[91] Mortgages made by different mortgagors can never be consolidated, even if both properties later come into the same hands. This is so even if X makes one mortgage and Y, as trustee for X, makes the other, or if A makes one mortgage and A and B jointly make the other.[92] But it is immaterial whether or not the mortgages were made to the same mortgagees.

(4) SIMULTANEOUS UNIONS OF MORTGAGES AND EQUITIES: there has been a time when both the mortgages have been vested in one person and simultaneously both the equities of redemption have been vested in another.[93] If this state of affairs exists at the time when redemption is sought, the mortgagee can consolidate, subject to the other conditions being fulfilled. Even if this state of affairs has ceased to exist when redemption is

[90] *Cummins* v. *Fletcher* (1880) 14 Ch.D. 699.
[91] *Sharp* v. *Rickards* [1909] 1 Ch. 109.
[92] *Thorneycroft* v. *Crockett* (1848) 2 H.L.C. 239.
[93] See *Pledge* v. *White* [1896] A.C. 187 at 198.

sought, and the equities of redemption are then owned by different persons, a mortgagee who holds both mortgages can consolidate.

(c) *Illustrations.* There is no need to illustrate (1) and (2), but the following examples may be given of the operation of (3) and (4).

(i)

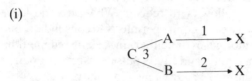

This represents the following steps:

(1) A mortgages one estate to X.
(2) B mortgages another estate to X.
(3) C purchases the equities of redemption of both properties.

There can be no consolidation here, even though Condition (4) is satisfied, for the mortgages were made by different mortgagors.

(ii)

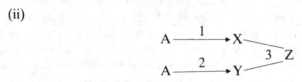

(1) A mortgages one estate to X.
(2) A mortgages another estate to Y.
(3) Z purchases both mortgages.

Here Z can consolidate, provided Conditions (1) and (2) are satisfied. Condition (3) is satisfied and so is Condition (4).

(iii)

(1) A mortgages one estate to X.
(2) A mortgages another estate to Y.
(3) C purchases the equity on the first estate.
(4) D purchases the equity on the second estate.
(5) Z purchases both mortgages.

There can be no consolidation here, for Condition (4) is not satisfied. It is true that at one stage (after Step (2)) both equities were in one person's hands, and that an another stage (Step (5)) both mortgages were in another person's hands; but at no one moment have both these conditions obtained. The equities separated before the mortgages came together.

If C instead of D had purchased the equity on the second estate, Z could have consolidated, even though at the time of C's purchase no right to consolidate had arisen; the purchaser of two or more equities takes subject to the risk of the mortgages coming into the same hand and so permitting consolidation.

(iv)

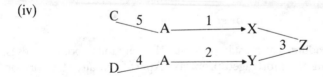

This represents the same position as the previous example, except that Steps (3) and (5) have changed places. As Z has now purchased both mortgages *before* A parted with either equity, Z may consolidate the mortgages provided Conditions (1) and (2) are satisfied. In this event, if C seeks to redeem his mortgage, Z can refuse redemption unless C purchases the mortgage on D's property as well as redeeming his own mortgage.

(d) *More than two mortgages.* These rules of consolidation apply equally when it is sought to consolidate more than two mortgages. Sometimes it will be found that while Mortgage I can be consolidated with Mortgages II and III, there is no right to consolidate Mortgages II and III with each other, *e.g.* if only Mortgage I contains a consolidation clause. Examples containing more than two mortgages are best worked out by taking the mortgages in pairs and applying the rules to each pair in turn.

(e) *Extent of doctrine.* The nature of the mortgages or the property mortgaged is immaterial. There can be consolidation even if one mortgage is legal and one equitable, or if both are equitable, or if one mortgage is of personalty and the other of realty,[94] or if both are mortgages of personalty. The doctrine has even been applied to two mortgages on the same property.[95] Further, it is immaterial whether the equity of redemption has been conveyed *in toto* or whether it has merely been mortgaged; a mortgagee of an equity of redemption is a purchaser *pro tanto*, *i.e.* to the extent of his interest. Thus if a mortgagee has a right of consolidation, it is effective against subsequent mortgagees of the property as well as the mortgagor.

(f) *Purchasers.* The doctrine of consolidation makes it dangerous to buy property subject to a mortgage without careful inquiry. If a right to consolidate has once arisen, a person who subsequently acquires one or both of the equities of redemption is liable to have the mortgages consolidated against him; and even if no right to consolidate has arisen, a person who acquires two equities of redemption is liable to have the mortgages consolidated if one person acquires both of them. But a person who acquires only one equity of redemption at a time when no right to consolidate has arisen normally suffers no risk of consolidation.[96]

[94] *Tassell* v. *Smith* (1858) 2 De G. & J. 713.
[95] *Re Salmon* [1903] 1 K.B. 147; *sed quaere.*
[96] *Harter* v. *Coleman* (1882) 19 Ch.D. 630.

5. Right to tack. This is considered below.[97]

Sect. 2. Rights Common to Both Parties

A. Power of Leasing

1. Leases not binding. The most important right common to both parties is the right of leasing the mortgaged property. Apart from any statutory or contractual provisions, the position of a mortgagor as soon as he has made a mortgage is that he has granted a long term of years to the mortgagee and retains merely the reversion on that lease, together with an equity of redemption. The mortgagor consequently has no right to possession of the land and so cannot grant a lease giving anyone else the right to possession. In practice, however, the mortgagor is usually left in possession of the land; and it was held before 1926, when mortgages were created by conveying the whole of the mortgagor's estate, that if the mortgagor granted a lease, he was unable subsequently to deny the validity of that lease and eject the tenant, for the lease bound both the mortgagor and the tenant under the doctrine of estoppel.[98] But the mortgagee is not bound, and in the same way that he can take possession from the mortgagor, he can take possession from a tenant of the mortgagor.[99] As to the mortgagee, although he is entitled to possession of the land at law, leases granted by him will cease to be binding on the mortgagor if he redeems the mortgage,[1] for in equity the mortgagor is entitled to redeem his property as free from incumbrances as it was when mortgaged.

It will thus be seen that once property had been mortgaged, a satisfactory lease could be made only if both mortgagor and mortgagee concurred in granting it, or if the mortgage gave either or both of the parties power to grant binding leases. However, statute has materially altered this position, and the following provisions apply to all mortgages made after 1881 if the parties have not expressed a contrary intention, either in the mortgage or otherwise in writing.[2] It is common for mortgages to preclude the mortgagor from exercising any power to grant leases or tenancies. A lease granted by the mortgagor in breach of the mortgage deed will not bind the mortgagee,[3] unless he subsequently adopts the tenancy, as by accepting rent from the tenant.[4]

2. Power to lease. A power to grant leases which will be binding on both mortgagor and mortgagee is exercisable—

---

[97] *Post*, pp. 487 *et seq*.
[98] *Cuthbertson* v. *Irving* (1859) 4 H. & N. 742 at 754; *ante* p. 321.
[99] *Rogers* v. *Humphreys* (1835) 4 A. & E. 299 at 313.
[1] See *Chapman* v. *Smith* [1907] 2 Ch. 97 at 102.
[2] L.P.A. 1925, s.99, replacing C.A. 1881, s.18.
[3] *Dudley & District Benefit B.S.* v. *Emerson* [1949] Ch. 707; *Britannia B.S.* v. *Earl* [1990] 1 W.L.R. 422.
[4] See *Stroud B.S.* v. *Delamont* [1960] 1 W.L.R. 431.

(1) by the mortgagee, if he is in possession or has appointed a receiver who is still acting; otherwise,
(2) by the mortgagor, if he is in possession.

3. Term of lease. A lease may be granted for the following terms—

(1) if the mortgage was made before 1926, for not more than—
    (i) 21 years for agricultural or occupation purposes; or
    (ii) 99 years for building;
(2) if the mortgage was made after 1925, for not more than—
    (i) 50 years for agricultural or occupation purposes; or
    (ii) 999 years for building.

4. Conditions of lease. To fall within the statutory powers, any lease granted must comply with the following conditions:

(1) It must be limited to take effect in possession not later than 12 months after its date.
(2) It must reserve the best rent reasonably obtainable, and with certain qualifications no fine may be taken.
(3) It must contain a covenant by the lessee for payment of rent and a condition of re-entry on the rent not being paid for a specified period not exceeding 30 days.
(4) A counterpart of the lease must be executed by the lessee and delivered to the lessor. A counterpart of any lease granted by the mortgagor must be delivered within one month to the mortgagee.[5]

These conditions do not preclude the grant of oral leases in exercise of the statutory power[6]; such leases need not comply with the last two conditions.[7] Neither the statutory power of leasing nor any provision in the mortgage excluding these powers (as is common in the case of the mortgagor) deprives either party of his common law right to grant a lease which will not bind the other unless adopted by him.[8] Further, the parties may extend the statutory powers by an agreement in writing, whether or not in the mortgage.[9]

B. Power of Accepting Surrenders of Leases

In the case of a mortgage made after 1911, if the parties have not expressed a contrary intention, either in the mortgage or otherwise in writing, statute[10] enables a surrender of any lease or tenancy to be effected, binding the parties to the mortgage, on the following terms.

1. Power to accept. The surrender may be accepted—

[5] See *Public Trustee* v. *Lawrence* [1912] 1 Ch. 789.
[6] L.P.A. 1925, s.99(17). For oral leases, see *ante*, p. 310.
[7] *Rhodes* v. *Dalby* [1971] 1 W.L.R. 1325 at 1331, 1332.
[8] *Rust* v. *Goodale* [1957] Ch. 33; contrast *Taylor* v. *Ellis* [1960] Ch. 368.
[9] L.P.A. 1925, s.99(14).
[10] *Ibid.* s.100, replacing C.A. 1911, s.3.

(1) by the mortgagee, if he is in possession or has appointed a receiver who is still acting; otherwise,

(2) by the mortgagor, if he is in possession.

2. Conditions of surrender. For the surrender to be valid—

(1) an authorised lease of the property must be granted to take effect in possession within one month of the surrender;

(2) the term of the new lease must not be shorter than the unexpired residue of the surrendered lease; and

(3) the rent reserved by the new lease must not be less than the rent reserved by the surrendered lease.

The statutory power of accepting a surrender is thus exercisable only for the purpose of replacing one lease by another[11]; but the power may be extended by an agreement in writing, whether or not in the mortgage.

Sect. 3. Rights of the Mortgagor

A. Right of Redemption

I. PROTECTION OF THE MORTGAGOR

One aspect of equity's protection of the mortgagor's equity of redemption is to be found in the maxim "once a mortgage, always a mortgage." This is applied in two ways.

1. The test of a mortgage is substance, not form: if a transaction is in substance a mortgage, equity will treat it as such, even if it is dressed up in some other guise, as by the documents being cast in the form of an absolute conveyance.[12] Thus if a mortgage is expressed in the form of a conveyance with an option for the mortgagor to repurchase the property in a year's time, the mortgagor is entitled to redeem it even after the year has expired.[13]

2. No clogs on the equity: there must be no clog or fetter on the equity of redemption. This means not only that the mortgagor cannot be prevented from eventually redeeming his property, but also that he cannot be prevented from redeeming it free from any conditions or stipulations in the mortgage.

(a) *No irredeemability.* It is impossible to provide that a mortgage shall be totally irredeemable[14] or that the right of redemption shall be confined to certain persons or to a limited period.[15] A provision in a mortgage that the property shall become the mortgagee's absolutely when some specified

[11] See *Barclays Bank Ltd.* v. *Stasek* [1957] Ch. 28.
[12] *Barnhart* v. *Greenshields* (1853) 9 Moo.P.C. 18.
[13] *Waters* v. *Mynn* (1850) 15 L.T.(o.s.) 157; and see *Grangeside Properties Ltd.* v. *Collingwoods Securities Ltd.* [1964] 1 W.L.R. 139.
[14] *Re Wells* [1933] Ch. 29 at 52.
[15] *Salt* v. *Marquess of Northampton* [1892] A.C. 1.

event occurs is void.[16] In all such cases, the owner of the equity of redemption may redeem as if there had been no such restriction. But once the mortgage has been made, equity will not intervene if the mortgagor, by a separate and independent transaction, gives the mortgagee an option of purchasing the property and thus of depriving the mortgagor of his equity of redemption.[17] While the mortgagor is in the defenceless position of seeking a loan, or arranging for a transfer of the mortgage,[18] equity will protect him; but once he has obtained the loan or secured the transfer, this protection is not needed.

A provision postponing the date of redemption until some future period longer than the customary six months, *e.g.* for 40 years, is valid, provided the mortgage as a whole is not so oppressive and unconscionable that equity would not enforce it, and provided it does not make the equitable right to redeem illusory.[19] In one case, a lease for 20 years was mortgaged on conditions which prevented its redemption until six weeks before the end of the term; such a provision rendered the equitable right to redeem illusory and so was held void.[20] Generally, however, the court will not interfere with a bargain made between two parties on an equal footing, even if this does postpone redemption for a considerable period.

Limited companies are not protected by this rule, for by statute a debenture may be made wholly or partly irredeemable, and even an ordinary mortgage by a company is a debenture.[21]

(b) *Redemption free from conditions in the mortgage.* The mortgagor cannot be prevented from redeeming exactly what he mortgaged, *i.e.* the property free from all conditions or stipulations in the mortgage. The essence of a mortgage is a loan of money in return for security. Sometimes terms are inserted in a mortgage which give the mortgagee some other advantage in addition to his security. If this advantage is obtained by fraud or oppression, it will be set aside, but otherwise there is no objection to an advantage which ceases whenever the mortgage is redeemed, such as a provision making the mortgaged property, a public-house, a "tied" house until redemption.[22] The general enforceability of advantages which end on redemption represents an advance on the attitude which the courts had at one time adopted, rendering all collateral advantages for the mortgagee void on the basis that they were a disguised form of interest contravening the usury laws.[23] After the last of the statutes dealing with usury was repealed in

[16] *Toomes* v. *Conset* (1745) 3 Atk. 261.
[17] *Reeve* v. *Lisle* [1902] A.C. 461 (option 12 days after mortgage, unlike *Samuel* v. *Jarrah Timber and Wood Paving Corporation Ltd.* [1904] A.C. 323, where the mortgage deed contained the option).
[18] *Lewis* v. *Frank Love Ltd.* [1961] 1 W.L.R. 261.
[19] *Knightsbridge Estates Trust Ltd.* v. *Byrne* [1939] Ch. 441 (affirmed on other grounds: *infra*, note 28). Both parties were bound to allow the full 40 year period.
[20] *Fairclough* v. *Swan Brewery Co. Ltd.* [1912] A.C. 565. Contrast *Santley* v. *Wilde* [1899] 2 Ch. 474, which seems unsound: see *Noakes & Co. Ltd.* v. *Rice* [1902] A.C. 24 at 31, 34.
[21] Companies Act 1985, s.193; *Knightsbridge Estates Trust Ltd.* v. *Byrne* [1940] A.C. 613.
[22] *Biggs* v. *Hoddinott* [1898] 2 Ch. 307; *Noakes & Co. Ltd.* v. *Rice* [1902] A.C. 24.
[23] See *Jennings* v. *Ward* (1705) 2 Vern. 520 at 521; *Noakes & Co. Ltd.* v. *Rice*, *supra*, at p. 33.

1854, the courts gradually became more liberal and it is now settled that in certain cases a collateral advantage may remain effective even after redemption.

The chief difficulty in stating the present position lies in trying to reconcile the clog held void in *Bradley* v. *Carritt*[24] with the collateral advantage held valid in *Kreglinger* v. *New Patagonia Meat and Cold Storage Co. Ltd.*[25] In *Bradley's* case the substance of the transaction was a mortgage of shares in which the mortgagor bound himself to endeavour to induce the company to employ the mortgagee as broker, and if the company did not, to pay the mortgagee an amount equivalent to the broker's fees. In *Kreglinger's* case the substance of the transaction was a loan of money to a meat company in return for an option for five years on any sheepskins which the company had for sale. The differing results in these cases can be explained in two ways. In *Bradley's* case the shares returned were fettered by the practical restriction that they could not be sold without retaining so much of the voting rights attached to them as allowed the mortgagor to continue to control the appointment, whereas in *Kreglinger's* case the property was returned unfettered. Alternatively it can be said that in *Bradley's* case the agreement fettering the mortgagor was a mere clause put in a mortgage, and so void, the basis of the agreement being a mortgage and nothing else; in *Kreglinger's* case, on the other hand, the transaction was substantially the grant of an option in return for a loan of money, with the result that the option was not merely a part of the mortgage but a separate and independent transaction and so valid.[26] The courts are reluctant to allow the doctrine which forbids clogs on the equity of redemption to upset a freely negotiated commercial contract.[27]

(c) *Unconscionable terms.* The court has a general jurisdiction to grant relief against terms in a mortgage which are oppressive or unconscionable.[28] Thus where a property company sold one of its houses to the tenant, lending him £2,900 on a mortgage of the house which required repayment of £4,553 over six years, the transaction was held to be unconscionable, and the tenant was held to be entitled to redeem the mortgage on paying £2,900 with interest of 7 per cent. as fixed by the court.[29] But if provisions in a mortgage, though unreasonable, are not initially unconscionable, subsequent events will not invalidate them. Thus where a commercial mortgage for ten years was indexed to the Swiss franc, and there was then an unforeseen fall in the value of the pound by two-thirds, the court refused to intervene.[30]

[24] [1903] A.C. 253.
[25] [1914] A.C. 25.
[26] See *Re Petrol Filling Station, Vauxhall Bridge Road, London* (1968) 20 P. & C.R. 1.
[27] *Kreglinger's Case, supra*, at p. 46; *Samuel* v. *Jarrah Timber and Wood Paving Corporation Ltd.* [1904] A.C. 323 at 327.
[28] *Knightsbridge Estates Trust Ltd.* v. *Byrne* [1939] Ch. 441 at 457; in H.L., [1940] A.C. 613.
[29] *Cityland and Property (Holdings) Ltd.* v. *Dabrah* [1968] Ch. 166, as explained in *Multiservice Bookbinding Ltd.* v. *Marden* [1979] Ch. 84 at 109, 110.
[30] *Multiservice Bookbinding Ltd.* v. *Marden* [1979] Ch. 84.

(d) *Regulated mortgages.* Mortgages under which the credit provided does not exceed £15,000[31] are regulated by the elaborate provisions of the Consumer Credit Act 1974 unless they fall within the list of "exempt agreements," which includes mortgages to building societies and local authorities.[32] Most commercial transactions and ordinary mortgages for house purchase are outside these provisions, which are aimed at improvident second mortgages by house owners for personal expenditure. There are detailed provisions requiring a mortgage within the Act to be in a prescribed form, signed by both parties, which makes the mortgagor aware of his rights and duties, and the protection given by the Act; and the mortgagor must be sent a copy of the proposed mortgage at least seven days before he is sent a copy for signature, thus giving him a "consideration period."[33] The mortgagor may repay the sums due at any time, despite any agreement to the contrary[34]; and mortgages within the Act are enforceable only on an order of the court.[35]

The Act also gives the court power to re-open extortionate credit bargains with individuals (but not companies), irrespective of the amount involved.[36]

(e) *Restraint of trade.* A provision in a mortgage which is not oppressive, unconscionable or extortionate nor a clog on the equity of redemption may nevertheless be void on other grounds. Thus it may be invalid under the ordinary law of contract as being in unreasonable restraint of trade.[37]

II. WHO CAN REDEEM

Redemption is usually sought by the mortgagor; but the right to redeem is not confined to him and may be exercised by any person interested in the equity of redemption.[38] Thus the right to redeem extends to assignees of the equity of redemption, subsequent mortgagees, and even a lessee under a lease granted by the mortgagor but not binding on the mortgagee.[39]

III. EFFECT OF REDEMPTION

Where redemption is effected by the only person interested in the equity of redemption, and the mortgage redeemed is the only incumbrance on the property, the effect of redemption is to discharge the mortgage and leave the property free from incumbrances. But if there are several mortgages on the property, the effect of redemption will normally be that the person paying the money takes a transfer of the mortgage, as where a second mortgagee redeems the first mortgage. If several incumbrancers seek to redeem a

---

[31] Consumer Credit Act 1974, ss.8(2), 189(1); S.I. 1983 No. 1878.
[32] Consumer Credit Act 1974, s.16.
[33] *Ibid.* ss.58–61.
[34] *Ibid.* ss.94, 173.
[35] *Ibid.* ss.126, 173(3).
[36] *Ibid.* ss.137–139, 189(1).
[37] *Esso Petroleum Co. Ltd.* v. *Harper's Garage (Stourport) Ltd.* [1968] A.C. 269.
[38] *Pearce* v. *Morris* (1869) 5 Ch.App. 227 at 229.
[39] *Tarn* v. *Turner* (1888) 39 Ch.D. 456.

mortgage, the first in order of priority has the best claim.[40] However, if the mortgagor redeems a mortgage which has priority over one or more subsequent mortgages, the redemption discharges the mortgage and the mortgagor cannot claim to have it kept alive to the prejudice of the subsequent mortgagees[41]; for his mortgage to them included all the rights he had, including those against the prior mortgagee. But no such rule binds his successors in title.[42]

An incumbrancer who is entitled to redeem a mortgage may usually, instead of redeeming, insist upon the mortgagee transferring the mortgage to the incumbrancer's nominee.[43]

IV. TERMS OF REDEMPTION

A mortgage may be redeemed either in court or out of court; the latter is the more usual. If a mortgagee unreasonably refuses to accept a proper tender of the money due and so makes an action for redemption necessary, he may be penalised in costs.[44]

The mortgagor may redeem on the legal date for redemption without giving notice of his intention to do so. After that date, when he is forced to rely upon his equitable right to redeem, it is a rule of practice that he must either give the mortgagee reasonable notice of his intention to redeem (six months usually sufficing), or else pay him six months' interest in lieu thereof[45]; it is only fair that the mortgagee should have a reasonable opportunity of finding another investment for his money. But the mortgagee is not entitled to any notice or interest in lieu thereof—

(i) if he has taken steps to enforce his security, as by taking possession, or commencing foreclosure proceedings, or giving the mortgagor notice to repay the loan so as to entitle the mortgagee to sell on default being made[46]; or

(ii) if the loan is merely of a temporary nature, as is usually the case in an equitable mortgage by deposit of title deeds.[47]

If the mortgagor gives six months' notice and fails to pay on the proper day, he must usually give a further six months' notice or pay six months' interest in lieu thereof,[48] unless he can give a reasonable explanation of his failure to pay, in which case it suffices to give reasonable notice, *e.g.* three months.[49]

---

[40] *Teevan* v. *Smith* (1882) 20 Ch.D. 724 at 730.
[41] *Otter* v. *Lord Vaux* (1856) 6 De G.M. & G. 638, recognised by L.P.A. 1925, s.115(3); *Parkash* v. *Irani Finance Ltd.* [1970] Ch. 101.
[42] *Whiteley* v. *Delaney* [1914] A.C. 132.
[43] L.P.A. 1925, s.95.
[44] *Graham* v. *Seal* (1918) 88 L.J.Ch. 31.
[45] *Johnson* v. *Evans* (1889) 61 L.T. 18. The mortgage deed may provide to the contrary.
[46] See *Bovill* v. *Endle* [1896] 1 Ch. 648.
[47] *Fitzgerald's Trustee* v. *Mellersh* [1892] 1 Ch. 385.
[48] *Re Moss* (1885) 31 Ch.D. 90 at 94.
[49] *Cromwell Property Investment Co. Ltd.* v. *Western* [1934] Ch. 322.

Even if the mortgage makes no provision for interest, the mortgagor must pay it at a rate which the court will, if necessary, fix.[50]

V. "REDEEM UP, FORECLOSE DOWN"

The maxim "Redeem up, foreclose down" applies where there are several incumbrancers and one of them seeks by action to redeem a superior mortgage. The effect is best shown by an example. X has mortgaged his property successively to A, B, C, D, and E, the mortgages ranking in that order; X thus ranks last, *e.g.* in claiming any surplus if the property is sold. Suppose that D wishes to redeem B, and owing to the complexity of the accounts or some other circumstance an action for redemption is commenced. Before B can be redeemed, the exact amount due to him must be settled by the court. This amount, however, does not affect only B and D, for C, E and X are all concerned with the amount which has priority to their interests; thus if the property were to be sold, C, E and X would all wish to know whether what B was entitled to was, say, £60,000 or £70,000, for upon that figure might depend their chances of receiving anything from the proceeds of sale. Consequently, the court will insist upon their being made parties to D's action for redemption so that they can be represented in the taking of the accounts between B and D, and thus be bound by the final result.

However, it would be unfair to give C, E and X the trouble and expense of taking part in the action merely to watch accounts being taken,[51] with the risk of a similar event taking place in the future, and so the court insists that the rights of all parties concerned in the action shall be settled once and for all. A is not concerned: it is immaterial to him what is due to B, for A's mortgage has priority to B's.[52] But all the other parties are concerned, and the order of the court will be that D shall redeem not only B, but also C, for both their mortgages have priority to D's. Further, E and X must be foreclosed: that is, each of them will have the opportunity of saving his rights by paying off the prior mortgages concerned in the action, but if he fails to do so, he will be foreclosed. Thus if E and X fail to redeem and are foreclosed, the final result will be that D, at the price of redeeming B and C, now holds the equity of redemption subject only to the first mortgage in favour of A.

The principle may be stated thus: a mortgagee who seeks to redeem a prior mortgage by action must not only redeem any mortgages standing between him and that prior mortgage,[53] but must also foreclose all subsequent mortgagees and the mortgagor[54]; in short, "redeem up, foreclose down."

---

[50] See *Cityland and Property (Holdings) Ltd.* v. *Dabrah* [1968] Ch. 166.
[51] *Ramsbottom* v. *Wallis* (1835) 5 L.J.Ch. 92.
[52] *Brisco* v. *Kenrick* (1832) 1 L.J.Ch. 11.
[53] *Teevan* v. *Smith* (1882) 20 Ch.D. 724 at 729.
[54] *Farmer* v. *Curtis* (1829) 2 Sim. 466.

It should be noted that this rule does not apply to redemptions out of court,[55] and that there is no rule "foreclose down, redeem up"; a mortgagee who forecloses is under no obligation to redeem any prior mortgages,[56] although he must foreclose all subsequent mortgagees as well as the mortgagor.[57] In other words, for foreclosure the rule is simply "foreclose down": a mortgagee cannot foreclose a subsequent mortgagee or the mortgagor unless he forecloses everyone beneath him.

VI. TERMINATION OF EQUITY OF REDEMPTION

An equity of redemption may be extinguished against the wishes of the mortgagor—

(i) by foreclosure[58];
(ii) by sale[59]; or
(iii) by lapse of time.[60]

In addition, the mortgagor may himself extinguish it by releasing it to the mortgagee, or by redeeming.

B. Other Rights

The mortgagor has various other rights, including the right to have the property sold by the court, the right to inspect the title deeds, the right to compel a transfer of the mortgage[61] and the right to bring actions. As to the right to bring actions, before 1926 the mortgagor normally had no legal estate in the land and so could bring no actions which depended on having such an estate, *e.g.* on the covenants of a lease or tenancy which had been granted before the mortgage was made, so that the legal reversion on it had passed to the mortgagee[62]; and after 1925 the mortgagor's only interest is normally a reversion upon a long lease. But by statute,[63] provided the mortgagee has not given notice of his intention to take possession or enter into receipt of the rents and profits, the mortgagor in possession may sue in his own name for possession or for the rents and profits; he may bring an action to prevent, or recover damages for, any trespass or other wrong; and he may enforce all covenants and conditions in any leases or tenancies of the property.

---

[55] See *Smith* v. *Green* (1844) 1 Coll.C.C. 555.
[56] *Richards* v. *Cooper* (1842) 5 Beav. 304.
[57] *Anderson* v. *Stather* (1845) 2 Coll.C.C. 209.
[58] *Ante*, pp. 449 *et seq.*
[59] *Ante*, pp. 451 *et seq.*
[60] *Post*, p. 498.
[61] L.P.A. 1925, ss.91, 95, 96.
[62] See, *e.g. Turner* v. *Walsh* [1909] 2 K.B. 484.
[63] L.P.A. 1925, ss.98, 141, replacing earlier legislation.

Part 4

TRANSFER OF RIGHTS

Sect. 1. Death of Mortgagor

On the death of a person who holds realty or personalty subject to a mortgage or charge, the person who is entitled under the will or intestacy will take the property subject to the mortgage or charge unless the deceased has shown a contrary intention[64] in any document, whether or not a will.[65] Formerly, the person entitled could call upon the personal representatives of the deceased to pay off the mortgage out of the estate as being a debt of the deceased[66]; but this applied only where the deceased was the original mortgagor, and thus liable on his personal covenant, and not where the deceased merely held subject to the mortgage or charge.[67] This rule was successively curtailed by the Real Estate Charges Acts 1854, 1867 and 1877 (known as Locke King's Acts), and was finally abolished by the Administration of Estates Act 1925.[68] The present law does not apply to a person who takes not as a legatee or devisee but, *e.g.* as a purchaser under an option given to him by the will.[69]

These provisions do not affect any rights the mortgagee may have against the estate of the mortgagor; they merely ensure that as between the person taking the mortgaged property and the other beneficiaries, the burden of the mortgage should fall upon the former, in the absence of any contrary intention.

Sect. 2. Death of Mortgagee

A. Death of Sole Mortgagee

Under the Administration of Estates Act 1925[70] the mortgagee's right to the money lent and his interest in the mortgaged property both pass to his personal representatives.

B. Death of One of Several Mortgagees

1. At law. Where two or more persons lent money on mortgage of freeholds or leaseholds, the legal estate was usually conveyed to them as joint tenants. On the death of one, his interest passed to the others by virtue

---

[64] See *Re Wakefield* [1943] 2 All E.R. 29; *Re Neeld* [1962] Ch. 643. See generally Parry & Clark, *The Law of Succession* (9th ed.), pp. 274–279.
[65] A.E.A. 1925, s.35.
[66] *Galton* v. *Hancock* (1743) 2 Atk. 427.
[67] *Butler* v. *Butler* (1800) 5 Ves. 534.
[68] s.35.
[69] *Re Fison's W.T.* [1950] Ch. 394.
[70] A.E.A. 1925, ss.1(1), 3(1).

of the *jus accrescendi*, and the survivors could reconvey the legal estate to the mortgagor when he redeemed.

2. In equity. In equity, however, there is a presumption of a tenancy in common where two or more together lend money on mortgage.[71] Accordingly, in the absence of any provision to the contrary, when one of the mortgagees died his share passed to his personal representatives, and if the mortgagor redeemed they would have to join in the transaction. If the mortgagees were trustees lending trust money, the disclosure of this fact would be sufficient to rebut the presumption, for trustees are always joint tenants[72]; but this would have the disadvantage of bringing the trusts on to the title.[73]

3. Joint account clause. The practice accordingly grew up of inserting a "joint account clause" in mortgages where two or more persons lent money. This clause rebutted the presumption of a tenancy in common so far as the mortgagor was concerned and made it safe for him to pay his money to the surviving mortgagees. Since 1881 such a clause is unnecessary, for statute[74] has provided that as between the mortgagor and the mortgagees, the mortgagees are deemed to have advanced the money on a joint account unless a contrary intention appears. The result is that the survivor or survivors can give a complete discharge for all moneys due, notwithstanding any notice of severance which the mortgagor may have. This, however, is mere conveyancing machinery; it does not affect the position of the mortgagees *inter se*, and if they are beneficially entitled and not trustees, the survivors must account to the personal representatives of the deceased mortgagee for his share.[75] Although a joint account clause in a mortgage today is thus strictly unnecessary, it is often inserted *ex abundanti cautela*.

Sect. 3. Transfer of Equity of Redemption Inter Vivos

A mortgagor may at any time without the mortgagee's consent make a conveyance of his property subject to the mortgage, and the mortgagee cannot prevent an order for sale being made under the court's discretionary power[75a] merely because the price is less than the sums due under the mortgage.[75b] Notwithstanding any such conveyance, the mortgagor remains personally liable on the covenant to pay the money.[76] He therefore usually takes an express covenant for indemnity from the transferee, although such an obligation is implied.[77]

---

[71] *Ante*, p. 287.
[72] *Ante*, p. 282.
[73] See, *e.g. Re Blaiberg and Abrahams* [1899] 2 Ch. 340.
[74] C.A. 1881, s.61, replaced by L.P.A. 1925, s.111.
[75] See *Re Jackson* (1887) 34 Ch.D. 732.
[75a] Under L.P.A. 1925, s.91(2); *ante*, p. 451.
[75b] *Palk* v. *Mortgage Services Funding Plc.* [1992] *The Times* Aug. 7.
[76] *Kinnaird* v. *Trollope* (1888) 39 Ch.D. 636.
[77] *Bridgman* v. *Daw* (1891) 40 W.R. 253.

A mortgagor who wishes to sell free from the mortgage may do so—

(i) if he redeems; or
(ii) if the mortgagee consents (as he may well do if the security is adequate or if some other property is substituted for the property in question); or
(iii) if the mortgagor takes advantage of the statutory provision enabling the court to declare property free from an incumbrance upon sufficient money being paid into court.[78]

An assignee of the equity of redemption in general steps into the shoes of the mortgagor; but he does not merely by the assignment become personally liable to the mortgagee to pay the mortgage debt.[79]

Sect. 4. Transfer of Mortgages Inter Vivos

1. In general. A mortgagee may transfer his mortgage at any time without the concurrence of the mortgagor. However, for various reasons it is advisable for the mortgagor's concurrence to be obtained, *e.g.* in order to obtain his admission of the state of accounts showing the amount still due under the mortgage.[80]

Once the transfer has been made, the transferee should give notice of it to the mortgagor, unless the mortgagor has notice already, *e.g.* because he was a party to the transfer. If the mortgagor has no actual or constructive notice, the transferee cannot complain if the mortgagor pays to the transferor money due under the mortgage.[81]

2. Sub-mortgages. A sub-mortgage is a mortgage of a mortgage. A mortgagee may, instead of transferring his mortgage, borrow money upon the security of it. A well-secured debt can itself be good security for a loan to the creditor. Thus if X has lent £20,000 upon a mortgage made by B, and X then wishes to raise a temporary loan of £2,000 himself, it would clearly be inadvisable for X to transfer the mortgage to Y for £20,000 or to call in the whole of his loan. Consequently, X would raise the money by mortgaging his mortgage, *i.e.* by making a sub-mortgage.

Before 1926, a sub-mortgage was effected by a transfer of the mortgage subject to a proviso for redemption. After 1925, this form is still available if the mortgage is equitable or is a legal charge; but where it has been created by the grant of a term of years, a legal sub-mortgage can be made only by the grant of a sub-term or by a legal charge.[82] In general, the sub-mortgagee takes over the mortgagee's rights of enforcing payment under the original mortgage; thus he may sell the property. Alternatively, he may exercise his remedies against the mortgage itself, as by selling it.[83]

---

[78] L.P.A. 1925, s.50, replacing C.A. 1881, s.5(1).
[79] *Re Errington* [1894] 1 Q.B. 11.
[80] See *Turner* v. *Smith* [1901] 1 Ch. 213.
[81] *Dixon* v. *Winch* [1900] 1 Ch. 736 at 742.
[82] L.P.A. 1925, s.86(1), (3).
[83] See generally Fisher & Lightwood, *Law of Mortgage* (10th ed. 1988), pp. 272–275.

Sect. 5. Discharge of Mortgages

1. Before 1926. Upon the redemption of a legal mortgage of a fee simple before 1926, the mortgagee had to execute a reconveyance of the fee simple. In the case of leaseholds, there was a reassignment or, if the mortgage had been made by subdemise, a surrender of the sub-lease. In each case, the document contained a receipt for the money paid. However, in the case of a mortgage to a building society, a mere receipt indorsed on the mortgage deed operated both as a discharge of the mortgage and a reconveyance of the estate[84]; and an equitable mortgage was sufficiently discharged by an indorsed receipt.

2. After 1925. In the case of any mortgage discharged after 1925, a receipt indorsed on or annexed to the mortgage deed, signed[85] by the mortgagee and stating the name of the person paying the money, normally operates as a surrender of the mortgage term or a reconveyance, as the case may be, and discharges the mortgage.[86] But if the receipt shows that the person paying the money was not entitled to the immediate equity of redemption and makes no provision to the contrary, it operates as a transfer of the mortgage to him.[87] Building society mortgages may still be discharged by a special form of receipt, indorsed on the mortgage, which does not state who paid the money and cannot operate as a transfer of the mortgage.[88] There are certain advantages in such a receipt.[89]

Apart from these provisions, once a mortgage by demise has been redeemed, the term becomes a satisfied term and ceases forthwith.[90] But although when coupled with this provision it might be thought that an ordinary receipt (*i.e.* one not complying with the conditions relating to indorsed receipts) would operate as a sufficient discharge, conveyancers do not in practice rely upon such a receipt, for it is only *prima facie* proof of payment.

3. Registered land. A registered charge is discharged by delivering the charge certificate to the Land Registry with a discharge in Form 53, or, in the case of a building society, with an indorsed certificate.[91] The charge is then deleted from the register.

Part 5

PRIORITY OF MORTGAGES

Where there are more mortgages than one on the same property it is

---

[84] Building Societies Acts 1836, s.5; 1874, s.42.
[85] See *Simpson* v. *Geoghegan* [1934] W.N. 232.
[86] L.P.A. 1925, s.115(1).
[87] *Ibid.* s.115(2). See *Cumberland Court (Brighton) Ltd.* v. *Taylor* [1964] Ch. 29.
[88] Building Societies Act 1986, Sched. 4, para. 2.
[89] Wurtzburg & Mills, *Building Society Law* (15th ed. 1989), pp. 6.44–6.46.
[90] L.P.A. 1925, ss.5, 116; *ante*, p. 441.
[91] Ruoff & Roper 24–19; Wurtzburg & Mills, *Building Society Law*, *supra*, at p. 6.50. For the certificate, see above.

sometimes necessary to determine the priority of the mortgages, as where the property is sold by one of the mortgagees and there is not enough money to satisfy all. Over the years, the courts evolved rules for determining priorities which were mainly particular applications of the rules relating to competing legal and equitable interests. These rules were (and are) subject to any agreement between the mortgagees, for they can alter them as they wish, without the mortgagor's consent, unless the mortgages otherwise provide.[92] Many of the rules evolved by the courts were greatly affected and largely (but far from entirely) superseded by the system of registration of land charges under the Land Charges Act 1925 (now 1972); and registered land has its own rules. In addition to these rules, there is also a process known as "tacking" which alters the priorities settled under the general rules.

Before 1926, there were two basic rules for mortgages of land:

(i) "*Qui prior est tempore, potior est jure*" (he who is first in time is stronger in law); mortgages primarily ranked in the order of their creation, or "First made, first paid"; but

(ii) "*Where the equities are equal, the law prevails*": if, apart from the order of their creation, a legal and an equitable mortgage had equal claims to be preferred, the legal mortgage took priority.

Today, there is no need to consider the rules for priority before 1926 in any detail, though parts of those rules are still relevant on certain points and will be considered in due course. The position after 1925 must, of course, be fully discussed. This will be done under the following heads.

Unregistered land will be considered first. Here, there are two basic rules, depending on what has been mortgaged. First, if a legal estate in land has been mortgaged, the rules depend on whether or not the mortgage has been protected by a deposit of documents relating to the legal estate affected; normally these are the title deeds. Mortgages protected in this way stand outside the system of registration of land charges, and depend for priority on the rules before 1926, subject to the law of land charges. Mortgages that are not protected in this way are registrable as land charges and depend on this system for their priority. Second, if an equitable interest in any property has been mortgaged, the rule in *Dearle* v. *Hall*[93] applies, so that priority depends on the dates on which notice of the mortgages was received by the trustees or other legal owner. Third, there are the rules for tacking.

For registered land, registered charges rank in the order in which they are entered on the register, subject to any tacking. Other mortgages rank in the order of creation, subject to any protection given by entries on the register or by deposit of the land certificate.

These rules will now be considered in turn.

---

[92] *Cheah Theam Swee* v. *Equiticorp Finance Group Ltd.* [1992] 1 A.C. 472.
[93] (1828) 3 Russ. 1.

Sect. 1. Unregistered Land

A. Mortgages of a Legal Estate

I. THE RULES

1. Mortgages included. This head includes all mortgages of a legal estate in land, whether the mortgage itself is legal or equitable. The question is "Has a legal estate been mortgaged?," not "Is the mortgage legal or equitable?"

2. Principles. The two main principles[94] are these:

(a) *Mortgages protected by deeds*: a mortgage protected "by a deposit of documents relating to the legal estate affected" is expressly excepted from the provisions of the 1925 legislation requiring registration of mortgages,[95] since the absence of the title deeds will proclaim the mortgage to anyone seeking to deal with the land.[96] Probably "protected" means "originally protected", and not "continuously protected."[97]

(b) *Mortgages not protected by deeds*: a mortgage made after 1925 and not protected by a deposit of documents relating to the legal estate affected should be registered as a land charge. If the mortgage is legal, it should be registered as a puisne mortgage (Class C(i)); if the mortgage is equitable, it should be registered as a general equitable charge (Class C(iii)).[98]

3. Reasons for registration. The reasons for registering a puisne mortgage or a general equitable charge are as follows:

(a) *Priority*. Section 97 of the Law of Property Act 1925 provides that every such mortgage "shall rank according to its date of registration as a land charge pursuant to the Land Charges Act 1925 or 1972."[99]

(b) *Void for want of registration*. Section 4(5) of the Land Charges Act 1972 provides that a Class C land charge created after 1925 shall "be void as against a purchaser of the land charged therewith, or of any interest in such land, unless the land charge is registered in the appropriate register before the completion of the purchase."[1] In the Act, unless the context otherwise requires, "purchaser" means "any person (including a mortgagee or lessee) who, for valuable consideration, takes any interest in land or in a charge of land."[2] Thus a puisne mortgage or a general equitable charge, if unregistered, is void against a purchaser of the legal fee simple even if he had actual

---

[94] There is a full discussion in (1940) 7 C.L.J. 243 (R.E.M.).
[95] L.C.A. 1972, s.2(4), replacing L.C.A. 1925, s.10. They are probably not registrable as Class C(iv) estate contracts: M. & W. 998.
[96] But see *ante*, p. 86, for leases.
[97] M. & W. 997.
[98] See *ante*, p. 78.
[99] See L.C.A. 1972, s.18(6).
[1] Formerly L.C.A. 1925, s.13(2).
[2] L.C.A. 1972, s.17(1).

knowledge of it; for where an interest is void for non-registration he is not prejudicially affected by notice of it.[3]

II. OPERATION OF THE RULES

The effect of these provisions must be considered under four possible heads.

1. Each mortgage protected by a deposit of deeds. A mortgage will be protected by a deposit of deeds if the documents deposited are material parts of the title, even if they are not all the title deeds.[4] Thus two or more mortgages protected by a deposit of deeds may be created, as where the mortgagor has secretly withheld some of the deeds when creating the first mortgage,[5] or where he recovers the deeds from the mortgagee on some pretext, such as obtaining them on a short loan to show the dimensions of the property to a person concerned with a rebuilding project.[6] In such cases, the mortgages are not registrable. Four categories have to be considered.

  (i) Where both mortgages are legal.
  (ii) Where the first is legal and the second equitable.
  (iii) Where the first is equitable and the second legal.
  (iv) Where both are equitable.

These will be considered in turn. Each is subject to the rules for loss of priority considered below.[7]

(a) *Both mortgages legal*. Where both mortgages are legal, priority will normally depend on the order of creation. Where two leases are granted, the second will take effect in reversion on the first,[8] and *qui prior est tempore, potior est jure*.

(b) *Legal mortgage followed by equitable mortgage*. Where a legal mortgage is followed by an equitable mortgage, the legal mortgage has a double claim to priority, both as being prior in time and because where the equities are equal, the law prevails.

(c) *Equitable mortgage followed by legal mortgage*. Where an equitable mortgage is followed by a legal mortgage, the primary rule is that the mortgages rank in the order of creation; but this priority may be displaced by the superiority of the legal estate. For this to occur, the legal mortgagee must show that he is a *bona fide* purchaser for value of a legal estate without notice of the prior equitable mortgage.[9] The inability of the mortgagor to produce all the title deeds will usually amount to notice to the legal mortgagee that

---

[3] *Ante*, p. 88.
[4] *Lacon* v. *Allen* (1856) 3 Drew. 579 (equitable mortgage).
[5] *Ibid.; Walker* v. *Linom* [1907] 2 Ch. 104.
[6] *Peter* v. *Russell* (1716) Gilb.Eq. 122 (the "Thatched House" case).
[7] *Post*, p. 480.
[8] *Jones* v. *Rhind* (1869) 17 W.R. 1091.
[9] *Pilcher* v. *Rawlins* (1872) 7 Ch.App. 259; *Att.-Gen.* v. *Biphosphated Guano Co.* (1879) 11 Ch.D. 327.

some prior mortgage already exists[10]; but if his inquiries for the deeds were met by a reasonable excuse, he can claim priority as having taken without notice. The court has accepted surprisingly frail excuses as being reasonable, such as that the mortgagor was busy but would produce the deeds later,[11] or that the deeds were in Ireland, where the property lay.[12] Instead of applying the normal rule that requires a purchaser to make a proper investigation of title, the courts have held that nothing save gross negligence will postpone the legal mortgagee[13]; and it is grossly negligent to accept the excuse that the deeds also relate to other property.[14]

(d) *Both mortgages equitable.* Where both mortgages are equitable, priority depends on the order in which they were created, provided that the equities are equal in other respects.[15] Accordingly, a first mortgagee who failed to ask for the title deeds, or who, having obtained them, redelivered them to the mortgagor without pressing for their early return, may be postponed to a second mortgagee who took all proper precautions but was nevertheless deceived.[16]

(e) *Loss of priority.* Before 1926 it was settled that even a legal mortgagee might lose his priority in three classes of case; and the principles appear to apply after 1925, though their application to the rules laid down by statute has yet to be considered. The cases, which are stated in terms of a legal mortgage, seem equally applicable to equitable mortgages.[17] They are as follows.

(1) FRAUD. If a legal mortgagee is guilty of some fraud whereby the equitable mortgagee is deceived into believing that there was no legal mortgage on the property, the legal mortgagee will be postponed to the equitable mortgagee.[18]

(2) ESTOPPEL. If the legal mortgagee either expressly or by implication made some misrepresentation by which the equitable mortgagee was deceived, the legal mortgagee will be estopped from asserting his priority.[19] Thus if a legal mortgagee indorses a receipt for his money on the mortgage and somebody is thereby induced to lend money on an equitable mortgage of the property, the legal mortgagee cannot afterwards claim priority for his loan if in fact it has not been discharged.[20] Again, if the legal mortgagee parts with the deeds to the mortgagor to enable him to raise money, he will be postponed to any subsequent mortgagee who lent money without notice of the first mortgage, even if the mortgagor had agreed to inform the second

---

[10] *Oliver* v. *Hinton* [1899] 2 Ch. 264 at 268.
[11] *Hewitt* v. *Loosemore* (1851) 9 Hare 449.
[12] *Agra Bank Ltd.* v. *Barry* (1874) L.R. 7 H.L. 135.
[13] *Hewitt* v. *Loosemore, supra; Oliver* v. *Hinton* [1899] 2 Ch. 264; see *post*, p. 481.
[14] *Oliver* v. *Hinton, supra.*
[15] *Rice* v. *Rice* (1853) 2 Drew. 73.
[16] *Farrand* v. *Yorkshire Banking Co.* (1888) 40 Ch.D. 182.
[17] See *Rimmer* v. *Webster* [1902] 2 Ch. 163; *Taylor* v. *Russell* [1902] A.C. 244.
[18] *Peter* v. *Russell* (1716) Gilb.Eq. 122.
[19] *Dixon* v. *Muckleston* (1872) 8 Ch.App. 155 at 160.
[20] *Rimmer* v. *Webster* [1902] 2 Ch. 163.

mortgagee of the first mortgage, or had agreed to borrow only a limited amount which in fact he exceeded.[21] Once the mortgagee clothes the mortgagor with apparent authority to deal with the property freely, he cannot afterwards claim the protection of any undisclosed limits set to this authority.

(3) GROSS NEGLIGENCE IN RELATION TO THE TITLE DEEDS. If the legal mortgagee is grossly negligent in failing to obtain the title deeds, he is postponed to a subsequent equitable mortgagee who exercises due diligence. Failure to ask for the deeds at all would postpone a legal mortgagee[22]; it is otherwise if he inquires for them and is given a reasonable excuse.[23]

If the legal mortgagee obtains the deeds, it appears that no amount of carelessness in failing to keep them in safe custody will postpone him, as where the deeds were kept in a safe to which the mortgagor had a key as manager working for the mortgagee.[24] But this seems questionable.[25]

2. Neither mortgage protected by a deposit of deeds. Where neither mortgage is protected by a deposit of title deeds, priority is determined by the Law of Property Act 1925 and the Land Charges Act 1972, subject to any question that may arise as to loss of priority.[26] The two statutes speak with united voice in some cases and discordant voices in others, depending on the order in which the competing mortgages have been made and registered.

(a) *Concord*. No difficulty arises if the first mortgage is duly registered before the second is made. Even if the first is equitable and the second legal, the first prevails, for section 97 of the Law of Property Act 1925 expressly provides that they shall rank in order of registration, and the provision that registration amounts to notice prevents the legal mortgagee from claiming to be a purchaser without notice. Nor is there any difficulty if neither mortgage is registered. Even if the first mortgage is legal and the second equitable, under section 4(5) of the Land Charges Act 1972 the first is void against the second for want of registration, and so the second has priority. Indeed, if there are several successive registrable mortgages, none of which has been registered, the priority accorded by the date of creation will be reversed, for the last will rank first and so on.

(b) *Discord*. The difficult case is where the first mortgage was registered after the creation of the second mortgage. For example:

January 1	A grants a mortgage to X
February 2	A grants a mortgage to Y
March 3	X registers
March 4	Y registers

---

[21] *Perry Herrick* v. *Attwood* (1857) 2 De G. & J. 21.
[22] *Walker* v. *Linom* [1907] 2 Ch. 104; and see *Colyer* v. *Finch* (1856) 5 H.L.C. 905.
[23] *Manners* v. *Mew* (1885) 29 Ch.D. 725.
[24] *Northern Counties, etc. Insurance Co.* v. *Whipp* (1884) 26 Ch.D. 482.
[25] M. & W. 989.
[26] *Supra.*

In such a case, the order according to section 97 is X, Y; according to section 4(5) it is Y, X, for X's mortgage is void against Y. It is not clear which section will prevail. In favour of section 97, the chief point is that it is expressly dealing with the priority of mortgages, whereas section 4(5) makes unregistered mortgages void against subsequent mortgages only by virtue of the provision that "purchaser" includes a mortgagee.[27] On the other hand, the provision in section 4(5) that an unregistered land charge is void against a subsequent purchaser makes it hard to see how the registration of X's mortgage can give priority to something which, as regards Y, has no existence.[28] The problem still awaits solution; probably section 4(5) will prevail, since Y will have been induced to lend his money by the fact that no earlier charge appeared to exist and X could easily have protected himself by speedier registration.[29] Even more complicated problems can be constructed, including cases of circularity, as where X has priority over Y who has priority over Z who has priority over X; but these need not be discussed here.[30]

(c) *Priority notices and official searches.* At the beginning of 1926, there was the difficulty that it was physically impossible to register a land charge the instant after it had been created; thus there was a dangerous gap between the creation of a mortgage and its registration. Further, even if a search for prior incumbrances was made, the mortgagee could not be sure that no incumbrance had been registered between the time of his search and the completion of the mortgage. These difficulties have been met by the devices of the priority notice and the official search, which have been dealt with earlier.[31]

3. First but not second mortgage protected by a deposit of deeds. In this case, the first mortgage, by taking its priority from the date of its creation, will normally have priority over the second mortgage.

4. Second but not first mortgage protected by a deposit of deeds. Here, sections 4(5) and 97 work in harmony. If the first mortgage is registered before the second is made, the first ranks for priority "according to its date of registration" (s.97), *i.e.* prior to the second mortgage, and section 4(5) has no application. If the first mortgage is not registered when the second mortgage is made, the first mortgage is void against the second for want of registration; and even if it is subsequently registered, it takes priority from the date of registration.

5. Summary

(a) *Deposit of deeds.* A mortgage protected by a deposit of deeds ranks

---

[27] L.P.A. 1925, s.205(1)(xxi).
[28] See *Kitney* v. *M.E.P.C. Ltd.* [1977] 1 W.L.R. 981.
[29] See M. & W. 1000; Fairest, *Mortgages*, (2nd ed.), pp. 146, 147.
[30] See M. & W. 1001, 1002; (1968) 32 Conv. 325 (W.A. Lee).
[31] *Ante*, p. 89.

according to the date on which it was created. The mortgagee may lose priority—

(i) by fraud, estoppel or gross negligence; or
(ii) if his mortgage is equitable, by a legal mortgage being made to a mortgagee for value without notice.

(b) *No deposit of deeds.* A mortgage not protected by deposit of deeds should be protected by registration. If the mortgagee fails to do this, he will not, it seems, be protected against a subsequent mortgagee (s.4(5)), unless, perhaps, he registers before him (s.97). If he does register he will be protected against all mortgages made thereafter.

6. Beneficial co-ownership. Apart from questions of priority between competing mortgagees, questions often occur as to whether a mortgagee is bound by adverse interests in the land. One particular instance of this arises where there is beneficial co-ownership, especially of a house. Often (but not always[32]) the question is between a married couple and the mortgagee.

Where H and W hold as trustees for sale, any proper mortgage by them will overreach the beneficial interests under the trust, usually their own, and so those interests will not concern the mortgagee.[33] But if W's signature to the mortgage has been obtained by H's misrepresentation or undue influence, the mortgagee may be unable to enforce the mortgage against her. There are three cases in which the mortgagee will be bound by H's conduct.

First, if when the mortgage is executed the mortgagee has actual or constructive notice that H has procured its execution by undue influence, W will not be bound by it if it is to her disadvantage.[34] Second, if the mortgagee entrusts H with the task of obtaining W's signature to the mortgage deed, H will be treated as being in some sense the mortgagee's agent, and so the mortgagee will be bound by his conduct.[35] An alternative and perhaps preferable view, rejecting agency, is that leaving H to obtain W's signature is an insufficient means of taking proper steps to ensure that W gets the explanation and advice that is required if she is to be held liable on the mortgage, even though there is no positive duty to take those steps.[36]

The third case is primarily that of married women, as being persons likely to be influenced by their husbands and to have some degree of reliance on them; but it also extends to other relationships (a "protected class") where a

---

[32] See, *e.g. Coldunell Ltd.* v. *Gallon* [1986] Q.B. 1184 (parents and son); *Bank of Baroda* v. *Shah* [1988] 3 All E.R. 24 (brother and sister); *Equity & Law Home Loans Ltd.* v. *Prestidge* [1992] 1 W.L.R. 137 (cohabitants).

[33] *City of London B.S.* v. *Flegg* [1988] A.C. 54; *ante*, p. 261.

[34] *Bank of Credit and Commerce International S.A.* v. *Aboody* [1990] 1 K.B. 923.

[35] *Kings North Trust Ltd.* v. *Bell* [1986] 1 W.L.R. 119 (misrepresentation); *Avon Finance Co. Ltd.* v. *Bridger* [1985] 2 All E.R. 281 and *Barclays Bank Plc.* v. *Kennedy* (1988) 58 P. & C.R. 221 (undue influence). Contrast *Midland Bank Plc.* v. *Perry* (1987) 56 P. & C.R. 202 (agency not established).

[36] *Barclays Bank Plc.* v. *O'Brien* [1992] *The Times* June 3, collecting and analysing most of the cases, though not *Lloyds Bank Plc.* v. *Egremont* [1990] 2 F.L.R. 351.

likelihood of influence and reliance is known to the mortgagee.[37] In such cases, quite apart from notice or agency, the wife's liability to the mortgagee will not exceed what she thought it to be (*e.g.* as being limited to £60,000 rather than unlimited) unless the mortgagee took reasonable steps to ensure that she understood the transaction, as by explaining it to her, or advising her (preferably in writing) to take independent advice.[37a]

Apart from co-ownership, where the legal estate is vested in H alone but W has an equitable interest in the land, a mortgagee will be bound by W's interest unless he lent the money without notice of W's rights; and mortgagees must be alert to the possible existence of such rights.[38] But where W knew that H could not buy the house without the aid of a mortgage, she will be taken to have authorised the mortgage, and so it will take priority over her beneficial interest.[39] Further, if without W's knowledge H replaces the mortgage by a larger mortgage, the new mortgagees will have priority over W to the extent of the original mortgage, but no further.[39a]

B. Mortgages of an Equitable Interest

The priority of mortgages of an equitable interest in any property, whether real or personal, depends on the rule in *Dearle* v. *Hall*.[40] Before 1926, the rule applied only to mortgages of an equitable interest in pure personalty, though this included an interest under a trust for sale of land[41]; but the Law of Property Act 1925[42] extended it to mortgages of equitable interests in land as well. The basic provision of the rule is that the priority of competing mortgages depends on the order in which notice of them is received by the trustees or other legal owner; but this is subject to the important qualification that a mortgagee who, when lending his money, has notice of a prior mortgage cannot gain priority over it by giving notice first.

Various reasons for the rule have been given, including the consideration that as between two equally innocent incumbrancers, priority should be accorded to the one who, by giving notice, had prevented the mortgagor from representing that he was the unincumbered owner of the interest mortgaged, and so deceiving third parties.[43] Whatever the reasons, the rule is now a rigid rule.[44] As amended by the Law of Property Act 1925, the rule falls under the following heads.

[37] *Avon Finance Co. Ltd.* v. *Bridger, supra; Barclays Bank Plc.* v. *O'Brien, supra,* which requires further consideration when fully reported.
[37a] *Barclays Bank Ltd.* v. *O'Brien, supra.*
[38] *Kingsnorth Finance Co. Ltd.* v. *Tizard* [1986] 1 W.L.R. 783; and see *ante,* p. 61.
[39] *Bristol and West B.S.* v. *Henning* [1985] 1 W.L.R. 778; *Paddington B.S.* v. *Mendelsohn* (1985) 50 P. & C.R. 244.
[39a] *Equity & Law Home Loans Ltd.* v. *Prestidge* [1992] 1 W.L.R. 137, criticised at [1992] Conv. 206 (M.P. Thompson).
[40] (1828) 3 Russ. 1.
[41] *Lee* v. *Howlett* (1856) 2 K. & J. 531.
[42] s.137(1).
[43] See *Ward* v. *Duncombe* [1893] A.C. 369 at 392.
[44] See *Re Dallas* [1904] 2 Ch. 385.

1. No notice of prior mortgage. A mortgagee who had notice of a prior mortgage when he lent his money cannot gain priority over it by giving notice first[45]; for he has not been prejudiced by the failure of the prior mortgagee to give notice and so it would be inequitable to give him priority. But if when he lent his money he had no notice of a prior mortgage, notice of it when he gives his notice is immaterial[46]; indeed, it is just what will impel him to give notice.[47]

2. Priority depends on notice being received, not given. Priority depends on the order in which notice is received by the trustees or other legal owner, and not on whether or when the mortgagees gave notice. Where notices are received simultaneously, the mortgages rank in the order of their creation, as where competing notices are delivered to a bank, one late at night and the other as soon as it opens the next day.[48] Notice from any reliable source suffices[49]; indeed, one first mortgagee kept his priority by virtue of notice of the mortgage given not by him but by a letter sent to the trustee by the second mortgagee before giving his own notice.[50]

3. Notice must be in writing. No notice given or received after 1925 will affect priorities unless it is in writing.[51] Before 1926, there was no such requirement, and clear and distinct oral notice sufficed,[52] though not something said in casual conversation.[53] Notice received through reading a notice in a newspaper sufficed to preserve priority against a subsequent mortgagee who then gave express notice,[54] though it would not gain priority for a later mortgage over an earlier mortgage[55]: less is required to preserve priority than to gain it. Whether such notice is effective after 1925 is doubtful, for although it is in writing it has not been "served."[56]

4. Service of notice

(a) *Persons to be served*. The persons "to be served" with notice are[57]—

   (i) in the case of settled land, the trustees of the settlement;
   (ii) in the case of a trust for sale, the trustees for sale; and
   (iii) in the case of any other land, the estate owner of the land affected.

The person to be served is normally the owner of the legal estate, except in

---

[45] *Re Holmes* (1885) 29 Ch.D. 786.
[46] *Mutual Life Assurance Society* v. *Langley* (1886) 32 Ch.D. 460.
[47] See *post*, p. 488.
[48] *Calisher* v. *Forbes* (1871) 7 Ch.App. 109.
[49] *Re Worcester* (1868) 3 Ch.App. 555.
[50] *Ipswich Permanent Money Club Ltd.* v. *Arthy* [1920] 2 Ch. 257.
[51] L.P.A. 1925, s.137(3).
[52] *Re Worcester* (1868) 3 Ch.App. 555.
[53] *Re Tichener* (1865) 35 Beav. 317.
[54] *Lloyd* v. *Banks* (1868) 3 Ch.App. 488.
[55] *Arden* v. *Arden* (1885) 29 Ch.D. 702.
[56] L.P.A. 1925, s.137(2).
[57] *Ibid.*

the case of settled land; notice to the tenant for life might well be no
protection, as where it is his life interest that is being mortgaged. No special
provision has been made for any other cases, and so in these notice must be
given to the legal owner, as before 1926.

(b) *Notice should be given to all the trustees.* It has always been advisable to
give notice to all the trustees for the following reasons.

  (i) Notice given to all the existing trustees remains effective even though
      they all retire or die without communicating the notice to their
      successors.[58]
 (ii) Notice given to one of several trustees is effective against all incum-
      brances created during his trusteeship, and remains effective despite
      his death or retirement.[58a]
(iii) On the other hand, notice given to one of several trustees is not
      effective against incumbrancers who advance money after the death
      or retirement of that trustee without having communicated the notice
      to one or more of the continuing trustees.[59]
 (iv) If the mortgagor is a trustee, priorities will not be affected by the
      notice of the mortgage that he has, for this will afford no protection to
      subsequent mortgages.[60] But if the mortgagee is a trustee, the notice
      of the mortgage that he has will affect priorities, for to protect his
      mortgage he will readily disclose its existence to any prospective
      incumbrancers.[61]

(c) *Notice by indorsement.* If for any reason a valid notice cannot be served
(*e.g.* where there are no trustees), or can be served only at unreasonable cost
or delay, a purchaser may require that a memorandum be indorsed on or
permanently annexed to the instrument creating the trust, and this has the
same effect as notice to the trustees. In the case of settled land, the trust
instrument, and in the case of a trust for sale, the instrument creating the
equitable interest, is the document to be used for this purpose.[62]

(d) *Notice to trust corporation.* The instrument creating the trust, the
trustees or the court may nominate a trust corporation to receive notices
instead of the trustees. In such cases, only notice to the trust corporation
affects priority; notice to the trustees has no effect until they deliver it to the
trust corporation, which they are bound to do forthwith. Provision is made
for the indorsement of notice of the appointment on the instrument upon
which notices may be indorsed, for the keeping of a register of notices, for
the inspection of the register, for the answering of inquiries and for the
payment of fees therefor.[63] In practice, little use is made of these provisions.

[58] *Re Wasdale* [1899] 1 Ch. 163.
[58a] *Ward* v. *Duncombe* [1893] A.C. 369.
[59] *Re Phillips' Trusts* [1903] 1 Ch. 183.
[60] *Lloyds Bank* v. *Pearson* [1901] 1 Ch. 865.
[61] *Browne* v. *Savage* (1859) 4 Drew. 635.
[62] L.P.A. 1925, s.137(4), (5).
[63] *Ibid.* s.138.

(e) *Production of notices*. Before 1926, the trustees were not bound to answer inquiries either by the beneficiaries or by a prospective mortgagee as to the extent to which a beneficiary's share was incumbered: "it is no part of the duty of a trustee to assist his *cestui que trust* in selling or mortgaging his beneficial interest and in squandering or anticipating his fortune."[64] But after 1925, on the application of any person interested in the equitable interest, the trustees must now produce any notices served on them or their predecessors.[65]

(f) *Distribution*. In addition to securing priority, notice to the trustees safeguards the mortgagee by ensuring that his claims will not be disregarded when the funds are distributed. Trustees are not liable if they distribute the trust funds to the prejudice of a mortgagee of whom they are unaware.[66]

C. Tacking

Tacking is a process whereby the rules relating to priorities can be modified, both for realty and for personalty. The process consists of allowing a mortgagee with inferior priority to "tack" (or attach) his mortgage to a mortgage with superior priority and thus to give it priority over any intervening mortgages. Before 1926, there were two forms of tacking:

(i) The *tabula in naufragio* ("the plank in the shipwreck"); and
(ii) The tacking of further advances.

After 1925, the first form of tacking no longer applies to mortgages. But the wider principle of which it forms part remains in force,[67] and so the doctrine will be considered here, before turning to the tacking of further advances.

I. THE TABULA IN NAUFRAGIO

1. The doctrine. If an equitable mortgagee lent money without notice of a prior equitable mortgage, he could gain priority over it if he subsequently acquired a legal estate in the land with priority over it.[68] This was so because, apart from the order of creation, the equities between the mortgagees were equal, and so the holder of a legal estate prevailed[69]; the subsequent mortgagee could tack his mortgage to the legal estate. Thus if A mortgaged his property to X by a legal mortgage and then to Y and Z by successive equitable mortgages, Z's mortgage would take priority over Y's if Z bought X's mortgage, provided Z had no notice of Y's mortgage when he advanced his money.[70] X's legal mortgage was the plank in the shipwreck, and whichever of Y and Z acquired it had the better chance of being saved if there was not enough money to pay both.

---

[64] *Low* v. *Bouverie* [1891] 3 Ch. 82 at 99, *per* Lindley L.J.
[65] L.P.A. 1925, s.137(8); and see subs. (9).
[66] *Phipps* v. *Lovegrove* (1873) L.R. 16 Eq. 80.
[67] See *post*, p. 488.
[68] *Marsh* v. *Lee* (1671) 2 Ventr. 337.
[69] *Wortley* v. *Birkhead* (1754) 2 Ves.Sen. 571 at 574.
[70] *Brace* v. *Duchess of Marlborough* (1728) 2 P.Wms. 491.

2. Notice. Although a mortgagee could not tack if he had notice of the prior equitable mortgage when he lent the money,[71] subsequent notice was no bar.[72] Indeed, if he had notice when he acquired the legal estate, that was "the very occasion, that shows the necessity of it."[73]

3. Legal estate. Normally the mortgagee seeking to tack actually took a transfer of the legal estate; but this was not essential, for he could tack if he had the best right to call for the legal estate,[74] as where the legal estate was held on trust for him. Further, if the mortgagee acquired a legal estate, it was not necessary that it should be the estate mortgaged; a mere term of years sufficed.[75] And even a legal estate created subsequently to the mortgage against which tacking was to be effected might suffice.[76] But a legal estate could not be used to alter priorities if it was acquired with notice that the conveyance was a breach of trust, for this made the mortgagee a trustee himself.[77]

4. Later mortgage. Although tacking under this head usually took place when a later mortgagee acquired a legal estate, the doctrine applied equally to a legal mortgagee who acquired a later mortgage without notice of an intervening incumbrancer.[78]

5. Abolition. Without prejudice to any priority gained before 1926, tacking by means of the *tabula in naufragio* was abolished at the end of 1925.[79] This, however, is confined to competing mortgages,[80] and does not affect the wider principle whereby priority for equitable interests may be obtained by acquiring a legal estate. Thus an equitable mortgagee may obtain priority over a prior unregistered[81] option to purchase the land if he obtains a legal charge on the land under a power in the mortgage, unless he had notice of the option when he lent the money.[82]

II. TACKING OF FURTHER ADVANCES

After lending the money, a mortgagee may make further advances to the mortgagor on the security of the same property. There are three cases in

---

[71] *Lacey* v. *Ingle* (1847) 2 Ph. 413.
[72] *Taylor* v. *Russell* [1892] A.C. 244 at 259.
[73] *Wortley* v. *Birkhead* (1754) 2 Ves.Sen. 571 at 574, *per* Lord Hardwicke L.C.; and see *ante*, p. 485.
[74] *Wilkes* v. *Bodington* (1707) 2 Vern. 599 at 600.
[75] *Willoughby* v. *Willoughby* (1756) 1 T.R. 763.
[76] *Cooke* v. *Wilton* (1860) 29 Beav. 100.
[77] *Saunders* v. *Dehew* (1692) 2 Vern. 271; *Taylor* v. *London and County Banking Co.* [1901] 2 Ch. 231 at 256.
[78] *Morret* v. *Paske* (1740) 2 Atk. 52 at 53.
[79] L.P.A. 1925, s.94(3).
[80] *McCarthy & Stone Ltd.* v. *Julian S. Hodge & Co. Ltd.* [1971] 1 W.L.R. 1547.
[81] Had the mortgage been legal, not equitable, the option would have been void against it for want of registration: *ante*, pp. 79, 88.
[82] *McCarthy & Stone Ltd.* v. *Julian S. Hodge & Co. Ltd.*, *supra*, where there was held to be notice. See also [1972A] C.L.J. 34 (P.B. Fairest).

which the mortgagee can tack his further advance to his original mortgage and claim priority over an intervening incumbrancer for both loans.[83] It is immaterial whether or not the prior mortgage was made expressly for securing further advances, or whether the subsequent mortgage is legal or equitable.[84]

1. Agreement of intervening incumbrancer. The mortgagee can tack if the intervening incumbrancer agrees. Building estates sometimes provide examples of this: the owner requires more money for further building on his estate, thereby making it a better security. The second mortgagee, not wishing to lend any more money, may agree to the first mortgagee making a further advance to be expended on further building and to rank in priority to the second mortgage.

2. No notice of intervening incumbrance. Any mortgagee, whether legal or equitable, may tack a further advance if it was made without notice of the intervening mortgage. Where the intervening mortgage is protected by a deposit of deeds and is thus not registrable, the normal rules as to notice operate. If the mortgage is not protected in this way and so is registrable, the rule that registration amounts to notice will apply and thus protect it if it is registered. In one case, however, registration is not deemed to be notice; if the prior mortgage was made expressly for securing further advances, such as on a current account (*e.g.* an overdraft at a bank, where the debt is increased and decreased as sums are drawn out or paid in), registration alone is not deemed to be notice, unless the intervening mortgage was registered when the last search was made by the mortgagee.[85] This applies to a spouse's right of occupation which is registered after a mortgage has been made.[86]

An example may make this clearer. Mortgages have been made to A (who took the deeds) and B, in that order, and A has made further advances. If when A made his further advances he had actual, constructive or imputed notice of B's mortgage, he cannot tack under this head even if his mortgage, without obliging him to make further advances, was stated to be security for any further advances he might choose to make. If he had no such notice of B's mortgage when he made his further advances, but B's mortgage was registered at that time, then if A's mortgage is silent as to further advances, the registration amounts to notice and prevents A from tacking. But if A's mortgage was expressed to be security for any further advances that he might make, the registration will not prevent him from tacking, and thus he need not search before making each further advance.

This points a practical moral. Even if a second mortgage has been duly

[83] L.P.A. 1925, s.94(1).
[84] *Ibid.*
[85] *Ibid.* s.94(2).
[86] Matrimonial Homes Act 1983, s.2(10). For the Act, see *ante*, p. 81.

registered, the mortgagee should give express notice of his mortgage to the first mortgagee, for this—

(i) prevents tacking under this head; and
(ii) compels the first mortgagee to hand over the deeds to him when the first mortgage is discharged.[87]

3. Obligation to make further advance. A further advance may be tacked if the prior mortgage imposes an obligation on the mortgagee to make it. In this case, not even express notice will prevent tacking.[88] If in return for a mortgage a bank binds itself to honour a customer's cheques up to an overdraft of £10,000 there is no question of the bank having to search before honouring each cheque, for not even express notice will prevent the bank from tacking each further advance.

Sect. 2. Registered Land

A. *Mortgages of a Legal Estate*

1. Categories. Mortgages of a legal estate in registered land are either registered charges or else minor interests.[89] For priorities, there are three main categories.

(a) *Registered charges*. Subject to any entry on the register,[90] registered charges rank in the order in which they are entered on the register, irrespective of the order of creation.[91] This rule applies only to registered charges, and not to minor interests.[92]

(b) *Protected minor interests*. A minor interest protected by an entry on the register or by a deposit of the land certificate will take priority over a subsequent mortgage, whether it is a registered charge or a minor interest.[93]

(c) *Unprotected minor interests*. Minor interests take effect as equitable interests,[94] and so as between competing minor interests the ordinary equitable rule applies. Thus the earlier minor interest will take priority over the later,[95] even if the later is protected by a notice or caution and the earlier is not.[96] But this priority may be displaced by fraud, estoppel or gross negligence.[97] By omitting to follow the normal practice of protecting the minor

---

[87] *Ante*, p. 460.
[88] L.P.A. 1925, s.94(1)(c), reversing *West* v. *Williams* [1899] 1 Ch. 132.
[89] See *ante*, pp. 447, 448.
[90] See Ruoff & Roper 23–39.
[91] L.R.A. 1925, s.29.
[92] Ruoff & Roper 8–09.
[93] *Parkash* v. *Irani Finance Ltd.* [1970] Ch. 101; Hayton 151–153.
[94] L.R.A. 1925, s.2(1); and see *ante*, p. 109.
[95] *Barclays Bank Ltd.* v. *Taylor* [1974] Ch. 137.
[96] *The Mortgage Corporation Ltd.* v. *Nationwide Credit Corporation Ltd.* [1992] *The Times* July 27.
[97] See *Abigail* v. *Lapin* [1934] A.C. 491; *Butler* v. *Fairclough* (1917) 23 C.L.R. 78; and see *ante*, pp. 480, 481.

interest, the earlier mortgagee enables the mortgagor to represent the land as being unincumbered, and so he should be precluded from asserting his natural priority against an innocent later mortgagee.[98] Further, statute gives a registered charge priority over even a prior minor interest which has not been protected by entry on the register or a deposit of the land certificate.[98a]

2. Deposit of the land certificate. The proprietor of registered land may create a lien on it by a deposit of the land certificate; and similarly for the proprietor of a registered charge.[99] Such a deposit is distinct from a deposit that is merely ancillary to a mortgage created by a document and creates no independent charge or lien.[1] Subject to any overriding interests and to any interests protected on the register at the date of the deposit, the lien is equivalent to a lien created by deposit of title deeds for unregistered land by a beneficial owner.[2] The inference seems to be that the lien is free from prior minor interests that were not protected on the register at the time of the deposit,[3] so that the lien will take priority over all unprotected mortgages, even if they were created before the deposit.[4]

B. Mortgages of an Equitable Interest

For mortgages of an equitable interest, the rule in *Dearle* v. *Hall*[5] now applies to registered land in the same way as it applies to unregistered land.[6] Formerly there was a Minor Interests Index in which entries were made in lieu of giving notice under the rule, but this has been abolished.[7]

C. Tacking

Provision for the tacking of further advances has been made only in the case of registered charges.[8] There are two categories.

1. Obligatory. Where the proprietor of a registered charge is under an obligation, noted on the register, to make a further advance, any subsequent registered charge will take effect subject to any such further advance.[9]

2. Optional. Where there is no obligation to make further advances but the registered charge is made for securing any further advances that may be

---

[98] Hayton 149.
[98a] L.R.A. 1925, ss.19(2), 20(1), 22(2), 23(1).
[99] *Ibid.* s.66.
[1] See *Re White Rose Cottage* [1964] Ch. 483 at 490, 491; in C.A. [1965] Ch. 941.
[2] L.R.A. 1925, s.66.
[3] See Hayton, p. 143.
[4] For difficulties, and for possible circularity (*ante*, p. 482), see Hayton 143, 153, 154, 160.
[5] (1828) 3 Russ. 1; *ante*, p. 484.
[6] Land Registration Act 1986, s.5(1); Ruoff & Roper 8–11, 12.
[7] *Ibid.*
[8] L.R.A. 1925, s.30.
[9] *Ibid.* s.30(3).

made, then before making any entry which would prejudicially affect the priority of any further advances, the registrar must give notice of it to the registered proprietor of the charge.[10] The entry will then not affect any further advance unless it is made after the notice should have been received in due course of post.[11] If in such cases the proprietor of the registered charge suffers any loss by reason of any failure by the registrar or the Post Office he is entitled to an indemnity as if a mistake had occurred in the register.[12]

[10] *Ibid.* s.30(1).
[11] *Ibid.*
[12] *Ibid.* s.30(2); see *ante*, p. 114.

CHAPTER 14

LIMITATION

THE fundamental principle of the Limitation Act 1980, which consolidates earlier legislation,[1] is that unless claims are enforced within a limited time, they become barred. It is more important that long and undisturbed possession of land should be protected, even if initially it was wrongful, than that the law should lend its aid to the enforcement of stale claims.

1. Limitation and prescription. Limitation must be distinguished from prescription.[2] Two differences may be mentioned.

(a) *Subject-matter.* Limitation often concerns the ownership of the land itself, whereas prescription is directed to the acquisition of easements and profits over the land of another.

(b) *Limitation negative.* Prescription operates positively so as to presume the grant of an easement or profit by the owner of the land; title is thus derived from him. Limitation, on the other hand, operates negatively so as to bar a claim to the land, thus leaving some other claimant to the land free from the competing claim. Limitation may operate differentially, barring one person but not another. Thus it may bar a tenant under a lease but not his landlord.

2. Possession as the basis of title. In English law, the basis of title to land is possession. Possession of land by itself gives a title to the land good against the whole world except a person with a better right to possession.[3] If X takes possession of A's land, X has a title which will avail against all save A; a title acquired by wrong is still a title. X has a fee simple, and so has A; but all titles are relative, and so although X's fee is good, A's is better.[4] If, however, A fails to take steps to recover the land in due time, his claim will be barred by limitation, and X's fee, freed from the superior claims of A's fee, will be good against all the world.

3. Elements of limitation. In every case of limitation, three points must be considered, namely—

(1) The length of the period;
(2) When time starts to run; and

---

[1] The Limitation Act 1939 as affecting land was amended by the Limitation Amendment Act 1980, and both were repealed and replaced by the present Act.
[2] *Ante*, pp. 386 *et seq.* See generally *Buckinghamshire C.C.* v. *Moran* [1990] Ch. 623 at 644.
[3] *Asher* v. *Whitlock* (1865) L.R. 1 Q.B. 1.
[4] See *Leach* v. *Jay* (1878) 9 Ch.D. 42 at 44, 45; *Ocean Estates Ltd.* v. *Pinder* [1969] 2 A.C. 19 at 24, 25.

(3) The effect of the elapse of time.

These will be taken in turn.

Part 1

THE LENGTH OF THE PERIOD

1. The main periods. There are two main periods of limitation:

(a) *Six years*: a period of six years for actions on simple contracts (*e.g.* for money lent without security) or claims for rent, and actions in tort.[5]

(b) *Twelve years*: a period of 12 years for the recovery of land or of money charged on land, as by a mortgage.[6] Under the Real Property Limitation Act 1833 the period was 20 years, but the Real Property Limitation Act 1874 reduced it to 12. Twelve years is also now the period for actions for money due upon a covenant, in place of the former period of 20 years.

2. Special provisions. There are also certain special provisions.

(a) *Crown land.* In the case of Crown land the period is now 30 years.[7] Formerly it was 60 years, a period which has been retained in the one case of foreshore owned by the Crown.[8]

(b) *Charitable corporation sole.* A spiritual or eleemosynary (*i.e.* charitable) corporation sole, such as a bishop or the master of a hospital, is barred after 30 years.[9]

Part 2

THE RUNNING OF TIME

The running of time falls under three heads: first, when time begins to run; second, what will postpone this date; and third, what will start time running afresh. In general,[10] once time has begun to run, it runs continuously.[11]

---

[5] Limitation Act 1980, ss.2, 5, 19. Claims in tort are subject to the Latent Damage Act 1986; and three years is the normal period for personal injuries: s.11.
[6] Limitation Act 1980, ss.15, 20.
[7] *Ibid.* s.15(1), Sched. 1, para. 10.
[8] *Ibid.* para. 11.
[9] *Ibid.* para. 10.
[10] Time is suspended during any period in which a party is an enemy or is detained in enemy territory: Limitation (Enemies and War Prisoners) Act 1945.
[11] *Bowring-Hanbury's Trustee* v. *Bowring-Hanbury* [1943] Ch. 104.

Sect. 1. When Time Begins to Run

In the case of actions for the recovery of land or capital sums charged on land, time begins to run in accordance with the following rules.

1. Owner entitled in possession. Time will begin to run against an owner of land who is entitled in possession only where—

(1) either he has been dispossessed or he has discontinued his possession, and also

(2) adverse possession of the land has been taken by some other person.[12]

(a) *Dispossession or discontinuance.* "Dispossessed" means that the owner has been driven out of possession by another,[13] though there may be dispossession even if the owner knows nothing of it.[14] "Discontinued" simply means that the owner has abandoned his possession,[15] though mere non-user will not necessarily be abandonment.[16] Neither dispossession nor discontinuance alone will start time running: there must be adverse possession as well, and it is this which is of paramount importance.[17]

(b) *Adverse possession.* Adverse possession is a somewhat complex concept. It depends on the squatter having possession of the land in fact, and also on his having the necessary *animus possidendi*; and in some cases these requirements may be affected by the owner's intended use for the land.

(1) POSSESSION. The squatter must establish that he has a degree of physical control of the land which amounts to possession in fact.[18] The nature of the requisite acts will vary with the nature of the land: they will not be the same for a house, a narrow strip of land, open fields, moorlands or a swamp.[19] For open land, "enclosure is the strongest possible evidence of adverse possession, but it is not indispensable,"[20] as where a fence or gates are erected merely in order to prevent invasions by the public.[21] Relatively trivial acts such as using the land for children to play on, or for tethering ponies or grazing goats will usually be insufficient,[22] though when land is virtually useless save for shooting, shooting over it may suffice.[23] In many

---

[12] Limitation Act 1980, Sched. 1, paras. 1, 8.
[13] *Rains* v. *Buxton* (1880) 14 Ch.D. 537 at 539.
[14] *Powell* v. *McFarlane* (1977) 38 P. & C.R. 452 at 480.
[15] *Rimington* v. *Cannon* (1853) 12 C.B. 18 at 33.
[16] *Tecbild Ltd.* v. *Chamberlain* (1969) 20 P. & C.R. 633.
[17] *Buckinghamshire C.C.* v. *Moran* [1990] Ch. 623 at 645.
[18] *Buckinghamshire C.C.* v. *Moran* [1990] Ch. 623.
[19] See *West Bank Estates Ltd.* v. *Arthur* [1967] 1 A.C. 665; *Treloar* v. *Nute* [1976] 1 W.L.R. 1295 at 1302.
[20] *Seddon* v. *Smith* (1877) 36 L.T. 168 at 169, *per* Cockburn C.J.; *Buckinghamshire C.C.* v. *Moran, supra.*
[21] *Littledale* v. *Liverpool Corporation* [1900] 1 Ch. 19; *George Wimpey & Co. Ltd.* v. *Sohn* [1967] Ch. 487.
[22] *Tecbild Ltd.* v. *Chamberlain* (1969) 20 P. & C.R. 633; *Boosey* v. *Davis* (1987) 55 P. & C.R. 83.
[23] *Red House Farms (Thorndon) Ltd.* v. *Catchpole* [1977] E.G.D. 798.

cases, in the nature of things, adverse possession cannot be continuous from day to day.[24] Acts may suffice even though they do not inconvenience or otherwise affect the owner[25]; and adverse possession may be subterranean, *e.g.* of a cellar.[26]

(2) "ADVERSE." Possession is "adverse" only if the squatter has an *animus possidendi*, intending to possess the land to the exclusion of all other persons, including the owner[27]; no intention to own or acquire ownership of the land is needed.[28] An intermittent though persistent trespasser who does not seek to dispossess the owner is not in adverse possession.[29] Nor is possession adverse if it is enjoyed under a contract with the owner,[30] or under a licence granted by him,[31] even if the licensee, without rejecting it, never in terms accepted it.[32] But possession will not cease to be adverse merely because the owner, in ignorance of his title, accepts a tenancy from the squatter.[33]

(3) OWNER'S INTENDED USE. Where the owner has no present use for the land, even very substantial acts of possession were formerly not accepted as constituting adverse possession if they did not interfere with the owner's intended future use of the land.[34] Thus in the circumstances of the case, using a strip of land as a dump for foundry refuse,[35] or cultivating the land and then erecting sheds and a fence on it for use in rearing greyhounds,[36] or using the land for farming and as part of a holiday camp,[37] have all been regarded as not constituting adverse possession as against owners whose respective intentions were to dedicate the strip as a highway in the future, to develop the land when that became possible, or to use the land as the site of a garage fronting on to a road if the road was ever constructed.

Today, these cases are not accepted as establishing any separate rule based on the owner's intention. Instead, they are explained in relation to the squatter. In such cases the court will readily treat the squatter's acts either as not manifesting a sufficient *animus possidendi* or else as not showing a sufficient degree of exclusive occupation to amount to possession.[38] In particular, if the squatter knows of the owner's future intentions for unbuilt land, that knowledge may prevent acts of the squatter that are not inconsis-

---

[24] *Bligh* v. *Martin* [1968] 1 W.L.R. 804 at 811.
[25] *Treloar* v. *Nute*, *supra*.
[26] *Rains* v. *Buxton* (1880) 14 Ch.D. 537.
[27] *Buckinghamshire C.C.* v. *Moran* [1990] Ch. 623.
[28] *Ibid.*
[29] *Powell* v. *McFarlane* (1977) 38 P. & C.R. 452 at 480.
[30] *Hyde* v. *Pearce* [1982] 1 W.L.R. 560.
[31] *Hughes* v. *Griffin* [1969] 1 W.L.R. 23.
[32] *B.P. Properties Ltd.* v. *Buckler* (1987) 55 P. & C.R. 337.
[33] *Bligh* v. *Martin* [1968] 1 W.L.R. 804.
[34] *Leigh* v. *Jack* (1879) 5 Ex.D. 264.
[35] *Ibid.*
[36] *Williams Brothers Direct Supply Ltd.* v. *Raftery* [1958] 1 Q.B. 159.
[37] *Wallis's Cayton Bay Holiday Camp Ltd.* v. *Shell-Mex and B.P. Ltd.* [1975] Q.B. 94. The doctrine of implied licence in this case has now been despatched: Limitation Act 1980, Sched. 1, para. 8(4).
[38] *Buckinghamshire C.C.* v. *Moran* [1990] Ch. 623; see at p. 639.

tent with those intentions from amounting to adverse possession, unless there is very clear evidence to the contrary.[39] The mere use of vacant land until the owner needs it is a frail foundation for a possessory title.

2. Future interests. A person entitled in reversion or in remainder at the time when adverse possession is taken has alternative periods: he has 12 years from adverse possession being taken or six years from the falling of his interest into possession, whichever is the longer.[40] Thus if land is settled on A for life with remainder to B, and X dispossesses A 10 years before A dies, B has six years from A's death in which to sue; but if X had dispossessed A three years before A's death, B would have 12 years from the dispossession of A. If X had not taken adverse possession until after A's death, B's interest would no longer have been a future interest, and he would have the normal period of 12 years from the taking of adverse possession. Further, if A's interest had been an entail, then if he had been dispossessed by X, B would have been barred 12 years later; the alternative six years' period does not extend to a reversioner or remainderman whose interest was liable to be barred by the barring of a prior interest in tail.[41]

3. Leaseholds. The above provisions do not apply to a reversioner on a lease for a term of years where the tenant has been ousted. Irrespective of when the dispossession occurred, time does not run against the reversioner until the lease expires, because, until then, he has no right to possession.[42] Thus if L grants T a lease for 99 years and T is dispossessed by X, the 12 year period runs against T from the dispossession but against L only from the determination of the lease.

A tenant cannot acquire a title to the land demised against his landlord during the currency of the lease, even by prolonged failure to pay rent. There is one exception to this in the case of a lease capable of enlargement into a fee simple. If a rent not exceeding £1 per annum reserved by such a lease has not been paid for a continuous period of 20 years, five of which have elapsed since 1925, the rent ceases to be payable; neither the arrears nor any future payment can be recovered, and the lease may be enlarged into a fee simple.[43] Further, where the tenant takes possession of adjoining land of the landlord, there is a rebuttable[44] presumption that he takes it as an extension of his lease,[45] and it becomes subject to the terms of the tenancy.[46] Similarly a tenant's adverse possession of adjoining land of a third party is *prima facie* for the benefit of the landlord as well as the tenant.[47]

[39] *Ibid.* at pp. 639, 643; and see *Pulleyn* v. *Hall Aggregates (Thames Valley) Ltd.* [1992] E.G.C.S. 102.
[40] Limitation Act 1980, s.15(2), Sched. 1, para. 4.
[41] *Ibid.* ss.15(3), 38(5).
[42] *Ibid.* Sched. 1, para. 4.
[43] L.P.A. 1925, s.153; *ante*, pp. 333, 334.
[44] See *Kingsmill* v. *Millard* (1855) 11 Exch. 313 at 318, 319.
[45] *Smirk* v. *Lyndale Developments Ltd.* [1975] Ch. 317, reversed on appeal but not on this point.
[46] *J.F. Perrott & Co. Ltd.* v. *Cohen* [1951] 1 K.B. 705.
[47] *King* v. *Smith* [1950] 1 All E.R. 554.

A landlord may be barred if adverse possession is taken not of the land but of the rent from it; for if for 12 years the tenant under a lease in writing at a rent of at least £10 per annum pays the rent to some person who wrongfully claims the reversion, and no rent is subsequently paid to the landlord, this bars the landlord's right to the reversion.[48]

4. Yearly or other periodic tenants. Where there is a yearly or other periodic tenancy under a lease in writing, time runs in the tenant's favour from the determination of the tenancy. If there is no lease in writing, time runs in the tenant's favour from the end of the first year or other period of the tenancy,[49] subject to extension[50] by written acknowledgement, or by payment of rent, in which case time runs from the last receipt of rent.[51]

5. Tenants at will and at sufferance, and licensees. Time begins to run in favour of a tenant at will on the determination of his tenancy,[52] and in favour of a tenant at sufferance on the commencement of his tenancy; for he has no true tenancy,[53] but is in adverse possession. Time does not run in favour of a licensee, for he holds by the owner's consent.[54]

6. Rentcharges. In the case of a rentcharge in possession, time runs from the last payment of rent to the owner of the rentcharge.[55] Thus the owner's rights are barred—

   (i) if no rent is paid for 12 years, in which case the rentcharge is extinguished; or

  (ii) if the rent is paid to a stranger for 12 years, in which case the rentcharge remains enforceable against the land but the former owner's claim to it is extinguished in favour of the stranger.

Similar rules apply to other rents not due under a lease.

7. Mortgages. As soon as a mortgagee goes into possession, time begins to run against subsequent mortgagees and the mortgagor so as to bar their rights to redeem.[56] As regards the mortgagee's right to recover the money charged on the land, or to foreclose, time runs against him from the date upon which the money was due[57]; and when he is barred, his mortgage ceases to exist.[58] In each case, any written acknowledgement or any payment on account of principal or interest starts time running afresh.[59]

---

[48] Limitation Act 1980, Sched. 1, para. 6.
[49] *Ibid.* para. 4, 5(1). See, *e.g. Jessamine Investment Co.* v. *Schwartz* [1978] Q.B. 264.
[50] *Post*, pp. 501, 502.
[51] Limitation Act 1980, Sched. 1, para. 5(2).
[52] Limitation Amendment Act 1980, s.3(1), repealing Limitation Act 1939, s.9(1); Limitation Act 1980, Sched. 1, para. 4.
[53] *Ante*, p. 319.
[54] *Hughes* v. *Griffin* [1969] 1 W.L.R. 23.
[55] Limitation Act 1980, s.38(8).
[56] *Ibid.* s.16; see, *e.g. Young* v. *Clarey* [1948] Ch. 191.
[57] Limitation Act 1980, s.20.
[58] *Cotterell* v. *Price* [1960] 1 W.L.R. 1097.
[59] Limitation Act 1980, s.29; *post*, pp. 501, 502.

8. Claims through Crown or corporation sole. It has been seen that the Crown is entitled to a 30 years' period instead of the usual 12.[60] If a person against whom time has started to run conveys his land to the Crown, the only change is that the limitation period becomes 30 years from the dispossession instead of 12. But in the converse case, where time has started to run against the Crown and the Crown then conveys the land to X, the rule is that X is barred at the expiration of 30 years from the original dispossession or 12 years from the conveyance to him, whichever is the shorter.[61] Thus X is entitled to 12 years from the date of the conveyance unless at that time there were less than 12 years of the Crown period unexpired, in which case he merely has the residue of that period.

Similar rules apply[62] to the 30 years' period for a spiritual or eleemosynary corporation sole.[63]

9. Trusts

(a) *Adverse possession by stranger.* Equitable interests in land or under trusts for sale of land are in general treated as "land," and so as subject to the 12 years' period.[64] But adverse possession of trust property by a stranger does not bar the trustee's title to the property until all the beneficiaries have been barred.[65] Thus if land is held on trust for A for life with remainder to B, 12 years' adverse possession of the land by X bars A's equitable interest and, but for the provision just mentioned, would bar the trustee's legal estate. But time will not start to run against B's equitable interest until A's death,[66] and the same accordingly applies to the trustee's legal estate. Consequently, after the 12 years have run, the trustee will hold the legal estate on trust for X for the life of A, and subject thereto on trust for B. This is so even if A is the trustee, as will normally be the case with settled land.

(b) *Adverse possession by trustee.* Trustees cannot obtain a title against their beneficiaries by adverse possession of the trust property; for there is no period of limitation for an action by a beneficiary to recover from his trustees the trust property or its proceeds in their possession or converted to their use, or in respect of any fraud by the trustees.[67] Thus if land is conveyed to X and Y as tenants in common, X cannot obtain a title to the land as against Y, no matter how long he excludes Y from the land or its rents and profits; for X and Y hold the legal estate on the statutory trusts for themselves as tenants in common,[68] and X is thus trustee for Y.[69] But subject to this, the period in

---

[60] *Ante*, p. 494.
[61] Limitation Act 1980, Sched. 1, para. 12.
[62] *Ibid.*
[63] *Ante*, p. 494.
[64] Limitation Act 1980, ss.18, 20.
[65] *Ibid.* s.18.
[66] *Ante*, p. 497.
[67] Limitation Act 1980, s.21(1).
[68] *Ante*, p. 289.
[69] See *Re Landi* [1939] Ch. 828.

respect of a breach of trust (*e.g.* for paying income to the wrong person) is six years.[70]

In one case a trustee's liability may be curtailed if he is also a beneficiary. If on a distribution of trust funds such a trustee receives or retains for himself trust property or its proceeds in excess of his proper share, his liability will be restricted to that excess, provided he acted honestly and reasonably.[71] Thus if in distributing the trust property T takes one-third of it for himself in the honest and reasonable belief that it is divisible equally between himself and two others, his liability on the subsequent appearance of a further beneficiary who is entitled to share equally will be limited to one-twelfth of the trust property, once the six years have run.

(c) *Adverse possession by beneficiary.* Time does not begin to run against the trustees or beneficiaries if settled land or land held on trust for sale is in the possession of a beneficiary who is not solely and absolutely entitled.[72]

Sect. 2. Postponement of the Period

The date from which time begins to run may be postponed for disability, fraud, deliberate concealment, or mistake.

1. Disability. If the owner of an interest in land is under disability when the right of action accrues, then even if the normal period of limitation expires, the period is extended to six years from the time when he ceases to be under a disability or dies, whichever happens first, with a maximum period in the case of land of 30 years from the date when the right of action first accrued.[73] Thus if X takes possession of A's land at a time when A is of unsound mind, A will have 12 years from the dispossession or six years from his recovery in which to bring his action, whichever period is the longer, subject to the limit of 30 years from the dispossession.

(a) *Meaning of "disability."* A person is under a disability for this purpose "while he is an infant or of unsound mind."[74] For brevity and uniformity, the terms "minor," and "insane" or "mental patient," will be used.

(b) *Supervening disability.* A disability is immaterial unless it existed at the time when the cause of action accrued. Thus if A becomes insane the day before he is dispossessed, the provisions for disability apply, whereas if he becomes insane the day after he has been dispossessed, they do not.

(c) *Successive disabilities.* In the case of successive disabilities, if a person is under one disability and before that ceases another disability begins, the period is extended until both disabilities cease, subject to the maximum of 30

[70] Limitation Act 1980, s.21(3).
[71] *Ibid.* s.21(2).
[72] *Ibid.* Sched. 1, para. 9.
[73] *Ibid.* s.28.
[74] *Ibid.* s.38(2).

years.[75] But if one disability comes to an end before another disability starts, or if the person under disability is succeeded by another person under disability, time runs from the ceasing of the first disability. For example, A is a minor when the cause of action accrues. If later, during his minority, he becomes insane, the six years does not start to run until he is both sane and of full age. But if he reaches full age before he becomes insane, or if he dies a minor, and B, a mental patient, becomes entitled to the land, the six years run from A's majority in the first case and his death in the second.[76]

2. Fraud, deliberate concealment and mistake. Where—

   (i) an action is based on the fraud of the defendant or his agent, or of any person through whom he claims, or his agent, or

 (ii) any fact relevant to the plaintiff's right of action has been deliberately concealed from him by any such person, or

(iii) the action is for relief from the consequences of a mistake,

then time does not begin to run against the landowner until he discovers the fraud, concealment or mistake, or could with reasonable diligence have discovered it.[77] The term "deliberately concealed" has removed the element of unconscionable conduct[78] that was required by the former words "concealed by . . . fraud."[79] The deliberate commission of a breach of duty in circumstances in which it is unlikely to be discovered for some time amounts to deliberate concealment of the facts involved in that breach of duty.[80]

The rule as to mistake applies only where mistake is the basis of the action, as where the action is to recover money paid under a mistake of fact. There is no general doctrine that making a mistake (*e.g.* as to the true position of a boundary) stops time running.[81]

Neither fraud nor mistake will postpone the running of time as against a subsequent purchaser for value who did not know or have reason to believe that there was fraud or mistake.[82]

Sect. 3. Starting Time Running Afresh

Time may be started running afresh by—

 (i) a signed acknowledgment in writing of the plaintiff's title; or

(ii) part payment of principal or interest.[83]

The acknowledgment or payment must be signed or made by the person in

---

[75] See Limitation Act 1980, s.28(1).
[76] *Ibid.* s.28(3).
[77] *Ibid.* s.32(1).
[78] See *Bartlett* v. *Barclays Bank Trust Co. Ltd.* [1980] Ch. 515 at 537.
[79] Limitation Act 1939, s.26(b).
[80] Limitation Act 1980, s.32(2).
[81] See *Phillips-Higgins* v. *Harper* [1954] 1 Q.B. 411.
[82] Limitation Act 1980, s.32(3).
[83] *Ibid.* s.29.

whose favour time is running, or by his agent, and it must be made to the person whose title is being barred, or to his agent.[84] The acknowledgment must be of existing liability[85] and not merely of facts which might give rise to liability,[86] or merely that there might be a claim.[87] An order for possession will start time running afresh,[88] but a mere demand for possession will not.[89] Once the full period has run, however, no payment or acknowledgment can revive a right to recover land, for the elapse of time will have extinguished not only the owner's remedies for recovering the land but also his right to it.[90] It is otherwise in the case of other actions, where lapse of time bars only the remedy and not the right. Yet by estoppel a squatter, like any other land-owner, may preclude himself from asserting his title.[91]

Part 3

THE EFFECT OF THE ELAPSE OF TIME

Sect. 1. Title to Land

1. The squatter's title

(a) *No "parliamentary conveyance".* The operation of the Limitation Act 1980 is negative, not positive: it transfers nothing but extinguishes the owner's title. The owner's title is not transferred to the squatter, and so there is no "parliamentary conveyance" to him[92]; instead, the squatter owns a new estate of his own which by limitation will progressively improve until all competing interests are barred and he has an unincumbered fee simple absolute.

Registered land may be different, in that the registration of a squatter as proprietor can be said to transfer the registered title to him[93]; but the point has yet to be settled.

(b) *Burdens binding the squatter.* Even if a squatter can show that the fee simple owner has been barred, he may not be able to take a clean title; for burdens which bound the land will continue to bind it in the hands of the squatter. For example, a squatter will be bound by a restrictive covenant attached to the land unless he can show that it is no longer enforceable, *e.g.*, by lapse of time since a breach of it; for until a breach occurs the covenantee

[84] *Ibid.* s.30.
[85] As in *Moodie* v. *Bannister* (1859) 4 Drew. 432; *Dungate* v. *Dungate* [1965] 1 W.L.R. 1477.
[86] *Re Flynn (No. 2)* [1969] 2 Ch. 403.
[87] *Good* v. *Parry* [1963] 2 Q.B. 418.
[88] *B.P. Properties Ltd.* v. *Buckler* (1987) 55 P. & C.R. 337.
[89] *Mount Carmel Investments Ltd.* v. *Peter Thurlow Ltd.* (1988) 57 P. & C.R. 396.
[90] Limitation Act 1980, s.17; *Nicholson* v. *England* [1962] 2 K.B. 93.
[91] *Colchester B.C.* v. *Smith* [1992] 2 W.L.R. 728; see *ante*, pp. 434 *et seq.*
[92] *Tichborne* v. *Weir* (1892) 67 L.T. 735 at 737.
[93] See *Spectrum Investment Co.* v. *Holmes* [1981] 1 W.L.R. 221; see also L.R.A. 1925, ss.9–11, 75; *Fairweather* v. *St. Marylebone Property Co. Ltd.* [1963] A.C. 510.

has no right of action and time does not run against him. A squatter without notice is not a purchaser without notice.[94] Again, a squatter on leasehold land who obtains a title against the tenant but not against the landlord is not in the position of an assignee of the lease.[95] An assignee is liable to be sued for a breach of covenant committed while he held the lease, even if at the time of the action the lease has expired[96]; but a squatter cannot be sued after the expiration of a lease for breaches of covenant committed while he was in possession of the land.[97] Yet during the term of the lease, he can be forced to pay the rent and perform the covenants by the threat of forfeiture, if the lease contains a forfeiture clause[98]; but he has no right to apply for relief against forfeiture,[99] and he is of course bound by any restrictive covenants.

If a squatter takes advantage of some clause in the lease, such as a proviso that the rent should be halved if the covenants are observed, he cannot "blow hot and cold"; if he accepts the benefits of the lease, he cannot reject the burdens. Consequently, he will be estopped from denying that he is bound by the lease.[1] But the mere payment of rent under a lease with no such clause will not operate as an estoppel.[2]

A squatter may also be bound by rights over the land that arise during the period of dispossession, as where the owner, by entering the land from time to time to trim a hedge and clear a drain,[3] or to repair and maintain his adjoining house,[4] acquires rights in the nature of easements.

(c) *Barred leaseholds.* If a squatter bars a tenant but not the freeholder, and the tenant then acquires the freehold, time begins to run against the freehold; but until it has run, the tenant, by virtue of owning the freehold, may evict the squatter, for the freehold is not barred, and the former tenancy has merged in the freehold.[5] Further, if instead the tenant surrenders his tenancy to the freeholder, this enables the freeholder to evict the squatter forthwith, for the surrender removes the only interest which prevented the freeholder from claiming possession of land that he owns.[6] But registered land is different. When the squatter has become the registered proprietor of the lease, the tenant no longer has a registered estate capable of surrender[7] or, it seems, of merger.

2. Proof of title. A good title cannot be shown merely by proving adverse

---

[94] *Re Nisbet & Pott's Contract* [1906] 1 Ch. 386.
[95] For registered land, see above.
[96] *Ante*, pp. 350, 354.
[97] *Tichborne* v. *Weir* (1892) 67 L.T. 735; and see *ante* p. 354.
[98] See *ante*, p. 349.
[99] *Tickner* v. *Buzzacott* [1965] Ch. 426.
[1] *Ashe* v. *Hogan* [1920] 1 I.R. 159; *Tito* v. *Waddell* (*No.* 2) [1977] Ch. 106 at 299–302.
[2] *Tichborne* v. *Weir, supra.*
[3] *Marshall* v. *Taylor* [1895] 1 Ch. 641; see at pp. 648, 651.
[4] *Williams* v. *Usherwood* (1981) 45 P. & C.R. 235.
[5] *Taylor* v. *Twinberrow* [1930] 2 K.B. 16.
[6] *Fairweather* v. *St. Marylebone Property Co. Ltd.* [1963] A.C. 510; but see (1962) 78 L.Q.R. 33 (H.W.R. Wade).
[7] *Spectrum Investment Co.* v. *Holmes* [1981] 1 W.L.R. 221.

possession of land, however long the period. If A and his predecessors in title have been in possession of land for 20, 50, or 100 years, that alone does not prove that A is entitled to it; for the true owner—

(i) might have been under disability at the time of dispossession; or
(ii) might have been the Crown; or
(iii) might have been the reversioner or remainderman under a settlement; or
(iv) might be the reversioner on a long lease.

Consequently, to establish a good title by the operation of the Act it must be shown—

(i) who was the true owner of the interest in land in question; and
(ii) that he has been barred by lapse of time.

A vendor who can do this can establish a title which the courts will force even an unwilling purchaser to accept.[8] However, in practice, it is comparatively unusual for a title to land to be acquired by limitation, except in the case of encroachments upon neighbouring land.

3. Successive squatters. Even before the statutory period has expired, a squatter has a title good against everyone except the true owner.[9] To hold otherwise would mean that a squatter who had not barred the true owner would have no remedy against a person who dispossessed him; this might lead to breaches of the peace by competing squatters. Consequently, if a squatter who has not barred the true owner sells the land he can give the purchaser a right to the land which is valid against all except the true owner. The same applies to devises, gifts or other dispositions by the squatter; in each case the person taking the squatter's interest can add the squatter's period of possession to his own.[10] Thus if X, who has occupied A's land for eight years, sells the land to Y, A will be barred after Y has held the land for a further four years. Again, if a squatter is himself dispossessed, the second squatter can add the former period of occupation to his own. For example, if land owned by A has been occupied by X for eight years, and Y dispossesses X, A will be barred when 12 years have elapsed from X first taking possession. But although at the end of that time A is barred, X will not be barred until 12 years from Y's first taking possession, for Y cannot claim to be absolutely entitled until he can show that everybody with any claim to the land has been barred by the elapse of the full period.

There is no right to add together two periods of adverse possession if a squatter abandons possession before the full period has run and some time elapses before another person takes possession of the land. During the interval, there is no person in adverse possession whom the true owner could

[8] *Re Atkinson & Horsell's Contract* [1912] 2 Ch. 1; contrast *George Wimpey & Co. Ltd.* v. *Sohn* [1967] Ch. 487. See M.P. Thompson, *Investigation and Proof of Title*, pp. 19, 20.
[9] *Perry* v. *Clissold* [1907] A.C. 73; *ante*, p. 493.
[10] *Asher* v. *Whitlock* (1865) L.R. 1 Q.B. 1. See also *Mount Carmel Investments Ltd.* v. *Peter Thurlow Ltd.* (1988) 57 P. & C.R. 396.

sue; thus time begins to run afresh when the second squatter takes possession of the land.[11]

Sect. 2. Arrears of Income

The recovery of arrears of income is distinct from the recovery of the land or capital money which produces it. The arrears of rent which the landlord or the owner of a rentcharge can recover by action or distress are limited to the arrears accrued due during the previous six years.[12] For agricultural holdings, distress is restricted to rent falling due during the previous year,[13] and for bankruptcy it is limited to six months' rent accruing due before the commencement of the bankruptcy.[14]

There is also a six years' period for arrears of mortgage interest.[15] But a mortgagee who exercises his power of sale may retain all arrears of interest out of the proceeds of sale, for this is not recovery by action[16]; and a mortgagor who seeks to redeem can do so only on the equitable terms of paying all arrears, however old.[17]

---

[11] *Trustees, Executors and Agency Co. Ltd.* v. *Short* (1888) 13 App. Cas. 793; Limitation Act 1980, Sched. 1, para. 8(2).
[12] Limitation Act 1980, ss.19, 38(1).
[13] Agricultural Holdings Act 1986, s.16.
[14] Insolvency Act 1986, s.347.
[15] Limitation Act 1980, s.20(5).
[16] *Re Marshfield* (1887) 34 Ch.D. 721.
[17] *Dingle* v. *Coppen* [1899] 1 Ch. 726; *Holmes* v. *Cowcher* [1970] 1 W.L.R. 834.

CHAPTER 15

OWNERSHIP AND ITS LIMITS

AT the beginning of this century, a landowner was very largely free to do as he pleased with his own. He could usually act with impunity despite any consequent injury to others or to the environment. Thus he could erect buildings on his land wherever he wished, use them for any purpose, and alter or demolish them at will; and he was equally free to open mines on his land, or change its use. He could also evict his tenants and increase their rents whenever he wished unless prevented by the terms of their tenancies.

Today, the position has been transformed. By a series of statutes, accelerated by the effects of two world wars, this freedom has, in the public interest, been greatly curtailed. Even in 1936 it was possible to say that "the fundamental assumption of modern statute law is that the landowner holds his land for the public good."[1] These statutes are many and complex, and they can be examined here only in outline: thus what takes over 1000 pages in a recent text-book[2] is summarised in 25 pages here.[3] There are exceptions and qualifications to most of what is stated in this chapter. But before considering these statutes, something must be said about the position of the landowner at common law; this is in Part 1. After that, Part 2 examines the general statutory control of ownership, and Part 3 considers the statutory protection of tenants.

Part 1

RIGHTS AND RESTRICTIONS AT COMMON LAW

Sect. 1. Rights

The owner of the largest estate known to the law, the fee simple absolute in possession, has traditionally enjoyed wide powers of control, disposition and use of the land in which his estate exists; and, subject to statute, he still does.

1. Ownership. The maxim is *cujus est solum, ejus est usque ad coelum et ad inferos*; he who owns the soil is presumed to own everything "up to the sky and down to the centre of the earth."[4] This *prima facie* includes all mines and

---

[1] (1936) 49 Harv.L.R. 426 at 436 (W.I. Jennings).
[2] Megarry's *Rent Acts* (11th ed. 1988–89).
[3] *Post*, pp. 531–556.
[4] *Corbett* v. *Hill* (1870) L.R. 9 Eq. 671 at 673; and see *Commissioner for Railways* v. *Valuer-General* [1974] A.C. 328 at 351, 352; *Grigsby* v. *Melville* [1974] 1 W.L.R. 80 (cellar). But see *post*, p. 509.

minerals,[5] and any chattel not the property of any known person[6] which is found under or attached to the land, *e.g.* in the bed of a canal[7]; but it probably does not include a chattel merely resting on the surface.[8] Where land is bounded by the sea or other water which over the years gradually and imperceptibly recedes or advances, then unless the title deeds show that the boundary is fixed and not moveable,[9] the area of the land in the title will be increased by accretion or reduced by diluvion.[10]

2. Disposition. The owner can dispose of his land or any part of it as he wishes. Thus he may sever it horizontally, as by disposing separately of an upper floor of a building, though such dispositions raise many problems, *e.g.* as to rights of access and support. The "flying freeholds" in Lincoln's Inn are regulated by statute.[11]

3. Use. The owner may in general use the land in the natural course of user in any way he thinks fit. He may waste or despoil it as he pleases and he is not liable merely because he neglects it.[12]

4. Wild animals. Although wild animals are not the subject of ownership,[13] a landowner has what is sometimes called a "qualified property" in them, consisting of the exclusive right to catch, kill and appropriate the animals on his land; and as soon as the animals are killed they fall into the ownership of the landowner, even if killed by a trespasser.[14]

5. Water. A landowner has no property in water which either percolates through his land or flows through it in a defined channel. In the case of percolating water, the landowner may draw off any or all of it without regard to the claims of neighbouring owners.[15] In the case of water flowing through a defined channel, the riparian owner (the owner of the land through which the water flows) cannot always take all the water, though he has certain valuable rights. The owner of only one bank of a stream *prima facie* may exercise riparian rights up to the middle of the stream.

(a) *Fishing.* As part of his natural right of ownership the owner has the sole right to fish in the water. Except in tidal waters, the public has no right of fishing even if there is a public right of navigation.[16]

---

[5] *Mitchell* v. *Mosley* [1914] 1 Ch. 438 at 450; for exceptions, see *post*, p. 509.
[6] See *Moffatt* v. *Kazana* [1969] 2 Q.B. 152 (bank notes hidden in flue).
[7] *Elwes* v. *Brigg Gas Co.* (1886) 33 Ch.D. 562.
[8] *Hannah* v. *Peel* [1945] K.B. 509; *Parker* v. *British Airways Board* [1982] Q.B. 1004.
[9] *Baxendale* v. *Instow Parish Council* [1982] Ch. 14.
[10] *Southern Centre of Theosophy Inc.* v. *State of South Australia* [1982] A.C. 706; see [1982] Conv. 208 (R.E. Annand); [1986] Conv. 247 (W. Howarth).
[11] See Lincoln's Inn Act 1860.
[12] *Giles* v. *Walker* (1890) 24 Q.B.D. 656 (thistles).
[13] *The Case of Swans* (1592) 7 Co.Rep. 15b at 17b.
[14] *Blade* v. *Higgs* (1865) 11 H.L.C. 621.
[15] *Chasemore* v. *Richards* (1859) 7 H.L.C. 349.
[16] See *Blount* v. *Layard* [1891] 2 Ch. 681.

(b) *Flow.* The owner is entitled to the flow of water through the land unaltered in volume or quality, subject to ordinary and reasonable use by the upper riparian owners; and he is bound by a corresponding obligation to the lower riparian owners.[17]

(c) *Abstraction.* The ordinary and reasonable use which a riparian owner was formerly entitled to make of the water flowing through his land was[18]—

- (i) the right to take and use all water necessary for ordinary purposes connected with his riparian tenement (such as for watering his cattle or for domestic purposes, or, possibly, in some manufacturing districts, for manufacturing purposes), even though this completely exhausted the stream; and
- (ii) the right to use the water for extraordinary purposes connected with his riparian tenement, provided the use was reasonable and the water was restored substantially undiminished in volume and unaltered in character. Such purposes include irrigation and, in all districts, manufacturing purposes, such as for cooling apparatus. The amount by which the flow might be diminished was a question of degree in each case.[19]

These rights have now been curtailed by statute. In general, nobody may now abstract water from any inland waters, whether river, stream, lake or pond, or from any underground strata, without the licence of the National Rivers Authority. Certain quantities, however are excepted:

(i) Not more than five cubic metres may be taken, provided this is not part of a continuous operation or series of operations[20] in which more than five cubic metres in all are taken; and

(ii) Not more than 20 cubic metres in any 24 hours may be taken from underground strata for the domestic purposes of an individual's household, or from inland waters for use on contiguous land for the domestic purposes of the occupier's household or for agricultural purposes other than spray irrigation.[21]

Sect. 2. Restrictions

1. Liability in tort. A landowner may be liable in tort for injuries caused to third parties by his acts and omissions in respect of things brought or artificially stored on the land, *e.g.* if water in a reservoir escapes, or if a lamp projecting over the highway gets into a dangerous state of repair and injures a passer-by. He may similarly be liable for nuisance, *e.g.* if he makes an

---

[17] *John Young & Co.* v. *The Bankier Distillery Co.* [1893] A.C. 691.
[18] *McCartney* v. *Londonderry and Lough Swilly Ry.* [1904] A.C. 301 at 306, 307.
[19] See *Rugby Joint Water Board* v. *Walters* [1967] Ch. 397.
[20] See *Cargill* v. *Gotts* [1981] 1 W.L.R. 441 ("series" judged by purposes of taking, not quantity or frequency).
[21] Water Resources Act 1991, ss.24, 27, 221, replacing provisions in the Water Resources Act 1963.

unusual and excessive collection of manure which attracts flies and causes a stink.[22]

2. Gold and silver. The Crown is entitled to all gold and silver occurring in any mine,[23] and is also entitled to all "treasure trove."[24] Objects amount to treasure trove only if—

(i) they consist of gold or silver,[25] whether in bullion, coin or some manufactured object;

(ii) they have been hidden in or on the land deliberately, and not merely lost[26]; and

(iii) the true owner is unknown.[27]

3. Air-space. Although for centuries a landowner's rights have been said to extend *usque ad coelum*,[28] the common law has restricted those rights to the air-space up to such a height as is necessary for the ordinary use and enjoyment of the land and the structures upon it.[29] Within these limits, the continued occupation of the air-space over land without the occupier's consent, as by telephone wires, or a cornice, or branches of a tree, is both a nuisance[30] and a trespass.[31] The intermittent presence of the jib of a tower crane 50 feet above the landowner's roof level has been admitted to be a trespass,[32] and the passage of dangerous projectiles 75 feet above the land has been held to be a nuisance.[33] Aircraft are protected by statute: for no action for trespass or nuisance lies by reason only of the flight of aircraft over land at a height which is reasonable in all the circumstances, provided the proper regulations have been observed.[34]

Part 2

STATUTORY RESTRICTIONS

In addition to the many types of statutory protection given to tenants and

[22] *Bland* v. *Yates* (1914) 58 S.J. 612.
[23] See *Att.-Gen.* v. *Morgan* [1891] 1 Ch. 432.
[24] See *Treasure Trove: Law Reform Issues* (Law Com., Sept. 1987).
[25] See *Att.-Gen. of the Duchy of Lancaster* v. *G.E. Overton (Farms) Ltd.* [1982] Ch. 277 (gold or silver content must be "substantial").
[26] See *R.* v. *Hancock* [1990] 2 Q.B. 242 at 247.
[27] See *Att.-Gen.* v. *Trustees of the British Museum* [1903] 2 Ch. 598 at 608–611.
[28] *Ante*, p. 506.
[29] *Baron Bernstein of Leigh* v. *Skyviews & General Ltd.* [1978] Q.B. 479; but consider the authorities *infra*.
[30] See McNair, *Law of the Air* (3rd ed. 1964), Ch. 3.
[31] *Kelsen* v. *Imperial Tobacco Co. (of Great Britain and Ireland) Ltd.* [1957] 2 Q.B. 334.
[32] *Wollerton & Wilson Ltd.* v. *Richard Costain Ltd.* [1970] 1 W.L.R. 411 (not followed in *John Trenberth Ltd.* v. *National Westminster Bank Ltd.* (1979) 39 P. & C.R. 104, but only on the remedy).
[33] *Clifton* v. *Viscount Bury* (1887) 4 T.L.R. 8.
[34] Civil Aviation Act 1982, s.76, replacing Civil Aviation Act 1949, s.40, previously Air Navigation Act 1920, s.9.

thus restricting their landlords, there are two main types of statute that curtail the rights of landowners. First, there are the statutory provisions which restrict the use and enjoyment of land, and its development, usually without compensation. Second, there are the statutes which authorise the expropriation of the land itself, usually on payment of compensation. Under the first head, there is the wide-ranging system of town and country planning, together with certain miscellaneous controls, while under the second head there is a wide variety of statutes authorising the compulsory acquisition of land. They will be taken in turn.

Sect. 1. Planning Control

A. Growth of Control

1. Control by schemes. At common law, any landowner was free to develop his land as he wished, provided he did not infringe the rights of others. He could erect whatever buildings he wished, however unsuitable they might be, and however injurious to the amenities of the district. Not until the Housing, Town Planning, etc., Act 1909 was enacted was there any general power for local authorities to control the development of land. Successive statutes strengthened and extended this control, culminating in the Town and Country Planning Act 1932, which for the first time conferred planning powers over land in the country, as distinct from towns. The essence of this and the earlier Acts was the preparation of a scheme. Each local authority was empowered to prepare a scheme showing what development would be permitted on each part of the land: and there were powers of enforcement against those who carried out development contravening the scheme.

2. Interim development control

(a) *Defects.* The system suffered from a number of defects. First, it was optional: there was no obligation for any local authority to prepare a scheme, and many did not. Second, there was the long period which usually elapsed between the decision of the local authority to prepare a scheme and the final approval of the scheme. During this period, the land was subject to "interim development control." Under this, any landowner could develop his land at his own risk: if when the scheme was at last approved the development accorded with the scheme, it was safe, whereas if it did not accord with it, the local authority could take enforcement action under the scheme and, for example, secure the removal of any offending buildings.

(b) *Permission.* To guard against this risk, an application for interim development permission could be made before carrying out the work. If this was given, the development was immune from enforcement action even if ultimately it was found to contravene the scheme. But if development was carried out without interim development permission, there was no power to take enforcement action against it during the interim development period; and some speculative developers relied successfully on the probability that no scheme would come into force until they had been able to reap the profits of their development.

3. The Act of 1943. This system continued until the Town and Country Planning (Interim Development) Act 1943 was passed. At that time, a mere 4 per cent. of England and Wales was subject to operative schemes; another 70 per cent. was subject to interim development control; and the remaining 26 per cent. was subject to no control. The Act imposed interim development control on all land in this last category, so that thenceforward the whole of the land in the country was under interim development control save for the 4 per cent. governed by schemes.[35] Second, the Act enabled local authorities to take enforcement proceedings against those who subsequently developed their land without obtaining interim development permission: unauthorised buildings could be demolished, and unauthorised uses penalised.[36]

These provisions transformed planning control. Formerly, over a quarter of the country was free from control, and all save some 4 per cent. of the rest was free from any control save the indefinite risk of a scheme ultimately being made which would be inconsistent with the development. After the Act of 1943, the whole of the country was subject to a system under which effective action could forthwith be taken against any future development carried out without permission.

B. Town and Country Planning Acts

1. Acts of 1947 to 1960. The Town and Country Planning Act 1947 was passed on August 6, 1947, and came into operation on the "appointed day," July 1, 1948.[37] It was subsequently amended extensively, notably by the Town and Country Planning Acts 1953, 1954 and 1959, and the Caravan Sites and Control of Development Act 1960. The Act of 1947, which was complex and far-reaching and repealed all the previous law, had two main objects: first, a general revision and strengthening of the existing systems of planning control; and second, the imposition of a new system of "development charges." The main object of development charges was to prevent landowners profiting from the great increase in value of their land which often accrued without effort on their part when, for example, the spread of a town transformed into valuable building land some meadows which had previously had only a low value for agricultural purposes. The system of development charges proved unworkable and was abolished by the Act of 1953; but the planning provisions of the Act of 1947 remained.

2. Acts of 1962 and 1968. In 1962 the previous legislation from the Act of

---

[35] s.1.
[36] s.5.
[37] S.I. 1948 No. 213.

1947 onwards was repealed and replaced and re-enacted in the consolidating Town and Country Planning Act 1962. This was successively amended,[38] and by the Land Commission Act 1967 a renewed attempt was made to secure for the State some of the increased value which accrues to land as a result of surrounding development. The new charge was known as "betterment levy," but after a change of government it too was abolished.[39]

3. Acts of 1971 to 1991. The Town and Country Planning Act 1971 consolidated the previous legislation, but it was soon amended and supplemented.[40] Yet another attempt was made to secure for the State some of the development value of land, this time by the rather more orthodox method of imposing a tax instead of creating a special kind of charge. The "development gains tax" under the Finance Act 1974 was soon replaced by a "development land tax" under the Development Land Tax Act 1976. This was designed to operate in conjunction with the Community Land Act 1975, which was intended to secure for local authorities the benefit of land ripe for development. On a change of government the Act of 1975 was repealed,[41] and the Finance Act 1985[42] abolished development land tax. There was then the Town and Country Planning Act 1990 ("Act of 1990"), which consolidated the previous legislation; and subject to important amendments made by the Planning and Compensation Act 1991 ("Act of 1991"), the Act of 1990 is now the governing Act, with certain supplementary Acts.[43] There are also many statutory instruments, dealing with much of the detail.

4. Administration. In general, the central administration of the Acts is under the Secretary of State for the Environment or, in Wales, the Secretary of State for Wales. Routine administration is carried out by the local planning authorities, namely, the district councils and the county councils.[44] For most purposes the local planning authority is the district council, but for some (*e.g.* the preparation of structure plans, as distinct from local plans[45]) it is the county council.

C. Control of Development

1. Development. The fundamental concept underlying the planning legislation is "development," which is defined as meaning—

---

[38] By the Town and Country Planning Acts 1963 and 1968, the Control of Office and Industrial Development Act 1965, and Part 3 of the Industrial Development Act 1966.
[39] By the Land Commission (Dissolution) Act 1971.
[40] By the Town and Country Planning (Amendment) Acts 1972 and 1977, the Town and Country Amenities Act 1974, the Community Land Act 1975, and the Control of Office Development Act 1977.
[41] By the Local Government, Planning and Land Act 1980, s.101, Sched. 17.
[42] s.93, Sched. 25.
[43] See Planning (Listed Buildings and Conservation Areas) Act 1990; Planning (Hazardous Substances) Act 1990 (see S.I. 1992 No. 656); Planning (Consequential Provisions) Act 1990.
[44] Act of 1990, s.1.
[45] See *post*, p. 514.

(i) "the carrying out of building, engineering, mining or other operations in, on, over or under land," or

(ii) "the making of any material change[46] in the use of any buildings or other land."[47]

Many of the expressions in the definition are themselves defined by the Act, though the only phrase which need be mentioned here is that "engineering operations" includes "the formation or laying out of means of access to highways."[48] The Act makes it clear that it is development to begin using one dwelling-house as two or more separate dwelling-houses,[49] or to extend dumps of refuse or waste materials. On the other hand, "development" does not include improvements or alterations to a building which do not materially affect its external appearance, the use of any buildings or other land within the curtilage of a dwelling-house for any purpose incidental to the enjoyment of the dwelling-house as such, the use of any land for agricultural purposes, and any change from one use to another use within the same class in the 16 classes of use set out in the Town and Country Planning (Use Classes) Order 1987.[50] The Act further provides in effect that the definition does not include certain cases of reverting to a former lawful use.[51]

2. Planning permission

(a) *Permission.* The general rule is that any person who proposes to develop land must first obtain planning permission from the local planning authority or from the Secretary of State on appeal; and such permission may be granted either unconditionally or subject to such conditions as are thought fit, or it may be refused.[52] Any conditions must reasonably relate to the proposed development.[53] Although the refusal of permission may be a very serious matter for the landowner, no compensation is payable except in a very limited class of cases.[54]

An applicant must give prior notice of his application to certain other persons owning interests in the property; and in a few cases of development likely to offend neighbours, he must first advertise his application, so that they may be able to object before permission is given.[55] An applicant for planning permission does not need to have a proprietary interest in the

---

[46] See *Guildford R.D.C.* v. *Fortescue* [1959] 2 Q.B. 112 (intensification of use not a change); *East Barnet U.D.C.* v. *British Transport Commission* [1962] 2 Q.B. 484; *Jennings Motors Ltd.* v. *Secretary of State for the Environment* [1982] Q.B. 541.
[47] Act of 1990, s.55(1).
[48] *Ibid.* s.336(1).
[49] *Ibid.* s.55(3); and see *Ealing Corporation* v. *Ryan* [1965] 2 Q.B. 486.
[50] Act of 1990, s.55(2)(f); S.I. 1987, No. 764, 1992 No. 610, 657.
[51] Act of 1990, s.57(4); and see *Young* v. *Secretary of State for the Environment* [1983] 2 A.C. 662.
[52] Act of 1990, s.70.
[53] See *Fawcett Properties Ltd.* v. *Buckinghamshire C.C.* [1961] A.C. 636; *R.* v. *Hillingdon L.B.C., ex p. Royco Homes Ltd.* [1974] Q.B. 720; *Newbury D.C.* v. *Secretary of State for the Environment* [1981] A.C. 578.
[54] Act of 1990, Pt. V.
[55] *Ibid.* ss.65, 66.

property concerned: applications are frequently made by prospective purchasers and lessees. Every local planning authority is bound to maintain a
register of applications for permission and the results of such applications[56];
this is quite distinct from the local land charges register.[57]

(b) *Development, structure and local plans.* Under the Act of 1947, each
local planning authority was bound to prepare a development plan by July 1,
1951, showing the proposed development of its area.[58] These plans, which
had to be reconsidered every five years, form a prophecy of the permissions
likely to be granted and those likely to be refused; but unlike planning
schemes under the old system, the plan itself authorises no development,
and it is as necessary to obtain planning permission after the plan has come
into force as before. All development plans were subject to amendment and
approval by the Minister after holding a public inquiry.

This system of development plans proved cumbersome, and so the Act of
1968 introduced a more flexible system, involving a gradual replacement of
development plans by less detailed "structure plans" which sketch the
general lines of development.[59] Despite its name, a structure plan does not
comprise a map: it is in the form of a written statement containing or
accompanied by diagrams, illustrations and descriptive matter. A structure
plan must formulate the planning authority's policy and general proposals in
respect of the development and other use of land in their area, including
measures for the improvement of the physical environment and the management of traffic. Structure plans require the approval of the Secretary of
State, and may be supplemented by local plans which will not normally be
under the Secretary of State's control.[60] A local plan, which consists of a map
and a written statement, provides a more detailed working out of aspects of
the structure plan. It may designate any part of the area which is to be
selected for comprehensive treatment at an early date. Such an area is
known as an "action area," and the local plan which is duly prepared for it as
an "action area plan." There are many types of local plan which can be
prepared under the overriding scheme of a structure plan.

(c) *Permitted development.* By the Town and Country Planning General
Development Order 1988[61] planning permission is given[62] for 28 classes of
development, subject to certain conditions, and so in these cases there is no
need to apply to the local planning authority for permission. The Order
includes such matters as minor alterations to dwellings, temporary uses, and
much development by gas, water, electricity and other undertakings.

(d) *Enterprise zones and S.P.Z.* Provision has been made for establishing

[56] *Ibid.* s.69.
[57] See *ante*, p. 91.
[58] Act of 1947, s.5.
[59] Act of 1968, Pt. I, now Act of 1990, Pt. II.
[60] Act of 1990, ss.36–45.
[61] S.I. 1988, No. 1813, as amended: see S.I. 1992 No. 609, 658.
[62] See *Cater* v. *Essex C.C.* [1960] 1 Q.B. 424.

schemes for "enterprise zones"[63] and "simplified planning zones" (or S.P.Z.)[64] The purpose of enterprise zones is to encourage business and industrial activities by granting planning permission for specified development or by making it easier to obtain permission, and by giving some tax advantages for 10 years: an example is London's Isle of Dogs. The object of S.P.Z. is to secure the regeneration of an area by encouraging the development of derelict or unused land by means similar to those in enterprise zones, though without the tax advantages.

(e) *Caravan sites.* Caravan sites proved very hard to control under the general law of town and country planning, the main difficulty being that the mere development of land without planning permission is not an offence. Sites could be exploited and the vans moved away before enforcement proceedings could be brought to a successful conclusion. To remedy this abuse, the Caravan Sites and Control of Development Act 1960[65] made it an offence in most cases to use land as a caravan site without a site licence granted by the local authority, and this is issued only if the requisite planning permission for the use of the land as a caravan site has been obtained. The licence will usually be subject to conditions relating to the physical use of the land, *e.g.* conditions aimed at preventing overcrowding.[66] The Caravan Sites Act 1968[67] is concerned with the duty of local authorities to provide caravan sites for gipsies, and deals with exemptions from the requirement for site licences.

3. Enforcement

(a) *Enforcement notices.* If any development is carried out without the requisite permission, or if any conditions to which a permission is subject have not been complied with, the local planning authority may serve an enforcement notice on the owner and occupier of the land, and on the owner of any interest in the land materially affected by the notice. The notice must specify the alleged breach of planning control and also the steps to be taken (or the activities that must cease) in order to remedy the breach, and the period within which this must be done. In addition, it must specify the date on which it is to take effect.[68] A notice is a nullity if it is defective on its face,[69] *e.g.* in failing to state the date on which it is to take effect. Other defects may make it invalid, and subject to appeal, though sometimes the defect can be cured. The notice must be served within 28 days of the date of issue, and at least 28 days before the date specified in it as the date when it is to take effect.[70] A local planning authority which suspects a breach of planning

---

[63] Local Government, Planning and Land Act 1980, Sched. 32; Act of 1990, ss.88, 89.
[64] Act of 1990, ss.82–87, Sched. 7; Act of 1991, s.28, Sched. 5.
[65] ss.1, 2, Sched. 1.
[66] *Ibid.* ss.3, 5.
[67] Amended by Local Government, Planning and Land Act 1980, Pt. XVII.
[68] Act of 1990, ss.172, 173, as substituted by Act of 1991, s.5.
[69] *East Riding C.C.* v. *Park Estate (Bridlington) Ltd.* [1957] A.C. 223.
[70] Act of 1990, s.172, as substituted by Act of 1991, s.5.

control may serve a "planning contravention notice," requiring information to be given as to activities on the land; and it is an offence to fail to comply with it.[71]

(b) *Time limit.* An enforcement notice cannot be served more than 10 years after the breach; but the period is four years if the breach consists of changing the use of a building to a single dwelling-house, or if it consists of building, engineering, mining or other operations, in which case time runs from the substantial completion of the operations.[72]

(c) *Appeal.* An appeal to the Secretary of State against an enforcement notice may be made at any time before it takes effect, and the notice then has no effect until the appeal is determined or withdrawn.[73] The Secretary of State has wide powers to grant permission for the development, or to vary or quash the notice[74]; and a further appeal lies to the High Court, though only on a point of law.[75]

(d) *Stop notices.* On or after serving an enforcement notice and before it takes effect a local planning authority may serve a stop notice. This prohibits the continuance of the alleged breach of planning control until the enforcement notice takes effect, thereby defeating the use of appeals as a delaying tactic. A stop notice cannot prohibit the use of any building as a dwelling-house, or the carrying on of any activity which has been continuing for four years or more. The notice must specify the date on which it takes effect, and this must be not later than 28 days after the date of service, and, in the absence of special reasons, at least three days after the date of service. In certain cases where, in the event, the notice is found not to be justified, compensation is payable.[76]

(e) *Non-compliance.* Failure to comply with an enforcement notice or a stop notice is an offence.[77] Further, the local planning authority may apply for an injunction to restrain any actual or apprehended breach of planning control.[78] Where any steps required by an enforcement notice have not been taken, the local planning authority may also enter the land and take them, and recover the expense from the landowner.[79]

(f) *Breach of condition notice.* An alternative, and simpler, procedure for breach of conditions is now available. If there is a breach of a condition in a planning permission, the local planning authority may serve a "breach of condition notice." This must require compliance with the condition, and

---

[71] Act of 1990, ss.171C, 171D, inserted by Act of 1991, s.1.
[72] Act of 1990, ss.171A, 171B, inserted by Act of 1991, s.4.
[73] Act of 1990, ss.174, 175; Act of 1991, s.6.
[74] Act of 1990, ss.176, 177.
[75] *Ibid.* s.289.
[76] *Ibid.* ss.183–186; Act of 1991, s.9. Registers of enforcement and stop notices must be kept in each area: Act of 1990, s.188.
[77] Act of 1990, ss.179, 187, as substituted by Act of 1991, ss.8, 9. Penalty, fine not exceeding £20,000 on summary conviction, or unlimited fine on conviction on indictment.
[78] Act of 1990, s.187B, inserted by Act of 1991, s.3.
[79] Act of 1990, s.178, as amended by Act of 1991, s.7.

specify the steps to be taken or the activities which must cease in order to secure compliance; and it must also specify the period for compliance, which must not be less than 28 days after service of the notice. Failure to comply with such a notice is a summary offence.[80] The time limit for serving a breach of condition notice is the same as for serving an enforcement notice.[81]

4. Additional controls. In addition to regulating development, legislation also provides a number of additional controls. Local planning authorities can make tree preservation orders which, in the interests of amenity, prohibit trees being felled, cut or otherwise damaged without the consent of the local planning authority.[82] The demolition or alteration of buildings of special architectural or historical interest without "listed building consent" will be prevented if they become "listed buildings" by being included in a list compiled by the Secretary of State.[83] Further, the local planning authority may designate any area of special architectural or historic interest as a "conservation area," whereupon the demolition of any building in that area requires a "conservation area consent,"[84] and the trees are protected as if they were subject to a tree preservation order.[85] There is also an elaborate system for controlling the display of advertisements on land.[86]

D. Effect on the Law of Property

When the Act of 1947 was enacted, some strange suggestions were made as to its fundamental effect on English land law. It was even contended that the fee simple in land no longer existed, but instead each landowner had merely a fee simple in the existing or permitted use of his land. This view appears to have been based on the need to obtain permission for any development, and on the obligation to pay a development charge to re-acquire the development rights which the State was acquiring. The substance of the first of these changes, however, had already been made by the Act of 1943 (which none had regarded as being epoch-making), and the second of the changes more resembled a tax on development than anything else. The subsequent betterment levy, development gains tax, and development land tax were even more purely fiscal measures and involved no element of purchasing rights in land from the State. Further, on this view, no purchaser of land in, say, 1950, received more than a fee simple in an existing use, and so today, despite the abolition of development charges, he still has no fee simple in the land. Yet again, it ignored "existing or permitted buildings" in which the landowner had the same kind of rights as in the "existing or permitted use."

In truth, the theory would not bear examination, and it has gained no

---

[80] Act of 1990, s.187A, added by Act of 1991, s.2: penalty, fine not exceeding £400.
[81] Act of 1990, ss.171A, 171B, added by Act of 1991, s.4; *ante*, p. 515.
[82] Act of 1990, ss.198–210; Act of 1991, s.23.
[83] Planning (Listed Buildings and Conservation Areas) Act 1990, Pt. I.
[84] *Ibid.* Pt. II.
[85] Act of 1990, ss.211–214.
[86] *Ibid.* ss.220–225; S.I. 1992 No. 666.

foothold in the courts or among practitioners. Planning control affects the use and enjoyment of land, but not the estates or interests in it; and the various charges, levies or taxes are a purely fiscal burden. Planning matters must be duly investigated for the protection of purchasers, but they are not technically matters of title. The right to use property in a particular way is not in itself property.[87] The fee simple in land remains the same fee simple as before. All that has happened is that the fruits of ownership have become less sweet; but that is nothing new in land law.

Sect. 2. Miscellaneous Controls

Apart from town and country planning legislation, there are various other statutes which control the use and enjoyment of land and buildings on it. The following are the most important.

1. Housing Act 1985. The Housing Act 1985[88] consolidates a number of statutes, beginning with the Housing of the Working Classes Act 1890, and today covering a wide range of provisions for the improvement of housing conditions. The purposes of the Act include securing the erection of houses; slum clearance; the repair or improvement of housing by means of serving repair or improvement notices, with provisions for making grants or loans for the purpose; abating overcrowding; and providing security of tenure for the tenants of dwellings let by local authorities or certain other bodies, and giving such tenants the right to buy the dwellings.[89]

2. Public Health Acts. The Public Health Acts 1936–61 are the principal Acts concerning public health. In relation to land, they deal with matters such as sewers, drains and public nuisances. Some of the provisions formerly made by these Acts, together with further provisions, are now dealt with by other Acts relating to particular aspects of public health and safety. These include the Planning (Hazardous Substances) Act 1990 (requiring "hazardous substances consents" to be obtained), the Environmental Protection Act 1990, the Water Industry Act 1991 and the Water Resources Act 1991; and under the Building Act 1984 there are Regulations[90] which control the design and construction of buildings. Other relevant legislation includes the Factories Act 1961 and the Offices, Shops and Railways Premises Act 1963.

3. Agricultural control. The Agriculture Act 1947 gave the Minister of Agriculture, Fisheries and Food (acting through the County Agricultural Executive Committees) wide powers of controlling farming operations and of securing a proper standard of good estate management, especially in the

---

[87] *Belfast Corporation* v. *O.D. Cars Ltd.* [1960] A.C. 490.
[88] See also Housing (Consequential Provisions) Act 1985, Housing Associations Act 1985 and L. & T.A. 1985.
[89] See *post*, pp. 546, 547.
[90] See S.I. 1985 No. 1065, as amended.

provision and maintenance of fixed equipment. These provisions were repealed by the Agriculture Act 1958. All that remains is a limited power for the Agricultural Land Tribunal (the successor to some of the functions of the County Agricultural Executive Committees) to direct a landlord to provide fixed equipment required to enable the tenant to comply with statutory provisions (*e.g.* for producing clean milk); but failure to comply is treated merely as a breach of the terms of the tenancy, giving the tenant the right to do the work himself and to recover the cost from the landlord.[91]

Sect. 3. Compulsory Purchase

1. Powers. A landowner is subject to what is sometimes called "eminent domain," namely, the right of Parliament, as part of its legislative omnipotence, to authorise the compulsory acquisition of land.

(a) *General.* There are many statutes, both general and specific, which authorise the compulsory purchase of land by various public and other bodies for specified purposes.[92] At first, each Act was usually self-contained, but then the Lands Clauses Consolidation Act 1845 laid down comprehensive codes of procedure and compensation. These provisions are now mainly contained in the Land Compensation Acts 1961 and 1973, the Compulsory Purchase Act 1965, the Acquisition of Land Act 1981, and the Planning and Compensation Act 1991. The individual Acts that authorise compulsory purchase are now primarily concerned with the purposes for which the land may be taken and the bodies which can take it.

(b) *Planning.* The Town and Country Planning Act 1947[93] extended the scope of compulsory acquisition from acquisitions for specified purposes to acquisitions made to secure the development of the land in accordance with the development plan. Under the present provisions, the Secretary of State may authorise local authorities to acquire any land in their areas which—

(i) is suitable for and required in order to secure the carrying out of development, re-development or improvement; or
(ii) is required for a purpose which it is necessary to achieve in the interests of the proper planning of an area in which the land is situated; or
(iii) adjoins such land and is required for executing works for facilitating its development or use.[94]

(c) *Useless and blighted land.* The Town and Country Planning Act 1947 introduced a process which enabled a landowner to require a local authority to purchase his land compulsorily if planning permission for it was refused or

---

[91] A.H.A. 1986, s.11.
[92] In 1962 over 70 "main Acts" could be listed (R.D. Stewart-Brown, *Guide to Compulsory Purchase and Compensation* (5th ed.)), and in 1974 the powers were summarised under 87 heads (A.S. Wisdom, *Local Authorities' Powers of Purchase* (5th ed.).
[93] s.38, foreshadowed by the more limited Town and Country Planning Act 1944, s.10.
[94] Town and Country Planning Act 1990, s.226; and see subs.(3)(b) (exchange for commons, open spaces etc.).

was granted subject to conditions. He can do this only if the land "has become incapable of reasonably beneficial use in its existing state,"[95] and cannot be rendered capable of such use by carrying out any permitted development.[96] There is also a similar right where land is "blighted" by planning proposals by public authorities contained in structure or local plans,[97] *e.g.* for the construction of highways.

2. Procedure. An Act which authorises the compulsory acquisition of land may of course make its own provisions governing procedure and compensation. But this is unusual, and normally the acquisition is governed by the general Acts that have been mentioned above.[98] Under these, the main steps are as follows.

(a) *Order.* When an authority wishes to make a specific purchase, it makes a compulsory purchase order. This does not take effect until it is confirmed by the appropriate Minister; and he must hear any objections to it, usually at a public local inquiry conducted by an inspector.

(b) *Notice to treat.* When confirmed, the order enables the acquiring authority to serve a "notice to treat" on the owner.[99] This does not by itself create a contract for sale, though it gives either party the right to have the compensation assessed by the Lands Tribunal in default of agreement. Once the compensation has been determined, the sale is specifically enforceable as a contract.

(c) *Entry.* Once the compensation has been determined, the acquiring authority can obtain possession by completing the purchase. Yet at any time after serving the notice to treat and before completion, the acquiring authority can enter the land on 14 days' notice, though in this case the authority must pay interest from the date of entry on the compensation when assessed.[1]

3. Compensation. For long, the general basis of compensation on a compulsory acquisition was the open market value of the land. The Town and Country Planning Act 1947 changed this by giving the owner only the value of the land for its existing use, without any potential development value, and leaving him with whatever claim he might have against a compensation fund for the loss of development values. After the abolition of the system of development charges,[2] this artificial basis for compensation was repealed by

[95] See *R. v. Minister of Housing and Local Government, ex p. Chichester R.D.C.* [1960] 1 W.L.R. 587.
[96] Town and Country Planning Act 1990, ss.137–148, replacing Town and Country Planning Act 1947, s.19.
[97] Town and Country Planning Act 1990, ss.149–160, Sched. 13.
[98] *Ante*, p. 519.
[99] Compulsory Purchase Act 1965, s.5; Planning and Compensation Act 1991, s.67.
[1] Compulsory Purchase Act 1965, s.11.
[2] *Ante*, p. 511.

the Town and Country Planning Act 1959, and the open market value was restored.

(a) *Open market value.* The open market value of land depends not only on the planning permissions that have been granted but also on those which might be granted. For these purposes it has to be assumed that planning permission will be granted—

(1) For the development for which the purchase is being made;
(2) For any development within the existing use of the land;
(3) For any development certified by the local planning authority as being likely to be granted planning permission;
(4) For any specified development as defined in the development plan; and
(5) For any development for which planning permission might reasonably be expected to be granted[3] if it either falls within a primary use for which the development plan allocates it, or else (if it is in an action area[4]) falls within the uses permitted in that area. Except for action areas, this and the last paragraph do not apply to land defined by the development plan as being subject to comprehensive development.[5]

Any enhancement in the value of the land that is due to the acquiring authority's proposals for other land must be excluded.[6]

(b) *Other provisions.* Apart from the market value, compensation may also be payable for injurious affection[7] (*i.e.* injury to other lands caused by the acquisition), and for disturbance, as well as "home loss payments."[8] Additional compensation is also payable to the former owner if the value of the land increases in consequence of a planning decision made within 10 years after completion.[9]

(c) *Equivalent reinstatement.* Where the land is devoted (and but for the acquisition would continue to be devoted) to a purpose for which there is no general demand or market, such as a church or school, compensation may be assessed on the basis of the reasonable cost of equivalent reinstatement[10] at the date when the work of reinstatement might reasonably be expected to begin.[11] But this basis can be adopted only where reinstatement in some other place is *bona fide* intended.[12]

---

[3] See *Provincial Properties (London) Ltd.* v. *Caterham and Warlingham U.D.C.* [1972] 1 Q.B. 453.
[4] See *ante*, p. 514.
[5] Land Compensation Act 1961, ss.15, 16, Pt. III.
[6] *Ibid.* ss.6–9, Sched. 1.
[7] See Land Compensation Act 1973, Pt. IV.
[8] *Ibid.* Pt. III.
[9] Land Compensation Act 1961, Pt. IV, repealed by Land Commission Act 1967, ss.86, 101, Sched. 17, but revived and amended by Planning and Compensation Act 1991, s.66, Sched. 14.
[10] Land Compensation Act 1961, s.5.
[11] *Birmingham Corporation* v. *West Midland Baptist (Trust) Association (Inc.)* [1970] A.C. 874.
[12] Land Compensation Act 1961, s.5.

Sect. 4. Minerals

As has been seen,[13] the Crown is entitled at common law to all gold and silver occurring in any mine. In addition, statute has deprived landowners of certain other minerals occurring in or under their land.

1. Petroleum and natural gas. Under the Petroleum (Production) Act 1934 there was vested in the Crown petroleum existing in its natural condition in strata, including any mineral oil or relative hydrocarbon and natural gas.[14]

2. Coal. Under the Coal Act 1938, all interests in coal (except interests arising under a coal-mining lease) were vested in the Coal Commission in return for compensation; and these interests (including coal-mining leases) are now vested in the British Coal Corporation.[15]

Part 3

PROTECTION OF TENANTS

The modern tendency has been to enact legislation designed to protect tenants against their landlords. At common law, the matter was in general one of contract: provided a landlord did not contravene the terms of his bargain, he might at will evict his tenant, or under the threat of eviction secure his agreement to pay an increased rent of whatever amount he could exact. Although a number of matters such as fixtures, emblements and the like are of importance, the two crucial matters in any scheme for protecting tenants are protection against eviction, and control of rent: and these subjects will be dealt with here.

Legislation has been piecemeal. Apart from some relatively mild provisions concerning agricultural land, beginning with the Agricultural Holdings (England) Act 1875, no real system of control existed until the first of the Rent Acts was enacted in 1915. There is little common design to be found in the various statutes: as will be seen, protection against eviction is provided by a wide variety of devices, and so is control of rent.

There are three main categories, depending on the nature of the tenancy. They are—

(1) Business premises;
(2) Agricultural holdings; and
(3) Dwellings.

Although the first two heads are not simple, they are relatively uncomplicated. The third head is highly complex. Both the application of the statutes

---

[13] *Ante*, p. 509.
[14] s.1; *Earl of Lonsdale* v. *Att.-Gen.* [1982] 1 W.L.R. 887.
[15] Coal Industry Nationalisation Act 1946; Coal Industry Act 1987, s.1.

and the extent of the protection that is given depend on matters such as the type of tenancy, its length, the value of the dwelling, the date when the tenancy was granted, and whether or not the landlord is a public body. Part of the complexity, though by no means all, is due to political considerations, with successive governments introducing legislation to increase or decrease the degree of protection. Outlines of the different systems will be considered in turn.

Sect. 1. Business Premises

1. The Act of 1927. Business premises were first protected[16] by Part I of the Landlord and Tenant Act 1927. This gave the tenant the right to a new lease (or compensation in lieu thereof) provided he could establish that by reason of the carrying on by him or his predecessors in title at the premises of a trade or business for not less than five years, goodwill had become attached to the premises by reason whereof they could be let at a higher rent than they otherwise would have realised.[17] The mere building up of goodwill was thus not enough, for often the tenant, on leaving, would carry much of it with him. What had to be shown was goodwill which remained adherent to the premises after the tenant had gone. This was usually difficult to prove and, indeed, normally impossible except in the case of shops; and tenancies of professional premises were outside these provisions. The procedural requirements for making a valid claim under the Act were complicated, too, and many claims failed on purely technical grounds. These relatively ineffectual provisions were replaced by the far-reaching terms of the Landlord and Tenant Act 1954, Part II, as amended in some details by the Law of Property Act 1969, Part I. The closely restricted right for business tenants to claim compensation for improvements, subject to certain conditions, continues in an amended form.[18]

2. The Act of 1954

(a) *Tenancies within the Act.* Part II of the Landlord and Tenant Act 1954 applies to any tenancy where the property comprised in it is or includes premises occupied by the tenant for the purposes of any trade, profession or employment[19]; there is no requirement of adherent goodwill. The principal exceptions from the Act are the following: agricultural holdings[20]; regulated tenancies under the Rent Act 1977[21] or assured tenancies under the Housing Act 1988[22]; mining leases; most licensed premises other than *bona fide* hotels and restaurants; and certain tenancies granted to a servant during his

---

[16] Apart from nearly a year's protection under the Rent Acts: Act of 1920, s.13.
[17] L. & T.A. 1927, ss.4, 5.
[18] *Post*, p. 526.
[19] L. & T.A. 1954, s.23.
[20] See *post*, p. 527.
[21] Rent Act 1977, s.24(3); *post*, p. 533.
[22] H.A. 1988, Sched. 1, para. 4; *post*, p. 541.

employment, or granted for not more than six months.[23] Tenancies at will or at sufferance are also outside the Act.[24]

(b) *Security of tenure.* Security of tenure is secured by the simple provision that a tenancy within Part II "shall not come to an end unless terminated in accordance with the provisions of this Part of this Act."[25] Thus a tenancy for a fixed term may continue indefinitely despite the expiration of the fixed term,[26] and an ordinary notice to quit given by the landlord will be inoperative; but the tenancy may still determine by notice to quit given by the tenant or by surrender or forfeiture.[27] In order to determine the tenancy the landlord must give not less than six nor more than 12 months' notice in the statutory form, to expire not earlier than the date when, apart from the Act, the tenancy could have been determined by notice to quit, or would have expired.[28] If within two months of receiving this notice the tenant gives the landlord notice that he is not willing to give up possession of the premises, he may, not less than two nor more than four months after the landlord's notice was given, apply to the court for a new tenancy.[29] For this purpose, the "corresponding date" rule[30] applies in determining whether the application was made too early[31] or too late.[32] Alternatively, a tenant holding for a fixed term (and not merely under a periodical tenancy) may serve on the landlord a statutory form of request for a new tenancy in place of the old, to begin not less than six nor more than 12 months later; and not less than two nor more than four months after serving this request he must apply to the court.[33]

(c) *Opposition to new tenancy.* The court is bound to grant the tenant a new tenancy unless the landlord establishes one of the seven statutory grounds of opposition. The landlord can rely only on the grounds stated in his statutory notice or in a notice served on the tenant within two months of receiving the request for a new tenancy. Some of the grounds are based on default by the tenant and others on the landlord's need; and only the first three and the fifth, by using the word "ought," give the court any discretion. The seven grounds are as follows.[34]

(1) REPAIR: that the tenant ought not to be granted a new tenancy in view of the state of the "holding" (*i.e.* the premises let, excluding any part not occupied by the tenant or a service tenant of his) due to the tenant's failure to comply with his repairing obligations.

[23] L. & T.A. 1954, s.43, as amended.
[24] *Wheeler* v. *Mercer* [1957] A.C. 416; *Hagee (London) Ltd.* v. *A.B. Erikson and Larson* [1976] Q.B. 209.
[25] Act of 1954, s.24.
[26] See *Herbert Duncan Ltd.* v. *Cluttons* [1992] 22 E.G. 110 (original lessee remains liable for rent during continuation).
[27] But see L.P.A. 1969, s.4 (ineffective if during first month of occupation).
[28] Act of 1954, s.25.
[29] *Ibid.* s.29.
[30] *Ante*, p. 317.
[31] *E.J. Riley Investments Ltd.* v. *Eurostyle Holdings Ltd.* [1985] 1 W.L.R. 1139.
[32] *Dodds* v. *Walker* [1981] 1 W.L.R. 1027.
[33] L. & T.A. 1954, ss.26, 29.
[34] *Ibid.* ss.29, 30.

(2) RENT: that the tenant ought not to be granted a new tenancy in view of his persistent delay in paying rent.

(3) OTHER BREACHES: that the tenant ought not to be granted a new tenancy in view of other substantial breaches by him of his obligations under the tenancy, or for any other reason connected with his use or management of the holding.

(4) ALTERNATIVE ACCOMMODATION: that the landlord has offered and is willing to provide or secure the provision of suitable alternative accommodation on reasonable terms.

(5) PART OF WHOLE: that the premises are part of larger premises held by the landlord and the tenant ought not to be granted a new tenancy because the landlord could obtain a substantially greater rent for the property as a whole than for the parts separately.

(6) DEMOLITION OR RECONSTRUCTION: "that on the termination of the current tenancy the landlord intends to demolish or reconstruct the premises comprised in the holding or a substantial part of those premises or to carry out substantial work of construction on the holding or part thereof and that he could not reasonably do so without obtaining possession of the holding." The landlord cannot succeed on this ground if he has a right under the current tenancy to enter and do the work,[35] or if the tenant is willing to give the landlord facilities for the work without unduly interfering with the tenant's business, or the tenant is willing to accept a tenancy of an economically separable part of the holding.[36]

(7) OWN OCCUPATION: "that on the termination of the current tenancy the landlord intends to occupy the holding for the purposes, or partly for the purposes, of a business to be carried on by him therein, or as his residence." But this head is not open to a landlord whose interest was purchased or created less than five years before the termination of the current tenancy.

The landlord cannot have the intention required by the last two heads unless at the date of the hearing he has not a mere hope but a firm, settled intention, not likely to be changed, to do something that he has a reasonable prospect of bringing about.[37] Normally an undertaking to the court given by a responsible person or body conclusively shows an intention to do what is undertaken, *e.g.* to demolish the premises.[38] A landlord who genuinely intends to reconstruct the premises and then occupy them himself is not affected by the five years rule, for the existence of Ground 7 does not prevent him from relying on Ground 6.[39]

(d) *Terms of new tenancy.* When premises are first let to a business tenant,

[35] *Heath* v. *Drown* [1973] A.C. 498.
[36] L. & T.A. 1954, s.31A, added by L.P.A. 1969, s.7.
[37] *Betty's Cafes Ltd.* v. *Phillips Furnishing Stores Ltd.* [1959] A.C. 20.
[38] *Espresso Coffee Machine Co. Ltd.* v. *Guardian Assurance Co. Ltd.* [1959] 1 W.L.R. 250.
[39] *Fisher* v. *Taylors Furnishing Stores Ltd.* [1956] 2 Q.B. 78.

there is no restriction on the amount of rent that may be charged. Nor is there any power to secure any revision of the rent as long as the initial tenancy continues, unless the tenancy provides for it, as by including a rent review clause. But if the tenant obtains a new tenancy under the Act, the rent will be the open market rent, and a rent review clause may be included; and in default of agreement the court will determine the rent and other terms of the tenancy, though new terms will be inserted only for good reason based on essential fairness.[40] The rent may thus be raised or lowered, but the tenant is protected against unreasonable demands by the landlord. The duration of any new tenancy is whatever the court thinks reasonable, not exceeding 14 years[41]; but there is no limit to the number of renewals. The basic idea of the Act is thus that a business tenant has a *prima facie* right to continue his business indefinitely in the premises, and although there is no restriction on the terms of the tenancy under which he first occupies the premises, any renewals are controlled by the court. The court may fix an interim rent to run until the new tenancy is granted.[42]

(e) *Compensation for eviction.* A tenant who does not obtain a new tenancy is entitled to no compensation unless this occurs because the landlord objects to the grant of a new tenancy solely by reason of one or more of the last three grounds set out above, all of which are for the landlord's benefit. In these cases, the landlord must pay the tenant compensation equal to the rateable value of the premises, or twice that sum if the tenant and his predecessors in the business have occupied the premises for business purposes for the previous 14 years.[43]

(f) *Compensation for improvements.* Under the Landlord and Tenant Act 1927,[44] if a tenant of premises used for a trade, business or profession carries out improvements to the premises which add to their letting value, the tenant may recover compensation from the landlord on leaving. But the tenant must satisfy a number of conditions: in addition to making his claim at the right time and in due form, he must give the landlord three months' notice of his intention to make the improvement. The landlord may then exclude the tenant's right to compensation if he successfully objects to the improvement, or carries it out himself in return for a reasonable increase of rent.

Sect. 2. Agricultural Holdings

1. Introduction. The Agricultural Holdings (England) Act 1875 was the

---

[40] L. & T.A. 1954, ss.32, 34, 35; *O'May* v. *City of London Real Property Co. Ltd.* [1983] 2 A.C. 726 at 741.

[41] L. & T.A. 1954, s.33.

[42] *Ibid.* s.24A, inserted by L.P.A. 1969, s.3, a difficult provision: see *Fawke* v. *Viscount Chelsea* [1980] Q.B. 441.

[43] L. & T.A. 1954, s.37, as amended by L.P.A. 1969, s.11.

[44] ss.1–3, as amended by L. & T.A. 1954, Pt. III. See (1989) Law Com. No. 178; (1991) 11 Legal Studies 119 (M. Haley).

first of a long series of Acts regulating agricultural holdings. At first, the Acts were mainly directed towards securing proper compensation for the tenant, initially for improvements and, latterly, also if his tenancy was determined without good cause.[45] The Agriculture Act 1947 first gave security of tenure and protection as to rent, in place of the limited security of tenure provided during the war by Defence Regulations. The principal Act today is the Agricultural Holdings Act 1986 which consolidates much previous legislation.[46]

2. Jurisdiction. The Act confers many powers on the Minister of Agriculture, Fisheries and Food, on Agricultural Land Tribunals, and on arbitrators. Under the Agriculture Act 1958 the powers of determining disputes which had been vested in the Minister and the former County Agricultural Executive Committee were transferred to the Agricultural Land Tribunals, which had previously had mainly appellate functions. Each of the eight areas into which England and Wales is divided has a Tribunal presided over by a lawyer appointed by the Lord Chancellor; and the Council on Tribunals supervises both the Tribunals and any arbitrators (unless appointed by agreement).[47]

3. "Agricultural holding." The Act applies to any "agricultural holding." This means the aggregate of land used for the trade or business of agriculture which is comprised in a contract of tenancy for years, or from year to year.[48] An agreement for value[49] granting a licence to occupy land for use as agricultural land, or letting it for an interest less than a tenancy from year to year, is treated as being a tenancy from year to year if the circumstances are such that the land would otherwise be an agricultural holding.[50] But this does not apply to agreements approved by the Minister, or to those made in contemplation of the use of the land only for grazing or mowing (or both) during some specified period of the year,[51] even if the period is 364 days[52] or there are successive periods of three months.[53] "Agriculture" is widely defined, and includes horticulture, fruit growing, seed growing and market gardening.[54] On a mixed letting, such as a tenancy of pasture, an orchard and an inn, the Act applies to all or none: the test is whether as a whole the tenancy is in substance a tenancy of agricultural land.[55]

---

[45] A.H.A. 1923, s.12.
[46] Principally A.H.A. 1948; Agricultural Holdings (Notice to Quit) Act 1977; A.H.A. 1984.
[47] See Agriculture Act 1947, s.73, Sched. 9; Tribunals and Inquiries Act 1971, s.1, Sched. 1; Agriculture (Miscellaneous Provisions) Act 1972, s.21 (abolishing the C.A.E. Committees); A.H.A. 1986, Sched. 14, para. 49.
[48] A.H.A. 1986, s.1.
[49] *Goldsack* v. *Shore* [1950] 1 K.B. 708.
[50] A.H.A. 1986, s.2.
[51] *Ibid.*
[52] *Reid* v. *Dawson* [1955] 1 Q.B. 214.
[53] *Scene Estate Ltd.* v. *Amos* [1957] 2 Q.B. 205; contrast *Rutherford* v. *Maurer* [1962] 1 Q.B. 16 ("six months periods").
[54] A.H.A. 1986, s.96.
[55] *Dunn* v. *Fidoe* [1950] 2 All E.R. 685; *Howkins* v. *Jardine* [1951] 1 K.B. 614; *Monson* v. *Bound* [1954] 1 W.L.R. 1321.

4. Notices to quit. On the expiry of a tenancy for two years or more, the tenancy continues as a tenancy from year to year unless either party has given notice to quit not less than a year nor more than two years before the date of expiration, or unless the tenant has died before that date.[56] This provision cannot be excluded by agreement unless the term is for at least two years but not more than five, and the Minister approves a joint application by both parties.[57] A notice to quit an agricultural holding (including a notice exercising an option of terminating the tenancy agreement[58]) is invalid if it purports to determine the tenancy before the expiry of one year from the end of the current tenancy[59]; and this is so despite any contrary provision in the tenancy agreement,[60] and even if the notice was given by the tenant.[61] But there are certain exceptions,[62] and the parties may agree to treat an invalid notice as being valid.[63] Curiously, a tenancy for more than 12 months and less than 24, although an "agricultural holding" for the purpose of business tenancies,[64] escapes the protection of these provisions.[65]

5. Security of tenure. The landlord's right to serve a notice to quit, as modified in this way, remains unaffected. But if he is given a counter-notice[66] by the tenant (or, for joint tenants, by all the tenants[67]) within one month of the tenant receiving a notice to quit, then, with eight exceptions,[68] the notice to quit becomes ineffective unless the Agricultural Land Tribunal consents to it taking effect; and only in six cases can the Tribunal give that consent.[69] There are thus three categories.

(a) *No security.* The notice to quit will be effective if either the tenant fails to serve a counter-notice in time, or else the case falls within one of the eight following heads and the notice to quit makes plain the head on which the landlord relies.[70]

CASE A: SMALLHOLDING: the holding is let as a smallholding; the tenant signed an acknowledgment in the tenancy agreement that it was subject to this head; he is 65 or more; and suitable alternative accommodation for him is available.

---

[56] A.H.A. 1986, ss.3, 4.
[57] *Ibid.* s.5. See, *e.g. Pahl* v. *Trevor* [1992] 25 E.G. 130 (five year term until deceased tenant's grandson is old enough to become tenant).
[58] See *Edell* v. *Dulieu* [1924] A.C. 38.
[59] A.H.A. 1986, s.25.
[60] *Ibid.*
[61] *Flather* v. *Hood* (1928) 44 T.L.R. 698.
[62] A.H.A. 1986, s.25.
[63] *Elsden* v. *Pick* [1980] 1 W.L.R. 898.
[64] *E.W.P. Ltd.* v. *Moore* [1992] 1 Q.B. 460; *ante,* p. 523.
[65] *Ibid.* applying *Gladstone* v. *Bower* [1960] 2 Q.B. 384.
[66] See *Mountford* v. *Hodkinson* [1956] 1 W.L.R. 422 (abusive letter), and contrast *Frankland* v. *Capstick* [1959] 1 W.L.R. 204.
[67] *Featherstone* v. *Staples* [1986] 1 W.L.R. 861.
[68] A.H.A. 1986, s.26, Sched. 3.
[69] *Ibid.* s.27.
[70] *Ibid.* Sched. 3; *Cowan* v. *Wrayford* [1953] 1 W.L.R. 1340.

CASE B: PLANNING PERMISSION: the land is required for some non-agricultural use for which planning permission has been given or (in certain cases) is not required.

CASE C: BAD HUSBANDRY: within the previous six months the Tribunal has certified that the tenant was not farming in accordance with the rules of good husbandry.

CASE D: UNREMEDIED BREACH: when the notice was given the tenant had failed to comply fully[71] with a written notice by the landlord in the prescribed form requiring him to remedy a breach of a term of his tenancy[72] within a specified time.

CASE E: IRREPARABLE BREACH: when the notice was given the landlord's interest in the holding had been materially prejudiced by an irreparable breach of a term of the tenancy.

CASE F: INSOLVENCY: the tenant was insolvent when the notice was given.

CASE G: DEATH: the notice is given within three months after the landlord receives written notice of the death of the tenant, or the sole surviving tenant. But there are elaborate provisions[73] which enable the Tribunal to direct, on an application made within three months of the death, that a tenancy of the holding should be given to one or more of certain near relations of the tenant who have lived by working on the holding for at least five years, and the notice to quit is subject to any such direction.

CASE H: MINISTER'S NOTICE: the notice to quit is given by the Minister for the purpose of an amalgamation or reshaping of any agricultural unit, and the tenant signed an acknowledgment in the tenancy agreement that it was subject to this head.

(b) *Security dependent on reasonableness.* In six cases the Tribunal must consent to the notice to quit taking effect unless it appears that "a fair and reasonable landlord would not insist on possession," in which case the Tribunal must withhold consent.[74] Each case except the fifth depends on the purpose for which the landlord proposes to terminate the tenancy; and any consent may be made subject to conditions (which may later be varied or revoked) to ensure that the land is used for the purpose stated by the landlord.[75] The six cases are as follows.

(1) GOOD HUSBANDRY: carrying out the purpose is desirable in the interests of the land as a separate unit;

(2) SOUND MANAGEMENT: carrying out the purpose is desirable in the interests of sound management of the estate.[76]

---

[71] *Price* v. *Romilly* [1960] 1 W.L.R. 1360.
[72] See *Lloyds Bank Ltd.* v. *Jones* [1955] 2 Q.B. 298 (personal residence).
[73] A.H.A. 1986, ss.34–48.
[74] *Ibid.* s.27(1), (2).
[75] *Ibid.* s.27(3), (4).
[76] See *Evans* v. *Roper* [1960] 1 W.L.R. 814.

(3) RESEARCH: carrying out the purpose is desirable for the purposes of agricultural research, education, experiment or demonstration, or for the purposes of the statutes relating to smallholdings.

(4) ALLOTMENTS: carrying out the purpose is desirable for the purposes of the statutes relating to allotments;

(5) GREATER HARDSHIP: withholding consent would cause greater hardship than granting it.

(6) NON-AGRICULTURAL USE: the purpose is to use the land for some non-agricultural use not within Case B above.

(c) *Full security:* Where the case does not fall within any of the foregoing heads, the notice to quit is ineffective, and the tenancy continues unaffected.

6. Protection as to rent. When an agricultural tenancy is first granted, the parties are free to agree whatever rent they please. However, not more frequently that once in every three years, either party may require the amount of rent to be submitted to arbitration by an arbitrator appointed by the parties or in default by the President of the Royal Institution of Chartered Surveyors.[77] The rent is to be the "rent properly payable" for the holding; and this is the rent at which it might reasonably be expected to be let, taking all relevant factors into account, including the current level of rents for comparable lettings, though disregarding any element in them that is due to an appreciable scarcity of comparable holdings.[78] Any increase or decrease awarded by the arbitrator takes effect as from the next day on which the tenancy could have been determined by a notice to quit given when the reference to arbitration was demanded.[79] Accordingly, apart from any agreement, no revision of rent is possible during a tenancy for a fixed term which is not determinable by a notice to quit. In addition, the landlord may increase the rent in respect of certain improvements carried out by him.[80]

7. Compensation for disturbance. If a tenant quits the holding in consequence of a notice to quit given by the landlord, he will usually be entitled to compensation from the landlord,[81] even if the notice to quit is in fact invalid.[82] "Basic compensation" is equal to one year's rent of the holding, or, subject to the tenant giving the landlord notice a month before the end of the tenancy and a reasonable opportunity of valuing the farming assets, either the actual loss or two years' rent, whichever is the smaller.[83] But in Cases C, D, E, F or G above, no compensation is payable.[84] In certain cases, as where

[77] A.H.A. 1986, ss.12, 84, Sched. 2.
[78] *Ibid.* s.12(2), Sched. 2.
[79] *Ibid.* s.12(2), (4). See *Sclater* v. *Horton* [1954] 2 Q.B. 1.
[80] A.H.A. 1986, s.13.
[81] *Ibid.* s.60.
[82] *Kestell* v. *Langmaid* [1950] 1 K.B. 233.
[83] A.H.A. 1986, s.60.
[84] *Ibid.* s.61.

the land is to be used otherwise than for agriculture, additional compensation equal to four years' rent may be payable.[85] No agreement can exclude either this or any other provision in the Act as to compensation,[86] and a provision which seeks to do this indirectly (*e.g.* by providing for the determination of the tenancy at such short notice as to leave no time to claim compensation) is void.[87]

8. Compensation for improvements. When an agricultural tenant quits his holding at the end of his tenancy, he is entitled to compensation for certain improvements carried out by him, provided he has observed the necessary requirements. For improvements begun on or after March 1, 1948, there are three categories.[88] First, there are long-term improvements for which the landlord's consent was obtained, such as planting orchards. Second, there are long-term improvements for which either the landlord's consent or the approval of the Tribunal was obtained, such as the erection of buildings. Third, there are short-term improvements for which no consent or approval is required, such as the liming or chalking of the land. The measure of compensation is the consequent increase in the value of the holding, or, for short-term improvements, their value to an incoming tenant. For "old improvements" (*i.e.* those commenced before March 1, 1948) there is a shorter list of improvements, including the erection of buildings and the reclaiming of waste land; and if they were made with the landlord's consent compensation is payable for the consequent increase in the value of the holding.[89]

Sect. 3. Dwellings

Not until 1915 were there any statutory provisions which protected tenants of dwellings. The first in a long line of Rent Acts[90] then established a system under which the rent of a dwelling could not be increased by more than a limited amount and the tenant could not be evicted except on specified grounds, even though at common law his tenancy had come to an end. In 1920 this system was consolidated and amended, and then, after various amendments which reduced the number of dwellings to which the system applied, in 1939 it was expanded so as to apply once more to all save the larger dwellings.[91] Many categories of tenancy were excluded from the system, including furnished dwellings, long tenancies (*i.e.* those for over 21 years), tenancies at a very low rent (*i.e.* less than two-thirds of the rateable value) and tenancies where the landlords were local authorities. But then,

---

[85] *Ibid.* ss.27(3)(f), 60(4), 61(4), (5).
[86] *Ibid.* s.78.
[87] *Coates* v. *Diment* [1951] 1 All E.R. 890.
[88] A.H.A. 1986, ss.64–66; Sched. 7, 8.
[89] *Ibid.* s.64, Sched. 9.
[90] Increase of Rent and Mortgage Interest (War Restrictions) Act 1915.
[91] Rent and Mortgage Interest Restrictions Acts 1920 to 1939.

from 1945 onwards, various statutes[92] were enacted which either applied the Acts to some of the types of tenancy which had been excluded or else provided some other form of protection for them; and with political changes in the government came variations in the maximum value of dwellings to which the Acts would apply.

Finally (at least for the time being) the Housing Act 1988 prevented the Rent Acts from applying to any tenancy granted on or after January 15, 1989, but instead gave such tenancies (called "assured tenancies") a more limited form of protection. For fifty years, tenancies protected by the Rent Acts were called "controlled tenancies"; but tenancies that the Rent Act 1965 brought into protection, with a different system for fixing the rent, were called "regulated tenancies," and the Rent Act 1977 called both types "protected tenancies." Under the Housing Act 1980 all controlled tenancies became regulated tenancies.

The best way of approaching the complex of systems protecting tenancies of dwellings seems to be to consider them in two main groups. The first group consists of protection for the tenant under the main systems of the Rent Acts, or some variant of them. Under this head there are four categories:

(1) The old general system of the Rent Acts which culminated in the system for regulated tenancies under the Rent Act 1977.
(2) The new general system for assured tenancies under the Housing Act 1988, with its lesser protection for tenants.
(3) The variant system of "agricultural occupancies" for "tied cottages."
(4) The variant and partial system of "secure tenancies" for lettings by local authorities.

The second main group consists of special systems for the protection of special categories, namely—

(5) Two alternative systems for long tenancies at a low rent.
(6) A special system for "restricted contracts" which fall outside the Rent Acts.

The broad picture is that all the systems except the first two were created in order to protect tenancies or contracts which had been excluded from the Rent Acts but were found to need protection; and this protection was given either by extending the ambit of the Rent Acts or by providing some new system. In addition to these systems, there are certain procedural provisions relating to eviction and harassment that are designed to ensure that no residential occupiers will be evicted from their dwellings except under an order of the court.

---

[92] The main Acts were Furnished Houses (Rent Control) Act 1946; Landlord and Tenant (Rent Control) Act 1949; Housing Repairs and Rents Act 1954; Rent Act 1957; Rent Act 1965; H.A. 1969; Housing Finance Act 1972; Counter-Inflation Act 1973; Rent Act 1974; Rent Act 1977; H.A. 1980; H.A. 1988.

A. The Rent Acts: Regulated Tenancies

No regulated tenancy can arise on a letting made on or after January 15, 1989[93]; but large numbers of regulated tenancies had arisen before that date, and these continue to be subject to the main Rent Acts. The present Act governing regulated tenancies is the Rent Act 1977, as amended.

1. Application of the Acts. The Rent Act 1977 applies to every "dwelling-house" of an appropriate rateable value[94] which satisfies certain conditions. "Dwelling-house" means any house (or part of a house) which is "let as a separate dwelling."[95] Thus the existence of a tenancy is essential; this requirement excludes a mere licence from the Acts, though not a tenant at will or at sufferance. Whether the premises are let "as" a dwelling depends on the use provided for or contemplated by the tenancy agreement, or, in default, by the *de facto* user at the time in question.[96] And the letting must be as "a" (*i.e.* one) dwelling and not as two or more dwellings.[97]

The word "separate" formerly excluded lettings where the tenant was required to share living accommodation such as a kitchen.[98] However, statute has modified the rule, so that where the sharing is with the landlord the tenant is given restricted contract protection,[99] and where the sharing is with other tenants, the tenant has normal protection, subject to certain modifications.[1] Often what is structurally a single dwelling-house contains many "dwelling-houses" for the purposes of the Rent Acts, even if it has not been physically divided into self-contained flats; for one or two rooms, with a right to share the bathroom and lavatory, may for this purpose constitute a "dwelling-house."

2. Exceptions. Certain tenancies which would otherwise fall within the Acts are nevertheless excluded. In some cases, the exception is personal to the landlord. Thus, the Crown is generally not bound by the Acts (though tenants are protected where the interest of the Crown is under the management of the Crown Estate Commissioners[2]), nor are local authorities, new town development corporations or certain housing associations or housing trusts,[3] though they are subject to a limit degree of control.[4] In such cases, the exemption does not operate in favour of other persons concerned with the property, such as sub-tenants or purchasers. Other exceptions depend on the nature of the tenancies. Thus the Acts do not apply where the letting

---

[93] H.A. 1988, s.1, Sched. 1.
[94] See *post*, p. 534.
[95] Act of 1977, s.1.
[96] *Wolfe* v. *Hogan* [1949] 2 K.B. 194.
[97] *Horford Investments Ltd.* v. *Lambert* [1976] Ch. 39; *St. Catherine's College* v. *Dorling* [1980] 1 W.L.R. 66.
[98] *Neale* v. *Del Soto* [1945] K.B. 144.
[99] Act of 1977, s.21. See *post*, p. 551.
[1] *Ibid.* s.22.
[2] *Ibid.* s.13, as substituted by H.A. 1980, s.73.
[3] Act of 1977, ss.14, 15, as amended by H.A. 1980, s.74.
[4] See *post*, p. 546.

is rent free or the rent is less than two-thirds of the rateable value.[5] Again, the Acts are excluded where the tenancy was granted in order to give the tenant the right to occupy the dwelling for a holiday, or if the tenant is pursuing or intends to pursue a course of study provided by a specified institution, and the tenancy was granted by that or some other specified body.[6] The Acts are also excluded where the rent includes payments in respect of board or, if they are substantial, attendance[7]; payments for the use of furniture formerly excluded the Acts but no longer do so.[8]

Most of the exceptions, however, depend on the nature or status of the premises themselves. Thus for diverse reasons, public houses,[9] and parsonage houses of the Church of England[10] (*e.g.* the ordinary rectory or vicarage), are outside the Act. Agricultural holdings occupied by the farmer are also outside the Acts, though, of course, within the Agricultural Holdings Act 1986.[11] Although in general any land or premises let together with a dwelling-house are treated as being part of the dwelling-house, if the dwelling-house is let together with more than two acres of agricultural land, both house and land are excluded from the Acts.[12]

A further exception is for a tenancy granted after August 13, 1974, by a "resident landlord," namely, a tenancy of part of a building granted by a landlord who throughout the tenancy occupies another part of the building as his residence. This does not apply to purpose-built blocks of flats unless the letting is of part of the landlord's flat, nor where the tenancy is granted to a protected or statutory tenant in the building.[13] A tenancy excluded from protection solely by this provision is treated as a restricted contract.[14]

3. Rateable value. A dwelling can be protected only if its rateable value does not exceed certain amounts. These amounts have varied over the years. The present amounts depend on the rateable value of the dwelling on the "appropriate day." This is March 23, 1965, or, if the rateable value of the dwelling first appeared in the valuation list after that date, the date when it first appeared.[15]

Appropriate day	*Greater London*	*Elsewhere*
A. After March 31, 1973	£1,500	£750
B. Between March 21 and April 1, 1973	£600	£300
C. Before March 22, 1973	£400	£200

[5] Act of 1977, s.5(1).
[6] *Ibid.* ss.8, 9.
[7] *Ibid.* s.7: see *Otter* v. *Norman* [1989] A.C. 129. Restricted contract protection may apply in some cases: *post*, p. 551.
[8] Rent Act 1974, s.1.
[9] Act of 1977, s.11.
[10] *Bishop of Gloucester* v. *Cunnington* [1943] K.B. 101.
[11] A.H.A. 1986, s.10.
[12] Act of 1977, s.26; and see s.6.
[13] *Ibid.* s.12, as amended by H.A. 1980, s.65.
[14] Act of 1977, s.20; *post*, p. 552.
[15] *Ibid.* s.25.

Cases in Class B must satisfy the amounts in Class A as well, and cases in Class C must also satisfy the amounts in Classes A and B,[16] so that the Acts are excluded if any relevant amount is exceeded. The striking increases in the values were due partly to the Acts being extended to larger dwellings and partly to a general reassessment and increase in rateable values. One result of the abolition of domestic rates is that for tenancies entered into after March 31, 1990, the test based on rateable values no longer applies, and the Acts are excluded only by a rent exceeding £25,000 a year.[17] Older tenancies are still governed by the rateable values.

4. Statutory tenancy. The Rent Acts protect a tenant from eviction by prohibiting the courts from making any order for possession except on specified grounds, and giving him the right to continue in possession of the premises despite the termination of the tenancy by notice to quit or otherwise.[18] The Acts thus bring into being what is usually called a "statutory tenancy": this is the right of the tenant to remain in possession, despite the determination of his contractual tenancy, on all the terms of the contractual tenancy which are not inconsistent with the Acts,[19] until the court makes an order for possession against him. A statutory tenancy is not really a "tenancy" at all, in the common law sense of the word; the tenant has no estate or interest in the land, but a mere personal right of occupation, or "status of irremovability."[20] He cannot dispose of his statutory tenancy by assignment[21] or by will, and it will not vest in his trustee in bankruptcy.

Further, a statutory tenancy will cease to exist if the tenant ceases to occupy the premises as his home[22] or one of his homes.[23] Mere temporary absences are immaterial; but once an absent tenant has lost either his *animus revertendi* (intention of returning)[24] or his *corpus possessionis* (visible indication of his *animus*, such as the presence on the premises of some caretaker on his behalf), his statutory tenancy is at an end.[25] If a house is totally destroyed, any statutory tenancy perishes with the house, whereas a contractual tenancy could continue to exist in the ruins.[26] A statutory tenancy is thus an anomaly which fits into no recognised category of property law.

5. Death of statutory tenant. When a statutory tenant dies, his tenancy does not pass under his will or intestacy, but his widow, if residing with him when he died, or otherwise any member of his family who resided with him for at least the previous six months (as decided by the court in default of

[16] *Ibid.* s.4.
[17] Local Government and Housing Act 1989, s.149; S.I. 1990, No. 434.
[18] Act of 1977, s.98.
[19] *Ibid.* s.3.
[20] *Jessamine Investment Co.* v. *Schwartz* [1978] Q.B. 264.
[21] But see Act of 1977, s.3(5), Sched. 1, para. 13.
[22] *Skinner* v. *Geary* [1931] 2 K.B. 546.
[23] *Hallwood Estates Ltd.* v. *Flack* (1950) 66(2) T.L.R. 368.
[24] *Colin Smith Music Ltd.* v. *Ridge* [1975] 1 W.L.R. 463 (tenant's deserted mistress).
[25] *Brown* v. *Brash* [1948] 2 K.B. 247; *Tickner* v. *Hearn* [1960] 1 W.L.R. 1406.
[26] *Ellis & Sons Amalgamated Properties Ltd.* v. *Sisman* [1948] 1 K.B. 653.

agreement), becomes statutory tenant in his place; and two such transmissions could take place.[27] For deaths after January 14, 1989, these rules have been modified.[28] They now apply to widowers as well as widows, and also to those merely cohabiting as man and wife; and the six months' period for residence by a member of the family is now two years' residence in the dwelling in question. But although a surviving spouse will still be fully protected as a statutory tenant, a member of the family will take only the lesser protection of an assured tenancy,[29] and so will a surviving spouse if the deceased tenant had already taken under these provisions. Further, these assured tenancies are subject to certain mandatory grounds for possession.

6. Grounds for possession. The court cannot make an order for possession unless the landlord satisfies one of the following two heads. First, that one of the discretionary grounds for possession exists, and also that in all the circumstances of the case, after considering the effect on both landlord and tenant of making or not making the order,[30] it is reasonable to make an order for possession.[31] Second, that one of the mandatory grounds for possession exists; here, there is no requirement of reasonableness. The two heads will be considered in turn.

(a) *Discretionary grounds.* Some of the discretionary grounds are based on misconduct by the tenant, others on the landlord's needs, or the existence of alternative accommodation. The heads are as follows.[32]

CASE 1: BREACH: rent lawfully due has not been paid, or some other obligation of the tenancy that is consistent with the Acts has been broken.

CASE 2: NUISANCE: the tenant, his lodger or sub-tenant has been guilty of conduct which is a nuisance to adjoining occupiers, or has been convicted of illegal or immoral user of the premises.

CASE 3: WASTE: the tenant, his lodger or sub-tenant has permitted the condition of the premises to deteriorate.

CASE 4: DAMAGE TO FURNITURE: the tenant, his lodger or sub-tenant has, by ill-treatment, caused the condition of furniture provided under the tenancy to deteriorate.

CASE 5: TENANT'S NOTICE TO QUIT: the tenant has given notice to quit and the landlord has acted upon it so as to be seriously prejudiced if he could not obtain possession.

CASE 6: ASSIGNING OR SUB-LETTING WITHOUT CONSENT: the tenant, without the landlord's consent, has assigned or sub-let the whole of the premises, or has sub-let part, the remainder being already sub-let.

[27] Act of 1977, s.2, Sched. 1, Pt. I, as amended by H.A. 1980, s.76.
[28] H.A. 1988, s.39, Sched. 4; and compare secure tenancies: *post*, p. 547.
[29] *Post*, p. 541.
[30] *Battlespring Ltd.* v. *Gates* (1983) 11 H.L.R. 6.
[31] Act of 1977, s.98.
[32] *Ibid.* Sched. 15, Pt. I.

CASE 8[33]: NEEDED FOR LANDLORD'S EMPLOYEE: the premises are reasonably required as a residence for a whole-time employee of the landlord, and they were let to the tenant in consequence of his former employment by the landlord or a previous landlord.

CASE 9: NEEDED FOR LANDLORD OR HIS FAMILY: the landlord reasonably requires the premises for occupation as a residence for himself, a child of his over 18 years old, or one of his parents or parents-in-law. There are two exceptions. First, this head is not available to a landlord who became landlord by purchasing[34] any interest in the premises after March 23, 1965. This prevents a landlord who buys the premises subject to an existing tenancy from evicting the tenant under this head.[35] Second, this head does not apply if the tenant satisfies the court that in all the circumstances "greater hardship" would be caused to all persons likely to be affected[36] by making the order for possession than by refusing it.

CASE 10: EXCESSIVE RENT ON SUB-LETTING: the tenant has sub-let part of the premises at an excessive rent.

CASE A.A.[37]: ALTERNATIVE ACCOMMODATION: suitable alternative accommodation is available for the tenant, or will be available when the order for possession takes effect. This accommodation need not be as suitable[38] as the existing accommodation and may even be part of it.[39]

(b) *Mandatory grounds.* A landlord who establishes one of the mandatory grounds for possession can obtain an order for possession as of right, irrespective of reasonableness.[40] But the grounds are available only if the tenant was given notice in writing not later than the relevant date (usually the commencement of the tenancy[41]) that the landlord might recover possession on the particular mandatory ground.[42] Further, in all the cases except the last three possession must be required for a particular purpose specified by the statute. In four cases the purpose is individually specified, but for three, several are available out of the following list, namely—

(a) the dwelling is required (*i.e.* genuinely desired[43]) as a residence for the owner or any member of his family who resided with him when he last occupied the dwelling;

(b) the owner has retired from regular employment and requires the dwelling as his residence;

[33] There is no longer a Case 7.
[34] See *Powell* v. *Cleland* [1948] 1 K.B. 262; *Thomas* v. *Fryer* [1970] 1 W.L.R. 845; *Mansukhani* v. *Sharkey* [1992] 33 E.G. 65 (gift of mortgaged flat not a purchase).
[35] See, *e.g. Wright* v. *Walford* [1955] 1 K.B. 363.
[36] See *Harte* v. *Frampton* [1948] 1 K.B. 73.
[37] Though not statutory, this heading is convenient.
[38] See *Siddiqui* v. *Rashid* [1980] 1 W.L.R. 1018; *Hill* v. *Rochard* [1983] 1 W.L.R. 478.
[39] *Parmee* v. *Mitchell* [1950] 2 K.B. 199; *Mykolyshyn* v. *Noah* [1970] 1 W.L.R. 1271.
[40] Act of 1977, s.98, Sched. 15, Pts. II, V, as amended by H.A. 1980, s.66.
[41] Act of 1977, s.98, Sched. 15, Pt. III.
[42] For Cases 11, 12, and 20, the court may dispense with this requirement.
[43] *Kennealy* v. *Dunne* [1977] Q.B. 837 (not "needed").

(c) the owner has died and the dwelling is required for a member of his family residing with him at the time of his death;

(d) the owner has died and the dwelling is required by a successor in title as his residence or for the purpose of disposing of it with vacant possession;

(e) the dwelling is subject to a mortgage which pre-dates the tenancy and the mortgagee requires the dwelling for the purpose of disposing of it with vacant possession, pursuant to his power of sale; and

(f) the dwelling is not suitably proximate to the owner's place of work and he needs the proceeds of a sale with vacant possession in order to acquire a dwelling more suitable to his needs.

The mandatory grounds are as follows[44]; they are here grouped not numerically but according to the purpose for which possession is required.

CASE 11: OWNER-OCCUPIER: the landlord was an owner-occupier of the dwelling when he let it, and he seeks possession for any purpose in the above list except (b).

CASE 12: RETIREMENT HOME: the landlord let the dwelling prior to his retirement and he seeks possession for any purpose in the above list except (a) or (f).

CASE 20: SERVICEMAN: the landlord was a member of the armed forces both when he acquired the dwelling and when he let it, and he requires it either as a residence or for any purpose in the above list except (a) or (b).

CASE 15: MINISTER OF RELIGION: the dwelling is held so as to be available for occupation by a minister of religion as a residence from which to perform his duties, and it is required for this purpose.

CASE 16: AGRICULTURAL WORKER: the dwelling was at any time occupied by an agricultural worker as such and it is required for such a worker.

CASE 17: REDUNDANT FARM-HOUSE: the dwelling is a farm-house which became redundant on amalgamation, but it is now required for an agricultural worker.

CASE 18: FARM-HOUSE REQUIRED FOR AGRICULTURE: the dwelling is a farm-house occupied by a non-agricultural tenant and it is required for occupation by a farmer or farm-worker.

CASE 13: HOLIDAY HOME: the tenancy was granted for a fixed term of not more than eight months, and at some time during the previous 12 months the dwelling had been occupied under a right to occupy it for a holiday. In this and the next two Cases there is no need for the landlord to show that he requires the dwelling for any particular purpose.

CASE 14: STUDENT RESIDENCE: the tenancy was granted for a fixed term of not more than 12 months and at some time during the previous 12 months

[44] Act of 1977, Sched. 15, Pt. II, as amended by H.A. 1980, ss.66, 67.

the dwelling was subject to a tenancy granted by a specified institution to a student at a specified educational institution.

CASE 19: PROTECTED SHORTHOLD TENANCIES. Protected shorthold tenancies were introduced by the Housing Act 1980[45] so as to encourage landlords to let dwellings by the assurance of possession being recoverable when the tenancy ended; but none could be created after January 14, 1989.[46] They were tenancies for fixed terms of from one to five years granted after giving the tenant notice that the letting was to be a protected shorthold tenancy. Once the tenancy ended, an order for possession under Case 19 was mandatory, provided (i) no further tenancy had been granted to anyone except the tenant; (ii) at least three months' notice had been given to the tenant stating that proceedings under this Case might be brought; (iii) the notice was at least three months long, and it was given during the three months immediately before the date when the tenancy ended, or an anniversary of that date; and (iv) proceedings for possession were brought within three months of the expiry of the notice.

OVERCROWDING: Although not listed as a "Case," an order for possession is mandatory as long as the dwelling is overcrowded within the meaning of the Housing Act 1985 in such circumstances as to render the occupier guilty of an offence[47]; and similarly for certain insanitary or dangerous premises.[48]

7. Rent limit

(a) *Systems.* There have been three stages in the control of rent. First, from 1915 to 1957, the "recoverable rent" for a dwelling within the Rent Acts consisted of the "standard rent" together with certain "permitted increases" (*e.g.* for improvements). The standard rent was normally the rent at which the dwelling was let on August 3, 1914, or on September 1, 1939, for newly controlled dwellings. Second, the Rent Act 1957 replaced the "recoverable rent" by a "rent limit," based on the gross value of the dwelling in 1956 for rating purposes. Third, the Rent Act 1965 continued this system for existing controlled tenancies, but applied a new system to the "regulated tenancies" that were newly brought within the Acts. Under this, "fair rents" were to be determined by "rent officers," and registered; but until that was done the maximum rent was to be the rent payable under the last regulated tenancy during the previous three years, or, if none, whatever rent was agreed under the tenancy in question. This is similar to the present system.

(b) *No registered rent.* Today, where there is no registered rent and a tenancy is being granted to a new tenant, there is no limit to the rent that can be charged: the tenant's safeguard is his right to apply to have a fair rent

[45] s.52.
[46] H.A. 1988, s.34.
[47] Act of 1977, s.101, as substituted by Housing (Consequential Provisions) Act 1985, Sched. 2.
[48] H.A. 1985, ss.264(5), 270(3), 276.

fixed and registered. But if the tenancy is granted to a sitting tenant who has security of tenure, an increased rent can be charged only under an agreement signed by both parties that boldly proclaims that refusal to sign it will not affect security of tenure and that the parties may at any time apply for the registration of a fair rent. Where the regulated tenancy has become statutory, the rent cannot exceed the rent for the last contractual period.[49]

(c) *Registration of rent.* An application to the rent officer for the registration of a fair rent may be made at any time by the landlord or the tenant. The rent officer, after giving the parties an opportunity to make representations, registers the rent if he thinks it fair, or, if not, determines and registers what he thinks would be a fair rent. There is a right of appeal to a rent assessment committee. For a period of two years after registration, neither party can apply for the registration of a different rent without the concurrence of the other, unless there have been changes in circumstances that make the registered rent no longer fair.[50] The landlord cannot recover more than the registered rent from a regulated tenant.[51]

(d) *Fair rent.* In determining what is a fair rent, regard must be had "to all the circumstances (other than personal circumstances) and in particular to . . . the age, character, locality and state of repair of the dwelling-house," any furniture provided under the tenancy, and also any premium paid for the tenancy. There must, however, be disregarded the effect of local shortages of accommodation, any disrepair or defect attributable to a failure by the tenant to comply with his obligations, any voluntary improvement carried out by the tenant, and any change in the condition of furniture.[52] The disregard of scarcity has often produced registered rents that are lower than market rents, sometimes strikingly so.

8. Premiums. There are wide provisions[53] prohibiting any person (whether landlord, tenant, agent or middleman[54]) from requiring a premium as a condition of the grant, renewal, continuance or assignment of any tenancy within the Act,[55] and preventing a statutory tenant (who has no assignable interest) from asking or receiving any consideration from any person except the landlord as a condition of giving up possession.[56]

9. Mortgages. Where the Acts restricted a landlord's rights against his tenant (*e.g.* to increase the rent) it was thought that the landlord ought to be correspondingly protected against his mortgagee. Today, there is no longer any automatic protection, but instead the landlord-mortgagor may some-

---

[49] See Megarry's *Rent Acts* (11th ed. 1988) vol. 1, pp. 541–551 for these rules and variants.
[50] Act of 1977, s.67, as amended by H.A. 1980, s.60: formerly the period was three years.
[51] Act of 1977, ss.44, 45.
[52] *Ibid.* s.70; Housing and Planning Act 1986, s.17.
[53] Rent Act 1977, s.103.
[54] *Farrell* v. *Alexander* [1977] A.C. 59.
[55] See *Elmdene Estates Ltd.* v. *White* [1960] A.C. 528.
[56] Act of 1977, s.3(5), Sched. 1, Pt. II.

times be granted relief by the court. He can apply for relief if the mortgage was created before certain dates when the Acts became applicable to the tenancy, and the mortgage is a legal mortgage of a dwelling let on a regulated tenancy that is binding on the mortgagee. If the rate of interest under the mortgage is increased, or steps are taken to enforce the mortgage, or a lower rent for the tenancy is registered, and this, coupled with the Act of 1977, causes the landlord-mortgagor "severe financial hardship," the court may grant relief by varying the mortgage or restricting the exercise of any remedies under it.[57]

B. *Housing Act 1988: Assured Tenancies*

1. Introduction. For the main body of dwellings, two separate but some-what similar systems of protecting tenants are now in operation. The long-established system under the Rent Acts which has been considered above continues to apply, with some variations, to tenancies created before January 15, 1989. Side by side with it, there is the new system under the Housing Act 1988 whereby tenancies created on or after January 15, 1989, may receive the lesser benefits of being assured tenancies. The two systems have much in common, but many differences.

2. Application of the Housing Act 1988

(a) *Date of tenancy.* A tenancy cannot be a protected tenancy under the old law if it was entered into on or after January 15, 1989, and it cannot be an assured tenancy under the new system if it was entered into before that date: the two categories are mutually exclusive.[58] Where a tenancy was entered into in pursuance of a contract, the date to be taken is that of the contract, not the tenancy. Further, a tenant protected under the old system does not lose his protection if he accepts a new tenancy after that date.[59]

(b) *Nature of tenancy.* As under the old system,[60] the Housing Act 1988 applies only if there is a tenancy under which a dwelling-house is let as a separate dwelling and the tenant occupies it as a home; but now it must be his "only or principal home."[61] With some modifications, the list of exceptions substantially follows the exceptions under the Act of 1977,[62] though the exception for board and attendance does not apply.

3. Types of assured tenancy. Under the Housing Act 1988 there are three main types of assured tenancy, namely, periodic tenancies, fixed term tenancies, and shorthold tenancies. An assured fixed term tenancy is any assured tenancy except a periodic tenancy.[63] An assured shorthold tenancy

---

[57] *Ibid.* Part X.
[58] See H.A. 1988, s.34(1), Sched. 1, para. 13(1).
[59] *Ibid.* s.34, Sched. 1, para. 1.
[60] *Ante,* p. 533.
[61] H.A. 1988, s.1.
[62] *Ante,* pp. 533, 534.
[63] H.A. 1988, s.45(1): thus for these purposes a tenancy at will is a fixed term tenancy.

is a special kind of fixed term tenancy. It is an assured tenancy granted for a fixed term of six months or more after a notice in the prescribed form has been served on the tenant stating that the tenancy will be a shorthold tenancy.[64]

4. Security of tenure. A landlord can bring an assured tenancy to an end only by obtaining an order of the court for possession, made on one of the statutory grounds.[65] A periodic tenancy will thus continue indefinitely despite any notice to quit given by the landlord; and when a fixed term tenancy comes to an end, then unless this was effected by the tenant (*e.g.* by surrender) or by an order of the court, the landlord is deemed to have granted the tenant a "statutory periodic tenancy" on the existing terms.[66] This tenancy is very different from a statutory tenancy under the old system,[67] for it is, by force of statute, a contractual tenancy and not a mere status of irremovability. In addition, no proceedings for possession can be brought unless the landlord has served on the tenant a "possession notice" in the prescribed form. This must state that within one year but not sooner than two weeks (or two months, in some cases) he intends to begin proceedings for possession on one or more of the grounds specified in the notice.[68]

5. Grounds for possession. The discretionary and mandatory grounds for possession have much in common with those under the Rent Act 1977, considered above[69]; but they are by no means identical. They are as follows.

(a) *Discretionary grounds.* If satisfied that any of the eight discretionary grounds for possession[70] is satisfied the court may make an order for possession if it considers it reasonable to do so.[71]

GROUND 9: ALTERNATIVE ACCOMMODATION. This is substantially the same as Case A.A.

GROUND 10: UNPAID RENT. This is a revised version of part of Case 1.

GROUND 11: PERSISTENT DELAY: even if no rent is in arrears, the tenant has persistently delayed in paying rent.

GROUND 12: BREACH OF OBLIGATION: an obligation of the tenancy (apart from rent) has been broken or not performed. This corresponds with the rest of Case 1.

GROUND 13: WASTE. This is a modified version of Case 3, expanded to include the common parts of any building that includes the dwelling.

[64] *Ibid.* s.20: tenancies granted to certain existing tenants are excluded.
[65] H.A. 1988, s.5.
[66] *Ibid.*
[67] *Ante*, p. 535.
[68] H.A. 1988, s.8.
[69] *Ante*, pp. 536–539.
[70] H.A. 1988, Sched. 2, Pt. II.
[71] *Ibid.* s.7(4).

GROUND 14: NUISANCE. This is almost identical with Case 2.

GROUND 15: DAMAGE TO FURNITURE. This is substantially the same as Case 3.

GROUND 16: LANDLORD'S EMPLOYEE: the dwelling was let to an employee of the landlord but his employment has ended. This matches the second limb of Case 8; the dwelling need not be required for another employee under this ground.

(b) *Mandatory grounds.* There are in effect nine mandatory grounds for possession.[72] The first five of them are available only if the tenant was given notice in writing not later than the beginning of the tenancy that possession might be recovered on the particular mandatory ground.[73]

GROUND 1: LANDLORD'S HOME: either (i) the landlord once occupied the dwelling as his only or principal home, or (ii) the landlord now requires the dwelling as the only or principal home for himself or his spouse, and he did not acquire the reversion on the tenancy for money or money's worth. There are elements of Cases 9 and 11 here.

GROUND 2: MORTGAGEE'S SALE: under a mortgage granted before the tenancy began, the mortgagee requires possession so that he can sell the dwelling with vacant possession under his power of sale.

GROUND 3: HOLIDAY HOME. This is substantially the same as Case 13.

GROUND 4: STUDENT RESIDENCE. This closely resembles Case 14.

GROUND 5: MINISTER OF RELIGION. This is substantially the same as Case 15.

GROUND 6: DEMOLITION OR SUBSTANTIAL WORKS: the landlord intends to demolish or reconstruct all or a substantial part of the dwelling, or to carry out substantial works on it, and he needs possession for this purpose. But this ground is not available to a landlord who acquired the reversion on the tenancy for money or money's worth.[74]

GROUND 7: DEATH OF TENANT: the tenancy is a periodic tenancy and the tenant has died; the tenancy has devolved under his will or intestacy; and proceedings for possession were commenced within a year of the tenant's death.

GROUND 8: PROLONGED NON-PAYMENT OF RENT: at least three months' rent is in arrears or unpaid, both when the possession notice is served and at the date of the hearing.

ASSURED SHORTHOLD TENANCIES. In addition to the eight numbered grounds, there is in effect an additional mandatory ground for assured

---

[72] *Ibid.* Sched. 2, Pt. I.
[73] See *ante*, p. 537. For Grounds 1 and 2 the court may dispense with this requirement.
[74] There is some parallel here with business tenancies: see *ante*, p. 525.

shorthold tenancies.[75] If the tenancy is for a fixed term which has ended, and before it ended the landlord gave the tenant at least two months' notice stating that he required possession of the dwelling, then provided no further assured tenancy (apart from a statutory periodic tenancy) is in existence, the landlord is entitled to a mandatory order for possession. If instead the tenancy is periodic, the landlord is entitled to his order if he has given the tenant at least two months' notice that he requires possession on a specified date, and this date is the last day of a period of the tenancy and also a day on which a notice to quit given at the same time could (apart from the Act) terminate the tenancy.

6. Death. On the death of an assured tenant, the provisions for transmission of the tenancy[76] are narrower than those for statutory tenants under regulated tenancies.[77] They apply only to periodic and not fixed term assured tenancies; they apply only to sole (and not joint) tenants; they apply only to a surviving spouse (as generously construed[78]) who occupied the dwelling as his or her only or principal home immediately before the tenant's death, though no period of occupation is required; members of the family have no rights of succession; and there can be only one transmission. If these requirements are satisfied, the tenancy, which is necessarily contractual, automatically vests in the spouse; otherwise it devolves under the tenant's will or intestacy.

7. Rent. Under an assured tenancy the rent will initially be whatever the parties have agreed: there is no system of registered rents or any other statutory restriction. Unless otherwise agreed, that rent will continue for as long as the tenancy exists. But for assured periodic tenancies and assured shorthold tenancies there is a limited degree of statutory control. This does not apply to other tenancies; under a tenancy for a fixed term (not being an assured shorthold) the rent payable is the rent agreed.

(a) *Assured periodic tenancies.* Under an assured periodic tenancy the initial rent will continue indefinitely unless the landlord serves a notice proposing an increased rent on the tenant. This increased rent will become the new rent unless the tenant refers the notice to the rent assessment committee, in which case the open market rent as determined by the committee will become the new rent. No such increase can be made during the first year of the tenancy, or if the tenancy makes its own provisions for increases.[79] Apart from this, the tenant has no right to apply to the committee.

(b) *Assured shorthold tenancies.* Under an assured shorthold tenancy the initial rent will continue indefinitely unless the tenant refers it to the rent

[75] H.A. 1988, s.21; *ante*, p. 541.
[76] *Ibid.* s.17.
[77] *Ante*, p. 535.
[78] *Ibid.*
[79] H.A. 1988, ss.13, 14.

assessment committee; he may do this at any time after the grant of the tenancy. The committee then determines the rent which the landlord might "reasonably be expected to obtain" under the tenancy; but there is no jurisdiction to do this unless there is a sufficiency of similar dwellings in the locality that are let on assured tenancies and the committee considers that the rent under the tenancy is "significantly higher" than the rent that the landlord might reasonably expect. The landlord cannot recover more than the rent thus determined.[80]

C. Agricultural Tied Dwellings: Protected and Assured Agricultural Occupancies

Many agricultural workers who occupied dwellings owned by their employers formerly had no statutory protection because they were mere licensees, or, if they were tenants, they paid little or no rent[81]; they occupied "tied cottages" or other dwellings which "went with the job." The Rent (Agriculture) Act 1976 gave such occupants the status of "protected occupiers," with much the same protection as under the Rent Acts, though with a number of variations.

1. Protected occupiers. A person is a "protected occupier" if he has a "relevant licence or tenancy" and is a "qualifying worker," and the dwelling is in "qualifying ownership."[82] A relevant licence or tenancy is one which would fall within the Rent Acts but for the exclusion of licences and tenancies at a low rent, and certain other matters. A qualifying worker is one who has worked full-time in agriculture for 91 out of the previous 104 weeks. A dwelling is in qualifying ownership if the occupier is employed in agriculture and his employer either owns the dwelling as the immediate landlord or licensor, or else has made arrangements with such a landlord or licensor for occupation by the employer's agricultural workers. When a protected occupier dies, his spouse or a member of his family may succeed to his occupancy, though there can be only one such succession.[83]

2. Possession. On the determination of a protected occupancy, the occupier, if in residence, becomes a statutory tenant, even if he is a mere licensee.[84] The grounds for possession are substantially the same as those under the Rent Acts, with the exclusion of the agricultural grounds and a reduction in the mandatory grounds.[85] One special provision is that if the landlord cannot reasonably provide suitable alternative accommodation for the occupier and the landlord requires vacant possession for another agricultural worker of his, then, if the interests of efficient agriculture require it, the

---

[80] *Ibid.* s.22.
[81] *Ante*, p. 534.
[82] Rent (Agriculture) Act 1976, ss.1, 2, Sched. 3, Pt. I.
[83] *Ibid.* s.3; and see *ante*, p. 535.
[84] *Ibid.* s.4.
[85] *Ibid.* ss.6, 7, Sched. 4; and see *ante*, pp. 536–539.

housing authority must use its best endeavours to provide suitable alternative accommodation for the displaced occupier.[86]

3. Rent. The system of fair rents for regulated tenancies applies in general
to protected occupiers.[87]

4. Assured agricultural occupancies. Normally, no new protected occupancy can arise on or after January 15, 1989. Instead, corresponding provisions are made for assured agricultural occupancies on similar lines.[88] These
are treated as being assured tenancies, though with variations: thus Ground
16 does not apply.[89]

D. Secure Tenancies: the Public Sector

Where the landlord is in the "public sector," tenancies of dwellings are
subject to only a partial application of statutory provisions which resemble
those which apply to other landlords. Until 1980, where a local authority was
the landlord, the tenant had no statutory protection either as to possession
or as to rent. The Housing Act 1980 introduced a system of "secure tenancies" which gave protection as to possession but not as to rent; and this is
now governed by the Housing Act 1985, Part IV.

1. Secure tenancies. A tenancy of a dwelling is a secure tenant only while
the "landlord condition" and the "tenant condition" are both satisfied. The
landlord condition is that the landlord is a local authority, new town corporation or one of certain other public bodies.[90] Housing associations and
housing trusts are no longer included. The tenant condition is that the tenant
is an individual who occupies the dwelling as his only or principal home.[91]

2. Security of tenure. A secure tenancy cannot be brought to an end except
by an order of the court. No such order can be made unless the landlord has
given the tenant a notice specifying the ground on which possession is
sought, and the landlord then establishes one of the 17 statutory grounds for
possession.[92] In eight cases the court must be satisfied that it is reasonable to
make the order, in four that suitable accommodation will be available for the
tenant, and in the remaining five both that such accommodation will be
available and that it is reasonable to make the order. The grounds have
much in common with those for protected and assured tenancies.[93]

There is also provision for succession to a secure tenancy on the death of

---

[86] *Ibid.* ss.27, 28.
[87] *Ibid.* s.13; *ante*, pp. 539, 540.
[88] H.A. 1988, s.24.
[89] *Ibid.* s.25; *ante*, p. 543.
[90] H.A. 1985, ss.79, 80, as amended. For numerous exceptions, see Sched. 1, and for an
example, see *Tower Hamlets L.B.C.* v. *Miah* [1992] 2 W.L.R. 761.
[91] *Ibid.* s.81. For joint tenants, occupation by one suffices.
[92] *Ibid.* ss.82–84, Sched. 2.
[93] *Ante*, pp. 536–539.

the tenant, unless he was himself a successor.[94] The tenant's spouse or, in default, a member of the tenant's family (as widely defined[95]) may take the tenancy by succession, provided that at the tenant's death he was occupying the dwelling as his only or principal home, and, in the case of a member of the tenant's family, he had also resided with the tenant for the year prior to his death,[96] whether in the dwelling or elsewhere.[97] The landlord (and not the court) selects the member of the family if they cannot agree.[98]

3. Rent. There is nothing to restrict the rent payable under a secure tenancy apart from the general provision which permits local authorities to make only "such reasonable charges" as they may determine.[99] Where the landlord is a housing association or housing trust, then although the tenancy will not be a secure tenancy, nor within the Rent Acts,[1] it will, if granted before January 15, 1989, be subject to a system of fair rents similar to the system applicable to protected and statutory tenancies.[2] If granted later, it will be an assured tenancy.

4. Right to buy. Elaborate statutory provisions[3] give a tenant who has been a secure tenant for two years or more a right to purchase either the reversion on his tenancy or a long lease at a low rent at its open market price less a discount. For a house, the discount ranges from 32 per cent. to 60 per cent., and for a flat from 44 per cent. to 70 per cent., depending in each case on the length of occupation. The discount has an upper limit of £50,000,[4] but the price may be left on mortgage.

E. Long Tenancies at a Low Rent

Originally there were no special provisions for long tenancies; but the Landlord and Tenant Act 1954, Part I, created a system under which long tenancies at a low rent were, on expiration, converted into statutory tenancies at a normal rent. The Rent Act 1957 extended this system to other long tenancies as well, but the Leasehold Reform Act 1967 restored them to the Rent Acts and once more confined the system to long tenancies at a low rent, many of which were building leases at a ground rent. In addition, the Leasehold Reform Act 1967 gave most tenants under such tenancies the alternative right to purchase the freehold or demand a long lease. These two heads will be taken in turn.

---

[94] H.A. 1985, ss.87, 88. Compare statutory tenancies: *ante*, pp. 535, 536.
[95] *Ibid.* s.113.
[96] *Ibid.* s.89.
[97] *Waltham Forest L.B.C.* v. *Thomas* [1992] 3 W.L.R. 131. Compare statutory tenancies: *ante*, p. 536.
[98] H.A. 1985, s.89.
[99] *Ibid.* s.24.
[1] *Ante*, p. 533.
[2] *Ante*, pp. 539, 540.
[3] H.A. 1985 (as amended by Housing and Planning Act 1986, Pt. I), Pt. V: see ss.118, 119, 127, 129.
[4] *Ibid.* s.131; S.I. 1989, No. 513.

I. LANDLORD AND TENANT ACT 1954, PART I

1. Conditions to be satisfied. A tenancy will fall within Part I of the Landlord and Tenant Act 1954 only if it is a "long tenancy" at a "low rent" which satisfies the "qualifying condition" of being a tenancy which, but for the lowness of the rent, would have fallen within the Rent Acts[5]; thus only residential tenants in occupation of dwellings of a type within the Rent Act 1977[6] will be protected. A long tenancy is a tenancy granted for more than 21 years, and a low rent is a rent that is less than two-thirds of the rateable value of the dwelling.[7]

2. The protection. Where Part I applies, the tenancy is automatically continued unless the tenant gives one month's notice to determine it.[8] The landlord may determine it in two ways. First, he may serve a "notice to resume possession." If the tenant fails to notify the landlord within two months that he is unwilling to give up possession, the tenancy ends on any date on or after the expiration of the term that is specified in the landlord's notice. Otherwise, the landlord may apply to the court on one of the statutory grounds for possession.[9] These are substantially the same as Cases 1, 2, 9 and A.A., and Ground 6, considered above,[10] though with some variations. Second, the landlord may serve a "landlord's notice proposing a statutory tenancy,"[11] in which case the rent and other terms of the tenancy will be as agreed by the parties or, in default, as determined by the county court.[12] The tenancy will be a regulated tenancy and will accordingly be subject to the provisions governing such tenancies, including the provisions as to fair rents.[13]

3. Housing Act 1988. A long tenancy at a low rent cannot fall within Part I if it was entered into on or after January 15, 1989, unless pursuant to a contract made before that date. The qualifying condition for Part I will not be satisfied because the tenancy is excluded from the Rent Acts both by the lowness of the rent and also by its date,[14] and not solely by the former. Nor can any tenancy at a low rent be an assured tenancy.[15] But the tenant may be able to claim the freehold or a new lease under the Leasehold Reform Act 1967.

---

[5] L. & T.A. 1954, ss.1, 2; Leasehold Reform Act 1967, s.39, Sched. 5; S.I. 1990 No. 434 (for dwellings with no rateable value).
[6] See *ante*, pp. 533–535.
[7] See n. 5, *supra*.
[8] L. & T.A. 1954, ss.5, 17.
[9] *Ibid.* ss.4, 12, 13, Sched. 3.
[10] See *ante*, pp. 536, 537, 543.
[11] L. & T.A. 1954, s.4.
[12] *Ibid.* ss.4, 6–9, as amended.
[13] Leasehold Reform Act 1967, Sched. 5, paras. 3, 4.
[14] *Ante*, p. 541.
[15] *Ante*, pp. 533, 541.

II. LEASEHOLD REFORM ACT 1967

The Leasehold Reform Act 1967 allows certain tenants under long leases at low rents to acquire the freehold or a new lease by paying for the land but not the house. The Act was based on the specious "principle" that under a building lease "the land belongs in equity to the landowner and the house belongs in equity to the occupying leaseholder."[16] Thus the purchaser of a building lease which had only a few years to run and so was worth little or nothing (because of the burden of repairs) suddenly found that "in equity" the house was his and not the landlord's, and that the landlord's valuable and appreciating asset in his ownership of the house subject only to the lease could be expropriated without compensation; but this has been held to be no infringement of human rights as being "in the public interest."[17]

1. Application of the Act. For the Act to apply, four conditions must be satisfied.[18]

(a) *Tenancy*: the tenancy must be a long tenancy at a low rent.[19]

(b) *Rateable value*: the rateable value of the house must fall within limits which are similar to those under the Rent Act 1977.[20]

(c) *Residence*: the tenant must have occupied the house as his only or main residence for the last three years, or for periods amounting to three years in the last 10.

(d) *House*: the premises must be a "house," including semi-detached and terraced houses but not flats; in effect, any division must be vertical. It suffices if the premises can reasonably be called a house, even if part is used as a shop.[21]

2. Claim. A tenant who wishes to claim the freehold or a lease must serve notice on the landlord in the prescribed form.[22] He can do this at any time during the continuance of his long tenancy, including any period while it is being automatically continued under Part I of the Act of 1954; but if the landlord serves a notice under that Act,[23] the tenant must serve his notice within two months or he will lose his rights.[24] When served, the tenant's notice takes effect as a contract for the conveyance of the freehold or the grant of the lease; it is registrable as an estate contract, or, for registered land, it may be protected by a notice or caution.[25] In default of agreement,

---

[16] White Paper on Leasehold Reform in England and Wales (1966, Cmnd. 2916), para. 4.
[17] *James* v. *United Kingdom* (1986) 8 E.H.R.R. 123, construing the European Convention on Human Rights 1950, Protocol No. 1 (1952), art. 1.
[18] Leasehold Reform Act 1967, ss.1–4.
[19] See *ante*, p. 548.
[20] See *ante*, p. 534.
[21] *Tandon* v. *Trustees of Spurgeons Homes* [1982] A.C. 755.
[22] Leasehold Reform Act 1967, s.22, Sched. 3.
[23] *Ante*, p. 548.
[24] Leasehold Reform Act 1967, Sched. 3, para. 2.
[25] *Ibid.* ss.1, 5, 8; see *ante*, pp. 79, 106.

the price, rent and other terms will be settled by a Leasehold Valuation Tribunal (constituted by a Rent Assessment Committee), with appeal to the Lands Tribunal; on other matters the county court has jurisdiction.[26]

3. Lease or freehold

(a) *Lease.* A tenant who claims a lease is entitled to a term of 50 years from the expiry of the existing lease, and on the same terms. The rent will be a ground rent, representing the rental value of the site without the buildings; but after 25 years the landlord may require the rent to be revalued. The tenant must pay the landlord's reasonable costs.[27]

(b) *Freehold.* The tenant is entitled to a conveyance in fee simple, subject to his tenancy but free from most incumbrances on the freehold.[28] The price is based on the open market value, as adjusted, but the method of valuation depends on the rateable value of the house on the appropriate day.[29] (i) If that rateable value is not more than £500 (or £1,000 in Greater London) the valuation is on the basis that the tenancy will be extended under the Act, but that the tenant and his family living with him in the house will not form part of the market.[30] (ii) If the rateable value exceeds the above figures (as adjusted for tenant's improvements) the valuation is on the basis of the house being subject to the tenancy and the tenant's right to remain as a statutory tenant without being liable for repairs, maintenance or redecoration, and with a reduction for any improvements made by the tenant, but with the market including the tenant and his family.[31] The tenant must pay the landlord's reasonable costs.[32]

4. Modifications. With some qualifications, any agreement excluding or modifying the statutory rights of the tenant is void.[33] But there are some statutory modifications.

(a) *Required for landlord.* If the tenant gives notice under the Act, and the landlord then seeks and obtains an order for possession of the house for occupation as the only or main residence for himself or an adult member of his family, the tenant has no right to the freehold or a lease, but is entitled to compensation instead. No such order can be made if the landlord obtained his interest after February 18, 1966, nor if in all the circumstances (including any other available accommodation) greater hardship would be caused by making the order than by refusing it.[34] Compensation is assessed on the basis

---

[26] *Ibid.* ss.20, 21; H.A. 1980, s.142.
[27] Leasehold Reform Act 1967, ss.14, 15; H.A. 1980, Sched. 22.
[28] Leasehold Reform Act 1967, s.8.
[29] *Ibid.* s.1(4): as under the Rent Act 1977: *ante*, p. 534.
[30] Leasehold Reform Act 1967, s.9(1), as amended by H.A. 1969, s.82.
[31] Leasehold Reform Act 1967, s.9(1A), (1B), added by H.A. 1974, s.118.
[32] Leasehold Reform Act 1967, s.9(4).
[33] *Ibid.* s.23.
[34] *Ibid.* s.18.

of the tenant having a 50 year extension of his tenancy, though with nothing for losing the right to obtain the freehold.[35]

(b) *Redevelopment.* A landlord can sometimes apply for an order for possession if he proposes to demolish or reconstruct the whole or a substantial part of the house for the purposes of redevelopment. If the tenant has already obtained a lease, the landlord can do this in the last year of the old tenancy or afterwards; but if the tenant has given notice only claiming a lease, the landlord must apply during the last year of the old tenancy. This head does not apply where the tenant is claiming the freehold. If an order for possession is made, the tenant is entitled to compensation as in (a) above.[36]

(c) *Development by public bodies.* If the landlord is a public body, and a Minister of the Crown certifies that within 10 years the house will be required for development for the purposes of that body, the tenant cannot obtain either the freehold or a lease, and the landlord will be entitled to possession when the tenancy expires. But if within two months of the service of the certificate the tenant claims the freehold or a lease, the provisions for possession and compensation under (b) above apply.[37]

(d) *The Crown.* The Act does not bind the Crown[38]; but usually, as of grace, freeholds or leaseholds will be granted to Crown tenants as if the Act applied.

(e) *Management.* An area occupied by tenants of houses under one landlord could formerly be made subject to a scheme under which the landlord retained powers of management over the houses, relating to matters such as repairs and development. This could be done only if the appropriate Minister certified, on an application to him made before 1970,[39] that this was in the general interest in order to maintain standards of appearance and amenity, and the High Court approved the scheme.[40] Such schemes, however, did not affect the right of tenants to obtain the freehold or a lease. Schemes thus made are still operative.

F. Restricted Contracts

Before the Furnished Houses (Rent Control) Act 1946, tenancies of dwellings that were let furnished or with services were wholly unprotected. The Act established a system of rent tribunals which could fix rents for such tenancies; and the Act conferred a limited and somewhat unsatisfactory degree of security of tenure. After various amendments, the present law is contained in the Rent Act 1977 as amended by the Housing Acts 1980 and

[35] *Ibid.* Sched. 2.
[36] *Ibid.* s.17.
[37] *Ibid.* s.28.
[38] See *ibid.* s.33.
[39] Or before August 1974 for houses brought within the Act by H.A. 1974: see s.118(2).
[40] Leasehold Reform Act 1967, s.19.

1988. The functions of rent tribunals are now discharged by rent assessment committees.[41]

1. Application. Originally the jurisdiction extended only to dwellings that were let furnished or with services, though it applied however great the value of the dwelling. The Rent Act 1957 then excluded dwellings with a rateable value outside the Rent Acts, and the Rent Act 1974 then excluded most furnished tenancies from it, transferring them to the full protection of the Rent Acts instead; but it also extended the jurisdiction to tenancies granted by a resident landlord.[42] The Rent Act 1977 further extended the jurisdiction to mere licences, though the Housing Act 1980 greatly curtailed the provisions for security of tenure. Finally, the Housing Act 1988 prevented the creation of any more restricted contracts. The subject will therefore be considered only briefly.

2. Restricted contract. A contract is a restricted contract only if the following conditions are satisfied.[43]

(a) *Rateable value*: the rateable value is within the limits for the Rent Acts.

(b) *Nature of contract*: the contract gives a person a right to occupy a dwelling as a residence, whether as tenant or licensee, at a rent which includes payment for the use of furniture or services. The scope of this provision is much reduced by the exclusion of regulated tenancies which include most furnished tenancies. Alternatively, the contract must be a tenancy which cannot be a protected tenancy either because the tenant shares some (but not all) of the accommodation with the landlord, or because there is a resident landlord.[44]

(c) *Not excepted*: the contract does not fall within any of the exceptions. These include regulated tenancies, cases where the rent includes substantial payment for board, holiday residences, and lettings by local authorities or certain other bodies.[45] In particular, no contract made on or after January 15, 1989, can be a restricted contract unless made pursuant to a contract made before that date.[46]

3. Rent. Either party may at any time refer the contract to the rent tribunal, which, after hearing the parties, may reduce or increase the rent to the amount which the tribunal considers reasonable, or may approve it.[47] The rent thus determined is registered with the local authority, whereupon it becomes an offence to require or receive more than that rent, or to charge any premium.[48] A registered rent may be reconsidered after two years, or if a

[41] H.A. 1980, s.72.
[42] *Ante*, p. 534.
[43] Rent Act 1977, ss.19–21; *ante*, p. 534.
[44] *Ibid.* ss.19–21; *ante*, p. 534.
[45] *Ibid.* s.19.
[46] H.A. 1988, s.36.
[47] Rent Act 1977, ss.77, 78.
[48] *Ibid.* ss.79, 81, 122.

change of circumstances has made the registered rent no longer reasonable, or if both parties make the application.[49] The tribunal must still consider a reference even if the tenant quits before the hearing.[50]

4. Security of tenure. There are two alternative systems for giving a limited degree of security of tenure, depending on whether the contract was made on or after November 28, 1980 ("new contracts") or before that date ("old contracts").[51]

(a) *New contracts.* On making an order for possession the court may stay or suspend execution of the order, or postpone the date of possession, for not more than three months, whether the occupier is a tenant or a licensee. But unless it would cause exceptional hardship or be unreasonable, the court must impose conditions for the payment of rent and arrears of rent, and may impose other conditions.[52]

(b) *Old contracts.* When an occupier has referred his contract to the tribunal, no subsequent notice to quit can take effect until six months after the tribunal's decision, unless the tribunal substitutes a shorter period.[53] This operates automatically, though it does not apply at all to a reference made after the notice to quit has been served. In that case, however, if an application to the tribunal for security of tenure is made while the notice to quit is still running, the tribunal may grant it for not more than six months, and may subsequently extend it by not more than six months at a time.[54] But this system can give no security of tenure where the contract expires by effluxion of time, without any notice to quit; nor does it apply to the recovery of dwellings under certain contracts with owner-occupiers.[55]

G. Eviction and Harassment

The various systems for protecting occupants of dwellings that have been considered above have been supplemented by the provisions of the Protection from Eviction Act 1977. The Act applies to all "residential occupiers," namely, persons who occupy premises as a residence under a contract or legal right[56]; and it protects them against eviction without an order of the court.

1. Eviction. Where premises are let as a dwelling and the tenancy is not within some statutory protection (*e.g.* under the Rent Acts), the Act, with

---

[49] *Ibid.* s.80; H.A. 1980, s.70.
[50] *R.* v. *West London Rent Tribunal, ex p. Napper* [1967] 1 Q.B. 169.
[51] Rent Act 1977, s.102A, added by H.A. 1980, s.69.
[52] Rent Act 1977, s.106A and Protection from Eviction Act 1977, s.3(2A), added by H.A. 1980, s.69.
[53] Rent Act 1977, s.103.
[54] *Ibid.* s.104.
[55] *Ibid.* s.105.
[56] Protection from Eviction Act 1977, s.1. For the details, see Megarry, *The Rent Acts* (11th ed.) Vol. 3, pp. 177–183.

some exceptions,[57] prohibits the eviction of an occupier who continues to reside in the premises when the tenancy has ended, except by an order of the court; and this now applies to licences as well as tenancies.[58] It also applies to the enforcement of any right of re-entry or forfeiture under a lease while any person is lawfully residing in the premises or any part of them.[59]

2. Criminal eviction. Any person who unlawfully deprives a residential occupier of his occupation of any or all of the premises, or attempts to do so, is guilty of an offence unless with reasonable cause he believed that the occupier had ceased to reside in the premises.[60] A residential occupier may now recover damages for the statutory tort of wrongful eviction.[60a]

3. Criminal harassment. The offence of criminal harassment is committed by a landlord or his agent who, without reasonable grounds, does certain specified acts with a specified knowledge. Those acts are acts likely to interfere with the peace or comfort of a residential occupier or members of his household, or the persistent withdrawing or withholding of services reasonably required for residential occupation. The requisite knowledge is knowing or having reasonable cause to believe that the acts are likely to cause the residential occupier to give up occupation of any or all of the premises or to refrain from exercising any right or remedy in respect of them.[61]

Sect. 4. Status

1. Evolution. Most tenants today are to some degree protected by statute. In early law, leasehold tenants were regarded as holding mere contracts; not until the sixteenth century were they recognised as owning estates,[62] though they had little protection beyond the terms of their tenancies. Today, most tenancies have some claim to having travelled from contract via estate to status: for many of their important rights depend in large part not on contract but on a positive statutory protection that overrides any contract. Yet the variations between the different forms of statutory protection are so great that it is difficult to find much common ground in them; and in recent years there has been a marked reduction in the degree of the protection.

2. Rent. There are many variants.

(a) *Initial control.* There is now no initial control of rent. Formerly, where a rent had been registered for a regulated tenancy or restricted contract, this restricted the rent under any subsequent tenancies or contracts of this kind; but such tenancies and contracts can no longer be created.

---

[57] "Excluded" tenancies and licences: see Protection from Eviction Act 1977, s.3A, inserted by H.A. 1988, s.31.
[58] Protection from Eviction Act 1977, ss.3, 3A; H.A. 1988, ss.30, 31.
[59] Protection from Eviction Act 1977, s.2.
[60] *Ibid.* s.1.
[60a] H.A. 1988, ss.27, 28.
[61] Protection from Eviction Act 1977, s.1; H.A. 1988, s.29.
[62] See *ante*, pp. 14, 28.

(b) *Subsequent control.* Control of rent may arise at any time (initial references of regulated tenancies, restricted contracts, protected occupancies, and long-low); on renewal of the tenancy (business); or after stated intervals (agriculture, regulated, assured periodic, reconsideration of regulated tenancies or restricted contracts).

(c) *Method.* The rent may be determined by the court (business, and long-low), by an arbitrator (agriculture), by a rent officer or rent assessment committee (regulated, and some assured), or by a tribunal (old restricted, and long-low 50 years).

(d) *Level.* The general level of rent is the market rent, though this is tempered in some cases by a requirement of reasonableness (secure, old restricted), and in others by a disregard of the effect of scarcity (regulated, protected occupancy, long-low, and to some extent agriculture).

3. Security of tenure. The many variants here have some degree of common ground. Security of tenure is in general provided in two stages. The tenant is, first, given the right to remain in possession in one way or another until, second, it is determined whether he can continue in possession, or whether the landlord has some statutory ground for claiming possession.

(a) *Initial.* The tenant's initial right to remain in possession may be given by making him a statutory tenant (regulated, and protected occupancies); by prolonging his contractual tenancy in some form until the determination of an application to the court (business, assured, assured occupancies, long-low), or until the landlord obtains an order for possession (secure); by enabling the tenant to give a notice that will make a notice to quit ineffective until the landlord obtains a tribunal's consent to it taking effect (agriculture); by providing that a reference to a tribunal will automatically suspend the operation of any subsequent notice to quit (old restricted); or by giving the court a limited and discretionary power to postpone the operation of an order for possession (new restricted).

(b) *Substantive.* The tenant's substantive right to continue in possession after the initial period of security may be provided by preventing an order for possession being made save on statutory grounds (regulated, assured, secure, protected and assured occupancies); by giving the tenant the right to a new tenancy unless statutory grounds preclude it (business); by continuing the ineffectiveness of a notice to quit (agriculture); by enabling the tenant to serve a notice requiring the grant of the freehold or a long lease (long-low, secure); or by enabling the tenant to apply to a tribunal for repeated extensions of the period while a notice to quit does not take effect (old restricted), or to ask the court for a limited postponement of the operation of an order for possession (new restricted).

4. Status. Both on major issues and on many minor matters, a tenant today will often look more to the rights conferred on him by the Statute

Book than to the terms of his tenancy. The diversity in the statutory rights is great, and recent years have seen some reduction in their ambit; yet it is perhaps true to say that there is still an indefinable and varied but nevertheless real status of protected tenant.

INDEX